THE BILL JAMES
PLAYER RATINGS BOOK 1994

Also by Bill James

The Baseball Abstract (1977–1988)
The Historical Baseball Abstract (1986)
The Baseball Book (1990–1992)
This Time Let's Not Eat the Bones (1989)
The Bill James Player Ratings Book 1993

THE BILL JAMES PLAYER RATINGS BOOK 1994

Collier Books
Macmillan Publishing Company
New York

Maxwell Macmillan Canada
Toronto

Maxwell Macmillan International
New York Oxford Singapore Sydney

Macmillan Publishing Company
866 Third Avenue
New York, NY 10022

Maxwell Macmillan Canada, Inc.
1200 Eglinton Avenue East
Suite 200
Don Mills, Ontario M3C 3N1

Macmillan Publishing Company is part of the Maxwell Communication Group of Companies.

ISBN 0-02-041564-8

Macmillan books are available at special discounts for bulk purchases for sales promotions, premiums, fund-raising, or educational use. For details, contact:

Special Sales Director
Macmillan Publishing Company
866 Third Avenue
New York, NY 10022

10 9 8 7 6 5 4 3 2 1

Printed in the United States of America

This book is for
my brother-in-law
STEVE METZLER,
whose Red Sox will be one of the surprise teams of 1994.

ACKNOWLEDGMENTS

I could not have written this book without my wife, who watches the kids and runs my life during the difficult period when I'm at the office almost 24 hours a day.

I could not have found all of the information I need about all 1200 or so players without John Sickels, who works with me, organizing the underlying research and writing draft comments for some players.

Almost all of the statistics in this book were produced by STATS Inc., in Chicago. Among the people who work with STATS Inc., and whose work therefore shows up in these pages, are John Dewan, Dick Cramer, Sue Dewan, Steve Moyer, Art Ashley, Bob Mecca, Ross Schaufelberger, Dave Pinto, Don Zminda, Craig Wright, Rob Neyer, Don Zminda, Michael Coulter, Kevin Davis, Alissa Hudson, Allan Spear, Jules Aquino, Jason Gumbs, Mike Hammer, Shawna Haskins, Chuck Miller, Jim Russo, Kenn Ruby, Michael Canter, Stephanie Armstrong, Steve Heinecke, Matt Greenberger, and others to humorous too mention.

I could not get the book printed without the help of Bill Rosen, of Macmillan Publishing, and Gillian Casey Sowell, of Bill Rosen's office. The book would not reach you without dozens of other Macmillan employees, who shall remain nameless because I don't know what their names are.

Much information in this book is taken from the media guides of the 28 teams, which were sent to me by the teams and their Media Relations Directors. Thank you, gentlemen and ladies.

Life would be scarcely worth living without my children, Rachel, age seven, Isaac, age five, and Reuben, who is now a few weeks old. The help of all of you is greatly appreciated.

Bill James

CONTENTS

INTRODUCTION

Hello, and welcome to the second annual *Bill James Player Ratings Book*.

This introduction is not required reading; if you read it last year, what I have to tell you this year is a lot of the same stuff. The guts of the book is the comments about players, which will begin in a few pages.

For those of you who haven't skipped immediately to the good stuff, the idea of this book is to take a quick look at every baseball player who

a) played in the majors in 1993, or

b) can reasonably be expected to play in the majors in 1994.

I have no operating assumption about *why* you are interested in baseball players. You may be a rotisserie player, fantasy league player, may be in an APBA league or a Strat-o-Matic League; hell, you may even be a baseball fan. I assume that however it is that you come to be interested in baseball, you will want to know who the players are, particularly the young players, and whether they're any good. It is my job, as the author of this book, to find out who every player in baseball is, where he came from, what he does well and what he does poorly, and to make an educated guess about what kind of a career he is going to have from now on.

The players are evaluated on a dollar scale. The best player in baseball, Barry Bonds, is worth $100. Players who have retired or have been released and clearly aren't coming back have no value. Everybody else is somewhere between zero and a hundred.

These values are entirely relative. Barry Bonds is worth a hundred dollars, so what is Ken Griffey Jr. worth? $98. What is Steve Finley worth? $40.

Why so low?

That's not low.

That's high?

That's pretty high.

The vast majority of players are valued at less than $50; only the very good players, proven quality players, are over $50. Good bullpen aces, like Aguilera and Tom Henke, are in the fifties. Here's the way the scale works:

$70–$100	The best players in baseball
$50–$70	All-Stars
$40–$50	Very good players, minor stars
$30–$40	Quality regulars
$20–$30	Run-of-the-mill regulars, good platoon players
$10–$20	Role players
Under $10	Players who probably won't be on a roster

At $40, Steve Finley is at the top of the "quality regulars" group, or at the edge of the "minor stars" group, depending on how you see it. In any case, he's got 90% of the baseball world looking up at him. He ranks below Juan Gonzalez ($88), Mark Langston ($66) and Gregg Jefferies ($52), but ahead of Moises Alou ($38), Steve Karsay ($28), Tim Bogar ($27), Phil Hiatt ($18), Steve Dreyer ($15), Keith Hughes ($13), Omar Daal ($11) and Drew Denson ($8).

The values are subjective; there is no "formula" which hides behind them. The value structure that I used this year is basically the same as it was last year, with one exception. In reviewing last year's book, I felt that there were far too many cases of players that I had valued at $1 to $9 who went on to play a significant amount, or even play regularly, or even play regularly and play well. A few examples:

- I had Junior Ortiz, veteran catcher, valued at $6, a figure you would give to someone who hardly ever plays. He batted 249 times.
- I had Mike Pagliarulo, who had been released after a poor season, valued at $4, assuming that he wouldn't play. He played 116 games and hit .303.
- I had Lee Guetterman, who was out of work at the time I wrote the book, valued at $3. He pitched 40 times, and pitched well.

My first thought was, how can I prevent that from happening again? How can I figure out more accurately who would and would not earn playing time? My second thought was that I couldn't. This book is written in October and early November, just after the World Series ends. No matter how hard I worked at it, it would be impossible for me to deduce with any real accuracy who will get the marginal jobs in baseball, the jobs which aren't decided until spring training. In attempting to guess who would be playing and who wouldn't, I had guessed wrong in a certain number of cases.

So what I did, instead, was to reduce the number of players with values under $10.

As a generalization, a roster spot in baseball is worth about $15. The last man on the roster, if he is in the majors all year, has a value of about $15, slightly higher on a good team (and less on a weak team). If I don't think a player is going to be on a major league roster all year, his value might be less than $15. This is very common. Look at it this way: if you allow 25 players for each of the 28 major league teams, that's 700 players. There are about 1,200 players in this book (I haven't actually counted. It's easier for you because by the time you see them they're laid out four to a page.) Anyway, that means that there are about 500 more players who might play or who will play part of the season than there are actual full-season roster spots. All of the 500 extra players are going to be valued under $20—so that's where the bulge in the population has got to be.

Last year, I would say "this guy's not going to play, I'll make him $4." This year, I left some of those guys at $10 or $12. I think that more realistically reflects the value of a marginal player with unknown playing time.

Last year was the first time I had done these values, and I got lucky in one respect: I picked the two MVPs at the top of the scale. I had Bonds valued at $100 last year, and he was the most productive player in his league, and I had Frank Thomas as the highest-valued player in the American League, at $98. That's just luck, of course; I won't hit both MVPs again if I do this for 20 years.

A few other points about the values:

1) The values look *forward*, not backward. Cliff Floyd is worth more than Eddie Murray, which, based on what they did last year or what they have done in the past, may seem odd—but Cliff Floyd is 17 years younger than Eddie Murray. Floyd, with luck, will do in the future what Murray has done in the past.

2) The values, to a degree, anticipate the rest of a player's career. Primarily, though, they are based on what I would expect of a player in 1994. A player who has 10 years ahead of him isn't worth 10 times as much as an older player who is still good, but who might just have one good year left. An older player who is still good, like Ozzie Smith, is still valuable.

3) The values do not imitate any specific game except baseball. There are many "shadow games" which are based on baseball, which I alluded to before—Rotisserie, Strat-O-Matic, APBA, Fantasy Games, Earl Weaver Baseball; they're all based on baseball, but they all give different approximations of a player's performance.

This poses a question: What game should I evaluate? Should I give a player extra value because he's a base stealer, and a rotisserie manager needs base stealers? Should I give closers extra value because some games place a premium on saves? Or should I assume, as some other games do, that David West is more valuable than Mitch Williams because of his innings and ERA, despite the fact that Williams got the saves?

There is only one answer to this: *the sum of all other images of the game of baseball must be the original game.*

I evaluate players based on how they performed in the real game of baseball, on their real value to their real teams—or actually, on what I believe that value will be in 1994.

This will not always fit your needs. You'll need to adjust the information I give you for your own game, your own interest.

I have, as I see it, three basic responsibilities in writing the player comments.

1) To do my research,
2) To tell the truth, and
3) To make it entertaining.

The research this year was intimidating. There are just a huge number of players, particularly in an expansion year, whose names do not set off bells—Huck Flener and Ken Greer and Rikkert Faneyte and Gar Finnvold and Roger Smithberg; who *are* these guys? I figure that you don't want to know that this pitcher had an injury of some kind some time during the season; you want to know what it was, when it was, what kind of shadow it casts over his future. What does he do well? Does he run? Does he throw? Can he hit lefthanders? Is he a lefthander? What role would he fit on a major league team? If he's a pitcher, what does he throw? Has he been consistent? Is he getting better? If so, why? Where does he come from?

There are 60 fundamental questions you can ask about each of those 1,200 players. I have to ask those questions, find the answers, and then chose from that file that which the reader most needs to know. That's basically what the book is about: background research. In a moment, a word from my sponsors.

I also have a responsibility, as I see it, to tell the truth. A few players—Ken Griffey and Chipper Jones—have more or less unlimited potential. Everybody else has limits. It is my responsibility to be sure that I don't mislead you about those limits.

And third, it has to be fun to read, or you're not going to read it. So if I'm hard on your favorite player, I hope you'll understand. If you're a Cecil Fielder fan and you don't like what I wrote about him, I hope you'll understand: it's the truth as I see it. I've got 60 to 79 words about each player; I've got to hit it and get out. Sometimes the prose is a little approximate.

And, of course, I'm going to make an error once in a while. I'm sure that somewhere in here there may be a lefthanded hitter who is identified as a switch hitter, and a fourth-round draft pick who is identified as an undrafted free agent, and a guy with an arm like a goose who is described as having a good arm. Believe me, I always have a source for these things—I don't make stuff up—but I know that that's no concilation to you if you are misled by an error. I take full responsibility for the accuracy of everything in the book, and I apologize for any such mistakes. And I promise you that there won't be many.

I don't claim to know more about every player than you do. If you're a Cleveland Indians fan, you're going to know more about the Cleveland players than I do. What I claim is what I said above: that I'll do my research and tell you honestly what I think. That's all.

Now, my sources:

1) *John Sickels*. John works with me; it's his job to round up media guides, to index articles about young players, and to provide me with files of information about each player. John also wrote draft comments for about 20% of the players in the book, and many times things that he wrote remained in the final book in some slightly altered form.

2) STATS *Inc*. STATS Inc. is the nation's largest and finest resource for statistical information about baseball. I work with STATS on dozens of different projects, and almost every stat in this book comes, in one way or another, from the home office in Chicago.

3) *Personal observation*. I go to games, I watch them on TV, and I make notes. I visit ballparks, minor league and major league and miscellaneous, and sometimes talk to managers and media people. Whatever I hear, I make a note of it.

4) *Friends*. I know dozens of people who live and breathe for the game of baseball, and I talk to them. I have at least one good friend who follows each of the 28 teams. Some of them are agents, some of them work for the teams. Most of them are just fans—but the things that they know are of great value to me.

5) *Media Guides*. We collect the media guides from all 28 teams, and these are invaluable to me. I also love them; I can spend hours just leafing through media guides. Best media guide of 1993: The Seattle Mariners.

6) *Baseball America*. I don't work regularly with *Baseball America*, although I do write an article for them a couple of times a year. BA is what *The Sporting News* used to be—the best source of information about minor league players. John Sickels reads and indexes all of their articles, so that when we need to find out something about some guy who played in the Montreal system, we can find the article.

7) *The Baseball Weekly*, from USA *Today*. Provides the other half of the picture that *The Sporting News* used to provide—the minutes and minutiae of major league baseball.

As to how all of this information is processed . . . well, I've been writing baseball books for a long time. I used to do what is called sabermetrics, which is a type of original baseball research. I did studies, thousands of studies over a period of ten-plus years, of baseball-related questions. Which elements of a pitcher's record predict future success? Which is a better predictor of next year's won-lost record: a pitcher's ERA, or his won-lost record? Who lasts longer, a power pitcher or a finesse pitcher? A lefthander or a righthander? What type of pitcher does well on artificial turf?

I don't do many of those studies anymore, and don't publish the ones I do; I retired from that in 1988. But I still know the things that I learned in doing that, and I still use that information to evaluate players. A few of the key things that I know (for those of you who want to skip ahead, this is exactly the same list that I ran in this article last year):

1) The number of runs a team scores is essentially a function of two things: the number of men on base and the team slugging percentage. Nothing else significantly changes the number of runs a team will score. Baserunning, base stealing, bunting, hitting behind the runner, making contact, going first-to-third on a single . . . it's worth the effort to keep track of it all, and we do, but the fact is that you can do everything else well, and if you're last in the league in the number of runners on base, you're still going to be last in runs scored most of the time.

2) The batting average is important, but it's not the whole game. It is not uncommon for a .250 hitter to contribute more runs to his team than a .300 hitter.

3) A player's offensive contribution can only be evaluated in the context of his defensive contribution, and vice versa. A shortstop who puts 70 runs on the scoreboard is worth more than a first baseman who creates 90 runs.

4) A player's minor league hitting statistics, ***if you know how to read them***, will predict his major league hitting ability in virtually every case.

5) A player's hitting or pitching statistics are very heavily colored by the park in which he plays. An ERA of 5.00 in Colorado is almost exactly equivalent to an ERA of 3.75 in the Astrodome.

6) The best predictor of future success by a pitcher is his strikeout to walk ratio. Make a list of pitchers with good strikeout/walk ratios but poor over-

all records—Mark Clark, Kevin Tapani, Greg Swindell, Doug Drabek, Rheal Cormier, even Melido Perez. You'll find that their overall record, as a group, will be better next year than it was this year. Do the opposite—pitchers with good records but bad strikeout/walk ratios—and check them next year. You'll see that, as a group, they've collapsed.

7) Power pitchers are vastly more durable and more consistent than finesse pitchers. Never bet on a finesse pitcher to sustain success, even when he has it. Always bet on a power pitcher; you'll load the odds in your favor.

8) Career length for batters is essentially a function of ability. Career length for a pitcher is primarily a function of two things: his ability to stay healthy, and how many strikeouts he gets.

9) An individual player may reach his peak at any age between 21 and 37, but any *group* of players will reach their peak value, as a group, at age 27. The only exceptions to this are a) knuckleballers, b) Tommy John–type pitchers, and c) those who are pre-selected because they had their best years at some other age.

10) In evaluating a prospect, the first thing you want to know is his age. Suppose you've got two rookies of the same ability: a 23-year-old and a 24-year-old. Suppose they each hit 15 home runs, same batting average and RBI. The 23-year-old can expect to hit, in his career, about 25% more home runs than the 24-year-old. If you compare a 23-year-old to a 25-year-old, the advantage of the 23-year-old is around 60 percent.

It's not that *all* young players improve; they don't. Many players level off about age 23. The key is that *some young players improve dramatically*. A 25-year-old player (non-pitcher) will never improve dramatically; a 22-year-old often will. The vast majority of players will be near their peak ability at age 25, and will retain that level for about five years.

11) A pitcher's won-lost record in an individual season doesn't mean much of anything.

There are a lot of other things that I believe as a consequence of my research or somebody else's, more minor things which may come into play in this comment or that one, but which aren't systematically important. A young player who strikes out a lot will always strike out a lot, although he will probably trim the totals in his prime seasons. I know that hitting ability changes astonishingly little after the age of 25, so that a player may *seem* to have totally lost his ability to hit, like Eric Davis now, only to re-discover it after several years.

Some of this is just entrenched skepticism. Whenever you read about a young player who is fast but doesn't steal bases, the inevitable next line is that he'll be able to steal bases once he learns to use his speed. On a small scale (increasing stolen bases from 10 to 20) this often does happen, and once in a blue moon (Lou Brock) it happens in a big way. Nine times in 10, what will happen instead is that the player will lose his speed.

On the other hand, if you ask me how I evaluate players, I won't tell you I evaluate them by research. I'll tell you that everything counts. In evaluating a player's defense, for example . . . the world has tended to divide into those who believe that defensive statistics tell the whole truth, and those who believe in evaluating defense by visual observation. I believe that everything counts. If a player has good defensive statistics, or bad defensive statistics, I want to know that. I want to know why. But if his defensive reputation is good or bad, I also want to know that, and I want to know why.

Most of the time, they're going to agree. If a player has bad defensive stats, most of the time he's going to have a bad defensive reputation as well. When they *don't* agree, as in the case of Roberto Alomar or Andy Van Slyke, then we need to look skeptically at *both*, the stats and the scouting reports, to figure out why. But here's the key point: that if a thing is true, you *must* be able to see it in different ways. If you can't explain *both* ends of it, then you don't understand it. That's my belief.

You will ask, sometime before the end of the book, "What exactly is a Grade A prospect?" I'm glad you asked me that. The term "Grade A prospect" means that *all* of the information about a young player is positive, or that the positive information about the player is much more weighty than the negative. Grade A prospects normally do carry small negatives. Manny Ramirez's defense is a mystery, and those unknowns have a way of leaping up to bite you. But the positive information about him is *so* positive that you just have to go with it.

What the term Grade A prospect does *not* mean is that the guy is going to be a star, and especially what it does not mean is that he is going to be a superstar. Many Grade A prospects will go on to become major league stars, but many will not. What we're saying with the term is that *there is no apparent reason* why this player should not become a star. When we look at his future, we don't see a limit.

Next, of course, are the Grade B prospects. The term "Grade B prospect" is intended as a compliment. The term Grade B prospect means that what we know about the player is mostly good, but with something that bothers you. A Grade B prospect is an exciting young player who strikes out too much, or a player who has hit extremely well in the minors, but started a year late.

There are Grade B prospects who will go on to become major league stars. Bob Gibson, evaluated at age 24, would have been a Grade B prospect. The term is *not* meant at all to say that the player *won't* be a major league star—only that there is something here to worry about.

The term "Grade C prospect" means that there is a

more or less even mix of information which makes you think that the player *will* be a good major league player, and information which makes you think that he won't.

The critical thing is the relationship between age and ability—where is the player at this age, compared to where he should be if he's going to be a good player?

A Grade A prospect is a player who tears up the Texas League when he is 22.

A Grade B prospect is a player who tears up the Texas League when he is 23.

A Grade C prospect is a player who tears up the Texas League when he is 24. You look at the record and say, "Gee, he looks great . . . but if he's really that good, why is he in the Texas League at age 24? Shouldn't he be in the majors by now?"

A Grade A prospect is a player who hits .300 in the Eastern League at age 22.

A Grade B prospect is a player who hits .275 in the Eastern League at age 22.

A Grade C prospect is a player who hits .250 in the Eastern League at age 22.

These are over-simplifications, of course. It's all a balancing act, and many times I really don't have the space, in a 79-word comment, to explain *why* I have classified the guy the way I have. You've usually got multiple seasons to deal with—one good, one not so good, one that you don't know what to do with. I will say two things, though:

1. It is almost always obvious how a player should be classified. Of the hundreds of players who were classified as Grade A, Grade B, Grade C, Grade D or no prospect in this book, in only a handful of cases was it difficult to decide where to put a player. I believe that anyone else, using the same system, would have classified most players the same way I did.

2. If you get out the first *Player Ratings Book* and look back at the classifications, you'll find that the vast majority of the players who went on to become stars were classified as Grade A prospects.

In last year's book there were about 30 players who were identified as Grade A prospects. That included both of the men who won the Rookie of the Year Award, Tim Salmon and Mike Piazza, and also included most of the other top candidates. The list also included Sam Militello and Brett Backlund, who did nothing. Can a Grade C prospect go on to become a major league star? Sure, it happens. It doesn't happen *a lot*, but it happens. But for every one who becomes a star, there's going to be 50 or 100 who disappear quicker than a greenhorn's wallet in Times Square.

The term "Grade D prospect" means that the indications about the player are *predominantly*, but not *overwhelmingly*, negative. The term Grade D prospect means that there is *something* here that you have to like. The only thing he's got is power, but gosh, he's got *real* power. Remember Rob Deer?

If I could identify young players who had a 100% chance to be major league stars, that would be great. I can't, and nobody else can. My guess is that a young player who is identified here as a Grade A prospect, like Alex Gonzalez or Javy Lopez, has probably a 40% chance to be a major league star, a 65% chance to be a good, solid regular (or better), and an 85% chance to be a major league regular of some stripe, at least for a few years. Those are just estimates, and that's for position players only.

A pitcher is a horse of a different color.

A Grade B prospect would have probably a 10 to 15 percent chance of becoming a major league star, a 40 to 50% chance of being a good player, and a 70% chance of being at least a marginal regular. Virtually all Grade A and Grade B prospects will at least play in the major leagues.

A Grade C prospect would have only a very slight chance of being a major league star, and perhaps a 50-50 chance of even playing regularly for a couple of years.

For a Grade D prospect to turn things around and become a major league star has probably happened, but it would be rare.

Those are for non-pitchers; for pitchers, everything is different. For a pitcher who is identified as a Grade A prospect, the probability that he will be a major league star, or superstar, or even a rotation starter, is dramatically lower. The reason for this is primarily injuries. *Whereas there are only a few young position players who have everything going their way, and almost all of those will go on to have good careers, there are many young pitchers who look tremendous, most of whom will hurt their arms before they finish their second major league season.* So the percentages for a top-line pitching prospect are much lower.

But on the other end, the Grade D prospects, the percentages for a pitcher are much *higher*. For a guy who can't hit to learn to hit is rare if the guy is 22, but it will happen. After age 25 it almost never happens. A *position player's level of ability very rarely takes a leap forward after the age of 25.*

But for a *pitcher* to make a great leap forward—that happens fairly regularly. I'm not talking about Alex Fernandez, who had great stuff all along and finally put it together. I'm talking about guys like Bob Tewksbury and Jeff Montgomery, who have had times in their careers when, to paraphrase Neil Young, any club in the world could have easily known them much better. If you wanted Bob Tewksbury five years ago, all you had to do was ask.

Pitchers, for many reasons, are *vastly* less predictable than position players; you really can't overstate that. Look at it this way: How many hitters in baseball history have won MVP Awards after their careers had bottomed out, after they had been released or been down so far that they were traded for basically nothing? I'm not sure that that has ever happened. If it has, I don't know about it.

But for a pitcher to win a Cy Young Award or even an MVP Award after his career appeared to be all but over—well, that's probably happened a dozen times. Mike Scott, John Denny, Steve Stone, Jim Perry, Mike McCormick, Jim Konstanty. Orel Hershiser was a Grade D prospect; the Dodgers offered him as a throw-in in several trades, and nobody took him. Look at the best pitchers around today, and you'll find that many of them have had periods in their career when nobody wanted them. So a pitcher who is a Grade D prospect has more value than a position player who is a Grade D prospect, just on the theory that you never know about a pitcher.

Another thing that I ought to explain here is how the two scales tie together, the dollar scale and the prospect scale. A Grade A prospect is worth, in general, $20 to $40, depending on three things:

a) Whether he is a pitcher or a position player. A shortstop who is a Grade A prospect is worth more than a pitcher with an equally impressive record.

b) Gradations of quality within the range described by the class.

c) Whether the player is ready to come to the major leagues right away.

A Grade B prospect is worth, in general, $10 to $25, depending on the same variables. A Grade C prospect is generally valued at anywhere up to $20, and a Grade D prospect is generally valued at $15 or less.

Another term that I will use a few hundred times, and ought to explain, is **secondary average.** Secondary average is a shorthand way of consolidating the *other* things that a hitter does, other than hit for average. The formula is Extra Bases on Hits, plus Walks, plus Stolen Bases, divided by At Bats.

The normal secondary average is about the same as the normal batting average, about .260. The National League batting average last year was .264; the secondary average was .249. The Phillies, who led the league in runs scored, hit .274 with a secondary average of .285. The Cubs hit for almost the same average (.270) but had a secondary average of .240—and thus scored 149 fewer runs.

If the book says that a player has hit .228 but has a secondary average of .389, this is just a somewhat more precise way of saying that even if he hits .228, the player will help his team score runs. If a player hits .300 but has a secondary average of .142, then he's *not* doing a lot to help the offense, despite his good batting average.

You will see hundreds of times in this book the term **MLE**, which stands for "Major League Equivalent." If a player hits .302 for Calgary, what is the equivalent major league batting average? It's .259.

If you're not familiar with the system, it would be a fool's errand for me to attempt to convince you that it works. It does work; MLEs match future major league performances just as well as past major league performances match future ones. But the only way to really convince you of that is to give it time, to let you see what Rondell White hits, compared to his MLE that I've given you here, and what Alan Zinter hits and what Midre Cummings hits, etc. When you see that the actual performance matches the MLE, then you'll be able to make your own decision.

I think those may be the only terms of my own invention that I used in this book; at any rate I can't think of any others. There's not a lot of jargon here. Occasionally I'll say something like "this player has an estimated 41% chance to get 3000 hits," which is based on a method I've explained in print many times before.

For some players, I will show the player's **projected 1994** batting stats. I make two claims for this system:

1) Sometimes it works, and
2) Sometimes it doesn't.

Here are a couple of the projections which appeared in this book last year, compared to what the player actually did:

MIKE GREENWELL

	G	AB	R	H	2B	3B	HR	RBI	BB	SB	AVG	OBP	SLG
PROJECTED LAST YR	146	543	71	162	30	4	13	77	54	10	.298	.362	.440
ACTUAL 1993 STATS	146	540	77	170	38	6	13	72	54	5	.315	.379	.480

GARY SHEFFIELD

	G	AB	R	H	2B	3B	HR	RBI	BB	SB	AVG	OBP	SLG
PROJECTED LAST YR	157	568	83	167	31	2	22	86	54	17	.294	.355	.472
ACTUAL 1993 STATS	140	494	67	145	20	5	20	73	47	17	.294	.361	.476

We're normally about that close, and if you believe that, you believe that the 1993 Tax Increase will cut into the National Debt. I also projected Andres Galarraga to hit .250 with 9 homers and 38 RBI, and projected that George Bell would drive in 98 runs.

I do these projections with John Dewan of STATS Inc.; we've run them for several years in another book, a reference book. We make no claims to being able to foresee the future. Essentially, we just project that a player will continue to do in the future something near the average of what he has done in the past, making adjustments for:

a) atypical performance in the recent past,
b) aging, and
c) maturity.

As a player matures, he adds power. As he ages, he loses speed. Sometimes we're right; sometimes we're wrong, and that's as much as I can say for the system.

There are no projections here for several groups of players—groups that, taken all together, could be described as "most of them." There are no projections for pitchers, because I don't know how to project pitchers stats, and also pitchers are unpredictable by nature. The are no projections for players who will probably spend most of the season in the minor leagues. There are no projections for players who have retired, and there are no projections for players in those cases when I simply don't trust the projection. In many cases, I'm going to know something about a player that the computer which creates the projections doesn't know. If that causes me to believe that the projection may be misleading, then it doesn't make sense for me to run the projection anyway.

When I have a projection, when that projection seems reasonable to me, then I'll run it. This leads into a general question, which is, how do I decide what information to run about each player?

What I try to do is choose the best available three lines of information about each player. For some players, we might have as many as nine lines of data to choose from. Those would include:

1991 Minor League Performance
1991 Major League Performance
1992 Minor League Performance
The 1992 MLE (Major League Equivalent)
1992 Major League Performance
1993 Minor League Performance
The 1993 MLE
1993 Major League Performance
Projected 1994 Major League Performance

Actually, there are more than that to choose from, because sometimes a player plays with two or three minor league teams in one season. Suppose that a player plays for both Jacksonville and Calgary. In that case, what shows above as one option is actually three: 1992 Jacksonville, 1992 Calgary, and 1992 combined minor league performance.

I tried to choose among those options, keeping this in mind:

1. This is not a reference book. If you want to know every stat in Jim Thome's minor league career, there are books for that. I can't do that here, so it's futile to try. I need to choose the three best lines to describe the players' major league skills.

2. Major league performance is preferred to minor league performance.

3. I don't like to run data in samples so small that they don't measure anything.

4. I don't run stats from A ball if there is any good alternative.

Well, I think that's it. Many of you, I suspect, are old friends, people who have been reading my books for years. I appreciate having you back. I've got another book coming out in a month or so, *The Politics of Glory*. It's about the Hall of Fame. Thanks for reading.

THE BILL JAMES PLAYER RATINGS BOOK 1994

PLAYERS

JIM ABBOTT

New York Yankees

Starting Pitcher

$28

The problems which plagued him last year are serious, which is not to say that they're irreversible. He's put on a lot of weight, and hardly resembles the trim young athlete of 1990. His strikeouts have slipped alarmingly over the last two years, while his control record has also gone a little bit in the wrong direction. The White Rat may have picked the right time to get rid of him.

YEAR	TEAM/LEVEL	G	IP	W-L	PCT.	HITS	SO	BB	ERA
1991	California	34	243	18-11	.621	222	158	73	2.89
1992	California	29	211	7-15	.318	200	130	68	2.77
1993	New York	32	214	11-14	.440	221	95	73	4.37

KURT ABBOTT

Oakland Athletics

Utility Player

$14

Another one of those shortstop/second baseman/outfielders that LaRussa has become so fond of in recent years, like Browne, Brosius, Bordick and Blankenship. He's 24 years old, and his play last year (see MLE) would suggest that he is capable of holding a major league job. Previous record was not nearly at the same level. Good speed, awful strikeout/walk ratios. Grade C prospect, no star potential.

YEAR	TEAM/LEVEL	G	AB	R	H	2B	3B	HR	RBI	BB	SB	AVG	OBP	SLG
1993	Tacoma AAA	133	480	75	153	36	11	12	79	33	19	.319	.363	.515
1993	MLE	133	450	56	123	28	6	8	59	24	14	.273	.310	.416
1993	Oakland	20	61	11	15	1	0	3	9	3	2	.246	.281	.410

KYLE ABBOTT

Philadelphia Phillies

Pitcher

$9

He's back where he was two years ago, only not quite. Abbott, a lefthander with fair stuff, was the Anthony Young of 1992, pitching just well enough to keep losing. He pitched all right for Scranton in '93, and might have earned a major league callup had the Phillies not been busy winning their division. There are worse pitchers around, but his next shot at a major league job probably won't be in the starting rotation. Grade D prospect.

YEAR	TEAM/LEVEL	G	IP	W-L	PCT.	HITS	SO	BB	ERA
1991	California	5	20	1-2	.333	22	12	13	4.58
1992	Philadelphia	31	133	1-14	.067	147	88	45	5.13
1993	Scranton AAA	27	173	12-10	.545	163	109	62	3.95

PAUL ABBOTT

Cleveland Indians

Righthanded Pitcher

$10

Power pitcher, has bounced up and down for the last three years; at times has pitched fairly well in the minors (never better than that) but has always been plagued by control trouble . . . Last year went 4-6 at Double- and Triple-A, but did strike out 98 men in 94 innings. . . . Has been prone to injuries, including shoulder separation and persistent shoulder strain. Weak Grade D prospect; almost no prospect.

YEAR	TEAM/LEVEL	G	IP	W-L	PCT.	HITS	SO	BB	ERA
1991	Minnesota	15	47	3-1	.750	38	43	36	4.75
1992	Minnesota	6	11	0-0	—	12	13	5	3.27
1993	Cleveland	5	18	0-1	.000	19	7	11	6.38

JUAN AGOSTO

Houston Astros

Lefthanded Spot Reliever

$4

There are a couple of indications in his record that he might have been miscast as a reliever—1, that he was more effective with the bases empty than with men on base, and 2, that he has been more effective after his first 15 pitches than he was when he first came into the game. He's 36 years old now, and his chance of having any more major league success is negligible.

YEAR	TEAM/LEVEL	G	IP	W-L	SAVES	HITS	SO	BB	ERA
1992	Two Teams	39	50	2-4	0	66	25	12	6.12
1993	Houston	6	6	0-0	0	8	3	0	6.00
1993	Two Teams AAA	51	51	7-3	3	66	33	29	5.29

RICK AGUILERA

Minnesota Twins

Closer

$52

Tom Kelly does a great job of keeping him within his workload limits, as a result of which he is one of the most consistent relievers in baseball. His save total dropped last year mostly because of the team's performance; Aguilera's performance was essentially the same as it has been for three years. Has a history of elbow problems, which will recur if he isn't carefully watched.

YEAR	TEAM/LEVEL	G	IP	W-L	SAVES	HITS	SO	BB	ERA
1991	Minnesota	63	69	4-5	42	44	61	30	2.35
1992	Minnesota	64	67	2-6	41	60	52	17	2.84
1993	Minnesota	65	72	4-3	34	60	59	14	3.11

SCOTT ALDRED

Montreal Expos

Pitcher of sorts

$5

A hard-throwing lefthander who knows as much about pitching as a giraffe knows about NAFTA. Aldred went on the disabled list in early May with tendonitis in his left elbow, and never came back. He has never been an effective pitcher even in the minor leagues, but at 25 it is still too early to say for sure that he won't come around some day.

YEAR	TEAM/LEVEL	G	IP	W-L	PCT.	HITS	SO	BB	ERA
1992	Toledo AAA	16	86	4-6	.400	92	81	47	5.13
1992	Detroit	16	65	3-8	.273	80	34	33	6.78
1993	Two Teams	8	12	1-0	1.000	19	9	10	9.00

MIKE (ALRIGHT) ALDRETE

Oakland Athletics

First Base

$19

Aldrete, who hit .325 in 126 games for San Francisco in 1987, had slipped back to the minors, where he was pounding the bejeezus out of the ball early in the year, when Mark McGwire went down with an injury, creating an opening for him. Lefthanded line drive hitter, not a .300 hitter but if there's a job in the majors for Cory Snyder, I'd sure as hell hope there was a job somewhere for Aldrete.

YEAR	TEAM/LEVEL	G	AB	R	H	2B	3B	HR	RBI	BB	SB	AVG	OBP	SLG
1992	Col. Sp. AAA	128	463	69	149	42	2	8	84	65	1	.322	.406	.473
1993	Tacoma AAA	37	122	20	39	11	2	7	21	26	2	.320	.439	.615
1993	Oakland	95	255	40	68	13	1	10	33	34	1	.267	.353	.443

MANNY ALEXANDER

Baltimore Orioles

Shortstop Prospect

$9

A shortstop from San Pedro de Macoris, defensively is probably ready for a major league job, but his bat still has some miles to go before he can push Ripken aside. He's only 23, so has time. Ripken, Reynolds and Pagliarulo were all born in 1960, so there should be an opening in the Oriole infield before too long. Grade C prospect; could become regular, but more likely to be a spear carrier.

YEAR	TEAM/LEVEL	G	AB	R	H	2B	3B	HR	RBI	BB	SB	AVG	OBP	SLG
1992	MLE	133	503	59	116	19	5	1	35	17	30	.231	.256	.294
1993	Rochestr AAA	120	471	55	115	23	8	6	51	22	19	.244	.283	.365
1993	MLE	120	454	43	98	19	5	4	40	17	13	.216	.244	.306

LUIS ALICEA

St. Louis Cardinals

Second Base

$22

Hit over .300 most of the year, but slipped at the end and reached October still locked in a battle for the second base job. I think he could be a very good second baseman. He's a switch hitter who runs well and won't chase bad pitches, witness the .362 on-base percentage, plus his range at second is among the best in the league. But he's 28, too old to be a prospect, and he's still fighting for the job.

YEAR	TEAM/LEVEL	G	AB	R	H	2B	3B	HR	RBI	BB	SB	AVG	OBP	SLG
1991	St. Louis	56	68	5	13	3	0	0	0	8	0	.191	.276	.235
1992	St. Louis	85	265	26	65	9	11	2	32	27	2	.245	.320	.385
1993	St. Louis	115	362	50	101	19	3	3	46	47	11	.279	.362	.373

ANDY ALLANSON

San Francisco Giants

Catcher

$6

Now 32 years old, just trying to build up his pension time. He's a righthanded hitter, a big guy but runs well for a catcher. He spent about two months on the Giants' roster in '93, despite the limited playing time. If you're going to use your backup catcher so little, it probably isn't a bad idea to move him up and down, give him some Triple-A playing time to keep him sharp.

YEAR	TEAM/LEVEL	G	AB	R	H	2B	3B	HR	RBI	BB	SB	AVG	OBP	SLG
1992	Milwaukee	9	25	6	8	1	0	0	0	1	3	.320	.346	.360
1993	Phoenix AAA	50	161	31	57	15	2	6	23	10	7	.354	.391	.584
1993	San Francisco	13	24	3	4	1	0	0	2	1	0	.167	.200	.208

ROBERTO ALOMAR

Toronto Blue Jays

Second Base

$92

He has accomplished so much already that it is difficult to remember that he is only 26, and the shape of his career is still to be determined. He's one of the most balanced hitters in baseball—hits for average **and** power **and** steals 50 bases a year **and** draws 80 walks a year **and** hits from both sides of the plate. His possibilities are endless—could get 4,000 hits or 400 homers or steal a thousand bases.

YEAR	TEAM/LEVEL	G	AB	R	H	2B	3B	HR	RBI	BB	SB	AVG	OBP	SLG
1992	Toronto	152	571	105	177	27	8	8	76	87	49	.310	.405	.427
1993	Toronto	153	589	109	192	35	6	17	93	80	55	.326	.408	.492
1994	**Projected**	**155**	**597**	**100**	**186**	**31**	**6**	**15**	**78**	**78**	**56**	**.312**	**.391**	**.459**

SANDY ALOMAR JR.

Cleveland Indians

Catcher

$22

The first thing you notice when you see him is that he's not built like a catcher. The first thing you notice in his record is that he's had three straight seasons of less than 300 at bats, because of injuries. This suggests that the traditional image of a catcher—a short, blocky guy with good padding—may have a solid basis in received wisdom. Alomar is a fine athlete, but as a catcher, just another player.

YEAR	TEAM/LEVEL	G	AB	R	H	2B	3B	HR	RBI	BB	SB	AVG	OBP	SLG
1992	Cleveland	89	299	22	75	16	0	2	26	13	3	.251	.293	.324
1993	Cleveland	64	215	24	58	7	1	6	32	11	3	.270	.318	.395
1994	**Projected**	**95**	**312**	**28**	**83**	**17**	**1**	**5**	**35**	**16**	**3**	**.266**	**.302**	**.375**

MOISES ALOU

Montreal Expos

Left Field

$38

He played somewhat better than I had projected for him in '93. I still don't see any reason to expect him to develop into a star. He's a Gary Matthews-type player—a little power, a little speed, can hit .280 to .300, can help a team win if they get enough guys around him having good years . . . The Alou family now has 5,332 hits among the four of them. I believe the Waners still hold the record.

YEAR	TEAM/LEVEL	G	AB	R	H	2B	3B	HR	RBI	BB	SB	AVG	OBP	SLG
1992	Montreal	115	341	53	96	28	2	9	56	25	16	.282	.328	.455
1993	Montreal	136	482	70	138	29	6	18	85	38	17	.286	.340	.483
1994	**Projected**	**146**	**529**	**75**	**148**	**27**	**4**	**15**	**81**	**43**	**22**	**.280**	**.334**	**.435**

TAVO ALVAREZ

Montreal Expos

Starting Pitcher

$9

A Grade A prospect a year ago, had a tough season at Ottawa, and would have to be significantly downgraded. I described him last year as a Mexican Bret Saberhagen—changes speeds, moves the ball in and out, seems to have been born knowing how to pitch. He's 22 years old. I suspect he will snap back from whatever was bothering him last year, and re-emerge as a prospect.

YEAR	TEAM/LEVEL	G	IP	W-L	PCT.	HITS	SO	BB	ERA
1992	West Palm Bea A	19	139	13-4	.765	124	83	24	1.49
1992	Harrisburg AA	7	47	4-1	.800	48	42	9	2.85
1993	Ottawa AAA	25	141	7-10	.412	163	77	55	4.22

WILSON ALVAREZ

Chicago White Sox

Starting Pitcher

$44

He wasn't having a great year in '93 until he went 5-0 with a 0.93 ERA in September. Anyone who has ever seen Alvarez pitch knows that his upside potential is unlimited: he could become the best pitcher in baseball—but he won't win consistently unless his control gets better than it was in '93 . . . Throws hard, and throws one of the best curveballs in baseball.

YEAR	TEAM/LEVEL	G	IP	W-L	PCT.	HITS	SO	BB	ERA
1991	Chicago	10	56	3-2	.600	47	32	29	3.51
1992	Chicago	34	100	5-3	.625	103	66	65	5.20
1993	Chicago	31	208	15-8	.652	168	155	122	2.95

RICH AMARAL

Seattle Mariners

Infielder

$23

One of the few utility infielders who can play a key offensive role. Most backup infielders are good glove/no hit guys who can also run; Amaral is a better hitter than most regular middle infielders and can also steal bases, but his glovework kept him out of a job until last year. His .290 average last year isn't a fluke, and he could have better years . . . Hit .372 against lefthanded pitchers, best in the major leagues.

YEAR	TEAM/LEVEL	G	AB	R	H	2B	3B	HR	RBI	BB	SB	AVG	OBP	SLG
1992	Seattle	35	100	9	24	3	0	1	7	5	4	.240	.276	.300
1993	Seattle	110	373	53	108	24	1	1	44	33	19	.290	.348	.367
1994	**Projected**	**78**	**244**	**34**	**67**	**15**	**1**	**1**	**19**	**25**	**15**	**.275**	**.342**	**.357**

RUBEN AMARO

Philadelphia Phillies

Utilityman

$14

A much better hitter than his .219 average in 1992 would lead people to believe, but is now 29 and has no clear role on a major league roster. Good defensive outfielder and good base runner, but doesn't hit enough to be the kind of fourth outfielder/pinch hitter that managers like to have available. Will probably continue to bounce up and down for several more years.

YEAR	TEAM/LEVEL	G	AB	R	H	2B	3B	HR	RBI	BB	SB	AVG	OBP	SLG
1992	Philadelphia	126	374	43	82	15	6	7	34	37	11	.219	.303	.348
1993	Scranton AAA	101	412	76	120	30	5	9	37	31	25	.291	.346	.454
1993	Philadelphia	25	48	7	16	2	2	1	6	6	0	.333	.400	.521

LARRY ANDERSEN

Philadelphia Phillies

Relief Pitcher

$26

The only 40-year-old pitcher I've ever seen who kicks his leg like a Radio City Rockette. He's still essentially a power pitcher, throws a hard slider 90% of the time; appears to be in great shape (which really stands out on the Phillies). I expect him to be effective for three or four more years, until elbow injuries take so much of his season that he just decides it's time to quit.

YEAR	TEAM/LEVEL	G	IP	W-L	SAVES	HITS	SO	BB	ERA
1991	San Diego	38	47	3-4	13	39	40	13	2.30
1992	San Diego	34	35	1-1	2	26	35	8	3.34
1993	Philadelphia	64	62	3-2	0	54	67	21	2.92

BRADY ANDERSON

Baltimore Orioles

Left Field

$45

What he did in 1993 is, in my opinion, a fair representation of his skills. Not a big star, but with a .363 on-base percentage, 57 extra-base hits, some stolen bases and good defense in left, he's the kind of multi-faceted player who wins championships. Now 30 years old, but probably won't lose his drive after just two years as a regular.

YEAR	TEAM/LEVEL	G	AB	R	H	2B	3B	HR	RBI	BB	SB	AVG	OBP	SLG
1992	Baltimore	159	623	100	169	28	10	21	80	98	53	.271	.373	.449
1993	Baltimore	142	560	87	147	36	8	13	66	82	24	.263	.363	.425
1994	**Projected**	**151**	**563**	**85**	**150**	**25**	**7**	**12**	**62**	**91**	**37**	**.266**	**.392**	**.400**

BRIAN ANDERSON

California Angels

Starting Pitcher

$22

A 22-year-old lefty, the Angels first-round pick in 1993, third overall, from Wright State University. Considered to be intelligent, throws hard, has exceptional control of four pitches . . . Walked six and struck out 110 in 93 college innings. Called up in September as part of his signing agreement. Hard to evaluate with little pro experience, but has good credentials.

YEAR	TEAM/LEVEL	G	IP	W-L	PCT.	HITS	SO	BB	ERA
1993	Midland AA	2	11	0-1	.000	16	9	0	3.38
1993	Vancouver AAA	2	8	0-1	.000	13	2	6	12.31
1993	California	4	11	0-0	—	11	4	2	3.97

MIKE ANDERSON

Cincinnati Reds

Pitching Prospect

$12

Minor league veteran, turns 28 in July. Signed by the Reds as a free agent in 1988, earned a major league look after minor league career record of 58-35, good strikeout/walk ratios and exceptional durability and consistency. He's 6-3, 200 pounds, but one can assume from the fact that he wasn't drafted and has made slow progress that he doesn't throw hard. There are worse pitchers with jobs, and Johnson may find a role for him.

YEAR	TEAM/LEVEL	G	IP	W-L	PCT.	HITS	SO	BB	ERA
1992	Chattanoga AA	28	172	13-7	.650	155	149	61	2.52
1993	AA and AAA	25	166	11-7	.611	160	125	57	3.52
1993	Cincinnati	3	5	0-0	—	12	4	3	18.56

SHANE ANDREWS

Montreal Expos

Third Base

$11

The Expos' first pick in the 1990 draft, from a New Mexico high school, so he's only 21 now. He's been overshadowed by more polished Expo prospects, but his hitting appears to be getting there. Big and strong, has had problems with weight, defense and strikeouts, but made substantial progress in AA at age 21. Probably will spend '94 at Ottawa, come to the majors in '95.

YEAR	TEAM/LEVEL	G	AB	R	H	2B	3B	HR	RBI	BB	SB	AVG	OBP	SLG
1992	Albany A	136	453	76	104	18	1	25	87	107	8	.230	.382	.439
1993	Harrisb AA	124	442	77	115	29	1	18	70	64	10	.260	.352	.452
1993	MLE	124	427	62	100	27	0	13	56	44	7	.234	.306	.389

ERIC ANTHONY

Houston Astros

Right Field

$29

Eric's enormously strong, and still capable of breaking loose with a 30-homer season. He's cut his strikeouts the last two years (only 88 strikeouts in '93), but he's done that by flattening out his swing, so he's hitting the ball on the ground (205 ground ball outs in 486 at bats), and frankly he's never going to make it big hitting ground balls. He's only 26, just entering his prime.

YEAR	TEAM/LEVEL	G	AB	R	H	2B	3B	HR	RBI	BB	SB	AVG	OBP	SLG
1992	Houston	137	440	45	105	15	1	19	80	38	5	.239	.298	.407
1993	Houston	145	486	70	121	19	4	15	66	49	3	.249	.319	.397
1994	Projected	144	480	61	123	20	2	17	71	43	6	.256	.317	.413

KEVIN APPIER

Kansas City Royals

Starting Pitcher

$83

Probably the best starting pitcher in the American League, if Clemens isn't 100%. He was second in the league in ERA in '92 (just behind Clemens) and led by a comfortable margin last year . . . Every year he changes. He vaults off the mound, and used to be vulnerable to the running game, but isn't now. Throws a running fastball; righthanders hit .184 against him last year. Gets more ground balls than fly balls.

YEAR	TEAM/LEVEL	G	IP	W-L	PCT.	HITS	SO	BB	ERA
1991	Kansas City	34	208	13-10	.565	205	158	61	3.42
1992	Kansas City	30	208	15-8	.652	167	150	68	2.46
1993	Kansas City	34	239	18-8	.692	183	186	81	2.56

TONY AQUINO

Florida Marlins

Pitcher

$17

Oddly consistent for a pitcher with no defined role, has moved back and forth between bullpen and starting assignments for six years, but has had 3.50 or better ERA in five of the six . . . Made 13 starts last year with a 3.36 ERA, was pushed out of the rotation by a minor injury and couldn't get back in when he was healthy. That's happened to him many times.

YEAR	TEAM/LEVEL	G	IP	W-L	PCT.	HITS	SO	BB	ERA
1991	Kansas City	38	157	8-4	.667	152	80	47	3.44
1992	Kansas City	15	68	3-6	.333	81	11	20	4.52
1993	Florida	38	111	6-8	.429	115	67	40	3.42

ALEX ARIAS

Florida Marlins

Infielder

$23

Started 29 games at second base, 18 at third base, 13 at shortstop. He played well and probably will continue to, but since Florida has good young players at all three positions (Barberie, Weiss and Sheffield), we can't foresee his developing into a regular. Should be one of the league's best backup infielders, and since all three regulars have injury histories, will probably bat 300-400 times.

YEAR	TEAM/LEVEL	G	AB	R	H	2B	3B	HR	RBI	BB	SB	AVG	OBP	SLG
1992	Chicago	32	99	14	29	6	0	0	7	11	0	.293	.375	.354
1993	Florida	96	249	27	67	5	1	2	20	27	1	.269	.344	.321
1994	**Projected**	**97**	**312**	**35**	**82**	**13**	**1**	**3**	**26**	**27**	**6**	**.263**	**.322**	**.340**

MARCOS ARMAS

Oakland Athletics

First Base

$8

Tony Armas's younger brother, Marcos was signed as a free agent out of Venezuela in 1987, fought various injuries until 1992. He is a similar player to his brother but not as good . . . Poor plate discipline, limited power, can't play the outfield. Grade D prospect; may spend the season in the minors if McGwire is healthy. Might hit better than MLEs show if he winds up with another team.

YEAR	TEAM/LEVEL	G	AB	R	H	2B	3B	HR	RBI	BB	SB	AVG	OBP	SLG
1992	MLE	132	488	70	123	25	3	12	72	29	7	.252	.294	.389
1993	MLE	117	409	52	101	21	4	10	67	26	3	.247	.292	.391
1993	Oakland	15	31	7	6	2	0	1	1	1	1	.194	.242	.355

JACK ARMSTRONG

Florida Marlins

Starting Pitcher

$19

One can't help but wonder about the record for consecutive seasons with a winning percentage around .350. He's 22-45 over the last three years, which qualifies him as the Losing Pitcher Mulcahy of the nineties. I'm sure his teams bear much of the responsibility for that, but he gave up 29 homers last year in a fair park, and your teammates can't help you when you do that.

YEAR	TEAM/LEVEL	G	IP	W-L	PCT.	HITS	SO	BB	ERA
1991	Cincinnati	27	140	7-13	.350	158	93	54	5.48
1992	Cleveland	35	167	6-15	.286	176	114	67	4.64
1993	Florida	36	196	9-17	.346	210	118	78	4.49

RENE AROCHA

St. Louis Cardinals

Starting Pitcher

$36

Ground ball pitcher . . . The attention given to Bob Tewksbury's control has overshadowed the rest of the staff, but Arocha and Cormier also have extremely fine control records. Arocha walked only 1.48 men per nine innings, a remarkable ratio for a rookie . . . Did not pitch well late in the year, but I'm high on him if he's healthy. He should win 14-17 games consistently for the next several years.

YEAR	TEAM/LEVEL	G	IP	W-L	PCT.	HITS	SO	BB	ERA
1991	(Not in Organized Baseball)								
1992	Louisville AAA	25	167	12-7	.632	145	128	67	2.70
1993	St. Louis	32	188	11-8	.579	197	96	31	3.78

ANDY ASHBY

San Diego Padres

Starting Pitcher

$9

He's in the major leagues because a) he has a good fastball, and b) some teams evaluate players not by what they can do, but by their "tools." His record in the minor leagues was 43-53, which should have given a pretty good indication that he wasn't going to be able to hold a rotation spot in the majors, but he throws hard, so people are determined to keep trying.

YEAR	TEAM/LEVEL	G	IP	W-L	PCT.	HITS	SO	BB	ERA
1992	Philadelphia	10	37	1-3	.250	42	24	21	7.54
1993	Col. Springs AAA	7	42	4-2	.667	45	35	12	4.10
1993	Two Teams	32	123	3-10	.231	168	77	56	6.80

BILLY ASHLEY

Los Angeles Dodgers

Outfielder

$9

A Frank Howard-, Dave Kingman-type player—tall, strong, righthanded batter with a sweeping swing; Eddie Epstein says he's just a tall Cory Snyder. He will probably strike out so much that his average will be below .240, with very few walks. He has no speed, isn't a good outfielder despite a strong arm, and I don't believe he will hit enough home runs to hold a roster spot, at least yet.

YEAR	TEAM/LEVEL	G	AB	R	H	2B	3B	HR	RBI	BB	SB	AVG	OBP	SLG
1993	Albuquer AAA	125	482	88	143	31	4	26	100	35	6	.297	.344	.539
1993	MLE	125	445	52	106	21	1	15	59	21	3	.238	.273	.391
1993	Los Angeles	14	37	0	9	0	0	0	0	2	0	.243	.282	.243

PAUL ASSENMACHER

New York Yankees

Relief Pitcher

$28

He remains, as he has always been, an underrated player. People don't take him seriously because he's ugly, looks sloppy on the mound and doesn't throw 90, but he's never been easy to hit. He uses a fastball early in the count, then uses his best pitch, which is an overhand curve. Doesn't walk many, doesn't give up many homers, gets a good many ground balls.

YEAR	TEAM/LEVEL	G	IP	W-L	SAVES	HITS	SO	BB	ERA
1991	Chicago NL	75	103	7-8	15	85	117	31	3.24
1992	Chicago NL	70	68	4-4	8	72	67	26	4.10
1993	Two Teams	72	56	4-3	0	54	45	22	3.38

PEDRO ASTACIO

Los Angeles Dodgers

Starting Pitcher

$40

He struggled some in the first half of '93, but pitched brilliantly over the second half (2.44 ERA, 72 strikeouts in 92 innings), and may be ready to emerge as the Dodgers' ace. He embodies most of the things you look for in a young pitcher—a power pitcher working in a pitcher's park, whose arm was not abused at an early age. Should be entering a fine period.

YEAR	TEAM/LEVEL	G	IP	W-L	PCT.	HITS	SO	BB	ERA
1992	Albuquerque AAA	24	99	6-6	.500	115	66	44	5.47
1992	Los Angeles	11	82	5-5	.500	80	43	20	1.98
1993	Los Angeles	31	186	14-9	.609	165	122	68	3.57

RICH AUDE

Pittsburgh Pirates

First Base

$14

A huge righthanded hitter who would like to be the Pirates' new first baseman. Despite his size (220 pounds listed) his power is limited, although that may develop as he ages (he's 22). He's already played 524 minor league games, but only 21 games at Triple-A . . . His defense needs work. He probably will spend 1994 in the minor leagues, but shouldn't be over-matched as a hitter if he does happen to get a job.

YEAR	TEAM/LEVEL	G	AB	R	H	2B	3B	HR	RBI	BB	SB	AVG	OBP	SLG
1993	Carolina AA	120	422	66	122	25	3	18	73	50	8	.289	.376	.491
1993	MLE	141	465	66	125	29	2	15	71	41	5	.269	.328	.437
1993	Pittsburgh	13	26	1	3	1	0	0	4	1	0	.115	.148	.154

BRAD AUSMUS

San Diego Padres

Catcher

$21

Ausmus was in the Yankees system, taken by Colorado in the expansion draft and traded to San Diego as part of the Harris deal. He had hit only eight home runs in six years in the minors, so his five homers in 49 games with San Diego were a surprise, or a fluke, depending on how you look at it. Ausmus does not have star potential, but is probably ready to play in the major leagues.

YEAR	TEAM/LEVEL	G	AB	R	H	2B	3B	HR	RBI	BB	SB	AVG	OBP	SLG
1993	MLE	76	228	21	52	8	2	1	23	18	6	.228	.285	.294
1993	San Diego	49	160	18	41	8	1	5	12	6	2	.256	.283	.412
1994	**Projected**	**101**	**300**	**34**	**71**	**11**	**1**	**7**	**34**	**25**	**11**	**.237**	**.295**	**.350**

JIM AUSTIN

Milwaukee Brewers

Relief Pitcher

$13

Righthanded middle reliever, 30 years old, was sent to New Orleans in July although he had pitched fairly well. Has had a chronic problem with his neck . . . Will never move into a key role, but if he's healthy should be on the major league roster in '94 . . . Good fielder, has extremely good move to first base. He has allowed only two stolen bases in his major league career (seven attempts).

YEAR	TEAM/LEVEL	G	IP	W-L	SAVES	HITS	SO	BB	ERA
1991	Milwaukee	5	9	0-0	0	8	3	11	8.31
1992	Milwaukee	47	58	5-2	0	38	30	32	1.85
1993	Milwaukee	31	33	1-2	0	28	15	13	3.82

STEVE AVERY

Atlanta Braves

Starting Pitcher

$66

He improved his control last year, which made 1993 his best major league season so far. You probably know as much about him as I do, since he's on the tube every October—throws hard, throws strikes, only weakness is that you can run on him . . . My guess is that he is in his prime now, and won't be as effective when he reaches 28.

YEAR	TEAM/LEVEL	G	IP	W-L	PCT.	HITS	SO	BB	ERA
1991	Atlanta	35	210	18-8	.692	189	137	65	3.38
1992	Atlanta	35	234	11-11	.500	216	129	71	3.20
1993	Atlanta	35	223	18-6	.750	216	125	43	2.94

BOBBY AYALA

Seattle Mariners

Pitcher

$23

Ayala spent most of the year in the bullpen, and was modestly effective there, but moved into the starting rotation in early August, and was beaten severely about the head and shoulders over the last two months (8.41 ERA in nine starts). He's 27 years old, will be 28 in April, righthander, but obviously Piniella knows something about him, or thinks he does, and intends to give him a key role.

YEAR	TEAM/LEVEL	G	IP	W-L	PCT.	HITS	SO	BB	ERA
1992	Cincinnati	5	29	2-1	.667	33	23	13	4.34
1993	Indianapolis AAA	5	27	0-2	.000	36	19	12	5.67
1993	Cincinnati	43	98	7-10	.412	106	65	45	5.60

BOB AYRAULT

Los Angeles Dodgers

Righthanded Relief Pitcher

$10

A survivor, a non-prospect who signed with an independant team several years ago, moved into the Phillies system, drifted slowly to the top, and earns occasional major league looks when everybody else around has had their shot. He pitched fairly well with the Mariners in mid-summer (June and July), but they sent him out anyway. He refused assignment, and wound up at Albuquerque. There probably aren't millions of dollars in his future.

YEAR	TEAM/LEVEL	G	IP	W-L	SAVES	HITS	SO	BB	ERA
1993	Philadelphia	10	10	2-0	0	18	8	10	9.58
1993	Seattle	14	20	1-1	0	18	7	6	3.20
1993	Albuquerque AAA	14	19	2-2	1	29	16	9	7.11

JEFF FASSERO

Montreal Expos

Lefthanded Pitcher

$30

Fassero is now a starting pitcher. Given up on by the Cardinals, White Sox and Indians, he signed with Montreal as a minor league free agent, and was a pleasant surprise in '91 and '92. Tried as a starter in mid-'93, he was brilliant, going 7-4 with a 2.29 ERA in 94 innings. Throws a fastball, slider and forkball; a fine pitcher, but we'll have to see if his arm will hold up to 200 innings.

YEAR	TEAM/LEVEL	G	IP	W-L	SAVES	HITS	SO	BB	ERA
1991	Montreal	51	55	2-5	8	39	42	17	2.44
1992	Montreal	70	86	8-7	1	81	63	34	2.84
1993	Montreal	56	150	12-5	1	119	140	54	2.29

MIKE FELDER

Seattle Mariners

Outfield

$23

Felder signed with Seattle as a free agent, and opened the season as their regular left fielder, in which role he was a miserable failure (surprise, surprise, isn't this like the fourth time we've learned this?) Felder, a switch hitter, could be compared to Brett Butler or Otis Nixon, and is a good man off the bench, but hasn't been able to keep his average above .250 when he's been put in the lineup every day.

YEAR	TEAM/LEVEL	G	AB	R	H	2B	3B	HR	RBI	BB	SB	AVG	OBP	SLG
1992	San Francisco	145	322	44	92	13	3	4	23	21	14	.286	.330	.382
1993	Seattle	109	342	31	72	7	5	1	20	22	15	.211	.262	.269
1994	**Projected**	**96**	**233**	**27**	**57**	**6**	**2**	**2**	**13**	**17**	**11**	**.245**	**.296**	**.313**

JUNIOR FELIX

Exiled

Center Field

$15

Bothered by a groin pull early in the year, Felix was sent to the minors a couple of times and didn't report the second time, leaving him with a murky future. Felix's listed age, 26, is believed to be a fiction, and his skills seem to slip another step backward every season. His health record is poor, and his attitude is the subject of frequent conversations, but it would be a mistake to *entirely* write him off.

YEAR	TEAM/LEVEL	G	AB	R	H	2B	3B	HR	RBI	BB	SB	AVG	OBP	SLG
1991	California	66	230	32	65	10	2	2	26	11	7	.283	.321	.370
1992	California	139	509	63	125	22	5	9	72	33	8	.246	.289	.361
1993	Florida	57	214	25	51	11	1	7	22	10	2	.238	.276	.397

FELIX FERMIN

Cleveland Indians

Shortstop

$24

Saw only 3.07 pitches per plate appearance, the lowest of any American League regular. Also put the ball in play 61% of the time when he swung, highest in the American League . . . Led American League in errors, with 23, was last in fielding percentage for a regular shortstop (.960) . . . His secondary average, .102, was the lowest of any major league regular, by far.

YEAR	TEAM/LEVEL	G	AB	R	H	2B	3B	HR	RBI	BB	SB	AVG	OBP	SLG
1992	Cleveland	79	58	27	58	7	2	0	13	18	0	.270	.326	.321
1993	Cleveland	140	480	48	126	16	2	2	45	24	4	.263	.303	.317
1994	**Projected**	**127**	**406**	**37**	**103**	**10**	**2**	**1**	**32**	**26**	**4**	**.254**	**.299**	**.296**

ALEX FERNANDEZ

Chicago White Sox
Starting Pitcher
$56

Handled 56 chances without an error, best in the American League . . . A powerfully built righthander with outstanding stuff, has been compared to Tom Seaver every day since he was an amateur, and finally delivered the goods in '93. He's piled up quite a few innings on an immature arm, but if he stays healthy there is every reason to assume that he'll win 150-170 games in the next 10 years.

YEAR	TEAM/LEVEL	G	IP	W-L	PCT.	HITS	SO	BB	ERA
1991	Chicago	34	192	9-13	.409	186	145	88	4.51
1992	Chicago	29	188	8-11	.421	199	95	50	4.27
1993	Chicago	34	247	18-9	.667	221	169	67	3.13

SID FERNANDEZ

New York Mets
(Free Agent)
Starting Pitcher
$28

A one-of-a-kind pitcher, an archetype, usually at the top or bottom of any list. Fernandez is an awfully good pitcher and is only 31 years old, but has trouble controlling his weight and has had serious knee injuries in 1991 and 1993. If he is not in Shea Stadium in '93 his strikeouts will decrease and his ERA will increase, but his won-lost record may improve. His durability will remain questionable.

YEAR	TEAM/LEVEL	G	IP	W-L	PCT.	HITS	SO	BB	ERA
1991	New York	8	44	1-3	.250	36	31	9	2.86
1992	New York	32	215	14-11	.560	162	193	67	2.73
1993	New York	18	120	5-6	.455	82	81	36	2.93

TONY FERNANDEZ

Toronto Blue Jays
Shortstop
$40

It is assumed at this writing that Fernandez will leave the Blue Jays for greener bank accounts, leaving Alex Gonzalez to play short for Toronto. It seems odd to describe Fernandez as "consistent" (Fernandez?), but he has hit .276, .272, .275 and .279 over the last four years, with on-base percentages grouped between .337 and .352 and slugging percentages between .359 and .394.

YEAR	TEAM/LEVEL	G	AB	R	H	2B	3B	HR	RBI	BB	SB	AVG	OBP	SLG
1992	San Diego	155	622	84	171	32	4	4	37	56	20	.275	.337	.359
1993	Two Teams	142	526	65	147	23	11	5	64	56	21	.279	.348	.394
1994	**Projected**	**146**	**563**	**74**	**152**	**27**	**5**	**5**	**45**	**56**	**21**	**.270**	**.336**	**.362**

MIKE FETTERS

Milwaukee Brewers
Relief Pitcher
$24

After a fine year in '92 he had a pulled groin muscle early last year, and didn't hit his stride until August. A first-round draft pick of the Angels in 1986, he was a starting pitcher in the minors, and might yet emerge as a starter in the majors. Standard repertoire—fastball/curve/slider; will be at least fairly effective if he is healthy.

YEAR	TEAM/LEVEL	G	IP	W-L	SAVES	HITS	SO	BB	ERA
1991	California	19	45	2-5	0	53	24	28	4.84
1992	Milwaukee	50	63	5-1	2	38	43	24	1.87
1993	Milwaukee	45	59	3-3	0	59	23	22	3.34

CECIL FIELDER
Detroit Tigers
First Base
$53

Has not hit a triple or stolen a base for three years, which I believe is unprecedented for a player playing this much. Also took extra bases (such as going first-to-third on a single or scoring from first on a double) only 12 times in 1993, the lowest percentage in the American League . . . There's a place for him on a baseball team, but he's basically a big fat guy who hits home runs.

YEAR	TEAM/LEVEL	G	AB	R	H	2B	3B	HR	RBI	BB	SB	AVG	OBP	SLG
1992	Detroit	155	594	80	145	22	0	35	124	73	0	.244	.325	.458
1993	Detroit	154	573	80	153	23	0	30	117	90	0	.267	.368	.464
1994	**Projected**	**156**	**593**	**87**	**152**	**21**	**0**	**36**	**120**	**84**	**0**	**.256**	**.349**	**.474**

CHUCK FINLEY
California Angels
Starting Pitcher
$55

A fine pitcher, snapped back after losing 1992 to a toe injury. Throws hard and mixes up five pitches without getting any of them in the red zone too often. He does have some trouble holding runners, although he is a lefty. Led American League in complete games . . . Now 31, he is fourth on the Angels' all-time pitching lists, behind Ryan, Tanana and Mike Witt. Has won 16 or more in four of the last five years.

YEAR	TEAM/LEVEL	G	IP	W-L	PCT.	HITS	SO	BB	ERA
1991	California	34	227	18-9	.667	205	171	101	3.80
1992	California	31	204	7-12	.368	212	124	98	3.96
1993	California	35	251	16-14	.533	243	187	82	3.15

STEVE FINLEY
Houston Astros
Center Field
$40

Finley had a broken wrist in late April, came back quickly but didn't start to play the way he is capable of playing until about July 1. A Brett Butler-type player, hits the ball harder than Butler, doesn't bunt as much or walk as much, but fast, durable, a good center fielder and a pretty good base stealer. Led National League in triples, with 13.

YEAR	TEAM/LEVEL	G	AB	R	H	2B	3B	HR	RBI	BB	SB	AVG	OBP	SLG
1992	Houston	162	607	84	177	29	13	5	55	58	44	.292	.355	.407
1993	Houston	142	545	69	145	15	13	8	44	28	19	.266	.304	.385
1994	**Projected**	**152**	**573**	**75**	**156**	**21**	**8**	**7**	**49**	**44**	**33**	**.272**	**.324**	**.373**

GAR FINNVOLD
Boston Red Sox
Starting Pitcher
$15

A 6-foot-5 inch righthander, the Red Sox sixth-round pick in 1990 out of Florida State, where he was an Academic All-American. Good health record. Has put in decent seasons at AA and AAA the last two years, although stuck with ugly won-lost records. Throws fastball in mid-80's, good breaking stuff . . . Grade C prospect, could emerge as fourth starter or long reliever in majors.

YEAR	TEAM/LEVEL	G	IP	W-L	PCT.	HITS	SO	BB	ERA
1991	New Britain AA	16	101	5-8	.385	97	80	36	3.82
1992	New Britain AA	25	165	7-13	.350	156	135	52	3.49
1993	Pawtucket AAA	24	136	5-9	.357	128	123	51	3.77

CARLTON FISK
Released
Catcher
No Value

The third sure Hall of Famer to retire in '93 . . . Did you see that incredibly stupid *Frontline* show last spring? The whole argument of the piece was that the game of baseball was in terrible trouble because Carlton Fisk couldn't get along with the White Sox management . . . Most-similar players in history: Bench and Berra. The chart below compares the career performance of Bench, Berra and Fisk per 150 games played.

	AB	R	H	2B	3B	HR	RBI	BB	SB	AVG	OBP	SLG
Bench per 150 games	532	76	142	26	2	27	96	62	5	.267	.345	.476
Fisk per 150 games	526	77	141	25	3	23	80	51	8	.269	.341	.457
Berra per 150 games	535	83	152	23	3	25	101	50	2	.285	.350	.482

JOHN FLAHERTY
Boston Red Sox
Catcher
$18

The departure of Eric Wedge, the precipitous decline of Tony Peña and his own improved play have created an opening for Flaherty, who a year ago seemed doomed to a career in Triple-A. He's a righthanded hitter, 26 years old, slow and doesn't have power, but his defense has always been well spoken of, and he's a better hitter than Bob Melvin or Peña. Could be a *part* of a catching solution.

YEAR	TEAM/LEVEL	G	AB	R	H	2B	3B	HR	RBI	BB	SB	AVG	OBP	SLG
1993	Pawtucket AAA	105	365	29	99	22	0	6	35	26	0	.271	.327	.381
1993	MLE	105	354	22	88	22	0	4	26	19	0	.249	.287	.345
1993	Boston	13	25	3	3	2	0	0	2	2	0	.120	.214	.200

DAVE FLEMING
Seattle Mariners
Starting Pitcher
$29

His season started late because of some tendonitis which showed up in spring training, and, to be honest, he didn't pitch as well as his 12-5 record might make you think. Righthanded hitters hit .298 against him (he's a lefthander), and he doesn't have the control or ground ball ratio to get by with that . . . Very effective at cutting off the running game.

YEAR	TEAM/LEVEL	G	IP	W-L	PCT.	HITS	SO	BB	ERA
1991	Seattle	9	18	1-0	1.000	19	11	3	6.62
1992	Seattle	33	228	17-10	.630	225	112	60	3.39
1993	Seattle	26	167	12-5	.706	189	75	67	4.36

HUCK FLENER
Toronto Blue Jays
Lefthanded Pitcher
$22

A 25-year-old lefthander, used as both a starter (16 games) and reliever at Knoxville. A ninth-round draft pick, his performance since has varied from "very good" to "spectacular" (1.82 ERA, 107 strikeouts in 79 innings at Myrtle Beach). I hope the Jays have the sense to a) decide whether he's a starter or reliever, and b) give him a full year at Syracuse, because he could be one of the better pitchers they've developed.

YEAR	TEAM/LEVEL	G	IP	W-L	PCT.	HITS	SO	BB	ERA
1992	Dunedin A	41	112	7-3	.700	70	93	50	2.24
1993	Knoxville AA	38	136	13-6	.684	130	114	39	3.30
1993	Toronto	6	7	0-0	—	7	2	4	4.05

DARRIN FLETCHER

Montreal Expos

Catcher

$26

After struggling with the bat early, Fletcher had a hot streak in early July, and took firm control of the Expos' catching job as the season went on. His RBI rate was very good for a catcher, and the Expos had a 3.22 ERA with Fletcher catching (4.10 with other catchers). He threw out only 14 of 113 opposing base stealers (12%), the poorest percentage of any major league regular catcher. Everybody else caught at least 19%.

YEAR	TEAM/LEVEL	G	AB	R	H	2B	3B	HR	RBI	BB	SB	AVG	OBP	SLG
1992	Montreal	83	222	13	54	10	2	2	26	14	0	.243	.289	.333
1993	Montreal	133	396	33	101	20	1	9	60	34	0	.255	.320	.379
1994	**Projected**	**128**	**380**	**29**	**93**	**18**	**1**	**7**	**48**	**26**	**1**	**.245**	**.293**	**.353**

PAUL FLETCHER

Philadelphia Phillies

Starting Pitcher

$7

Was called up and pitched one-third of one inning in July, which required me to put him in the book despite his generally miserable season. A righthander, 40th-round draft pick in 1988, but won the Paul Owens award as the best pitcher in the Phillies' minor league system in '92. His good strikeout/walk ratios suggest that he may have some ability. Grade D prospect.

YEAR	TEAM/LEVEL	G	IP	W-L	PCT.	HITS	SO	BB	ERA
1992	Reading AA	22	127	9-4	.692	103	103	47	2.83
1992	Scranton AAA	4	23	3-0	1.000	17	26	2	2.78
1993	Scranton AAA	34	140	4-12	.250	146	116	60	5.66

SCOTT FLETCHER

Boston Red Sox

Second Base

$28

He was released by Milwaukee, signed with the Red Sox and had his best season since 1987. His .402 slugging percentage was a career high; his 16-for-19 performance as a base stealer was by far his career best. He's 35 now, but one player in a hundred is better in his mid- to late-thirties than he was in his late twenties, and you never know: he might be the one.

YEAR	TEAM/LEVEL	G	AB	R	H	2B	3B	HR	RBI	BB	SB	AVG	OBP	SLG
1992	Milwaukee	123	386	53	106	18	3	3	51	30	17	.275	.335	.360
1993	Boston	121	480	81	137	31	5	5	45	37	16	.285	.341	.402
1994	**Projected**	**117**	**380**	**47**	**97**	**17**	**2**	**3**	**39**	**29**	**11**	**.255**	**.311**	**.334**

CLIFF FLOYD

Montreal Expos

First Base/Outfield

$44

A big lefthanded hitter, also throws left, Floyd was a highly regarded prospect a year ago, and dominated Double-A at age 20, pushing him near the top among the super-prospects. He runs well enough to be a 30-30 man, although in view of his size, he will probably lose his speed by age 28. **Grade A prospect;** probably the number-one candidate for NL Rookie of the Year, but may be a year early.

YEAR	TEAM/LEVEL	G	AB	R	H	2B	3B	HR	RBI	BB	SB	AVG	OBP	SLG
1993	AA and AAA	133	505	94	155	19	6	28	119	70	33	.307	.396	.535
1993	MLE	133	482	75	132	17	3	20	94	49	23	.274	.341	.446
1994	**Projected**	**155**	**530**	**81**	**144**	**18**	**3**	**22**	**99**	**51**	**24**	**.272**	**.336**	**.442**

TOM FOLEY

Pittsburgh Pirates

Utilityman

$18

Foley spent seven years as a backup infielder in Montreal, but wasn't invited back after hitting .174 in '92. He signed a one-year contract with Pittsburgh; Leyland used him often as a pinch hitter (33 times, mostly pinch hitting for pitchers) and played him at second base about once a week. He had his best year since 1988, and probably will return in '94. He's 34.

YEAR	TEAM/LEVEL	G	AB	R	H	2B	3B	HR	RBI	BB	SB	AVG	OBP	SLG
1992	Montreal	72	115	7	20	3	1	0	5	8	3	.174	.230	.217
1993	Pittsburgh	86	194	18	49	11	1	3	22	11	0	.253	.287	.366
1994	**Projected**	**89**	**157**	**13**	**35**	**10**	**1**	**2**	**15**	**11**	**1**	**.223**	**.274**	**.338**

BROOK FORDYCE

New York Mets

Catcher

$15

Fordyce is projected as the Mets catcher of the future, if Hundley doesn't make progress with the bat. Drafted out of high school, he has played 522 minor league games already, although he's only 23. His defense gets excellent reviews, and he's probably going to hit enough to have at least some kind of a career. Grade C prospect; still has to develop, as a hitter, if he's going to hold a regular job.

YEAR	TEAM/LEVEL	G	AB	R	H	2B	3B	HR	RBI	BB	SB	AVG	OBP	SLG
1992	MLE	118	412	49	105	26	0	8	51	26	0	.255	.299	.376
1993	Norfolk AAA	116	409	33	106	21	2	2	40	26	2	.259	.307	.335
1993	MLE	116	397	27	94	18	1	1	33	21	1	.237	.275	.295

TONY FOSSAS

Boston Red Sox

Relief Pitcher

$12

Lefthanded one-out reliever, comes in to pitch to Kent Hrbek, or Ken Griffey, or Rafael Palmeiro, or whoever the big lefty coming up is. He does this well, limiting lefties to a .129 batting average last year (9-for-70) and .196 over the last four years. You need to get him out of the game quickly, because righthanded hitters hit about .320 against him, with a slugging percentage up around .500.

YEAR	TEAM/LEVEL	G	IP	W-L	SAVES	HITS	SO	BB	ERA
1991	Boston	64	57	3-2	1	49	29	28	3.47
1992	Boston	60	30	1-2	2	31	19	14	2.43
1993	Boston	71	40	1-1	0	38	39	15	5.18

KEVIN FOSTER

Philadelphia Phillies

Relief Pitcher

$12

Foster pitched well in the Expos system in 1991 (10-4, 2.74 ERA at Sumter) and 1992 (7-2, 1.95 ERA at West Palm Beach), but without becoming a hot prospect, from which we may infer that his fastball does not explode. He was traded to the Phillies last June, pitched OK in his first look at Triple-A, and got into two games in September. Grade C prospect.

YEAR	TEAM/LEVEL	G	IP	W-L	PCT.	HITS	SO	BB	ERA
1993	Jacksonville AA	12	66	4-4	.500	53	72	29	3.97
1993	Scranton AAA	17	71	1-1	.500	63	59	29	3.93
1993	Philadelphia	2	7	0-1	.000	13	6	7	14.85

STEVE FOSTER

Cincinnati Reds

Relief Pitcher

$15

Foster, never a red-hot prospect, has posted a 2.41 ERA through 59 major league games, but his career took a turn for the worse last June, when he had shoulder surgery, and went on the 60-day disabled list. Righthander, not big, has excellent control, is described by the papers as a bulldog. He can pitch, but don't assume he'll be healthy, even if he's healthy in spring training.

YEAR	TEAM/LEVEL	G	IP	W-L	SAVES	HITS	SO	BB	ERA
1991	Cincinnati	11	14	0-0	0	7	11	4	1.93
1992	Cincinnati	31	50	1-1	2	52	34	13	2.88
1993	Cincinnati	17	26	2-2	0	23	16	5	1.75

ERIC FOX

Oakland Athletics

Outfield

$13

A 30-year-old switch hitter who runs well, opened the season playing almost every game, either as the starting center fielder or a defensive sub, but was sent to the minor leagues on May 18 after failing to collect more than an occasional hit. His performance back at Tacoma was very good (.312, MLE of .268), much better than his previous standards. He's not going to be a regular, but he might be around.

YEAR	TEAM/LEVEL	G	AB	R	H	2B	3B	HR	RBI	BB	SB	AVG	OBP	SLG
1992	MLE	96	346	47	74	14	1	3	16	31	15	.214	.279	.286
1992	Oakland	51	143	24	34	5	2	3	13	13	3	.238	.299	.364
1993	Oakland	29	56	5	8	1	0	1	5	2	0	.143	.172	.214

JOHN FRANCO

New York Mets

Relief Pitcher

$22

The ultimate Met, earns a big salary based on his performance over the years, while in the real and present world he is the league's sorriest excuse for a closer. He is famous for crashing and burning in September, and did it again last year, posting a 13.50 ERA in September and blowing four out of five save opportunities. The Mets will be looking for a new closer.

YEAR	TEAM/LEVEL	G	IP	W-L	SAVES	HITS	SO	BB	ERA
1991	New York	52	55	5-9	30	61	45	18	2.93
1992	New York	31	33	6-2	15	24	20	11	1.64
1993	New York	35	36	4-3	10	46	29	19	5.20

JULIO FRANCO

Texas Rangers

Designated Hitter

$37

Franco returned from a serious injury (a ruptured tendon in his knee) to play at a level comparable to what he had done before the injury . . . He hit .329 after August 1, suggesting that he might be back even further in '93. Also hit .338 with men in scoring position. . . .Never a great second baseman, he was used by Texas as their fulltime DH . . . Has a reasonable shot at 3,000 career hits.

YEAR	TEAM/LEVEL	G	AB	R	H	2B	3B	HR	RBI	BB	SB	AVG	OBP	SLG
1991	Texas	146	589	108	201	27	3	15	78	65	36	.342	.408	.474
1992	Texas	35	107	19	25	7	0	2	8	15	1	.234	.328	.355
1993	Texas	144	532	85	154	31	3	14	84	62	9	.289	.360	.438

LOU FRAZIER

Montreal Expos

Outfield/Pinch Hitter

$19

A veteran of the Astros and Tigers systems, he hooked on with the Expos as a minor league free agent. He made the club in spring training, and had a fine season off the bench. Switch hitter, excellent speed, draws walks, can play outfield or infield, most often used in left . . . A useful player, but unlikely to hit anywhere near .286 in most seasons.

YEAR	TEAM/LEVEL	G	AB	R	H	2B	3B	HR	RBI	BB	SB	AVG	OBP	SLG
1992	MLE	129	464	76	107	12	2	0	30	73	42	.231	.335	.265
1993	Montreal	112	189	27	54	7	1	1	16	16	17	.286	.340	.349
1994	**Projected**	**90**	**170**	**25**	**38**	**3**	**0**	**1**	**12**	**24**	**14**	**.224**	**.320**	**.259**

SCOTT FREDERICKSON

Colorado Rockies

Relief Pitcher

$10

Another pitcher from the University of Texas, like Clemens, Swindell, etc. Well, not *too* much like them . . . Didn't come out of college until he was almost 23 (1990), but pitched well in the San Diego system from 1990 to 1992, as a reward for which he was taken by Colorado in the expansion draft. Grade D prospect; there isn't a lot here to make you think he's going to succeed.

YEAR	TEAM/LEVEL	G	IP	W-L	SAVES	HITS	SO	BB	ERA
1992	Wichita AA	56	73	4-7	5	50	66	38	3.19
1993	Colorado Spr AAA	23	26	1-3	7	26	20	19	5.47
1993	Colorado	25	29	0-1	0	33	20	17	6.21

MARVIN FREEMAN

Colorado Rockies

Relief Pitcher

$19

Released by the Braves after the season; the Rockies signed him. Freeman struggled through the first half of last year, and went on the DL in early June with a sore arm. He returned in late August and pitched well, posting a 2.53 ERA in 10 games, with 14 strikeouts and one walk. A 6-foot-7 righthander with intimidating equipment; suspect he has good years ahead, if not great ones.

YEAR	TEAM/LEVEL	G	IP	W-L	SAVES	HITS	SO	BB	ERA
1991	Atlanta	34	48	1-0	1	37	34	13	3.00
1992	Atlanta	58	64	7-5	3	61	41	29	3.22
1993	Atlanta	21	24	2-0	0	24	25	10	6.08

STEVE FREY

California Angels

Relief Pitcher

$22

One of several California pitchers who took a turn as the closer. His turn was in June, and was ended by a streak of wildness in early July, leading to a couple of blown saves . . . A little lefthander, he throws a hard-breaking curve as his bread-and-butter pitch, and is generally assumed to be more along the lines of a lefthanded spot reliever, rather than a closer.

YEAR	TEAM/LEVEL	G	IP	W-L	SAVES	HITS	SO	BB	ERA
1991	Montreal	31	45	0-1	1	43	21	23	4.99
1992	California	51	45	4-2	4	39	24	22	3.57
1993	California	55	48	2-3	13	41	22	26	2.98

TODD FROHWIRTH

Baltimore Orioles

Relief Pitcher

$22

His career has degenerated to a puzzling extent over the last two years; I suspect he is not getting the support he needs from his organization. A pitcher like this (a Tekulve-type pitcher) can give up line drive after line drive and still be effective, but he has to throw strikes and work ahead of the hitters. Frohwirth did that in '91, but didn't in '93: 50-50 chance of snapping back to form.

YEAR	TEAM/LEVEL	G	IP	W-L	SAVES	HITS	SO	BB	ERA
1991	Baltimore	51	96	7-3	3	64	77	29	1.87
1992	Baltimore	65	106	4-3	4	97	58	41	2.46
1993	Baltimore	70	96	6-7	3	91	50	44	3.83

JEFF FRYE

Texas Rangers

Second Base

$19

After playing well as the Rangers second baseman in the second half of '92 he missed all of '93 with a knee injury, casting his future into doubt. The Rangers have a comparable young player, Jon Shave, plus Doug Strange, who played well there in '93. I liked Frye a lot before the injury, but that's what happens to young middle infielders.

YEAR	TEAM/LEVEL	G	AB	R	H	2B	3B	HR	RBI	BB	SB	AVG	OBP	SLG
1992	MLE	87	323	50	87	22	1	1	22	39	7	.269	.348	.353
1992	Texas	67	199	24	51	9	1	1	12	16	1	.256	.320	.327
1993	Texas	(On Disabled List)												

TRAVIS FRYMAN

Detroit Tigers

Shortstop/Third Base

$70

Signed a five-year, $25 million contract after the season. Fryman is still young (25) and has been amazingly consistent, building his on-base percentage from .309 in 1991 to .379 last year, improving his walks and batting average while posting almost exactly the same numbers in the other categories. He hasn't improved as a shortstop, and the Tigers may move him permanently to third base. One of the best players in baseball over the next five years.

YEAR	TEAM/LEVEL	G	AB	R	H	2B	3B	HR	RBI	BB	SB	AVG	OBP	SLG
1992	Detroit	161	659	87	175	31	4	20	96	45	8	.266	.316	.416
1993	Detroit	151	607	98	182	37	5	22	97	77	9	.300	.379	.486
1994	**Projected**	**156**	**617**	**85**	**170**	**35**	**3**	**22**	**95**	**58**	**10**	**.276**	**.338**	**.449**

GARY GAETTI

Kansas City Royals

Third Base

$17

Had a .477 slugging percentage after joining Kansas City in mid-season, which, from my standpoint as a Royals fan, will keep his miserable carcass in the lineup another year. He embodies the basic weaknesses of the Royals: he is old, slow, and doesn't get on base. It's a question of *when* he will go into a slump and force the team through a mid-season transition, not if.

YEAR	TEAM/LEVEL	G	AB	R	H	2B	3B	HR	RBI	BB	SB	AVG	OBP	SLG
1992	California	130	456	41	103	13	2	12	48	21	3	.226	.267	.342
1993	Two Teams	102	331	40	81	20	1	14	50	21	1	.245	.300	.438
1994	**Projected**	**121**	**425**	**42**	**99**	**21**	**1**	**13**	**50**	**24**	**3**	**.233**	**.274**	**.379**

GREG GAGNE
Kansas City Royals
Shortstop
$40

Watching him almost every day, I couldn't believe what a good player he was—a wonderful shortstop (he led AL shortstops in fielding percentage, .986), a good baserunner (despite a poor stolen base ratio), a surprising hitter. I've never been more surprised by any player the Royals have ever acquired. After seeing him for a season, I understand now how the Twins were able to win a couple of World Championships.

YEAR	TEAM/LEVEL	G	AB	R	H	2B	3B	HR	RBI	BB	SB	AVG	OBP	SLG
1992	Minnesota	146	439	53	108	23	0	7	39	19	6	.246	.280	.346
1993	Kansas City	159	540	66	151	32	3	10	57	33	10	.280	.319	.406
1994	**Projected**	**148**	**511**	**60**	**129**	**28**	**3**	**10**	**56**	**29**	**10**	**.260**	**.299**	**.379**

JAY GAINER
Colorado Rockies
First Base
$13

Thickset lefthanded first baseman, doesn't have quite enough material to be a major league regular. He has some power, more power than reflected in his '93 record, but not Fred McGriff power, isn't going to hit for average, no speed, poor strikeout/walk ratios. Mile High Stadium may help his numbers for a year, and let him get established as a role player.

YEAR	TEAM/LEVEL	G	AB	R	H	2B	3B	HR	RBI	BB	SB	AVG	OBP	SLG
1993	Colo Spri AAA	86	293	51	86	11	3	10	74	22	4	.294	.341	.454
1993	MLE	86	273	31	66	8	1	6	45	13	2	.242	.276	.344
1993	Colorado	23	41	4	7	0	0	3	6	4	1	.171	.244	.390

ANDRES GALARRAGA
Colorado Rockies
First Base
$40

Saw only 2.97 pitches per plate appearance, the lowest of any major league regular . . . Hit .462 when he put the first pitch in play. The only other National Leaguer over .400 was Dante Bichette . . . Olerud also led his league in this category . . . Galarraga and Bichette were the only major league players who swung at 60% of the pitches they saw, Galarraga leading with 62.5%.

YEAR	TEAM/LEVEL	G	AB	R	H	2B	3B	HR	RBI	BB	SB	AVG	OBP	SLG
1993	Colorado	120	470	71	174	35	4	22	98	24	2	.370	.403	.602
1993	REAL PARK	120	461	56	156	33	2	19	78	24	2	.339	.374	.542
1994	**Projected**	**135**	**500**	**58**	**144**	**27**	**2**	**17**	**70**	**25**	**6**	**.288**	**.322**	**.452**

DAVE GALLAGHER
New York Mets
Utility Outfielder
$16

A useful player in the Henry Cotto/Stan Javier/Doug Dascenzo mold; when you have one you think they're a dime a dozen, but when you don't have one you'll notice it in a hurry. He does not have a contract for '94, and the Mets may be looking to purge the locker room, so it's anybody's guess where he will be playing.

YEAR	TEAM/LEVEL	G	AB	R	H	2B	3B	HR	RBI	BB	SB	AVG	OBP	SLG
1992	New York	98	175	20	42	11	1	1	21	19	4	.240	.307	.331
1993	New York	99	201	34	55	12	2	6	28	20	1	.274	.338	.443
1994	**Projected**	**108**	**233**	**29**	**61**	**13**	**1**	**2**	**27**	**23**	**3**	**.262**	**.328**	**.362**

MIKE GALLEGO

New York Yankees

Seccond Base/Shortstop

$30

His good on-base percentage and ability to play three positions make him an invaluable part of the Yankee roster. He started 46 games last year at shortstop, 41 at second, 24 at third, played all three positions well and hit .283 with a secondary average of .261. He probably won't hit .283 again, but he's one of the most underrated players in baseball.

YEAR	TEAM/LEVEL	G	AB	R	H	2B	3B	HR	RBI	BB	SB	AVG	OBP	SLG
1992	New York	53	173	24	44	7	1	3	14	20	0	.254	.343	.358
1993	New York	119	403	63	114	20	1	10	54	50	3	.283	.364	.412
1994	**Projected**	**118**	**370**	**48**	**88**	**11**	**1**	**6**	**36**	**49**	**4**	**.238**	**.327**	**.322**

RON GANT

Atlanta Braves

Left Field

$66

Most-similar season ever: Dale Murphy, 1982 . . . His .962 fielding percentage was the lowest for any regular outfielder in the majors, not that fielding percentage means a lot for an outfielder, but his range factor was also the worst of any regular left fielder (Cory Snyder was worse in right) . . . His defense won't cost him his job, and he has many good years ahead of him with the bat.

YEAR	TEAM/LEVEL	G	AB	R	H	2B	3B	HR	RBI	BB	SB	AVG	OBP	SLG
1992	Atlanta	153	544	74	141	22	6	17	80	45	32	.259	.321	.415
1993	Atlanta	157	606	113	166	27	4	36	117	67	26	.274	.345	.510
1994	**Projected**	**157**	**579**	**97**	**148**	**29**	**4**	**27**	**98**	**65**	**32**	**.256**	**.331**	**.459**

RICH GARCES

Minnesota Twins

Relief Pitcher

$7

A hot prospect three years ago, he's been plagued since by minor injuries and serious weight problems. He got off to a good start at Portland, was called up in late April when the Twins were struggling, sent back down in mid-May despite having pitched OK, and didn't throw two strikes in a row the rest of the season. Still throws hard, but has lost all semblance of command. His future is very cloudy.

YEAR	TEAM/LEVEL	G	IP	W-L	SAVES	HITS	SO	BB	ERA
1992	Orlando AA	58	73	3-3	13	76	72	39	4.54
1993	Minnesota	3	4	0-0	0	4	3	2	0.00
1993	Portland AAA	35	54	1-3	0	70	48	64	8.33

CARLOS GARCIA

Pittsburgh Pirates

Second Base

$36

Garcia was exactly what he was advertised as being—a .270 range hitter with more power than the average second baseman, a little speed, a pretty good second baseman for a rookie who was new to the position. He creates more runs than Chico Lind. His 1993 season was exactly what I would expect him to do again, but he might be able to improve it.

YEAR	TEAM/LEVEL	G	AB	R	H	2B	3B	HR	RBI	BB	SB	AVG	OBP	SLG
1992	MLE	113	407	56	110	24	6	9	54	18	14	.270	.301	.425
1993	Pittsburgh	141	546	77	147	25	5	12	47	31	18	.269	.316	.399
1994	**Projected**	**140**	**530**	**68**	**138**	**23**	**5**	**10**	**56**	**29**	**21**	**.260**	**.309**	**.379**

MIKE GARDINER

Detroit Tigers

Relief Pitcher

$5

One of countless rejects collected by the Tigers in their effort to patch the pitching. Gardiner has been in the majors four years and has posted four losing records, so he was released by Montreal in late August, having registered a 5.21 ERA for them. The Tigers signed him and took a look, but he didn't pitch as well as Boever or Storm Davis, and probably will not make the team out of spring training.

YEAR	TEAM/LEVEL	G	IP	W-L	PCT.	HITS	SO	BB	ERA
1991	Boston	22	130	9-10	.474	140	91	47	4.85
1992	Boston	28	131	4-10	.286	126	79	58	4.75
1993	Two Teams	34	49	2-3	.400	52	25	26	4.93

JEFF GARDNER

San Diego Padres

Second Base

$28

Finally got a chance to play with a major league team—well, *kind of* a major league team—after almost a thousand minor league games. He was essentially an average National League second baseman. He will have to improve in two areas to hold his job: his strikeout/walk ratio, which was sensational in the minors, just OK last year, and his double play rate, which was expected to be good but was actually poor.

YEAR	TEAM/LEVEL	G	AB	R	H	2B	3B	HR	RBI	BB	SB	AVG	OBP	SLG
1992	MLE	120	402	50	110	22	2	0	31	40	4	.274	.339	.338
1993	San Diego	140	404	53	106	21	7	1	24	45	2	.262	.337	.356
1994	**Projected**	**135**	**400**	**49**	**103**	**15**	**2**	**1**	**31**	**51**	**4**	**.258**	**.341**	**.313**

MARK GARDNER

Kansas City Royals

Starting Pitcher

$12

Had a one-year contract with KC, and probably will be somewhere else in '94. He couldn't put two good outings together, and the bad ones got worse until a strained shoulder put him on the DL in early July. On his return he went to Omaha, where he pitched well. Gardner has a high leg kick, and has worked on reducing this with men on base, with disastrous results: his batting average allowed jumped 62 points with men on.

YEAR	TEAM/LEVEL	G	IP	W-L	PCT.	HITS	SO	BB	ERA
1991	Montreal	27	168	9-11	.450	139	107	75	3.85
1992	Montreal	33	180	12-10	.545	179	132	60	4.36
1993	Kansas City	17	92	4-6	.400	92	54	36	6.19

BRENT GATES

Oakland Athletics

Second Base

$42

He had a rookie-of-the-year season, not that anybody noticed. An argument can be made that a good second baseman who hits .290 with collateral contributions has had a better rookie season than an outfielder who hits 30 homers. Gates, the A's first-round pick in 1991, played A ball in 1992, but went through Double-A and Triple-A in 12 games apiece at the start of 1993. Outstanding potential—but he has to stay healthy.

YEAR	TEAM/LEVEL	G	AB	R	H	2B	3B	HR	RBI	BB	SB	AVG	OBP	SLG
1993	AA and AAA	24	89	14	30	11	0	1	15	11	2	.337	.412	.494
1993	Oakland	139	535	64	155	29	2	7	69	56	7	.290	.357	.391
1994	**Projected**	**145**	**547**	**68**	**162**	**34**	**2**	**9**	**74**	**59**	**7**	**.296**	**.365**	**.415**

BOB GEREN
San Diego Padres
Catcher
$8

Returned to the majors after a year at Pawtucket, where he hit .207. His argument is defense, in that he's no kind of a hitter. In 1993 his argument was good: he made only two errors, and the Padres had a 3.55 ERA when he was catching, 4.45 without him (he caught 360 innings). Despite this he was outrighted to Las Vegas at the end of July, and his major league career is probably over.

YEAR	TEAM/LEVEL	G	AB	R	H	2B	3B	HR	RBI	BB	SB	AVG	OBP	SLG
1991	New York AL	64	128	7	28	3	0	2	12	9	0	.219	.270	.289
1992	Pawtuck AAA	66	213	28	44	7	0	9	25	17	0	.207	.265	.366
1993	San Diego	58	145	8	31	6	0	3	6	13	0	.214	.278	.317

KIRK GIBSON
Detroit Tigers
Left Field
$22

Returned to the game after a year's retirement, and alternated between being the best player in the league one week and the worst the next. In April he hit .407 with a .661 slugging percentage; in June he hit .115. He's a platoon player now, and on balance he was productive enough to keep that job if he chooses to do it.

YEAR	TEAM/LEVEL	G	AB	R	H	2B	3B	HR	RBI	BB	SB	AVG	OBP	SLG
1992	Pittsburgh	16	56	6	11	0	0	2	5	3	3	.196	.237	.304
1993	Detroit	116	403	62	105	18	6	13	62	44	15	.261	.337	.433
1994	**Projected**	**86**	**281**	**43**	**69**	**13**	**2**	**9**	**36**	**36**	**10**	**.246**	**.331**	**.402**

PAUL GIBSON
New York Yankees
Relief Pitcher
$21

Pitched for the two New York teams, also went to Norfolk and Columbus. He struck out 37 in 44 innings in the majors, also 36 in 28 innings in Triple-A, remarkable totals for a guy who doesn't throw hard enough to smoosh a doughnut. He's a con artist, always getting the hitter out on his front foot, always jerking the chain. With a little luck, he could have a Larry Andersen-type season—65 games, 1.85 ERA.

YEAR	TEAM/LEVEL	G	IP	W-L	SAVES	HITS	SO	BB	ERA
1991	Detroit	68	96	5-7	8	112	52	48	4.59
1992	New York NL	43	62	0-1	0	70	49	25	5.23
1993	Two Teams	28	44	3-1	0	45	37	11	3.47

BENJI GIL
Texas Rangers
Shortstop
$24

A promising young shortstop, was called up and put in the lineup in April after Manuel Lee's injury. Gil, born in Mexico and raised in California, is very young (turned 21 in October), and was over-matched in his major league trial, but in view of his youth and the fact that he hadn't played Double-A or Triple-A, that's not surprising, and not damning. He played well in the field. **Grade A prospect.**

YEAR	TEAM/LEVEL	G	AB	R	H	2B	3B	HR	RBI	BB	SB	AVG	OBP	SLG
1993	Tulsa AA	101	342	45	94	9	1	17	59	35	20	.275	.351	.456
1993	MLE	101	330	36	82	8	0	13	47	24	14	.248	.299	.391
1993	Texas	22	57	3	7	0	0	0	2	5	1	.123	.194	.123

BERNARD GILKEY
St. Louis Cardinals
Left Field
$47

The third-best left fielder in the National League last year, behind Bonds and Gant—actually, Luis Gonzalez was about the same, and the Philadelphia platoon was better, taken as a whole. Gilkey has made two giant steps in the last two years, and is about a half-step away from emerging as a star . . . Not much of an outfielder, but he did lead the league in baserunner kills, with 19.

YEAR	TEAM/LEVEL	G	AB	R	H	2B	3B	HR	RBI	BB	SB	AVG	OBP	SLG
1992	St. Louis	131	384	56	116	19	4	7	43	39	18	.302	.364	.427
1993	St. Louis	137	557	99	170	40	5	16	70	56	15	.305	.370	.481
1994	**Projected**	**142**	**489**	**73**	**144**	**27**	**4**	**10**	**53**	**57**	**19**	**.294**	**.368**	**.427**

JOE GIRARDI
Colorado Rockies
Catcher
$21

A pretty awful player, even for an expansion team. He hit .290, but that's .266 if you adjust for the park, and there was no production there—no power, no walks, no runs, no RBI. His defense isn't anything special, and in view of his age (he's 29) he's not likely to get any better. He missed two months in mid-season following surgery on his right hand, which kept him from driving in 40 or even 45 runs.

YEAR	TEAM/LEVEL	G	AB	R	H	2B	3B	HR	RBI	BB	SB	AVG	OBP	SLG
1992	Chicago	91	270	19	73	3	1	1	12	19	3	.270	.320	.300
1993	Colorado	86	310	35	90	14	5	3	31	24	6	.290	.346	.397
1993	REAL PARK	86	304	28	81	13	3	3	25	24	6	.266	.322	.359

DAN GLADDEN
Detroit Tigers
Left Field
$19

He missed almost all of April and May with a torn quadricep, but became a full-time player when Deer was traded, at least until the Tigers acquired Eric Davis. Established a career high in home runs, despite the injury, and drove in runs at a 100-RBI pace for the 91 games he played. He's about the same age as the other Tigers—Gibson, Trammell, Whitaker, Phillips, Barnes—and it is assumed that they can't go on forever.

YEAR	TEAM/LEVEL	G	AB	R	H	2B	3B	HR	RBI	BB	SB	AVG	OBP	SLG
1992	Detroit	113	417	57	106	20	1	7	42	30	4	.254	.304	.357
1993	Detroit	91	356	52	95	16	2	13	56	21	8	.267	.312	.432
1994	**Projected**	**102**	**312**	**41**	**79**	**13**	**2**	**5**	**36**	**22**	**7**	**.253**	**.302**	**.356**

TOM GLAVINE
Atlanta Braves
Starting Pitcher
$59

Through most of last year he didn't pitch all that well, but continued to roll up wins due to the superb team behind him, good luck, and his own survival skills. In late August he found himself, going 6-1 with a 31-8 strikeout/walk ratio after September 1. I'm not wild about him, and wouldn't rate him among the top five pitchers in the league for '94, but you have to respect his won-lost records.

YEAR	TEAM/LEVEL	G	IP	W-L	PCT.	HITS	SO	BB	ERA
1991	Atlanta	34	246	20-11	.645	201	192	69	2.56
1992	Atlanta	33	225	20-8	.714	197	129	70	2.76
1993	Atlanta	36	239	22-6	.786	236	120	90	3.20

JERRY GOFF
Pittsburgh Pirates
Catcher/Third Base
$18

Pirates signed him as a six-year minor league free agent. He put in a decent year at Buffalo, and got a late season callup. A catcher and third baseman in the minors, he won't hit for average, but will probably take Tom Prince's job or Lloyd McClendon's. He has the advantage of being lefthanded, a comparable hitter to McClendon, better than Prince, plus he's OK defensively.

YEAR	TEAM/LEVEL	G	AB	R	H	2B	3B	HR	RBI	BB	SB	AVG	OBP	SLG
1993	Buffalo AAA	104	362	52	91	27	3	14	69	55	1	.251	.346	.459
1993	MLE	104	346	37	75	24	1	9	49	39	0	.217	.296	.370
1993	Pittsburgh	14	37	5	11	2	0	2	6	8	0	.297	.422	.514

GREG GOHR
Detroit Tigers
Starting Pitcher
$12

The new Scott Aldred, Exhibit B in the Grand Jury investigation concerning the murder of the Detroit minor league system. Gohr was a first-round draft pick in 1989, and the Tigers have considered him their top pitching prospect ever since, despite a lack of supporting evidence. He does throw fairly hard, and might eventually emerge as some sort of a middle reliever or something.

YEAR	TEAM/LEVEL	G	IP	W-L	PCT.	HITS	SO	BB	ERA
1992	Toledo AAA	22	131	8-10	.444	124	94	46	3.99
1993	Toledo AAA	18	107	3-10	.231	127	77	38	5.80
1993	Detroit	16	23	0-0	—	26	23	14	5.96

CHRIS GOMEZ
Detroit Tigers
Shortstop
$26

An All-American shortstop at Long Beach State, he was the Tigers' third pick in '92, went straight to Double-A and held his own, was so-so at Triple-A, then came to the majors when the Tigers decided Fryman wasn't a shortstop. The funny thing is he hit only .274 at Long Beach State, but has stayed near there as he stepped up. Not fast, not flashy, could be good but could be the new Chris Pittaro.

YEAR	TEAM/LEVEL	G	AB	R	H	2B	3B	HR	RBI	BB	SB	AVG	OBP	SLG
1993	Toledo AAA	87	277	29	68	12	2	0	20	23	6	.245	.308	.303
1993	MLE	87	271	27	62	10	1	0	19	22	4	.229	.287	.273
1993	Detroit	46	128	11	32	7	1	0	11	9	2	.250	.304	.320

LEO GOMEZ
Baltimore Orioles
Third Base
$26

He took a giant step backward at a critical moment, when he needed to show that he was a little bit *better* than he had played in '92. He was troubled by tendonitis and a cyst on his right wrist, plus his manager doesn't seem to believe in him, which often resolves itself by a trade. On the other hand Pagliarulo has filed for free agency . . . Gomez could drive in a hundred runs, but can't afford another off year.

YEAR	TEAM/LEVEL	G	AB	R	H	2B	3B	HR	RBI	BB	SB	AVG	OBP	SLG
1991	Baltimore	118	391	40	91	17	2	16	45	40	1	.233	.302	.409
1992	Baltimore	137	468	62	124	24	0	17	64	63	2	.265	.356	.425
1993	Baltimore	71	244	30	48	7	0	10	25	32	0	.197	.295	.348

PAT GOMEZ

San Diego Padres

Relief Pitcher

$9

Gomez was in the Atlanta system for several years, was traded to San Diego by way of Texas. He's a 26-year-old lefthander who doesn't throw hard and doesn't throw strikes, has started as much as he has relieved in the minors, showing occasional flashes of light as a starter, but never as a reliever. He missed some time in mid-summer with a strained left elbow, and was returned to a minor league roster at season's end.

YEAR	TEAM/LEVEL	G	IP	W-L	SAVES	HITS	SO	BB	ERA
1992	Greenville AA	8	48	7-0	0	25	38	19	1.13
1992	Richmond AAA	23	71	3-5	0	79	48	42	5.45
1993	San Diego	27	32	1-2	0	35	26	19	5.12

LARRY GONZALES

California Angels

Catcher

$6

A 27-year-old righthanded hitting catcher, he got a couple of at bats in June as an emergency backup. Has hit .300 several times in the minors, but didn't last year. Chris Turner is the organization's catching prospect, although Gonzales has hit about as well as Turner at each minor league stop. A big guy with no power, probably has no future, although he may fool us. And the Angels.

YEAR	TEAM/LEVEL	G	AB	R	H	2B	3B	HR	RBI	BB	SB	AVG	OBP	SLG
1992	Edmonton	80	241	37	79	10	0	3	47	38	2	.328	.422	.407
1993	Vancouver AAA	81	264	30	69	9	0	2	27	26	5	.261	.329	.318
1993	MLE	81	251	21	56	6	0	1	19	18	3	.223	.275	.259

RENE GONZALES

California Angels

Infield

$20

Wears number 88, the highest number in the league . . . Had a big surprise season in 1992, and was following through in 1993 until a September slump (12 for 67) cut about 20 points off his average. He played mostly third base, after the wipeouts of Gaetti and Gruber; that place was taken by Perez, which throws him back into a utility role. He's 31 years old, good backup player who will never be a regular.

YEAR	TEAM/LEVEL	G	AB	R	H	2B	3B	HR	RBI	BB	SB	AVG	OBP	SLG
1992	California	104	329	47	91	17	1	7	38	41	7	.277	.363	.398
1993	California	118	335	34	84	17	0	2	31	49	5	.251	.346	.319
1994	**Projected**	**98**	**249**	**28**	**59**	**8**	**0**	**3**	**22**	**33**	**4**	**.237**	**.326**	**.305**

ALEX GONZALEZ

Toronto Blue Jays

Shortstop

$34

A 21-year-old product of the Miami Cuban community, Gonzalez was taken by the Blue Jays in the 14th round in 1991, and is now regarded by some people as the best prospect in the minors today. He has real speed, some power, and is a solid, unspectacular shortstop with a strong arm. If Tony Fernandez leaves Toronto as a free agent, Gonzalez is expected to step into his shoes.

YEAR	TEAM/LEVEL	G	AB	R	H	2B	3B	HR	RBI	BB	SB	AVG	OBP	SLG
1992	Myrtle Bea A	134	535	82	145	22	9	10	62	38	26	.271	.322	.402
1993	Knoxville AA	142	561	93	162	29	7	16	69	39	38	.289	.339	.451
1993	MLE	142	544	75	145	27	5	14	55	26	27	.267	.300	.412

JUAN GONZALEZ

Texas Rangers

Left Field

$88

Most-similar season: Orlando Cepeda, 1961 . . . Absolutely the only issues which stand between Gonzalez and Cooperstown are health and conduct. If he is healthy, he is *going* to hit 500 home runs, probably 600, possibly 700 . . . Homered 80% more often with men on base than with the bases empty . . . Has homered more often on the road than he has at home, so the move to a new park probably won't cost him home runs.

YEAR	TEAM/LEVEL	G	AB	R	H	2B	3B	HR	RBI	BB	SB	AVG	OBP	SLG
1992	Texas	155	584	77	152	24	2	43	109	35	0	.260	.304	.529
1993	Texas	140	536	105	166	33	1	46	118	37	4	.310	.368	.632
1994	**Projected**	**149**	**567**	**89**	**158**	**32**	**2**	**37**	**109**	**41**	**3**	**.279**	**.327**	**.538**

LUIS GONZALEZ

Houston Astros

Left Field

$47

1993 was the first time in his professional career that he has hit higher than .286 in more than 39 games. That said, there is no obvious reason that he shouldn't remain a .300 hitter. He's a lefthanded hitter with a good, level stroke who makes contact, doesn't chase pitches over his head or a foot outside, doesn't bail out against lefties, runs well and hits the ball hard. . .Led National League in sacrifice flies, with ten.

YEAR	TEAM/LEVEL	G	AB	R	H	2B	3B	HR	RBI	BB	SB	AVG	OBP	SLG
1992	Houston	122	387	40	94	19	3	10	55	24	7	.243	.289	.385
1993	Houston	154	540	82	162	34	3	15	72	47	20	.300	.361	.457
1994	**Projected**	**155**	**550**	**69**	**151**	**30**	**5**	**17**	**78**	**46**	**16**	**.275**	**.331**	**.440**

DWIGHT GOODEN

New York Mets

Starting Pitcher

$36

His skills have been diminished by injury, but he is still a fairly good pitcher. A 12-15 record for a 100-loss team is nothing to be ashamed of, and his control, strikeout rates and hits/innings ratios remain above average. If the shoulder problem which ended his season isn't serious, he still has the chance to have some good years. Still well positioned with respect to the Hall of Fame.

YEAR	TEAM/LEVEL	G	IP	W-L	PCT.	HITS	SO	BB	ERA
1991	New York	27	190	13-7	.650	185	150	56	3.60
1992	New York	31	206	10-13	.435	197	145	70	3.67
1993	New York	29	209	12-15	.444	188	149	61	3.45

TOM GOODWIN

Los Angeles Dodgers

Outfielder

$11

Goodwin spent most of the season at Albuquerque, after appearing in 73 games for the Dodgers in '92. He's a grade D prospect—a lefthanded hitter who can run and can be used for defense in the outfield, but doesn't do anything else well. He's never going to be a regular, and getting those 25th-man slots is as much a matter of luck and personality as it is skill. He can hit .260.

YEAR	TEAM/LEVEL	G	AB	R	H	2B	3B	HR	RBI	BB	SB	AVG	OBP	SLG
1992	Los Angeles	73	80	15	17	1	1	0	3	6	8	.233	.291	.274
1993	MLE	85	270	28	56	3	2	0	16	18	12	.207	.257	.233
1993	Los Angeles	30	17	6	5	1	0	0	1	1	1	.294	.333	.353

KEITH GORDON

Cincinnati Reds

Outfield

$11

A second-round draft pick in 1990, he has made slow progress, passing through the levels not quite slowly enough to be written off. He played Double-A at age 24 in '93, and hit .291, which is amazing in view of his strikeout/walk ratio (132-19). He is big enough to hit for power, but doesn't, and fast enough to be a base stealer, but isn't. Grade C prospect; could be .270 hitter, 20-homer man.

YEAR TEAM/LEVEL	G	AB	R	H	2B	3B	HR	RBI	BB	SB	AVG	OBP	SLG
1993 Chattanooga	118	419	69	122	26	3	14	59	19	13	.291	.327	.468
1993 MLE	118	405	55	108	23	1	13	47	13	9	.267	.289	.425
1993 Cincinnati	3	6	0	1	0	0	0	0	0	0	.167	.167	.167

TOM GORDON

Kansas City Royals

Relief Pitcher

$35

Gordon, who won 17 games as a 21-year-old rookie in 1989, apparently has his career moving in the right direction after several years of drifting. He pitched well in long relief, then moved into the rotation in late July, and was 8-4 with a 3.36 ERA in 14 starts. Only 26, throws hard, excellent breaking ball; still has a good chance to be an outstanding pitcher.

YEAR	TEAM/LEVEL	G	IP	W-L	SAVES	HITS	SO	BB	ERA
1991	Kansas City	45	158	9-14	1	129	167	87	3.87
1992	Kansas City	40	118	6-10	0	116	98	55	4.59
1993	Kansas City	48	156	12-6	1	125	143	77	3.58

GOOSE GOSSAGE

Oakland Athletics

Relief Pitcher

$17

Your basic 42-year-old power pitcher. In the early part of '93 he pitched effectively, but in the second half of the season he had injuries, and his record was ruined because he stayed in the game to absorb the punishment a couple of times when the A's were getting blown out. His most serious injury was a broken wrist, late August. He's still a major league pitcher if he doesn't retire.

YEAR	TEAM/LEVEL	G	IP	W-L	SAVES	HITS	SO	BB	ERA
1991	Texas	44	41	4-2	1	33	28	16	3.57
1992	Oakland	30	38	0-2	0	32	26	19	2.84
1993	Oakland	39	48	4-5	1	49	40	26	4.53

JIM GOTT

Los Angeles Dodgers

Relief Pitcher

$38

Reclaimed the closer role for the first time since 1988, and pitched well most of the year, getting saves in 25 of 29 opportunities. He developed tendonitis in early September, which ended his season. My guess is that Lasorda will keep him in the closer role, rather than moving Pedro Martinez there, because a) Gott pitched well, and b) Lasorda, like many managers, prefers a veteran in that role.

YEAR	TEAM/LEVEL	G	IP	W-L	SAVES	HITS	SO	BB	ERA
1991	Los Angeles	55	76	4-3	2	63	73	32	2.96
1992	Los Angeles	68	88	3-3	6	72	75	41	2.45
1993	Los Angeles	62	78	4-8	25	71	67	17	2.32

MAURO GOZZO

New York Mets
Starting Pitcher
$15

A survivor of 10 years and more than a thousand innings in the minor leagues, although he's only 28. He was originally signed by the Mets, traded to the Royals in the David Cone deal, and has pitched in the majors for Toronto (1989), Cleveland (1990-1991) and Minnesota (1992). His strong points are his control and his durability—in 10 years of pitching he has had no major injuries.

YEAR	TEAM/LEVEL	G	IP	W-L	PCT.	HITS	SO	BB	ERA
1992	Portland AAA	37	156	10-9	.526	155	108	50	3.35
1993	Norfolk AAA	28	190	8-11	.421	208	97	49	3.45
1993	New York	10	14	0-1	.000	11	6	5	2.57

MARK GRACE

Chicago Cubs
First Base
$58

He's a negative image of Sammie Sosa: He has everything *except* power and speed. In the first three months of '93 he hit over .300 with slugging percentages over .500; the last three months he hit over .300 but slugged under .500 . . . Tied for the major league lead in grounding into double plays, with 25 . . . Fine first baseman, good baserunner. Hit .453 in the late innings of close games, best in the major leagues by far.

YEAR	TEAM/LEVEL	G	AB	R	H	2B	3B	HR	RBI	BB	SB	AVG	OBP	SLG
1992	Chicago	158	603	72	185	37	5	9	79	72	6	.307	.380	.430
1993	Chicago	155	594	86	193	39	4	14	98	71	8	.325	.393	.475
1994	**Projected**	**158**	**604**	**81**	**180**	**32**	**3**	**11**	**77**	**74**	**6**	**.298**	**.375**	**.416**

JOE GRAHE

California Angels
Closer
$26

Grahe opened and closed the year as the Angels' closer. In between he had tendonitis in his right rotator cuff, which gave about a dozen other people a shot at the role . . . Throws sinking fastball, curve, and slider; not everyone is convinced he has closer stuff, but he saved 11 in 13 chances and allowed 32% of inherited runners to score, acceptable numbers. Gets 72% ground balls.

YEAR	TEAM/LEVEL	G	IP	W-L	SAVES	HITS	SO	BB	ERA
1991	California	18	73	3-7	0	84	40	33	4.81
1992	California	46	95	5-6	21	85	39	39	3.52
1993	California	45	57	4-1	11	54	31	25	2.86

JEFF GRANGER

Kansas City Royals
Starting Pitcher
$23

Granger was the Royals' number-one draft pick, a lefthander from Texas A&M. The Royals started him in A ball, which frankly is silly for a first-round pick who has pitched in the College World Series, and he struck out 14 men a game there, which doesn't mean much of anything. His contract required that he be recalled in September, and he was, and pitched one inning. Intelligent, poised, throws hard and was a college quarterback.

YEAR	TEAM/LEVEL	G	IP	W-L	PCT.	HITS	SO	BB	ERA
1993	Texas A & M		107	14-3	.824		114		2.72
1993	Eugene A	8	36	3-3	.500	28	56	10	3.00
1993	Kansas City	1	1	0-0	—	3	1	2	27.00

MARK GRANT

Colorado Rockies

Reliever

$6

Originally from the Giants system, has now pitched for the Giants, Padres, Braves, Mariners, Astros and Rockies, which may tell you all that you need to know about him. A finesse pitcher, had a strained rib cage and a strained shoulder in '93. Last year I reported that lefthanded hitters had hit .336 against him, which went up to .395 in '93. He's only 30, but there's no indication of any ability here.

YEAR	TEAM/LEVEL	G	IP	W-L	SAVES	HITS	SO	BB	ERA
1991	Two Teams	59	91	2-3	3	108	69	37	4.73
1992	Seattle	23	81	2-4	0	100	42	22	3.89
1993	Two Teams	20	25	0-1	1	34	14	11	7.46

MARK GRATER

Detroit Tigers

Relief Pitcher

$8

See Mike Gardiner comment, and here's another one. Grater must have been hurt or something, as he pitched well for Louisville in '91 and '92 (ERAs of 2.02 and 2.13), and had pitched well in the Cardinal system for years, but just couldn't get anybody out in '93 (see stats below). He turned 30 during the winter, and is probably thinking deeply about his future.

YEAR	TEAM/LEVEL	G	IP	W-L	SAVES	HITS	SO	BB	ERA
1993	Toledo AAA	28	31	1-2	4	42	31	12	8.13
1993	Calgary AAA	9	12	0-1	0	19	4	6	7.71
1993	Detroit	6	5	0-0	0	6	4	4	5.40

CRAIG GREBECK

Chicago White Sox

Shortstop/Second Base

$21

One of my favorite players, a little tiny guy who takes advantage of his size by forcing the pitchers to pitch to him, and is also strong enough to drive the ball. He had a disappointing year, as the second base job became open and Joey Cora grabbed it, then his season was ended by a broken foot in August. He's an overqualified reserve infielder, and good enough to play every day for somebody.

YEAR	TEAM/LEVEL	G	AB	R	H	2B	3B	HR	RBI	BB	SB	AVG	OBP	SLG
1992	Chicago	88	287	24	77	21	2	3	35	30	0	.268	.341	.387
1993	Chicago	72	190	25	43	5	0	1	12	26	1	.226	.319	.268
1994	**Projected**	**90**	**226**	**28**	**58**	**12**	**1**	**3**	**25**	**32**	**2**	**.257**	**.349**	**.358**

SHAWN GREEN

Toronto Blue Jays

Outfielder

$12

A tall skinny lefthanded batter from California, the Blue Jays first-round draft pick in 1991. It is too early to conclude that this was a wasted draft pick, since he just turned 21 in November, but he has work to do. He hit .283 at Knoxville, which is not quite like hitting .350, but counts as his strong point. His weak points were power, speed, and command of the strike zone.

YEAR	TEAM/LEVEL	G	AB	R	H	2B	3B	HR	RBI	BB	SB	AVG	OBP	SLG
1993	Knoxville AA	99	360	40	102	14	2	4	34	26	4	.283	.339	.367
1993	MLE	99	348	32	90	13	1	3	27	17	2	.259	.293	.328
1993	Toronto	3	6	0	0	0	0	0	0	0	0	.000	.000	.000

TYLER GREEN

Philadelphia Phillies

Starting Pitcher

$16

I'm glad that we have players like Tyler Green around, so that I get to use time-honored baseball adjectives such as "much-ballyhooed" and "injury-plagued." Green, the Phillies first-round pick in 1991, is a big righthander who throws hard and has pitched fairly well, but is probably on a first-name basis with Dr. Jobe's secretary. Grade B prospect.

YEAR	TEAM/LEVEL	G	IP	W-L	PCT.	HITS	SO	BB	ERA
1992	Reading AA	12	62	6-3	.667	46	67	20	1.88
1992	Scranton AAA	2	10	0-1	.000	7	15	12	6.10
1993	Scranton AAA	28	118	6-10	.375	102	87	43	3.95

TOMMY GREENE

Philadelphia Phillies

Starting Pitcher

$59

Led the National League in wild pitches, with 15. The two pitchers who led their leagues in wild pitches, between them, won 30 games and lost only 7, go figure . . . It is too early to start talking about the Hall of Fame, but if this guy stays healthy he is going to win 200+ games. I'd compare him to Jim Palmer in '69, when Palmer came off several years of arm injuries to go 16-4.

YEAR	TEAM/LEVEL	G	IP	W-L	PCT.	HITS	SO	BB	ERA
1991	Philadelphia	36	208	13-7	.650	177	154	66	3.38
1992	Philadelphia	13	64	3-3	.500	75	39	34	5.32
1993	Philadelphia	31	200	16-4	.800	175	167	62	3.42

WILLIE GREENE

Cincinnati Reds

Third Base

$30

A **Grade A prospect**, a trim lefthanded hitter with 30-home-run power, has the feet and arm to be a good major league third baseman, if not a shortstop. Doesn't have outstanding speed, but not slow; has been in several organizations and has received some criticism for his intensity, but nothing like what people used to say about Albert Belle. I recommend him highly . . . Season was ended with a dislocated thumb. He's only 22.

YEAR	TEAM/LEVEL	G	AB	R	H	2B	3B	HR	RBI	BB	SB	AVG	OBP	SLG
1992	MLE	96	340	38	88	17	1	15	54	34	5	.259	.326	.447
1993	MLE	98	332	49	82	17	0	20	46	42	1	.247	.332	.479
1993	Cincinnati	15	50	7	8	1	1	2	5	2	0	.160	.189	.340

MIKE GREENWELL

Boston Red Sox

Left Field

$37

Like his boyhood hero, George Brett, he often starts slowly, and drives his batting average upward. Last year he hit .400 in September (42-for-105), making his final numbers surprisingly strong . . . He doesn't run as well as he did, and frankly he was never a Gold Glove candidate, although I think he has improved in the outfield. But if a man can hit .315 and slug up around .500, there's a place for him.

YEAR	TEAM/LEVEL	G	AB	R	H	2B	3B	HR	RBI	BB	SB	AVG	OBP	SLG
1992	Boston	49	180	16	42	2	0	2	18	18	2	.233	.307	.278
1993	Boston	146	540	77	170	38	6	13	72	54	5	.315	.379	.480
1994	**Projected**	**146**	**538**	**74**	**160**	**31**	**4**	**13**	**78**	**51**	**9**	**.297**	**.358**	**.442**

KEN GREER

New York Mets
Righthanded Pitcher
$9

The Mets' compensation for donating Frank Tanana to the Yankees down the stretch. A minor league veteran, 27 years old, good size. As sometimes happens in the Yankee system he spent year after year at A ball, even though he sometimes pitched well, and didn't get any real experience until he was 25. He's been in middle relief since 1990, pitched well in that role in '92 at Albany, not so well in '93 at Columbus. Grade D prospect.

YEAR	TEAM/LEVEL	G	IP	W-L	SAVES	HITS	SO	BB	ERA
1991	Ft. Lauderd A	31	57	4-3	0	49	46	22	4.24
1992	Albany AA	40	69	4-1	4	48	53	30	1.83
1993	Columbus AAA	46	79	9-4	6	78	50	36	4.42

TOMMY GREGG

Cincinnati Reds
Pinch Hitter
$12

Spent most of the summer at Indianapolis, re-establishing his ability to batter minor league pitchers. He could help somebody as a pinch hitter—a lefthanded line-drive hitter who could hit .270, won't chase bad pitches, and has just a little bit of power. To this point in his career he's been hurt every time he's got a chance to play in the majors, and time is running out on him.

YEAR	TEAM/LEVEL	G	AB	R	H	2B	3B	HR	RBI	BB	SB	AVG	OBP	SLG
1992	Atlanta	18	19	1	5	0	0	1	1	1	1	.263	.300	.421
1993	Indianapol AAA	71	198	34	63	12	5	7	30	26	3	.318	.398	.535
1993	Cincinnati	10	12	1	2	0	0	0	1	0	0	.167	.154	.167

KEN GRIFFEY JR.

Seattle Mariners
Center Field
$98

Before 1993 no player since 1970 had hit 35 doubles and 45 homers in the same season. Both Bonds and Griffey did it last year . . . That's been done 14 times now—three times by Ruth, four times by Gehrig, once each by Foxx, DiMaggio, Mays, Reggie and Bench . . . Hit only .239 with runners in scoring position, but historically has done OK in that category. The most-comparable players in history are Mays and Aaron.

YEAR	TEAM/LEVEL	G	AB	R	H	2B	3B	HR	RBI	BB	SB	AVG	OBP	SLG
1992	Seattle	142	565	83	174	39	4	27	103	44	10	.308	.361	.535
1993	Seattle	156	582	113	180	38	3	45	109	96	17	.309	.408	.617
1994	**Projected**	**154**	**577**	**93**	**162**	**37**	**3**	**32**	**105**	**75**	**16**	**.315**	**.394**	**.556**

ALFREDO GRIFFIN

Toronto Blue Jays
Shortstop
$11

Now 37 years old; might or might not return for a third season as Toronto's backup shortstop. What his .211 average doesn't show is that in May, when a couple of other guys failed or got hurt and Fernandez was in New York, Griffin stepped in and played well, holding shortstop together and hitting .255. That, and the fact that he is regarded as a clubhouse positive, may earn him an invitation to return.

YEAR	TEAM/LEVEL	G	AB	R	H	2B	3B	HR	RBI	BB	SB	AVG	OBP	SLG
1991	Los Angeles	109	350	27	85	6	2	0	27	22	5	.243	.286	.271
1992	Toronto	63	150	21	35	7	0	0	10	9	3	.233	.273	.280
1993	Toronto	46	95	15	20	3	0	0	3	3	0	.211	.235	.242

JASON GRIMSLEY

Cleveland Indians

Starting Pitcher

$15

Was released by Houston in spring training, signed with Cleveland, and spent the warm months at Charlotte. Although his major league record doesn't show it, Grimsley is closer to being a pitcher now than he was three or four years ago, when the Phillies were trying to rush him into the rotation. He's gained some command of his breaking pitch, and he's not trying as hard to make perfect, unhittable pitches. Grade C prospect.

YEAR	TEAM/LEVEL	G	IP	W-L	PCT.	HITS	SO	BB	ERA
1992	Tucson AAA	26	125	8-7	.533	152	90	55	5.05
1993	Charlotte AAA	28	135	6-6	.500	138	102	49	3.39
1993	Cleveland	10	42	3-4	.429	52	27	20	5.31

MARQUIS GRISSOM

Montreal Expos

Center Field

$65

He is having a textbook career, getting a little bit better every year than he was the year before. His batting averages since he came up: .257, .257, .267, .276, .298. His slugging percentages: .324, .351, .373, .418, .438. His runs scored: 16, 42, 73, 99, 104. It's unlikely he'll get **too** much better—he might have one or two steps left—but he's an 85% base stealer, a fine center fielder, and a .280 hitter with power.

YEAR	TEAM/LEVEL	G	AB	R	H	2B	3B	HR	RBI	BB	SB	AVG	OBP	SLG
1992	Montreal	159	653	99	180	39	6	14	66	42	78	.276	.322	.418
1993	Montreal	157	630	104	188	27	2	19	95	52	53	.298	.351	.438
1994	**Projected**	**159**	**629**	**93**	**175**	**29**	**5**	**13**	**68**	**46**	**74**	**.278**	**.327**	**.402**

BUDDY GROOM

Detroit Tigers

Starting Pitcher

$14

His real name is "Wedsel," which is a good excuse to skip Mother's Day. Groom is 28, old for a prospect, and his major league record is 0-7 with an ERA of 5.97, but I like him a lot. He works ahead of the hitters, has been consistently successful in the minor leagues, and he gets ground balls. He's a Tommy John-type pitcher, and John-type pitchers are rarely successful with bad teams.

YEAR	TEAM/LEVEL	G	IP	W-L	PCT.	HITS	SO	BB	ERA
1992	Toledo AAA	16	109	7-7	.500	102	71	23	2.80
1993	Toledo AAA	16	102	9-3	.750	98	78	30	2.74
1993	Detroit	19	37	0-2	.000	48	15	13	6.14

KEVIN GROSS

Los Angeles Dodgers

Starting Pitcher

$32

Pitched .500 ball for the first time since 1986, when he was 12-12; he hasn't had a *winning* record since 1985. There is no indication that time is running out on him. He is 32, but he hasn't had a sore arm in several years, and his strikeout rate is still good. I know it is too late to be saying this, but I still half-expect him to break loose with a big year.

YEAR	TEAM/LEVEL	G	IP	W-L	PCT.	HITS	SO	BB	ERA
1991	Los Angeles	46	116	10-11	.476	123	95	50	3.58
1992	Los Angeles	34	205	8-13	.381	182	158	77	3.17
1993	Los Angeles	33	202	13-13	.500	224	150	74	4.14

KIP GROSS

Los Angeles Dodgers

Relief Pitcher

$20

A 29-year-old righthander, has been on the border of breaking through for several years, and may finally have done it in '93, when he pitched well at Albuquerque (a 4.05 ERA at Albuquerque in a hitter's year is good) and then was almost perfect in a September callup. His strikeout rate at Albuquerque improved dramatically. May be in the Dodger bullpen in '94.

YEAR	TEAM/LEVEL	G	IP	W-L	SAVES	HITS	SO	BB	ERA
1992	Los Angeles	16	24	1-1	0	32	14	10	4.18
1993	Albuquerque AAA	59	124	13-7	13	115	96	41	4.05
1993	Los Angeles	10	15	0-0	0	13	12	4	0.60

KELLY GRUBER

Released

Third Base

$14

Acquired from Toronto in a trade for Luis Sojo, he started the year on the DL following surgery on his left shoulder, also suffering from bulging discs in his neck. He returned June 3, played very well for three weeks, then went out for the year with an injury to his left shoulder. He was released in September; his ability to get another job will depend on convincing somebody that he is truly healthy. Now 32.

YEAR	TEAM/LEVEL	G	AB	R	H	2B	3B	HR	RBI	BB	SB	AVG	OBP	SLG
1991	Toronto	113	429	58	108	18	2	20	65	31	12	.252	.308	.443
1992	Toronto	120	446	42	102	16	3	11	43	26	7	.229	.275	.352
1993	California	18	65	10	18	3	0	3	9	2	0	.277	.309	.462

EDDIE GUARDADO

Minnesota Twins

Starting Pitcher

$14

Young lefthander, rushed to the majors after a quick start at Double-A, got pounded but stayed the rest of the season. The league hit .369 against him when there were men on base. That's not too good . . . A 21st-round pick in 1990, has very good control, but his fastball won't tie anybody in knots. Short, pudgy, nice mechanics, has good curve and changeup. Probably will have better years.

YEAR	TEAM/LEVEL	G	IP	W-L	PCT.	HITS	SO	BB	ERA
1992	Two Teams A	25	150	12-10	.545	153	142	40	3.47
1993	Nashville AA	10	65	4-0	1.000	53	57	10	1.24
1993	Minnesota	19	95	3-8	.273	123	46	36	6.18

MARK GUBICZA

Kansas City Royals

Reliever/Starter

$18

Opened the year in the starting rotation, and was hit hard (7.03 ERA through six starts). He moved to the bullpen then and pitched fairly well in relief. Gubicza still throws a major league fastball, has good control and is now an extreme ground-ball pitcher. Doesn't have a contract for '94, but will have a job somewhere, and may pitch well.

YEAR	TEAM/LEVEL	G	IP	W-L	PCT.	HITS	SO	BB	ERA
1991	Kansas City	26	133	9-12	.429	168	89	42	5.68
1992	Kansas City	18	111	7-6	.538	110	81	36	3.72
1993	Kansas City	49	104	5-8	.385	128	80	43	4.66

LEE GUETTERMAN

St. Louis Cardinals

Relief Pitcher

$18

Released by the Mets, he signed with the Cardinals and started the year at Louisville, where he pitched well (2.94 ERA). The Cardinals called him up in late June to be the lefthanded one-out guy, and he pitched, if anything, a little better in the majors, had his best season since 1990. I guess you know about him—a tall, thin dart thrower, now 35 years old.

YEAR	TEAM/LEVEL	G	IP	W-L	SAVES	HITS	SO	BB	ERA
1991	New York	64	88	3-4	6	91	35	25	3.68
1992	Two Teams	58	66	4-5	2	92	20	27	7.09
1993	St. Louis	40	46	3-3	1	41	19	16	2.93

OZZIE GUILLEN

Chicago White Sox

Shortstop

$32

Missed the 1992 season after ripping a couple of tendons in a collision with Tim Raines, but returned in '93 to play at more or less the same level as before. He's 30; should be good for at least one more year of the same . . . Doesn't it seem strange to you that nobody could ever convince Guillen, who is intelligent and approachable, to stop chasing bad pitches?

YEAR	TEAM/LEVEL	G	AB	R	H	2B	3B	HR	RBI	BB	SB	AVG	OBP	SLG
1992	Chicago	12	40	5	8	4	0	0	7	1	1	.200	.214	.300
1993	Chicago	134	457	44	128	23	4	4	50	10	5	.280	.292	.374
1994	**Projected**	**136**	**471**	**45**	**124**	**18**	**5**	**3**	**47**	**11**	**13**	**.263**	**.280**	**.342**

BILL GULLICKSON

Detroit Tigers

Starting Pitcher

$18

Opened the season on the disabled list following off-season surgery to both his knee and his shoulder, and struggled most of the year. He saved his season with a 6-0 record, 2.68 ERA in August (then was hammered in September.) The Tigers scored 6.9 runs/nine innings for him, which gave him a winning record despite his 5.37 ERA and horrible rate of home runs allowed (28 in 159 innings).

YEAR	TEAM/LEVEL	G	IP	W-L	PCT.	HITS	SO	BB	ERA
1991	Detroit	35	226	20-9	.690	256	91	44	3.90
1992	Detroit	34	222	14-13	.519	228	64	50	4.34
1993	Detroit	28	159	13-9	.591	186	70	44	5.37

MARK GUTHRIE

Minnesota Twins

Relief Pitcher

$29

Could be a steal in any '94 draft. Guthrie struggled with a shoulder problem early last year, which turned out to be a blood clot. His season ended in May, but he is expected to be healthy for spring training. Roberto Hernandez had a similar problem in 1991 . . . Guthrie was a fine pitcher in 1992, and there is little reason to think he won't be in '94, but some people will forget about him because of the lost season.

YEAR	TEAM/LEVEL	G	IP	W-L	SAVES	HITS	SO	BB	ERA
1991	Minnesota	41	98	7-5	2	116	72	41	4.32
1992	Minnesota	54	75	2-3	5	59	76	23	2.88
1993	Minnesota	22	21	2-1	0	20	15	16	4.71

RICKY GUTIERREZ
San Diego Padres
Shortstop
$32

Another of the good young players collected by San Diego while they have been circling the wagons. Gutierrez, from the Baltimore system, has Gold Glove potential at shortstop, although he's not there yet, plus he runs well and is not a wild swinger. None of that would keep him in the lineup if he hit .220, which seemed possible a year ago, but he hit .251 and scored more runs per at bat than Jay Bell.

YEAR	TEAM/LEVEL	G	AB	R	H	2B	3B	HR	RBI	BB	SB	AVG	OBP	SLG
1992	Rocheste AAA	125	431	54	109	9	3	0	41	53	14	.253	.331	.288
1993	San Diego	133	438	76	110	10	5	5	26	50	4	.251	.334	.331
1994	**Projected**	**140**	**472**	**56**	**115**	**10**	**3**	**3**	**37**	**57**	**9**	**.244**	**.325**	**.297**

JOSE GUZMAN
Chicago Cubs
Starting Pitcher
$36

Classic four-pitch pitcher, throws fastball, curve, slider and changeup. He was out in mid-summer with back trouble, and took time off in September, as Lefebvre looked at younger pitchers, which kept him under 200 innings . . . In my opinion, Guzman will continue to be a fine pitcher for several years, but the Cubs need to be careful not to push him when the back acts up . . . Has a multi-year record of pitching well late in the season.

YEAR	TEAM/LEVEL	G	IP	W-L	PCT.	HITS	SO	BB	ERA
1991	Texas	25	170	13-7	.650	152	125	84	3.08
1992	Texas	33	224	16-11	.593	229	179	73	3.66
1993	Chicago	30	191	12-10	.545	188	163	74	4.34

JUAN GUZMAN
Toronto Blue Jays
Starting Pitcher
$40

You should not take seriously the fact that his career winning percentage (.784) is the highest in history. That's the kind of record which is held by many people in turn, each of whom surrenders it as soon as he has a tough season . . . Guzman hasn't really harnessed his ability yet, and didn't pitch all that well in '93. The Blue Jays saved his butt about 15 times in 33 starts.

YEAR	TEAM/LEVEL	G	IP	W-L	PCT.	HITS	SO	BB	ERA
1991	Toronto	23	139	10-3	.769	98	123	66	2.99
1992	Toronto	28	181	16-5	.762	135	165	72	2.64
1993	Toronto	33	221	14-3	.824	211	194	110	3.99

CHRIS GWYNN
Kansas City Royals
Left Field
$26

I like him a little better every year. He's a lefthanded line drive hitter, hits a lot of hard ground balls. He doesn't have power or speed, and hardly ever goes to bat against a lefthanded pitcher, but is a pretty good outfielder. Still, in the last three years he has batted 510 times with 64 runs scored, 54 RBI—unimpressive run production for an outfielder.

YEAR	TEAM/LEVEL	G	AB	R	H	2B	3B	HR	RBI	BB	SB	AVG	OBP	SLG
1992	Kansas City	34	84	10	24	3	2	1	7	3	0	.286	.303	.405
1993	Kansas City	103	287	36	86	14	4	1	25	24	0	.300	.354	.387
1994	**Projected**	**115**	**318**	**39**	**89**	**14**	**3**	**5**	**35**	**24**	**1**	**.280**	**.330**	**.390**

TONY GWYNN

San Diego Padres

Right Field

$59

A lefthanded hitter, he led the National League in batting against lefthanded pitchers, at .359. Also led in innumerable other splits . . . Now has 11 consecutive .300 seasons, a lifetime .329 average, and 2,000+ hits with at least five years left. Was 14-for-15 as a base stealer last year, set a career high in doubles despite missing 40 games, and plays right field as well as anyone, although he may move to first.

YEAR	TEAM/LEVEL	G	AB	R	H	2B	3B	HR	RBI	BB	SB	AVG	OBP	SLG
1992	San Diego	128	520	77	165	27	3	6	41	46	3	.317	.371	.415
1993	San Diego	122	489	70	175	41	3	7	59	36	14	.358	.398	.497
1994	**Projected**	**130**	**514**	**67**	**164**	**25**	**4**	**6**	**50**	**40**	**8**	**.319**	**.369**	**.412**

DAVE HAAS

Detroit Tigers

Relief Pitcher

$9

He started the year as a well-regarded pitching prospect, but the league hit .375 against him, with 20% of the hits being home runs. He went on the disabled list in June with the ever-popular tendonitis, which is a baseball term meaning "His arm hurts and we don't know what the hell is wrong with it." A 28-year-old righthander, a .500 pitcher in the minor leagues, Grade D prospect.

YEAR	TEAM/LEVEL	G	IP	W-L	SAVES	HITS	SO	BB	ERA
1992	Toledo AAA	22	149	9-8	0	149	112	53	4.18
1992	Detroit	12	62	5-3	0	68	29	16	3.94
1993	Detroit	20	28	1-2	0	45	17	8	6.11

JOHN HABYAN

Kansas City Royals

Relief Pitcher

$21

A competent middle reliever, acquired by the Royals in late July, when they were losing games in the middle innings. Has always pitched well, and sometimes brilliantly, the first half of the season, but has had trouble in the hot months and late in the year. A sinker/slider pitcher with good control, no chance of moving into the closer role, would expect him to remain effective as a setup man.

YEAR	TEAM/LEVEL	G	IP	W-L	SAVES	HITS	SO	BB	ERA
1991	New York AL	66	90	4-2	2	73	70	20	2.30
1992	New York AL	56	73	5-6	7	84	44	21	3.84
1993	Two Teams	48	56	2-1	1	59	39	20	4.15

CHIP HALE

Minnesota Twins

Second Base/Third Base

$23

Hit .515 in September (17-for-33). The Twins second baseman of the future before the emergence of Knoblauch, Hale was trapped in AAA for four and a half years. He's not really a .300 hitter, but he'll hit .260-.280, with some doubles and walks, and can do the job at second and third. He won't budge Knoblauch, but he is a good backup for the Twins and could help somebody as a regular.

YEAR	TEAM/LEVEL	G	AB	R	H	2B	3B	HR	RBI	BB	SB	AVG	OBP	SLG
1992	MLE	132	463	61	124	23	7	0	42	59	3	.268	.351	.348
1993	Portland AAA	55	211	37	59	15	3	1	24	21	2	.280	.343	.393
1993	Minnesota	69	186	25	62	6	1	3	27	18	2	.333	.408	.425

BOB HAMELIN

Kansas City Royals

Designated Lumbering Slugger

$20

I used to describe Hamelin as a Kent Hrbek type, but I was afraid Hrbek would sue. Hamelin has a long swing, is slow and such a bad first baseman that it's hard to play him there. Has extensive history of injuries, because of his weight and a bad back. The Royals needed a lefthanded bat, and with Brett retired they *really* need a lefthanded bat, so I suppose he's it. Can hit better than .225.

YEAR	TEAM/LEVEL	G	AB	R	H	2B	3B	HR	RBI	BB	SB	AVG	OBP	SLG
1993	MLE	137	458	56	103	17	2	17	62	59	5	.225	.313	.382
1993	Kansas City	16	49	2	11	3	0	2	5	6	0	.224	.309	.408
1994	**Projected**	**109**	**321**	**37**	**76**	**13**	**2**	**11**	**44**	**42**	**2**	**.237**	**.325**	**.393**

DARRYL HAMILTON

Milwaukee Brewers

Outfielder

$43

Hamilton plays all three outfield positions for the Brewers, more in right field than anywhere else. He's kind of the unknown .300 hitter, has hit .295, .311, .298 and .310 over the last four years, plus it's not all singles and he can steal a base. Was hitting .325 last year until a September slump . . . Good player. Hit .364 on an 0-2 count (8 for 22). That was the best in the American League.

YEAR	TEAM/LEVEL	G	AB	R	H	2B	3B	HR	RBI	BB	SB	AVG	OBP	SLG
1992	Milwaukee	128	470	67	140	19	7	5	62	45	41	.298	.356	.400
1993	Milwaukee	135	520	74	161	21	1	9	48	45	21	.310	.367	.406
1994	**Projected**	**140**	**506**	**72**	**151**	**20**	**3**	**5**	**57**	**47**	**28**	**.298**	**.358**	**.379**

JOEY HAMILTON

San Diego Padres

Starting Pitcher

$17

Hamilton was the Padres' first pick in 1991 and was considered the top pitching prospect in their organization a year ago, but had a poor season and didn't get called up. He's a righthander, good size and a good fastball, doesn't walk five men a game and get beat that way, but needs to develop his second and third pitches. I suspect that he and the Padres' organization don't get along too well.

YEAR	TEAM/LEVEL	G	IP	W-L	PCT.	HITS	SO	BB	ERA
1992	Wichita AA	6	35	3-0	1.000	33	26	11	2.86
1993	Wichita AA	15	91	4-9	.308	101	50	36	3.97
1993	Las Vegas AAA	8	47	3-2	.600	49	33	22	4.40

CHRIS HAMMOND

Florida Marlins

Starting Pitcher

$23

The Marlins acquired him in a trade for Gary Scott, an exchange of former pheenoms, and it looked like one of the best trades ever made, as Hammond was 10-4 at the All-Star break. He was pounded senseless the second half, which has been his habit—in his career he is 22-14 before the break, but 3-17 after. Lefthanded finesse pitcher, a type of pitcher who rarely does well with a bad team.

YEAR	TEAM/LEVEL	G	IP	W-L	PCT.	HITS	SO	BB	ERA
1991	Cincinnati	20	100	7-7	.500	92	50	48	4.06
1992	Cincinnati	28	147	7-10	.412	149	79	55	4.21
1993	Florida	32	191	11-12	.478	207	108	66	4.66

JEFF HAMMONDS

Baltimore Orioles

Outfielder

$27

The fourth player taken in the '92 draft, an outfielder from Stanford; received reported $975,000 to sign. Might have gone higher in the draft if he wasn't expected to cost so much. Has been compared to Rickey Henderson, except he never walks, which is like being called a flat-chested Dolly Parton, or Randy Johnson without the fastball. Has power and speed, might be able to play center but his arm is a question. Has a back problem.

YEAR	TEAM/LEVEL	G	AB	R	H	2B	3B	HR	RBI	BB	SB	AVG	OBP	SLG
1993	MLE	60	232	29	62	9	0	6	26	9	6	.267	.295	.384
1993	Baltimore	33	105	10	32	8	0	3	19	2	4	.305	.312	.467
1994	**Projected**	**137**	**531**	**61**	**148**	**27**	**0**	**14**	**71**	**17**	**16**	**.279**	**.301**	**.409**

MIKE HAMPTON

Seattle Mariners

Starting Pitcher

$15

A small lefthander who will probably spend 1993 in Triple-A, but who has considerable promise. Florida native, drafted out of high school. Has above-average fastball, changes speeds well, curve and slider are in the development stage but work sometimes. Has thrown strikes in the minors, although his control left him when he got the call, as it often does. Grade B prospect.

YEAR	TEAM/LEVEL	G	IP	W-L	PCT.	HITS	SO	BB	ERA
1992	San Bernadino A	25	170	13-8	.619	163	132	66	3.12
1993	Jacksonville AA	15	87	6-4	.600	71	84	33	3.71
1993	Seattle	13	17	1-3	.250	28	8	17	9.53

CHRIS HANEY

Kansas City Royals

Starting Pitcher

$23

On balance, he pitched much better than the 6.02 ERA would suggest. He's a funny pitcher. Some days he looks like a finished product, like Bud Black or Terry Mulholland; other times he looks like he would never get anybody out. No star potential, but could be third-starter type. His father, I suspect, is a pretty good pitching coach, and that may be the little edge he needs to get over the hump.

YEAR	TEAM/LEVEL	G	IP	W-L	PCT.	HITS	SO	BB	ERA
1992	Two Teams	16	80	4-6	.400	75	54	26	4.61
1993	Omaha AAA	8	48	6-1	.857	43	32	14	2.27
1993	Kansas City	23	124	9-9	.500	141	65	53	6.02

DAVE HANSEN

Los Angeles Dodgers

Third Base

$25

Had a great year as a pinch hitter, and may have earned another shot at the third base job, which has been up for grabs since Ron Cey was traded in 1983. He's only 25 years old, and would not be the first player to have a good career after punting one chance. Lefthanded line drive hitter, good plate discipline, was slowed in '92 by a back injury. Hit .492 with runners on base (29-for-59).

YEAR	TEAM/LEVEL	G	AB	R	H	2B	3B	HR	RBI	BB	SB	AVG	OBP	SLG
1992	Los Angeles	132	341	30	73	11	0	6	22	34	0	.214	.286	.299
1993	Los Angeles	84	105	13	38	3	0	4	30	21	0	.362	.465	.505
1994	**Projected**	**116**	**247**	**25**	**63**	**10**	**1**	**4**	**28**	**30**	**2**	**.255**	**.336**	**.352**

ERIK HANSON

Cincinnati Reds

Starting Pitcher

$35

If you're looking at me to explain the trade, look somewhere else. I don't understand either part of it. Hanson-for-Ayala is a trade I wouldn't make, but a) Hanson could be a free agent in a year, and b) Lou Piniella knows these guys better than I do. But Bret Boone for Dan Wilson? It brings to mind Ryne Sandberg as partial payment for Ivan DeJesus.

YEAR	TEAM/LEVEL	G	IP	W-L	PCT.	HITS	SO	BB	ERA
1991	Seattle	27	175	8-8	.500	182	143	56	3.81
1992	Seattle	31	187	8-17	.320	209	112	57	4.82
1993	Seattle	31	215	11-12	.478	215	163	60	3.47

MIKE HARKEY

Chicago Cubs

Starting Pitcher

$19

After pitching well in April (3-0, 1.77 ERA) he developed tendonitis in his shoulder, and struggled the rest of the year, having ERAs of 5.10 to 6.46 in each of the other months. While it is perhaps premature to bury him, he has now battled serious injuries for three years, and it is very questionable whether he will ever win with any consistency.

YEAR	TEAM/LEVEL	G	IP	W-L	PCT.	HITS	SO	BB	ERA
1991	Chicago	4	19	0-2	.000	34	15	6	5.30
1992	Chicago	7	38	4-0	1.000	38	21	15	1.89
1993	Chicago	28	157	10-10	.500	187	67	43	5.26

PETE HARNISCH

Houston Astros

Starting Pitcher

$69

Led the National League in shutouts (4), opposition batting average (.214), fewest hits per nine innings (171 in 217.2, 7.07), also had the lowest ratio of ground balls to fly balls in the National League (240-263) . . . Speaking of lopsided trades, the Orioles traded Harnisch *and* Curt Schilling *and* Steve Finley for Glenn Davis . . . Always bet on a power pitcher. You'll win more than you lose.

YEAR	TEAM/LEVEL	G	IP	W-L	PCT.	HITS	SO	BB	ERA
1991	Houston	33	217	12-9	.571	169	172	83	2.70
1992	Houston	34	207	9-10	.474	182	164	64	3.70
1993	Houston	33	218	16-9	.640	171	185	79	2.98

BRIAN HARPER

Free Agent

Catcher

$38

He will probably be leaving a park in which he has hit 30-40 points better than he hit on the road, so his average will probably dip a few points in '94. He's 34 years old, and his defense has never been good. Still, he's hit .294 or better six straight times, and there aren't many catchers who do that . . . There was a 1930s catcher named Spud Davis who had exactly the same combination of talents as Harper.

YEAR	TEAM/LEVEL	G	AB	R	H	2B	3B	HR	RBI	BB	SB	AVG	OBP	SLG
1992	Minnesota	140	502	58	154	25	0	9	73	26	0	.307	.343	.410
1993	Minnesota	147	530	52	161	26	1	12	73	29	1	.304	.347	.425
1994	**Projected**	**136**	**484**	**50**	**141**	**24**	**1**	**9**	**67**	**23**	**1**	**.291**	**.323**	**.401**

DONALD HARRIS

Texas Rangers

Center Field

$8

A born-again football player, a free safety from Texas Tech who was almost good enough to turn pro. Harris is said to be an exceptional center fielder with an arm, and he is strong enough to hit home runs if he can make contact, which seems like a major longshot. Didn't have a good year at Oklahoma City (his MLE from 1992 was better), but was called up to cover center during Hulce's injury. Grade D prospect.

YEAR	TEAM/LEVEL	G	AB	R	H	2B	3B	HR	RBI	BB	SB	AVG	OBP	SLG
1993	Ok City AAA	96	367	48	93	13	9	6	40	23	4	.253	.301	.387
1993	MLE	96	353	36	79	11	5	4	30	17	2	.224	.259	.317
1993	Texas	40	76	10	15	2	0	1	8	5	0	.197	.253	.263

GENE HARRIS

San Diego Padres

Relief Pitcher

$29

After a bad slump in July he converted his last seven save opportunities, regaining control of the Padres' closer spot. He is not well-qualified to do that job. He had never had an ERA below 4.00 until last year, and even last year his peripheral stats were poor, and he gave up seven unearned runs in 59 innings. Still, the big money job is his to lose.

YEAR	TEAM/LEVEL	G	IP	W-L	SAVES	HITS	SO	BB	ERA
1991	Seattle	8	13	0-0	1	15	6	10	4.05
1992	Two Teams	22	30	0-2	0	23	25	15	4.15
1993	San Diego	59	59	6-6	23	57	39	37	3.03

GREG HARRIS

Boston Red Sox

Relief Pitcher

$30

Hardworking reliever, led the American League in games pitched and led the major leagues in relief innings, with 112. He pitched OK overall, but attempted to move into the closer role while Russell was out with an ankle injury, and that went very badly. He blew most of his leads, which contributed to the team's miserable pennant drive . . . Harris is a solid middle reliever, and should continue to be.

YEAR	TEAM/LEVEL	G	IP	W-L	SAVES	HITS	SO	BB	ERA
1991	Boston	53	173	11-12	2	157	127	69	3.85
1992	Boston	70	108	4-9	4	82	73	60	2.51
1993	Boston	80	112	6-7	8	95	103	60	3.77

GREG W. HARRIS

Colorado Rockies

Starting Pitcher

$26

Some guys just aren't born lucky. Harris could easily have been 17-11 with a 3.59 ERA in '93. A pitcher's record reflects the park and embodies his team, not only in wins. If an infielder doesn't reach a ground ball, that's a base hit. Harris led the league in runs allowed (127) home runs (33), and slugging percentage (.455), but Greg Maddux would have a hard time posting a good record for this team in this park.

YEAR	TEAM/LEVEL	G	IP	W-L	PCT.	HITS	SO	BB	ERA
1991	San Diego	20	133	9-5	.643	116	95	27	2.23
1992	San Diego	20	118	4-8	.333	113	66	35	4.12
1993	Two Teams	35	225	11-17	.393	239	123	69	4.59

LENNY HARRIS
Free Agent
Utilityman
$21

Harris had hit well for three years (.304, .287 and .271) before failing to hit much in 160 at bats last year. Harris very much wants to play regularly, and he is *almost* there—another 10 points on his average, another 10 stolen bases a year, a few more walks and he's Bip Roberts or Tony Phillips. He's an awfully good bench player—a lefthanded line drive hitter who can run and play third base or second.

YEAR	TEAM/LEVEL	G	AB	R	H	2B	3B	HR	RBI	BB	SB	AVG	OBP	SLG
1992	Los Angeles	135	347	28	94	11	0	0	30	24	19	.271	.318	.303
1993	Los Angeles	107	160	20	38	6	1	2	11	15	3	.238	.303	.325
1994	**Projected**	**122**	**191**	**22**	**51**	**7**	**1**	**1**	**17**	**16**	**7**	**.267**	**.324**	**.330**

MIKE HARTLEY
Free Agent
Relief Pitcher
$20

The Twins tried to outright Hartley to Portland, but he refused the assignment and has become a free agent. Hartley went through the Dodger system very slowly, and was pushing 30 before he surfaced; he's now 32, and still not *really* established, although he's not a bad pitcher. Posted a 2.61 ERA after the All-Star break . . . Nobody who has him seems to want to keep him, which probably should tell us something.

YEAR	TEAM/LEVEL	G	IP	W-L	SAVES	HITS	SO	BB	ERA
1991	Two Teams	58	83	4-1	2	74	63	47	4.21
1992	Philadelphia	46	55	7-6	0	54	53	23	3.44
1993	Minnesota	53	81	1-2	1	86	57	36	4.00

BRYAN HARVEY
Florida Marlins
Closer
$66

He had a wonderful season, from which we should learn this: that the bullpen is **not** the key to success in baseball. The Marlins' bullpen was vastly better than that of any other expansion team in history—yet the team's won-lost record was 64-98, a typical expansion-type record . . . Limited lefthanded hitters to a .132 batting average, lowest in the major leagues . . . Allowed only 7.6 baserunners per nine innings, the best in the majors.

YEAR	TEAM/LEVEL	G	IP	W-L	SAVES	HITS	SO	BB	ERA
1991	California	67	79	2-4	46	51	101	17	1.60
1992	California	25	29	0-4	13	22	34	11	2.83
1993	Florida	59	69	1-5	45	45	73	13	1.70

BILL (WHATTA) HASELMAN
Seattle Mariners
Catcher
$18

Got his first chance to play a little, and showed OK with the bat. With the acquisition of Dan Wilson, another righthanded hitting catcher, his position on the team is unclear. His arm is weak, plus teams prefer to carry a lefthanded hitting backup catcher when they can, so if he hadn't hit his career would have ended quickly. But if you hit, they'll work you in somewhere.

YEAR	TEAM/LEVEL	G	AB	R	H	2B	3B	HR	RBI	BB	SB	AVG	OBP	SLG
1992	MLE	105	340	36	71	15	1	12	40	35	1	.209	.283	.365
1993	Seattle	58	137	21	35	8	0	5	16	12	2	.255	.316	.423
1993	**Projected**	**72**	**211**	**25**	**50**	**13**	**0**	**7**	**28**	**22**	**2**	**.237**	**.309**	**.398**

JOHN CANDELARIA

Released

Relief Pitcher

No Value

Was released by the Pirates on July 10. His career began brilliantly and ground to an agonizing halt; he was a month away from being released for five years . . . The puzzle about Candelaria was that while almost everyone who had to deal with him regarded him as a fool, he was a very heady pitcher. When he had ordinary stuff he was still a fine pitcher; when he had nothing he was still getting people out.

YEAR	TEAM/LEVEL	G	IP	W-L	SAVES	HITS	SO	BB	ERA
1991	Los Angeles	59	34	1-1	2	31	38	11	3.74
1992	Los Angeles	50	25	2-5	5	20	23	13	2.84
1993	Pittsburgh	24	20	0-3	1	25	17	9	8.24

TOM CANDIOTTI

Los Angeles Dodgers

Starting Pitcher

$54

The Dodgers, for the second straight year, stuck him with an undeserved won-lost record although he pitched very well. His offensive support, 2.53 runs per nine innings, was easily the worst in the major leagues. He had a terrible slump in September, which may have been from frustration/trying to be perfect, or may indicate something more serious. I suspect he's got five good years left.

YEAR	TEAM/LEVEL	G	IP	W-L	PCT.	HITS	SO	BB	ERA
1991	Two Teams	34	238	13-13	.500	202	167	73	2.65
1992	Los Angeles	32	204	11-15	.423	177	152	63	3.00
1993	Los Angeles	33	214	8-10	.444	192	155	71	3.12

JOSE CANSECO

Texas Rangers

Right Field/Relief Pitcher

$28

He is probably all but done. He's hit one triple in two years and is 12-for-25 as a base stealer. His range is limited and he grounds into double plays, which confirms what we see: he can't run anymore. His chance to be a star now is to be Cecil Fielder, to hit 50 homers and drive in 130, but he has to stay healthy to do that, and he needs to grow up to stay healthy.

YEAR	TEAM/LEVEL	G	AB	R	H	2B	3B	HR	RBI	BB	SB	AVG	OBP	SLG
1991	Oakland	154	572	115	152	32	1	44	122	78	26	.266	.359	.556
1992	Two Teams	119	439	74	107	15	0	26	87	63	6	.244	.344	.456
1993	Texas	60	231	30	59	14	1	10	46	16	6	.255	.308	.455

OZZIE CANSECO

Released

Outfielder

$14

Quit the game in mid-summer, frustrated that the Cardinals would not recall him although he was hitting some home runs. His skills now are similar to his brother's, still not quite as good—a low-average power hitter who is capable of hitting quite a few home runs. If he comes out of retirement he needs to sign with someone like Seattle or San Diego, where there is opportunity for a hitter in a good park.

YEAR	TEAM/LEVEL	G	AB	R	H	2B	3B	HR	RBI	BB	SB	AVG	OBP	LG
1992	MLE	98	295	39	69	16	0	16	42	33	0	.234	.311	.451
1993	St. Louis	6	17	0	3	0	0	0	0	1	0	.176	.222	.176
1993	Louisvill AAA	44	154	20	37	6	1	13	33	15	1	.240	.306	.545

RAMON CARABALLO
Atlanta Braves
Second Base
$9

A 24-year-old marginal prospect who was called up to pinch run in September, although he's been less than a 60 percent base stealer in Triple-A. He's a Joey Cora-type, a tiny switch-hitting second baseman. Mark Lemke is not exactly Roberto Alomar, but Caraballo's batting average wouldn't be a lot better than Lemke's, he has no power, and his poor strikeout/walk ratio and poor stolen base percentages are significant liabilities.

YEAR	TEAM/LEVEL	G	AB	R	H	2B	3B	HR	RBI	BB	SB	AVG	OBP	SLG
1992	Richmond AAA	101	405	42	114	20	3	2	40	22	19	.281	.323	.360
1993	Richmond AAA	126	470	73	128	25	9	3	41	30	20	.272	.322	.383
1993	MLE	126	452	54	110	21	4	2	30	21	12	.243	.277	.321

PAUL CAREY
Baltimore Orioles
Utility Player
$18

I would compare him to a lefthanded Francisco Cabrera. A huge outfielder/first baseman/catcher, was signed in 1990 by an independent minor league team, then purchased by Baltimore. He doesn't run and doesn't have a position, so will have to make his mark as a hitter, but it appears he might. Erroneously listed as a righthanded hitter in many sources, 26 years old; can do what Glenn Davis did and save the Orioles $3 million.

YEAR	TEAM/LEVEL	G	AB	R	H	2B	3B	HR	RBI	BB	SB	AVG	OBP	SLG
1993	Rochester AAA	96	325	63	101	20	4	12	50	65	0	.311	.431	.508
1993	MLE	96	311	49	87	16	2	10	39	51	0	.280	.381	.441
1993	Baltimore	18	47	1	10	1	0	0	3	5	0	.213	.288	.234

CRIS CARPENTER
Texas Rangers
Relief Pitcher
$24

A pretty good middle reliever, acquired by the Rangers (for two good prospects) as part of a mid-summer effort to build up their bullpen. Has no star potential . . . Throws fastball most of the time, which people say makes him ineffective the second time through the lineup, although actually the data do not show this . . . A good hitter, not that that will help much if he stays in the American League.

YEAR	TEAM/LEVEL	G	IP	W-L	SAVES	HITS	SO	BB	ERA
1991	St. Louis	59	66	10-4	0	53	47	20	4.23
1992	St. Louis	73	88	5-4	1	69	46	27	2.97
1993	Two Teams	56	69	4-2	1	64	53	25	3.50

CHUCK CARR
Florida Marlins
Outfielder
$33

His skills should be one of the solid building blocks of a rapidly improving Florida team, and some form of minor stardom cannot be ruled out. A true center fielder is something that expansion teams historically have had trouble coming up with, and often they have played left or right fielders in center for several years. Carr needs to boost his on-base percentage to the .350 range to be a championship-quality player.

YEAR	TEAM/LEVEL	G	AB	R	H	2B	3B	HR	RBI	BB	SB	AVG	OBP	SLG
1992	MLE	124	468	68	125	13	6	2	26	30	46	.267	.311	.333
1992	St. Louis	22	64	8	14	3	0	0	3	9	10	.219	.315	.266
1993	Florida	142	551	75	147	19	2	4	41	49	58	.267	.327	.330

MARK CARREON
San Francisco Giants
Outfielder
$26

He signed with the Giants as a free agent, and was one of the best pinch hitter/fifth outfielders in baseball. Two-thirds of his at bats were against lefthanded pitching, which seemed to be the edge he needed to get his slugging percentage out of the mid-.300s, where he was of limited value. Doesn't provide any defense and doesn't run real well, but should remain valuable if he stays in his role.

YEAR	TEAM/LEVEL	G	AB	R	H	2B	3B	HR	RBI	BB	SB	AVG	OBP	SLG
1991	New York NL	106	254	18	66	6	0	4	21	12	2	.260	.297	.331
1992	Detroit	101	336	34	78	11	1	10	41	22	3	.232	.278	.360
1993	S. Francisco	78	150	22	49	9	1	7	33	13	1	.327	.373	.540

MATIAS CARRILLO
Florida Marlins
Right Field
$11

Is 31 years old, a lefthanded batter and thrower, born in Mexico and played in the Mexican League for many years, hitting .353 with 20 homers, 102 RBI for Mexico City in 1985. He was signed by the Pirates in 1986 and taken by the Brewers in a minor league draft in 1987, but made slow progress, and was eventually released. Florida signed him as a free agent. Probably has no future, but played OK.

YEAR	TEAM/LEVEL	G	AB	R	H	2B	3B	HR	RBI	BB	SB	AVG	OBP	SLG
1991	Denver AAA	120	421	56	116	18	5	8	56	32	11	.276	.325	.399
1991	MLE	120	400	40	95	15	2	5	40	23	7	.238	.279	.323
1993	Florida	24	55	4	14	6	0	0	3	1	0	.255	.281	.364

JOE CARTER
Toronto Blue Jays
Right Field
$63

Hits the ball in the air more consistently than any other major league player . . . Joe is the kind of player that statistical analysts will tell you is badly overrated, but no GM will ever be able to resist. You might assume that he is going to skate into the Hall of Fame as easily as he can pass through Canadian customs, and you might well be right, but the Hall of Fame has never been kind to RBI men.

YEAR	TEAM/LEVEL	G	AB	R	H	2B	3B	HR	RBI	BB	SB	AVG	OBP	SLG
1992	Toronto	158	622	97	164	30	7	34	119	36	12	.264	.309	.498
1993	Toronto	155	603	92	153	33	5	33	121	47	8	.254	.312	.489
1994	**Projected**	**157**	**612**	**83**	**152**	**31**	**3**	**27**	**101**	**44**	**13**	**.248**	**.299**	**.441**

CHUCK CARY
Chicago White Sox
Lefthanded Pitcher
$6

Note the strikeout-to-walk ratio at South Bend: 28 to 1. Cary, who was in the Yankees starting rotation in 1990, was out of baseball in 1992, and came back apparently determined to throw more strikes. He was still troubled by the injuries which drove him from the game, and made two trips to the disabled list after signing with the White Sox in January. Limited future, probably.

YEAR	TEAM/LEVEL	G	IP	W-L	SAVES	HITS	SO	BB	ERA
1991	New York AL	10	53	1-6	0	61	34	32	5.91
1993	South Bend A	8	18	1-1	1	13	28	1	2.00
1993	Chicago	16	21	1-0	0	22	10	11	5.23

LARRY CASIAN

Minnesota Twins

Lefthanded Relief Pitcher

$24

A minor league veteran, he converted to the bullpen in 1991, had an excellent year at Portland in '92, and came out of spring training with a job. His first almost-full season in the majors was a qualified success. Lefthanders, whom he is supposed to get out above all else, hit .289 against him, but his stats were generally good, and only 10 of 47 inherited runners crossed the plate (norm: 32%).

YEAR	TEAM/LEVEL	G	IP	W-L	SAVES	HITS	SO	BB	ERA
1992	Portland AAA	58	62	4-0	11	54	43	13	2.32
1992	Minnesota	6	7	1-0	0	7	2	1	2.70
1993	Minnesota	54	57	5-3	1	59	31	14	3.02

PEDRO (ANDRE) CASTELLANO

Colorado Rockies

Third Base

$9

He is unlikely to move immediately into the majors in view of a) his youth (he's 24), b) Charlie Hayes's fine season, and c) his poor offensive and defensive performance in his trials. A native of Venezuela, he was taken from the Cubs in the third round of the expansion draft. 1993 would normally have been his Double-A season, but the Rockies didn't have a Double-A team yet. Grade C prospect.

YEAR	TEAM/LEVEL	G	AB	R	H	2B	3B	HR	RBI	BB	SB	AVG	OBP	SLG
1993	Colo Spr AAA	90	304	61	95	21	2	12	60	36	3	.313	.387	.513
1993	MLE	90	285	37	76	16	1	8	37	22	1	.267	.319	.414
1993	Colorado	34	71	12	13	2	0	3	7	8	1	.183	.266	.338

VINNY CASTILLA

Colorado Rockies

Shortstop

$18

He hit .297 before the All-Star break (60 for 202), but .193 afterward. My description of him last year, as a Todd Cruz-type player, still seems accurate; he's a decent shortstop with a strong arm, has some power but not Power, doesn't run well enough to count for much, and swings at everything. I predict a six- to eight-year career punctuated by flashes of brilliance, but never developing consistency. (Lay off the watches, kid.)

YEAR	TEAM/LEVEL	G	AB	R	H	2B	3B	HR	RBI	BB	SB	AVG	OBP	SLG
1992	Richmond AAA	127	449	49	113	29	1	7	44	21	1	.252	.288	.367
1993	Colorado	105	337	36	86	9	7	9	30	13	2	.255	.283	.404
1994	**Projected**	**100**	**300**	**28**	**71**	**12**	**2**	**6**	**30**	**11**	**1**	**.237**	**.264**	**.350**

FRANK CASTILLO

Chicago Cubs

Starting Pitcher

$20

Had a miserable year, for no really obvious reason, and his future is in doubt. He was dropped from the rotation in September, to allow the Cubs to look at other pitchers; with a new manager, he might or might not be chosen for the 1994 starting rotation. If he comes out of spring training with a starting job, I would recommend that you draft him. He's a better pitcher than his 1993 or career record shows.

YEAR	TEAM/LEVEL	G	IP	W-L	PCT.	HITS	SO	BB	ERA
1991	Chicago	18	112	6-7	.462	107	73	37	4.35
1992	Chicago	33	205	10-11	.476	179	135	63	3.46
1993	Chicago	29	141	5-8	.385	162	84	39	4.84

TONY CASTILLO

Toronto Blue Jays

Lefthanded Relief Pitcher

$16

Another Blue Jays' prodigal son, like Griffin and Fernandez. Castillo was traded to Atlanta some years ago, was the Braves lefthanded one-out man in '90, wasn't great, went to the minors in '91 in an effort to convert to a starting role, was traded to the Mets and Tigers, and came back to the Blue Jays as a minor league free agent. He's 31 years old, just a modest, serviceable talent.

YEAR	TEAM/LEVEL	G	IP	W-L	SAVES	HITS	SO	BB	ERA
1991	Richmond AAA	23	118	5-6	0	89	78	32	2.90
1992	Toledo AAA	12	45	2-3	2	48	24	14	3.63
1993	Toronto	51	51	3-2	0	44	28	22	3.38

ANDUJAR CEDENO

Houston Astros

Shortstop

$42

In view of his youth (he's only 24) we might assume that his fine season at bat represents real development. If so, he's going to be one of the highest-paid players in baseball in three years. On the other hand, it is possible that his ability has matured at a level somewhere between 1992 and 1993, in which case he is still going to have a job. He has yet to play consistently well in the field.

YEAR	TEAM/LEVEL	G	AB	R	H	2B	3B	HR	RBI	BB	SB	AVG	OBP	SLG
1991	Houston	67	251	27	61	13	2	9	36	9	4	.243	.270	.418
1992	Houston	71	220	15	38	13	2	2	13	14	2	.173	.232	.277
1993	Houston	149	505	69	143	24	4	11	56	48	9	.283	.346	.412

DOMINGO CEDENO

Toronto Blue Jays

Shortstop

$12

If Tony Fernandez departs the World Champions as a free agent, Cedeno will be second in line for the shortstop job, behind Alex Gonzalez. He is said to be an exceptional fielder, and he is coming off his best season with the bat. I could not state with any confidence that he will hit above .220 in the majors, and I am fairly confident that his secondary average will be under .200. Grade C prospect.

YEAR	TEAM/LEVEL	G	AB	R	H	2B	3B	HR	RBI	BB	SB	AVG	OBP	SLG
1992	MLE	124	387	29	80	9	5	2	21	15	6	.207	.236	.271
1993	MLE	103	374	50	96	15	9	2	24	28	11	.257	.308	.361
1993	Toronto	15	46	5	8	0	0	0	7	1	1	.174	.188	.174

WES CHAMBERLAIN

Philadelphia Phillies

Right Field

$29

The Eisenreich/Chamberlain combination was among the most effective platoons in the majors last year, along with Incaviglia/Thompson and Wilkins/Lake. Chamberlain also played very well in the field, defying his reputation . . . His chance of being a star is probably gone, but he is young enough to work back into an everyday job, with luck. Eisenreich may not return, which should help him.

YEAR	TEAM/LEVEL	G	AB	R	H	2B	3B	HR	RBI	BB	SB	AVG	OBP	SLG
1992	Philadelphia	76	275	26	71	18	0	9	41	10	4	.258	.285	.422
1993	Philadelphia	96	284	34	80	20	2	12	45	17	2	.282	.320	.493
1994	**Projected**	**108**	**368**	**41**	**95**	**20**	**2**	**11**	**52**	**24**	**7**	**.258**	**.304**	**.413**

NORM CHARLTON

Seattle Mariners

Relief Ace

$15

He blew out the ligament in his pitching elbow. He has had the Tommy John surgery, but is expected to be out at least until the All-Star break in '94, probably all year. Always pitches well . . . He was 18-for-21 in save opportunities last year and struck out 12.5 men per nine innings before the elbow finished his season in early July . . . Throws 90-plus, mixes in slider and split-finger.

YEAR	TEAM/LEVEL	G	IP	W-L	SAVES	HITS	SO	BB	ERA
1991	Cincinnati	39	108	3-5	1	92	77	34	2.91
1992	Cincinnati	64	81	4-2	26	79	90	26	2.99
1993	Seattle	34	35	1-3	18	22	48	17	2.34

MIKE CHRISTOPHER

Cleveland Indians

Relief Pitcher

$14

A 30-year-old minor league veteran. He has saved 64 games in three years in Triple-A and has pitched well in his callups (2.94 ERA in 22 games), so frankly it is hard for me to understand why the Indians have not shown more interest in letting him pitch. There is, of course, a pervasive prejudice in favor of guys who throw hard, which Christopher doesn't. He deserves a better deal.

YEAR	TEAM/LEVEL	G	IP	W-L	SAVES	HITS	SO	BB	ERA
1992	Cleveland	10	18	0-0	0	17	13	10	3.00
1993	Charlotte AAA	50	50	3-6	22	51	36	6	3.22
1993	Cleveland	9	12	0-0	0	14	8	2	3.86

ARCHI CIANFROCCO

San Diego Padres

First/Third Base

$19

The Padres acquired him from the Expos the day before the Sheffield trade. They wanted Cianfrocco to play third, but he doesn't look anything like a third baseman, and, as Dan Rather said, if it walks like a duck, talks like a duck, and quacks like a duck, it can't play third base. He doesn't hit quite enough to be a regular first baseman, but should have a substantial career off the bench.

YEAR	TEAM/LEVEL	G	AB	R	H	2B	3B	HR	RBI	BB	SB	AVG	OBP	SLG
1992	Montreal	86	232	25	56	5	2	6	16	11	3	.241	.276	.358
1993	San Diego	96	296	30	72	11	2	12	48	17	2	.243	.287	.416
1994	**Projected**	**109**	**345**	**38**	**87**	**15**	**3**	**8**	**46**	**18**	**4**	**.252**	**.289**	**.383**

JEFF CIRILLO

Milwaukee Brewers

Third Base

$20

An 11th-round pick in 1991, Cirillo has made a name for himself by hitting .350 in the Pioneer League, .304 in the Midwest League, .341 in the Texas League and .293 in the American Association. His MLE shows that he is probably a better hitter right now than B. J. Surhoff, and while I haven't seen him, his defensive statistics and his rapid progress would both suggest that his glovework is not anything too awful. Grade B prospect.

YEAR	TEAM/LEVEL	G	AB	R	H	2B	3B	HR	RBI	BB	SB	AVG	OBP	SLG
1993	El Paso AA	67	249	53	85	16	2	9	41	26	2	.341	.410	.530
1993	New Orl AAA	58	215	31	63	13	2	3	32	29	2	.293	.385	.414
1993	MLE	125	442	66	126	25	2	9	58	39	2	.285	.343	.412

DAVE CLARK

Pittsburgh Pirates

Outfielder/Pinch Hitter

$22

Well, I'm happy. I've been arguing for years that Clark could hit .270-.280 with a .400-plus slugging percentage in the majors, and Jim Leyland finally gave him a chance to do it. A lefthanded hitter, had 94% of his at bats against righthanders. He's 31, so he won't move out of the platoon role, but should keep his job. Defense isn't great, not fast but not Mike Lavalliere.

YEAR	TEAM/LEVEL	G	AB	R	H	2B	3B	HR	RBI	BB	SB	AVG	OBP	SLG
1992	MLE	78	241	33	65	15	4	7	42	26	4	.270	.341	.452
1992	Pittsburgh	23	33	3	7	0	0	2	7	6	0	.212	.325	.394
1993	Pittsburgh	110	277	43	75	11	2	11	46	38	1	.271	.358	.444

JERALD CLARK

Colorado Rockies

Left Field

$22

I figured the "Real Park Equivalent" for some of the Colorado players; Clark's stats are equivalent to .258 with 11 homers, 53 RBI in a real park. In other words, his season is about like his performance in San Diego, which is to say, not really good enough to play . . . The Rockies need to avoid being fooled by the stats, and try to get a real player out there as quickly as they can.

YEAR	TEAM/LEVEL	G	AB	R	H	2B	3B	HR	RBI	BB	SB	AVG	OBP	SLG
1992	San Diego	146	496	45	120	22	6	12	58	22	3	.242	.278	.383
1993	Colorado	140	478	65	135	26	6	13	67	20	9	.282	.324	.444
1993	REAL PARK	140	469	52	121	25	3	11	53	20	9	.258	.300	.397

MARK CLARK

Cleveland Indians

Starting Pitcher

$25

He spent six weeks on the disabled list, just after the All-Star game. Before going on the DL he had a 5.70 ERA; afterward (six starts) it was 2.09 . . . Base stealers were 8-for-18 against him last year, after going 22-for-25 before last year. 8-for-18, from the pitcher's standpoint, is far better than 0-for-0 . . . Throws hard sinking fastball, has good control. Could be Cleveland's number-one starter.

YEAR	TEAM/LEVEL	G	IP	W-L	PCT.	HITS	SO	BB	ERA
1992	Louisville AAA	9	61	4-4	.500	56	38	15	2.80
1992	St. Louis	20	113	3-10	.231	117	44	36	4.45
1993	Cleveland	26	109	7-5	.583	119	57	25	4.28

PHIL CLARK

San Diego Padres

All-around Hitter

$23

Was used by San Diego as a catcher, first baseman, third baseman, left fielder and right fielder, collecting 55% of his at bats against lefties. Right field might be his best position, at a guess . . . A far better hitter than his brother Jerald, he is one of the many fine young players collected by the Padres while they've been taking their licks. He doesn't have superstar potential, but he can drive in some runs.

YEAR	TEAM/LEVEL	G	AB	R	H	2B	3B	HR	RBI	BB	SB	AVG	OBP	SLG
1993	Detroit	23	54	3	22	4	0	1	5	6	1	.407	.467	.537
1993	San Diego	102	240	33	75	17	0	9	33	8	2	.313	.345	.496
1994	**Projected**	**97**	**275**	**32**	**76**	**14**	**1**	**7**	**35**	**15**	**3**	**.276**	**.314**	**.411**

WILL CLARK

San Francisco Giants

First Base

$52

A free agent at this writing. The top group of NL first basemen is now McGriff, Grace and Bagwell; the middle group—you rank 'em—is Clark, Kruk, Jefferies, Galarraga and Murray. Drove in 95 to 116 runs a year from 1987 to 1991, but 73 a year the last two years . . . He's 30; many or most players' best years are behind them at 30, but certainly if he's healthy, he's going to drive in more than 73.

YEAR	TEAM/LEVEL	G	AB	R	H	2B	3B	HR	RBI	BB	SB	AVG	OBP	SLG
1992	San Francisco	144	513	69	154	40	1	16	73	73	12	.300	.384	.476
1993	San Francisco	132	491	82	139	27	2	14	73	63	2	.283	.367	.432
1994	**Projected**	**143**	**525**	**79**	**156**	**30**	**4**	**21**	**88**	**66**	**6**	**.297**	**.376**	**.490**

ROYAL CLAYTON

New York Yankees

Starter/Reliever

$7

Minor league veteran, Royce Clayton's older brother, Yankees 18th-round pick out of UC-Irvine in 1987. He is not a true prospect but has been consistent in the swingman role for three years in AAA. A minor league free agent . . . Someone who needs pitching might give him a look. Doesn't throw hard, but is healthy, versatile, and deserves a shot in the majors.

YEAR	TEAM/LEVEL	G	IP	W-L	PCT.	HITS	SO	BB	ERA
1991	Columbus AAA	32	150	11-7	.611	152	100	53	3.84
1992	Columbus AAA	36	131	10-5	.667	132	72	45	3.58
1993	Columbus AAA	47	117	7-6	.538	119	66	31	3.54

ROYCE CLAYTON

San Francisco Giants

Shortstop

$31

Not to deprive him of credit for contributing to the Giants' fine season, but his record is less impressive under a microscope. His average was good and your stats look better when you get 550 at bats, but his stolen base percentage was in the negative range (11 of 21), his strikeout/walk ratio was poor, and his fielding percentage was below average. He drove in 70 runs, but he batted 173 times with men in scoring position.

YEAR	TEAM/LEVEL	G	AB	R	H	2B	3B	HR	RBI	BB	SB	AVG	OBP	SLG
1992	San Francisco	98	321	31	72	7	4	4	24	26	8	.224	.281	.308
1993	San Francisco	153	549	54	155	21	5	6	70	38	11	.282	.331	.372
1994	**Projected**	**154**	**540**	**65**	**139**	**19**	**5**	**7**	**61**	**44**	**20**	**.257**	**.313**	**.350**

ROGER CLEMENS

Boston Red Sox

Starting Pitcher

$64

Missed a month with a groin pull, and had his poorest season . . . It is common for great power pitchers to have seasons like this around age 30 (Clemens was 30 last year). Seaver at age 29 was 11-11; Nolan Ryan at 31 was 10-13. It is very likely that Clemens will bounce back and have more 20-win seasons. It is less likely that he will be dominant year-in and year-out, as he has been.

YEAR	TEAM/LEVEL	G	IP	W-L	PCT.	HITS	SO	BB	ERA
1991	Boston	35	271	18-10	.643	219	241	65	2.62
1992	Boston	32	247	18-11	.621	203	208	62	2.41
1993	Boston	29	192	11-14	.440	175	160	67	4.46

CRAIG COLBERT

San Francisco Giants

Catcher

$8

A 29-year-old backup catcher; the Giants like to run their second-string catchers back and forth to Phoenix so that they get some playing time, which enables two or three players to share what is essentially one job. Colbert is a righthanded hitter, doesn't run or hit, plays pretty good defense. His future involves more of the same.

YEAR	TEAM/LEVEL	G	AB	R	H	2B	3B	HR	RBI	BB	SB	AVG	OBP	SLG
1992	Phoenix AAA	36	140	16	45	8	1	1	12	3	0	.321	.336	.414
1992	San Francisco	49	126	10	29	5	2	1	16	9	1	.230	.277	.325
1993	San Francisco	23	37	2	6	2	0	1	5	3	0	.162	.225	.297

GREG COLBRUNN

Florida Marlins

First Base

$14

Colbrunn just two years ago was a highly regarded catching prospect, but was troubled by bursitis in his right elbow, which forced a move to first base. Although he hits well for a catcher he doesn't hit enough to be a regular first baseman, and when Cliff Floyd showed up the Expos released him. He signed immediately with the Marlins; it is unclear what their plans for him are. He's only 24, and could have a good career.

YEAR	TEAM/LEVEL	G	AB	R	H	2B	3B	HR	RBI	BB	SB	AVG	OBP	SLG
1992	MLE	57	204	23	54	16	0	7	35	5	0	.265	.282	.446
1992	Montreal	52	168	12	45	8	0	2	18	6	3	.268	.294	.351
1993	Montreal	70	153	15	39	9	0	4	23	6	4	.255	.282	.392

ALEX COLE

Colorado Rockies (Released)

Center Field

$11

Being released by an expansion team certainly can't do much for your career, but I would be surprised in Cole's career is completely over. The Rockies were platooning him in center field (he's a lefthanded hitter), but he's not much of a center fielder and didn't have a good year with the bat, although he did hit .315 with men in scoring position. He may come back to life as a pinch hitter/pinch runner/ fifth outfielder.

YEAR	TEAM/LEVEL	G	AB	R	H	2B	3B	HR	RBI	BB	SB	AVG	OBP	SLG
1991	Cleveland	122	387	58	114	17	3	0	21	58	16	.295	.386	.354
1992	Two Teams	105	302	44	77	4	7	0	15	28	16	.255	.318	.315
1993	Colorado	126	348	50	89	9	4	0	24	43	30	.256	.339	.305

VINCE COLEMAN

California Penal League

Left Felon

$13

His reprehensible behavior in the Dodger Stadium parking lot may have ended his career. He was one of the most overrated players of the last decade. He was a great base stealer, and his plate discipline improved the last few years in St. Louis, but he was never truly a star. It cost the Mets a lot of money to find that out, and I don't know whether anyone else will risk the same conclusion.

YEAR	TEAM/LEVEL	G	AB	R	H	2B	3B	HR	RBI	BB	SB	AVG	OBP	SLG
1991	New York NL	72	278	45	71	7	5	1	17	39	37	.255	.347	.327
1992	New York NL	71	229	37	63	11	1	2	21	27	24	.275	.355	.358
1993	New York NL	92	373	64	104	14	8	2	25	21	38	.279	.316	.375

DARNELL COLES
Toronto Blue Jays
Outfielder/Third Baseman
$18

Has settled into a backup role now after a couple of years as a regular, then a trip to the minors. Righthanded hitter whose best position is left field, can throw well enough to fill in at third base or in right. Essentially, he's the same player as Hubie Brooks, except Hubie was 20% better, which means that since Coles is now 31 and Hubie's 37, they're about even. Coles is probably a better bet for '94.

YEAR	TEAM/LEVEL	G	AB	R	H	2B	3B	HR	RBI	BB	SB	AVG	OBP	SLG
1991	Phoenix AAA	83	328	43	95	23	2	6	65	27	0	.290	.352	.433
1992	Cincinnati	55	141	16	44	11	2	3	18	3	1	.312	.322	.482
1993	Toronto	64	194	26	49	9	1	4	26	16	1	.253	.319	.371

CRIS COLON
Texas Rangers
Third Base
$9

Colon (the name, I am told, means "Christopher Columbus") is a major league hitter and has at least some of the attributes of a major league shortstop—a lithe, greyhound body and a strong arm. The Rangers, who have been looking for a shortstop since they moved to Texas in 1972, have apparently given up on him at that position, and moved him to third base, where his bat is less of an asset. Grade C prospect.

YEAR	TEAM/LEVEL	G	AB	R	H	2B	3B	HR	RBI	BB	SB	AVG	OBP	SLG
1992	Texas	14	36	5	6	0	0	0	1	1	0	.167	.189	.167
1993	Tulsa AA	124	490	63	147	27	3	11	47	13	6	.300	.322	.435
1993	MLE	124	472	51	129	24	2	9	38	8	4	.273	.285	.390

DAVID CONE
Kansas City Royals
Starting Pitcher
$62

He pitched very well, but the Royals scored only 83 runs for him all year, the poorest offensive support in the league (2.94 runs per nine innings), and stuck him with a losing record . . . Throws constantly to first base (288 times), but still has trouble with stolen bases . . . Over a four-year period with three teams he has a 2.53 ERA on the road, but 3.80 in his home parks . . . Will bounce back strong in '94.

YEAR	TEAM/LEVEL	G	IP	W-L	PCT.	HITS	SO	BB	ERA
1991	New York NL	34	233	14-14	.500	204	241	73	3.29
1992	Two Teams	35	250	17-10	.630	201	261	111	2.81
1993	Kansas City	34	254	11-14	.440	205	191	114	3.33

JEFF CONINE
Florida Marlins
Outfielder/First Base
$37

Was the only National Leaguer to play 162 games last year . . . The Marlins were using him in left field, which is a new position for him and not really a natural one. Would be a Gold Glove candidate at first base . . . His chance to be a star is his chance to hit .320 with 20-25 home runs, but since he struck out 135 times, I don't see that as real likely. A solid player.

YEAR	TEAM/LEVEL	G	AB	R	H	2B	3B	HR	RBI	BB	SB	AVG	OBP	SLG
1992	Kansas City	28	91	10	23	5	2	0	9	8	0	.253	.313	.352
1993	Florida	162	595	75	174	24	3	12	79	52	2	.292	.351	.403
1994	**Projected**	**158**	**583**	**74**	**163**	**29**	**4**	**13**	**75**	**59**	**3**	**.280**	**.346**	**.410**

JIM CONVERSE

Seattle Mariners

Starting Pitcher

$12

A 16th-round draft pick in 1990, he became the Mariners' top pitching prospect after a) he had a big year at Double-A and b) Roger Salkeld was hurt. He had a brief try at the rotation last May, didn't pitch well there and didn't pitch well at Calgary after going back down. Throws 90-plus. Grade C prospect; will get more chances as soon as he gets some people out in Triple-A.

YEAR	TEAM/LEVEL	G	IP	W-L	PCT.	HITS	SO	BB	ERA
1992	Jacksonville AA	27	159	12-7	.632	134	157	82	2.66
1993	Calgary AAA	23	122	7-8	.467	144	78	64	5.40
1993	Seattle	4	20	1-3	.250	23	10	14	5.31

ANDY COOK

New York Yankees (Released)

Relief Pitcher

$6

A 26-year-old righthander with unimpressive stuff, will have to scramble to have a career. After pitching very well at Columbus in '91 and '92 he got a brief look by the Yankees in May, but his control, which is his major asset, betrayed him, and he returned to Columbus, where things went from bad to worse. Grade D prospect; probably will sign with another organization.

YEAR	TEAM/LEVEL	G	IP	W-L	SAVES	HITS	SO	BB	ERA
1992	Columbus AAA	32	100	7-5	2	85	58	36	3.16
1993	Columbus AAA	21	118	6-7	0	149	47	49	6.54
1993	New York	4	5	0-1	0	4	4	7	5.06

DENNIS COOK

Cleveland Indians

Starter/Reliever

$8

Cook is a lefthander who rarely throws the ball below the belt, and who gives up a tremendous number of home runs. He made six starts for the Indians in May and June, with a 7.43 ERA. Although he pitched much better in relief (3.95 ERA) he was sent down about the All-Star break, and didn't pitch well in Triple-A, either (5.06 ERA in 43 innings). Future is in doubt.

YEAR	TEAM/LEVEL	G	IP	W-L	PCT.	HITS	SO	BB	ERA
1991	Los Angeles	20	18	1-0	1.000	12	8	7	0.51
1992	Cleveland	32	158	5-7	.417	156	96	50	3.82
1993	Cleveland	25	54	5-5	.500	62	34	16	5.67

MIKE COOK

Baltimore Orioles

Relief Pitcher

$7

A 30-year-old minor league veteran, spent several eons in the California system, one year in the Cardinal camp before coming to Baltimore. Has had major league looks since 1986. Has been tried as a starter and reliever, but his control has always been a problem. There are probably pitchers who have had careers after this kind of a struggle, but I don't think I could name three of them.

YEAR	TEAM/LEVEL	G	IP	W-L	SAVES	HITS	SO	BB	ERA
1992	Louisville AAA	43	59	3-2	0	58	56	31	4.60
1993	Rochester AAA	57	81	6-7	13	77	74	48	3.10
1993	Baltimore	2	3	0-0	0	1	3	2	0.00

STEVE COOKE

Pittsburgh Pirates

Starting Pitcher

$33

A 35th-round draft pick in 1989, he cleared the minors in two-and-a-half seasons, and is coming off an impressive rookie season. As a pitcher I'd compare him to Jim Abbott, except that he's bigger (6-foot-6) and has more hands (2). Doesn't have an explosive fastball, but has good movement and locates it very well, mixes in his other pitches as if he'd been doing it for years. Looks very good.

YEAR	TEAM/LEVEL	G	IP	W-L	PCT.	HITS	SO	BB	ERA
1992	Minors 2 Levels	19	110	8-5	.615	102	90	48	3.51
1992	Pittsburgh	11	23	2-0	1.000	22	10	4	3.52
1993	Pittsburgh	32	211	10-10	.500	207	132	59	3.89

RON COOMER

Chicago White Sox

Third Base

$13

It's hard to know what to make of him. A 27-year-old infielder, he was drafted by the A's in 1987 and hit fairly well in their system, but didn't impress defensively and was released, apparently after an injury, in 1990. His 1993 record strongly suggests that he can hit, but as a righthanded hitter with no walks, no speed and no defense, he is probably not going to be handed a position. Grade C prospect.

YEAR	TEAM/LEVEL	G	AB	R	H	2B	3B	HR	RBI	BB	SB	AVG	OBP	SLG
1993	Birmingh AA	69	262	44	85	18	0	13	50	15	1	.324	.358	.542
1993	Nashvill AAA	59	211	34	66	19	0	13	51	10	1	.313	.342	.588
1993	MLE	128	454	61	132	31	0	20	80	17	0	.291	.316	.491

SCOTT COOPER

Boston Red Sox

Third Base

$33

One of my favorite players, for no obvious reason; he just looks like a ballplayer to me. An August slump cost him 10 points off his average, and he had a disappointing year defensively at third base, making more errors than double plays. Lefthanded batter, fine arm, no speed, charges the bunt well. For those of you over 40, I'd describe him as the Don Wert of the '90s.

YEAR	TEAM/LEVEL	G	AB	R	H	2B	3B	HR	RBI	BB	SB	AVG	OBP	SLG
1992	Boston	123	337	34	93	21	0	5	33	37	1	.276	.346	.383
1993	Boston	156	526	67	147	29	3	9	63	58	5	.279	.355	.397
1994	**Projected**	**155**	**550**	**59**	**153**	**26**	**2**	**11**	**63**	**57**	**3**	**.278**	**.346**	**.393**

JOEY CORA

Chicago White Sox

Second Base

$39

Led the American League in sacrifice bunts, with 19, and was second in triples . . . Another refugee from the San Diego system, played second for the Padres in 1988, when he was 22. He played OK, but they sent him back to the minors, anyway . . . If he stays healthy, will hold his job for several years, and will score more than 100 runs in his best seasons.

YEAR	TEAM/LEVEL	G	AB	R	H	2B	3B	HR	RBI	BB	SB	AVG	OBP	SLG
1991	Chicago	100	228	37	55	2	3	0	18	20	11	.241	.313	.276
1992	Chicago	68	122	27	30	7	1	0	9	22	10	.246	.371	.320
1993	Chicago	153	579	95	155	15	13	2	51	67	20	.268	.351	.349

WILFREDO CORDERO

Montreal Expos

Shortstop

$40

Explain this: Cordero struck out *less than half as often* as we had expected based on his minor league record, but still hit for *more* power but with a *lower* batting average . . . He's probably going to be a major league shortstop for 15 years, so we've got time to figure him out. His defense as a rookie was poor, but he has the ability to play the position, and his bat should keep him around until he learns.

YEAR	TEAM/LEVEL	G	AB	R	H	2B	3B	HR	RBI	BB	SB	AVG	OBP	SLG
1992	Montreal	45	126	17	38	4	1	2	8	9	0	.302	.353	.397
1993	Montreal	138	475	56	118	32	2	10	58	34	12	.248	.308	.387
1994	**Projected**	**144**	**501**	**59**	**127**	**25**	**2**	**10**	**55**	**37**	**10**	**.253**	**.305**	**.371**

RHEAL CORMIER

St. Louis Cardinals

Starting Pitcher

$25

Cormier opened the season in the Cardinals' rotation, dropped out of it in May, returned in late May but didn't pitch well and went back to the bullpen, returned to the rotation in August and finished the season pitching quite well. He's had trouble staying 100% healthy and hasn't pitched well when he's not 100%, but I like him. A ground ball pitcher with a 3-1 strikeout/walk ratio has got to win more than he loses.

YEAR	TEAM/LEVEL	G	IP	W-L	PCT.	HITS	SO	BB	ERA
1992	St. Louis	11	68	4-5	.444	74	38	8	4.12
1992	St.Louis	31	186	10-10	.500	194	117	33	3.68
1993	St. Louis	38	145	7-6	.538	163	75	27	4.33

ROD CORREIA

California Angels

Infielder

$15

Was called up in late June, after playing well at Vancouver, and wound up the year playing regularly while DiSarcina was hurt. He looks good—a trim athlete who plays with confidence and aggressiveness—but his record does not suggest that he will hit at the .266 level of 1993. Listed at 5-11, but looks smaller. Grade D prospect; doubt that he will hit enough to stay in the lineup.

YEAR	TEAM/LEVEL	G	AB	R	H	2B	3B	HR	RBI	BB	SB	AVG	OBP	SLG
1992	MLE	123	445	43	103	16	0	3	33	13	10	.231	.253	.288
1993	Vancouver AAA	60	207	43	56	10	4	4	28	15	11	.271	.316	.415
1993	California	64	128	12	34	5	0	0	9	6	2	.266	.319	.305

JIM CORSI

Florida Marlins

Relief Pitcher

$2

His season was ended in early July by torn cartilage in his right shoulder, and I suspect that his career may be over. A heavyset 32-year-old who pitched well with Oakland in middle relief, he has always been a marginal pitcher, and his ability to come back from a serious injury is questionable. Ground ball pitcher, righthander.

YEAR	TEAM/LEVEL	G	IP	W-L	SAVES	HITS	SO	BB	ERA
1991	Houston	47	78	0-5	0	76	53	23	3.71
1992	Oakland	32	44	4-2	0	44	19	18	1.43
1993	Florida	15	20	0-2	0	28	7	10	6.64

TIM COSTO

Cincinnati Reds

Outfielder

$16

A massive righthanded hitter who played in the Cincinnati outfield because of injuries to the regular outfielders, but whose best chance to play in the majors might be as a platoon partner for Hal Morris. He would be OK in that role—might hit close to .300, or might hit for more power but less average. Was once a hot prospect in the Cleveland system. At 25, it's time to see what he can do.

YEAR	TEAM/LEVEL	G	AB	R	H	2B	3B	HR	RBI	BB	SB	AVG	OBP	SLG
1992	MLE	121	417	52	95	16	1	28	58	35	2	.228	.288	.472
1993	MLE	106	347	38	103	27	1	10	45	18	2	.297	.332	.467
1993	Cincinnati	31	98	13	22	5	0	3	12	4	0	.224	.250	.367

HENRY COTTO

Florida Marlins

Outfield

$17

A fine fourth outfielder, traded to the Marlins in late June. He can play all three outfield positions fairly well, is an excellent baserunner, and has hit .293 against lefthanded pitchers over the last four years (177 for 605). On the down side, his on-base percentage is poor, and he can't hit righthanders (.228 over the last four years). Should continue in his present role for several years.

YEAR	TEAM/LEVEL	G	AB	R	H	2B	3B	HR	RBI	BB	SB	AVG	OBP	SLG
1991	Seattle	66	177	35	54	6	2	6	23	10	16	.305	.347	.463
1992	Seattle	108	294	42	76	11	1	5	27	14	23	.259	.294	.354
1993	Two Teams	108	240	25	60	8	0	5	21	5	16	.250	.269	.346

DANNY COX

Toronto Blue Jays

Relief Pitcher

$26

Joining Toronto as a free agent, he pitched his best ball since 1987, indicating that his recovery from ligament transplant surgery is now complete. He allowed only 11.0 baserunners per nine innings, one of the best rates in the league, and limited the first batters he saw to a .140 batting average (6-for-43), the best figure in the American League. Should be effective over the next few years.

YEAR	TEAM/LEVEL	G	IP	W-L	SAVES	HITS	SO	BB	ERA
1991	Philadelphia	23	102	4-6	0	98	46	39	4.57
1992	Two Teams	25	63	5-3	3	66	48	27	4.60
1993	Toronto	44	84	7-6	2	73	84	29	3.12

CHUCK CRIM

Released

Relief Pitcher

$1

Released by the Angels in May after several years of ineffective performance. Crim, whose minor league record was so-so, led the American League in game appearances in 1988 and 1989, when he was the setup man for Dan Plesac. When Plesac lost his effectiveness Crim got a shot at the closer, but was burned out by then, and never could solidify the job. A pitcher with a low strikeout rate almost always has a short career.

YEAR	TEAM/LEVEL	G	IP	W-L	SAVES	HITS	SO	BB	ERA
1991	Milwaukee	66	91	8-5	3	115	39	25	4.63
1992	California	57	87	7-6	1	100	30	29	5.17
1993	California	11	15	2-2	0	17	10	5	5.87

TRIPP CROMER

St. Louis Cardinals

Shortstop

$13

His real name is Roy Bunyan Cromer the Third. A third-round pick in 1989, he has always been regarded as a defensive shortstop who had to prove he could hit. He made some progress in that regard at Louisville in '93, hitting far better than he had before, but then went 2-for-23 after being called up. His glovework will get him to a major league bench; anything more would be a gamble.

YEAR	TEAM/LEVEL	G	AB	R	H	2B	3B	HR	RBI	BB	SB	AVG	OBP	SLG
1992	MLE	116	354	28	77	14	4	5	29	17	3	.218	.253	.322
1992	Louisvil AAA	86	309	39	85	8	4	11	33	15	1	.275	.313	.434
1993	MLE	86	297	30	73	7	2	8	25	11	0	.246	.273	.364

JOHN CUMMINGS

Seattle Mariners

Starting Pitcher

$13

An eighth-round draft pick, Cummings had a big year at Peninsula in 1992 (16-6, led the league in strikeouts with 144). The Mariners, showing the bad judgment for which they have long been famous, decided to skip Double-A and Triple-A, and put him in the rotation at the start of the season. He was completely ineffective, and now nobody knows what to make of him. Grade B prospect; probably a year away.

YEAR	TEAM/LEVEL	G	IP	W-L	PCT.	HITS	SO	BB	ERA
1993	Jacksonvi AA	7	46	2-2	.500	50	35	9	3.15
1993	Calgary AAA	11	65	3-4	.429	69	42	21	4.13
1993	Seattle	10	46	0-6	.000	59	19	16	6.02

MIDRE CUMMINGS

Pittsburgh Pirates

Outfielder

$21

The Pirates got him from the Twins in the Smiley trade. Switch hitter, has speed and line-drive power, consistent .300 hitter in the low minors. He held his own at Triple-A at age 21, which strongly suggests that he has major league ability if not star ability, but there have been questions raised about his attitude, effort, and work ethic. Below average plate discipline, poor percentage base stealer. Grade B prospect.

YEAR	TEAM/LEVEL	G	AB	R	H	2B	3B	HR	RBI	BB	SB	AVG	OPB	SLG
1993	AA and AAA	123	469	69	134	29	3	15	47	36	10	.286	.337	.456
1993	MLE	123	448	53	113	25	1	10	37	25	6	.252	.292	.379
1993	Pittsburgh	13	36	5	4	1	0	0	3	4	0	.111	.195	.139

CHAD CURTIS

California Angels

Center Field

$42

A fine young player with multiple skills, he is apparently emphasizing his speed at the expense of his power. He has more speed than power, but it is all but impossible to steal bases effectively on the California playing surface, and Curtis tied for the league lead in caught stealing . . . good defensive center fielder, excellent hustle. I anticipate a long and productive career for him . . . was married in his baseball uniform in 1990.

YEAR	TEAM/LEVEL	G	AB	R	H	2B	3B	HR	RBI	BB	SB	AVG	OBP	SLG
1992	California	139	441	59	114	16	2	10	46	51	43	.259	.341	.372
1993	California	152	583	94	166	25	3	6	59	70	48	.285	.361	.369
1994	**Projected**	**151**	**571**	**84**	**158**	**23**	**3**	**10**	**61**	**64**	**51**	**.277**	**.350**	**.380**

MILT CUYLER

Detroit Tigers

Center Field

$14

Appears to be suffering from Jerome Walton's Disease, played very well as a rookie but has failed to hold his ground. Only 25 years old; has time to recover, but the Tigers' outfield picture is crowded. Has better chance of coming back if traded, particularly to a turf park . . . Very fine outfielder and baserunner, which would make him an OK reserve; needs to have .300 on-base percentage if he's going to be in the starting lineup.

YEAR	TEAM/LEVEL	G	AB	R	H	2B	3B	HR	RBI	BB	SB	AVG	OBP	SLG
1991	Detroit	154	475	77	122	15	7	3	33	52	41	.257	.335	.337
1992	Detroit	89	291	39	70	11	1	3	28	10	8	.241	.275	.316
1993	Detroit	82	249	46	53	11	7	0	19	19	13	.213	.276	.313

OMAR DAAL

Los Angeles Dodgers

Lefthanded Relief Pitcher

$11

A skinny Venezuelan who pitched brilliantly in the Dominican Summer League, but hasn't gotten anybody out in the States yet. He's very young (22 now), and when Candelaria wiped out and the Dodgers were looking for a lefthanded one-out guy, they called him up. There are a million guys wanting that job, so I really can't understand rushing up a kid who can't get anybody out at Albuquerque, but then, that's the Dodgers. Grade C prospect.

YEAR	TEAM/LEVEL	G	IP	W-L	SAVES	HITS	SO	BB	ERA
1992	San Antonio AA	35	57	2-6	5	60	52	33	5.02
1992	Albuquerque AAA	12	10	0-2	0	14	9	11	7.84
1993	Los Angeles	47	35	2-3	0	36	19	21	5.09

RON DARLING

Oakland Athletics

Starting Pitcher

$14

Failed to follow up on his fine 1992 season, winning only five of 29 starts, and might be through as a rotation starter. Throws a mix of pitches which look a lot alike—fastball, cut fastball, split-finger fastball, forkball . . . Who knows if he really throws all of these, or just uses them in post-game interviews. He doesn't strike people out or get consistent ground balls, and his control is not good.

YEAR	TEAM/LEVEL	G	IP	W-L	PCT.	HITS	SO	BB	ERA
1991	Three Teams	32	194	8-15	.348	185	129	71	4.26
1992	Oakland	33	206	15-10	.600	198	99	72	3.66
1993	Oakland	31	178	5-9	.357	198	95	72	5.16

DANNY DARWIN

Boston Red Sox

Starting Pitcher

$38

Last year I wrote that "He *could* go 16-11." Unfortunately, I then encouraged you to believe that he probably *wouldn't* . . . His 15 wins and 229 innings were career highs. His control, always good, was exceptional, and he allowed only 9.7 baserunners per nine innings, best of any American League starter . . . Now 38 years old, which has to worry you, but what I would essentially expect from him next year is another 14 to 17 wins.

YEAR	TEAM/LEVEL	G	IP	W-L	PCT.	HITS	SO	BB	ERA
1991	Boston	12	68	3-6	.333	71	42	15	5.16
1992	Boston	51	161	9-9	.500	159	124	53	3.96
1993	Boston	34	229	15-11	.577	196	130	49	3.26

DOUG DASCENZO
Texas Rangers
Center Field
$13

The surprising development of David Hulce took most of the job he was signed to do, and his batting average was in the mid-ones until a September drive. Doesn't hit enough to play left/right field or be of much use as a pinch hitter, but can pinch run and play the outfield, which will keep him in the league if he can hit .250. Good hustle, not much future.

YEAR	TEAM/LEVEL	G	AB	R	H	2B	3B	HR	RBI	BB	SB	AVG	OBP	SLG
1991	Chicago	118	239	40	61	11	0	1	18	24	14	.255	.327	.314
1992	Chicago	139	376	37	96	13	4	0	20	27	6	.255	.304	.311
1993	Texas	76	146	20	29	5	1	2	10	8	2	.199	.239	.288

JACK DAUGHERTY
Cincinnati Reds
Outfield
$9

Started the year in the majors but not playing, went to Tucson, where he hit .390 through 42 games, came back up to help Cincinnati through their omnipresent injuries. A singles hitter who can't run and has hit .204 over the last three years . . . Basically I think he's a terrible player who shouldn't be in the league, and I have enough confidence in Davey Johnson to assume that he will figure this out.

YEAR	TEAM/LEVEL	G	AB	R	H	2B	3B	HR	RBI	BB	SB	AVG	OBP	SLG
1991	Texas	58	144	8	28	3	2	1	11	16	1	.194	.270	.264
1992	Texas	59	127	13	26	9	0	0	9	16	2	.205	.295	.276
1993	Cincinnati	50	62	7	14	2	0	2	9	11	0	.226	.338	.355

DARREN DAULTON
Philadelphia Phillies
Catcher
$62

How many catchers have had consecutive 100-RBI seasons? I don't know, but I'd be astonished if it was 10. I know there are a lot of catchers in the Hall of Fame who didn't . . . Secondary average of .465 last year, .365 in his career . . . Batted 136 times in double-play situations, but grounded into only two double plays (1.5%), by far the lowest percentage in the National League . . . Is an 82% base stealer for his career.

YEAR	TEAM/LEVEL	G	AB	R	H	2B	3B	HR	RBI	BB	SB	AVG	OBP	SLG
1991	Philadelphia	89	285	36	56	12	0	12	42	41	5	.196	.297	.365
1992	Philadelphia	145	485	80	131	32	5	27	109	88	11	.270	.385	.524
1993	Philadelphia	147	510	90	131	35	4	24	105	117	5	.257	.392	.482

BUTCH (WARM FRONT) DAVIS
Texas Rangers
Outfield/Designated Hitter
$10

One of several minor league veterans Kennedy brought to Texas. Davis, 35, played with the Royals in late 1983 and hit .344 in 122 at bats. He hit .147 in 116 at bats the next year, hung around AAA for eight years, getting an occasional cup of coffee but never impressing. Good athlete, still runs well, poor plate discipline, weak arm. The Chico Walker of the American League.

YEAR	TEAM/LEVEL	G	AB	R	H	2B	3B	HR	RBI	BB	SB	AVG	OBP	SLG
1991	MLE	91	263	36	68	13	4	4	28	12	7	.259	.291	.385
1992	MLE	135	519	45	123	24	4	7	50	22	12	.237	.268	.339
1993	Texas	62	159	24	39	10	4	3	20	5	3	.245	.273	.415

CHILI DAVIS
California Angels
Designated Hitter
$32

A full-time DH, Davis drove in a hundred runs for the first time in his career, which effectively prevented people from talking about all of the things that he can't do. He did his best work with men on base, hitting .192 with 10 homers with the bases empty, but .294 with 17 homers with men on base, his at bats perfectly divided between the two. With men in scoring position he hit .325.

YEAR	TEAM/LEVEL	G	AB	R	H	2B	3B	HR	RBI	BB	SB	AVG	OBP	SLG
1992	Minnesota	138	444	63	128	27	2	12	66	73	4	.288	.386	.439
1993	California	153	573	74	139	32	0	27	112	71	4	.243	.327	.440
1994	**Projected**	**151**	**562**	**73**	**140**	**27**	**2**	**19**	**86**	**88**	**5**	**.249**	**.351**	**.406**

ERIC DAVIS
Detroit Tigers
Left Field
$29

Was 33-for-38 as a base stealer for the Dodgers, the best percentage in the National League. His career stolen base percentage, 87%, is still a major league record . . . His 1993 playing time (131 games and 451 at bats) almost set career highs for him (135 and 474) . . . He struck out less than he used to (only 106 times), but didn't seem to reap any rewards from it. A big season now would be a big surprise.

YEAR	TEAM/LEVEL	G	AB	R	H	2B	3B	HR	RBI	BB	SB	AVG	OBP	SLG
1992	Los Angeles	76	267	21	61	8	1	5	32	36	19	.228	.325	.322
1993	Two Teams	131	451	71	107	18	1	20	68	55	35	.237	.319	.415
1994	**Projected**	**120**	**420**	**57**	**103**	**17**	**2**	**18**	**61**	**59**	**28**	**.245**	**.338**	**.424**

GLENN DAVIS
Released
First Base/Designated Hitter
$3

He came to the majors within a few weeks of Eric Davis in 1984, and has played 48 games fewer than Eric . . . His tremendous power has disappeared (14 homers in 511 at bats over the last two years), and he doesn't have any peripheral skills to build on. The power was his game. If he doesn't convince somebody that his power has come back, his career is over.

YEAR	TEAM/LEVEL	G	AB	R	H	2B	3B	HR	RBI	BB	SB	AVG	OBP	SLG
1991	Baltimore	49	176	29	40	9	1	10	28	16	4	.227	.307	.460
1992	Baltimore	106	398	46	110	15	2	13	48	37	1	.276	.338	.422
1993	Baltimore	30	113	8	20	3	0	1	9	7	0	.177	.230	.230

MARK DAVIS
San Diego Padres
Relief Pitcher
$12

He gave the world another of his patented flashes of brilliance late in the season, posting an 0.61 ERA in 12 games in September. He still throws hard and his curve is still nearly unhittable . . . If you draft him this year you are *probably* wasting the draft pick, but if he gets enough of his confidence back, he could also save about 40 games.

YEAR	TEAM/LEVEL	G	IP	W-L	SAVES	HITS	SO	BB	ERA
1991	Kansas City	29	63	6-3	1	55	47	39	4.45
1992	Two Teams	27	53	2-3	0	64	34	41	7.13
1993	Two Teams	60	70	1-5	4	79	70	44	4.26

RUSS DAVIS

New York Yankees

Third Base

$12

A prototype of a marginal prospect, a power-hitting third baseman who could hit 20 homers in the majors, but has a catalogue of nattering negatives: slow, righthanded, poor strikeout/walk ratio, won't hit for average (although he was hitting close to .300 at Columbus until a late-season slump). He's not a lot different from Sean Berry or Gary Gaetti or Mike Blowers or Ed Sprague, so will probably have a major league career eventually.

YEAR	TEAM/LEVEL	G	AB	R	H	2B	3B	HR	RBI	BB	SB	AVG	OBP	SLG
1992	MLE	132	473	63	122	20	2	17	58	34	2	.258	.308	.416
1993	Columbus AAA	113	424	63	108	24	1	26	83	40	1	.255	.319	.500
1993	MLE	113	410	52	94	21	0	21	68	33	0	.229	.287	.434

STORM DAVIS

Detroit Tigers

Relief Pitcher

$23

Has added a new pitch or something, and may be gearing up for a career-saving big year. His '93 strikeout rate was the best of his career, and he struck out more than one per inning after joining Detroit in July. I saw him pitch in August, and had the impression that he was throwing harder than he had in 10 years. Be realistic in your expectations for him, but his best years could be coming up.

YEAR	TEAM/LEVEL	G	IP	W-L	SAVES	HITS	SO	BB	ERA
1991	Kansas City	51	114	3-9	2	140	53	46	4.96
1992	Baltimore	48	89	7-3	4	79	53	36	3.43
1993	Two Teams	43	98	2-8	4	93	73	48	5.05

ANDRE DAWSON

Boston Red Sox

Designated Hitter/Right Field

$26

He needs 370 more hits to reach 3,000, which looks like a thousand. He's 39 years old, and needs a comeback. He can't run and he doesn't play the outfield much, so that means he's got to do it all with his bat. As a hitter, although I admire Andre, he always was overrated. I'm not saying he *won't* drive in 100 runs—but if it's my team, I'd rather take a chance on somebody else.

YEAR	TEAM/LEVEL	G	AB	R	H	2B	3B	HR	RBI	BB	SB	AVG	OBP	SLG
1992	Chicago	143	542	60	150	27	2	22	90	30	6	.277	.316	.456
1993	Boston	121	461	44	126	29	1	13	67	17	2	.273	.313	.425
1994	**Projected**	**107**	**392**	**40**	**104**	**18**	**2**	**14**	**61**	**18**	**3**	**.265**	**.308**	**.429**

KEN DAYLEY

Los Angeles Dodgers

Relief Pitcher

$1

If this guy gets a World Series ring, I'm going to have one made for my wife. Dayley signed with the Blue Jays as a free agent in November, 1990, but pitched only four and two-thirds innings for them in three years due to elbow trouble, and was released (in exasperation) in April. He signed with the Dodger system, but pitched only 10 innings for Albuquerque. Career is probably over.

YEAR	TEAM/LEVEL	G	IP	W-L	SAVES	HITS	SO	BB	ERA
1990	St. Louis	58	73	4-4	2	63	51	30	3.56
1991	Toronto	8	4	0-0	0	7	3	5	6.23
1993	Toronto	2	.2	0-0	0	1	2	4	0.00

STEVE DECKER

Florida Marlins

Catcher

$3

Taken by the Marlins in the expansion draft, he opened the season in the majors, but after going 0-for-15 was sent to the minors. He had a back injury, which kept him from reporting to the minors . . . Almost nothing is left of the player that I liked so well in 1990, after a big year at Shreveport and a brilliant performance in a late-season look. You can trade him now for Andy Allanson.

YEAR	TEAM/LEVEL	G	AB	R	H	2B	3B	HR	RBI	BB	SB	AVG	OBP	SLG
1991	San Francisco	79	233	16	48	7	1	5	24	16	0	.206	.262	.309
1992	MLE	125	422	32	99	17	1	5	48	29	1	.235	.284	.315
1993	Florida	8	15	0	0	0	0	0	1	3	0	.000	.158	.000

ROB DEER

Boston Red Sox

Right Field

$25

I wish somebody would let him play 162 games, just to see how many times he could strike out. Playing 128 games last year he led the majors in strikeouts by a comfortable margin, striking out 169 times . . . Also had the lowest batting average of any major league regular . . . Over the last four years has hit .263 with 48 homers in 498 at bats against lefthanded pitching, but just .190 with .367 slugging percentage against righthanders.

YEAR	TEAM/LEVEL	G	AB	R	H	2B	3B	HR	RBI	BB	SB	AVG	OBP	SLG
1992	Detroit	110	393	66	97	20	1	32	64	51	4	.247	.337	.547
1993	Two Teams	128	466	66	98	17	1	21	55	58	5	.210	.303	.386
1994	**Projected**	**106**	**361**	**51**	**74**	**13**	**1**	**18**	**46**	**56**	**3**	**.205**	**.312**	**.396**

JOSE DeLEON

Chicago White Sox

Long Reliever/Spot Starter

$20

Has lost a bit off his fastball, but still throws hard enough, and nobody has better movement on his fastball. He pitched well in a limited role for the Phillies, who traded him in early August for fellow enigma Bobby Thigpen . . . I'd speculate on why they made the trade, but who wants to get sued? . . . Isn't going to crack the White Sox rotation, but he can still pitch.

YEAR	TEAM/LEVEL	G	IP	W-L	PCT.	HITS	SO	BB	ERA
1991	St. Louis	28	163	5-9	.357	144	118	61	2.71
1992	Two Teams	32	117	2-8	.200	111	79	48	4.37
1993	Two Teams	35	57	3-0	1.000	44	40	30	2.98

CARLOS DELGADO

Toronto Blue Jays

Catcher

$39

One of four super-prospects in the minors right now, with Ramirez, Chipper Jones and Cliff Floyd. His defense is an unknown, but he's going to be an awesome hitter . . . Delgado has already played 504 minor league game. No other outstanding catching prospect in history has ever played that many minor league games. Bench made the majors after 265 minor league games, Berra after 188, Cochrane, 164, Dickey, 249, Hartnett, 100.

YEAR	TEAM/LEVEL	G	AB	R	H	2B	3B	HR	RBI	BB	SB	AVG	OBP	SLG
1992	Dunedin A	133	485	83	157	30	2	30	100	59	2	.324	.402	.579
1993	Knoxville AA	140	468	91	142	28	0	25	102	102	10	.303	.430	.524
1993	MLE	140	454	73	128	26	0	22	82	70	6	.282	.378	.485

RICH DeLUCIA

Seattle Mariners

Reliever/Starter

$12

Mike Boddicker-type righthander, changes speeds off a fastball that itself would make a fine changeup. After pitching well at times as a rookie in '91 he had an inflamed right elbow in '92, a strained right shoulder in '93 . . . Spent August at Calgary; was 1-5 with a 5.73 ERA there . . . If healthy, will eventually have some excellent seasons in middle relief.

YEAR	TEAM/LEVEL	G	IP	W-L	PCT.	HITS	SO	BB	ERA
1991	Seattle	32	182	12-13	.480	176	98	78	5.09
1992	Seattle	30	84	3-6	.333	100	66	35	5.49
1993	Seattle	30	43	3-6	.333	46	48	23	4.64

DREW DENSON

Chicago White Sox

First Base/Designated Hitter

$8

A huge righthanded batter, was in the Braves system years ago and is now 28. He has as much chance of taking Frank Thomas's job as you do, but isn't a bad hitter. He could do George Bell's job better than Bell did in '93, at least . . . Would have much better shot at playing time if he was lefthanded. Doubt that he will ever land an everyday job in the majors.

YEAR	TEAM/LEVEL	G	AB	R	H	2B	3B	HR	RBI	BB	SB	AVG	OBP	SLG
1992	Vancouver AAA	105	340	43	94	7	3	13	70	36	1	.276	.358	.429
1993	Nashville AAA	136	513	82	144	36	0	24	103	46	0	.281	.361	.491
1993	MLE	136	494	64	125	30	0	19	81	36	0	.253	.304	.429

JIM DESHAIES (HIT DEFAN)

San Francisco Giants

Lefthanded Starting Pitcher

$22

His ground ball/fly ball ratio, .66 to one, was the lowest in the majors. This counts only outs, which is to say that it doesn't count those Big Flies, of which he had plenty—26, to be exact, plus 39 doubles. He started the year red-hot, but had only intermittent victories after mid-May. He's 33 years old, never did throw hard and is now 29-46 over the last four years.

YEAR	TEAM/LEVEL	G	IP	W-L	PCT.	HITS	SO	BB	ERA
1991	Houston	28	161	5-12	.294	156	98	72	4.98
1992	San Diego	15	96	4-7	.364	92	46	33	3.28
1993	Two Teams	32	184	13-15	.464	183	85	57	4.39

DELINO DeSHIELDS

Montreal Expos

Second Base

$61

Baseball history is littered with second basemen who *would* have been great, if they could just have stayed healthy. DeShields could be as devastating a player as Robbie Alomar, but he missed time in '93 with chicken pox and a broken thumb suffered sliding into second base . . . Swung at only 35% of the pitches he saw in '93, the lowest percentage of any major league player except Rickey Henderson.

YEAR	TEAM/LEVEL	G	AB	R	H	2B	3B	HR	RBI	BB	SB	AVG	OBP	SLG
1992	Montreal	135	530	82	155	19	8	7	56	54	46	.292	.359	.398
1993	Montreal	123	481	75	142	17	7	2	29	72	43	.295	.389	.372
1994	**Projected**	**136**	**519**	**82**	**146**	**19**	**6**	**6**	**48**	**77**	**51**	**.281**	**.374**	**.376**

JOHN DeSILVA

Los Angeles Dodgers

Starting Pitcher

$20

DeSilva was the best pitching prospect in the Tigers system, although they never realized this, and traded him to the Dodgers for Eric Davis. I'd compare him to Chris Bosio—a pitcher with a decent arm, changes speeds well, gets ahead of the hitters, has had trouble staying healthy . . . Out pitch is a slider. It's unclear how the Dodgers plan to use him. Grade B prospect.

YEAR	TEAM/LEVEL	G	IP	W-L	PCT.	HITS	SO	BB	ERA
1992	Toledo AAA	7	19	0-3	.000	26	21	8	8.53
1992	London AA	9	52	2-4	.333	51	53	13	4.13
1993	Toledo AAA	25	161	7-10	.412	145	136	60	3.69

ORESTES DESTRADE

Florida Marlins

First Base/Hometown Hero

$25

Looked like a major disappointment after a poor first half, but got hot in August and saved his job. Whether this was just a hot streak or represents adjustment to major league pitching, who knows . . . He's 31 now, near the end of a player's prime, so we wouldn't ordinarily expect anything more . . . Took extra bases on hits only six times all season, by far the lowest percentage in baseball . . . Made 19 errors, most of any major league first baseman.

YEAR	TEAM/LEVEL	G	AB	R	H	2B	3B	HR	RBI	BB	SB	AVG	OBP	SLG
1991	Seibu (Japan)	130	437	90	117	21	0	39	92	100	0	.268	.404	.584
1992	Seibu (Japan)	128	448	87	119	19	0	41	87	95	12	.266	.394	.583
1993	Florida	153	569	61	145	20	3	20	87	58	0	.255	.324	.406

MIKE DEVEREAUX

Baltimore Orioles

Center Field

$33

Has been a good player over the last three years, but be wary of drafting him in '94. He's 31 years old, and probably not a good enough player to play regularly until he reaches, let's say, 33. His speed has evaporated due to some leg problems, and he's not the center fielder or baserunner that he was two or three years ago (he stole 22 bases in 1989).

YEAR	TEAM/LEVEL	G	AB	R	H	2B	3B	HR	RBI	BB	SB	AVG	OBP	SLG
1992	Baltimore	156	653	76	180	29	11	24	107	44	10	.276	.321	.464
1993	Baltimore	131	527	72	132	31	3	14	75	43	3	.250	.306	.400
1994	**Projected**	**147**	**598**	**71**	**151**	**25**	**4**	**17**	**73**	**48**	**10**	**.253**	**.306**	**.393**

MARK DEWEY

Pittsburgh Pirates

Relief Pitcher

$24

A 29-year-old righthander without an impressive fastball, was the property of the Giants and then the Mets, but didn't get much of a trial with either organization despite pitching well. The Pirates, desperate for pitching help, gave him a shot at the closer role, but he blew five out of 12 save chances, so couldn't be said to have a grip on the job. He should be in the majors to stay, however.

YEAR	TEAM/LEVEL	G	IP	W-L	SAVES	HITS	SO	BB	ERA
1992	New York NL	20	33	1-0	0	37	24	10	4.32
1993	Buffalo AAA	22	29	2-0	6	21	17	5	1.23
1993	Pittsburgh	21	27	1-2	7	14	14	10	2.36

ALEX DIAZ

Milwaukee Brewers

Pinch Runner/Outfield

$12

Diaz's father played in the Brewers' system, which I suppose means the Brewers are officially no longer an expansion team. A Brooklyn native who signed originally with the Mets, Diaz is a switch-hitter with speed and a good percentage base stealer, but has never hit higher than .268 in the minors, with the exception of a few games here and there. The Brewers used him mostly for his legs, but he's only 25, so could develop.

YEAR	TEAM/LEVEL	G	AB	R	H	2B	3B	HR	RBI	BB	SB	AVG	OBP	SLG
1992	MLE	106	433	49	100	14	2	0	30	17	31	.231	.260	.273
1992	Milwaukee	22	9	5	1	0	0	0	1	0	3	.111	.111	.111
1993	Milwaukee	32	69	9	22	2	0	0	1	0	5	.319	.319	.348

MARIO DIAZ

Texas Rangers

Shortstop

$18

A singles-hitting shortstop who has been around for years, is now 32 years old; the Rangers used him as their regular shortstop between the time that their prospects failed and the time they decided to give up and point to next year. He's an average or better hitter for a shortstop, and it's hard to say why, specifically, he hasn't gotten more playing time over the years. He played well for the Rangers.

YEAR	TEAM/LEVEL	G	AB	R	H	2B	3B	HR	RBI	BB	SB	AVG	OBP	SLG
1991	Texas	96	182	24	48	7	0	1	22	15	0	.264	.318	.319
1992	Texas	19	31	2	7	1	0	0	1	1	0	.226	.250	.258
1993	Texas	71	205	24	56	10	1	2	24	8	1	.273	.297	.361

ROB DIBBLE

Cincinnati Reds

Closer?

$25

Had 19 saves in 28 opportunities, the poorest percentage of any NL pitcher with 20 chances . . . May finally have gone nuts . . . Had injuries and lost some off his fastball, got burned on changeups and bad sliders, finally lost command of the strike zone altogether. Ryne Duren, who was one of the few pitchers who was comparable to Dibble, had a similar season in 1960. Duren never really came back. Dick Radatz burned out quickly; he never came back either.

YEAR	TEAM/LEVEL	G	IP	W-L	SAVES	HITS	SO	BB	ERA
1991	Cincinnati	67	82	3-5	31	67	124	25	3.17
1992	Cincinnati	63	70	3-5	25	48	110	31	3.07
1993	Cincinnati	45	42	1-4	19	34	49	42	6.48

FRANK DiPINO

Released

Relief Pitcher

No Value

Has been troubled over the last two years by a sore left elbow and strained muscles in his neck. He is 37 years old, was the Astros' closer in 1983 and part of '84, but settled then into a spot role, where he remained for most of 10 years. The Royals released him on July 25, probably bringing his long career to an end.

YEAR	TEAM/LEVEL	G	IP	W-L	SAVES	HITS	SO	BB	ERA
1992	Louisville AAA	18	23	0-3	0	28	10	8	3.97
1992	St. Louis	9	11	0-0	0	9	8	3	1.64
1993	Kansas City	11	16	1-1	0	21	5	6	6.89

JERRY DiPOTO

Cleveland Indians

Relief Pitcher

$26

Appears to be the Indians closer, for now. A third-round draft pick in 1990, DiPoto was a starter through most of his minor league career, and was just good enough to keep drifting upward in a weak system. He converted to the bullpen in 1992, earned the closer role after a hot start at Charlotte in '93, then moved up to Cleveland. Pitched 32 times after August 1, with 10 saves and a 1.42 ERA.

YEAR	TEAM/LEVEL	G	IP	W-L	SAVES	HITS	SO	BB	ERA
1992	Colorado Sp AAA	50	122	9-9	2	148	62	66	4.94
1993	Charlotte AAA	34	47	6-3	12	34	44	13	1.93
1993	Cleveland	46	56	4-4	11	57	41	30	2.40

GARY DISARCINA

California Angels

Shortstop

$25

He's pretty much Dick Schofield all over again, a good defensive shortstop but a .240 hitter without too much else to brag about. He doesn't walk as much as Schofield did . . . As a rookie he hit .132 in the late innings of close games. Last year, .176 . . . He broke his right thumb in August, and it is possible that Correia may take his job, although I doubt it.

YEAR	TEAM/LEVEL	G	AB	R	H	2B	3B	HR	RBI	BB	SB	AVG	OBP	SLG
1992	California	157	518	48	128	19	0	3	42	20	9	.247	.283	.301
1993	California	126	416	44	99	20	1	3	45	15	5	.238	.273	.313
1994	**Projected**	**132**	**423**	**42**	**103**	**16**	**1**	**3**	**40**	**18**	**8**	**.243**	**.274**	**.307**

STEVE DIXON

St.Louis Cardinals

Relief Pitcher

$9

A 31st-round draft pick in 1989, he earned the closer role at Louisville with a good year in 1992, but seems more likely destined for a role as a lefthanded situation pitcher, if in fact he has a career. Good curve, mediocre fastball, throws with funky sidearm motion. Joe Torre's fondness for pitchers with good control might suggest that Dixon's will have to improve before he gets the job he wants.

YEAR	TEAM/LEVEL	G	IP	W-L	SAVES	HITS	SO	BB	ERA
1992	AA and AAA	58	69	3-3	4	54	81	34	2.75
1993	Louisville AAA	57	68	5-7	20	57	61	33	4.92
1993	St. Louis	4	3	0-0	0	7	2	5	33.75

JOHN DOHERTY

Detroit Tigers

Starting Pitcher

$22

A pitcher with 14 wins and 63 strikeouts, as a rule, is about as good an investment as a store with 14 employees and 63 customers. Such pitchers almost always fall apart in the following season, although you have to note Doherty's exceptional control and increased strikeouts late in the year . . . His ground ball/fly ball ratio, 2.63 to one, was the highest in the American League . . . Threw only 86 pitches per start, lowest in the league.

YEAR	TEAM/LEVEL	G	IP	W-L	PCT.	HITS	SO	BB	ERA
1991	London AA	53	65	3-3	.500	62	42	21	2.22
1992	Detroit	47	116	7-4	.636	131	37	25	3.88
1993	Detroit	32	185	14-11	.560	205	63	48	4.44

CHRIS DONNELS
Houston Astros
Third Base
$18

Spelled Caminiti at third base most of the year, then played every day at first when Bagwell was hurt in September. He hit all right, although he didn't draw the large number of walks that would be indicated by his minor league records (417 walks in 586 games in the minors) . . . He'll be 28 in late April, so getting a regular job is probably out, but could have a good career as a pinch hitter/extra infielder.

YEAR	TEAM/LEVEL	G	AB	R	H	2B	3B	HR	RBI	BB	SB	AVG	OBP	SLG
1992	MLE	81	267	27	72	12	2	3	24	45	8	.270	.375	.363
1992	New York NL	45	121	8	21	4	0	0	6	17	1	.174	.275	.207
1993	Houston	88	179	18	46	14	2	2	24	19	2	.257	.327	.391

JOHN DOPSON
Boston Red Sox
Starting Pitcher
$16

Two straight 7-11 seasons may get him an endorsement contract with a convenience store company, but otherwise could not be considered lucky. He's actually a good pitcher when healthy, but tries to pitch through fatigue and minor injuries, and gets hammered. His 14-22 record over the last two years breaks down as 13-9 before the All-Star break, but 1-13 with an awful ERA after the break.

YEAR	TEAM/LEVEL	G	IP	W-L	PCT.	HITS	SO	BB	ERA
1991	Boston	1	1	0-0	—	2	0	1	18.00
1992	Boston	25	141	7-11	.389	159	55	38	4.08
1993	Boston	34	156	7-11	.389	170	89	59	4.97

BILLY DORAN
Milwaukee Brewers
Second Base
$3

Doran, who is a switch hitter, opened the season as a righthanded platoon player, which is very strange since he hasn't hit a lick against lefthanders for years and years. (Could the Brewers have mixed up his numbers, and confused what he did *against lefthanders* with what he did *as a lefthander*? More likely they just never checked). Anyway, a shoulder injury ended his season, if not his career, in May. He's almost 36.

YEAR	TEAM/LEVEL	G	AB	R	H	2B	3B	HR	RBI	BB	SB	AVG	OBP	SLG
1991	Cincinnati	111	361	51	101	12	2	6	35	46	5	.280	.359	.374
1992	Cincinnati	132	387	48	91	16	2	8	47	64	7	.235	.342	.349
1993	Milwaukee	28	60	7	13	4	0	0	6	6	1	.217	.284	.283

BRIAN DORSETT
Cincinnati Reds
Catcher
$13

A veteran righthanded catcher who followed up a big year at Buffalo in 1992 (35 doubles, 21 homers, 102 RBI) with a big first half at Indianapolis (below), and was called up just before the All-Star break. He is 33 years old and has never been confused with Ron Karkovice, but is probably a better hitter than Oliver or the Reds' other catchers, so there should be a role for him somewhere.

YEAR	TEAM/LEVEL	G	AB	R	H	2B	3B	HR	RBI	BB	SB	AVG	OBP	SLG
1993	Indianap AAA	77	278	38	83	27	0	18	57	28	2	.299	.363	.590
1993	MLE	77	266	30	71	24	0	13	45	22	1	.267	.323	.504
1993	Cincinnati	25	63	7	16	4	0	2	12	3	0	.254	.288	.413

KELLY DOWNS

Oakland Athletics

Pitcher

$10

Started 12 times for LaRussa, with ghastly results (0-6, 7.02 ERA) and pitched 30 times in the bullpen, with unimpressive results (4.30 ERA, poor peripheral stats). At this point, four years after rotator cuff surgery, there really isn't *anything* here to like. He doesn't throw hard, doesn't have good control, hasn't been consistently successful . . . Still capable of pitching well for a few weeks at a time, but I'd hate to be counting on him.

YEAR	TEAM/LEVEL	G	IP	W-L	PCT.	HITS	SO	BB	ERA
1991	San Francisco	45	112	10-4	.714	99	62	53	4.19
1992	Two Teams	37	144	6-7	.462	137	71	70	3.37
1993	Oakland	42	120	5-10	.333	135	66	60	5.64

DOUG DRABEK

Houston Astros

Starting Pitcher

$53

Pitched a lot of close games and didn't win them, thus leading the league in losses. His stats in terms of innings, hits allowed, walks allowed, and home runs allowed were very similar in 1993 to 1991, when he won 15 games and had a good 3.07 ERA, suggesting that there is nothing really much wrong with him. He'll bounce back with another 15- to 18-win season in '94.

YEAR	TEAM/LEVEL	G	IP	W-L	PCT.	HITS	SO	BB	ERA
1991	Pittsburgh	35	235	15-14	.517	245	142	62	3.07
1992	Pittsburgh	34	257	15-11	.577	218	177	54	2.77
1993	Houston	34	238	9-18	.333	242	157	60	3.79

BRIAN DRAHMAN

Chicago White Sox

Relief Pitcher

$17

A big fat guy, 27 years old; the White Sox got him in a trade for Jerry Reuss, sometime during the Truman administration. His career had been idling for years until he took the closer role for the Sox' Triple-A team, but after two straight good years in that role, he has to be seen as somebody who is ready for a major league job.

YEAR	TEAM/LEVEL	G	IP	W-L	SAVES	HITS	SO	BB	ERA
1992	Vancouver AAA	48	58	2-4	30	44	34	31	2.01
1993	Nashville AAA	54	56	9-4	20	59	49	19	2.91
1993	Chicago	5	5	0-0	1	7	3	2	0.00

MIKE DRAPER

New York Mets

Relief Pitcher

$14

The Yankees didn't keep him on their roster despite 37 saves for Columbus in '92, and the Mets took him in the Rule V draft. He didn't pitch very well. The league hit .327 against him, and at 26 (now 27) he is rather old to be thought of as a project. His control is good and he gets some ground balls, which puts him in the same class as John Doherty.

YEAR	TEAM/LEVEL	G	IP	W-L	SAVES	HITS	SO	BB	ERA
1991	AA and AAA	40	160	11-9	2	161	84	52	3.38
1992	Columbus AAA	57	80	5-6	37	70	42	28	3.60
1993	New York	29	42	1-1	0	53	16	14	4.25

STEVE DREYER

Texas Rangers

Starting Pitcher

$15

The Rangers eighth-round pick in 1990 out of the University of Northern Iowa, he went through the minors in three years by being consistently adequate. Called up August 6, he moved immediately into the rotation, where he wasn't the worst pitcher in the league, quite. Doesn't throw major league hard, has had excellent control in the minors, although (like many pitchers) he got a little timid when he got to the majors. Grade C prospect.

YEAR	TEAM/LEVEL	G	IP	W-L	PCT.	HITS	SO	BB	ERA
1992	Charlotte A	26	169	11-7	.611	164	111	37	2.40
1993	AA and AAA	21	138	6-8	.429	134	86	39	3.19
1993	Texas	10	41	3-3	.500	48	23	20	5.71

ROB DUCEY

Texas Rangers

Outfield

$24

There is something strange here. This guy runs well, is a promising lefthanded hitter and a good enough outfielder, but here he is almost 29 years old, and just now getting a chance to play. Toronto wanted to keep him, for some reason, but they didn't want to let him play . . . I'm not suggesting that he's Dave Parker, but I think he's as good a player as, let's say, Wes Chamberlain.

YEAR	TEAM/LEVEL	G	AB	R	H	2B	3B	HR	RBI	BB	SB	AVG	OBP	SLG
1992	Two Teams	54	80	7	15	4	0	0	2	5	2	.188	.233	.238
1993	MLE	105	364	46	93	12	4	12	38	30	10	.255	.312	.409
1993	Texas	27	85	15	24	6	3	2	9	10	2	.282	.351	.494

MARIANO DUNCAN

Philadelphia Phillies

Second Base/Shortstop

$32

Started 61 games at second base in '93, 49 games at shortstop. As a second baseman he is OK but Morandini is a lot better; as a shortstop he's just a stopgap (shortstopgap?), but he doesn't panic no matter where you put him, and he hits better than most middle infielders. His hitting has improved dramatically since he stopped switch hitting a few years ago. . . .

YEAR	TEAM/LEVEL	G	AB	R	H	2B	3B	HR	RBI	BB	SB	AVG	OBP	SLG
1992	Philadelphia	142	574	74	153	40	3	8	50	17	23	.267	.292	.389
1993	Philadelphia	124	496	68	140	26	4	11	73	12	6	.282	.304	.417
1994	**Projected**	**129**	**490**	**69**	**126**	**21**	**3**	**10**	**52**	**15**	**12**	**.255**	**.277**	**.371**

SHAWON DUNSTON

Chicago Cubs

Shortstop

$27

Has been out for almost two years after back surgery in May, 1992. He tried to come back too quickly last year, and went two steps backward . . . If he is healthy, it is generally thought that he may be traded. The Cubs have Sanchez, who has played well at short, and Vizcaino, who has played *very* well. Dunston is 31; he should still be a major league player.

YEAR	TEAM/LEVEL	G	AB	R	H	2B	3B	HR	RBI	BB	SB	AVG	OBP	SLG
1992	Chicago	18	73	8	23	3	1	0	2	3	2	.315	.342	.384
1993	Chicago	7	10	3	4	2	0	0	2	0	0	.400	.400	.600
1994	**Projected**	**120**	**410**	**48**	**108**	**19**	**3**	**9**	**37**	**19**	**16**	**.263**	**.296**	**.390**

LENNY DYKSTRA

Philadelphia Phillies

Center Field

$79

Established a major league record for plate appearances, with 772 . . . His season was almost certainly the greatest year by any leadoff man in National League history, and better than many, many MVP seasons, although not quite at the same level as Bonds's. Established career highs in runs scored (by 37), hits (by 2), doubles (by 9), home runs (by 9), RBI (by 6), walks (by 40) and stolen bases (by 4).

YEAR	TEAM/LEVEL	G	AB	R	H	2B	3B	HR	RBI	BB	SB	AVG	OBP	SLG
1992	Philadelphia	85	345	53	104	18	0	6	39	40	30	.301	.375	.406
1993	Philadelphia	161	637	143	194	44	6	19	66	129	37	.305	.420	.482
1994	**Projected**	**145**	**570**	**107**	**162**	**34**	**3**	**12**	**51**	**98**	**41**	**.284**	**.389**	**.418**

DAMION EASLEY

California Angels

Infielder

$24

Eighty percent of his playing time was at second base. He won the second base job and played regularly through the end of May, hitting in my opinion more than he ought to, but was stopped then by chronic shin splints, which eventually put him on the disabled list . . . Probably will hit enough and field well enough to be a regular second baseman. Only 24; could emerge as a star, but needs to stay healthy.

YEAR	TEAM/LEVEL	G	AB	R	H	2B	3B	HR	RBI	BB	SB	AVG	OBP	SLG
1992	California	47	151	14	39	5	0	1	12	8	9	.258	.307	.311
1993	California	73	230	33	72	13	2	2	22	28	6	.313	.392	.413
1994	**Projected**	**89**	**293**	**34**	**74**	**12**	**1**	**3**	**26**	**22**	**11**	**.253**	**.305**	**.331**

DENNIS ECKERSLEY

Oakland Athletics

Closer

$53

It is my opinion that he will come back from his "off season," that he will save 35-50 games again this year. Eckersley comes from third base, and in 1993 developed a weakness of the type: lefthanders. They hit .323 against him, with a .538 slugging percentage. He has not historically had this trouble, and I think that it was just something that happened, that he didn't get the At'em balls.

YEAR	TEAM/LEVEL	G	IP	W-L	SAVES	HITS	SO	BB	ERA
1991	Oakland	67	76	5-4	43	60	87	9	2.96
1992	Oakland	69	80	7-1	51	62	93	11	1.91
1993	Oakland	64	67	2-4	36	67	80	13	4.16

TOM EDENS

Houston Astros

Relief Pitcher

$22

Edens was not one of the Twins' 15 protected players after a fine year in the Minnesota bullpen in '92. Florida took him in the expansion draft and traded him to the Astros, who were trying to build a championship-quality pitching staff. Edens started the year on the DL with a minor injury, but pitched fairly well after joining the team in early May. He's 32 years old, no star potential.

YEAR	TEAM/LEVEL	G	IP	W-L	SAVES	HITS	SO	BB	ERA
1991	Minnesota	8	33	2-2	0	34	19	10	4.09
1992	Minnesota	52	76	6-3	3	65	57	36	2.83
1993	Houston	38	49	1-1	0	47	21	19	3.12

JIM EDMONDS

California Angels

Right Field

$15

A September callup after hitting well at Vancouver. A lefthanded line-drive hitter, 23 years old. His arm is said to be very good, and he could play for the Angels in '94 if Polonia doesn't return to the team, in which case Salmon might move to left, Edmonds in right. He would probably hit around .270, which isn't enough for a player without power or speed, but he is young enough to improve substantially.

YEAR	TEAM/LEVEL	G	AB	R	H	2B	3B	HR	RBI	BB	SB	AVG	OBP	SLG
1993	Vancouv AAA	95	356	59	112	28	4	9	74	41	6	.315	.382	.492
1993	MLE	95	334	41	90	21	1	6	52	28	3	.269	.326	.392
1993	California	18	61	5	15	4	1	0	4	2	0	.246	.270	.344

MARK EICHHORN

Toronto Blue Jays

Relief Pitcher

$29

Has modified his motion so that he is more sidearm and not as much underhand as he once was, but is still essentially a Tekulve-type pitcher—gets many ground balls, has excellent control, doesn't give up home runs, gets hit hard by lefthanded hitters (.326 last year; ground ball/fly ball ratio was 134-56). Every good organization should have one.

YEAR	TEAM/LEVEL	G	IP	W-L	SAVES	HITS	SO	BB	ERA
1991	California	70	82	3-3	1	63	49	13	1.98
1992	Two Teams	65	88	4-4	2	86	61	25	3.08
1993	Toronto	54	73	3-1	0	76	47	22	2.72

DAVE EILAND

San Diego

Starting Pitcher

$10

His career doesn't seem to be going very well. A seventh-round 1987 pick, Eiland has a won-lost log of 58-28 in the minors, including a 16-5 record for Columbus in 1990, which earned him a shot at the Yankees' rotation in 1991. He wasn't awful but didn't win, and has since been troubled by back spasms and bruised ankles . . . Hit a major league home run in his first professional at bat, against Bob Ojeda.

YEAR	TEAM/LEVEL	G	IP	W-L	PCT.	HITS	SO	BB	ERA
1991	New York AL	18	73	2-5	.286	87	18	23	5.33
1992	San Diego	7	27	0-2	.000	33	10	5	5.67
1993	San Diego	10	48	0-3	.000	58	14	17	5.21

JIM EISENREICH

Philadelphia Phillies

Utility Outfield

$26

He had the odd record—153 games, only 362 at bats—because he was a platoon player who would be used as a defensive substitute if the Phillies were ahead and a pinch hitter if they were behind. The Phillies didn't pick up his option, despite his fine season, and he is a free agent at this writing. The Royals' MVP in 1989, has hit .301 and .318 since—unusual consistency for a part-time player.

YEAR	TEAM/LEVEL	G	AB	R	H	2B	3B	HR	RBI	BB	SB	AVG	OBP	SLG
1992	Kansas City	113	353	31	95	13	3	2	28	24	11	.269	.313	.340
1993	Philadelphia	153	362	51	115	17	4	7	54	26	5	.318	.363	.445
1994	**Projected**	**132**	**355**	**41**	**99**	**21**	**3**	**4**	**41**	**23**	**6**	**.279**	**.303**	**.389**

CAL ELDRED

Milwaukee Brewers

Starting Pitcher

$37

Led AL in innings, 258, and batters faced, 1087, led majors in pitches thrown, 4,250 . . . Appears to be tracing the career of Jim Nash, who was called up in mid-season 1966 and went 12-1 with a 2.06 ERA. Nash pitched well for a lousy team in '67 and '68, but was burned out before his team improved . . . Eldred is capable of having a big season if he gets a little more help from his team.

YEAR	TEAM/LEVEL	G	IP	W-L	PCT.	HITS	SO	BB	ERA
1992	Denver AAA	19	141	10-6	.625	122	99	42	3.00
1992	Milwaukee	14	100	11-2	.846	76	62	23	1.79
1993	Milwaukee	36	258	16-16	.500	232	180	91	4.01

SCOTT ERICKSON

Minnesota Twins

Starting Pitcher

$26

Led American League in all the good categories, like losses (19), hits allowed (266), runs allowed (138) and stolen base percentage allowed (87.5%) . . . Has lost velocity on his sinking fastball, and has had trouble adjusting, but his strikeouts, walks and homers allowed weren't a lot different from his big season. 1993 was a tough year for a lot of ground ball pitchers; if 1994 is a more normal season, he'll be better. If he's still in the rotation.

YEAR	TEAM/LEVEL	G	IP	W-L	PCT.	HITS	SO	BB	ERA
1991	Minnesota	32	204	20-8	.714	189	108	71	3.18
1992	Minnesota	32	212	13-12	.520	197	101	83	3.40
1993	Minnesota	34	219	8-19	.296	266	116	71	5.19

ALVARO ESPINOZA

Cleveland Indians

Third Base/Shortstop

$17

The worst example of redundancy in modern baseball is a) Cleveland having both Alvaro Expinoza and Felix Fermin, b) the Royals having both Gary Gaetti and Hubie Brooks, or c) the Yankees having George Steinbrenner and being surrounded by a giant slum . . . Did you ever notice that Espinoza can rifle the ball across the infield with just a flick of his wrist? How does he do that.

YEAR	TEAM/LEVEL	G	AB	R	H	2B	3B	HR	RBI	BB	SB	AVG	OBP	SLG
1992	Colo Spr AAA	122	483	64	145	36	6	9	79	21	2	.300	.333	.455
1993	Cleveland	129	263	34	73	15	0	4	27	8	2	.278	.298	.380
1994	**Projected**	**100**	**286**	**28**	**72**	**13**	**1**	**3**	**25**	**9**	**2**	**.252**	**.276**	**.336**

CECIL ESPY

Cincinnati Reds

Outfield

$9

A 31-year-old sixth-outfielder type, was taken from the Pirates on a waiver claim (they still have those?), but was released in July. He's a tall, skinny .250 hitter with no power, runs well and is a switch hitter. No arm; can be used as pinch hitter, pinch runner or defense in the outfield. He'll be in spring training somewhere as a non-roster player, and might wind up with a job.

YEAR	TEAM/LEVEL	G	AB	R	H	2B	3B	HR	RBI	BB	SB	AVG	OBP	SLG
1991	Pittsburgh	43	82	7	20	4	0	1	11	5	4	.244	.281	.329
1992	Pittsburgh	112	194	21	50	7	3	1	20	15	6	.258	.310	.340
1993	Cincinnati	40	60	6	14	2	0	0	5	14	2	.233	.368	.267

MARK ETTLES

San Diego Padres

Pitcher

$12

A 27-year-old Australian; I have it on good authority that, in all the Padres' mid-summer trade talks, his name never came up. He's a modest talent, not big and doesn't blow anybody away, but he's sneaky fast with good control, and might slide into a Joe Boever-type career. Grade C prospect . . . First major league player whose name rhymes with "Nettles."

YEAR	TEAM/LEVEL	G	IP	W-L	SAVES	HITS	SO	BB	ERA
1992	Wichita AA	54	68	3-8	22	54	86	23	2.77
1993	Las Vegas AAA	47	50	3-6	15	58	29	22	4.71
1993	San Diego	14	18	1-0	0	23	9	4	6.50

CARL "POOCHY" EVERETT

Florida Marlins

Center Field

$23

A raw athletic talent, taken from the Yankees in the expansion draft, and had a very successful season. He hadn't hit much before, and home runs at High Desert are as common as fast food joints, but his .596 slugging percentage in Triple-A, even though it's Edmonton, will get your attention. The Marlins don't need a center fielder, but how you gonna keep them down on the farm, after they slug .600? Grade B prospect.

YEAR	TEAM/LEVEL	G	AB	R	H	2B	3B	HR	RBI	BB	SB	AVG	OBP	SLG
1993	High Des A	59	253	48	73	12	6	10	52	22	24	.289	.358	.502
1993	Edmonton AAA	35	136	28	42	13	4	6	16	19	12	.309	.401	.596
1993	Florida	11	19	0	2	0	0	0	0	1	1	.105	.150	.105

HECTOR FAJARDO

Texas Rangers

Pitcher

$10

Big Mexican righthander who is impossible to evaluate because, having been in pro ball since 1989, he has never pitched more than 11 games or 61 innings at any stop before moving on, usually to the disabled list (he has chronic bursitis). In '93 he pitched six games in a Rookie League and five innings of A ball, plus two-thirds of one inning in the majors. This is a typical season for him. Grade C prospect.

YEAR	TEAM/LEVEL	G	IP	W-L	SAVES	HITS	SO	BB	ERA
1993	Rangers R	6	30	3-1	0	21	27	5	1.80
1993	Charlotte A	2	5	0-0	0	5	3	1	1.80
1993	Texas	1	1	0-0	0	0	1	0	0.00

RIKKERT FANEYTE

San Francisco Giants

Outfield

$14

A native of the Netherlands who still lists Amsterdam as his residence, Faneyte played college ball in Dade County, then was drafted by the Giants. He's a righthanded hitter with good to outstanding defensive skills, and some modest offensive ability. He skipped Double-A and hit well at Phoenix, but will be 25 in May, so probably isn't going to get a lot better as a hitter. Grade C prospect, will have a career.

YEAR	TEAM/LEVEL	G	AB	R	H	2B	3B	HR	RBI	BB	SB	AVG	OBP	SLG
1993	Phoenix AAA	115	426	71	133	23	2	11	71	40	15	.312	.379	.453
1993	MLE	115	398	49	105	18	1	7	49	26	9	.264	.309	.367
1993	San Francisco	7	15	2	2	0	0	0	0	2	0	.133	.235	.133

PAUL FARIES

San Francisco Giants

Infield

$12

Faries, who is basically a second baseman, led the Pacific Coast League in runs scored and hits in 1990. Time has run out on him as a prospect (he's 29), but he still hopes to find a position as a backup infielder, and is certainly a good enough player to do that job. His 1993 MLE is fairly typical—he's a .260-range hitter, and runs well.

YEAR	TEAM/LEVEL	G	AB	R	H	2B	3B	HR	RBI	BB	SB	AVG	OBP	SLG
1993	Phoenix AAA	78	327	56	99	14	5	2	32	22	18	.303	.348	.394
1993	MLE	78	308	39	80	11	2	1	22	15	12	.260	.294	.318
1993	San Francisco	15	36	6	8	2	1	0	4	1	2	.222	.237	.333

MONTY FARISS

Florida Marlins

Outfield

$10

Farriss's career has gone into a fiery tailspin, although at 26 he may still be able to save some of it. An all-American shortstop in college, he is too big to be a shortstop (6-4, 205) unless he had Cal Ripken's skills, which he doesn't. The Rangers kept wanting him to solve their shortstop problem, so that messed up his career, and now he has stopped hitting. Grade D prospect.

YEAR	TEAM/LEVEL	G	AB	R	H	2B	3B	HR	RBI	BB	SB	AVG	OBP	SLG
1992	Texas	67	166	13	36	7	1	3	21	17	0	.217	.297	.325
1993	MLE	74	242	22	53	9	2	4	26	30	0	.219	.305	.322
1993	Florida	18	29	3	5	2	1	0	2	5	0	.172	.294	.310

STEVE FARR

New York Yankees

Closer

$29

After several consecutive outstanding seasons he was troubled in '93 by a strained back and a tender elbow, which may leave the Yankees looking for a new closer. Farr is 37 years old, and he never did have obvious closer stuff—no Goose Gossage fastball, no Bruce Sutter splitter—but made exceptionally good use of what he has by jamming hitters and working ahead in the count. A quality pitcher if healthy.

YEAR	TEAM/LEVEL	G	IP	W-L	SAVES	HITS	SO	BB	ERA
1991	New York	60	70	5-5	23	57	60	20	2.19
1992	New York	50	52	2-2	30	34	37	19	1.56
1993	New York	49	47	2-2	25	44	39	28	4.21

JOHN FARRELL

California Angels

Starting Pitcher

$13

A rotation starter for the Indians in the late 1980s, he blew out his elbow and spent two years on the DL. He threw the ball well in spring training, made the Angels rotation, and had made 12 starts for the Angels by early June, being regularly clobbered. The Angels sent him to Vancouver, where he made 12 starts and pitched well, came back to start five more times and was as bad as before. Could still come back.

YEAR	TEAM/LEVEL	G	IP	W-L	PCT.	HITS	SO	BB	ERA
1992	(On Disabled List)								
1993	Vancouver AAA	12	86	4-5	.444	83	71	28	3.99
1993	California	21	91	3-12	.200	110	45	44	7.35

JEFF FASSERO
Montreal Expos
Lefthanded Pitcher
$30

Fassero is now a starting pitcher. Given up on by the Cardinals, White Sox and Indians, he signed with Montreal as a minor league free agent, and was a pleasant surprise in '91 and '92. Tried as a starter in mid-'93, he was brilliant, going 7-4 with a 2.29 ERA in 94 innings. Throws a fastball, slider and forkball; a fine pitcher, but we'll have to see if his arm will hold up to 200 innings.

YEAR	TEAM/LEVEL	G	IP	W-L	SAVES	HITS	SO	BB	ERA
1991	Montreal	51	55	2-5	8	39	42	17	2.44
1992	Montreal	70	86	8-7	1	81	63	34	2.84
1993	Montreal	56	150	12-5	1	119	140	54	2.29

MIKE FELDER
Seattle Mariners
Outfield
$23

Felder signed with Seattle as a free agent, and opened the season as their regular left fielder, in which role he was a miserable failure (surprise, surprise, isn't this like the fourth time we've learned this?) Felder, a switch hitter, could be compared to Brett Butler or Otis Nixon, and is a good man off the bench, but hasn't been able to keep his average above .250 when he's been put in the lineup every day.

YEAR	TEAM/LEVEL	G	AB	R	H	2B	3B	HR	RBI	BB	SB	AVG	OBP	SLG
1992	San Francisco	145	322	44	92	13	3	4	23	21	14	.286	.330	.382
1993	Seattle	109	342	31	72	7	5	1	20	22	15	.211	.262	.269
1994	**Projected**	**96**	**233**	**27**	**57**	**6**	**2**	**2**	**13**	**17**	**11**	**.245**	**.296**	**.313**

JUNIOR FELIX
Exiled
Center Field
$15

Bothered by a groin pull early in the year, Felix was sent to the minors a couple of times and didn't report the second time, leaving him with a murky future. Felix's listed age, 26, is believed to be a fiction, and his skills seem to slip another step backward every season. His health record is poor, and his attitude is the subject of frequent conversations, but it would be a mistake to *entirely* write him off.

YEAR	TEAM/LEVEL	G	AB	R	H	2B	3B	HR	RBI	BB	SB	AVG	OBP	SLG
1991	California	66	230	32	65	10	2	2	26	11	7	.283	.321	.370
1992	California	139	509	63	125	22	5	9	72	33	8	.246	.289	.361
1993	Florida	57	214	25	51	11	1	7	22	10	2	.238	.276	.397

FELIX FERMIN
Cleveland Indians
Shortstop
$24

Saw only 3.07 pitches per plate appearance, the lowest of any American League regular. Also put the ball in play 61% of the time when he swung, highest in the American League . . . Led American League in errors, with 23, was last in fielding percentage for a regular shortstop (.960) . . . His secondary average, .102, was the lowest of any major league regular, by far.

YEAR	TEAM/LEVEL	G	AB	R	H	2B	3B	HR	RBI	BB	SB	AVG	OBP	SLG
1992	Cleveland	79	58	27	58	7	2	0	13	18	0	.270	.326	.321
1993	Cleveland	140	480	48	126	16	2	2	45	24	4	.263	.303	.317
1994	**Projected**	**127**	**406**	**37**	**103**	**10**	**2**	**1**	**32**	**26**	**4**	**.254**	**.299**	**.296**

ALEX FERNANDEZ

Chicago White Sox
Starting Pitcher
$56

Handled 56 chances without an error, best in the American League . . . A powerfully built righthander with outstanding stuff, has been compared to Tom Seaver every day since he was an amateur, and finally delivered the goods in '93. He's piled up quite a few innings on an immature arm, but if he stays healthy there is every reason to assume that he'll win 150-170 games in the next 10 years.

YEAR	TEAM/LEVEL	G	IP	W-L	PCT.	HITS	SO	BB	ERA
1991	Chicago	34	192	9-13	.409	186	145	88	4.51
1992	Chicago	29	188	8-11	.421	199	95	50	4.27
1993	Chicago	34	247	18-9	.667	221	169	67	3.13

SID FERNANDEZ

New York Mets
(Free Agent)
Starting Pitcher
$28

A one-of-a-kind pitcher, an archetype, usually at the top or bottom of any list. Fernandez is an awfully good pitcher and is only 31 years old, but has trouble controlling his weight and has had serious knee injuries in 1991 and 1993. If he is not in Shea Stadium in '93 his strikeouts will decrease and his ERA will increase, but his won-lost record may improve. His durability will remain questionable.

YEAR	TEAM/LEVEL	G	IP	W-L	PCT.	HITS	SO	BB	ERA
1991	New York	8	44	1-3	.250	36	31	9	2.86
1992	New York	32	215	14-11	.560	162	193	67	2.73
1993	New York	18	120	5-6	.455	82	81	36	2.93

TONY FERNANDEZ

Toronto Blue Jays
Shortstop
$40

It is assumed at this writing that Fernandez will leave the Blue Jays for greener bank accounts, leaving Alex Gonzalez to play short for Toronto. It seems odd to describe Fernandez as "consistent" (Fernandez?), but he has hit .276, .272, .275 and .279 over the last four years, with on-base percentages grouped between .337 and .352 and slugging percentages between .359 and .394.

YEAR	TEAM/LEVEL	G	AB	R	H	2B	3B	HR	RBI	BB	SB	AVG	OBP	SLG
1992	San Diego	155	622	84	171	32	4	4	37	56	20	.275	.337	.359
1993	Two Teams	142	526	65	147	23	11	5	64	56	21	.279	.348	.394
1994	**Projected**	**146**	**563**	**74**	**152**	**27**	**5**	**5**	**45**	**56**	**21**	**.270**	**.336**	**.362**

MIKE FETTERS

Milwaukee Brewers
Relief Pitcher
$24

After a fine year in '92 he had a pulled groin muscle early last year, and didn't hit his stride until August. A first-round draft pick of the Angels in 1986, he was a starting pitcher in the minors, and might yet emerge as a starter in the majors. Standard repertoire—fastball/curve/slider; will be at least fairly effective if he is healthy.

YEAR	TEAM/LEVEL	G	IP	W-L	SAVES	HITS	SO	BB	ERA
1991	California	19	45	2-5	0	53	24	28	4.84
1992	Milwaukee	50	63	5-1	2	38	43	24	1.87
1993	Milwaukee	45	59	3-3	0	59	23	22	3.34

CECIL FIELDER

Detroit Tigers

First Base

$53

Has not hit a triple or stolen a base for three years, which I believe is unprecedented for a player playing this much. Also took extra bases (such as going first-to-third on a single or scoring from first on a double) only 12 times in 1993, the lowest percentage in the American League . . . There's a place for him on a baseball team, but he's basically a big fat guy who hits home runs.

YEAR	TEAM/LEVEL	G	AB	R	H	2B	3B	HR	RBI	BB	SB	AVG	OBP	SLG
1992	Detroit	155	594	80	145	22	0	35	124	73	0	.244	.325	.458
1993	Detroit	154	573	80	153	23	0	30	117	90	0	.267	.368	.464
1994	**Projected**	**156**	**593**	**87**	**152**	**21**	**0**	**36**	**120**	**84**	**0**	**.256**	**.349**	**.474**

CHUCK FINLEY

California Angels

Starting Pitcher

$55

A fine pitcher, snapped back after losing 1992 to a toe injury. Throws hard and mixes up five pitches without getting any of them in the red zone too often. He does have some trouble holding runners, although he is a lefty. Led American League in complete games . . . Now 31, he is fourth on the Angels' all-time pitching lists, behind Ryan, Tanana and Mike Witt. Has won 16 or more in four of the last five years.

YEAR	TEAM/LEVEL	G	IP	W-L	PCT.	HITS	SO	BB	ERA
1991	California	34	227	18-9	.667	205	171	101	3.80
1992	California	31	204	7-12	.368	212	124	98	3.96
1993	California	35	251	16-14	.533	243	187	82	3.15

STEVE FINLEY

Houston Astros

Center Field

$40

Finley had a broken wrist in late April, came back quickly but didn't start to play the way he is capable of playing until about July 1. A Brett Butler-type player, hits the ball harder than Butler, doesn't bunt as much or walk as much, but fast, durable, a good center fielder and a pretty good base stealer. Led National League in triples, with 13.

YEAR	TEAM/LEVEL	G	AB	R	H	2B	3B	HR	RBI	BB	SB	AVG	OBP	SLG
1992	Houston	162	607	84	177	29	13	5	55	58	44	.292	.355	.407
1993	Houston	142	545	69	145	15	13	8	44	28	19	.266	.304	.385
1994	**Projected**	**152**	**573**	**75**	**156**	**21**	**8**	**7**	**49**	**44**	**33**	**.272**	**.324**	**.373**

GAR FINNVOLD

Boston Red Sox

Starting Pitcher

$15

A 6-foot-5 inch righthander, the Red Sox sixth-round pick in 1990 out of Florida State, where he was an Academic All-American. Good health record. Has put in decent seasons at AA and AAA the last two years, although stuck with ugly won-lost records. Throws fastball in mid-80's, good breaking stuff . . . Grade C prospect, could emerge as fourth starter or long reliever in majors.

YEAR	TEAM/LEVEL	G	IP	W-L	PCT.	HITS	SO	BB	ERA
1991	New Britain AA	16	101	5-8	.385	97	80	36	3.82
1992	New Britain AA	25	165	7-13	.350	156	135	52	3.49
1993	Pawtucket AAA	24	136	5-9	.357	128	123	51	3.77

CARLTON FISK
Released
Catcher
No Value

The third sure Hall of Famer to retire in '93 . . . Did you see that incredibly stupid *Frontline* show last spring? The whole argument of the piece was that the game of baseball was in terrible trouble because Carlton Fisk couldn't get along with the White Sox management . . . Most-similar players in history: Bench and Berra. The chart below compares the career performance of Bench, Berra and Fisk per 150 games played.

	AB	R	H	2B	3B	HR	RBI	BB	SB	AVG	OBP	SLG
Bench per 150 games	532	76	142	26	2	27	96	62	5	.267	.345	.476
Fisk per 150 games	526	77	141	25	3	23	80	51	8	.269	.341	.457
Berra per 150 games	535	83	152	23	3	25	101	50	2	.285	.350	.482

JOHN FLAHERTY
Boston Red Sox
Catcher
$18

The departure of Eric Wedge, the precipitous decline of Tony Peña and his own improved play have created an opening for Flaherty, who a year ago seemed doomed to a career in Triple-A. He's a righthanded hitter, 26 years old, slow and doesn't have power, but his defense has always been well spoken of, and he's a better hitter than Bob Melvin or Peña. Could be a *part* of a catching solution.

YEAR	TEAM/LEVEL	G	AB	R	H	2B	3B	HR	RBI	BB	SB	AVG	OBP	SLG
1993	Pawtucket AAA	105	365	29	99	22	0	6	35	26	0	.271	.327	.381
1993	MLE	105	354	22	88	22	0	4	26	19	0	.249	.287	.345
1993	Boston	13	25	3	3	2	0	0	2	2	0	.120	.214	.200

DAVE FLEMING
Seattle Mariners
Starting Pitcher
$29

His season started late because of some tendonitis which showed up in spring training, and, to be honest, he didn't pitch as well as his 12-5 record might make you think. Righthanded hitters hit .298 against him (he's a lefthander), and he doesn't have the control or ground ball ratio to get by with that . . . Very effective at cutting off the running game.

YEAR	TEAM/LEVEL	G	IP	W-L	PCT.	HITS	SO	BB	ERA
1991	Seattle	9	18	1-0	1.000	19	11	3	6.62
1992	Seattle	33	228	17-10	.630	225	112	60	3.39
1993	Seattle	26	167	12-5	.706	189	75	67	4.36

HUCK FLENER
Toronto Blue Jays
Lefthanded Pitcher
$22

A 25-year-old lefthander, used as both a starter (16 games) and reliever at Knoxville. A ninth-round draft pick, his performance since has varied from "very good" to "spectacular" (1.82 ERA, 107 strikeouts in 79 innings at Myrtle Beach). I hope the Jays have the sense to a) decide whether he's a starter or reliever, and b) give him a full year at Syracuse, because he could be one of the better pitchers they've developed.

YEAR	TEAM/LEVEL	G	IP	W-L	PCT.	HITS	SO	BB	ERA
1992	Dunedin A	41	112	7-3	.700	70	93	50	2.24
1993	Knoxville AA	38	136	13-6	.684	130	114	39	3.30
1993	Toronto	6	7	0-0	—	7	2	4	4.05

DARRIN FLETCHER

Montreal Expos

Catcher

$26

After struggling with the bat early, Fletcher had a hot streak in early July, and took firm control of the Expos' catching job as the season went on. His RBI rate was very good for a catcher, and the Expos had a 3.22 ERA with Fletcher catching (4.10 with other catchers). He threw out only 14 of 113 opposing base stealers (12%), the poorest percentage of any major league regular catcher. Everybody else caught at least 19%.

YEAR	TEAM/LEVEL	G	AB	R	H	2B	3B	HR	RBI	BB	SB	AVG	OBP	SLG
1992	Montreal	83	222	13	54	10	2	2	26	14	0	.243	.289	.333
1993	Montreal	133	396	33	101	20	1	9	60	34	0	.255	.320	.379
1994	**Projected**	**128**	**380**	**29**	**93**	**18**	**1**	**7**	**48**	**26**	**1**	**.245**	**.293**	**.353**

PAUL FLETCHER

Philadelphia Phillies

Starting Pitcher

$7

Was called up and pitched one-third of one inning in July, which required me to put him in the book despite his generally miserable season. A righthander, 40th-round draft pick in 1988, but won the Paul Owens award as the best pitcher in the Phillies' minor league system in '92. His good strikeout/walk ratios suggest that he may have some ability. Grade D prospect.

YEAR	TEAM/LEVEL	G	IP	W-L	PCT.	HITS	SO	BB	ERA
1992	Reading AA	22	127	9-4	.692	103	103	47	2.83
1992	Scranton AAA	4	23	3-0	1.000	17	26	2	2.78
1993	Scranton AAA	34	140	4-12	.250	146	116	60	5.66

SCOTT FLETCHER

Boston Red Sox

Second Base

$28

He was released by Milwaukee, signed with the Red Sox and had his best season since 1987. His .402 slugging percentage was a career high; his 16-for-19 performance as a base stealer was by far his career best. He's 35 now, but one player in a hundred is better in his mid- to late-thirties than he was in his late twenties, and you never know: he might be the one.

YEAR	TEAM/LEVEL	G	AB	R	H	2B	3B	HR	RBI	BB	SB	AVG	OBP	SLG
1992	Milwaukee	123	386	53	106	18	3	3	51	30	17	.275	.335	.360
1993	Boston	121	480	81	137	31	5	5	45	37	16	.285	.341	.402
1994	**Projected**	**117**	**380**	**47**	**97**	**17**	**2**	**3**	**39**	**29**	**11**	**.255**	**.311**	**.334**

CLIFF FLOYD

Montreal Expos

First Base/Outfield

$44

A big lefthanded hitter, also throws left, Floyd was a highly regarded prospect a year ago, and dominated Double-A at age 20, pushing him near the top among the super-prospects. He runs well enough to be a 30-30 man, although in view of his size, he will probably lose his speed by age 28. **Grade A prospect;** probably the number-one candidate for NL Rookie of the Year, but may be a year early.

YEAR	TEAM/LEVEL	G	AB	R	H	2B	3B	HR	RBI	BB	SB	AVG	OBP	SLG
1993	AA and AAA	133	505	94	155	19	6	28	119	70	33	.307	.396	.535
1993	MLE	133	482	75	132	17	3	20	94	49	23	.274	.341	.446
1994	**Projected**	**155**	**530**	**81**	**144**	**18**	**3**	**22**	**99**	**51**	**24**	**.272**	**.336**	**.442**

TOM FOLEY

Pittsburgh Pirates

Utilityman

$18

Foley spent seven years as a backup infielder in Montreal, but wasn't invited back after hitting .174 in '92. He signed a one-year contract with Pittsburgh; Leyland used him often as a pinch hitter (33 times, mostly pinch hitting for pitchers) and played him at second base about once a week. He had his best year since 1988, and probably will return in '94. He's 34.

YEAR	TEAM/LEVEL	G	AB	R	H	2B	3B	HR	RBI	BB	SB	AVG	OBP	SLG
1992	Montreal	72	115	7	20	3	1	0	5	8	3	.174	.230	.217
1993	Pittsburgh	86	194	18	49	11	1	3	22	11	0	.253	.287	.366
1994	**Projected**	**89**	**157**	**13**	**35**	**10**	**1**	**2**	**15**	**11**	**1**	**.223**	**.274**	**.338**

BROOK FORDYCE

New York Mets

Catcher

$15

Fordyce is projected as the Mets catcher of the future, if Hundley doesn't make progress with the bat. Drafted out of high school, he has played 522 minor league games already, although he's only 23. His defense gets excellent reviews, and he's probably going to hit enough to have at least some kind of a career. Grade C prospect; still has to develop, as a hitter, if he's going to hold a regular job.

YEAR	TEAM/LEVEL	G	AB	R	H	2B	3B	HR	RBI	BB	SB	AVG	OBP	SLG
1992	MLE	118	412	49	105	26	0	8	51	26	0	.255	.299	.376
1993	Norfolk AAA	116	409	33	106	21	2	2	40	26	2	.259	.307	.335
1993	MLE	116	397	27	94	18	1	1	33	21	1	.237	.275	.295

TONY FOSSAS

Boston Red Sox

Relief Pitcher

$12

Lefthanded one-out reliever, comes in to pitch to Kent Hrbek, or Ken Griffey, or Rafael Palmeiro, or whoever the big lefty coming up is. He does this well, limiting lefties to a .129 batting average last year (9-for-70) and .196 over the last four years. You need to get him out of the game quickly, because righthanded hitters hit about .320 against him, with a slugging percentage up around .500.

YEAR	TEAM/LEVEL	G	IP	W-L	SAVES	HITS	SO	BB	ERA
1991	Boston	64	57	3-2	1	49	29	28	3.47
1992	Boston	60	30	1-2	2	31	19	14	2.43
1993	Boston	71	40	1-1	0	38	39	15	5.18

KEVIN FOSTER

Philadelphia Phillies

Relief Pitcher

$12

Foster pitched well in the Expos system in 1991 (10-4, 2.74 ERA at Sumter) and 1992 (7-2, 1.95 ERA at West Palm Beach), but without becoming a hot prospect, from which we may infer that his fastball does not explode. He was traded to the Phillies last June, pitched OK in his first look at Triple-A, and got into two games in September. Grade C prospect.

YEAR	TEAM/LEVEL	G	IP	W-L	PCT.	HITS	SO	BB	ERA
1993	Jacksonville AA	12	66	4-4	.500	53	72	29	3.97
1993	Scranton AAA	17	71	1-1	.500	63	59	29	3.93
1993	Philadelphia	2	7	0-1	.000	13	6	7	14.85

STEVE FOSTER

Cincinnati Reds

Relief Pitcher

$15

Foster, never a red-hot prospect, has posted a 2.41 ERA through 59 major league games, but his career took a turn for the worse last June, when he had shoulder surgery, and went on the 60-day disabled list. Righthander, not big, has excellent control, is described by the papers as a bulldog. He can pitch, but don't assume he'll be healthy, even if he's healthy in spring training.

YEAR	TEAM/LEVEL	G	IP	W-L	SAVES	HITS	SO	BB	ERA
1991	Cincinnati	11	14	0-0	0	7	11	4	1.93
1992	Cincinnati	31	50	1-1	2	52	34	13	2.88
1993	Cincinnati	17	26	2-2	0	23	16	5	1.75

ERIC FOX

Oakland Athletics

Outfield

$13

A 30-year-old switch hitter who runs well, opened the season playing almost every game, either as the starting center fielder or a defensive sub, but was sent to the minor leagues on May 18 after failing to collect more than an occasional hit. His performance back at Tacoma was very good (.312, MLE of .268), much better than his previous standards. He's not going to be a regular, but he might be around.

YEAR	TEAM/LEVEL	G	AB	R	H	2B	3B	HR	RBI	BB	SB	AVG	OBP	SLG
1992	MLE	96	346	47	74	14	1	3	16	31	15	.214	.279	.286
1992	Oakland	51	143	24	34	5	2	3	13	13	3	.238	.299	.364
1993	Oakland	29	56	5	8	1	0	1	5	2	0	.143	.172	.214

JOHN FRANCO

New York Mets

Relief Pitcher

$22

The ultimate Met, earns a big salary based on his performance over the years, while in the real and present world he is the league's sorriest excuse for a closer. He is famous for crashing and burning in September, and did it again last year, posting a 13.50 ERA in September and blowing four out of five save opportunities. The Mets will be looking for a new closer.

YEAR	TEAM/LEVEL	G	IP	W-L	SAVES	HITS	SO	BB	ERA
1991	New York	52	55	5-9	30	61	45	18	2.93
1992	New York	31	33	6-2	15	24	20	11	1.64
1993	New York	35	36	4-3	10	46	29	19	5.20

JULIO FRANCO

Texas Rangers

Designated Hitter

$37

Franco returned from a serious injury (a ruptured tendon in his knee) to play at a level comparable to what he had done before the injury . . . He hit .329 after August 1, suggesting that he might be back even further in '93. Also hit .338 with men in scoring position. . . .Never a great second baseman, he was used by Texas as their fulltime DH . . . Has a reasonable shot at 3,000 career hits.

YEAR	TEAM/LEVEL	G	AB	R	H	2B	3B	HR	RBI	BB	SB	AVG	OBP	SLG
1991	Texas	146	589	108	201	27	3	15	78	65	36	.342	.408	.474
1992	Texas	35	107	19	25	7	0	2	8	15	1	.234	.328	.355
1993	Texas	144	532	85	154	31	3	14	84	62	9	.289	.360	.438

LOU FRAZIER

Montreal Expos

Outfield/Pinch Hitter

$19

A veteran of the Astros and Tigers systems, he hooked on with the Expos as a minor league free agent. He made the club in spring training, and had a fine season off the bench. Switch hitter, excellent speed, draws walks, can play outfield or infield, most often used in left . . . A useful player, but unlikely to hit anywhere near .286 in most seasons.

YEAR	TEAM/LEVEL	G	AB	R	H	2B	3B	HR	RBI	BB	SB	AVG	OBP	SLG
1992	MLE	129	464	76	107	12	2	0	30	73	42	.231	.335	.265
1993	Montreal	112	189	27	54	7	1	1	16	16	17	.286	.340	.349
1994	**Projected**	**90**	**170**	**25**	**38**	**3**	**0**	**1**	**12**	**24**	**14**	**.224**	**.320**	**.259**

SCOTT FREDERICKSON

Colorado Rockies

Relief Pitcher

$10

Another pitcher from the University of Texas, like Clemens, Swindell, etc. Well, not *too* much like them . . . Didn't come out of college until he was almost 23 (1990), but pitched well in the San Diego system from 1990 to 1992, as a reward for which he was taken by Colorado in the expansion draft. Grade D prospect; there isn't a lot here to make you think he's going to succeed.

YEAR	TEAM/LEVEL	G	IP	W-L	SAVES	HITS	SO	BB	ERA
1992	Wichita AA	56	73	4-7	5	50	66	38	3.19
1993	Colorado Spr AAA	23	26	1-3	7	26	20	19	5.47
1993	Colorado	25	29	0-1	0	33	20	17	6.21

MARVIN FREEMAN

Colorado Rockies

Relief Pitcher

$19

Released by the Braves after the season; the Rockies signed him. Freeman struggled through the first half of last year, and went on the DL in early June with a sore arm. He returned in late August and pitched well, posting a 2.53 ERA in 10 games, with 14 strikeouts and one walk. A 6-foot-7 righthander with intimidating equipment; suspect he has good years ahead, if not great ones.

YEAR	TEAM/LEVEL	G	IP	W-L	SAVES	HITS	SO	BB	ERA
1991	Atlanta	34	48	1-0	1	37	34	13	3.00
1992	Atlanta	58	64	7-5	3	61	41	29	3.22
1993	Atlanta	21	24	2-0	0	24	25	10	6.08

STEVE FREY

California Angels

Relief Pitcher

$22

One of several California pitchers who took a turn as the closer. His turn was in June, and was ended by a streak of wildness in early July, leading to a couple of blown saves . . . A little lefthander, he throws a hard-breaking curve as his bread-and-butter pitch, and is generally assumed to be more along the lines of a lefthanded spot reliever, rather than a closer.

YEAR	TEAM/LEVEL	G	IP	W-L	SAVES	HITS	SO	BB	ERA
1991	Montreal	31	45	0-1	1	43	21	23	4.99
1992	California	51	45	4-2	4	39	24	22	3.57
1993	California	55	48	2-3	13	41	22	26	2.98

TODD FROHWIRTH

Baltimore Orioles

Relief Pitcher

$22

His career has degenerated to a puzzling extent over the last two years; I suspect he is not getting the support he needs from his organization. A pitcher like this (a Tekulve-type pitcher) can give up line drive after line drive and still be effective, but he has to throw strikes and work ahead of the hitters. Frohwirth did that in '91, but didn't in '93: 50-50 chance of snapping back to form.

YEAR	TEAM/LEVEL	G	IP	W-L	SAVES	HITS	SO	BB	ERA
1991	Baltimore	51	96	7-3	3	64	77	29	1.87
1992	Baltimore	65	106	4-3	4	97	58	41	2.46
1993	Baltimore	70	96	6-7	3	91	50	44	3.83

JEFF FRYE

Texas Rangers

Second Base

$19

After playing well as the Rangers second baseman in the second half of '92 he missed all of '93 with a knee injury, casting his future into doubt. The Rangers have a comparable young player, Jon Shave, plus Doug Strange, who played well there in '93. I liked Frye a lot before the injury, but that's what happens to young middle infielders.

YEAR	TEAM/LEVEL	G	AB	R	H	2B	3B	HR	RBI	BB	SB	AVG	OBP	SLG
1992	MLE	87	323	50	87	22	1	1	22	39	7	.269	.348	.353
1992	Texas	67	199	24	51	9	1	1	12	16	1	.256	.320	.327
1993	Texas	(On Disabled List)												

TRAVIS FRYMAN

Detroit Tigers

Shortstop/Third Base

$70

Signed a five-year, $25 million contract after the season. Fryman is still young (25) and has been amazingly consistent, building his on-base percentage from .309 in 1991 to .379 last year, improving his walks and batting average while posting almost exactly the same numbers in the other categories. He hasn't improved as a shortstop, and the Tigers may move him permanently to third base. One of the best players in baseball over the next five years.

YEAR	TEAM/LEVEL	G	AB	R	H	2B	3B	HR	RBI	BB	SB	AVG	OBP	SLG
1992	Detroit	161	659	87	175	31	4	20	96	45	8	.266	.316	.416
1993	Detroit	151	607	98	182	37	5	22	97	77	9	.300	.379	.486
1994	**Projected**	**156**	**617**	**85**	**170**	**35**	**3**	**22**	**95**	**58**	**10**	**.276**	**.338**	**.449**

GARY GAETTI

Kansas City Royals

Third Base

$17

Had a .477 slugging percentage after joining Kansas City in mid-season, which, from my standpoint as a Royals fan, will keep his miserable carcass in the lineup another year. He embodies the basic weaknesses of the Royals: he is old, slow, and doesn't get on base. It's a question of *when* he will go into a slump and force the team through a mid-season transition, not if.

YEAR	TEAM/LEVEL	G	AB	R	H	2B	3B	HR	RBI	BB	SB	AVG	OBP	SLG
1992	California	130	456	41	103	13	2	12	48	21	3	.226	.267	.342
1993	Two Teams	102	331	40	81	20	1	14	50	21	1	.245	.300	.438
1994	**Projected**	**121**	**425**	**42**	**99**	**21**	**1**	**13**	**50**	**24**	**3**	**.233**	**.274**	**.379**

GREG GAGNE
Kansas City Royals
Shortstop
$40

Watching him almost every day, I couldn't believe what a good player he was—a wonderful shortstop (he led AL shortstops in fielding percentage, .986), a good baserunner (despite a poor stolen base ratio), a surprising hitter. I've never been more surprised by any player the Royals have ever acquired. After seeing him for a season, I understand now how the Twins were able to win a couple of World Championships.

YEAR	TEAM/LEVEL	G	AB	R	H	2B	3B	HR	RBI	BB	SB	AVG	OBP	SLG
1992	Minnesota	146	439	53	108	23	0	7	39	19	6	.246	.280	.346
1993	Kansas City	159	540	66	151	32	3	10	57	33	10	.280	.319	.406
1994	**Projected**	**148**	**511**	**60**	**129**	**28**	**3**	**10**	**56**	**29**	**10**	**.260**	**.299**	**.379**

JAY GAINER
Colorado Rockies
First Base
$13

Thickset lefthanded first baseman, doesn't have quite enough material to be a major league regular. He has some power, more power than reflected in his '93 record, but not Fred McGriff power, isn't going to hit for average, no speed, poor strikeout/walk ratios. Mile High Stadium may help his numbers for a year, and let him get established as a role player.

YEAR	TEAM/LEVEL	G	AB	R	H	2B	3B	HR	RBI	BB	SB	AVG	OBP	SLG
1993	Colo Spri AAA	86	293	51	86	11	3	10	74	22	4	.294	.341	.454
1993	MLE	86	273	31	66	8	1	6	45	13	2	.242	.276	.344
1993	Colorado	23	41	4	7	0	0	3	6	4	1	.171	.244	.390

ANDRES GALARRAGA
Colorado Rockies
First Base
$40

Saw only 2.97 pitches per plate appearance, the lowest of any major league regular . . . Hit .462 when he put the first pitch in play. The only other National Leaguer over .400 was Dante Bichette . . . Olerud also led his league in this category . . . Galarraga and Bichette were the only major league players who swung at 60% of the pitches they saw, Galarraga leading with 62.5%.

YEAR	TEAM/LEVEL	G	AB	R	H	2B	3B	HR	RBI	BB	SB	AVG	OBP	SLG
1993	Colorado	120	470	71	174	35	4	22	98	24	2	.370	.403	.602
1993	REAL PARK	120	461	56	156	33	2	19	78	24	2	.339	.374	.542
1994	**Projected**	**135**	**500**	**58**	**144**	**27**	**2**	**17**	**70**	**25**	**6**	**.288**	**.322**	**.452**

DAVE GALLAGHER
New York Mets
Utility Outfielder
$16

A useful player in the Henry Cotto/Stan Javier/Doug Dascenzo mold; when you have one you think they're a dime a dozen, but when you don't have one you'll notice it in a hurry. He does not have a contract for '94, and the Mets may be looking to purge the locker room, so it's anybody's guess where he will be playing.

YEAR	TEAM/LEVEL	G	AB	R	H	2B	3B	HR	RBI	BB	SB	AVG	OBP	SLG
1992	New York	98	175	20	42	11	1	1	21	19	4	.240	.307	.331
1993	New York	99	201	34	55	12	2	6	28	20	1	.274	.338	.443
1994	**Projected**	**108**	**233**	**29**	**61**	**13**	**1**	**2**	**27**	**23**	**3**	**.262**	**.328**	**.362**

MIKE GALLEGO
New York Yankees
Seccond Base/Shortstop
$30

His good on-base percentage and ability to play three positions make him an invaluable part of the Yankee roster. He started 46 games last year at shortstop, 41 at second, 24 at third, played all three positions well and hit .283 with a secondary average of .261. He probably won't hit .283 again, but he's one of the most underrated players in baseball.

YEAR	TEAM/LEVEL	G	AB	R	H	2B	3B	HR	RBI	BB	SB	AVG	OBP	SLG
1992	New York	53	173	24	44	7	1	3	14	20	0	.254	.343	.358
1993	New York	119	403	63	114	20	1	10	54	50	3	.283	.364	.412
1994	**Projected**	**118**	**370**	**48**	**88**	**11**	**1**	**6**	**36**	**49**	**4**	**.238**	**.327**	**.322**

RON GANT
Atlanta Braves
Left Field
$66

Most-similar season ever: Dale Murphy, 1982 . . . His .962 fielding percentage was the lowest for any regular outfielder in the majors, not that fielding percentage means a lot for an outfielder, but his range factor was also the worst of any regular left fielder (Cory Snyder was worse in right) . . . His defense won't cost him his job, and he has many good years ahead of him with the bat.

YEAR	TEAM/LEVEL	G	AB	R	H	2B	3B	HR	RBI	BB	SB	AVG	OBP	SLG
1992	Atlanta	153	544	74	141	22	6	17	80	45	32	.259	.321	.415
1993	Atlanta	157	606	113	166	27	4	36	117	67	26	.274	.345	.510
1994	**Projected**	**157**	**579**	**97**	**148**	**29**	**4**	**27**	**98**	**65**	**32**	**.256**	**.331**	**.459**

RICH GARCES
Minnesota Twins
Relief Pitcher
$7

A hot prospect three years ago, he's been plagued since by minor injuries and serious weight problems. He got off to a good start at Portland, was called up in late April when the Twins were struggling, sent back down in mid-May despite having pitched OK, and didn't throw two strikes in a row the rest of the season. Still throws hard, but has lost all semblance of command. His future is very cloudy.

YEAR	TEAM/LEVEL	G	IP	W-L	SAVES	HITS	SO	BB	ERA
1992	Orlando AA	58	73	3-3	13	76	72	39	4.54
1993	Minnesota	3	4	0-0	0	4	3	2	0.00
1993	Portland AAA	35	54	1-3	0	70	48	64	8.33

CARLOS GARCIA
Pittsburgh Pirates
Second Base
$36

Garcia was exactly what he was advertised as being—a .270 range hitter with more power than the average second baseman, a little speed, a pretty good second baseman for a rookie who was new to the position. He creates more runs than Chico Lind. His 1993 season was exactly what I would expect him to do again, but he might be able to improve it.

YEAR	TEAM/LEVEL	G	AB	R	H	2B	3B	HR	RBI	BB	SB	AVG	OBP	SLG
1992	MLE	113	407	56	110	24	6	9	54	18	14	.270	.301	.425
1993	Pittsburgh	141	546	77	147	25	5	12	47	31	18	.269	.316	.399
1994	**Projected**	**140**	**530**	**68**	**138**	**23**	**5**	**10**	**56**	**29**	**21**	**.260**	**.309**	**.379**

MIKE GARDINER
Detroit Tigers
Relief Pitcher
$5

One of countless rejects collected by the Tigers in their effort to patch the pitching. Gardiner has been in the majors four years and has posted four losing records, so he was released by Montreal in late August, having registered a 5.21 ERA for them. The Tigers signed him and took a look, but he didn't pitch as well as Boever or Storm Davis, and probably will not make the team out of spring training.

YEAR	TEAM/LEVEL	G	IP	W-L	PCT.	HITS	SO	BB	ERA
1991	Boston	22	130	9-10	.474	140	91	47	4.85
1992	Boston	28	131	4-10	.286	126	79	58	4.75
1993	Two Teams	34	49	2-3	.400	52	25	26	4.93

JEFF GARDNER
San Diego Padres
Second Base
$28

Finally got a chance to play with a major league team—well, *kind of* a major league team—after almost a thousand minor league games. He was essentially an average National League second baseman. He will have to improve in two areas to hold his job: his strikeout/walk ratio, which was sensational in the minors, just OK last year, and his double play rate, which was expected to be good but was actually poor.

YEAR	TEAM/LEVEL	G	AB	R	H	2B	3B	HR	RBI	BB	SB	AVG	OBP	SLG
1992	MLE	120	402	50	110	22	2	0	31	40	4	.274	.339	.338
1993	San Diego	140	404	53	106	21	7	1	24	45	2	.262	.337	.356
1994	**Projected**	**135**	**400**	**49**	**103**	**15**	**2**	**1**	**31**	**51**	**4**	**.258**	**.341**	**.313**

MARK GARDNER
Kansas City Royals
Starting Pitcher
$12

Had a one-year contract with KC, and probably will be somewhere else in '94. He couldn't put two good outings together, and the bad ones got worse until a strained shoulder put him on the DL in early July. On his return he went to Omaha, where he pitched well. Gardner has a high leg kick, and has worked on reducing this with men on base, with disastrous results: his batting average allowed jumped 62 points with men on.

YEAR	TEAM/LEVEL	G	IP	W-L	PCT.	HITS	SO	BB	ERA
1991	Montreal	27	168	9-11	.450	139	107	75	3.85
1992	Montreal	33	180	12-10	.545	179	132	60	4.36
1993	Kansas City	17	92	4-6	.400	92	54	36	6.19

BRENT GATES
Oakland Athletics
Second Base
$42

He had a rookie-of-the-year season, not that anybody noticed. An argument can be made that a good second baseman who hits .290 with collateral contributions has had a better rookie season than an outfielder who hits 30 homers. Gates, the A's first-round pick in 1991, played A ball in 1992, but went through Double-A and Triple-A in 12 games apiece at the start of 1993. Outstanding potential—but he has to stay healthy.

YEAR	TEAM/LEVEL	G	AB	R	H	2B	3B	HR	RBI	BB	SB	AVG	OBP	SLG
1993	AA and AAA	24	89	14	30	11	0	1	15	11	2	.337	.412	.494
1993	Oakland	139	535	64	155	29	2	7	69	56	7	.290	.357	.391
1994	**Projected**	**145**	**547**	**68**	**162**	**34**	**2**	**9**	**74**	**59**	**7**	**.296**	**.365**	**.415**

BOB GEREN
San Diego Padres
Catcher
$8

Returned to the majors after a year at Pawtucket, where he hit .207. His argument is defense, in that he's no kind of a hitter. In 1993 his argument was good: he made only two errors, and the Padres had a 3.55 ERA when he was catching, 4.45 without him (he caught 360 innings). Despite this he was outrighted to Las Vegas at the end of July, and his major league career is probably over.

YEAR	TEAM/LEVEL	G	AB	R	H	2B	3B	HR	RBI	BB	SB	AVG	OBP	SLG
1991	New York AL	64	128	7	28	3	0	2	12	9	0	.219	.270	.289
1992	Pawtuck AAA	66	213	28	44	7	0	9	25	17	0	.207	.265	.366
1993	San Diego	58	145	8	31	6	0	3	6	13	0	.214	.278	.317

KIRK GIBSON
Detroit Tigers
Left Field
$22

Returned to the game after a year's retirement, and alternated between being the best player in the league one week and the worst the next. In April he hit .407 with a .661 slugging percentage; in June he hit .115. He's a platoon player now, and on balance he was productive enough to keep that job if he chooses to do it.

YEAR	TEAM/LEVEL	G	AB	R	H	2B	3B	HR	RBI	BB	SB	AVG	OBP	SLG
1992	Pittsburgh	16	56	6	11	0	0	2	5	3	3	.196	.237	.304
1993	Detroit	116	403	62	105	18	6	13	62	44	15	.261	.337	.433
1994	**Projected**	**86**	**281**	**43**	**69**	**13**	**2**	**9**	**36**	**36**	**10**	**.246**	**.331**	**.402**

PAUL GIBSON
New York Yankees
Relief Pitcher
$21

Pitched for the two New York teams, also went to Norfolk and Columbus. He struck out 37 in 44 innings in the majors, also 36 in 28 innings in Triple-A, remarkable totals for a guy who doesn't throw hard enough to smoosh a doughnut. He's a con artist, always getting the hitter out on his front foot, always jerking the chain. With a little luck, he could have a Larry Andersen-type season—65 games, 1.85 ERA.

YEAR	TEAM/LEVEL	G	IP	W-L	SAVES	HITS	SO	BB	ERA
1991	Detroit	68	96	5-7	8	112	52	48	4.59
1992	New York NL	43	62	0-1	0	70	49	25	5.23
1993	Two Teams	28	44	3-1	0	45	37	11	3.47

BENJI GIL
Texas Rangers
Shortstop
$24

A promising young shortstop, was called up and put in the lineup in April after Manuel Lee's injury. Gil, born in Mexico and raised in California, is very young (turned 21 in October), and was over-matched in his major league trial, but in view of his youth and the fact that he hadn't played Double-A or Triple-A, that's not surprising, and not damning. He played well in the field. **Grade A prospect.**

YEAR	TEAM/LEVEL	G	AB	R	H	2B	3B	HR	RBI	BB	SB	AVG	OBP	SLG
1993	Tulsa AA	101	342	45	94	9	1	17	59	35	20	.275	.351	.456
1993	MLE	101	330	36	82	8	0	13	47	24	14	.248	.299	.391
1993	Texas	22	57	3	7	0	0	0	2	5	1	.123	.194	.123

BERNARD GILKEY
St. Louis Cardinals
Left Field
$47

The third-best left fielder in the National League last year, behind Bonds and Gant—actually, Luis Gonzalez was about the same, and the Philadelphia platoon was better, taken as a whole. Gilkey has made two giant steps in the last two years, and is about a half-step away from emerging as a star . . . Not much of an outfielder, but he did lead the league in baserunner kills, with 19.

YEAR	TEAM/LEVEL	G	AB	R	H	2B	3B	HR	RBI	BB	SB	AVG	OBP	SLG
1992	St. Louis	131	384	56	116	19	4	7	43	39	18	.302	.364	.427
1993	St. Louis	137	557	99	170	40	5	16	70	56	15	.305	.370	.481
1994	**Projected**	**142**	**489**	**73**	**144**	**27**	**4**	**10**	**53**	**57**	**19**	**.294**	**.368**	**.427**

JOE GIRARDI
Colorado Rockies
Catcher
$21

A pretty awful player, even for an expansion team. He hit .290, but that's .266 if you adjust for the park, and there was no production there—no power, no walks, no runs, no RBI. His defense isn't anything special, and in view of his age (he's 29) he's not likely to get any better. He missed two months in mid-season following surgery on his right hand, which kept him from driving in 40 or even 45 runs.

YEAR	TEAM/LEVEL	G	AB	R	H	2B	3B	HR	RBI	BB	SB	AVG	OBP	SLG
1992	Chicago	91	270	19	73	3	1	1	12	19	3	.270	.320	.300
1993	Colorado	86	310	35	90	14	5	3	31	24	6	.290	.346	.397
1993	REAL PARK	86	304	28	81	13	3	3	25	24	6	.266	.322	.359

DAN GLADDEN
Detroit Tigers
Left Field
$19

He missed almost all of April and May with a torn quadricep, but became a full-time player when Deer was traded, at least until the Tigers acquired Eric Davis. Established a career high in home runs, despite the injury, and drove in runs at a 100-RBI pace for the 91 games he played. He's about the same age as the other Tigers—Gibson, Trammell, Whitaker, Phillips, Barnes—and it is assumed that they can't go on forever.

YEAR	TEAM/LEVEL	G	AB	R	H	2B	3B	HR	RBI	BB	SB	AVG	OBP	SLG
1992	Detroit	113	417	57	106	20	1	7	42	30	4	.254	.304	.357
1993	Detroit	91	356	52	95	16	2	13	56	21	8	.267	.312	.432
1994	**Projected**	**102**	**312**	**41**	**79**	**13**	**2**	**5**	**36**	**22**	**7**	**.253**	**.302**	**.356**

TOM GLAVINE
Atlanta Braves
Starting Pitcher
$59

Through most of last year he didn't pitch all that well, but continued to roll up wins due to the superb team behind him, good luck, and his own survival skills. In late August he found himself, going 6-1 with a 31-8 strikeout/walk ratio after September 1. I'm not wild about him, and wouldn't rate him among the top five pitchers in the league for '94, but you have to respect his won-lost records.

YEAR	TEAM/LEVEL	G	IP	W-L	PCT.	HITS	SO	BB	ERA
1991	Atlanta	34	246	20-11	.645	201	192	69	2.56
1992	Atlanta	33	225	20-8	.714	197	129	70	2.76
1993	Atlanta	36	239	22-6	.786	236	120	90	3.20

JERRY GOFF

Pittsburgh Pirates

Catcher/Third Base

$18

Pirates signed him as a six-year minor league free agent. He put in a decent year at Buffalo, and got a late season callup. A catcher and third baseman in the minors, he won't hit for average, but will probably take Tom Prince's job or Lloyd McClendon's. He has the advantage of being lefthanded, a comparable hitter to McClendon, better than Prince, plus he's OK defensively.

YEAR	TEAM/LEVEL	G	AB	R	H	2B	3B	HR	RBI	BB	SB	AVG	OBP	SLG
1993	Buffalo AAA	104	362	52	91	27	3	14	69	55	1	.251	.346	.459
1993	MLE	104	346	37	75	24	1	9	49	39	0	.217	.296	.370
1993	Pittsburgh	14	37	5	11	2	0	2	6	8	0	.297	.422	.514

GREG GOHR

Detroit Tigers

Starting Pitcher

$12

The new Scott Aldred, Exhibit B in the Grand Jury investigation concerning the murder of the Detroit minor league system. Gohr was a first-round draft pick in 1989, and the Tigers have considered him their top pitching prospect ever since, despite a lack of supporting evidence. He does throw fairly hard, and might eventually emerge as some sort of a middle reliever or something.

YEAR	TEAM/LEVEL	G	IP	W-L	PCT.	HITS	SO	BB	ERA
1992	Toledo AAA	22	131	8-10	.444	124	94	46	3.99
1993	Toledo AAA	18	107	3-10	.231	127	77	38	5.80
1993	Detroit	16	23	0-0	—	26	23	14	5.96

CHRIS GOMEZ

Detroit Tigers

Shortstop

$26

An All-American shortstop at Long Beach State, he was the Tigers' third pick in '92, went straight to Double-A and held his own, was so-so at Triple-A, then came to the majors when the Tigers decided Fryman wasn't a shortstop. The funny thing is he hit only .274 at Long Beach State, but has stayed near there as he stepped up. Not fast, not flashy, could be good but could be the new Chris Pittaro.

YEAR	TEAM/LEVEL	G	AB	R	H	2B	3B	HR	RBI	BB	SB	AVG	OBP	SLG
1993	Toledo AAA	87	277	29	68	12	2	0	20	23	6	.245	.308	.303
1993	MLE	87	271	27	62	10	1	0	19	22	4	.229	.287	.273
1993	Detroit	46	128	11	32	7	1	0	11	9	2	.250	.304	.320

LEO GOMEZ

Baltimore Orioles

Third Base

$26

He took a giant step backward at a critical moment, when he needed to show that he was a little bit *better* than he had played in '92. He was troubled by tendonitis and a cyst on his right wrist, plus his manager doesn't seem to believe in him, which often resolves itself by a trade. On the other hand Pagliarulo has filed for free agency . . . Gomez could drive in a hundred runs, but can't afford another off year.

YEAR	TEAM/LEVEL	G	AB	R	H	2B	3B	HR	RBI	BB	SB	AVG	OBP	SLG
1991	Baltimore	118	391	40	91	17	2	16	45	40	1	.233	.302	.409
1992	Baltimore	137	468	62	124	24	0	17	64	63	2	.265	.356	.425
1993	Baltimore	71	244	30	48	7	0	10	25	32	0	.197	.295	.348

PAT GOMEZ

San Diego Padres

Relief Pitcher

$9

Gomez was in the Atlanta system for several years, was traded to San Diego by way of Texas. He's a 26-year-old lefthander who doesn't throw hard and doesn't throw strikes, has started as much as he has relieved in the minors, showing occasional flashes of light as a starter, but never as a reliever. He missed some time in mid-summer with a strained left elbow, and was returned to a minor league roster at season's end.

YEAR	TEAM/LEVEL	G	IP	W-L	SAVES	HITS	SO	BB	ERA
1992	Greenville AA	8	48	7-0	0	25	38	19	1.13
1992	Richmond AAA	23	71	3-5	0	79	48	42	5.45
1993	San Diego	27	32	1-2	0	35	26	19	5.12

LARRY GONZALES

California Angels

Catcher

$6

A 27-year-old righthanded hitting catcher, he got a couple of at bats in June as an emergency backup. Has hit .300 several times in the minors, but didn't last year. Chris Turner is the organization's catching prospect, although Gonzales has hit about as well as Turner at each minor league stop. A big guy with no power, probably has no future, although he may fool us. And the Angels.

YEAR	TEAM/LEVEL	G	AB	R	H	2B	3B	HR	RBI	BB	SB	AVG	OBP	SLG
1992	Edmonton	80	241	37	79	10	0	3	47	38	2	.328	.422	.407
1993	Vancouver AAA	81	264	30	69	9	0	2	27	26	5	.261	.329	.318
1993	MLE	81	251	21	56	6	0	1	19	18	3	.223	.275	.259

RENE GONZALES

California Angels

Infield

$20

Wears number 88, the highest number in the league . . . Had a big surprise season in 1992, and was following through in 1993 until a September slump (12 for 67) cut about 20 points off his average. He played mostly third base, after the wipeouts of Gaetti and Gruber; that place was taken by Perez, which throws him back into a utility role. He's 31 years old, good backup player who will never be a regular.

YEAR	TEAM/LEVEL	G	AB	R	H	2B	3B	HR	RBI	BB	SB	AVG	OBP	SLG
1992	California	104	329	47	91	17	1	7	38	41	7	.277	.363	.398
1993	California	118	335	34	84	17	0	2	31	49	5	.251	.346	.319
1994	**Projected**	**98**	**249**	**28**	**59**	**8**	**0**	**3**	**22**	**33**	**4**	**.237**	**.326**	**.305**

ALEX GONZALEZ

Toronto Blue Jays

Shortstop

$34

A 21-year-old product of the Miami Cuban community, Gonzalez was taken by the Blue Jays in the 14th round in 1991, and is now regarded by some people as the best prospect in the minors today. He has real speed, some power, and is a solid, unspectacular shortstop with a strong arm. If Tony Fernandez leaves Toronto as a free agent, Gonzalez is expected to step into his shoes.

YEAR	TEAM/LEVEL	G	AB	R	H	2B	3B	HR	RBI	BB	SB	AVG	OBP	SLG
1992	Myrtle Bea A	134	535	82	145	22	9	10	62	38	26	.271	.322	.402
1993	Knoxville AA	142	561	93	162	29	7	16	69	39	38	.289	.339	.451
1993	MLE	142	544	75	145	27	5	14	55	26	27	.267	.300	.412

JUAN GONZALEZ
Texas Rangers
Left Field
$88

Most-similar season: Orlando Cepeda, 1961 . . . Absolutely the only issues which stand between Gonzalez and Cooperstown are health and conduct. If he is healthy, he is *going* to hit 500 home runs, probably 600, possibly 700 . . . Homered 80% more often with men on base than with the bases empty . . . Has homered more often on the road than he has at home, so the move to a new park probably won't cost him home runs.

YEAR	TEAM/LEVEL	G	AB	R	H	2B	3B	HR	RBI	BB	SB	AVG	OBP	SLG
1992	Texas	155	584	77	152	24	2	43	109	35	0	.260	.304	.529
1993	Texas	140	536	105	166	33	1	46	118	37	4	.310	.368	.632
1994	**Projected**	**149**	**567**	**89**	**158**	**32**	**2**	**37**	**109**	**41**	**3**	**.279**	**.327**	**.538**

LUIS GONZALEZ
Houston Astros
Left Field
$47

1993 was the first time in his professional career that he has hit higher than .286 in more than 39 games. That said, there is no obvious reason that he shouldn't remain a .300 hitter. He's a lefthanded hitter with a good, level stroke who makes contact, doesn't chase pitches over his head or a foot outside, doesn't bail out against lefties, runs well and hits the ball hard. . .Led National League in sacrifice flies, with ten.

YEAR	TEAM/LEVEL	G	AB	R	H	2B	3B	HR	RBI	BB	SB	AVG	OBP	SLG
1992	Houston	122	387	40	94	19	3	10	55	24	7	.243	.289	.385
1993	Houston	154	540	82	162	34	3	15	72	47	20	.300	.361	.457
1994	**Projected**	**155**	**550**	**69**	**151**	**30**	**5**	**17**	**78**	**46**	**16**	**.275**	**.331**	**.440**

DWIGHT GOODEN
New York Mets
Starting Pitcher
$36

His skills have been diminished by injury, but he is still a fairly good pitcher. A 12-15 record for a 100-loss team is nothing to be ashamed of, and his control, strikeout rates and hits/innings ratios remain above average. If the shoulder problem which ended his season isn't serious, he still has the chance to have some good years. Still well positioned with respect to the Hall of Fame.

YEAR	TEAM/LEVEL	G	IP	W-L	PCT.	HITS	SO	BB	ERA
1991	New York	27	190	13-7	.650	185	150	56	3.60
1992	New York	31	206	10-13	.435	197	145	70	3.67
1993	New York	29	209	12-15	.444	188	149	61	3.45

TOM GOODWIN
Los Angeles Dodgers
Outfielder
$11

Goodwin spent most of the season at Albuquerque, after appearing in 73 games for the Dodgers in '92. He's a grade D prospect—a lefthanded hitter who can run and can be used for defense in the outfield, but doesn't do anything else well. He's never going to be a regular, and getting those 25th-man slots is as much a matter of luck and personality as it is skill. He can hit .260.

YEAR	TEAM/LEVEL	G	AB	R	H	2B	3B	HR	RBI	BB	SB	AVG	OBP	SLG
1992	Los Angeles	73	80	15	17	1	1	0	3	6	8	.233	.291	.274
1993	MLE	85	270	28	56	3	2	0	16	18	12	.207	.257	.233
1993	Los Angeles	30	17	6	5	1	0	0	1	1	1	.294	.333	.353

KEITH GORDON
Cincinnati Reds
Outfield
$11

A second-round draft pick in 1990, he has made slow progress, passing through the levels not quite slowly enough to be written off. He played Double-A at age 24 in '93, and hit .291, which is amazing in view of his strikeout/walk ratio (132-19). He is big enough to hit for power, but doesn't, and fast enough to be a base stealer, but isn't. Grade C prospect; could be .270 hitter, 20-homer man.

YEAR TEAM/LEVEL	G	AB	R	H	2B	3B	HR	RBI	BB	SB	AVG	OBP	SLG
1993 Chattanooga	118	419	69	122	26	3	14	59	19	13	.291	.327	.468
1993 MLE	118	405	55	108	23	1	13	47	13	9	.267	.289	.425
1993 Cincinnati	3	6	0	1	0	0	0	0	0	0	.167	.167	.167

TOM GORDON
Kansas City Royals
Relief Pitcher
$35

Gordon, who won 17 games as a 21-year-old rookie in 1989, apparently has his career moving in the right direction after several years of drifting. He pitched well in long relief, then moved into the rotation in late July, and was 8-4 with a 3.36 ERA in 14 starts. Only 26, throws hard, excellent breaking ball; still has a good chance to be an outstanding pitcher.

YEAR	TEAM/LEVEL	G	IP	W-L	SAVES	HITS	SO	BB	ERA
1991	Kansas City	45	158	9-14	1	129	167	87	3.87
1992	Kansas City	40	118	6-10	0	116	98	55	4.59
1993	Kansas City	48	156	12-6	1	125	143	77	3.58

GOOSE GOSSAGE
Oakland Athletics
Relief Pitcher
$17

Your basic 42-year-old power pitcher. In the early part of '93 he pitched effectively, but in the second half of the season he had injuries, and his record was ruined because he stayed in the game to absorb the punishment a couple of times when the A's were getting blown out. His most serious injury was a broken wrist, late August. He's still a major league pitcher if he doesn't retire.

YEAR	TEAM/LEVEL	G	IP	W-L	SAVES	HITS	SO	BB	ERA
1991	Texas	44	41	4-2	1	33	28	16	3.57
1992	Oakland	30	38	0-2	0	32	26	19	2.84
1993	Oakland	39	48	4-5	1	49	40	26	4.53

JIM GOTT
Los Angeles Dodgers
Relief Pitcher
$38

Reclaimed the closer role for the first time since 1988, and pitched well most of the year, getting saves in 25 of 29 opportunities. He developed tendonitis in early September, which ended his season. My guess is that Lasorda will keep him in the closer role, rather than moving Pedro Martinez there, because a) Gott pitched well, and b) Lasorda, like many managers, prefers a veteran in that role.

YEAR	TEAM/LEVEL	G	IP	W-L	SAVES	HITS	SO	BB	ERA
1991	Los Angeles	55	76	4-3	2	63	73	32	2.96
1992	Los Angeles	68	88	3-3	6	72	75	41	2.45
1993	Los Angeles	62	78	4-8	25	71	67	17	2.32

MAURO GOZZO

New York Mets

Starting Pitcher

$15

A survivor of 10 years and more than a thousand innings in the minor leagues, although he's only 28. He was originally signed by the Mets, traded to the Royals in the David Cone deal, and has pitched in the majors for Toronto (1989), Cleveland (1990-1991) and Minnesota (1992). His strong points are his control and his durability—in 10 years of pitching he has had no major injuries.

YEAR	TEAM/LEVEL	G	IP	W-L	PCT.	HITS	SO	BB	ERA
1992	Portland AAA	37	156	10-9	.526	155	108	50	3.35
1993	Norfolk AAA	28	190	8-11	.421	208	97	49	3.45
1993	New York	10	14	0-1	.000	11	6	5	2.57

MARK GRACE

Chicago Cubs

First Base

$58

He's a negative image of Sammie Sosa: He has everything *except* power and speed. In the first three months of '93 he hit over .300 with slugging percentages over .500; the last three months he hit over .300 but slugged under .500 . . . Tied for the major league lead in grounding into double plays, with 25 . . . Fine first baseman, good baserunner. Hit .453 in the late innings of close games, best in the major leagues by far.

YEAR	TEAM/LEVEL	G	AB	R	H	2B	3B	HR	RBI	BB	SB	AVG	OBP	SLG
1992	Chicago	158	603	72	185	37	5	9	79	72	6	.307	.380	.430
1993	Chicago	155	594	86	193	39	4	14	98	71	8	.325	.393	.475
1994	**Projected**	**158**	**604**	**81**	**180**	**32**	**3**	**11**	**77**	**74**	**6**	**.298**	**.375**	**.416**

JOE GRAHE

California Angels

Closer

$26

Grahe opened and closed the year as the Angels' closer. In between he had tendonitis in his right rotator cuff, which gave about a dozen other people a shot at the role . . . Throws sinking fastball, curve, and slider; not everyone is convinced he has closer stuff, but he saved 11 in 13 chances and allowed 32% of inherited runners to score, acceptable numbers. Gets 72% ground balls.

YEAR	TEAM/LEVEL	G	IP	W-L	SAVES	HITS	SO	BB	ERA
1991	California	18	73	3-7	0	84	40	33	4.81
1992	California	46	95	5-6	21	85	39	39	3.52
1993	California	45	57	4-1	11	54	31	25	2.86

JEFF GRANGER

Kansas City Royals

Starting Pitcher

$23

Granger was the Royals' number-one draft pick, a lefthander from Texas A&M. The Royals started him in A ball, which frankly is silly for a first-round pick who has pitched in the College World Series, and he struck out 14 men a game there, which doesn't mean much of anything. His contract required that he be recalled in September, and he was, and pitched one inning. Intelligent, poised, throws hard and was a college quarterback.

YEAR	TEAM/LEVEL	G	IP	W-L	PCT.	HITS	SO	BB	ERA
1993	Texas A & M		107	14-3	.824		114		2.72
1993	Eugene A	8	36	3-3	.500	28	56	10	3.00
1993	Kansas City	1	1	0-0	—	3	1	2	27.00

MARK GRANT

Colorado Rockies

Reliever

$6

Originally from the Giants system, has now pitched for the Giants, Padres, Braves, Mariners, Astros and Rockies, which may tell you all that you need to know about him. A finesse pitcher, had a strained rib cage and a strained shoulder in '93. Last year I reported that lefthanded hitters had hit .336 against him, which went up to .395 in '93. He's only 30, but there's no indication of any ability here.

YEAR	TEAM/LEVEL	G	IP	W-L	SAVES	HITS	SO	BB	ERA
1991	Two Teams	59	91	2-3	3	108	69	37	4.73
1992	Seattle	23	81	2-4	0	100	42	22	3.89
1993	Two Teams	20	25	0-1	1	34	14	11	7.46

MARK GRATER

Detroit Tigers

Relief Pitcher

$8

See Mike Gardiner comment, and here's another one. Grater must have been hurt or something, as he pitched well for Louisville in '91 and '92 (ERAs of 2.02 and 2.13), and had pitched well in the Cardinal system for years, but just couldn't get anybody out in '93 (see stats below). He turned 30 during the winter, and is probably thinking deeply about his future.

YEAR	TEAM/LEVEL	G	IP	W-L	SAVES	HITS	SO	BB	ERA
1993	Toledo AAA	28	31	1-2	4	42	31	12	8.13
1993	Calgary AAA	9	12	0-1	0	19	4	6	7.71
1993	Detroit	6	5	0-0	0	6	4	4	5.40

CRAIG GREBECK

Chicago White Sox

Shortstop/Second Base

$21

One of my favorite players, a little tiny guy who takes advantage of his size by forcing the pitchers to pitch to him, and is also strong enough to drive the ball. He had a disappointing year, as the second base job became open and Joey Cora grabbed it, then his season was ended by a broken foot in August. He's an over-qualified reserve infielder, and good enough to play every day for somebody.

YEAR	TEAM/LEVEL	G	AB	R	H	2B	3B	HR	RBI	BB	SB	AVG	OBP	SLG
1992	Chicago	88	287	24	77	21	2	3	35	30	0	.268	.341	.387
1993	Chicago	72	190	25	43	5	0	1	12	26	1	.226	.319	.268
1994	**Projected**	**90**	**226**	**28**	**58**	**12**	**1**	**3**	**25**	**32**	**2**	**.257**	**.349**	**.358**

SHAWN GREEN

Toronto Blue Jays

Outfielder

$12

A tall skinny lefthanded batter from California, the Blue Jays first-round draft pick in 1991. It is too early to conclude that this was a wasted draft pick, since he just turned 21 in November, but he has work to do. He hit .283 at Knoxville, which is not quite like hitting .350, but counts as his strong point. His weak points were power, speed, and command of the strike zone.

YEAR	TEAM/LEVEL	G	AB	R	H	2B	3B	HR	RBI	BB	SB	AVG	OBP	SLG
1993	Knoxville AA	99	360	40	102	14	2	4	34	26	4	.283	.339	.367
1993	MLE	99	348	32	90	13	1	3	27	17	2	.259	.293	.328
1993	Toronto	3	6	0	0	0	0	0	0	0	0	.000	.000	.000

TYLER GREEN

Philadelphia Phillies

Starting Pitcher

$16

I'm glad that we have players like Tyler Green around, so that I get to use time-honored baseball adjectives such as "much-ballyhooed" and "injury-plagued." Green, the Phillies first-round pick in 1991, is a big righthander who throws hard and has pitched fairly well, but is probably on a first-name basis with Dr. Jobe's secretary. Grade B prospect.

YEAR	TEAM/LEVEL	G	IP	W-L	PCT.	HITS	SO	BB	ERA
1992	Reading AA	12	62	6-3	.667	46	67	20	1.88
1992	Scranton AAA	2	10	0-1	.000	7	15	12	6.10
1993	Scranton AAA	28	118	6-10	.375	102	87	43	3.95

TOMMY GREENE

Philadelphia Phillies

Starting Pitcher

$59

Led the National League in wild pitches, with 15. The two pitchers who led their leagues in wild pitches, between them, won 30 games and lost only 7, go figure . . . It is too early to start talking about the Hall of Fame, but if this guy stays healthy he is going to win 200+ games. I'd compare him to Jim Palmer in '69, when Palmer came off several years of arm injuries to go 16-4.

YEAR	TEAM/LEVEL	G	IP	W-L	PCT.	HITS	SO	BB	ERA
1991	Philadelphia	36	208	13-7	.650	177	154	66	3.38
1992	Philadelphia	13	64	3-3	.500	75	39	34	5.32
1993	Philadelphia	31	200	16-4	.800	175	167	62	3.42

WILLIE GREENE

Cincinnati Reds

Third Base

$30

A **Grade A prospect**, a trim lefthanded hitter with 30-home-run power, has the feet and arm to be a good major league third baseman, if not a shortstop. Doesn't have outstanding speed, but not slow; has been in several organizations and has received some criticism for his intensity, but nothing like what people used to say about Albert Belle. I recommend him highly . . . Season was ended with a dislocated thumb. He's only 22.

YEAR	TEAM/LEVEL	G	AB	R	H	2B	3B	HR	RBI	BB	SB	AVG	OBP	SLG
1992	MLE	96	340	38	88	17	1	15	54	34	5	.259	.326	.447
1993	MLE	98	332	49	82	17	0	20	46	42	1	.247	.332	.479
1993	Cincinnati	15	50	7	8	1	1	2	5	2	0	.160	.189	.340

MIKE GREENWELL

Boston Red Sox

Left Field

$37

Like his boyhood hero, George Brett, he often starts slowly, and drives his batting average upward. Last year he hit .400 in September (42-for-105), making his final numbers surprisingly strong . . . He doesn't run as well as he did, and frankly he was never a Gold Glove candidate, although I think he has improved in the outfield. But if a man can hit .315 and slug up around .500, there's a place for him.

YEAR	TEAM/LEVEL	G	AB	R	H	2B	3B	HR	RBI	BB	SB	AVG	OBP	SLG
1992	Boston	49	180	16	42	2	0	2	18	18	2	.233	.307	.278
1993	Boston	146	540	77	170	38	6	13	72	54	5	.315	.379	.480
1994	**Projected**	**146**	**538**	**74**	**160**	**31**	**4**	**13**	**78**	**51**	**9**	**.297**	**.358**	**.442**

KEN GREER

New York Mets

Righthanded Pitcher

$9

The Mets' compensation for donating Frank Tanana to the Yankees down the stretch. A minor league veteran, 27 years old, good size. As sometimes happens in the Yankee system he spent year after year at A ball, even though he sometimes pitched well, and didn't get any real experience until he was 25. He's been in middle relief since 1990, pitched well in that role in '92 at Albany, not so well in '93 at Columbus. Grade D prospect.

YEAR	TEAM/LEVEL	G	IP	W-L	SAVES	HITS	SO	BB	ERA
1991	Ft. Lauderd A	31	57	4-3	0	49	46	22	4.24
1992	Albany AA	40	69	4-1	4	48	53	30	1.83
1993	Columbus AAA	46	79	9-4	6	78	50	36	4.42

TOMMY GREGG

Cincinnati Reds

Pinch Hitter

$12

Spent most of the summer at Indianapolis, re-establishing his ability to batter minor league pitchers. He could help somebody as a pinch hitter—a lefthanded line-drive hitter who could hit .270, won't chase bad pitches, and has just a little bit of power. To this point in his career he's been hurt every time he's got a chance to play in the majors, and time is running out on him.

YEAR	TEAM/LEVEL	G	AB	R	H	2B	3B	HR	RBI	BB	SB	AVG	OBP	SLG
1992	Atlanta	18	19	1	5	0	0	1	1	1	1	.263	.300	.421
1993	Indianapol AAA	71	198	34	63	12	5	7	30	26	3	.318	.398	.535
1993	Cincinnati	10	12	1	2	0	0	0	1	0	0	.167	.154	.167

KEN GRIFFEY JR.

Seattle Mariners

Center Field

$98

Before 1993 no player since 1970 had hit 35 doubles and 45 homers in the same season. Both Bonds and Griffey did it last year . . . That's been done 14 times now—three times by Ruth, four times by Gehrig, once each by Foxx, DiMaggio, Mays, Reggie and Bench . . . Hit only .239 with runners in scoring position, but historically has done OK in that category. The most-comparable players in history are Mays and Aaron.

YEAR	TEAM/LEVEL	G	AB	R	H	2B	3B	HR	RBI	BB	SB	AVG	OBP	SLG
1992	Seattle	142	565	83	174	39	4	27	103	44	10	.308	.361	.535
1993	Seattle	156	582	113	180	38	3	45	109	96	17	.309	.408	.617
1994	**Projected**	**154**	**577**	**93**	**162**	**37**	**3**	**32**	**105**	**75**	**16**	**.315**	**.394**	**.556**

ALFREDO GRIFFIN

Toronto Blue Jays

Shortstop

$11

Now 37 years old; might or might not return for a third season as Toronto's backup shortstop. What his .211 average doesn't show is that in May, when a couple of other guys failed or got hurt and Fernandez was in New York, Griffin stepped in and played well, holding shortstop together and hitting .255. That, and the fact that he is regarded as a clubhouse positive, may earn him an invitation to return.

YEAR	TEAM/LEVEL	G	AB	R	H	2B	3B	HR	RBI	BB	SB	AVG	OBP	SLG
1991	Los Angeles	109	350	27	85	6	2	0	27	22	5	.243	.286	.271
1992	Toronto	63	150	21	35	7	0	0	10	9	3	.233	.273	.280
1993	Toronto	46	95	15	20	3	0	0	3	3	0	.211	.235	.242

JASON GRIMSLEY

Cleveland Indians

Starting Pitcher

$15

Was released by Houston in spring training, signed with Cleveland, and spent the warm months at Charlotte. Although his major league record doesn't show it, Grimsley is closer to being a pitcher now than he was three or four years ago, when the Phillies were trying to rush him into the rotation. He's gained some command of his breaking pitch, and he's not trying as hard to make perfect, unhittable pitches. Grade C prospect.

YEAR	TEAM/LEVEL	G	IP	W-L	PCT.	HITS	SO	BB	ERA
1992	Tucson AAA	26	125	8-7	.533	152	90	55	5.05
1993	Charlotte AAA	28	135	6-6	.500	138	102	49	3.39
1993	Cleveland	10	42	3-4	.429	52	27	20	5.31

MARQUIS GRISSOM

Montreal Expos

Center Field

$65

He is having a textbook career, getting a little bit better every year than he was the year before. His batting averages since he came up: .257, .257, .267, .276, .298. His slugging percentages: .324, .351, .373, .418, .438. His runs scored: 16, 42, 73, 99, 104. It's unlikely he'll get **too** much better—he might have one or two steps left—but he's an 85% base stealer, a fine center fielder, and a .280 hitter with power.

YEAR	TEAM/LEVEL	G	AB	R	H	2B	3B	HR	RBI	BB	SB	AVG	OBP	SLG
1992	Montreal	159	653	99	180	39	6	14	66	42	78	.276	.322	.418
1993	Montreal	157	630	104	188	27	2	19	95	52	53	.298	.351	.438
1994	**Projected**	**159**	**629**	**93**	**175**	**29**	**5**	**13**	**68**	**46**	**74**	**.278**	**.327**	**.402**

BUDDY GROOM

Detroit Tigers

Starting Pitcher

$14

His real name is "Wedsel," which is a good excuse to skip Mother's Day. Groom is 28, old for a prospect, and his major league record is 0-7 with an ERA of 5.97, but I like him a lot. He works ahead of the hitters, has been consistently successful in the minor leagues, and he gets ground balls. He's a Tommy John-type pitcher, and John-type pitchers are rarely successful with bad teams.

YEAR	TEAM/LEVEL	G	IP	W-L	PCT.	HITS	SO	BB	ERA
1992	Toledo AAA	16	109	7-7	.500	102	71	23	2.80
1993	Toledo AAA	16	102	9-3	.750	98	78	30	2.74
1993	Detroit	19	37	0-2	.000	48	15	13	6.14

KEVIN GROSS

Los Angeles Dodgers

Starting Pitcher

$32

Pitched .500 ball for the first time since 1986, when he was 12-12; he hasn't had a *winning* record since 1985. There is no indication that time is running out on him. He is 32, but he hasn't had a sore arm in several years, and his strikeout rate is still good. I know it is too late to be saying this, but I still half-expect him to break loose with a big year.

YEAR	TEAM/LEVEL	G	IP	W-L	PCT.	HITS	SO	BB	ERA
1991	Los Angeles	46	116	10-11	.476	123	95	50	3.58
1992	Los Angeles	34	205	8-13	.381	182	158	77	3.17
1993	Los Angeles	33	202	13-13	.500	224	150	74	4.14

KIP GROSS

Los Angeles Dodgers

Relief Pitcher

$20

A 29-year-old righthander, has been on the border of breaking through for several years, and may finally have done it in '93, when he pitched well at Albuquerque (a 4.05 ERA at Albuquerque in a hitter's year is good) and then was almost perfect in a September callup. His strikeout rate at Albuquerque improved dramatically. May be in the Dodger bullpen in '94.

YEAR	TEAM/LEVEL	G	IP	W-L	SAVES	HITS	SO	BB	ERA
1992	Los Angeles	16	24	1-1	0	32	14	10	4.18
1993	Albuquerque AAA	59	124	13-7	13	115	96	41	4.05
1993	Los Angeles	10	15	0-0	0	13	12	4	0.60

KELLY GRUBER

Released

Third Base

$14

Acquired from Toronto in a trade for Luis Sojo, he started the year on the DL following surgery on his left shoulder, also suffering from bulging discs in his neck. He returned June 3, played very well for three weeks, then went out for the year with an injury to his left shoulder. He was released in September; his ability to get another job will depend on convincing somebody that he is truly healthy. Now 32.

YEAR	TEAM/LEVEL	G	AB	R	H	2B	3B	HR	RBI	BB	SB	AVG	OBP	SLG
1991	Toronto	113	429	58	108	18	2	20	65	31	12	.252	.308	.443
1992	Toronto	120	446	42	102	16	3	11	43	26	7	.229	.275	.352
1993	California	18	65	10	18	3	0	3	9	2	0	.277	.309	.462

EDDIE GUARDADO

Minnesota Twins

Starting Pitcher

$14

Young lefthander, rushed to the majors after a quick start at Double-A, got pounded but stayed the rest of the season. The league hit .369 against him when there were men on base. That's not too good . . . A 21st-round pick in 1990, has very good control, but his fastball won't tie anybody in knots. Short, pudgy, nice mechanics, has good curve and changeup. Probably will have better years.

YEAR	TEAM/LEVEL	G	IP	W-L	PCT.	HITS	SO	BB	ERA
1992	Two Teams A	25	150	12-10	.545	153	142	40	3.47
1993	Nashville AA	10	65	4-0	1.000	53	57	10	1.24
1993	Minnesota	19	95	3-8	.273	123	46	36	6.18

MARK GUBICZA

Kansas City Royals

Reliever/Starter

$18

Opened the year in the starting rotation, and was hit hard (7.03 ERA through six starts). He moved to the bullpen then and pitched fairly well in relief. Gubicza still throws a major league fastball, has good control and is now an extreme ground-ball pitcher. Doesn't have a contract for '94, but will have a job somewhere, and may pitch well.

YEAR	TEAM/LEVEL	G	IP	W-L	PCT.	HITS	SO	BB	ERA
1991	Kansas City	26	133	9-12	.429	168	89	42	5.68
1992	Kansas City	18	111	7-6	.538	110	81	36	3.72
1993	Kansas City	49	104	5-8	.385	128	80	43	4.66

LEE GUETTERMAN

St. Louis Cardinals

Relief Pitcher

$18

Released by the Mets, he signed with the Cardinals and started the year at Louisville, where he pitched well (2.94 ERA). The Cardinals called him up in late June to be the lefthanded one-out guy, and he pitched, if anything, a little better in the majors, had his best season since 1990. I guess you know about him—a tall, thin dart thrower, now 35 years old.

YEAR	TEAM/LEVEL	G	IP	W-L	SAVES	HITS	SO	BB	ERA
1991	New York	64	88	3-4	6	91	35	25	3.68
1992	Two Teams	58	66	4-5	2	92	20	27	7.09
1993	St. Louis	40	46	3-3	1	41	19	16	2.93

OZZIE GUILLEN

Chicago White Sox

Shortstop

$32

Missed the 1992 season after ripping a couple of tendons in a collision with Tim Raines, but returned in '93 to play at more or less the same level as before. He's 30; should be good for at least one more year of the same . . . Doesn't it seem strange to you that nobody could ever convince Guillen, who is intelligent and approachable, to stop chasing bad pitches?

YEAR	TEAM/LEVEL	G	AB	R	H	2B	3B	HR	RBI	BB	SB	AVG	OBP	SLG
1992	Chicago	12	40	5	8	4	0	0	7	1	1	.200	.214	.300
1993	Chicago	134	457	44	128	23	4	4	50	10	5	.280	.292	.374
1994	**Projected**	**136**	**471**	**45**	**124**	**18**	**5**	**3**	**47**	**11**	**13**	**.263**	**.280**	**.342**

BILL GULLICKSON

Detroit Tigers

Starting Pitcher

$18

Opened the season on the disabled list following off-season surgery to both his knee and his shoulder, and struggled most of the year. He saved his season with a 6-0 record, 2.68 ERA in August (then was hammered in September.) The Tigers scored 6.9 runs/nine innings for him, which gave him a winning record despite his 5.37 ERA and horrible rate of home runs allowed (28 in 159 innings).

YEAR	TEAM/LEVEL	G	IP	W-L	PCT.	HITS	SO	BB	ERA
1991	Detroit	35	226	20-9	.690	256	91	44	3.90
1992	Detroit	34	222	14-13	.519	228	64	50	4.34
1993	Detroit	28	159	13-9	.591	186	70	44	5.37

MARK GUTHRIE

Minnesota Twins

Relief Pitcher

$29

Could be a steal in any '94 draft. Guthrie struggled with a shoulder problem early last year, which turned out to be a blood clot. His season ended in May, but he is expected to be healthy for spring training. Roberto Hernandez had a similar problem in 1991 . . . Guthrie was a fine pitcher in 1992, and there is little reason to think he won't be in '94, but some people will forget about him because of the lost season.

YEAR	TEAM/LEVEL	G	IP	W-L	SAVES	HITS	SO	BB	ERA
1991	Minnesota	41	98	7-5	2	116	72	41	4.32
1992	Minnesota	54	75	2-3	5	59	76	23	2.88
1993	Minnesota	22	21	2-1	0	20	15	16	4.71

RICKY GUTIERREZ

San Diego Padres

Shortstop

$32

Another of the good young players collected by San Diego while they have been circling the wagons. Gutierrez, from the Baltimore system, has Gold Glove potential at shortstop, although he's not there yet, plus he runs well and is not a wild swinger. None of that would keep him in the lineup if he hit .220, which seemed possible a year ago, but he hit .251 and scored more runs per at bat than Jay Bell.

YEAR	TEAM/LEVEL	G	AB	R	H	2B	3B	HR	RBI	BB	SB	AVG	OBP	SLG
1992	Rocheste AAA	125	431	54	109	9	3	0	41	53	14	.253	.331	.288
1993	San Diego	133	438	76	110	10	5	5	26	50	4	.251	.334	.331
1994	**Projected**	**140**	**472**	**56**	**115**	**10**	**3**	**3**	**37**	**57**	**9**	**.244**	**.325**	**.297**

JOSE GUZMAN

Chicago Cubs

Starting Pitcher

$36

Classic four-pitch pitcher, throws fastball, curve, slider and changeup. He was out in mid-summer with back trouble, and took time off in September, as Lefebvre looked at younger pitchers, which kept him under 200 innings . . . In my opinion, Guzman will continue to be a fine pitcher for several years, but the Cubs need to be careful not to push him when the back acts up . . . Has a multi-year record of pitching well late in the season.

YEAR	TEAM/LEVEL	G	IP	W-L	PCT.	HITS	SO	BB	ERA
1991	Texas	25	170	13-7	.650	152	125	84	3.08
1992	Texas	33	224	16-11	.593	229	179	73	3.66
1993	Chicago	30	191	12-10	.545	188	163	74	4.34

JUAN GUZMAN

Toronto Blue Jays

Starting Pitcher

$40

You should not take seriously the fact that his career winning percentage (.784) is the highest in history. That's the kind of record which is held by many people in turn, each of whom surrenders it as soon as he has a tough season . . . Guzman hasn't really harnessed his ability yet, and didn't pitch all that well in '93. The Blue Jays saved his butt about 15 times in 33 starts.

YEAR	TEAM/LEVEL	G	IP	W-L	PCT.	HITS	SO	BB	ERA
1991	Toronto	23	139	10-3	.769	98	123	66	2.99
1992	Toronto	28	181	16-5	.762	135	165	72	2.64
1993	Toronto	33	221	14-3	.824	211	194	110	3.99

CHRIS GWYNN

Kansas City Royals

Left Field

$26

I like him a little better every year. He's a lefthanded line drive hitter, hits a lot of hard ground balls. He doesn't have power or speed, and hardly ever goes to bat against a lefthanded pitcher, but is a pretty good outfielder. Still, in the last three years he has batted 510 times with 64 runs scored, 54 RBI—unimpressive run production for an outfielder.

YEAR	TEAM/LEVEL	G	AB	R	H	2B	3B	HR	RBI	BB	SB	AVG	OBP	SLG
1992	Kansas City	34	84	10	24	3	2	1	7	3	0	.286	.303	.405
1993	Kansas City	103	287	36	86	14	4	1	25	24	0	.300	.354	.387
1994	**Projected**	**115**	**318**	**39**	**89**	**14**	**3**	**5**	**35**	**24**	**1**	**.280**	**.330**	**.390**

TONY GWYNN
San Diego Padres
Right Field
$59

A lefthanded hitter, he led the National League in batting against lefthanded pitchers, at .359. Also led in innumerable other splits . . . Now has 11 consecutive .300 seasons, a lifetime .329 average, and 2,000+ hits with at least five years left. Was 14-for-15 as a base stealer last year, set a career high in doubles despite missing 40 games, and plays right field as well as anyone, although he may move to first.

YEAR	TEAM/LEVEL	G	AB	R	H	2B	3B	HR	RBI	BB	SB	AVG	OBP	SLG
1992	San Diego	128	520	77	165	27	3	6	41	46	3	.317	.371	.415
1993	San Diego	122	489	70	175	41	3	7	59	36	14	.358	.398	.497
1994	**Projected**	**130**	**514**	**67**	**164**	**25**	**4**	**6**	**50**	**40**	**8**	**.319**	**.369**	**.412**

DAVE HAAS
Detroit Tigers
Relief Pitcher
$9

He started the year as a well-regarded pitching prospect, but the league hit .375 against him, with 20% of the hits being home runs. He went on the disabled list in June with the ever-popular tendonitis, which is a baseball term meaning "His arm hurts and we don't know what the hell is wrong with it." A 28-year-old righthander, a .500 pitcher in the minor leagues, Grade D prospect.

YEAR	TEAM/LEVEL	G	IP	W-L	SAVES	HITS	SO	BB	ERA
1992	Toledo AAA	22	149	9-8	0	149	112	53	4.18
1992	Detroit	12	62	5-3	0	68	29	16	3.94
1993	Detroit	20	28	1-2	0	45	17	8	6.11

JOHN HABYAN
Kansas City Royals
Relief Pitcher
$21

A competent middle reliever, acquired by the Royals in late July, when they were losing games in the middle innings. Has always pitched well, and sometimes brilliantly, the first half of the season, but has had trouble in the hot months and late in the year. A sinker/slider pitcher with good control, no chance of moving into the closer role, would expect him to remain effective as a setup man.

YEAR	TEAM/LEVEL	G	IP	W-L	SAVES	HITS	SO	BB	ERA
1991	New York AL	66	90	4-2	2	73	70	20	2.30
1992	New York AL	56	73	5-6	7	84	44	21	3.84
1993	Two Teams	48	56	2-1	1	59	39	20	4.15

CHIP HALE
Minnesota Twins
Second Base/Third Base
$23

Hit .515 in September (17-for-33). The Twins second baseman of the future before the emergence of Knoblauch, Hale was trapped in AAA for four and a half years. He's not really a .300 hitter, but he'll hit .260-.280, with some doubles and walks, and can do the job at second and third. He won't budge Knoblauch, but he is a good backup for the Twins and could help somebody as a regular.

YEAR	TEAM/LEVEL	G	AB	R	H	2B	3B	HR	RBI	BB	SB	AVG	OBP	SLG
1992	MLE	132	463	61	124	23	7	0	42	59	3	.268	.351	.348
1993	Portland AAA	55	211	37	59	15	3	1	24	21	2	.280	.343	.393
1993	Minnesota	69	186	25	62	6	1	3	27	18	2	.333	.408	.425

BOB HAMELIN
Kansas City Royals
Designated Lumbering Slugger
$20

I used to describe Hamelin as a Kent Hrbek type, but I was afraid Hrbek would sue. Hamelin has a long swing, is slow and such a bad first baseman that it's hard to play him there. Has extensive history of injuries, because of his weight and a bad back. The Royals needed a lefthanded bat, and with Brett retired they *really* need a lefthanded bat, so I suppose he's it. Can hit better than .225.

YEAR	TEAM/LEVEL	G	AB	R	H	2B	3B	HR	RBI	BB	SB	AVG	OBP	SLG
1993	MLE	137	458	56	103	17	2	17	62	59	5	.225	.313	.382
1993	Kansas City	16	49	2	11	3	0	2	5	6	0	.224	.309	.408
1994	**Projected**	**109**	**321**	**37**	**76**	**13**	**2**	**11**	**44**	**42**	**2**	**.237**	**.325**	**.393**

DARRYL HAMILTON
Milwaukee Brewers
Outfielder
$43

Hamilton plays all three outfield positions for the Brewers, more in right field than anywhere else. He's kind of the unknown .300 hitter, has hit .295, .311, .298 and .310 over the last four years, plus it's not all singles and he can steal a base. Was hitting .325 last year until a September slump . . . Good player. Hit .364 on an 0-2 count (8 for 22). That was the best in the American League.

YEAR	TEAM/LEVEL	G	AB	R	H	2B	3B	HR	RBI	BB	SB	AVG	OBP	SLG
1992	Milwaukee	128	470	67	140	19	7	5	62	45	41	.298	.356	.400
1993	Milwaukee	135	520	74	161	21	1	9	48	45	21	.310	.367	.406
1994	**Projected**	**140**	**506**	**72**	**151**	**20**	**3**	**5**	**57**	**47**	**28**	**.298**	**.358**	**.379**

JOEY HAMILTON
San Diego Padres
Starting Pitcher
$17

Hamilton was the Padres' first pick in 1991 and was considered the top pitching prospect in their organization a year ago, but had a poor season and didn't get called up. He's a righthander, good size and a good fastball, doesn't walk five men a game and get beat that way, but needs to develop his second and third pitches. I suspect that he and the Padres' organization don't get along too well.

YEAR	TEAM/LEVEL	G	IP	W-L	PCT.	HITS	SO	BB	ERA
1992	Wichita AA	6	35	3-0	1.000	33	26	11	2.86
1993	Wichita AA	15	91	4-9	.308	101	50	36	3.97
1993	Las Vegas AAA	8	47	3-2	.600	49	33	22	4.40

CHRIS HAMMOND
Florida Marlins
Starting Pitcher
$23

The Marlins acquired him in a trade for Gary Scott, an exchange of former phee-noms, and it looked like one of the best trades ever made, as Hammond was 10-4 at the All-Star break. He was pounded senseless the second half, which has been his habit—in his career he is 22-14 before the break, but 3-17 after. Lefthanded finesse pitcher, a type of pitcher who rarely does well with a bad team.

YEAR	TEAM/LEVEL	G	IP	W-L	PCT.	HITS	SO	BB	ERA
1991	Cincinnati	20	100	7-7	.500	92	50	48	4.06
1992	Cincinnati	28	147	7-10	.412	149	79	55	4.21
1993	Florida	32	191	11-12	.478	207	108	66	4.66

JEFF HAMMONDS
Baltimore Orioles
Outfielder
$27

The fourth player taken in the '92 draft, an outfielder from Stanford; received reported $975,000 to sign. Might have gone higher in the draft if he wasn't expected to cost so much. Has been compared to Rickey Henderson, except he never walks, which is like being called a flat-chested Dolly Parton, or Randy Johnson without the fastball. Has power and speed, might be able to play center but his arm is a question. Has a back problem.

YEAR	TEAM/LEVEL	G	AB	R	H	2B	3B	HR	RBI	BB	SB	AVG	OBP	SLG
1993	MLE	60	232	29	62	9	0	6	26	9	6	.267	.295	.384
1993	Baltimore	33	105	10	32	8	0	3	19	2	4	.305	.312	.467
1994	**Projected**	**137**	**531**	**61**	**148**	**27**	**0**	**14**	**71**	**17**	**16**	**.279**	**.301**	**.409**

MIKE HAMPTON
Seattle Mariners
Starting Pitcher
$15

A small lefthander who will probably spend 1993 in Triple-A, but who has considerable promise. Florida native, drafted out of high school. Has above-average fastball, changes speeds well, curve and slider are in the development stage but work sometimes. Has thrown strikes in the minors, although his control left him when he got the call, as it often does. Grade B prospect.

YEAR	TEAM/LEVEL	G	IP	W-L	PCT.	HITS	SO	BB	ERA
1992	San Bernadino A	25	170	13-8	.619	163	132	66	3.12
1993	Jacksonville AA	15	87	6-4	.600	71	84	33	3.71
1993	Seattle	13	17	1-3	.250	28	8	17	9.53

CHRIS HANEY
Kansas City Royals
Starting Pitcher
$23

On balance, he pitched much better than the 6.02 ERA would suggest. He's a funny pitcher. Some days he looks like a finished product, like Bud Black or Terry Mulholland; other times he looks like he would never get anybody out. No star potential, but could be third-starter type. His father, I suspect, is a pretty good pitching coach, and that may be the little edge he needs to get over the hump.

YEAR	TEAM/LEVEL	G	IP	W-L	PCT.	HITS	SO	BB	ERA
1992	Two Teams	16	80	4-6	.400	75	54	26	4.61
1993	Omaha AAA	8	48	6-1	.857	43	32	14	2.27
1993	Kansas City	23	124	9-9	.500	141	65	53	6.02

DAVE HANSEN
Los Angeles Dodgers
Third Base
$25

Had a great year as a pinch hitter, and may have earned another shot at the third base job, which has been up for grabs since Ron Cey was traded in 1983. He's only 25 years old, and would not be the first player to have a good career after punting one chance. Lefthanded line drive hitter, good plate discipline, was slowed in '92 by a back injury. Hit .492 with runners on base (29-for-59).

YEAR	TEAM/LEVEL	G	AB	R	H	2B	3B	HR	RBI	BB	SB	AVG	OBP	SLG
1992	Los Angeles	132	341	30	73	11	0	6	22	34	0	.214	.286	.299
1993	Los Angeles	84	105	13	38	3	0	4	30	21	0	.362	.465	.505
1994	**Projected**	**116**	**247**	**25**	**63**	**10**	**1**	**4**	**28**	**30**	**2**	**.255**	**.336**	**.352**

ERIK HANSON

Cincinnati Reds

Starting Pitcher

$35

If you're looking at me to explain the trade, look somewhere else. I don't understand either part of it. Hanson-for-Ayala is a trade I wouldn't make, but a) Hanson could be a free agent in a year, and b) Lou Piniella knows these guys better than I do. But Bret Boone for Dan Wilson? It brings to mind Ryne Sandberg as partial payment for Ivan DeJesus.

YEAR	TEAM/LEVEL	G	IP	W-L	PCT.	HITS	SO	BB	ERA
1991	Seattle	27	175	8-8	.500	182	143	56	3.81
1992	Seattle	31	187	8-17	.320	209	112	57	4.82
1993	Seattle	31	215	11-12	.478	215	163	60	3.47

MIKE HARKEY

Chicago Cubs

Starting Pitcher

$19

After pitching well in April (3-0, 1.77 ERA) he developed tendonitis in his shoulder, and struggled the rest of the year, having ERAs of 5.10 to 6.46 in each of the other months. While it is perhaps premature to bury him, he has now battled serious injuries for three years, and it is very questionable whether he will ever win with any consistency.

YEAR	TEAM/LEVEL	G	IP	W-L	PCT.	HITS	SO	BB	ERA
1991	Chicago	4	19	0-2	.000	34	15	6	5.30
1992	Chicago	7	38	4-0	1.000	38	21	15	1.89
1993	Chicago	28	157	10-10	.500	187	67	43	5.26

PETE HARNISCH

Houston Astros

Starting Pitcher

$69

Led the National League in shutouts (4), opposition batting average (.214), fewest hits per nine innings (171 in 217.2, 7.07), also had the lowest ratio of ground balls to fly balls in the National League (240-263) . . . Speaking of lopsided trades, the Orioles traded Harnisch *and* Curt Schilling *and* Steve Finley for Glenn Davis . . . Always bet on a power pitcher. You'll win more than you lose.

YEAR	TEAM/LEVEL	G	IP	W-L	PCT.	HITS	SO	BB	ERA
1991	Houston	33	217	12-9	.571	169	172	83	2.70
1992	Houston	34	207	9-10	.474	182	164	64	3.70
1993	Houston	33	218	16-9	.640	171	185	79	2.98

BRIAN HARPER

Free Agent

Catcher

$38

He will probably be leaving a park in which he has hit 30-40 points better than he hit on the road, so his average will probably dip a few points in '94. He's 34 years old, and his defense has never been good. Still, he's hit .294 or better six straight times, and there aren't many catchers who do that . . . There was a 1930s catcher named Spud Davis who had exactly the same combination of talents as Harper.

YEAR	TEAM/LEVEL	G	AB	R	H	2B	3B	HR	RBI	BB	SB	AVG	OBP	SLG
1992	Minnesota	140	502	58	154	25	0	9	73	26	0	.307	.343	.410
1993	Minnesota	147	530	52	161	26	1	12	73	29	1	.304	.347	.425
1994	**Projected**	**136**	**484**	**50**	**141**	**24**	**1**	**9**	**67**	**23**	**1**	**.291**	**.323**	**.401**

DONALD HARRIS

Texas Rangers

Center Field

$8

A born-again football player, a free safety from Texas Tech who was almost good enough to turn pro. Harris is said to be an exceptional center fielder with an arm, and he is strong enough to hit home runs if he can make contact, which seems like a major longshot. Didn't have a good year at Oklahoma City (his MLE from 1992 was better), but was called up to cover center during Hulce's injury. Grade D prospect.

YEAR	TEAM/LEVEL	G	AB	R	H	2B	3B	HR	RBI	BB	SB	AVG	OBP	SLG
1993	Ok City AAA	96	367	48	93	13	9	6	40	23	4	.253	.301	.387
1993	MLE	96	353	36	79	11	5	4	30	17	2	.224	.259	.317
1993	Texas	40	76	10	15	2	0	1	8	5	0	.197	.253	.263

GENE HARRIS

San Diego Padres

Relief Pitcher

$29

After a bad slump in July he converted his last seven save opportunities, regaining control of the Padres' closer spot. He is not well-qualified to do that job. He had never had an ERA below 4.00 until last year, and even last year his peripheral stats were poor, and he gave up seven unearned runs in 59 innings. Still, the big money job is his to lose.

YEAR	TEAM/LEVEL	G	IP	W-L	SAVES	HITS	SO	BB	ERA
1991	Seattle	8	13	0-0	1	15	6	10	4.05
1992	Two Teams	22	30	0-2	0	23	25	15	4.15
1993	San Diego	59	59	6-6	23	57	39	37	3.03

GREG HARRIS

Boston Red Sox

Relief Pitcher

$30

Hardworking reliever, led the American League in games pitched and led the major leagues in relief innings, with 112. He pitched OK overall, but attempted to move into the closer role while Russell was out with an ankle injury, and that went very badly. He blew most of his leads, which contributed to the team's miserable pennant drive . . . Harris is a solid middle reliever, and should continue to be.

YEAR	TEAM/LEVEL	G	IP	W-L	SAVES	HITS	SO	BB	ERA
1991	Boston	53	173	11-12	2	157	127	69	3.85
1992	Boston	70	108	4-9	4	82	73	60	2.51
1993	Boston	80	112	6-7	8	95	103	60	3.77

GREG W. HARRIS

Colorado Rockies

Starting Pitcher

$26

Some guys just aren't born lucky. Harris could easily have been 17-11 with a 3.59 ERA in '93. A pitcher's record reflects the park and embodies his team, not only in wins. If an infielder doesn't reach a ground ball, that's a base hit. Harris led the league in runs allowed (127) home runs (33), and slugging percentage (.455), but Greg Maddux would have a hard time posting a good record for this team in this park.

YEAR	TEAM/LEVEL	G	IP	W-L	PCT.	HITS	SO	BB	ERA
1991	San Diego	20	133	9-5	.643	116	95	27	2.23
1992	San Diego	20	118	4-8	.333	113	66	35	4.12
1993	Two Teams	35	225	11-17	.393	239	123	69	4.59

LENNY HARRIS

Free Agent

Utilityman

$21

Harris had hit well for three years (.304, .287 and .271) before failing to hit much in 160 at bats last year. Harris very much wants to play regularly, and he is *almost* there—another 10 points on his average, another 10 stolen bases a year, a few more walks and he's Bip Roberts or Tony Phillips. He's an awfully good bench player—a lefthanded line drive hitter who can run and play third base or second.

YEAR	TEAM/LEVEL	G	AB	R	H	2B	3B	HR	RBI	BB	SB	AVG	OBP	SLG
1992	Los Angeles	135	347	28	94	11	0	0	30	24	19	.271	.318	.303
1993	Los Angeles	107	160	20	38	6	1	2	11	15	3	.238	.303	.325
1994	**Projected**	**122**	**191**	**22**	**51**	**7**	**1**	**1**	**17**	**16**	**7**	**.267**	**.324**	**.330**

MIKE HARTLEY

Free Agent

Relief Pitcher

$20

The Twins tried to outright Hartley to Portland, but he refused the assignment and has become a free agent. Hartley went through the Dodger system very slowly, and was pushing 30 before he surfaced; he's now 32, and still not *really* established, although he's not a bad pitcher. Posted a 2.61 ERA after the All-Star break . . . Nobody who has him seems to want to keep him, which probably should tell us something.

YEAR	TEAM/LEVEL	G	IP	W-L	SAVES	HITS	SO	BB	ERA
1991	Two Teams	58	83	4-1	2	74	63	47	4.21
1992	Philadelphia	46	55	7-6	0	54	53	23	3.44
1993	Minnesota	53	81	1-2	1	86	57	36	4.00

BRYAN HARVEY

Florida Marlins

Closer

$66

He had a wonderful season, from which we should learn this: that the bullpen is **not** the key to success in baseball. The Marlins' bullpen was vastly better than that of any other expansion team in history—yet the team's won-lost record was 64-98, a typical expansion-type record . . . Limited lefthanded hitters to a .132 batting average, lowest in the major leagues . . . Allowed only 7.6 baserunners per nine innings, the best in the majors.

YEAR	TEAM/LEVEL	G	IP	W-L	SAVES	HITS	SO	BB	ERA
1991	California	67	79	2-4	46	51	101	17	1.60
1992	California	25	29	0-4	13	22	34	11	2.83
1993	Florida	59	69	1-5	45	45	73	13	1.70

BILL (WHATTA) HASELMAN

Seattle Mariners

Catcher

$18

Got his first chance to play a little, and showed OK with the bat. With the acquisition of Dan Wilson, another righthanded hitting catcher, his position on the team is unclear. His arm is weak, plus teams prefer to carry a lefthanded hitting backup catcher when they can, so if he hadn't hit his career would have ended quickly. But if you hit, they'll work you in somewhere.

YEAR	TEAM/LEVEL	G	AB	R	H	2B	3B	HR	RBI	BB	SB	AVG	OBP	SLG
1992	MLE	105	340	36	71	15	1	12	40	35	1	.209	.283	.365
1993	Seattle	58	137	21	35	8	0	5	16	12	2	.255	.316	.423
1993	**Projected**	**72**	**211**	**25**	**50**	**13**	**0**	**7**	**28**	**22**	**2**	**.237**	**.309**	**.398**

BILLY HATCHER

Boston Red Sox

Center Field

$24

Over the last four years has hit .333 in May, but .216 in September (about 300 at bats in each group) . . . Hatcher is coming off of his best season since 1987, and the Red Sox have nobody else to put in center, so despite his age (33) and some health concerns, it must be assumed that he will open the season as the Red Sox center fielder . . . He is one of the first players I would want to avoid.

YEAR	TEAM/LEVEL	G	AB	R	H	2B	3B	HR	RBI	BB	SB	AVG	OBP	SLG
1992	Two Teams	118	409	47	102	19	2	3	33	22	9	.249	.290	.328
1993	Boston	136	508	71	146	24	3	9	57	28	14	.287	.336	.400
1994	**Projected**	**133**	**456**	**62**	**117**	**22**	**2**	**5**	**42**	**26**	**10**	**.257**	**.297**	**.346**

HILLY HATHAWAY

California Angels

Lefthanded Starting Pitcher

$15

A pitcher who has had exceptional control in the minor leagues, but has tried to make perfect pitches during his major league trials, with predictable results: major league hitters don't bite, he gets behind, has to come in and BOOM. Getting past this stage is probably more a matter of when than if, and time is on his side at age 24. Had 1993 bout with tendonitis; Grade B prospect.

YEAR	TEAM/LEVEL	G	IP	W-L	PCT.	HITS	SO	BB	ERA
1992	Midland	14	95	7-2	.778	90	69	10	3.21
1993	Vancouver AAA	12	70	7-0	1.000	60	44	27	4.09
1993	California	11	57	4-3	.571	71	11	26	5.02

CHARLIE HAYES

Colorado Rockies

Third Base

$48

Maybe they should trade him again; he seems to get 10 percent better every time he is traded. Not *all* of his improved stats are attributable to Mile High Stadium. He improved his strikeout/walk ratio and stole more bases with a better percentage, which the park doesn't explain, plus he hit almost as many doubles on the road last year (22) as his previous career high for a season (23).

YEAR	TEAM/LEVEL	G	AB	R	H	2B	3B	HR	RBI	BB	SB	AVG	OBP	SLG
1992	New York AL	142	509	52	131	19	2	18	66	28	3	.257	.297	.409
1993	Colorado	157	573	89	175	45	2	25	98	43	11	.305	.355	.522
1993	REAL PARK	157	562	71	157	42	1	22	78	43	11	.279	.331	.475

NEAL HEATON

New York Yankees

Relief Pitcher

$1

Released by the Yankees on June 27, presumably bringing his 12-year career to an end. Heaton was the Freddie Kruger of pitchers, dead and buried a dozen times, but he would get a chance somewhere, rip off five quick wins and extend his career for three more years while people tried to figure out what to make of that hot streak. He had ERAs below 4.00 only twice in 12 years.

YEAR	TEAM/LEVEL	G	IP	W-L	PCT.	HITS	SO	BB	ERA
1991	Pittsburgh	42	69	3-3	.500	72	34	21	4.33
1992	Two Teams	32	42	3-1	.750	43	31	23	4.07
1993	New York	18	27	1-0	1.000	34	15	11	6.00

ERIC HELFAND

Oakland Athletics

Catcher

$5

A second-round draft pick in 1991, the A's let him go in the expansion draft, and then traded Walt Weiss to get him back. They must see something in him that I don't, which I would suppose was defense. He's a lefthanded hitter, but he didn't hit at Double-A at the age of 24, and 99 times in 100 that means he won't hit in the majors at 27 or 30.

YEAR	TEAM/LEVEL	G	AB	R	H	2B	3B	HR	RBI	BB	SB	AVG	OBP	SLG
1993	Huntsville AA	100	302	38	69	15	2	10	48	43	1	.228	.333	.391
1993	MLE	100	290	30	57	12	1	7	38	29	0	.197	.270	.317
1993	Oakland	8	13	1	3	0	0	0	1	0	0	.231	.231	.231

RICKEY HELLING

Texas Rangers

Starting Pitcher

$27

He was rated the number-seven prospect in the Texas League by *Baseball America*, about which I would say that if there are six better prospects in the league than this guy, that was some league. He struck out 188 men in 177 innings, the highest strikeout total in the league since Sid Fernandez went through, plus his control was good. His ERA wasn't great, but that's a good park for a hitter. May make the Rangers' rotation.

YEAR	TEAM/LEVEL	G	IP	W-L	PCT.	HITS	SO	BB	ERA
1992	Charlotte A	3	20	1-1	.500	13	20	4	2.29
1993	Tulsa AA	26	177	12-8	.600	150	188	46	3.60
1993	Okl City AAA	2	11	1-1	.500	5	17	3	1.64

SCOTT HEMOND

Oakland Athletics

Catcher

$21

Was hitting barely over .200 going into September, but got playing time with Steinbach hurt and put on a push. He had a .414 slugging percentage in '93; if he could sustain that, which is unlikely, he might emerge as a regular. Runs unusually well for a catcher, in part because he has played all over the field through the minors, rather than catching every game. Will be on the roster, anyway.

YEAR	TEAM/LEVEL	G	AB	R	H	2B	3B	HR	RBI	BB	SB	AVG	OBP	SLG
1991	MLE	92	310	37	72	13	1	2	33	35	8	.232	.298	.313
1993	Oakland	91	215	31	55	16	0	6	26	32	14	.256	.353	.414
1994	**Projected**	**92**	**232**	**31**	**55**	**13**	**1**	**3**	**21**	**26**	**9**	**.237**	**.314**	**.341**

DAVE HENDERSON

Oakland Athletics

Center Field

$24

Hit .161 with runners in scoring position, the worst of any major league player with 100 tries . . . On the good side, batted 90 times in double play situtations and grounded into only one double play, the best rate in the major leagues . . . The A's are still playing him in center field, which is a joke, and still letting him bat cleanup. He doesn't have those kind of skills anymore; might be OK in a platoon role.

YEAR	TEAM/LEVEL	G	AB	R	H	2B	3B	HR	RBI	BB	SB	AVG	OBP	SLG
1992	Oakland	20	63	1	9	1	0	0	2	2	0	.143	.169	.159
1993	Oakland	107	382	37	84	19	0	20	53	32	0	.220	.275	.427
1994	**Projected**	**90**	**313**	**35**	**74**	**16**	**1**	**11**	**39**	**28**	**2**	**.236**	**.299**	**.399**

RICKEY HENDERSON

Toronto Blue Jays

Left Field

$62

He took 70% of his pitches in '93 (1840 of 2636), by far the highest percentage in the major leagues, and thus looked over 4.3 pitches per plate appearance, also the most . . . His .528 secondary average was the best in the American League, as was his power/speed number (30.1) . . . Now has 1,586 career runs scored, 39 less than Ty Cobb at the same age. Cobb holds the career record for runs scored.

YEAR	TEAM/LEVEL	G	AB	R	H	2B	3B	HR	RBI	BB	SB	AVG	OBP	SLG
1992	Oakland	117	396	77	112	18	3	15	46	95	48	.283	.426	.457
1993	Two Teams	134	481	114	139	22	2	21	59	120	53	.289	.432	.474
1994	**Projected**	**129**	**444**	**94**	**120**	**22**	**2**	**13**	**50**	**105**	**51**	**.270**	**.410**	**.417**

TOM HENKE

Texas Rangers

Closer

$55

Henke was born in the same month as Lee Smith (December 1957), and is of similar size (6-5, 225—Smith is 6-6 but weighs more). He doesn't have as many saves as Smith, but he has 260, which is seventh on the all-time list, and is a better pitcher now than Lee. His 2.91 ERA last year was his highest in seven years, and he now has eight straight seasons of 20 or more saves.

YEAR	TEAM/LEVEL	G	IP	W-L	SAVES	HITS	SO	BB	ERA
1991	Toronto	49	50	0-2	32	33	53	11	2.32
1992	Toronto	57	56	3-2	34	40	46	22	2.26
1993	Texas	66	74	5-5	40	55	79	27	2.91

MIKE HENNEMAN

Detroit Tigers

Closer

$32

Had a 1.44 ERA in April and May, 2.45 in June/July, 4.68 in August/September, which had Sparky experimenting with other closers in the last weeks. His position seems fairly safe. Anderson doesn't use him like a modern closer, giving him a lot of one-inning and one-out saves, but uses him more like Elroy Face was used, so it's hard to compare his stats with those of guys like Montgomery and Ward.

YEAR	TEAM/LEVEL	G	IP	W-L	SAVES	HITS	SO	BB	ERA
1991	Detroit	60	84	10-2	21	81	61	34	2.88
1992	Detroit	60	77	2-6	24	75	58	20	3.96
1993	Detroit	63	72	5-3	24	69	58	32	2.64

BUTCH HENRY

Montreal Expos

Starting Pitcher

$15

Henry, after pitching over his head in 1992, was dragooned by the Rockies. He pitched 85 innings for Colorado, with a Mile-High ERA, after which he was traded to Montreal and sent to Ottawa. He pitched 31 good innings there, was called up in mid-August and posted a 3.93 ERA in 10 games for Montreal. He's never going to be *consistently* successful, but he'll have better years.

YEAR	TEAM/LEVEL	G	IP	W-L	PCT.	HITS	SO	BB	ERA
1992	Houston	28	165	6-9	.400	185	96	41	4.02
1993	Ottawa AAA	5	31	3-1	.750	34	25	1	3.73
1993	Two Teams	30	103	3-9	.250	135	47	28	6.12

DOUG HENRY

Milwaukee Brewers

Relief Pitcher

$15

Started the year as the Brewers' savemeister, and had a 10.00 ERA in April, but five saves in five opportunities. He pitched better for a while, and held his job until mid-July. Had 17 saves but seven blown saves, the poorest percentage (71%) in the American League (for a pitcher with 20 save opportunities) . . . Was utterly ineffective over the second half the season, and may not be even be in the majors in '94.

YEAR	TEAM/LEVEL	G	IP	W-L	SAVES	HITS	SO	BB	ERA
1991	Milwaukee	32	36	2-1	15	16	28	14	1.00
1992	Milwaukee	60	77	2-6	24	75	58	20	3.96
1993	Milwaukee	54	55	4-4	17	67	38	25	5.56

DWAYNE HENRY

Seattle Mariners

Relief Pitcher

$15

The three relief pitchers named "Henry" had an aggregate ERA of 3.84 in 1992 (3.33 to 4.02) and 6.06 in '93 (5.56 to 6.44). Does anybody know for sure that there *are* three of these guys? Has anybody seen them together? . . . This Henry, actually, is the opposite of Butch. Butch is a control pitcher who gets hit hard, Dwayne has good stuff but has never been able to locate the strike zone.

YEAR	TEAM/LEVEL	G	IP	W-L	SAVES	HITS	SO	BB	ERA
1991	Houston	52	68	3-2	2	51	51	39	3.19
1992	Cincinnati	60	84	3-3	0	59	72	44	3.33
1993	Two Teams	34	59	2-2	2	62	37	39	6.44

PAT HENTGEN

Toronto Blue Jays

Starting Pitcher

$30

My best guess is that Hentgen is a one-year wonder, that he will not be able to win consistently. I base this on four concerns—1) his ratio of strikeouts to wins is very low, 2) his minor league record is poor, 3) he started fast but faded, and 4) he has a history of elbow trouble. But the Blue Jays will help his record; an average pitcher with the Jays is going to pitch .550 baseball.

YEAR	TEAM/LEVEL	G	IP	W-L	PCT.	HITS	SO	BB	ERA
1991	Syracuse	31	171	8-9	.471	146	155	90	4.47
1992	Toronto	28	50	5-2	.714	49	39	32	5.36
1993	Toronto	34	216	19-9	.679	215	122	74	3.87

GIL HEREDIA

Montreal Expos

Righthanded Pitcher

$24

Heredia pitched brilliantly in the lower ranges of the Giants system, but was worked hard at a young age, and developed a fragile arm. He had bone chips removed after the 1992 season, and may be on the way back. In nine starts for Montreal last year he was 4-2 with a 3.67 ERA, and his strikeout/walk ratio is excellent. Montreal has *many* good candidates for the starting rotation, and he's one of them.

YEAR	TEAM/LEVEL	G	IP	W-L	PCT.	HITS	SO	BB	ERA
1992	Two ML Teams	20	44	2-3	.400	44	22	20	4.23
1993	Ottawa AAA	16	103	8-4	.667	97	66	26	2.98
1993	Montreal	20	57	4-2	.667	66	40	14	3.92

CARLOS HERNANDEZ

Los Angeles Dodgers

Catcher

$17

He's buried behind Piazza, but a fine young catcher in his own right. Only 27; his minor league records show him to be a better hitter than the .252 average he has put up so far. He is short, solidly built (like a catcher), defense is OK but probably not quite as good as Piazza's. Can be expected to remain as the Dodgers' backup catcher for several years.

YEAR	TEAM/LEVEL	G	AB	R	H	2B	3B	HR	RBI	BB	SB	AVG	OBP	SLG
1992	Los Angeles	69	173	11	45	4	0	3	17	11	0	.260	.316	.335
1993	Los Angeles	50	99	6	25	5	0	2	7	2	0	.253	.267	.364
1994	**Projected**	**55**	**105**	**9**	**29**	**4**	**0**	**2**	**10**	**5**	**1**	**.276**	**.309**	**.371**

CESAR HERNANDEZ

Cincinnati Reds

Outfielder

$9

Opened the season on the Reds' roster after playing well during some injuries in late 1992. He runs very well and is supposed to be a demon of a center fielder, but was 1-for-3 as a base stealer and hit .083, which earned him a ticket to Indianapolis. I'll say the same thing this year that I said last year: he's never going to hit.

YEAR	TEAM/LEVEL	G	AB	R	H	2B	3B	HR	RBI	BB	SB	AVG	OBP	SLG
1992	Cincinnati	34	51	6	14	4	0	0	4	0	6	.275	.375	.353
1993	Cincinnati	27	24	3	2	0	0	0	1	1	1	.083	.120	.083
1993	MLE	84	263	23	61	10	2	4	17	7	3	.232	.252	.331

JEREMY HERNANDEZ

Cleveland Indians

Relief Pitcher

$23

He was traded to Cleveland on June 1 and anointed the Indians' closer, did the job fairly well for a month and fell into a slump, which meant it was somebody else's chance. He was a starter in the minor leagues, converted to relief at Triple-A. Good control, ground ball pitcher, good health record. I suspect that he's going to be one of the better middle relievers in the game over the next two-three years.

YEAR	TEAM/LEVEL	G	IP	W-L	SAVES	HITS	SO	BB	ERA
1992	Las Vegas	42	55	2-4	11	53	38	20	2.91
1992	San Diego	26	36	1-4	1	39	25	11	4.17
1993	Two Teams	70	112	6-7	8	116	70	34	3.63

ROBERTO HERNANDEZ

Chicago White Sox

Relief Pitcher

$60

Among the better relievers in the league in '93, probably not quite on a level with Montgomery and Ward, but close. He should remain effective. His control is excellent, which means you're not afraid to put him in to start an inning, and he's equally sharp against lefthanded or righthanded hitters, which simplifies the manager's job. Bread-and-butter pitch is a hard, sinking fastball. Real hard.

YEAR	TEAM/LEVEL	G	IP	W-L	SAVES	HITS	SO	BB	ERA
1991	AA and AAA	11	67	6-2	0	52	65	29	2.81
1992	Chicago	43	71	7-3	12	45	68	20	1.65
1993	Chicago	70	79	3-4	38	66	71	20	2.29

XAVIER HERNANDEZ

Houston Astros

Relief Pitcher

$34

Although his ERA rose a little, he was as effective last year as he was in '92, when he went 9-1. He pitched three days every week, limited hitters to a .212 average, and struck out more than one an inning. Takes a long stride and whips the ball in a long loop, which seems to mesmerize batters . . . With a new manager and Doug Jones's off season, he could receive a full trial as the closer.

YEAR	TEAM/LEVEL	G	IP	W-L	SAVES	HITS	SO	BB	ERA
1991	Houston	32	63	2-7	3	66	55	32	4.71
1992	Houston	77	111	9-1	7	81	96	42	2.11
1993	Houston	72	97	4-5	9	75	101	28	2.61

OREL HERSHISER

Los Angeles Dodgers

Starting Pitcher

$32

He stopped hitting late, and his batting average wound up at .356 . . . Has led the NL in intentional walks issued in each of the last two years (13 each year). I don't understand it, either . . . A ground-ball pitcher; over the last four years he is 2-11 on artificial turf. He's 35 years old but shows no obvious signs of decay. Still capable of winning 15-17 games.

YEAR	TEAM/LEVEL	G	IP	W-L	PCT.	HITS	SO	BB	ERA
1991	Los Angeles	21	112	7-2	.778	112	73	32	3.46
1992	Los Angeles	33	211	10-15	.400	209	130	69	3.67
1993	Los Angeles	33	216	12-14	.462	201	141	72	3.59

JOE HESKETH

Boston Red Sox

Lefthanded Pitcher

$15

Opened 1993 as a starting pitcher, but returned to bullpen after 8.44 ERA through five starts. Posted 2.81 ERA as a reliever (32 innings) and 0.68 in eight games after the All-Star break, but then developed tendonitis in his elbow, and missed the last six weeks. His hold on a job is rather tenuous, and more so because the Red Sox have another lefthanded one-out guy (Fossas) and several young pitchers.

YEAR	TEAM/LEVEL	G	IP	W-L	SAVES	HITS	SO	BB	ERA
1991	Boston	39	153	12-4	0	142	104	53	3.29
1992	Boston	30	149	8-9	1	162	104	58	4.36
1993	Boston	28	53	3-4	1	62	34	29	5.06

PHIL HIATT

Kansas City Royals

Third Base

$18

Hit well in spring training, and wound up with a roster spot when Miller was hurt, then led the Royals in home runs and RBI in the opening weeks. He fell slowly to earth, striking out 82 times in 238 at bats, and hitting .104 when he had two strikes on him, the lowest of any major league player. Has similar equipment to Gaetti—excellent arm, slow feet, real power but low on-base percentage. Might develop.

YEAR	TEAM/LEVEL	G	AB	R	H	2B	3B	HR	RBI	BB	SB	AVG	OBP	SLG
1992	MLE	134	485	60	106	19	4	19	71	18	3	.219	.247	.392
1993	Kansas City	81	238	30	52	12	1	7	36	16	6	.218	.285	.366
1994	**Projected**	**102**	**331**	**41**	**75**	**13**	**2**	**11**	**46**	**15**	**5**	**.227**	**.280**	**.378**

GREG HIBBARD

Chicago Cubs

Starting Pitcher

$38

I'm beginning to believe in him. Tommy John-type pitchers have four defining characteristics: they're lefthanded, have excellent control, get 70% ground balls, and cut off the running game. There are only a few such pitchers in the game; Hibbard is one. Because of these traits, John-type pitchers a) can win if the batting average against them is very high, even .290, and b) usually have their best years in their thirties. Hibbard is 29.

YEAR	TEAM/LEVEL	G	IP	W-L	PCT.	HITS	SO	BB	ERA
1991	Chicago AL	32	194	11-11	.500	196	71	57	4.31
1992	Chicago AL	31	176	10-7	.588	187	69	57	4.40
1993	Chicago NL	31	191	15-11	.577	209	82	47	3.96

BRYAN HICKERSON

San Francisco Giants

Lefthanded Pitcher

$29

Had a difficult assignment in '93, stepping into and out of the starting rotation when other pitchers failed. As a starting pitcher he was 7-3, although his ERA wasn't good (4.63); as a reliever he was on and off. He's a lefthander, and righthanded batters hit .307 against him. Nobody is predicting big things for him, but he's done well for three years in a row.

YEAR	TEAM/LEVEL	G	IP	W-L	SAVES	HITS	SO	BB	ERA
1991	San Francisco	17	50	2-2	0	53	43	17	3.60
1992	San Francisco	61	87	5-3	0	74	68	21	3.09
1993	San Francisco	47	120	7-5	0	137	69	39	4.26

KEVIN HIGGINS

San Diego Padres

Catcher

$15

A 27-year-old lefthanded hitter, he reached Triple-A in 1991 but had stalled out after hitting less than .300 at Las Vegas, a hitter's haven. With Santiago gone he saw daylight and hit it, hitting .359 at Vegas, which led to his recall in late May. Through June and July he was a platoon regular, losing that status when a) he didn't hit, and b) the Padres acquired Brad Ausmus. Bench player.

YEAR	TEAM/LEVEL	G	AB	R	H	2B	3B	HR	RBI	BB	SB	AVG	OBP	SLG
1993	Las Vegas AAA	40	142	22	51	8	0	1	22	18	1	.359	.429	.437
1993	San Diego	71	181	17	40	4	1	0	13	16	0	.221	.294	.254
1994	**Projected**	**75**	**201**	**19**	**48**	**6**	**0**	**1**	**17**	**17**	**1**	**.239**	**.298**	**.284**

TED HIGUERA

Milwaukee Brewers

Starting Pitcher

$2

Higuera, who was a consistent winner from 1985 through 1988 (15-8, 20-11, 18-10 and 16-9), had a back problem in 1988 and a torn rotator cuff in 1990. He signed a big contract just before the rotator cuff, and so has spent most of the last several years on the disabled list. He tried to come back and pitch at the end of last year, but was utterly ineffective. He is probably finished.

YEAR	TEAM/LEVEL	G	IP	W-L	PCT.	HITS	SO	BB	ERA
1991	Milwaukee	7	36	3-2	.600	37	33	10	4.46
1992	Milwaukee	(On major league disabled list)							
1993	Milwaukee	8	30	1-3	.250	43	27	16	7.20

GLENALLEN HILL
Chicago Cubs
Left Field
$27

Had a .770 slugging percentage in 31 games after joining the Cubs, who traded Candy Maldonado to get him. He's 29, not fundamentally a good ballplayer and certainly not a great player, but still very capable of busting loose with a 35-homer season. The prototype of the "raw tools" player, the kind of player a scout loves, but has been slow to convert the tools into production.

YEAR	TEAM/LEVEL	G	AB	R	H	2B	3B	HR	RBI	BB	SB	AVG	OBP	SLG
1992	Cleveland	102	369	38	89	16	1	18	49	20	9	.241	.287	.436
1993	Two Teams	97	261	33	69	14	2	15	47	17	8	.264	.307	.506
1994	**Projected**	**116**	**353**	**42**	**90**	**18**	**4**	**16**	**50**	**27**	**10**	**.255**	**.308**	**.456**

KEN HILL
Montreal Expos
Starting Pitcher
$32

He missed some time in mid-summer with a groin injury, which prevented him from pulling near his 16-win season of '92. He didn't pitch the best ball of his career when he returned, walking as many as he struck out, and probably wasn't 100% until the end of the season . . . Allowed only seven home runs in '93, the best home run rate in the National League.

YEAR	TEAM/LEVEL	G	IP	W-L	PCT.	HITS	SO	BB	ERA
1991	St. Louis	30	182	11-10	.524	147	121	67	3.57
1992	Montreal	33	218	16-9	.640	187	150	75	2.68
1993	Montreal	28	184	9-7	.563	163	90	74	3.23

MILT HILL
Cincinnati Reds
Relief Pitcher
$11

Had a fine year at Nashville in '92, saving 18 games, then pitched well in a late-season look. This put him on the bubble, and he opened the season shuttling between Cincinnati and Indianapolis. He didn't pitch well either place, and was sent down to stay in late June . . . Righthander, doesn't throw hard. Nothing marks him as a prospect except that, until last year, he had always pitched well. I think he'll be back.

YEAR	TEAM/LEVEL	G	IP	W-L	SAVES	HITS	SO	BB	ERA
1991	Cincinnati	22	33	1-1	0	36	20	8	3.78
1992	Cincinnati	14	20	0-0	1	15	10	5	3.15
1993	Cincinnati	19	29	3-0	0	34	23	9	5.65

SHAWN HILLEGAS
Oakland Athletics
Starting Pitcher
$4

A truly dreadful pitcher, having none of the attributes of a major league hurler except for what they say is a live arm. He doesn't have a breaking pitch, his control is poor, and his record is consistently bad for a long period of time. To be honest, I really have no idea what in the hell he is doing in the major leagues.

YEAR	TEAM/LEVEL	G	IP	W-L	PCT.	HITS	SO	BB	ERA
1991	Cleveland	51	83	3-4	.429	67	66	46	4.34
1992	Two Teams	26	86	1-8	.111	104	49	37	5.23
1993	Oakland	18	61	3-6	.333	78	29	33	6.97

ERIC HILLMAN

New York Mets

Lefthanded Pitcher

$15

A 6-foot 10-inch lefty, has more in common with Lee Guetterman than with Randy Johnson. He had control troubles at first, and went through the minors slowly, spending three and a half years in A ball. Now his control is superb, and he throws mostly ground balls, which gives him a chance to win if the team becomes more respectable. He looks OK, but a one-of-a-kind player is hard to evaluate.

YEAR	TEAM/LEVEL	G	IP	W-L	PCT.	HITS	SO	BB	ERA
1992	New York	11	52	2-2	.500	67	16	10	5.33
1993	Norfolk AAA	10	61	6-2	.750	52	27	12	2.21
1993	New York	27	145	2-9	.182	173	60	24	3.97

STERLING HITCHCOCK

New York Yankees

Starting Pitcher

$20

A ninth-round draft pick in 1989, he vaulted to prospect status immediately by going 9-1 with a 1.64 ERA at Sarasota. He hasn't had a winning record anywhere since then, since 1989, but has continued to strike out more than a man an inning, with reasonably good control. Lefthander, best pitch is a split-finger fastball. Grade B prospect.

YEAR	TEAM/LEVEL	G	IP	W-L	PCT.	HITS	SO	BB	ERA
1992	Albany	24	146	6-9	.400	116	155	42	2.58
1993	Columbus AAA	16	77	3-5	.375	80	85	28	4.81
1993	New York	6	31	1-2	.333	32	26	14	4.65

DENNY HOCKING

Minnesota Twins

Shortstop

$15

Drafted in 1989 as a catcher, he was converted to shortstop in 1990. He's erratic defensively, and there's been occasional talk of moving him again, to the outfield. He has some pop in his bat, and is an excellent athlete. His competition for the shortstop job is Pat Meares, Jeff Reboulet and Scott Leius, so one would say that he has an opportunity. Grade C prospect, slowed in 1993 by a broken ankle in spring training.

YEAR	TEAM/LEVEL	G	AB	R	H	2B	3B	HR	RBI	BB	SB	AVG	OBP	SLG
1993	Nashvill AA	107	409	54	109	9	4	8	50	34	15	.267	.327	.367
1993	MLE	107	399	43	99	9	4	6	40	24	11	.248	.291	.336
1993	Minnesota	15	36	7	5	1	0	0	0	6	1	.139	.262	.167

TREVOR HOFFMAN

San Diego Padres

Relief Pitcher

$25

Hoffman started his career as an infielder, and converted to the mound in 1991. He had a modestly impressive rookie season in '93, striking out 79 in 90 innings while walking only 26 (not counting intentional walks). Taken by Florida in the expansion draft, he was included in the Sheffield trade, and was one of several pitchers who had an opportunity to take the closer role away from Gene Harris, but failed. Throws very hard.

YEAR	TEAM/LEVEL	G	IP	W-L	SAVES	HITS	SO	BB	ERA
1992	Chattanoga AA	6	30	3-0	0	22	31	11	1.52
1992	Nashville AAA	42	65	4-6	6	57	63	32	4.27
1993	Two Teams	67	90	4-6	5	80	79	39	3.90

CHRIS HOILES
Baltimore Orioles
Catcher
$69

Wow. And we thought 1992 was an impressive year . . . A .585 slugging percentage, for a catcher? Johnny Bench never did that. Yogi Berra and Carlton Fisk and Gary Carter never did that. His on-base percentage was .416; I'm not sure that any of those guys ever matched that, either. He threw out 41% of opposing base stealers; that's very, very good. How good can this guy be?

YEAR	TEAM/LEVEL	G	AB	R	H	2B	3B	HR	RBI	BB	SB	AVG	OBP	SLG
1992	Baltimore	96	310	49	85	10	1	20	40	55	0	.274	.384	.506
1993	Baltimore	126	419	80	130	28	0	29	82	69	1	.310	.416	.585
1994	**Projected**	**138**	**450**	**69**	**122**	**23**	**0**	**22**	**62**	**67**	**1**	**.271**	**.366**	**.469**

DAVE HOLLINS
Philadelphia Phillies
Third Base
$54

Has scored exactly 104 runs and driven in exactly 93 in each of the last two years . . . Took 77% of the available bases as a baserunner (such as going first to third on a single), the best figure in the National League . . . Made 27 errors at third base, which defined a role for Kim Batiste . . . The third- or fourth-best third baseman in the league, behind Matt Williams, Terry Pendleton, possibly Charlie Hayes.

YEAR	TEAM/LEVEL	G	AB	R	H	2B	3B	HR	RBI	BB	SB	AVG	OBP	SLG
1992	Philadelphia	156	586	104	158	28	4	27	93	76	9	.270	.369	.469
1993	Philadelphia	143	543	104	148	30	4	18	93	85	2	.273	.372	.442
1994	**Projected**	**151**	**530**	**89**	**139**	**26**	**3**	**19**	**78**	**79**	**5**	**.262**	**.358**	**.430**

BRAD HOLMAN
Seattle Mariners
Relief Pitcher
$15

Brian Holman's little brother, was originally taken by the Royals but released by them in 1991. Signed by the Mariners, he went through their system like a shot, reaching the majors in early August He hit five batters with pitches in 36 major league innings . . . The Mariners really have *no* proven relievers at this moment—none—so Holman can pitch 80 times this year if he's just OK.

YEAR	TEAM/LEVEL	G	IP	W-L	SAVES	HITS	SO	BB	ERA
1992	Jacksonvill AA	35	74	3-3	4	67	75	21	2.57
1993	Calgary AAA	21	99	8-4	0	109	54	42	4.74
1993	Seattle	19	36	1-3	3	27	17	16	3.72

BRIAN HOLMAN
Seattle Mariners
Starting Pitcher
$8

Holman, acquired by Seattle along with Randy Johnson as part of the Mark Langston deal, pitched as well as Johnson did from 1989 through 1991, going 8-10, 11-11 and 13-14. A torn rotator cuff was diagnosed at the end of the 1991 season, and he hasn't pitched since. He's a free agent now, and may or may not return to Seattle. The Mariners current management doesn't even *remember* when he was good.

YEAR	TEAM/LEVEL	G	IP	W-L	PCT.	HITS	SO	BB	ERA
1991	Seattle	30	195	13-14	.481	199	108	77	3.69
1992	Seattle	(On Disabled List)							
1993	Seattle	(More of the Same)							

DARREN HOLMES

Colorado Rockies

Relief Pitcher

$38

After a poor beginning he had an impressive season as the Rockies' first closer. He had 25 saves in 29 chances, among the better percentages in the league. Jim Gott had the same totals, and it's a lot different doing that in Denver than in Dodger Stadium. His ERA on the road was 2.10. His strikeout/walk ratio was excellent. After the All-Star break he had 17 saves in 18 chances, and a 2.25 ERA.

YEAR	TEAM/LEVEL	G	IP	W-L	SAVES	HITS	SO	BB	ERA
1991	Milwaukee	40	76	1-4	3	90	59	27	4.72
1992	Milwaukee	41	42	4-4	6	35	31	11	2.55
1993	Colorado	62	67	3-3	25	56	60	20	4.05

MARK HOLZEMER

California Angels

Starting Pitcher

$9

A fourth-round draft pick in 1987, he has somehow survived and become a prospect through years of uninspired performance. His minor league career record is 36-40, his ERA 4.66, and he has walked 4.6 men per nine innings. Lefthander, throws OK fastball but no breaking pitch. Called up August 20, in time to get pasted to the center field wall a few times. Grade D prospect.

YEAR	TEAM/LEVEL	G	IP	W-L	PCT.	HITS	SO	BB	ERA
1992	AA and AAA	24	134	7-12	.368	159	85	68	5.72
1993	Vancouver AAA	24	146	9-6	.600	158	80	70	4.82
1993	California	5	23	0-3	.000	34	10	13	8.87

RICK HONEYCUTT

Oakland Athletics

Lefthanded Reliever

$25

Forty years old, has been in the Oakland bullpen since 1987. He was originally in the Pirates' system, and pitched for the Mariners in their expansion season, 1977 . . . Despite his age he is still pitching well, leading the American League in holds last year, with 20, and giving up only 30 hits in 42 innings. I would expect him to be open for business next year at the same address.

YEAR	TEAM/LEVEL	G	IP	W-L	SAVES	HITS	SO	BB	ERA
1991	Oakland	43	38	2-4	0	37	26	20	3.58
1992	Oakland	54	39	1-4	3	41	32	10	3.69
1993	Oakland	52	42	1-4	1	30	21	20	2.81

JOHN HOPE

Pittsburgh Pirates

Righthanded Pitcher

$16

The Pirates third-round draft pick in 1989, he hasn't really pitched Triple-A yet, just four games with a 6.33 ERA. The newspapers say he has throws 90, but if that's true he must not have any breaking pitch at all, because he gets a strikeout about as often as a pig gets caviar. Excellent control, history of serious injuries . . . Grade D prospect.

YEAR	TEAM/LEVEL	G	IP	W-L	PCT.	HITS	SO	BB	ERA
1992	Salem A	27	176	11-8	.579	169	106	46	3.47
1993	AA and AAA	25	133	11-5	.688	133	72	31	4.68
1993	Pittsburgh	7	38	0-2	.000	47	8	8	4.03

SAM HORN
Cleveland Indians
Designated Hitter
$19

Horn played '93 for Charlotte, the Indians Triple-A affiliate, where he walloped 38 homers in 122 games. Called up, he compiled a neat .848 slugging percentage for the big team, 33 at bats . . . I know I've said this before, but Horn is pretty much the same player as Cecil Fielder; he's just lefthanded and can't catch a break. The Indians have Ramirez, Sorrento, Jefferson and Milligan, so there's no job for him here.

YEAR	TEAM/LEVEL	G	AB	R	H	2B	3B	HR	RBI	BB	SB	AVG	OBP	SLG
1992	Baltimore	63	152	13	38	10	1	5	19	21	0	.235	.326	.401
1993	MLE	122	386	45	92	13	0	30	70	44	0	.238	.316	.505
1993	Cleveland	12	33	8	15	1	0	4	8	1	0	.455	.472	.848

VINCE HORSMAN
Oakland Athletics
Relief Pitcher
$14

The A's second lefthander in the bullpen, pitched well in 1992 but not so well last year. Lefthanders hit .203 against him in '92, but .304 last year . . . Horsman, a native of Nova Scotia, was signed by Toronto as part of their unending effort to find Canadian players who can actually play. He bounced between Knoxville and Dunedin from 1988 to 1991, before the Jays finally gave up on him . . . Best pitch is his curve.

YEAR	TEAM/LEVEL	G	IP	W-L	SAVES	HITS	SO	BB	ERA
1992	Oakland	58	43	2-1	1	39	18	21	2.49
1993	Tacoma AAA	26	34	1-2	3	37	23	9	4,28
1993	Oakland	40	25	2-0	0	25	17	15	5.40

DWAYNE HOSEY
San Diego Padres
Outfielder
$12

An outfielder who has been in several other systems (White Sox, Oakland, Milwaukee); he didn't play in the majors and isn't a big prospect, but I decided to put him in the book because the Padres need players, and I think he is now close to finding a niche. A 27-year-old switch hitter, small, steals 20 or more bases a year in the minors. No star material but can play a little.

YEAR	TEAM/LEVEL	G	AB	R	H	2B	3B	HR	RBI	BB	SB	AVG	OBP	SLG
1993	Wichita AA	86	326	52	95	19	2	18	61	25	13	.291	.342	.528
1993	Las Vegas AAA	32	110	21	29	4	2	3	12	11	7	.264	.352	.455
1993	MLE	118	418	55	106	17	2	19	56	24	13	.254	.294	.440

STEVE HOSEY
San Francisco Giants
Outfielder
$13

Also had two at bats with the Giants in '93, which don't show in the chart below. A big guy who can run, he was a number-one draft pick in 1989, and has received the press attention which accompanies that. I've always been skeptical about his future and still am, but he had a better year in his second year at Triple-A, and is close to being a useful player now. Grade C prospect.

YEAR	TEAM/LEVEL	G	AB	R	H	2B	3B	HR	RBI	BB	SB	AVG	OBP	SLG
1992	MLE	125	433	42	103	22	3	6	42	24	9	.238	.278	.344
1992	San Fran NL	21	56	6	14	1	0	1	6	0	1	.250	.241	.321
1993	MLE	129	428	48	106	32	2	11	58	44	10	.248	.318	.409

CHARLIE HOUGH
Florida Marlins
Starting Pitcher
$27

Before '93 Benito Santiago had not been charged with a passed ball in 263 games. He had 23 last year—all of them when Hough was pitching . . . Led National League in pickoff throws per baserunner (1.77) . . . Pitched as well last year as he had in several years, and is expected to re-sign with the Marlins . . . Has an awful record on artificial turf. Is still capable of producing a better record than 9-16. Is 73 years old.

YEAR	TEAM/LEVEL	G	IP	W-L	PCT.	HITS	SO	BB	ERA
1991	Chicago	31	199	9-10	.474	167	107	94	4.02
1992	Chicago	27	176	7-12	.368	160	76	66	3.93
1993	Florida	34	204	9-16	.360	202	126	71	4.27

WAYNE HOUSIE
Milwaukee Brewers
Outfielder
$10

No prospect probably, a small 28-year-old switch hitter who can run. He has played almost a thousand minor league games since signing with the Tigers system in 1986. His minor league batting average is .252, his slugging percentage .342, his strikeout/walk ratio is poor and has degenerated in recent seasons. The Brewers, who love fast guys more than ballplayers, got him in exchange for Josias Manzanillo.

YEAR	TEAM/LEVEL	G	AB	R	H	2B	3B	HR	RBI	BB	SB	AVG	OBP	SLG
1992	Pawtucket AAA	134	456	53	100	22	5	2	28	32	20	.219	.274	.309
1993	N Orleans AAA	64	113	18	31	6	1	0	7	18	6	.274	.379	.345
1993	New York NL	18	16	2	3	1	0	0	1	1	0	.188	.235	.250

CHRIS HOWARD
Seattle Mariners
Catcher
$8

A 28-year-old catcher who has carried the good field/no hit label for many years, but who hit .320 at Calgary in '93. He had never before hit higher than .253, anywhere, and it assumed that his 1993 performance is a fluke. On the other hand, it's always possible that he figured something out . . . The acquisition of Dan Wilson, who is a similar type of player, probably freezes him out in Seattle.

YEAR	TEAM/LEVEL	G	AB	R	H	2B	3B	HR	RBI	BB	SB	AVG	OBP	SLG
1993	Calgary AAA	94	331	40	106	23	0	6	55	23	1	.320	.371	.444
1993	MLE	94	309	26	84	19	0	3	37	15	0	.272	.306	.362
1993	Seattle	4	1	0	0	0	0	0	0	1	0	.143	.250	.286

CHRIS HOWARD
Chicago White Sox
Pitcher
$14

Howard is a lefthander, looking for a shot as a member of the bullpen staff. He was undrafted, signed with the Yankees as a free agent and made it as far as Albany, then was released in 1990. The White Sox signed him as a roster filler, but he has pitched efficiently for several years, and at 28 is almost ready to get a good shot at the job he wants. Grade D prospect.

YEAR	TEAM/LEVEL	G	IP	W-L	SAVES	HITS	SO	BB	ERA
1992	Vancouver AAA	20	25	3-1	0	18	23	22	2.92
1993	Nashville AAA	43	67	4-3	3	55	53	16	3.38
1993	Chicago	3	2	1-0	0	2	1	3	0.00

DAVID HOWARD
Kansas City Royals
Infield
$14

Howard is a much better player now than he was three years ago, when the Royals rushed him into a major league job. He has had back and knee trouble and a bout with Bell's Palsey, plus he should never have been considered as someone who could play regularly, but he's an excellent bunter, a pretty good baserunner and can play shortstop better than a typical backup infielder. There's a place for him as a utility infielder.

YEAR	TEAM/LEVEL	G	AB	R	H	2B	3B	HR	RBI	BB	SB	AVG	OBP	SLG
1992	Kansas City	74	219	19	49	6	2	1	18	15	3	.224	.271	.283
1993	Kansas City	15	24	5	8	0	1	0	2	2	1	.333	.370	.417
1994	**Projected**	**76**	**138**	**12**	**30**	**3**	**1**	**1**	**11**	**9**	**2**	**.217**	**.265**	**.275**

THOMAS HOWARD
Cincinnati Reds
Left Field/Center Field
$16

I don't remember what I wrote about Mike Felder, but whatever it was, it probably applies here, too. Howard is a switch hitter, runs well, and can hit .300 for about two months at a time. He's a good player in a supporting role, but for some reason there is always some manager who is trying to make him a regular, and he just doesn't create enough runs to hold the job. Played '93 with Cleveland and Cincinnati.

YEAR	TEAM/LEVEL	G	AB	R	H	2B	3B	HR	RBI	BB	SB	AVG	OBP	SLG
1992	Two Teams	122	361	37	100	15	2	2	32	17	15	.277	.308	.346
1993	Two Teams	112	319	48	81	15	3	7	36	24	10	.254	.302	.386
1994	**Projected**	**111**	**313**	**41**	**82**	**17**	**2**	**4**	**32**	**23**	**13**	**.262**	**.313**	**.367**

STEVE HOWE
New York Yankees
Relief Pitcher
$13

After years of pitching brilliantly while bouncing on and off the ineligible list, he finally got in a full season, but pitched poorly. I will be surprised if he comes back. He is, after all, 36 years old, and he struck out only 19 men in 51 innings, 3.35 per game (almost nobody can pitch effectively under four). Assuming that he does come back, then you've got to worry about his 178th relapse. Forget about him.

YEAR	TEAM/LEVEL	G	IP	W-L	SAVES	HITS	SO	BB	ERA
1991	New York	37	48	3-1	3	39	34	7	1.68
1992	New York	20	22	3-0	6	9	12	3	2.45
1993	New York	51	51	3-5	4	58	19	10	4.97

JAY HOWELL
Atlanta Braves
Relief Pitcher
$29

Removed from the closer role there was less pressure to get him in the game when he wasn't 100%, and he pitched more games and innings than he had since 1989 . . . Posted 0.41 ERA in 20 games after August first . . . Now 38 years old, has had knee and elbow troubles for most of the last 10 years, but still a fine pitcher. And still the worst All-Star selection of all time, by John McNamara in 1987.

YEAR	TEAM/LEVEL	G	IP	W-L	SAVES	HITS	SO	BB	ERA
1991	Los Angeles	44	51	6-5	16	39	40	11	3.18
1992	Los Angeles	41	47	1-3	4	41	36	18	1.54
1993	Atlanta	54	58	3-3	0	48	37	16	2.31

DANN HOWITT
Seattle Mariners
Outfielder
$6

Howitt, a perennial prospect because of his size and strength, spent most of the 1993 season at Calgary, where he hit 21 homers but averaged just .279. I've never believed in him, and since he is now 30 I'm not likely to change my mind. A lefthanded hitter, runs all right, but doesn't control the strike zone and doesn't read breaking pitches.

YEAR	TEAM/LEVEL	G	AB	R	H	2B	3B	HR	RBI	BB	SB	AVG	OBP	SLG
1992	Two AL Teams	35	85	7	16	4	1	2	10	8	1	.188	.250	.329
1993	MLE	95	314	38	74	17	0	14	51	26	4	.236	.294	.424
1993	Seattle	32	76	6	16	3	1	2	8	4	0	.211	.250	.355

KENT HRBEK
Minnesota Twins
First Base
$30

Hit very well in April and September, but nagging injuries to shoulders and knees ruined the rest of the season for him. Hrbek, who hit .300 three times when he was younger, has hit under .250 twice in a row, but his power and walks still generate a good number of runs. His best years are clearly behind him, his contract expires at the end of 1994, and he has expressed a willingness to retire.

YEAR	TEAM/LEVEL	G	AB	R	H	2B	3B	HR	RBI	BB	SB	AVG	OBP	SLG
1992	Minnesota	112	394	52	96	20	0	15	58	71	5	.244	.357	.409
1993	Minnesota	123	392	60	95	11	1	25	83	71	4	.242	.357	.467
1994	**Projected**	**126**	**421**	**63**	**111**	**22**	**1**	**18**	**78**	**72**	**4**	**.264**	**.371**	**.449**

MIKE HUFF
Chicago White Sox
Right Field
$17

Thirty-year-old fifth-outfielder type, has Rickey Henderson's skills but in faint colors. He's a righthanded hitter who runs well and could hit around .270, walk 80 or 100 times a year and hit an occasional homer. He spent most of the year at Nashville, where he had .411 on-base percentage. He was close to breaking through a year or two ago, but broke his shoulder instead, and went back to point A.

YEAR	TEAM/LEVEL	G	AB	R	H	2B	3B	HR	RBI	BB	SB	AVG	OBP	SLG
1992	Chicago	60	115	13	24	5	0	0	8	10	1	.209	.273	.252
1993	MLE	92	331	51	88	10	3	6	25	50	12	.266	.362	.369
1993	Chicago	43	44	4	8	2	0	1	6	9	1	.182	.321	.295

KEITH HUGHES
Cincinnati Reds
Outfield
$13

Time is running out on him (he's 30), but he is too good a player to be trapped in the minors. His assets: He's big (6-3, 210), a lefthanded hitter, and had a .551 slugging percentage at Indianapolis, where 45 of his 81 hits were for extra bases. He runs fairly well, and is said to be a good baserunner. He doesn't throw well, and failed in his one good shot, with Baltimore in 1988.

YEAR	TEAM/LEVEL	G	AB	R	H	2B	3B	HR	RBI	BB	SB	AVG	OBP	SLG
1992	MLE	89	216	29	55	10	2	4	20	20	4	.255	.318	.375
1993	MLE	82	278	46	76	28	3	11	35	34	3	.273	.353	.514
1993	Cincinnati	3	4	0	0	0	0	0	0	0	0	.000	.000	.000

TIM HULETT

Baltimore Orioles
Utilityman
$16

A veteran reserve, well-liked. He got a chance to play at third last year when Gomez was hurt (and not playing well), and hit .300 (with a secondary average of .173). There are other guys I'd rather have as a backup infielder. He doesn't run well, so he can't pinch run. He doesn't have power and doesn't walk much, plus he's righthanded, so he's not much use as a pinch hitter. He can't play short.

YEAR	TEAM/LEVEL	G	AB	R	H	2B	3B	HR	RBI	BB	SB	AVG	OBP	SLG
1992	Baltimore	57	142	11	41	7	2	2	21	10	0	.289	.340	.408
1993	Baltimore	85	260	40	78	15	0	2	23	23	1	.300	.361	.381
1994	**Projected**	**91**	**234**	**28**	**55**	**12**	**1**	**4**	**22**	**18**	**1**	**.235**	**.290**	**.346**

DAVID HULSE

Texas Rangers
Center Field
$29

One of the better newcomers in the American League in '93. A 26-year-old lefthanded hitter, his positives are his speed and the possibility that he could hit .300; his negatives are his lack of power, his lack of plate discipline, a just-fair arm and a long history of hamstring pulls. He'll be in the lineup for several years, but I don't expect to see him on the All-Star team.

YEAR	TEAM/LEVEL	G	AB	R	H	2B	3B	HR	RBI	BB	SB	AVG	OBP	SLG
1992	Texas	32	92	14	28	4	0	0	2	3	3	.304	.326	.348
1993	Texas	114	407	71	118	9	10	1	29	26	29	.290	.333	.369
1994	**Projected**	**129**	**472**	**69**	**134**	**14**	**6**	**3**	**34**	**24**	**26**	**.284**	**.319**	**.358**

MIKE HUMPHREYS

New York Yankees
Outfield
$10

Marginal prospect, a righthanded hitter with no power and just enough speed to get caught stealing a lot (he was 18-for-33 as a base stealer at Columbus). He's been at Columbus for three years, hitting .283, .282 and .288, plus he walks enough to have a good on-base percentage, up in the high threes. The Yankees have better young outfielders; may have a short career as a bench player.

YEAR	TEAM/LEVEL	G	AB	R	H	2B	3B	HR	RBI	BB	SB	AVG	OBP	SLG
1993	Columbus AAA	92	330	59	95	16	2	6	42	52	18	.288	.388	.403
1993	MLE	92	318	48	83	14	1	4	34	42	13	.261	.347	.349
1993	New York	25	35	6	6	2	1	1	6	4	2	.171	.250	.371

TODD HUNDLEY

New York Mets
Catcher
$26

Finished with a strong September, giving him significantly better stats than in his first year—his batting average up 19 points, his slugging percentage up 41 points. His batting average with runners in scoring position jumped from .157 to .276. He is still very young, 25 in May. On the down side, his defense has not been everything that was advertised in advance. With the Mets' fondness for veteran free agents, his job is not safe.

YEAR	TEAM/LEVEL	G	AB	R	H	2B	3B	HR	RBI	BB	SB	AVG	OBP	SLG
1992	New York	123	358	32	75	17	0	7	32	19	3	.209	.256	.316
1993	New York	130	417	40	95	17	2	11	53	23	1	.228	.269	.357
1994	**Projected**	**131**	**424**	**44**	**98**	**19**	**2**	**9**	**48**	**31**	**1**	**.231**	**.284**	**.349**

BRIAN HUNTER
Atlanta Braves
First Base
$18

Exiled to Richmond after the McGriff trade, almost sent to Expos as part of the deal that Denny Martinez vetoed. He has no future in Atlanta with Crime Dog and Klesko around, so it can be assumed he will be somewhere else next year. Like Sam Horn, could drive in 100 runs if he gets his bat started, but also could be a washout. Good defensive first baseman.

YEAR	TEAM/LEVEL	G	AB	R	H	2B	3B	HR	RBI	BB	SB	AVG	OBP	SLG
1992	Atlanta	102	238	34	57	13	2	14	41	21	1	.229	.292	.487
1993	Atlanta	37	80	4	11	3	1	0	8	2	0	.138	.153	.200
1994	**Projected**	**80**	**200**	**23**	**46**	**8**	**1**	**8**	**29**	**14**	**4**	**.230**	**.277**	**.400**

BRIAN HUNTER
Houston Astros
Outfield
$15

A second-round pick in '89, tall and elegant, and Ffast. *Baseball America* tabbed him the second-best prospect in the Texas League, quoting a manager that "the guy is one of the best at getting from first to third that I've seen. Good attitude, too . . . He played hard." He's young, and may be a hell of a player five years from now, but he's already played 560 minor league games, and still has things to work on.

YEAR	TEAM/LEVEL	G	AB	R	H	2B	3B	HR	RBI	BB	SB	AVG	OBP	SLG
1992	Osceola A	131	489	62	146	18	9	1	62	31	39	.299	.344	.378
1993	Jackson AA	133	523	84	154	22	5	10	52	34	35	.294	.338	.413
1993	MLE	133	502	68	133	19	3	7	42	23	27	.265	.297	.357

BRUCE HURST
Colorado Rockies
Starting Pitcher
$5

He made one start in May, one in June, one in August and two in September. In between all that activity he made at least three visits to the disabled list, all of them attributable to shoulder trouble, and was traded to the Black Hole of Calcutta, also known as Mile High Stadium. This put an end to a string of seven straight winning seasons, and he is 36 years old. He faces the odds grimly.

YEAR	TEAM/LEVEL	G	IP	W-L	PCT.	HITS	SO	BB	ERA
1991	San Diego	31	222	15-8	.652	201	141	59	3.29
1992	San Diego	32	217	14-9	.609	223	131	51	3.85
1993	Colorado	5	13	0-2	.000	15	9	6	7.62

BUTCH HUSKEY
New York Mets
Third Base
$15

A 245-pound power hitter, has hit 79 homers in the minors over the last three years, but has yet to try Triple-A. The Mets think he's a third baseman. I've seen a dozen guys that big try to play third base, and none of them could do it, so I'm skeptical. Grade C prospect; *Baseball America* made him the number-five prospect in the Eastern League, which is reasonable in view of his youth (22) and power.

YEAR	TEAM/LEVEL	G	AB	R	H	2B	3B	HR	RBI	BB	SB	AVG	OBP	SLG
1993	Binghmton AA	139	526	72	132	23	1	25	98	48	11	.251	.312	.441
1993	MLE	139	509	58	115	20	0	19	79	33	8	.226	.273	.377
1993	New York	13	41	2	6	1	0	0	3	1	0	.146	.159	.171

JEFF HUSON

Texas Rangers

Infielder

$14

Huson's 1993 season was destroyed by a broken toe, which he tried to come back from too quickly and re-injured. He had been a good utility infielder for the Rangers in two of the previous three years, and will get an opportunity to show that he can still do that job. Lefthanded hitter with a reasonable on-base percentage, runs well, doesn't have a shortstop's arm.

YEAR	TEAM/LEVEL	G	AB	R	H	2B	3B	HR	RBI	BB	SB	AVG	OBP	SLG
1991	Texas	119	268	36	57	8	3	2	26	39	8	.213	.312	.287
1992	Texas	123	318	49	83	14	3	4	24	41	18	.261	.342	.362
1993	Texas	23	45	3	6	1	1	0	2	0	0	.133	.133	.200

MARK HUTTON

New York Yankees

Starting Pitcher

$25

A 6-foot-6, 245-pound Australian; his nickname is "Mate." He's a Don Drysdale type—a big, strong righthander with a real fastball, pitches inside and hits a lot of batters (33 over the last three years). *Baseball America* listed him among the top prospects in his league each of the last two years. There is every reason to think that he'll be good, except that the Yankees are so inept at bringing along a young pitcher.

YEAR	TEAM/LEVEL	G	IP	W-L	PCT.	HITS	SO	BB	ERA
1992	Albany AA	25	165	13-7	.650	146	128	66	3.59
1993	Columbus AAA	21	133	10-4	.714	98	112	53	3.18
1993	New York	7	22	1-1	.500	24	12	17	5.73

MIKE IGNASIAK

Milwaukee Brewers

Relief Pitcher

$25

Since he entered pro ball in 1988 he has pitched well or brilliantly at every stop except for four games with Milwaukee in '91. As a starter from '88 to '91 he was 33-19. Converted to the bullpen, he posted a 2.93 ERA at Denver, Mile High Stadium, then posted eye-popping numbers at New Orleans—1.09 ERA, 26 hits allowed in 58 innings. I believe he may be the Brewers closer within 2-3 years.

YEAR	TEAM/LEVEL	G	IP	W-L	SAVES	HITS	SO	BB	ERA
1992	Denver AAA	62	92	7-4	10	83	64	33	2.93
1993	New Orleans AAA	35	58	6-0	9	26	61	20	1.09
1993	Milwaukee	27	37	1-1	0	32	28	21	3.65

PETE INCAVIGLIA

Philadelphia Phillies

Left Field

$29

One of the most amazing statistics of the 1993 season: Philadelphia sixth-place hitters—*sixth-place hitters*—drove in 133 runs in '93. No other NL team got that many RBI from any spot in the batting order. San Francisco cleanup hitters were second, driving in 132 . . . Philadelphia left fielders drove in 120 runs; their right fielders hit .316 and drove in 105 . . . Platooning remains an under-used strategy in modern baseball.

YEAR	TEAM/LEVEL	G	AB	R	H	2B	3B	HR	RBI	BB	SB	AVG	OBP	SLG
1992	Houston	113	349	31	93	22	1	11	44	25	2	.266	.319	.430
1993	Philadelphia	116	368	60	101	16	3	24	89	21	1	.274	.318	.530
1994	**Projected**	**96**	**358**	**45**	**92**	**17**	**2**	**16**	**57**	**29**	**2**	**.257**	**.313**	**.450**

JEFF INNIS

New York Mets

Relief Pitcher

$22

Here's a question for you: did ground-ball pitchers, as a group, have a poor year in 1993? It seems to me that they did, that the league ERA rode up on the backs of ground-ball pitchers. But I can't prove that. I can prove that the *Mets* had an off year . . . Struggled early, but finished the season pitching well. Won't move up, but should regain his effectiveness this year.

YEAR	TEAM/LEVEL	G	IP	W-L	SAVES	HITS	SO	BB	ERA
1991	New York	69	85	0-2	0	66	47	23	2.66
1992	New York	76	88	6-9	1	85	39	36	2.86
1993	New York	67	77	2-3	3	81	36	38	4.11

BO JACKSON

Free Agent

Designated Hitter

$19

The Sox elected to decline his option, leaving him free to pursue another team (Bo Knows Rejection). White Sox designated hitters hit 22 homers and drove in 103, but averaged just .214 and scored only 64 runs. They have released both DHs, Jackson and Bell, apparently intending to scoot Thomas into the role . . . I have always felt that the "Bo Show" was irrelevant to and a distraction from what the team should be trying to do.

YEAR	TEAM/LEVEL	G	AB	R	H	2B	3B	HR	RBI	BB	SB	AVG	OBP	SLG
1991	Chicago	23	71	8	16	4	0	3	14	12	0	.225	.333	.408
1992	Chicago	(Out for season—Installing a new hip)												
1993	Chicago	85	284	32	66	9	0	16	45	23	0	.232	.289	.433

DANNY JACKSON

Philadelphia Phillies

Starting Pitcher

$30

His stats for the last two years almost perfectly mirror his career numbers, an ERA of 3.80 for the last two years (3.82 career), a won-lost record of 20-24 (career 93-103), suggesting that his value has finally stabilized after years of bouncing up and down. He probably won't last more than one or two more years. He's been injured several times, and his next injury will finish him.

YEAR	TEAM/LEVEL	G	IP	W-L	PCT.	HITS	SO	BB	ERA
1991	Chicago NL	17	71	1-5	.167	89	31	48	6.75
1992	Two Teams	34	201	8-13	.381	211	97	77	3.84
1993	Philadelphia	32	210	12-11	.522	214	120	80	3.77

DARRIN JACKSON

New York Mets

Center Field

$21

If the Mets truly believe that Darrin Jackson is in the same range of value as Tony Fernandez, it is easy to undertsand how they lost 103 games. Here's a rule of thumb for you: if a guy has as many GIDP (double play balls) as walks, you don't want him on your team. Jackson in the last two seasons has been almost even . . . Has modest power and speed, which creates some rotisserie value, but can't really play.

YEAR	TEAM/LEVEL	G	AB	R	H	2B	3B	HR	RBI	BB	SB	AVG	OBP	SLG
1992	San Diego	155	587	72	146	23	5	17	70	26	14	.249	.283	.392
1993	Two Teams	77	263	19	55	9	0	6	26	10	0	.209	.237	.312
1994	**Projected**	**77**	**254**	**29**	**80**	**8**	**1**	**8**	**29**	**14**	**4**	**.236**	**.276**	**.370**

MIKE JACKSON

San Francisco Giants

Relief Pitcher

$28

Led the major leagues in game appearances, with 81, and holds, with 34. No one else had more than 25 holds . . . The presence of Rod Beck on the team, along with some other quality relievers, has finally allowed him to escape from the curse of unlimited potential, and settle into just being a good pitcher . . . Only 29, he must have pitched about as many major league games as anybody in history has pitched by the same age.

YEAR	TEAM/LEVEL	G	IP	W-L	SAVES	HITS	SO	BB	ERA
1991	Seattle	72	89	7-7	14	64	74	34	3.25
1992	San Francisco	67	82	6-6	2	76	80	33	3.73
1993	San Francisco	81	77	6-6	1	58	70	24	3.03

JOHN JAHA

Milwaukee Brewers

First Base

$33

He ended the season hot, hitting 14 homers and driving in 39 runs after August 1. A little quick math will show you that he hadn't done much of anything *before* August 1, leaving open the question: is he the kind of guy who can hit seven homers a month, or isn't he? He isn't, but he could hit a little better than '93—could hit .280 with 25-30 homers . . . OK baserunner and first baseman.

YEAR	TEAM/LEVEL	G	AB	R	H	2B	3B	HR	RBI	BB	SB	AVG	OBP	SLG
1992	Milwaukee	47	133	17	30	3	1	2	10	12	10	.226	.291	.308
1993	Milwaukee	153	515	78	136	21	0	19	70	51	13	.264	.337	.416
1994	**Projected**	**151**	**514**	**88**	**144**	**27**	**1**	**21**	**85**	**58**	**14**	**.280**	**.353**	**.459**

CHRIS JAMES

Texas Rangers

Left Field

$18

Spent most of the year with Houston; was traded to Texas in mid-September and had one of his famous hot streaks in late September, giving his season's stats an entirely different look. James has tremendous bat speed, and could be valuable as a righthanded platoon player/pinch hitter. Originally thought to be a good outfielder, has had some shoulder injuries which left him with bad-glove reputation, but played better last year.

YEAR	TEAM/LEVEL	G	AB	R	H	2B	3B	HR	RBI	BB	SB	AVG	OBP	SLG
1992	San Francisco	111	248	25	60	10	4	5	32	14	2	.242	.285	.375
1993	Two Teams	73	160	24	44	11	1	9	26	18	2	.275	.348	.525
1994	**Projected**	**72**	**157**	**15**	**39**	**7**	**1**	**4**	**18**	**9**	**1**	**.248**	**.289**	**.382**

DION JAMES

New York Yankees

Left Field

$27

He was platooning, sort of, with Jim Leyritz; against a lefthanded pitcher Leyritz or Tartabull would go into right field, O'Neill switching to left. It was an extremely productive platoon, one of the best in baseball, and a classic instruction on the intelligent use of a limited player. By playing James in left field and sitting him down against righthanders, Showalter hid the things that he doesn't do well.

YEAR	TEAM/LEVEL	G	AB	R	H	2B	3B	HR	RBI	BB	SB	AVG	OBP	SLG
1992	New York	67	145	24	38	8	0	3	17	22	1	.262	.359	.379
1993	New York	115	343	62	114	21	2	7	36	31	0	.332	.390	.466
1994	**Projected**	**112**	**291**	**48**	**84**	**18**	**2**	**5**	**30**	**32**	**0**	**.289**	**.359**	**.416**

STAN JAVIER
California Angels
Utility Outfielder
$23

An exceptionally good fourth outfielder—a switch hitter who can play any outfield position, fair arm, outstanding baserunner (lifetime 84% base stealer, 95 for 113). He falls asleep on the field once in a while, and doesn't have the power of a regular left/right fielder, but has good on-base percentages. Can be used as pinch hitter either way, pinch runner, defensive outfielder.

YEAR	TEAM/LEVEL	G	AB	R	H	2B	3B	HR	RBI	BB	SB	AVG	OBP	SLG
1992	Two Teams	130	334	42	83	17	1	1	29	37	18	.249	.327	.314
1993	California	92	237	33	69	10	4	3	28	27	12	.291	.362	.405
1994	**Projected**	**119**	**254**	**33**	**62**	**11**	**3**	**2**	**24**	**29**	**12**	**.244**	**.322**	**.335**

DOMINGO JEAN
New York Yankees
Starting Pitcher
$19

My guess, and it is strictly a guess, is that Jean is *not* ready to win at the major league level. He has pitched only 151 innings above A ball, counting the 40 innings with the Yankees. I think four or five hundred innings of good competition would be more appropriate. I'm also a big believer in one of Earl Weaver's Rules: the best place for a rookie pitcher is long relief. Obviously, Jean's equipment is first rate.

YEAR	TEAM/LEVEL	G	IP	W-L	PCT.	HITS	SO	BB	ERA
1993	Albany AA	11	61	5-3	.625	42	41	33	2.51
1993	Columbus AAA	7	45	2-2	.500	40	39	13	2.82
1993	New York	10	40	1-1	.500	37	20	19	4.46

GREGG JEFFERIES
St. Louis Cardinals
First Base
$52

The two stories which tell you most about the collapse of the Mets are not Strawberry and Gooden and not Coleman and Saberhagen, but Dykstra and Jefferies. If you create a situation in which a young player cannot thrive even if he has MVP ability, then how can you expect the *team* to deal successfully with that environment? . . . 1993 was the first of a string of outstanding seasons for Jefferies.

YEAR	TEAM/LEVEL	G	AB	R	H	2B	3B	HR	RBI	BB	SB	AVG	OBP	SLG
1992	Kansas City	152	604	66	172	36	3	10	75	43	19	.285	.329	.404
1993	St. Louis	142	544	89	186	24	3	16	83	62	46	.342	.408	.485
1994	**Projected**	**150**	**567**	**77**	**171**	**31**	**3**	**15**	**80**	**55**	**32**	**.302**	**.363**	**.446**

REGGIE JEFFERSON
Cleveland Indians
First Base
$24

What Jefferson did in '93 is a fair estimate of what he might be expected to do in the future, allowing that he will probably improve some with experience, and his numbers would be more impressive with another 200 at bats. I've never believed he had star potential, and since he is now competing for playing time with Manny Ramirez, who *does* have star potential, it may be a couple of years before he becomes a full-time player.

YEAR	TEAM/LEVEL	G	AB	R	H	2B	3B	HR	RBI	BB	SB	AVG	OBP	SLG
1992	Cleveland	24	89	8	30	6	2	1	6	1	0	.337	.352	.483
1993	Cleveland	113	366	35	91	11	2	10	34	28	1	.249	.310	.372
1994	**Projected**	**110**	**350**	**43**	**94**	**15**	**2**	**10**	**43**	**26**	**1**	**.269**	**.319**	**.409**

DOUG JENNINGS

Chicago Cubs

First Base/Pinch Hitter

$13

Small lefthanded power hitter, looks shorter than his listed size (5-10) but generates tremendous bat speed. Is 29 years old; has been trying for years to find a spot on a major league roster, and helped his cause with a couple of pinch-hit home runs after being called up in June. No chance of taking Mark Grace's job, but will probably have Gerald Perry-type assignment this season.

YEAR	TEAM/LEVEL	G	AB	R	H	2B	3B	HR	RBI	BB	SB	AVG	OBP	SLG
1993	Iowa AAA	65	228	38	67	20	1	7	37	29	3	.294	.380	.482
1993	MLE	65	217	29	56	16	0	5	28	22	2	.258	.326	.401
1993	Chicago	42	52	8	13	3	1	2	8	3	0	.250	.316	.462

MIGUEL JIMINEZ

Oakland Athletics

Starting Pitcher

$10

A 24-year-old New Yorker, graduated from Fordham in 1991, apparently with a degree in pitching behind the hitters. He has walked 203 men in 305 minor league innings so far, pitching about .500 ball despite this. With the A's he added 16 walks in 27 innings, surviving with a decent record anyway, but in the long run that will get you every time. I don't see any way he'll be a successful major league pitcher in '94.

YEAR	TEAM/LEVEL	G	IP	W-L	PCT.	HITS	SO	BB	ERA
1993	Huntsville AA	20	107	10-6	.625	92	105	64	2.94
1993	Tacoma AAA	8	38	2-3	.400	32	34	24	4.78
1993	Oakland	5	27	1-0	1.000	27	13	16	4.00

DAVE JOHNSON

Detroit Tigers

Pitcher

$6

If you were wondering exactly how low Detroit had sunk in their search for pitching, this is the answer. Johnson won 13 for Baltimore in 1990, and was noted for being impossible to run against. His control is willing but his arm is weak, and he disappeared from the league after a 7.07 ERA in '91. He pitched well at Toledo in April, got called up, but wound up on the 60-day DL with an eye infection.

YEAR	TEAM/LEVEL	G	IP	W-L	PCT.	HITS	SO	BB	ERA
1991	Baltimore	22	84	4-8	.333	127	38	24	7.07
1992	Toledo AAA	25	53	4-4	.500	60	29	17	4.27
1993	Detroit	6	8	1-1	.500	13	7	5	12.96

ERIC JOHNSON

San Francisco Giants

Infielder

$2

A 28-year-old infielder, he was called up for 10 days in July, and got into four games. He hasn't hit a home run in two years, is a 37% base stealer over those two seasons and is a career .235 hitter in the minor leagues. Apart from that, he looks pretty good . . . Doesn't walk. Grounds into a few two many double plays. No prospect.

YEAR	TEAM/LEVEL	G	AB	R	H	2B	3B	HR	RBI	BB	SB	AVG	OBP	SLG
1992	Phoenix AAA	90	229	24	55	5	1	0	19	20	8	.240	.306	.271
1993	Phoenix AAA	101	363	33	90	8	5	0	33	29	3	.248	.303	.298
1993	MLE	101	344	22	71	6	2	0	22	19	1	.206	.248	.235

HOWARD JOHNSON

New York Mets

Third Base

$37

His last two seasons have been ruined by a broken right wrist, a virus and a broken thumb. There's no reason he shouldn't be Comeback Player of the Year. He is only 33, and a good enough player that he *should* have several years left. The injuries are the kind that should heal. If he leaves the Mets that's a positive for him, because Shea Stadium is a tough place to hit.

YEAR	TEAM/LEVEL	G	AB	R	H	2B	3B	HR	RBI	BB	SB	AVG	OBP	SLG
1991	New York	156	564	108	146	34	4	38	117	78	30	.259	.342	.535
1992	New York	100	350	48	78	19	0	7	43	55	22	.223	.329	.337
1993	New York	72	235	32	56	8	2	7	26	43	6	.238	.354	.379

JEFF JOHNSON

New York Yankees

Starting Pitcher

$7

He pitched two and two/thirds innings with the Yankees in '93, giving up nine earned runs (30.38 ERA). This lifted his career earned run average, for almost two hundred innings, to 6.47. His career batting average allowed with runners in scoring position is .374. He didn't pitch well last year with Columbus, giving up more than a hit an inning, and walking almost as many as he struck out. I don't see much here to like.

YEAR	TEAM/LEVEL	G	IP	W-L	PCT.	HITS	SO	BB	ERA
1992	Columbus AAA	11	58	2-1	.667	41	36	18	2.17
1993	Columbus AAA	19	115	7-6	.538	125	59	47	3.45
1992	New York	13	53	2-3	.400	71	14	23	6.66

LANCE JOHNSON

Chicago White Sox

Center Field

$33

The only major league regular who didn't hit a home run in '93—and then he hit one in the playoffs. Regularly leads the league in triples . . . Had the highest ground ball/fly ball ratio in the American League (265-110) . . . An ordinary hitter, scores 70-75 runs every year and drives in 45-50, but an exceptional fielder. Usually bats seventh for the White Sox . . . Should have six-eight more years of performance at this level.

YEAR	TEAM/LEVEL	G	AB	R	H	2B	3B	HR	RBI	BB	SB	AVG	OBP	SLG
1991	Chicago	160	588	72	161	14	13	0	49	26	26	.274	.304	.342
1992	Chicago	157	567	67	158	15	12	3	47	34	41	.279	.318	.363
1993	Chicago	147	540	75	168	18	14	0	47	36	35	.311	.354	.396

RANDY JOHNSON

Seattle Mariners

Starting Pitcher

$76

He threw 124 pitches per start, the highest of any major league pitcher . . . His strikeouts have gone up every year since he came to the majors: 25, 130, 194, 228, 241, 308. His control has improved dramatically, his walks per game dropping by 49% in the last two years . . . He almost never faces a lefthanded batter, only 71 at bats by lefties last year. Lefthanders just don't play against him.

YEAR	TEAM/LEVEL	G	IP	W-L	PCT.	HITS	SO	BB	ERA
1991	Seattle	33	201	13-10	.565	151	228	152	3.98
1992	Seattle	31	210	12-14	.462	154	241	144	3.77
1993	Seattle	35	255	19-8	.704	185	308	99	3.24

JOEL JOHNSTON

Pittsburgh Pirates

Relief Pitcher

$18

He was pitching horribly at Buffalo when Leyland, for some reason, decided to go and get him. It seemed to work out . . . Maybe Leyland had sent him to Buffalo to work on one key pitch or something. The Pirates have been collecting young pitchers with good arms, and he certainly qualifies. He is big and strong and throws hard; could emerge as a closer if he develops a strikeout pitch.

YEAR	TEAM/LEVEL	G	IP	W-L	SAVES	HITS	SO	BB	ERA
1992	Omaha AAA	42	75	5-2	2	80	48	45	6.39
1993	Buffalo AAA	26	31	1-3	1	30	26	25	7.76
1993	Pittsburgh	33	53	2-4	2	38	31	19	3.38

JOHN JOHNSTONE

Florida Marlins

Pitcher

$11

Taken from the Mets in the third round of the expansion draft, Johnstone didn't have a good year at Triple-A, but was called up in September anyway because, hey, who else were the Marlins going to take a look at? Unless something surprising happens, he'll begin 1994 back at Edmonton. Grade C prospect, a good arm and good control.

YEAR	TEAM/LEVEL	G	IP	W-L	PCT.	HITS	SO	BB	ERA
1992	Binghamton AA	24	149	7-7	.500	132	121	36	3.74
1993	Edmonton AAA	30	144	4-15	.211	167	126	59	5.18
1993	Florida	7	11	0-2	.000	16	5	7	5.91

BARRY JONES

Chicago White Sox

Relief Pitcher

$5

Jones had a real good year pitching middle relief for the White Sox in 1990 (11-4, 2.31 ERA). He was traded to Montreal in the Tim Raines deal, and had flamed out of the league, being released by Philadelphia and the Mets. He signed with the White Sox as a free agent, and was called up in late April, but was hit hard again. His career is probably over.

YEAR	TEAM/LEVEL	G	IP	W-L	SAVES	HITS	SO	BB	ERA
1992	Two Teams	61	70	7-6	1	85	30	35	5.68
1993	Nashville AAA	7	17	0-0	2	16	19	2	2.60
1993	Chicago	6	7	0-1	0	14	7	3	8.59

BOBBY J. JONES

New York Mets

Starting Pitcher

$30

The only thing about him that's *not* to like is that he pitches for a bad team, which may mean, if the Mets continue to reek, that he won't be able to pile up wins. Other than that, everything is good news—went to the same high school as Tom Seaver in Fresno, California, drafted as a sandwich pick between first and second rounds, throws hard, throws strikes, has pitched well everywhere he has been. **Grade A prospect.**

YEAR	TEAM/LEVEL	G	IP	W-L	PCT.	HITS	SO	BB	ERA
1992	Binghamton AA	23	180	11-4	.733	113	137	42	1.98
1993	Norfolk AAA	24	166	12-10	.545	149	126	32	3.63
1993	New York	9	62	2-4	.333	61	35	22	3.65

CHIPPER JONES
Atlanta Braves
Shortstop
$40

Unless something tremendously unexpected happens, this guy is going to be a major league star. His defense at short doesn't draw rave reviews, but he has the equipment to play the position, and is probably going to hit enough to become a star second baseman, third baseman or outfielder if need be. Could play short this year if Blauser leaves, or third base if Pendleton is traded, or could take Lemke's job. **Grade A prospect.**

YEAR	TEAM/LEVEL	G	AB	R	H	2B	3B	HR	RBI	BB	SB	AVG	OBP	SLG
1992	MLE	67	258	35	84	15	5	9	35	7	9	.326	.343	.527
1993	Richmond	139	536	97	174	31	12	13	89	57	23	.325	.387	.500
1993	MLE	139	512	71	150	26	5	11	65	40	14	.293	.344	.428

CHRIS JONES
Colorado Rockies
Center Field
$17

Cut from the same mold as Galarraga, Hayes, and Bichette—a righthanded hitter with some power and an awful strikeout/walk ratio. The group seems to like Mile High Stadium, or Don Baylor's management, or Amos Otis's hitting instruction, or something. Jones actually hit better on the road than in Colorado . . . 28-year-old minor league veteran, runs well and may benefit from the release of Alex Cole, but doubt that he can hold a regular job.

YEAR	TEAM/LEVEL	G	AB	R	H	2B	3B	HR	RBI	BB	SB	AVG	OBP	SLG
1992	Houston	54	63	7	12	2	1	1	4	7	3	.190	.271	.302
1993	Colorado	86	209	29	57	11	4	6	31	10	9	.273	.305	.450
1994	**Projected**	**97**	**245**	**28**	**55**	**10**	**2**	**5**	**26**	**15**	**7**	**.224**	**.269**	**.343**

DOUG JONES
Houston Astros
Closer
$20

When Jones's effectiveness left him in Cleveland in '91 it was believed that he had developed a "tell," that he was tipping his pitches. Whatever the gremlin was, it returned last year, and the league hit .298 against him, not really what you're looking for in a closer. He is 36 years old, 37 in mid-summer, and he has worked awfully hard over the last two years. I suspect the Astros will have to replace him.

YEAR	TEAM/LEVEL	G	IP	W-L	SAVES	HITS	SO	BB	ERA
1991	Cleveland	36	63	4-8	7	87	48	17	5.54
1992	Houston	80	112	11-8	36	96	93	17	1.85
1993	Houston	71	85	4-10	26	102	66	21	4.54

JIMMY JONES
Montreal Expos
Starting Pitcher
$14

Has managed to keep his career record over .500 so far (43-39), and if he wants to keep it that way I would say it is probably time for him to retire. Jones signed with the Expos as a free agent and opened the season in their rotation, but made two trips to the disabled list with an inflamed elbow, and was sent to the minors in July. Marginal pitcher, useful as a long reliever/spot starter.

YEAR	TEAM/LEVEL	G	IP	W-L	PCT.	HITS	SO	BB	ERA
1991	Houston	26	135	6-8	.429	143	88	51	4.39
1992	Houston	25	139	10-6	.625	135	69	39	4.07
1993	Montreal	12	40	4-1	.800	47	21	9	6.35

TIM JONES

St. Louis Cardinals

Shortstop/Second Base

$15

Spent most of the '93 season at Louisville, and had a good year there (.289, MLE of .260). Jones is a good infielder, and might be as good a hitter as the Dick Schofield/Spike Owen types, but the Cardinals have never had a place for him to play, what with Ozzie at short and a cast of thousands vying for the second base job. Lefthanded bat, runs well, doesn't chase bad pitches, now 31 years old.

YEAR	TEAM/LEVEL	G	AB	R	H	2B	3B	HR	RBI	BB	SB	AVG	OBP	SLG
1991	St. Louis	16	24	1	4	2	0	0	2	2	0	.167	.222	.250
1992	St. Louis	67	145	9	29	4	0	0	3	11	5	.200	.256	.228
1993	St. Louis	29	61	13	16	6	0	0	1	9	2	.262	.366	.361

TODD JONES

Houston Astros

Relief Pitcher

$17

Excessive walks have dogged him through most of his career, but he made the majors in early July, and his major league control record was the best of his career. A sandwich pick in 1989 (the Astros got him as compensation for the loss of Nolan Ryan), he's been moved steadily up through the minors although he's never really pitched very well. Grade C prospect.

YEAR	TEAM/LEVEL	G	IP	W-L	SAVES	HITS	SO	BB	ERA
1992	Jackson AA	61	66	3-7	25	53	60	44	3.14
1993	Tucson AAA	41	49	4-2	12	49	45	31	4.44
1993	Houston	27	37	1-2	2	28	25	15	3.13

BRIAN JORDAN

St. Louis Cardinals

Outfielder

$34

With some obvious differences, I would compare him to a young Kirk Gibson. In 122 major league games, 416 at bats, he's hit 15 homers, 10 triples, has stolen 13 bases, driven in 66, averaged .262. One *has* to believe, based on that, that he's going to be at least a minor star, a 20-homer, 20-stolen-base guy. The Cardinals have four outfielders who have to play, but that will work itself out somehow.

YEAR	TEAM/LEVEL	G	AB	R	H	2B	3B	HR	RBI	BB	SB	AVG	OBP	SLG
1992	St. Louis	55	193	17	40	9	4	5	22	10	7	.207	.250	.373
1993	Louisville AAA	38	144	24	54	13	2	5	35	16	9	.375	.442	.597
1993	St. Louis	67	223	33	69	10	6	10	44	12	6	.309	.351	.510

RICKY JORDAN

Philadelphia Phillies

First Base

$20

He's the odd man out on a team that drew 665 walks last year, most in the National League. He doesn't create enough runs to be a regular first baseman, plus he has a weak arm which is a liability in the field, but is a consistent .280 hitter with a little bit of power. Also has a career average of .307 as a pinch hitter, with 39 pinch hits.

YEAR	TEAM/LEVEL	G	AB	R	H	2B	3B	HR	RBI	BB	SB	AVG	OBP	SLG
1991	Philadelphia	101	301	38	82	21	3	9	49	14	0	.272	.304	.452
1992	Philadelphia	94	276	33	84	19	0	4	34	5	3	.304	.313	.417
1993	Philadelphia	90	159	21	46	4	1	5	18	8	0	.289	.324	.421

TERRY JORGENSEN
Minnesota Twins
Third Base
$16

If he's going to be a regular, two things are going to have to happen: 1) he's going to have to show that he can play third base *well*, and 2) he's needs to start hitting right now. Jorgensen's MLEs say that he should hit enough to be a regular third baseman, and he has played OK at that position, but he took a couple of left turns before getting to the majors, and the clock is running on him.

YEAR	TEAM/LEVEL	G	AB	R	H	2B	3B	HR	RBI	BB	SB	AVG	OBP	SLG
1992	MLE	135	491	61	135	31	1	10	56	43	1	.275	.333	.403
1993	MLE	61	229	27	64	17	1	2	33	14	0	.279	.321	.389
1993	Minnesota	59	152	15	34	7	0	1	12	10	1	.224	.270	.299

FELIX JOSE
Kansas City Royals
Right Field
$29

Had a shoulder problem all year which didn't allow him to bat righthanded, thus he hit .094 against lefthanded pitchers (6 for 61). A fast runner and tremendously strong, but pushing 30 and has never hit more than 14 homers. Poor outfielder (his .970 fielding percentage was the lowest of any AL right fielder) although he gives a good effort. He is muscle-bound, and subject to the injuries, but I expect him to bounce back.

YEAR	TEAM/LEVEL	G	AB	R	H	2B	3B	HR	RBI	BB	SB	AVG	OBP	SLG
1992	St. Louis	131	509	62	150	22	3	14	75	40	28	.295	.347	.432
1993	Kansas City	149	499	64	126	24	3	6	43	36	31	.253	.303	.349
1994	**Projected**	**153**	**529**	**64**	**144**	**28**	**3**	**10**	**63**	**44**	**27**	**.272**	**.328**	**.393**

WALLY JOYNER
Kansas City Royals
First Base
$35

Rates about even with Don Mattingly. Had a problem with his lower back, which may explain why he has stopped running out ground balls. He's as good a defensive first baseman as you'll see, and he's a surprising hitter, often looks overmatched for two or three pitches in a row, and then will turn on the pitch and hit it hard somewhere. I would be surprised if he has more than one or two good years left.

YEAR	TEAM/LEVEL	G	AB	R	H	2B	3B	HR	RBI	BB	SB	AVG	OBP	SLG
1992	Kansas City	149	572	66	154	36	2	9	66	55	11	.269	.336	.386
1993	Kansas City	141	497	83	145	36	3	15	65	66	5	.292	.375	.467
1994	**Projected**	**144**	**538**	**71**	**148**	**31**	**1**	**16**	**72**	**59**	**6**	**.275**	**.347**	**.426**

JEFF JUDEN
Houston Astros
Starting Pitcher
$21

Only 23 years old, he has bounced onto and off of the prospect lists so many times I've lost count. *Baseball America* didn't put him among the top 10 prospects in the Pacific Coast League in '93, but I'd rather have Juden than the man they listed first (Darrell Whitmore). Juden is a 6-7 righthander with a history of weight problems, but I'll take anybody who is this close to Randy Johnson's size and strikeout rates.

YEAR	TEAM/LEVEL	G	IP	W-L	PCT.	HITS	SO	BB	ERA
1992	Tucson AAA	26	147	9-10	.474	149	120	71	4.04
1993	Tucson AAA	27	169	11-6	.647	174	156	76	4.63
1993	Houston	2	5	0-1	.000	4	7	4	5.40

DAVE JUSTICE

Atlanta Braves

Right Field

$63

Fifth player in history to hit 40 homers with 15 or fewer doubles. The others were Babe Ruth (at age 37), Henry Aaron (at 39), Harmon Killebrew and Frank Howard . . . His stats are extremely similar to those of Jeff Burroughs in Burroughs's first season in Atlanta (41 homers, 115 RBI, .271). Justice is a year older than Burroughs was. That was Burroughs's last good year . . . He's good, but be careful. He's slow and awkward, and he probably won't last.

YEAR	TEAM/LEVEL	G	AB	R	H	2B	3B	HR	RBI	BB	SB	AVG	OBP	SLG
1992	Atlanta	144	484	78	124	19	5	21	72	79	2	.256	.359	.446
1993	Atlanta	157	585	90	158	15	4	40	120	78	3	.270	.357	.515
1994	**Projected**	**155**	**553**	**90**	**146**	**25**	**3**	**29**	**100**	**88**	**6**	**.264**	**.365**	**.477**

JEFF KAISER

New York Mets

Lefty

$5

A 33-year-old reliever who has had trials with Oakland, Cleveland, and Detroit, and who hasn't been regarded as a prospect since Watergate. He had a good year with Toledo in '92, and thus made the Mets' roster in the spring. He went on the DL with an "abrasion of the left index finger" on May 18, which may have ended his last opportunity to be a major league pitcher.

YEAR	TEAM/LEVEL	G	IP	W-L	SAVES	HITS	SO	BB	ERA
1992	Toledo AAA	28	31	1-0	5	25	33	12	2.35
1993	Norfolk AAA	21	22	1-1	9	23	23	6	5.64
1993	New York	9	8	0-0	0	10	9	5	7.88

SCOTT KAMIENIECKI

New York Yankees

Starting Pitcher

$25

Moved back into the Yankees rotation in June, after spending about 10 days at Columbus, and pitched well through the warm months. Kamieniecki throws hard and mixes it up with a curve, slider and changeup. His control is good, and he showed dramatic improvement in cutting off the running game last year . . . In my opinion, he will never get beyond the stage of third/fourth starter.

YEAR	TEAM/LEVEL	G	IP	W-L	PCT.	HITS	SO	BB	ERA
1991	New York	9	55	4-4	.500	54	34	22	3.90
1992	New York	28	188	6-14	.300	193	88	74	4.36
1993	New York	30	154	10-7	.588	163	72	59	4.08

RON KARKOVICE

Chicago White Sox

Catcher

$32

Karkovice is 30 years old, having served a six-year apprenticeship to Carlton Fisk. He finally got the number-one shinguards last year, and did what he should do: hit 20 homers and cut off the running game. He threw out 50% of opposing base stealers (48 of 96), the best percentage for a regular catcher . . . In his career has hit three times as many home runs on the road (42) as he has in Chicago (14).

YEAR	TEAM/LEVEL	G	AB	R	H	2B	3B	HR	RBI	BB	SB	AVG	OBP	SLG
1992	Chicago	123	342	39	81	12	1	13	50	30	10	.237	.302	.392
1993	Chicago	128	403	60	92	17	1	20	54	29	2	.228	.287	.424
1994	**Projected**	**125**	**401**	**53**	**91**	**18**	**1**	**18**	**57**	**34**	**5**	**.227**	**.287**	**.411**

ERIC KARROS

Los Angeles Dodgers

First Base

$29

In a hitter's year he went backward, rather than forward, and hit only .213 after the All-Star break. He may have been swinging for the fences, as his power did increase, or he may have been trying to play through an injury . . . I would see him as a minor star, at best, and I suspect that he might be better cast as a platoon player. This is the key year if he's going to prove me wrong.

YEAR	TEAM/LEVEL	G	AB	R	H	2B	3B	HR	RBI	BB	SB	AVG	OBP	SLG
1992	Los Angeles	149	545	63	140	30	1	20	88	37	2	.257	.304	.429
1993	Los Angeles	158	619	74	153	27	2	23	80	34	0	.247	.287	.409
1994	**Projected**	**151**	**549**	**68**	**145**	**31**	**2**	**20**	**81**	**38**	**2**	**.264**	**.312**	**.437**

STEVE KARSAY

Oakland Athletics

Starting Pitcher

$28

Toronto's first pick in 1990, was pitching well at Knoxville when Toronto felt an overwhelming desire for Rickey Henderson. Karsay went to Oakland, in a trade that Pat Gillick soon regretted. Karsay joined Huntsville (more Double-A) and struck out 22 in two starts, at which moment the A's decided to point to '94. They put him in the major league rotation, and he pitched fairly well. Looks good; I expect him to win 12-15 games this year.

YEAR	TEAM/LEVEL	G	IP	W-L	PCT.	HITS	SO	BB	ERA
1993	Knoxville AA	19	104	8-4	.667	98	100	32	3.38
1993	Huntsville AA	2	14	0-0	—	13	22	3	5.14
1993	Oakland	8	49	3-3	.500	49	33	16	4.04

PAT KELLY

New York Yankees

Second Base

$29

The Yankees first home-grown second baseman since Horace Clarke, has emerged with the job after a couple of years of confusion, injuries, competition, etc. . . . Has always been regarded as having the ability to be an outstanding glove, and in '93, he was at least above-average at the position. He's not Hall of Fame material, but he was a good player last year, and he will have better years.

YEAR	TEAM/LEVEL	G	AB	R	H	2B	3B	HR	RBI	BB	SB	AVG	OBP	SLG
1992	New York	106	318	38	72	22	2	7	27	25	8	.226	.301	.374
1993	New York	127	406	49	111	24	1	7	51	24	14	.273	.317	.389
1994	**Projected**	**131**	**407**	**53**	**107**	**22**	**3**	**7**	**44**	**27**	**15**	**.263**	**.309**	**.383**

BOBBY KELLY

Cincinnati Reds

Center Field

$38

Was acquired in exchange for Paul O'Neill (in New York he was Roberto), and quickly proved himself a true Cincinnati Red: he spent half the season on the disabled list. Having an all-star season, he went out in July with a separated shoulder. Should be at full strength in '94 . . . He's 29, too old to talk about his potential, but I still think he hasn't had his best year yet.

YEAR	TEAM/LEVEL	G	AB	R	H	2B	3B	HR	RBI	BB	SB	AVG	OBP	SLG
1992	New York AL	152	580	81	158	31	2	10	66	41	28	.272	.322	.384
1993	Cincinnati	78	320	44	102	17	3	9	35	17	21	.319	.354	.475
1994	**Projected**	**118**	**452**	**53**	**129**	**21**	**2**	**12**	**55**	**35**	**28**	**.285**	**.337**	**.420**

JEFF KENT
New York Mets
Second Base
$34

Made 18 errors at second base, most in the National League . . . His .969 fielding percentage was the lowest in the majors for a second baseman with 100 or more games . . . More disappointing than that was his walk total, 30. He was supposed to be a guy who could get on base. I don't believe he's a bad second baseman, and a good second baseman who can hit 20-25 homers is a valuable player. He ain't there yet.

YEAR	TEAM/LEVEL	G	AB	R	H	2B	3B	HR	RBI	BB	SB	AVG	OBP	SLG
1992	Two Teams	102	305	52	73	21	2	11	50	27	2	.239	.312	.430
1993	New York	140	496	65	134	24	0	21	80	30	4	.270	.320	.446
1994	**Projected**	**145**	**525**	**75**	**135**	**32**	**1**	**19**	**78**	**49**	**11**	**.257**	**.321**	**.430**

KEITH KESSINGER
Cincinnati Reds
Shortstop
$6

A switch-hitting shortstop, like his daddy, Dr. Henry. Kessinger is 27 and had never hit a lick until '93, for which reason he had never gotten out of A ball. The Reds tried him at Double-A, and he got hot and wound up earning a September look by the new administration. If his improvement with the bat is real he has a chance to hang around as a backup infielder, but that's as optimistic as I could be.

YEAR	TEAM/LEVEL	G	AB	R	H	2B	3B	HR	RBI	BB	SB	AVG	OBP	SLG
1993	AA and AAA	91	281	41	84	18	0	5	43	38	0	.299	.384	.416
1993	MLE	91	270	32	73	16	0	5	33	30	0	.270	.343	.385
1993	Cincinnati	11	27	4	7	1	0	1	3	4	0	.259	.344	.407

JIMMY KEY
New York Yankees
Starting Pitcher
$70

He led the American League in fewest walks per nine innings (1.6) and strikeout to walk ratio (4.02 to 1) . . . In a 10-year major league career his only losing records are 4-5, as a rookie relief pitcher, and 13-14 in 1989. His strikeout rates have gone *upward* as he has aged; last year was his career high in strikeouts and strikeouts/game. He's a terrific pitcher, and a joy to watch.

YEAR	TEAM/LEVEL	G	IP	W-L	PCT.	HITS	SO	BB	ERA
1991	Toronto	33	209	16-12	.571	207	125	44	3.05
1992	Toronto	33	217	13-13	.500	205	117	59	3.53
1993	New York	34	237	18-6	.750	219	173	43	3.00

MARK KIEFER
Milwaukee Brewers
Pitcher
$15

Pitched nine good innings in a September callup, to the surprise of everybody. He's been a starting pitcher in the minor leagues, with records that don't look very good on a superficial level, but then, no pitcher looks great at El Paso or Denver . . . He's had his elbow scoped once or twice. Grade C prospect, but could be a surprise player, particularly if he's moved to the bullpen . . . His brother, Steve, also played for the Brewers.

YEAR	TEAM/LEVEL	G	IP	W-L	PCT.	HITS	SO	BB	ERA
1992	Denver AAA	27	163	7-13	.350	168	145	65	4.59
1993	AA and AAA	16	80	6-6	.500	76	67	36	4.39
1993	Milwaukee	6	9	0-0	—	3	7	5	0.00

JOHN (CLAUDE) KIELY

Detroit Tigers

Relief Pitcher

$13

After posting a 2.13 ERA in '92 he encountered some rough sledding at the start of the '93 season, and was sent to Toledo on May 7. He pitched OK for Toledo, working middle relief, but the Tigers, who were looking over guys like Storm Davis and Joe Boever, didn't call him back up in September. Grade C prospect, throws sidearm. He would benefit from being in an organization which can distinguish between a pitcher and a kumquat.

YEAR	TEAM/LEVEL	G	IP	W-L	SAVES	HITS	SO	BB	ERA
1992	Detroit	39	55	4-2	0	44	18	28	2.13
1993	Toledo AAA	37	58	3-4	4	65	48	25	3.88
1993	Detroit	8	12	0-2	0	13	5	13	7.71

DARRYL KILE

Houston Astros

Starting Pitcher

$42

"His" improvement in '93 is chiefly attributable to the Astros hitters, who scored 6.4 runs per nine innings when he was pitching. He had it coming, as the bats had stiffed him in previous years, and he did make some real progress . . . Led the National League in hit batsmen, with 15 . . . He's only 25, and will be a Cy Young candidate in a year or two if he's able to remain healthy and throw 230-250 innings.

YEAR	TEAM/LEVEL	G	IP	W-L	PCT.	HITS	SO	BB	ERA
1991	Houston	37	154	7-11	.389	144	100	84	3.69
1992	Houston	22	125	5-10	.333	124	90	63	3.95
1993	Houston	32	172	15-8	.652	152	141	69	3.51

PAUL KILGUS

St. Louis Cardinals

Lefthanded Pitcher

$19

Thirty-two years old, was in the majors 1987-1991, never posting an ERA under 4.13. He went 12-15 with Texas in 1988, after which he was one of the key players exchanged for Rafael Palmeiro. Released by St. Louis last spring, he re-signed, went to Louisville and earned a recall in June. He missed two and half months then with a sprained foot, but got everybody out when he was able to pitch.

YEAR	TEAM/LEVEL	G	IP	W-L	SAVES	HITS	SO	BB	ERA
1992	Louisville AAA	27	168	9-8	0	189	90	28	3.80
1993	Louisville AAA	9	68	7-1	0	59	54	19	2.65
1993	St. Louis	22	29	1-0	1	18	21	8	0.63

JEFF KING

Pittsburgh Pirates

Infielder

$44

I knew he was a better hitter than he had shown before '93. He drove in 45 runs after the All-Star break in '92, then drove in just about 50 in each half last year. His control of the strike zone improved dramatically in '93, as he struck out 24% less often, and walked 72% more often. His defense at third is among the three or four best in the league.

YEAR	TEAM/LEVEL	G	AB	R	H	2B	3B	HR	RBI	BB	SB	AVG	OBP	SLG
1992	Pittsburgh	130	480	56	111	21	2	14	65	27	4	.231	.272	.371
1993	Pittsburgh	158	611	82	180	35	3	9	98	59	8	.295	.356	.406
1994	**Projected**	**152**	**560**	**70**	**142**	**24**	**3**	**13**	**78**	**50**	**7**	**.254**	**.315**	**.377**

KEVIN KING

Seattle Mariners

Lefthanded Pitcher

$13

He was rushed to the majors a few weeks out of A Ball, with predictable results. A starter until 1993, he had gone 7-16 with San Bernandino in 1992, posting a 5.32 ERA. The Mariners moved him to the bullpen and that seemed to work, so they hurried him from Riverside to Jacksonville to Seattle . . . Grade C prospect. Piniella knows how to build a bullpen, and I wouldn't discount King's chance to be a part of it.

YEAR	TEAM/LEVEL	G	IP	W-L	SAVES	HITS	SO	BB	ERA
1993	Riverside A	25	46	3-2	5	37	28	20	1.57
1993	Jacksonville AA	16	29	2-0	1	25	13	7	3.14
1993	Seattle	13	12	0-1	0	9	8	4	6.17

WAYNE KIRBY

Cleveland Indians

Right Field

$24

Finished fourth in the A.L. Rookie-of-the-Year voting, two spots ahead of Brent Gates. How in the hell could anybody have voted for Wayne Kirby over Brent Gates? Are there *really* sportswriters around who are that ignorant? . . . Led the American League in outfield assists, with 19 . . . Good outfielder, could hit .300, but will be pushed to a part-time role by the competition with younger and more talented players.

YEAR	TEAM/LEVEL	G	AB	R	H	2B	3B	HR	RBI	BB	SB	AVG	OBP	SLG
1992	MLE	123	441	65	133	15	8	7	48	23	31	.302	.336	.420
1993	Cleveland	131	458	71	123	19	5	6	60	37	17	.269	.323	.371
1994	**Projected**	**95**	**288**	**42**	**76**	**10**	**3**	**3**	**30**	**20**	**16**	**.264**	**.312**	**.351**

RYAN KLESKO

Atlanta Braves

First Base

$28

A young, white Fred McGriff—a lefthanded power-hitting first baseman, capable of hitting 25-30 home runs in a season. He's certainly not Fred McGriff at this point, in that his batting average would be lower and he would have half as many walks, hence a much lower on-base percentage. In view of his youth (he's only 22) he might improve substantially by the time he has a chance to play. **Grade A prospect.**

YEAR	TEAM/LEVEL	G	AB	R	H	2B	3B	HR	RBI	BB	SB	AVG	OBP	SLG
1993	Richmond AAA	98	343	59	94	14	2	22	74	47	4	.274	.361	.519
1993	MLE	98	331	43	82	12	1	17	54	34	2	.248	.318	.444
1993	Atlanta	22	17	3	6	1	0	2	5	3	0	.353	.450	.765

JOE KLINK

Florida Marlins

Relief Pitcher

$9

Klink missed all of the 1992 season with a sore left elbow, on which surgery was enacted in late June. He signed with the Marlins as a free agent, and pitched well enough to earn a spot as the second lefthander out of the bullpen, and was effective in getting out lefthanders (.216 average), but was in big trouble if he had to face a righthander (.323). Limited future.

YEAR	TEAM/LEVEL	G	IP	W-L	SAVES	HITS	SO	BB	ERA
1991	Oakland	62	62	10-3	2	60	34	21	4.35
1992	Oakland	Unable to perform due to injury							
1993	Florida	59	38	0-2	0	37	22	24	5.02

JOE KMAK
Milwaukee Brewers
Catcher
$10

A kmember of the Onomatopoeia All-Stars, where he shares the catcher's position with Steve Swisher. Kmak is a 30-year-old righthanded batter, originally from the St. Louis system. He fits in with Phil Garner's scheme because he runs unusually well for a catcher, but doesn't have enough Kpop in his bat to require what one might call a serious analysis.

YEAR	TEAM/LEVEL	G	AB	R	H	2B	3B	HR	RBI	BB	SB	AVG	OBP	SLG
1991	Denver AAA	100	294	34	70	17	2	1	33	28	7	.238	.314	.320
1992	Denver AAA	67	225	27	70	11	4	3	31	19	6	.311	.369	.436
1993	Milwaukee	51	110	9	24	5	0	0	7	14	6	.218	.317	.264

CHUCK KNOBLAUCH
Minnesota Twins
Second Base
$64

A wonderful player, he had his poorest major league season in his third year up, though as to that, the distance between the best and the worst is hardly worth the measuring. I mention it only to suggest that he might not be getting *better*, which is important because if he gets any better he's going to be an MVP candidate. A great number-two hitter, a classic second baseman. And he's only 25.

YEAR	TEAM/LEVEL	G	AB	R	H	2B	3B	HR	RBI	BB	SB	AVG	OBP	SLG
1992	Minnesota	155	600	104	178	19	6	2	56	88	34	.297	.384	.358
1993	Minnesota	153	602	82	167	27	4	2	41	65	29	.277	.354	.346
1994	**Projected**	**156**	**599**	**92**	**172**	**26**	**6**	**3**	**54**	**75**	**31**	**.287**	**.366**	**.366**

RANDY KNORR
Toronto Blue Jays
Catcher
$22

Knorr is 26, one day older than Pat Hentgen. Two years ago the Blue Jays were awash in catchers and catching prospects—Myers, Maksudian, Delgado, Borders, Sprague. Myers and Maksudian are gone, Borders may be leaving, Sprague's a third baseman, and Knorr is positioned to take a good share of the job. I think the Blue Jays probably made a smart decision. Knorr is either going to be a solid regular or an awfully good backup catcher.

YEAR	TEAM/LEVEL	G	AB	R	H	2B	3B	HR	RBI	BB	SB	AVG	OBP	SLG
1992	MLE	61	219	20	53	11	0	8	20	12	0	.242	.281	.402
1993	Toronto	39	101	11	25	3	2	4	20	9	0	.248	.309	.436
1994	**Projected**	**62**	**195**	**18**	**50**	**8**	**0**	**6**	**23**	**14**	**0**	**.266**	**.306**	**.390**

KURT KNUDSEN
Detroit Tigers
Relief Pitcher
$12

Was sent out in spring training, called up in May, sent down in July, called up in August, went on the DL a week after that, re-activated in mid-September. The slugging percentage against him was .500, and lefthanded batters hit him at a .392 clip, with a .725 slugging percentage. He's done some good things in the minors, and may do something right in the majors some day—but it won't be for Detroit.

YEAR	TEAM/LEVEL	G	IP	W-L	SAVES	HITS	SO	BB	ERA
1992	Detroit	48	71	2-3	5	70	51	41	4.58
1993	Toledo AAA	23	33	2-2	6	24	39	11	3.78
1993	Detroit	30	38	3-2	2	41	29	16	4.78

MARK KNUDSON

Colorado Rockies

Pitcher

$3

Signed with the Rockies as a free agent, having been released by everybody else, and started the year at Colorado Springs. He pitched well there and was called up in early May. This was a horrible experience for everybody involved, and he was sent back down in mid-May, but didn't pitch the rest of the year. I'm not sure if he is hurt or has retired or what.

YEAR	TEAM/LEVEL	G	IP	W-L	PCT.	HITS	SO	BB	ERA
1992	Las Vegas AAA	37	147	11-7	.611	184	79	47	4.47
1993	Colo Spr AAA	5	28	3-1	.750	30	15	8	2.25
1993	Colorado	4	6	0-0	—	16	3	5	22.24

BRIAN KOELLING

Cincinnati Reds

Infielder

$12

A shortstop until last year, he was moved to second base because of the vacancy there, which is now filled with the acquisition of Bret Boone. Koelling is a righthanded hitter who chases bad pitches and strikes out, for no apparent gain, since he doesn't hit for power, but he runs well and is suspected of being a good second baseman. In a perfect world he would spend '94 in Triple-A.

YEAR	TEAM/LEVEL	G	AB	R	H	2B	3B	HR	RBI	BB	SB	AVG	OBP	SLG
1993	Chattanooga AA	110	430	64	119	17	6	4	47	32	34	.277	.328	.372
1993	MLE	112	422	51	104	15	3	3	38	23	24	.246	.285	.318
1993	Cincinnati	7	15	2	1	0	0	0	0	0	0	.067	.125	.067

KEVIN KOSLOFSKI

Kansas City Royals

Outfielder

$15

As a Royals fan, I couldn't understand why he wasn't in the majors last year, since he provides a combination of things that the Royals need—speed, a lefthanded bat on the bench, and a defensive outfielder. He isn't going to be a major league regular, probably, but is capable of hitting .250 or a little better, which makes him a viable reserve.

YEAR	TEAM/LEVEL	G	AB	R	H	2B	3B	HR	RBI	BB	SB	AVG	OBP	SLG
1992	Kansas City	55	133	20	33	0	2	3	13	12	2	.248	.313	.346
1993	MLE	111	380	42	94	20	4	4	33	31	10	.247	.304	.353
1993	Kansas City	15	26	4	7	0	0	1	2	4	0	.269	.387	.385

TOM KRAMER

Cleveland Indians

Starting Pitcher

$21

Kramer was a starter in the low minors and pitched consistently well, but the organization never had any faith in him. They moved him to middle relief in 1991, and forgot about him until their need for pitching became deperate. He wasn't great—as a starter he was 5-2 in 16 starts, 4.34 ERA—plus he had some tenderness in his elbow, but should be good enough to remain in the rotation.

YEAR	TEAM/LEVEL	G	IP	W-L	PCT.	HITS	SO	BB	ERA
1991	Canton AA	35	79	7-3	.700	61	61	34	2.38
1992	Colorado Sp AAA	38	76	8-3	.727	88	72	43	4.88
1993	Cleveland	39	121	7-3	.700	126	71	59	4.02

CHAD KREUTER
Detroit Tigers
Catcher
$32

The top surprise player of 1993, to me at least (I had written that he would go back to .220) . . . Kreuter seems to have discovered late in life that he was born to be a lefthanded hitter. He was a righthanded hitter who converted to switch hitting a few years ago, and in both '92 and '93 has hit *far* better lefthanded than righthanded. Defense is good, throws extremely well.

YEAR	TEAM/LEVEL	G	AB	R	H	2B	3B	HR	RBI	BB	SB	AVG	OBP	SLG
1992	Detroit	67	190	22	48	9	0	2	16	20	0	.253	.321	.332
1993	Detroit	119	374	59	107	23	3	15	51	49	2	.286	.371	.484
1994	**Projected**	**117**	**343**	**50**	**85**	**15**	**1**	**8**	**37**	**52**	**1**	**.248**	**.347**	**.367**

BILL KRUEGER
Detroit Tigers
Starting Pitcher
$25

He started seven times, four in April and three at the end of the season, and was OK as a starter, 3-2 with a 3.52 ERA. It would be my guess, based on that, that he will open the season in the Tigers' rotation. If that happens, the key to keeping him productive is to limit his innings. If he pitches 100 innings before the All-Star break, he won't win two games after the break.

YEAR	TEAM/LEVEL	G	IP	W-L	PCT.	HITS	SO	BB	ERA
1991	Seattle	35	175	11-8	.579	194	91	60	3.60
1992	Two Teams	36	179	10-8	.556	189	99	53	4.53
1993	Detroit	32	82	6-4	.600	90	60	30	3.40

JOHN KRUK
Philadelphia Phillies
First Base
$58

You probably know as much about him as I do, a fun guy with a bad body and a chaw of tobacco that would choke a T-Rex. He is always going to be able to hit, even when he's 40 years old and unable to play the field and unable to stay in the lineup because of injuries, he'll still be able to hit. His .430 on-base percentage last year was one of the keys to the Phillies' season.

YEAR	TEAM/LEVEL	G	AB	R	H	2B	3B	HR	RBI	BB	SB	AVG	OBP	SLG
1992	Philadelphia	144	507	86	164	30	4	10	70	92	3	.323	.423	.458
1993	Philadelphia	150	535	100	169	33	5	14	85	111	6	.316	.430	.475
1994	**Projected**	**146**	**515**	**81**	**161**	**23**	**3**	**13**	**72**	**90**	**5**	**.293**	**.398**	**.425**

STEVE LAKE
Chicago Cubs
Backup Catcher
$16

Platooned with Wilkins and had a decent year with the bat, slugging .400. Although Lake is regarded as a strong defensive catcher, almost all of the Cub pitchers were more effective when Wilkins was catching than when Lake was catching. Hibbard, for example, had a 3.69 ERA with Wilkins, 4.63 with Lake, Morgan was 3.43 and 5.94, Harkey 5.18 and 5.49, and Guzman 4.15 and 5.82.

YEAR	TEAM/LEVEL	G	AB	R	H	2B	3B	HR	RBI	BB	SB	AVG	OBP	SLG
1991	Philadelphia	58	158	12	36	4	1	1	11	2	0	.228	.238	.285
1992	Philadelphia	20	53	3	13	2	0	1	2	1	0	.245	.255	.340
1993	Chicago	44	120	11	27	6	0	5	13	4	0	.225	.250	.400

TIM LAKER

Montreal Expos

Catcher

$15

A young catcher who will probably never hit. A year ago Laker was regarded as possibly the Expos catcher of the future, but Fletcher had a good year and Laker didn't, which, since Laker is only three years younger than Fletcher, gives him a rather narrow window to possess the job. Laker is big and has hit as many as 15 homers in a season, but his minor league career average is .230.

YEAR	TEAM/LEVEL	G	AB	R	H	2B	3B	HR	RBI	BB	SB	AVG	OBP	SLG
1992	MLE	117	394	43	84	17	2	10	53	25	2	.213	.260	.343
1992	Montreal	28	46	8	10	3	0	0	4	2	1	.217	.250	.283
1993	Montreal	43	86	3	17	2	1	0	7	2	2	.198	.222	.244

TOM LAMPKIN

Milwaukee

Catcher

$14

Like Joe Kmak, he runs well for a catcher, and thus fits in with Phil Garner's plan to see how many bases he can steal with a last-place team (the answer, as it turned out, was 138). Lampkin is a better hitter than his .190 averages show, but not a whole lot, and is a better defensive catcher than Nilsson, which isn't saying a whole lot. Secondary average was .290, RBI rate was excellent.

YEAR	TEAM/LEVEL	G	AB	R	H	2B	3B	HR	RBI	BB	SB	AVG	OBP	SLG
1991	San Diego	38	58	4	11	3	1	0	3	3	0	.190	.230	.276
1992	MLE	108	314	27	78	12	1	2	29	32	9	.248	.318	.312
1993	Milwaukee	73	162	22	32	8	0	4	25	20	7	.198	.280	.321

LES LANCASTER

St. Louis Cardinals

Relief Pitcher

$21

Lancaster spent five years with the Chicago Cubs, mostly as a reliever, and posted a 1.36 ERA with them in 1989 (73 innings). He had fallen on mediocre times, and was released twice in 1992, once by the Cubs (in spring training) and once by the Tigers (in the fall). The Cardinals gave him a chance, and he'll probably be back with them again. Mixes up five pitches, usually throws strikes. Is prone to a sore elbow.

YEAR	TEAM/LEVEL	G	IP	W-L	SAVES	HITS	SO	BB	ERA
1991	Chicago NL	64	156	9-7	3	150	102	49	3.52
1992	Detroit	41	87	3-4	0	101	35	51	6.33
1993	St. Louis	50	61	4-1	0	56	36	21	2.93

BILL LANDRUM

Cincinnati Reds

Relief Pitcher

$5

An ersatz closer for the Pirates from 1989 to 1991, during which three years he saved 56 games and had ERAs of 1.67, 2.13 and 3.18. He was released by the Pirates in '92. There was a debate about whether he was healthy at the time he was released, but in any case he hasn't been since, and in '93 went out for the season in early June, inflammation in his right elbow. Minimal value.

YEAR	TEAM/LEVEL	G	IP	W-L	SAVES	HITS	SO	BB	ERA
1991	Pittsburgh	61	76	4-4	17	76	45	19	3.18
1992	Montreal	18	20	1-1	0	27	7	9	7.20
1993	Cincinnati	18	22	0-2	0	18	14	6	3.74

CED LANDRUM
New York Mets
Outfielder
$10

A tiny outfielder who played for the Cubs in 1991, and stole 27 bases for them in only 56 games, mostly as a pinch runner. He is 30, and no threat to crash the Mets' lineup or anybody else's, but may be on a roster. His MLE from '93 is consistent with what he has done in previous years, meaning that he is probably as good a player as Vince Coleman, plus he's a lot cheaper and virtually unarmed.

YEAR	TEAM/LEVEL	G	AB	R	H	2B	3B	HR	RBI	BB	SB	AVG	OBP	SLG
1993	Norfolk AA	69	275	39	80	13	5	5	29	19	16	.291	.339	.429
1993	MLE	73	271	34	72	12	3	4	25	16	14	.266	.307	.376
1993	New York NL	22	19	2	5	1	0	0	1	0	0	.263	.263	.316

MARK LANGSTON
California Angels
Starting Pitcher
$66

A marvelous pitcher, has pitched 220+ innings for eight straight years. He now has a career record of 144-126 despite pitching his entire career with bad teams. He's a better pitcher now than he's ever been, still throws very hard and has put his control troubles behind him. Needs to win 20 games a couple of times to get the respect that he deserves . . . Picked off 13 runners, tying Jack McDowell for most in the American League.

YEAR	TEAM/LEVEL	G	IP	W-L	PCT.	HITS	SO	BB	ERA
1991	California	34	246	19-8	.704	190	183	96	3.00
1992	California	32	229	13-14	.481	206	174	74	3.66
1993	California	35	256	16-11	.593	220	196	85	3.20

RAY LANKFORD
St. Louis Cardinals
Center Field
$38

May be traded this winter, with the Cardinals having Gilkey, Jordan and Whiten. He was bothered by a sore wrist, which put him on the DL for a time in mid-summer, and gave him a slow trigger the rest of the year. He couldn't get around on a lefthander, and his .233 slugging percentage against lefties was the lowest in the National League by almost 50 points . . . Has a 75 to 80% chance of bouncing back.

YEAR	TEAM/LEVEL	G	AB	R	H	2B	3B	HR	RBI	BB	SB	AVG	OBP	SLG
1992	St. Louis	153	598	87	175	40	6	20	86	72	42	.293	.371	.480
1993	St. Louis	127	407	64	97	17	3	7	45	81	14	.238	.366	.346
1994	**Projected**	**142**	**516**	**77**	**134**	**27**	**7**	**12**	**65**	**67**	**35**	**.260**	**.345**	**.409**

MIKE LANSING
Montreal Expos
Shortstop
$32

Won a job in spring training without having played above Double-A, and was one of the better rookies in the league. Lansing was a member of the Wichita State team which won the College World Series in '89. He was drafted by the Miami Miracle, an independant team, and sold to the Expos after two years. Fast and a smart baserunner, he is a hell of a third baseman and a better shortstop at this point than Cordero.

YEAR	TEAM/LEVEL	G	AB	R	H	2B	3B	HR	RBI	BB	SB	AVG	OBP	SLG
1992	Harrisburg AA	128	483	66	135	20	6	6	54	52	46	.280	.352	.383
1993	Montreal	141	491	64	141	29	1	3	45	46	23	.287	.352	.369
1994	**Projected**	**111**	**388**	**49**	**107**	**19**	**2**	**4**	**39**	**35**	**23**	**.276**	**.336**	**.366**

BARRY LARKIN

Cincinnati Reds

Shortstop

$60

His season was ended in early August by a thumb injury. Since his first full season, 1987, Larkin has missed 21% of the Reds games, or 34 games a year, with various injuries. When in the lineup he is a faultless player, a .300 hitter with line drive power, excellent speed. He's a good shortstop with a good strikeout/walk ratio, and a smart baserunner . . . Rivals Concepcion as the best shortstop the Reds have ever had.

YEAR	TEAM/LEVEL	G	AB	R	H	2B	3B	HR	RBI	BB	SB	AVG	OBP	SLG
1992	Cincinnati	140	533	76	162	32	6	12	78	63	15	.304	.377	.454
1993	Cincinnati	100	384	57	121	20	3	8	51	51	14	.315	.394	.445
1994	**Projected**	**128**	**473**	**72**	**137**	**23**	**4**	**11**	**62**	**61**	**18**	**.290**	**.371**	**.425**

GENE LARKIN

Minnesota Twins

Right Field/First Base

$15

Continues to chug along as the most consistently mediocre player in the major leagues. His season ended in August, due to a heel injury, but the Twins talk as if they want him back. He's a switch hitter; the Twins need lefties on the bench because all their big hitters except Hrbek are righthanded. He draws a few walks, but what he does really well is take at bats away from guys who can actually play.

YEAR	TEAM/LEVEL	G	AB	R	H	2B	3B	HR	RBI	BB	SB	AVG	OBP	SLG
1992	Minnesota	115	337	38	83	18	1	6	42	28	7	.246	.308	.359
1993	Minnesota	56	144	17	38	7	1	1	19	21	0	.264	.347	.357
1994	**Projected**	**75**	**194**	**22**	**48**	**12**	**1**	**2**	**21**	**20**	**2**	**.261**	**.333**	**.370**

MIKE LAVALLIERE

Chicago White Sox

Catcher

$19

Released by the Pirates because he, and his paychecks, had grown too fat. The White Sox signed him and sent to the Florida State League to lose weight, and he backed up Karkovice on his return. He threw out 75% of runners attempting to steal, which is unbelievable (24 of 32), and played errorless ball behind the plate. Is 33 years old, could last as backup/platoon catcher for several years.

YEAR	TEAM/LEVEL	G	AB	R	H	2B	3B	HR	RBI	BB	SB	AVG	OBP	SLG
1992	Pittsburgh	95	293	22	75	13	1	2	29	44	0	.256	.350	.328
1993	Two Teams	38	102	6	26	2	0	0	8	4	0	.255	.278	.275
1994	**Projected**	**77**	**176**	**12**	**46**	**7**	**0**	**1**	**18**	**20**	**1**	**.261**	**.337**	**.318**

TIM LAYANA

San Francisco Giants

Relief Pitcher

$10

Pitched two innings with the Giants, and otherwise spent the season at Phoenix. Layana began in the Yankee system, but didn't make the 40-man roster after a big year at Albany (1.73 ERA with 17 saves), thus was taken by Cincinnati under Rule V. He had a 3.49 ERA in 55 games with the Reds in 1990, but was hit hard in '91, went back to the minors, and is almost out of chances at age 30.

YEAR	TEAM/LEVEL	G	IP	W-L	SAVES	HITS	SO	BB	ERA
1992	Rochester AAA	41	72	3-3	4	79	47	38	5.35
1993	Phoenix AAA	55	67	3-2	9	80	55	24	4.81
1993	San Francisco	1	2	0-0	0	7	1	1	22.50

TERRY LEACH

Chicago White Sox
Relief Pitcher
$15

A 40-year-old sidearm/submarine reliever, was pitching effectively last year, as he always has, but went on the disabled list in April with tendonitis in his elbow, and went out for the year in mid-June, same cause. Tendonitis, as I have pointed out before, is used as a catchall for some non-specific pain, and what is originally diagnosed as tendonitis will often turn out to be something serious. Has 50-50 chance of coming back.

YEAR	TEAM/LEVEL	G	IP	W-L	SAVES	HITS	SO	BB	ERA
1991	Minnesota	50	67	1-2	0	82	32	14	3.61
1992	Chicago	51	74	6-5	0	57	22	20	1.95
1993	Chicago	14	16	0-0	1	15	3	2	2.81

TIM LEARY

Seattle Mariners
Starting Pitcher
$9

The league hit .300 against him and he posted his third consecutive ERA over 5.00, which moves him, in all likelihood, within a few innings of the end of his career. He is 35 years old and his strikeout rates have declined steadily, from 7.1 per nine innings in 1988 to 3.6 last year. This kind of strikeout rate would concern me if he was a *good* pitcher.

YEAR	TEAM/LEVEL	G	IP	W-L	PCT.	HITS	SO	BB	ERA
1991	New York AL	28	121	4-10	.286	150	83	57	6.49
1992	Two Teams	26	141	8-10	.444	131	46	87	5.36
1993	Seattle	33	169	11-9	.550	202	68	58	5.05

DEREK LEE

Minnesota Twins
Outfielder
$17

A veteran of the White Sox minor league system, he played very well for the Twins in spring training, but was the last man cut (he lost out to Randy Bush). When Bush was released, Lee was recalled but did not impress, got demoted, and didn't return, despite playing well in Triple-A. He'd make a good fourth outfielder . . . Some speed, can hit doubles, draws walks, good defense, lefthanded hitter. He's Wayne Kirby with a bit more patience.

YEAR	TEAM/LEVEL	G	AB	R	H	2B	3B	HR	RBI	BB	SB	AVG	OBP	SLG
1993	Portland AAA	106	381	79	120	30	7	10	80	60	16	.315	.410	.509
1993	MLE	106	361	58	100	24	4	7	59	44	10	.277	.356	.424
1993	Minnesota	15	33	3	5	1	0	0	4	1	0	.152	.176	.182

MANUEL LEE

Texas Rangers
Shortstop
$26

A good gamble in '94. Signed as a free agent a year ago, he was expected to solve the Texas shortstop problem, but his season was ruined by hand and thumb injuries, leaving him with a .168 average going into September. He finished hot, lifting his average out of the nether regions, and he is a good shortstop, although he has made some famous errors. He has a guaranteed '94 contract with an option for '95.

YEAR	TEAM/LEVEL	G	AB	R	H	2B	3B	HR	RBI	BB	SB	AVG	OBP	SLG
1992	Toronto	128	396	49	104	10	1	3	39	50	6	.263	.343	.316
1993	Texas	73	205	31	45	3	1	1	12	22	2	.220	.300	.259
1994	**Projected**	**115**	**386**	**46**	**94**	**12**	**3**	**3**	**32**	**37**	**6**	**.244**	**.310**	**.313**

CRAIG LEFFERTS

Texas Rangers

Lefthanded Pitcher

$18

Lefferts, a career reliever, lost the closer role when San Diego acquired Randy Myers. He asked for the chance to start and pitched well, then signed as a free agent with Texas. He began '93 in the Ranger rotation, and couldn't have been worse: he was 1-5 with an 8.54 ERA. He went on the DL with strained neck muscles, went to the bullpen on his return and posted a 3.86 ERA in 44 games.

YEAR	TEAM/LEVEL	G	IP	W-L	PCT.	HITS	SO	BB	ERA
1991	San Diego	54	69	1-6	.143	74	48	14	3.91
1992	Two Teams	32	196	14-12	.538	214	104	41	3.76
1993	Texas	52	83	3-9	.250	102	58	28	6.05

PHIL LEFTWICH

California Angels

Starting Pitcher

$25

A 6-5, 205-pound righthander, just like Aaron Sele. He isn't Aaron Sele, but his record is better than it might look at a glance. Midland is a tough place to pitch. He wasn't great in the PCL in '93, but struck out 7.3 per nine innings. He pitched pretty well after being called up, certainly better than Hathaway or Springer did in their trials, and is penciled in as the Angels' third starter.

YEAR	TEAM/LEVEL	G	IP	W-L	PCT.	HITS	SO	BB	ERA
1992	Midland AA	21	121	6-9	.400	156	85	37	5.88
1993	Vancouver AAA	20	126	7-7	.500	138	102	45	4.64
1993	California	12	81	4-6	.400	81	31	27	3.79

CHARLIE LEIBRANDT

Texas Rangers

Starting Pitcher

$23

One of the "three Ls" acquired by Texas to solve specific problems which stood between them and the pennant, Lee, Lefferts and Leibrandt. All three failed. Leibrandt, acquired in exchange for Jose Oliva, pitched brilliantly through the end of May (6-2, 2.54 ERA) but developed tendonitis in his shoulder, and was ineffective the rest of the year. Is 37 years old; can come back, but the team will need to monitor his work load.

YEAR	TEAM/LEVEL	G	IP	W-L	PCT.	HITS	SO	BB	ERA
1991	Atlanta	36	230	15-13	.536	212	128	56	3.49
1992	Atlanta	32	193	15-7	.682	191	104	42	3.36
1993	Texas	26	150	9-10	.474	169	89	45	4.55

AL LEITER

Toronto Blue Jays

Pitcher

$25

His real name is "Alois" . . . To recap: Leiter was in the Yankees' system years ago, became a hot prospect for no obvious reason, and was traded to Toronto for Jesse Barfield. For several years following he was plagued by blisters, and lost his control in the battle, sinking to non-prospect status. He re-emerged last year, at 27, and went 5-1 with a 2.75 ERA after the All-Star break. 1994 might be his best season.

YEAR	TEAM/LEVEL	G	IP	W-L	PCT.	HITS	SO	BB	ERA
1991	Dunedin A	4	10	0-0	—	5	5	7	1.86
1992	Syracuse AAA	27	163	8-9	.471	159	108	64	3.86
1993	Toronto	34	105	9-6	.600	93	66	56	4.11

MARK LEITER

Detroit Tigers

Starter/Reliever

$25

Has shuttled between starting and relieving for three years, with 13-15 starts each year and consistent results, ERAs in the fours and at least as many wins as losses . . . Actually, you can throw his brother's 1993 season in the mix, and it looks just the same. The brothers are the same size and look alike . . . Righthander, throws fastball with good movement, slider and changeup. I wouldn't know what to expect from him except more of the same.

YEAR	TEAM/LEVEL	G	IP	W-L	PCT.	HITS	SO	BB	ERA
1991	Detroit	38	135	9-7	.563	125	103	50	4.21
1992	Detroit	35	112	8-5	.615	116	75	43	4.18
1993	Detroit	27	107	6-6	.500	111	70	44	4.73

SCOTT LEIUS

Minnesota Twins

Shortstop/Third Base

$26

Started off the year as the Twins shortstop, but went down quickly with a torn rotator cuff. Doubts already existed about his range on artificial turf, and it is likely that Meares or Hocking will take the shortstop job. If healthy, Leius could return to third in platoon role with Stahoviak, or as utility infielder with reliable glove and good punch against lefthanded pitchers. Kelly is very loyal to his players, and will give him every chance.

YEAR	TEAM/LEVEL	G	AB	R	H	2B	3B	HR	RBI	BB	SB	AVG	OBP	SLG
1991	Minnesota	109	199	35	57	7	2	5	20	30	5	.286	.378	.417
1992	Minnesota	129	409	50	102	18	2	2	35	34	6	.249	.309	.318
1993	Minnesota	10	18	4	3	0	0	0	2	2	0	.167	.227	.167

MARK LEMKE

Atlanta Braves

Second Base

$31

An exceptional defensive second baseman, and finally in '93 hit more the way he is capable of hitting. His job is under some pressure because of the emergence of Chipper Jones and because there is still some skepticism about his bat, but a Gold Glove-type second baseman who hits .250, has a little power and draws 65 walks . . . Well, that's a winning player.

YEAR	TEAM/LEVEL	G	AB	R	H	2B	3B	HR	RBI	BB	SB	AVG	OBP	SLG
1992	Atlanta	155	427	38	97	7	4	6	26	50	0	.227	.307	.304
1993	Atlanta	151	493	52	124	19	2	7	49	65	1	.252	.335	.341
1994	**Projected**	**145**	**480**	**52**	**113**	**18**	**3**	**6**	**41**	**61**	**2**	**.235**	**.322**	**.323**

MARK LEONARD

Baltimore Orioles

Left Field

$15

One of my favorite players, which is not to be taken to mean that I think he is Babe Ruth. I think that he can hit enough to help a team as a designated hitter/extra outfielder. The Orioles acquired him last spring, but he got only 15 at bats with the major league team (1-for-15), and spent the summer at Rochester. No kind of a fielder; will soon be able to choose his own organization.

YEAR	TEAM/LEVEL	G	AB	R	H	2B	3B	HR	RBI	BB	SB	AVG	OBP	SLG
1992	San Francisco	55	128	13	30	7	0	4	16	16	0	.234	.331	.383
1993	Rochester AAA	97	330	57	91	23	1	17	58	60	0	.276	.397	.506
1993	MLE	97	313	41	74	19	0	12	41	42	0	.236	.327	.412

CURTIS LESKANIC

Colorado Rockies

Starting Pitcher

$12

Flakey righthander, shaves his pitching arm before each start to make it more aerodynamic. A teammate of Ben McDonald at LSU, he was drafted by the Indians in 1989, and went 15-8 in A ball in 1991. He went to the Twins in the Sorrento deal, then was drafted by Colorado in the expansion draft. Good arm, smooth mechanics, good strikeout rate in minors. Grade C prospect; won't break through in '94.

YEAR	TEAM/LEVEL	G	IP	W-L	PCT.	HITS	SO	BB	ERA
1992	AA and AAA	31	168	10-13	.435	174	140	72	4.82
1993	Colo Spr AAA	9	44	4-3	.571	39	38	23	4.47
1993	Colorado	18	57	1-5	.167	59	30	27	5.37

JESSE LEVIS

Cleveland Indians

Catcher

$16

Why Hargrove decided to play Ortiz all summer and shuttle Levis up and down is one of the mysteries of the Indians' little universe. Levis hit .364 at Colorado Springs in '92, but has yet to prove he can hit major league pitching. Ortiz has proven that he can't. Levis's fielding percentage and percentage of runners caught stealing were better than Ortiz's, and the Indians' ERA with Levis catching was better than with Ortiz (3.82 to 4.27).

YEAR	TEAM/LEVEL	G	AB	R	H	2B	3B	HR	RBI	BB	SB	AVG	OBP	SLG
1992	MLE	87	237	25	76	16	0	4	28	24	0	.321	.383	.439
1992	Cleveland	28	43	2	12	4	0	1	3	0	0	.279	.279	.442
1993	Cleveland	31	63	7	11	2	0	0	4	2	0	.175	.197	.206

DARREN LEWIS

San Francisco Giants

Center Field

$28

Has never been charged with an error in the majors . . . At one time it looked like Lewis would walk maybe 100 times a season. In '91 he walked 36 times in 72 games, but as he has moved up in the lineup the walks have magically disappeared, dropping his OBP from .358 (good) to .302 (bad). He steals bases, and he may have some good seasons yet, but just based on what he has done lately, I wouldn't want him.

YEAR	TEAM/LEVEL	G	AB	R	H	2B	3B	HR	RBI	BB	SB	AVG	OBP	SLG
1992	San Francisco	100	320	38	74	8	1	1	18	29	28	.231	.295	.272
1993	San Francisco	136	522	84	132	17	7	2	48	30	46	.253	.302	.324
1994	**Projected**	**140**	**515**	**77**	**130**	**14**	**5**	**3**	**43**	**46**	**41**	**.252**	**.314**	**.317**

MARK LEWIS

Cleveland Indians

Shortstop

$29

Lewis was one of the hottest prospects in the world three years ago, but played regularly in '92 and didn't set the world on fire, winding up back at Charlotte. He's still very young (24), and I think his future is still very bright. One of the things he *didn't* do the first time around was hit for power, but he hit 17 homers at Charlotte, so that may be coming around. **Recommended.**

YEAR	TEAM/LEVEL	G	AB	R	H	2B	3B	HR	RBI	BB	SB	AVG	OBP	SLG
1992	Cleveland	122	413	44	109	21	0	5	30	25	4	.264	.308	.351
1993	MLE	126	486	71	123	26	2	13	51	26	6	.253	.291	.395
1993	Cleveland	14	52	6	13	2	0	1	5	0	3	.250	.250	.346

RICHIE LEWIS

Florida Marlins

Pitcher

$29

Lewis is looking now like one of the shrewdest picks of the expansion draft, a short righthander taken from Baltimore, for no better reason than that he was pitching well. His elbow has been scoped out more times than the girls' locker room, but he still throws hard. He may move to the starting rotation, but starting or relieving, I'd bet on him to have better seasons than '93, and he pitched well in '93.

YEAR	TEAM/LEVEL	G	IP	W-L	PCT.	HITS	SO	BB	ERA
1992	Rochester AAA	24	159	10-9	.526	136	154	61	3.28
1992	Baltimore	2	7	1-1	.500	13	4	7	10.80
1993	Florida	57	77	6-3	.667	68	65	43	3.26

SCOTT LEWIS

California Angels

Pitcher

$20

The Angels obviously don't have any faith in him, and who am I to tell them they should, but if they evaluated their young pitchers by performance, rather than radar guns, they'd give Lewis more opportunity and stop wasting time with guys like Holzemer and Swingle. Lewis reached Triple-A in 1990 and has a 9-8 record in the majors, but didn't shine in a 1991 shot at the rotation, is trying to fit in in middle relief.

YEAR	TEAM/LEVEL	G	IP	W-L	SAVES	HITS	SO	BB	ERA
1992	California	21	38	4-0	0	36	18	14	3.99
1993	VancouverAAA	24	39	3-1	9	31	38	9	1.37
1993	California	15	32	1-2	0	37	10	12	4.22

JIM LEYRITZ

New York Yankees

Utilityman

$22

Was used by the Yankees at catcher, first base, left and right field and designated hitter, playing regularly against lefthanders, and playing some against righthanders. He was one of the best platoon players in baseball, hitting .336 with a .600 slugging percentage against lefthanders. There isn't much in his history which would suggest that he is really that good, but on the other hand, he doesn't have to be *that* good in order to help.

YEAR	TEAM/LEVEL	G	AB	R	H	2B	3B	HR	RBI	BB	SB	AVG	OBP	SLG
1992	New York	63	144	17	37	6	0	7	26	14	0	.257	.341	.444
1993	New York	95	259	43	80	14	0	14	53	37	0	.309	.410	.525
1994	**Projected**	**104**	**279**	**40**	**72**	**16**	**0**	**9**	**41**	**38**	**1**	**.258**	**.347**	**.412**

MARK LIEBERTHAL

Philadelphia Phillies

Catcher

$20

The Phillies future catcher, perhaps, a number-one draft pick in 1990 who has moved through the system by the numbers. He played all of 1993 at Scranton/Wilkes Barre, where he wasn't great but wasn't terrible. Righthanded hitter, throws well, moves around well, and has some potential as a hitter . . . Darren Daulton is a great player, but Lieberthal has 10 years on him, which will come into play at some point.

YEAR	TEAM/LEVEL	G	AB	R	H	2B	3B	HR	RBI	BB	SB	AVG	OBP	SLG
1992	MLE	102	341	26	84	14	0	1	31	13	2	.246	.274	.296
1993	Scranton AAA	112	382	35	100	17	0	7	40	24	2	.262	.313	.361
1993	MLE	112	376	32	94	17	0	6	37	22	1	.250	.291	.343

DEREK LILLIQUIST

Cleveland Indians

Relief Pitcher

$29

Has had two straight good seasons as the Indians' top lefthanded reliever, although 1993 did not end well. Lilliquist had a 1.75 ERA in '92 and 1.22 through the end of July in '93. The Indians tried to make him their closer, and that didn't work; he blew three of four save chances, and his ERA ballooned. I would assume that he will bounce back . . . Looks a little bit chubby.

YEAR	TEAM/LEVEL	G	IP	W-L	SAVES	HITS	SO	BB	ERA
1991	San Diego	6	14	0-2	0	25	7	4	8.79
1992	Cleveland	71	62	5-3	6	39	47	18	1.75
1993	Cleveland	56	64	4-4	10	64	40	19	2.25

JOSE LIND

Kansas City Royals

Second Base

$23

Led major league second basemen in fielding percentage, .994 . . . He's a fine second baseman, fairly good range and turns the double play as well as the next guy, but is a complete cipher with the bat. He never walks, has no power and doesn't steal bases. His secondary average was .077. When one guy doesn't hit at all, somebody has got to hit twice as much to make up for it, and the Royals don't have any Barry Bonds.

YEAR	TEAM/LEVEL	G	AB	R	H	2B	3B	HR	RBI	BB	SB	AVG	OBP	SLG
1992	Pittsburgh	135	468	38	110	14	1	0	39	26	3	.235	.275	.269
1993	Kansas City	136	431	33	107	13	2	0	37	13	3	.248	.303	.349
1994	**Projected**	**122**	**402**	**37**	**100**	**16**	**3**	**1**	**39**	**21**	**4**	**.249**	**.286**	**.311**

JIM LINDEMAN

Houston Astros

Outfielder

$12

He has been released, despite mounting evidence that he is a better hitter now than he has been over the years. Over the last three seasons he has hit .318 in the majors. That is only 157 at bats, but his MLE at Tucson last year was vastly better than his MLEs when he was in the minors before, which suggested that he would be a .230 hitter (which he was). He's 32, but might yet salvage his career.

YEAR	TEAM/LEVEL	G	AB	R	H	2B	3B	HR	RBI	BB	SB	AVG	OBP	SLG
1993	Tucson AAA	101	390	72	141	28	7	12	88	41	5	.362	.422	.562
1993	MLE	101	367	52	118	25	4	8	63	29	3	.322	.371	.477
1993	Houston	9	23	2	8	3	0	0	0	0	0	.348	.348	.478

DOUG LINDSEY

Chicago White Sox

Catcher

$8

Acquired in a trade with the Phillies; you may have missed the headlines. Lindsey is a career .217 hitter in the minors; we must assume from the fact that he has played in the majors that he is a megasuperlative defensive player, although the nature of official statistics leaves us limited ability to confirm this . . . The Phillies media guide says that he threw out 46.3% of opposing base stealers in 1990, and 46 of 100 in 1991.

YEAR	TEAM/LEVEL	G	AB	R	H	2B	3B	HR	RBI	BB	SB	AVG	OBP	SLG
1992	Scranton AAA	87	274	28	57	9	0	4	27	37	0	.208	.303	.285
1993	Scranton AAA	38	121	9	21	4	1	2	7	5	0	.174	.206	.273
1993	Two Teams	4	3	0	1	0	0	0	0	0	0	.333	.333	.333

DOUG LINTON

California Angels (Released)

Relief Pitcher

$8

After three-and-a-half years at Syracuse (Toronto system) he was called up, pitched 11 innings and was released. The Angels signed him for bullpen help, but he wasn't much help and was released by them on September 13. A righthander, he pitched around .500 ball in Triple-A, with reasonably good strikeout/walk rates. Grade D prospect; could catch on somewhere.

YEAR	TEAM/LEVEL	G	IP	W-L	PCT.	HITS	SO	BB	ERA
1992	Syracuse	25	171	12-10	.545	176	126	70	3.74
1993	Syracuse	13	47	2-6	.250	48	42	14	5.32
1993	Two Teams	23	37	2-1	.667	46	23	23	7.36

NELSON LIRIANO

Colorado Rockies

Second Base/Shortstop

$25

Not to be an I-told-you-so, but I've been saying for years that this guy was too good a hitter to be in the minors. The Rockies used him mostly at shortstop, and it will be a tremendous surprise if he turns out to be a major league shortstop, but as a second baseman, his bat carries his glove. A switch hitter, but probably a better lefthanded than righthanded hitter.

YEAR	TEAM/LEVEL	G	AB	R	H	2B	3B	HR	RBI	BB	SB	AVG	OBP	SLG
1993	Colo Spr AAA	79	293	48	105	23	6	6	46	32	9	.358	.419	.539
1993	MLE	79	273	33	85	19	3	4	31	22	6	.311	.363	.447
1993	Colorado	48	151	28	46	6	3	2	15	18	4	.305	.376	.424

PAT LISTACH

Milwaukee Brewers

Shortstop

$32

He had a series of health problems in '93, beginning with a "root canal cyst" in spring training (I don't know what that is, but I don't think I want one) and progressing through the more usual hamstring pulls, etc. There are two things to worry about here—1, that he was never a good hitter in the minors, and 2, that hamstring pulls are a recurring injury. I do not regard his superb rookie season as a fluke.

YEAR	TEAM/LEVEL	G	AB	R	H	2B	3B	HR	RBI	BB	SB	AVG	OBP	SLG
1992	Milwaukee	149	579	93	168	19	6	1	47	55	54	.290	.352	.349
1993	Milwaukee	98	356	50	87	15	1	3	30	37	18	.244	.319	.317
1994	**Projected**	**135**	**520**	**81**	**137**	**18**	**4**	**2**	**44**	**54**	**39**	**.263**	**.333**	**.325**

GREG LITTON

Seattle Mariners

Utilityman

$22

Played left field, first base, second base and DH for the Mariners, also a few innings at other positions. His fine season and the trade of Bret Boone will increase his playing time in '94 (second base is probably his best position) . . . Appears to have larger-than-normal platoon differential. He's a career .272 hitter with a .428 slugging percentage against lefthanded pitchers, just .212/.280 the other way.

YEAR	TEAM/LEVEL	G	AB	R	H	2B	3B	HR	RBI	BB	SB	AVG	OBP	SLG
1992	San Francisco	68	140	9	32	5	0	4	15	11	0	.229	.285	.350
1993	Seattle	72	174	25	52	17	0	3	25	18	0	.299	.366	.448
1994	**Projected**	**94**	**225**	**26**	**55**	**12**	**1**	**4**	**27**	**22**	**1**	**.244**	**.312**	**.360**

SCOTT LIVINGSTONE

Detroit Tigers

Third Base

$27

The odd man out in the Detroit infield, where Gomez has taken over at shortstop, Fryman and Trammell both play third when they can't play short and Tony Phillips is liable to play anywhere. Through 259 major league games he has hit a rock-steady .288, although the secondary contributions are limited. Despite this, his playing time won't increase, and may decrease, unless he is traded. If I was running the Tigers, I'd trade him for a pitcher.

YEAR	TEAM/LEVEL	G	AB	R	H	2B	3B	HR	RBI	BB	SB	AVG	OBP	SLG
1991	Detroit	44	127	19	37	5	0	2	11	10	2	.291	.341	.378
1992	Detroit	117	354	43	100	21	0	4	46	21	1	.282	.319	.376
1993	Detroit	98	304	39	89	10	2	2	39	19	1	.293	.328	.359

GRAEME LLOYD

Milwaukee Brewers

Relief Pitcher

$19

A 6-foot-7 lefthanded Australian, more in the Eric Hillman/Lee Guetterman tradition than the Randy Johnson mold. He didn't make Toronto's 40-man roster despite excellent performances in '91 and '92, and the Brewers took him in the Rule V draft. Lefthanded hitters found him undecipherable, hitting .192 against him (15 for 78), but he was vulnerable to the majority of the population.

YEAR	TEAM/LEVEL	G	IP	W-L	SAVES	HITS	SO	BB	ERA
1991	Dunedin A	50	60	2-5	24	54	39	25	2.24
1992	Knoxville AA	49	92	4-8	14	79	65	25	1.96
1993	Milwaukee	55	64	3-4	0	64	31	13	2.83

KENNY LOFTON

Cleveland Indians

Center Field

$65

Has led the league in stolen bases twice in a row, and is only 355 stolen bases behind Rickey Henderson at the same age . . . Also took 81% of the available extra bases on hits (such as going first to third on a single), the best of any major league player . . . A devastating player. In the two years he has been in the lineup he's never really gone into a slump.

YEAR	TEAM/LEVEL	G	AB	R	H	2B	3B	HR	RBI	BB	SB	AVG	OBP	SLG
1992	Cleveland	148	576	96	164	15	8	5	42	68	66	.285	.362	.365
1993	Cleveland	148	569	116	185	28	8	1	42	81	70	.325	.408	.408
1994	**Projected**	**152**	**588**	**100**	**173**	**21**	**8**	**3**	**46**	**68**	**59**	**.294**	**.367**	**.372**

TONY LONGMIRE

Philadelphia Phillies

Outfielder

$18

A pinch hitter type, a lefthanded line drive hitter. He was originally in the Pirates' system; the Phillies got him, along with Wes Chamberlain and another guy, for Carmelo Martinez (put me down for two of those, won't you?). He probably isn't really a .293 hitter (his 1993 MLE) but is close enough to get some chances at a major league job.

YEAR	TEAM/LEVEL	G	AB	R	H	2B	3B	HR	RBI	BB	SB	AVG	OBP	SLG
1993	Scranton AAA	120	447	63	136	36	4	6	67	41	12	.304	.364	.443
1993	MLE	120	440	58	129	36	3	5	62	38	9	.293	.349	.423
1993	Philadelphia	11	13	1	3	0	0	0	1	0	0	.231	.231	.231

BRIAN (MULL) LOONEY

Montreal Expos

Lefthanded Pitcher

$18

The second coming of Brian Barnes (keeping in mind that I *like* Brian Barnes, and still half-expect him to turn out to be good). Looney is a short lefthander who doesn't throw real hard but has struck out more than one per inning in the minor leagues, walking hardly anyone. The Expos called him up with only 57 innings of Double-A work, for no obvious reason . . . Grade B prospect, could be Jimmy Key.

YEAR	TEAM/LEVEL	G	IP	W-L	PCT.	HITS	SO	BB	ERA
1993	West Palm B A	18	106	4-6	.400	108	109	29	3.14
1993	Harrisburg AA	8	57	3-2	.600	36	76	17	2.38
1993	Montreal	3	6	0-0	—	8	7	2	3.00

ALBIE LOPEZ

Cleveland Indians

Starting Pitcher

$20

Lopez, a 20th-round draft pick, pitched well in Rookie Ball, both levels of A ball and in a half-season of Double-A, so the Indians called him up. He wasn't effective, although he was 3-1, so was sent to do some Triple-A work, which, to be frank, should have been taken care of first. Only 22 years old, has a great opportunity with a team short of pitching. Grade B prospect.

YEAR	TEAM/LEVEL	G	IP	W-L	PCT.	HITS	SO	BB	ERA
1993	Canton-Akr AA	16	110	9-4	.692	79	80	47	3.11
1993	Charlotte AAA	3	12	1-0	1.000	8	7	2	2.25
1993	Cleveland	9	50	3-1	.750	49	25	32	5.98

JAVIER LOPEZ

Atlanta Braves

Catcher

$33

One of the best prospects in the minors today, an active, athletic catcher who should hit .275-.300 in the majors with some power, although he never walks. The Braves are understandably reluctant to turn the catching job over to him, because they think they can win without him, so putting him in the lineup (or making any other change) is an opportunity to *lose* the pennant, not an opportunity to win it. **Grade A prospect.**

YEAR	TEAM/LEVEL	G	AB	R	H	2B	3B	HR	RBI	BB	SB	AVG	OBP	SLG
1993	Richmond AAA	100	380	56	116	23	2	17	74	12	1	.305	.334	.511
1993	MLE	100	365	41	101	19	1	13	54	8	0	.277	.292	.441
1993	Atlanta	8	16	1	6	1	1	1	2	0	0	.375	.412	.750

LUIS LOPEZ

San Diego Padres

Infield

$22

Grade B prospect, a 23-year-old middle infielder who has hit .300 in Triple-A. The Padres have shifted him back and forth between shortstop and second base, but the emergence of Gutierrez probably nails him to second. He's a switch hitter from Puerto Rico. What's not to like: a) he has no power, b) he doesn't walk, c) his hitting record is up and down. He has a chance to be good.

YEAR	TEAM/LEVEL	G	AB	R	H	2B	3B	HR	RBI	BB	SB	AVG	OBP	SLG
1993	Las Vegas AAA	131	491	52	150	36	6	6	58	27	8	.305	.346	.440
1993	MLE	131	458	33	117	26	2	4	37	17	5	.255	.282	.347
1993	San Diego	17	43	1	5	1	0	0	1	0	0	.116	.114	.140

TOREY LOVULLO

California Angels

Second Base

$24

A switch-hitting infielder who had a chance years ago, he got another shot last year and played well enough to keep him in the league. He was used by California as a lefthanded platoon player; early in the year he played third, then second, then Easley got the second base job, then he got it back when Easley was out. He played surprisingly well at second base, and should play as much again this year.

YEAR	TEAM/LEVEL	G	AB	R	H	2B	3B	HR	RBI	BB	SB	AVG	OBP	SLG
1992	MLE	131	449	54	119	29	2	16	70	50	6	.265	.339	.445
1993	California	116	367	42	92	20	0	6	30	36	7	.251	.318	.354
1994	**Projected**	**99**	**321**	**41**	**78**	**19**	**1**	**8**	**41**	**38**	**4**	**.243**	**.323**	**.383**

LARRY LUEBBERS

Cincinnati Reds

Pitcher

$17

A tall, gangly righthander who was called up by the Reds in early July. He wasn't pitching all that well at Indianapolis and didn't pitch very well for Cincinnati, and I really don't see any reason to believe that he will develop into a big winner, or even remain a rotation starter . . . Throws fairly hard, but needs an out pitch.

YEAR	TEAM/LEVEL	G	IP	W-L	PCT.	HITS	SO	BB	ERA
1992	Chattanooga AA	14	87	6-5	.545	86	56	34	2.27
1993	Indianapolis AAA	15	84	4-7	.364	81	51	47	4.16
1993	Cincinnati	14	77	2-5	.286	74	38	38	4.54

MITCH LYDEN

Florida Marlins

Catcher

$5

A 29-year-old catcher, a big guy with a seven-to-one strikeout/walk ratio in the minor leagues. Having belonged to the Yankees, Indians, Tigers and Mets, he signed with Edmonton as a minor league free agent, and was used as the backup catcher there. He was called up June 2, didn't play until June 16, hit a home run that day—and got sent back down after playing one more game. No prospect.

YEAR	TEAM/LEVEL	G	AB	R	H	2B	3B	HR	RBI	BB	SB	AVG	OBP	SLG
1992	Tidewater AAA	91	299	34	77	13	0	14	52	12	1	.258	.289	.441
1993	Edmonton AAA	50	160	34	49	15	1	8	31	5	1	.306	.323	.563
1993	Florida	6	10	2	3	0	0	1	1	0	0	.300	.300	.600

SCOTT LYDY

Oakland Athletics

Outfielder

$16

Given a chance to play by the A's injuries and general shortage of talent, he struck out 39 times in 102 at bats, an unacceptable rate. His minor league record suggests that this will be a persistent problem for him—he's a big guy (6-foot-5), and that gives him a big strike zone. He runs very well, and has 20-20 potential, but the strikeouts may keep him from fulfilling it.

YEAR	TEAM/LEVEL	G	AB	R	H	2B	3B	HR	RBI	BB	SB	AVG	OBP	SLG
1993	Tacoma AAA	95	341	70	100	22	6	9	41	50	12	.293	.382	.472
1993	MLE	95	321	52	80	17	3	6	30	37	8	.249	.327	.377
1993	Oakland	41	102	11	23	5	0	2	7	8	2	.225	.288	.333

STEVE LYONS

Boston Red Sox

Utilityman

$2

Signed with the Red Sox on May 6 as a free agent, was sent to the minors in July and recalled in September. I would guess he has played his last major league game. In any case, he is 34 and clearly, as Frank Sullivan said, in the twilight of a mediocre career, but seems to be the type who may be around another 20 or 30 years as a coach and manager.

YEAR	TEAM/LEVEL	G	AB	R	H	2B	3B	HR	RBI	BB	SB	AVG	OBP	SLG
1991	Boston	87	212	15	51	10	1	4	17	11	10	.241	.277	.354
1992	Three Teams	48	55	5	11	0	2	0	4	3	1	.200	.241	.273
1993	Boston	28	23	4	3	1	0	0	0	2	1	.130	.200	.174

KEVIN MAAS

New York Yankees

Designated Hitter/First Base

$19

He has slipped from regular to bit player and doesn't seem likely to reverse the trend, but he was one of many Yankees who was productive in limited at bats in '94. He hit just .205, but his secondary average was .371, and he drove in more runs per at bat than Don Mattingly or Eddie Murray . . . Would benefit from nailing the first pitch once in a while.

YEAR	TEAM/LEVEL	G	AB	R	H	2B	3B	HR	RBI	BB	SB	AVG	OBP	SLG
1992	New York	98	286	35	71	12	0	11	35	25	3	.248	.305	.406
1993	New York	59	151	20	31	4	0	9	25	24	1	.205	.316	.411
1994	**Projected**	**76**	**227**	**31**	**54**	**10**	**0**	**10**	**31**	**34**	**2**	**.238**	**.337**	**.414**

BOB MacDONALD

Detroit Tigers

Lefthanded Relief Pitcher

$11

He was in danger of not making the Blue Jays roster at the end of spring training, so a trade was arranged to send him to Detroit, where he led the staff in appearances. A short reliever, pitches to one or two lefties and will never get beyond that role, if he can even keep it . . . The Toronto media guide says that his career high for strikeouts in a game is three. And he's only done that once.

YEAR	TEAM/LEVEL	G	IP	W-L	SAVES	HITS	SO	BB	ERA
1991	Toronto	45	54	3-3	0	51	24	25	2.85
1992	Toronto	27	47	1-0	0	50	26	16	4.37
1993	Detroit	68	66	3-3	3	67	39	33	5.35

MIKE MACFARLANE

Kansas City Royals

Catcher

$41

Brent Mayne won the starting catching job in spring training, '93, but the Royals weren't scoring any runs, and Macfarlane is their best power hitter, so he got back in the lineup, and had his best season. Has real power. In a kinder park he could hit 25-30 homers a year; playing another position, you could add five or 10 on to that. Slow, throws well, average defense.

YEAR	TEAM/LEVEL	G	AB	R	H	2B	3B	HR	RBI	BB	SB	AVG	OBP	SLG
1992	Kansas City	127	402	51	94	28	3	17	48	30	1	.234	.310	.445
1993	Kansas City	117	388	55	106	27	0	20	67	40	2	.273	.360	.497
1994	**Projected**	**131**	**417**	**52**	**103**	**26**	**2**	**15**	**55**	**36**	**3**	**.247**	**.307**	**.427**

SHANE MACK

Minnesota Twins

Center Field

$47

Dislocated his shoulder in spring training and never fully recovered, aggravated the injury several times and didn't play the last two weeks. The injury hampered his swing, and he is scheduled for off-season surgery. He may be traded, and if he is that might cut a few points off his average; otherwise, he will rebound strongly. As a hitter he is similar to Hal McRae, who had his best season late in his career after he had shoulder surgery.

YEAR	TEAM/LEVEL	G	AB	R	H	2B	3B	HR	RBI	BB	SB	AVG	OBP	SLG
1992	Minnesota	156	600	101	189	31	6	16	75	64	26	.315	.394	.467
1993	Minnesota	128	503	66	139	30	4	10	61	41	15	.276	.335	.412
1994	**Projected**	**144**	**517**	**78**	**151**	**22**	**4**	**13**	**65**	**49**	**20**	**.292**	**.353**	**.426**

LONNIE MACLIN

St. Louis Cardinals

Outfield

$12

A minor league veteran, has spent three-plus years at Louisville, mostly as a backup outfielder, and got a courtesy callup last year. He's a singles hitter with a little bit of speed. On the basis of what I know, he doesn't look a lot different from Dave Gallagher or Gary Varsho or Doug Dascenzo, guys who do the same job at the major league level. Lefthanded hitter, Grade D prospect, will never be a regular.

YEAR	TEAM/LEVEL	G	AB	R	H	2B	3B	HR	RBI	BB	SB	AVG	OBP	SLG
1991	MLE	84	315	28	82	11	1	3	30	13	14	.260	.290	.330
1992	MLE	111	276	21	80	14	2	0	28	16	2	.290	.329	.355
1993	MLE	62	211	22	52	8	2	3	14	12	2	.246	.287	.346

GREG MADDUX

Atlanta Braves

Starting Pitcher

$95

With Clemens's off season, he obviously has to rank as the best starting pitcher in the majors today. His consistency is beyond nature, pitching 263 to 268 innings every year with 197 to 199 strikeouts . . . Has led the league in games started for four straight years, and in innings and batters faced for three. He's won 15 or more games for six straight years . . . Was charged with seven errors, the most of any major league pitcher.

YEAR	TEAM/LEVEL	G	IP	W-L	PCT.	HITS	SO	BB	ERA
1991	Chicago NL	37	263	15-11	.577	232	198	66	3.35
1992	Chicago NL	35	268	20-11	.645	201	199	70	2.18
1993	Atlanta	36	267	20-10	.667	228	197	52	2.36

MIKE MADDUX

New York Mets

Relief Pitcher

$28

He struggled early in the year, while the Mets were establishing themselves as the baseball world's answer to Strom Thurmond, but pitched well after the All-Star break . . . One of the best middle relievers in the game, would be more useful on a good team . . . Can you name the only other Cy Young Award winners whose brothers also pitched? There were two of them. Gaylord and Jim Perry each had a brother who won the award.

YEAR	TEAM/LEVEL	G	IP	W-L	SAVES	HITS	SO	BB	ERA
1991	San Diego	64	99	7-2	5	78	57	27	2.46
1992	San Diego	50	80	2-2	5	71	60	24	2.37
1993	New York	58	75	3-8	5	67	57	27	3.60

DAVE MAGADAN

Florida Marlins

Third Base/First Base

$29

One of at least five major league players right now whose manager is also a relative . . . Magadan was not a great player when he hit .328 in 1990, and is marginal at .270. On the other hand, his career on-base percentage is .389. A good manager *ought* to be able to use that. Take the guy with the .389 OBP and bat him ahead of Ken Griffey. You'll be amazed at how many runs he'll score.

YEAR	TEAM/LEVEL	G	AB	R	H	2B	3B	HR	RBI	BB	SB	AVG	OBP	SLG
1991	New York NL	124	418	58	108	23	0	4	51	83	1	.258	.378	.342
1992	New York NL	99	321	33	91	9	1	3	28	56	1	.283	.390	.346
1993	Two Teams	137	455	49	124	23	0	5	50	80	2	.273	.378	.356

MIKE MAGNANTE

Kansas City Royals

Pitcher

$14

Lefthanded finesse pitcher, made six starts for the Royals in August and September. Is 29 years old, no fastball, good control; will compete for a spot in the rotation with Pichardo, Haney, possibly others. Grade D prospect; when you see him pitch it is hard to understand why he is even in the majors, but I have occasionally seen pitchers like him who could keep the hitters constantly off stride.

YEAR	TEAM/LEVEL	G	IP	W-L	PCT.	HITS	SO	BB	ERA
1992	Kansas City	44	89	4-9	.308	115	35	31	4.94
1993	Omaha AAA	33	105	2-6	.250	97	74	29	3.67
1993	Kansas City	7	35	1-2	.333	37	16	11	4.08

JOE MAGRANE

California Angels

Starting Pitcher

$21

Spent most of the year in St. Louis, where he went 8-10 with a 4.97 ERA. Released, he signed with California August 19, and made eight starts, pitching much better (3.94 ERA), which led to a nice contract to remain with California . . . He was a good pitcher before his injury, and if he just needed a couple of years to build his arm back up, could be again. I wouldn't want to be counting on it.

YEAR	TEAM/LEVEL	G	IP	W-L	PCT.	HITS	SO	BB	ERA
1990	St. Louis	31	203	10-17	.370	204	100	59	3.59
1992	St. Louis	5	31	1-2	.333	34	20	15	4.02
1993	Two Teams	30	164	11-12	.478	175	62	58	4.66

PAT MAHOMES

Minnesota Twins

Starting Pitcher

$20

I recommended that you draft him last year, for which I must express my sincere regrets (Sam's Law: Young pitchers will break your heart). He opened the season in the Twins rotation, but couldn't get anybody out and was sent to Portland in late May. He did not return, despite leading the PCL in ERA. Still young, throws hard, throws strikes, has a good slider . . . There is no reason that he shouldn't be a very good major league pitcher.

YEAR	TEAM/LEVEL	G	IP	W-L	PCT.	HITS	SO	BB	ERA
1992	Minnesota	14	70	3-4	.429	73	44	37	5.04
1993	Minnesota	12	37	1-5	.167	47	23	16	7.71
1993	Portland AAA	17	116	11-4	.733	89	94	54	3.03

MIKE MAKSUDIAN
Minnesota Twins
First Base/Catcher
$15

Signed with the Twins as a free agent, and it looked like he might make the roster, but he had a sore elbow. A sore elbow is not a good thing for a catcher, and he spent the summer in Portland. With Harper probably leaving as a free agent, Hrbek increasingly prone to injuries and Randy Bush released, there is a place for Maksudian on the Minnesota bench if he can convince Tom Kelly that he can play.

YEAR	TEAM/LEVEL	G	AB	R	H	2B	3B	HR	RBI	BB	SB	AVG	OBP	SLG
1992	MLE	101	326	28	82	14	0	10	43	23	2	.252	.301	.387
1993	Portland	76	264	57	83	16	7	10	49	45	5	.314	.409	.542
1993	MLE	76	255	44	74	14	5	8	38	35	3	.290	.376	.478

CANDY MALDONADO
Cleveland Indians
Left Field
$16

An August trade for Glenallen Hill brought him back to Cleveland, where he had his best year in 1990 (22 homers, 95 RBI). He picked up where he had left off, driving in 20 runs in just 81 at bats for the Indians. He's now 33, and not a good enough player that he is likely to last much longer than 35, plus the Indians have other players who will squeeze his playing time.

YEAR	TEAM/LEVEL	G	AB	R	H	2B	3B	HR	RBI	BB	SB	AVG	OBP	SLG
1992	Toronto	137	489	64	133	25	4	20	66	59	2	.272	.357	.462
1993	Two Teams	98	221	19	46	7	0	8	35	24	0	.208	.287	.348
1994	**Projected**	**75**	**214**	**24**	**49**	**11**	**1**	**7**	**29**	**26**	**1**	**.229**	**.313**	**.388**

CARLOS MALDONADO
Milwaukee Brewers
Pitcher
$14

I would compare Maldonado to Juan Berenguer pre-1984 or Aurelio Lopez pre-1979. He's very strong, and he has a fastball. His control is fair, but he needs something to set up the fastball or finish it off, just some little slip pitch or something that doesn't go in the dirt or up in the batter's eyes. He might be a good pitcher, but he may bounce through two or three more stops before he finds himself.

YEAR	TEAM/LEVEL	G	IP	W-L	SAVES	HITS	SO	BB	ERA
1992	Omaha AAA	47	75	7-4	16	61	60	35	3.60
1993	New Orleans AAA	12	19	1-0	7	13	14	7	0.47
1993	Milwaukee	29	37	2-2	1	40	18	17	4.58

JEFF MANTO
Philadelphia Phillies
Third Base/First Base
$12

Expansion has come and gone and he still doesn't have a job, so what now? Manto was the Phillies' Triple-A cleanup hitter, hit over .400 the last six weeks there to earn a brief shot with the league champions (he went 1-for-18). He could hit .270 and has a little power, which should give him a job, but there's no third asset. He can't run, isn't lefthanded, can't really play third.

YEAR	TEAM/LEVEL	G	AB	R	H	2B	3B	HR	RBI	BB	SB	AVG	OBP	SLG
1992	MLE	127	439	52	120	21	0	11	54	43	0	.273	.338	.396
1993	Scranton AAA	106	388	62	112	30	1	17	88	55	4	.289	.379	.503
1993	MLE	106	377	49	101	26	0	14	69	42	2	.268	.341	.448

KIRT MANWARING

San Francisco Giants

Catcher

$31

The NL's Gold Glove catcher, led the majors in fielding percentage, .998, and was second in the league in the percentage of baserunners thrown out (42%) . . . I still don't believe he is any kind of a hitter, but the Giants had a great year with him catching, so it will take him years to play himself out of a job. He's not a .275 hitter, plus his secondary average was .171, and that was inflated by intentional walks.

YEAR	TEAM/LEVEL	G	AB	R	H	2B	3B	HR	RBI	BB	SB	AVG	OBP	SLG
1992	San Francisco	109	349	24	85	10	5	4	26	29	2	.244	.311	.335
1993	San Francisco	130	432	48	119	15	1	5	49	41	1	.275	.345	.350
1994	**Projected**	**125**	**400**	**35**	**96**	**13**	**2**	**4**	**39**	**34**	**2**	**.240**	**.300**	**.313**

JOSIAS MANZANILLO

New York Mets

Pitcher

$10

A native of San Pedro de Macoris, he entered the Red Sox system when he was 16 (assuming that his listed age is correct) and has pitched about a jillion innings since then, despite missing whole seasons with shoulder injuries. He's 26, has a live arm, but his record is hard to evaluate, since he has bounced around. Pitched well for Norfolk, despite the 1-5 record. Grade D prospect; the "Two Teams" below are the Mets and Brewers.

YEAR	TEAM/LEVEL	G	IP	W-L	PCT.	HITS	SO	BB	ERA
1992	Omaha AAA	26	136	7-10	.412	138	114	71	4.36
1993	Norfolk AAA	14	84	1-5	.167	82	79	25	3.11
1993	Two Teams	16	29	1-1	.500	30	21	19	6.83

ORESTE MARRERO

Montreal Expos

First Base

$14

The Expos could have won the East last year if their first baseman had hit anything, but they averaged .225 with 69 RBI. The "A" plan to fix this problem is Cliff Floyd. Plan "B" is Derrick White, and Plan "C" is Marrero. He's a 24-year-old lefthanded hitter who has played 636 minor league games, mostly in the Brewers system, but has never played Triple-A and only 103 games of Double-A. Grade C prospect.

YEAR	TEAM/LEVEL	G	AB	R	H	2B	3B	HR	RBI	BB	SB	AVG	OBP	SLG
1993	Harrisburg AA	85	255	39	85	18	1	10	49	22	3	.333	.381	.529
1993	MLE	85	243	31	73	16	0	7	39	15	2	.300	.341	.453
1993	Montreal	32	81	10	17	5	1	1	4	14	1	.210	.326	.333

AL MARTIN

Pittsburgh Pirates

Outfielder

$33

Martin had been in the minors a long time before 1992, but hadn't hit. He hit well in 1992, but at the time I didn't know if this was real improvement (he was 24) or just a fluke. His 1993 major league performance almost exactly matched his MLE, establishing that it was real improvement, and creating the possibility that bigger things may be in store for him. With luck, he could hit .300 with 25 homers, 25 steals.

YEAR	TEAM/LEVEL	G	AB	R	H	2B	3B	HR	RBI	BB	SB	AVG	OBP	SLG
1992	MLE	125	400	66	108	14	10	14	45	26	13	.270	.315	.460
1993	Pittsburgh	143	480	85	135	26	8	18	64	42	16	.281	.338	.481
1994	**Projected**	**141**	**482**	**71**	**124**	**21**	**6**	**14**	**56**	**36**	**19**	**.257**	**.309**	**.413**

NORBERTO MARTIN
Chicago White Sox
Second Base
$11

His full name is Norberto Edonal Martin; he's a 27-year-old veteran of 866 minor league games, and would be over a thousand except that he missed the 1986 season with a separated shoulder and the 1989 season with an ankle injury. Small, looks like a major league player based on his 1993 MLE, but hasn't hit nearly as well in the past. Grade C prospect; was 31-for-36 as a base stealer.

YEAR	TEAM/LEVEL	G	AB	R	H	2B	3B	HR	RBI	BB	SB	AVG	OBP	SLG
1993	Nashville AAA	137	580	87	179	21	6	9	74	26	31	.309	.337	.412
1993	MLE	137	557	68	156	17	3	7	58	20	21	.280	.305	.359
1993	Chicago	8	14	3	5	0	0	0	2	1	0	.357	.400	.357

CARLOS MARTINEZ
Cleveland Indians
Third Base
$13

Has hit four or five home runs for five straight years . . . Martinez was used by the Indians primarily at third base (35 games); he also played first and was used as the DH. He can play third base about as well as he can perform brain surgery, and the addition of the Indians' young players (Thome and Ramirez, in particular) will probably push him off the roster. Will play somewhere, but he's really not much use.

YEAR	TEAM/LEVEL	G	AB	R	H	2B	3B	HR	RBI	BB	SB	AVG	OBP	SLG
1992	Cleveland	69	228	23	60	9	1	5	35	7	1	.263	.283	.377
1993	Cleveland	80	262	26	64	10	0	5	31	20	1	.244	.295	.340
1994	**Projected**	**73**	**218**	**24**	**60**	**10**	**1**	**5**	**31**	**11**	**3**	**.275**	**.310**	**.399**

CHITO MARTINEZ
Baltimore Orioles
Right Field
$12

The Orioles had six players competing for the right field job in spring training, '93. Martinez won the competition, and opened the season as the Orioles right fielder against righthanded pitchers, platooning with Obando. He didn't get a hit, however—he has never in his career had a hit in April—and was shipped to Double-A by the end of the month. No draft.

YEAR	TEAM/LEVEL	G	AB	R	H	2B	3B	HR	RBI	BB	SB	AVG	OBP	SLG
1991	Baltimore	67	216	32	58	12	1	13	33	11	1	.269	.303	.514
1992	Baltimore	83	198	26	53	10	1	5	25	31	0	.268	.366	.404
1993	Baltimore	8	15	4	0	0	0	0	0	4	0	.000	.211	.000

DAVE MARTINEZ
San Francisco Giants
Center Field
$22

Rates in a group with Stan Javier, Henry Cotto, Daryl Boston—the best reserve outfielders in the major leagues who do that job every year. He runs well, is an average/above average center fielder or right fielder, a decent lefthanded hitter whose secondary average is better than his batting average. He signed with the Giants as a free agent, and wasn't under a lot of pressure in '93, since their outfielders were healthy.

YEAR	TEAM/LEVEL	G	AB	R	H	2B	3B	HR	RBI	BB	SB	AVG	OBP	SLG
1992	Cincinnati	135	393	47	100	20	5	7	31	42	12	.254	.323	.354
1993	San Francisco	91	241	28	58	12	1	5	27	27	6	.241	.317	.361
1994	**Projected**	**120**	**349**	**42**	**94**	**14**	**4**	**6**	**36**	**31**	**12**	**.269**	**.329**	**.384**

DENNIS MARTINEZ
Montreal Expos
Starting Pitcher
$55

Opponents stole 49 bases against him, 17 *more* than any other National League pitcher. The stolen base percentage against him (89.1%, 49 of 55) was also the worst in the major leagues, but he limited opponents to a .174 batting average after runners were in scoring position, the best in the major leagues . . . Has won 208 games in his career, but never more than 16 in a season. No one else in history has done that.

YEAR	TEAM/LEVEL	G	IP	W-L	PCT.	HITS	SO	BB	ERA
1991	Montreal	31	222	14-11	.560	187	123	62	2.39
1992	Montreal	32	226	16-11	.593	172	147	60	2.47
1993	Montreal	35	225	15-9	.625	211	138	64	3.85

DOMINGO MARTINEZ
Toronto Blue Jays
First Base
$18

Martinez has been at Syracuse for three years and was at Knoxville for three before that; altogether he has played 1,065 minor league games at age 26, probably more than anybody in 30 years. He's obviously not going to take Olerud's job, but the Jays are going to have to let him play now or turn him loose. The MLEs below assume he would be playing in Toronto; his stats will be somewhat different in another park.

YEAR	TEAM/LEVEL	G	AB	R	H	2B	3B	HR	RBI	BB	SB	AVG	OBP	SLG
1991	MLE	126	453	49	132	14	1	15	67	33	4	.291	.340	.426
1992	MLE	116	421	40	103	19	0	17	46	24	4	.254	.323	.354
1993	MLE	127	456	43	118	23	1	22	68	26	3	.259	.299	.458

EDGAR MARTINEZ
Seattle Mariners
Third Base
$54

Martinez, one of the best hitters in baseball, severely pulled his hamstring in April, tried to come back too quickly, and then a) didn't hit, and b) re-injured the hamstring. He may be bothered periodically by hamstring pulls for the rest of his career, but he has not and will not lose his hitting ability; he'll be up around .300, with a .400 on-base percentage.

YEAR	TEAM/LEVEL	G	AB	R	H	2B	3B	HR	RBI	BB	SB	AVG	OBP	SLG
1992	Seattle	135	528	100	181	46	3	18	73	54	14	.343	.404	.544
1993	Seattle	42	135	20	32	7	0	4	13	28	0	.237	.366	.378
1994	**Projected**	**140**	**527**	**90**	**160**	**35**	**1**	**14**	**57**	**74**	**6**	**.304**	**.389**	**.454**

PEDRO A. MARTINEZ
San Diego Padres
Lefthanded Pitcher
$20

A starting pitcher in the minor leagues, with a career record of 57-44, he moved to long relief after coming to the majors in June. He has a good arm, not the kind of mitt-popping fastball that will move a pitcher through the minors in two or three years, but an OK fastball, and a standard mix—curve, slider, change. A lean, flexible body, should remain healthy. Grade B prospect; might succeed as starter or reliever.

YEAR	TEAM/LEVEL	G	IP	W-L	PCT.	HITS	SO	BB	ERA
1992	Wichita AA	26	168	11-7	.611	153	142	52	2.99
1993	Las Vegas AAA	15	88	3-5	.375	94	65	40	4.72
1993	San Diego	32	37	3-1	.750	23	32	13	2.43

PEDRO J. MARTINEZ

Los Angeles Dodgers
Righthanded Pitcher
$38

Just a kid, just 22 years old, he struck out 10 men per nine innings, and was the only major league pitcher to win 10 games in relief . . . The Dodgers starting rotation is ancient (Hershiser, Gross and Candiotti) and Martinez may get a starting job alongside his brother, or even get his brother's spot. On the other hand, the bullpen is old, too (Gott and McDowell), and Martinez could be in line for the closer's role.

YEAR	TEAM/LEVEL	G	IP	W-L	PCT.	HITS	SO	BB	ERA
1992	Albuquerque AAA	20	125	7-6	.538	104	124	57	3.81
1992	Los Angeles	2	8	0-1	.000	6	8	1	2.25
1993	Los Angeles	65	107	10-5	.667	76	119	57	2.61

RAMON MARTINEZ

Los Angeles Dodgers
Starting Pitcher
$28

Martinez battled his control but survived most of the season, then had a terrible slump in September, leaving his career about where it was a year ago: something is wrong with his arm, he's trying to work his way back and may eventually do it, but as of right now he's not a very good pitcher . . . Led the National League in walks, 104 . . . Pitches substantially better with long rest than on four days rest.

YEAR	TEAM/LEVEL	G	IP	W-L	PCT.	HITS	SO	BB	ERA
1991	Los Angeles	33	220	17-13	.567	190	150	69	3.27
1992	Los Angeles	25	151	8-11	.421	141	101	69	4.00
1993	Los Angeles	32	212	10-12	.455	202	127	104	3.44

TINO MARTINEZ

Seattle Mariners
First Base
$19

His season was ended in August by a serious knee injury, which may cost him much or all of the 1994 season. Absent the injury, he is about the most average first baseman one would ever see—a .260, .270 hitter with 20-25 home run power, an average number of walks, no speed. His defense is good. When he returns from the injury he'll play regularly for three or four years and might have one big season.

YEAR	TEAM/LEVEL	G	AB	R	H	2B	3B	HR	RBI	BB	SB	AVG	OBP	SLG
1991	Seattle	36	112	11	23	2	0	4	9	11	0	.205	.272	.330
1992	Seattle	136	460	53	118	19	2	16	66	42	2	.257	.316	.411
1993	Seattle	109	408	48	108	25	1	17	60	45	0	.265	.343	.456

ROGER MASON

Philadelphia Phillies
Relief Pitcher
$24

Lost 12 games in relief, the most of any major league pitcher . . . also tied Pedro Martinez for the NL lead in relief innings, with 99.2 . . . He pitched 34 games, 50 innings for San Diego, was traded to Philadelphia and pitched 34 games, 49.2 innings. With San Diego he had a 3.24 ERA but was 0-7; with Philly he had a 4.89 ERA but went 5-5 . . . A fairly good middle reliever, no star potential.

YEAR	TEAM/LEVEL	G	IP	W-L	SAVES	HITS	SO	BB	ERA
1991	Pittsburgh	24	30	3-2	3	21	21	6	3.03
1992	Pittsburgh	65	88	5-7	8	80	56	33	4.09
1993	Two Teams	68	100	5-12	0	90	71	34	4.06

BILLY MASSE

New York Yankees

Outfielder

$18

A member of the 1988 Olympic team, he has yet to play a major league game, although he is not a bad hitter. The Yankees' Double-A and Triple-A parks are pitchers' parks, so their young pitchers always have great stats, while their hitters' stats don't knock your eyes out . . . 27-year-old righthanded batter, is never listed as a prospect but he can hit, runs OK, and I'm told he throws OK.

YEAR	TEAM/LEVEL	G	AB	R	H	2B	3B	HR	RBI	BB	SB	AVG	OBP	SLG
1991	MLE	108	343	55	92	15	1	8	50	52	7	.268	.365	.388
1992	MLE	110	343	41	81	11	1	9	47	40	5	.236	.316	.353
1993	MLE	117	386	66	111	31	1	15	75	67	12	.288	.393	.490

DON MATTINGLY

New York Yankees

First Base

$35

In his best year, 1986, he was 88% better than an average American League hitter. Last year he was 20% better. This is a normal rate of aging . . . Led major league first basemen in fielding percentage, .998 . . . Moved from 10th to seventh on the Yankees' all-time hit list in '93, from 1,754 to 1,908. He needs 61 more hits to pass Bill Dickey . . . Also moved from tenth to seventh in homers, but remained ninth in RBI.

YEAR	TEAM/LEVEL	G	AB	R	H	2B	3B	HR	RBI	BB	SB	AVG	OBP	SLG
1992	New York	157	640	89	184	40	0	14	86	39	3	.288	.327	.416
1993	New York	134	530	78	154	27	2	17	86	61	0	.291	.364	.445
1994	**Projected**	**145**	**574**	**76**	**166**	**35**	**1**	**16**	**82**	**49**	**1**	**.289**	**.345**	**.437**

TIM MAUSER

San Diego Padres

Relief Pitcher

$20

I like this guy. A third-round draft pick of the Phillies in 1988, he was sometimes overpowering in the low minors (a 15-strikeout game, a no-hitter) but just another pitcher once he got to Double-A. He moved to the bullpen in '92, had a good year in long relief, became the closer in '93 and made the majors after two months of being Dennis Eckersley. Philly traded him for Roger Mason . . . Could have bright future.

YEAR	TEAM/LEVEL	G	IP	W-L	SAVES	HITS	SO	BB	ERA
1992	Scranton AA	45	100	8-6	4	87	75	45	2.97
1993	Scranton AA	19	21	2-0	10	10	25	5	0.87
1993	Two Teams	36	54	0-1	0	51	46	24	4.00

DERRICK MAY

Chicago Cubs

Left Field

$29

May had a fine season, even a breakthrough season, until stopped by a hamstring in early September. He's a good young outfielder, but his position is **not** secure. The Cubs have *many* fine young outfielders, and May's secondary offensive skills (speed, power, walks) are very limited. He is not a defensive outfielder. He's a guy that if he hits .300 he's OK, but if he hits .260 he's useless. Could emerge as platoon player, could be traded.

YEAR	TEAM/LEVEL	G	AB	R	H	2B	3B	HR	RBI	BB	SB	AVG	OBP	SLG
1992	Chicago	124	351	33	96	11	0	8	45	14	5	.274	.306	.373
1993	Chicago	128	465	62	137	25	2	10	77	31	10	.295	.336	.422
1994	**Projected**	**140**	**482**	**58**	**137**	**24**	**2**	**9**	**68**	**27**	**9**	**.284**	**.322**	**.398**

BRENT MAYNE

Kansas City Royals

Catcher

$28

It's hard to explain this, but he's a special player, a player who does things that don't show up in the records. He guards the basepaths like a Doberman; he'll decide he can't make a play at the plate, rush out and get the throw, then throw behind the runner. You never know what he'll do, which makes him dangerous . . . Made some progress as a hitter, isn't going to be a big hitter but might hit enough to play.

YEAR	TEAM/LEVEL	G	AB	R	H	2B	3B	HR	RBI	BB	SB	AVG	OBP	SLG
1992	Kansas City	82	213	16	48	10	0	0	18	11	0	.225	.260	.272
1993	Kansas City	71	205	22	52	9	1	2	22	18	3	.254	.317	.337
1994	**Projected**	**97**	**255**	**25**	**64**	**11**	**1**	**2**	**28**	**21**	**3**	**.251**	**.308**	**.325**

MATT MAYSEY

Milwaukee Brewers

Relief Pitcher

$14

He is big and stays healthy. This pretty much exhausts the positive things we can say about him, as he has rarely pitched well anywhere. He was born in Canada, went to high school in Houston and was drafted by San Diego. The Padres released him after a few years; Montreal signed him and took a look, and they released him. He made the Brewers as a non-roster player . . . One can't foresee anything good in store for him.

YEAR	TEAM/LEVEL	G	IP	W-L	SAVES	HITS	SO	BB	ERA
1992	Indianapolis AAA	35	67	5-3	5	63	38	28	4.30
1993	New Orleans AAA	29	52	0-3	2	48	40	14	4.13
1993	Milwaukee	23	22	1-2	1	28	10	13	5.73

DAVE McCARTY

Minnesota Twins

Outfielder/First Base

$25

A good draft value. McCarty is a tall, skinny righthanded batter, Minnesota's first pick in 1991. He played well at Double-A and tore up the Pacific Coast League, but regressed alarmingly while in the majors. He'll hit; the minor league hitter who can't hit major league pitching is a myth. The only real concern is that Kelly is very unpredictable in who he plays, but he doesn't have a world of talent, and he needs McCarty to develop.

YEAR	TEAM/LEVEL	G	AB	R	H	2B	3B	HR	RBI	BB	SB	AVG	OBP	SLG
1992	MLE	137	475	70	129	17	2	15	75	45	4	.272	.335	.411
1993	Portland AAA	40	143	42	55	11	0	8	31	27	5	.385	.477	.629
1993	Minnesota	98	350	36	75	15	2	2	21	19	2	.214	.257	.286

KIRK McCASKILL

Chicago White Sox

Starting Pitcher

$28

He may be poised for a comeback. McCaskill has not been an effective pitcher for years, and probably would be out of work by now except that he looks good on the mound. But his strikeout/walk ratio in '93 was his best since 1986, and was far better than recent years. Also, he finished the season pitching well, posting a 2.43 ERA after August 1, 29-6 strikeout/walk ratio.

YEAR	TEAM/LEVEL	G	IP	W-L	PCT.	HITS	SO	BB	ERA
1991	California	30	178	10-19	.345	193	71	66	4.26
1992	Chicago	34	209	12-13	.480	193	109	95	4.18
1993	Chicago	30	114	4-8	.333	144	65	36	5.23

LLOYD McCLENDON

Pittsburgh Pirates

Right Field

$13

It would be an understatement to say that McClendon's career is under pressure. He is 35 and has hit poorly for two years. He has few assets other than his bat. He doesn't run, used to be a third catcher but doesn't catch anymore. In the past, when his career has been in jeopardy he has come through with a big season, but that's harder to do at 35.

YEAR	TEAM/LEVEL	G	AB	R	H	2B	3B	HR	RBI	BB	SB	AVG	OBP	SLG
1991	Pittsburgh	85	163	24	47	7	0	7	24	18	2	.288	.366	.460
1992	Pittsburgh	84	190	26	48	8	1	3	20	28	1	.253	.350	.353
1993	Pittsburgh	88	181	21	40	11	1	2	19	23	0	.221	.306	.326

BOB McCLURE

Released

Relief Pitcher

No Value

His remarkable career has finally come to an end, apparently. McClure was like a guy who sits down in a high-stakes poker game with $1.75, and is down to his last chip time and time again, but somehow manages to stay in the game until it breaks up. He never did go to spring training with a job, but he had a 19-year career in the major leagues, and pitched almost 700 games.

YEAR	TEAM/LEVEL	G	IP	W-L	SAVES	HITS	SO	BB	ERA
1991	Two Teams	45	33	1-1	0	37	20	13	4.96
1992	St Louis	71	54	1-0	0	52	24	25	3.17
1993	Florida	14	6	1-1	0	13	6	5	7.11

RAY McDAVID

San Diego Padres

Outfielder

$14

A 22-year-old lefthanded hitting outfielder with exceptional secondary skills, has had secondary averages of .541 (Charleston, 1991), .563 (High Desert) and .372 (Wichita). He produces all three elements of secondary average—power, speed and walks. He was a ninth-round draft pick and will have to hit better than .244 to get a good job, but time is on his side.

YEAR	TEAM/LEVEL	G	AB	R	H	2B	3B	HR	RBI	BB	SB	AVG	OBP	SLG
1992	High Desert A	123	428	94	118	22	5	24	94	94	43	.276	.409	.519
1993	Wichita AA	126	441	65	119	18	5	11	55	70	33	.270	.371	.408
1993	MLE	126	426	52	104	15	3	9	44	48	22	.244	.321	.357

BEN McDONALD

Baltimore Orioles

Starting Pitcher

$45

If you're skeptical I can understand, but I intend to acquire him for '94. His strikeout rates, since his brief trial in '89: 3.7 per nine innings, 4.9, 6.1, 6.3, 7.0. This is consistent with the belief that a) he is learning to pitch, and b) his arm was not 100% coming out of college. He cut his home runs allowed in half in '93. He could be ready to have a big year.

YEAR	TEAM/LEVEL	G	IP	W-L	PCT.	HITS	SO	BB	ERA
199	Baltimore	21	126	6-8	.429	126	85	43	4.84
1992	Baltimore	35	227	13-13	.500	213	158	74	4.24
1993	Baltimore	34	220	13-14	.482	185	171	86	3.39

JACK McDOWELL

Chicago White Sox

Starting Pitcher

$74

He struggled in September, but he has normally done that, so I suppose it isn't anything to worry about. Otherwise, there's not much to say about him, assuming that you all know he is one of the best starting pitchers in baseball . . . A short list of quality pitchers who had musical careers on the side: Denny McLain, Mudcat Grant, Nelson Briles . . . Picked seven runners off first in '93, and allowed only 10 stolen bases.

YEAR	TEAM/LEVEL	G	IP	W-L	PCT.	HITS	SO	BB	ERA
1991	Chicago	35	254	17-10	.630	212	191	82	3.41
1992	Chicago	34	261	20-10	.667	247	178	75	3.18
1993	Chicago	34	257	22-10	.688	261	158	69	3.37

ROGER McDOWELL

Los Angeles Dodgers

Relief Pitcher

$18

McDowell was a free agent a year ago, and it was something of a surprise that the Dodgers re-signed him after a dismal second half in '92. His ERA for '93 looks good, but what this doesn't tell you is that he gave up 15 *un*-earned runs, so that altogether he was giving up 4.24 runs per nine innings. The batting average against him was .288. Minimal value.

YEAR	TEAM/LEVEL	G	IP	W-L	SAVES	HITS	SO	BB	ERA
1991	Two Teams	71	101	9-9	10	100	50	48	2.93
1992	Los Angeles	65	84	6-10	14	103	50	42	4.09
1993	Los Angeles	54	68	5-3	2	76	27	30	2.25

CHUCK McELROY

Chicago Cubs

Lefthanded Relief Pitcher

$17

His heavy workload of 1991 and 1992, or something, caught up with him. He wasn't throwing as hard, and his slider lacked bite. His strikeout rate dropped from 8.89 strikeouts per nine innings to 5.94, and his batting average allowed shot through the roof. The first batters he faced hit .381, worst in the National League. He could rebound, but I'd be wary of him until we know for sure that his arm is healthy.

YEAR	TEAM/LEVEL	G	IP	W-L	SAVES	HITS	SO	BB	ERA
1991	Chicago	71	101	6-2	3	73	92	57	1.95
1992	Chicago	72	84	4-7	6	73	83	51	3.55
1993	Chicago	49	47	2-2	0	51	31	25	4.56

WILLIE McGEE

San Francisco Giants

Right Field

$24

Hit 3.5 times as many ground balls as fly balls, the highest ratio in the major leagues by far (253-73). No one else was over 2.6 . . . Willie isn't my kind of player. He's a .300 hitter, a good baserunner, a good outfielder, has played on more than his share of good teams. Over the last five years he has hit .315 with men in scoring position, .335 in the late innings of close games.

YEAR	TEAM/LEVEL	G	AB	R	H	2B	3B	HR	RBI	BB	SB	AVG	OBP	SLG
1992	San Francisco	138	474	56	141	20	2	1	36	29	13	.297	.339	.354
1993	San Francisco	130	475	53	143	28	1	4	46	38	10	.301	.353	.389
1994	**Projected**	**129**	**461**	**53**	**130**	**23**	**4**	**4**	**39**	**33**	**12**	**.282**	**.330**	**.375**

KEVIN McGEHEE
Baltimore Orioles
Starting Pitcher
$27

A righthanded pitcher, acquired from the San Francisco Giants in exchange for Luis Mercedes. His 1993 performance in Rochester, a hitter's park, is merely the latest in a series of strong seasons; one might generally say that he has pitched well everywhere since he entered pro ball, except for 17 poor innings in the majors. Throws a hard sinking fastball, curve and change. Will be a fine pitcher if he stays healthy.

YEAR	TEAM/LEVEL	G	IP	W-L	PCT.	HITS	SO	BB	ERA
1992	Shreveport AA	25	158	9-7	.563	146	140	42	2.96
1993	Rochester AAA	20	134	7-6	.538	124	92	37	2.96
1993	Baltimore	5	17	0-0	—	18	7	7	5.94

FRED McGRIFF
Atlanta Braves
First Base
$78

There are 621 seasons in baseball history in which a player has hit 30 home runs. McGriff has done it six times in a row. So Fred McGriff, by himself, accounts for about 1% of all the 30-home run seasons there have ever been . . . Has hit 228 career home runs, driven in 616. McCovey at the same age had 232 homers, 628 RBI. McGriff's batting average is five points better; McCovey's slugging percentage was five points better.

YEAR	TEAM/LEVEL	G	AB	R	H	2B	3B	HR	RBI	BB	SB	AVG	OBP	SLG
1992	San Diego	152	531	79	152	30	4	35	104	96	8	.286	.394	.494
1993	Two Teams	151	557	111	162	29	2	37	101	76	5	.291	.375	.549
1994	**Projected**	**154**	**545**	**92**	**153**	**26**	**2**	**33**	**101**	**98**	**6**	**.281**	**.390**	**.517**

TERRY McGRIFF
Florida Marlins
Catcher
$7

A 30-year-old backup catcher, he'd like to get a hit this year, so that he can say that he hit safely in two decades. (He hasn't had a hit in the major leagues since 1989.) He had a wonderful year at Edmonton, the best season of his long minor league career, and could be back in the majors this year as a backup catcher . . . His wife's maiden name was Raquel Payroll, so he shouldn't need the money.

YEAR	TEAM/LEVEL	G	AB	R	H	2B	3B	HR	RBI	BB	SB	AVG	OBP	SLG
1993	Edmonton AAA	105	339	62	117	29	2	7	55	49	2	.345	.426	.504
1993	MLE	105	321	44	99	25	1	5	39	35	1	.308	.376	.439
1993	Florida	3	7	0	0	0	0	0	0	1	0	.000	.125	.000

MARK McGWIRE
Oakland Athletics
First Base
$59

He missed five-sixths of the season due to an injury affecting his left heel. The problem wasn't originally believed serious, but refused to heal, being eventually diagnosed as a bruise and a tearing of the tissue in the heel. Assuming he's healthy, he's one of the best power hitters in baseball, and a good first baseman with an exceptional arm . . . How does a guy 6'5" draw 100 walks a year?

YEAR	TEAM/LEVEL	G	AB	R	H	2B	3B	HR	RBI	BB	SB	AVG	OBP	SLG
1992	Oakland	139	467	87	125	22	0	42	104	90	0	.268	.385	.585
1993	Oakland	27	84	16	28	6	0	9	24	21	0	.333	.467	.726
1994	**Projected**	**141**	**521**	**83**	**125**	**22**	**1**	**34**	**94**	**108**	**2**	**.240**	**.370**	**.482**

TIM McINTOSH
Montreal Expos
Catcher
$8

Released by Milwaukee and signed by the Expos, who had lost Rob Natal and Jerry Goff, and needed an extra catcher so they could send Tim Laker to the minors for a while. McIntosh is a converted outfielder, an outfielder who didn't hit quite enough to make it that way. These conversions take years to pay off if they ever do, and McIntosh hasn't hit enough (yet) to make him an attractive option as a third catcher. He's 29.

YEAR	TEAM/LEVEL	G	AB	R	H	2B	3B	HR	RBI	BB	SB	AVG	OBP	SLG
1991	MLE	122	437	50	110	16	5	12	66	26	1	.252	.294	.394
1992	Milwaukee	35	77	7	14	3	0	0	6	3	1	.182	.229	.221
1993	Two Teams	21	21	2	2	1	0	0	2	0	0	.095	.095	.143

JEFF McKNIGHT
New York Mets
Utilityman
$17

Spent a full season in the major leagues for the first time in his 11-year pro career, and played well enough to hold his job. McKnight is a better hitter than your typical backup middle infielder, and is also a switch hitter. He didn't impress anyone with his glovework, and at 31 has no chance of moving into a regular job.

YEAR	TEAM/LEVEL	G	AB	R	H	2B	3B	HR	RBI	BB	SB	AVG	OBP	SLG
1992	MLE	102	336	33	92	17	0	2	33	39	2	.274	.349	.342
1992	New York	31	85	10	23	3	1	2	13	2	0	.271	.287	.400
1993	New York	105	164	19	42	3	1	2	13	13	0	.256	.311	.323

MARK McLEMORE
Baltimore Orioles
Right Field
$27

He started the year on the Orioles bench but got hot, while the Martinez/Obando platoon didn't do Chito, and McLemore got the right field job. His .284 batting average and 72 RBI were major surprises, plus he proved to be an astonishingly good right fielder. He grounded into 21 double plays and was caught stealing 15 times, so there's 36 baserunners out the window, and he doesn't have any power. Doubt that he can hold the job.

YEAR	TEAM/LEVEL	G	AB	R	H	2B	3B	HR	RBI	BB	SB	AVG	OBP	SLG
1992	Baltimore	101	228	40	56	7	2	0	27	21	11	.246	.308	.294
1993	Baltimore	148	581	81	165	27	5	4	72	64	21	.284	.353	.368
1994	**Projected**	**109**	**350**	**47**	**90**	**12**	**2**	**2**	**36**	**38**	**13**	**.257**	**.330**	**.320**

GREG McMICHAEL
Atlanta Braves
Relief Pitcher
$30

Came out of nowhere to become one of the better relievers in the National League. A seventh-round pick of the Indians in 1988, he was a starter until his release in 1990. He hooked on with the Braves and converted to relief, then made the big club out of spring training as a non-roster player. Excellent control, decent stuff; may not hold the closer role but can expect successful career as set-up man.

YEAR	TEAM/LEVEL	G	IP	W-L	SAVES	HITS	SO	BB	ERA
1991	Durham A	36	80	5-6	2	83	82	29	3.62
1992	AA and AAA	34	137	10-7	3	126	139	47	3.36
1993	Atlanta	74	92	2-3	19	68	89	29	2.06

JIM McNAMARA
San Francisco Giants
Catcher
$5

McNamara, who wouldn't be considered a good-hitting pitcher if he was a pitcher, is a backup catcher at Phoenix who somehow got into a few major league games. He's a .220 hitter in the minors, a big guy whose defense is supposed to be extraordinary . . . Attended North Carolina State. According to the Giants media guide, his father was a CIA agent.

YEAR	TEAM/LEVEL	G	AB	R	H	2B	3B	HR	RBI	BB	SB	AVG	OBP	SLG
1992	San Francisco	30	74	6	16	1	0	1	9	6	0	.216	.275	.270
1993	Phoenix AAA	50	158	10	31	5	0	1	23	12	1	.196	.250	.247
1993	San Francisco	4	7	1	1	0	0	0	1	0	0	.143	.143	.143

JEFF McNEELY
Boston Red Sox
Center Field
$17

A second-round pick in the 1989 draft, McNeely is now 24. He runs too well to be a Red Sock, and still needs some work with the bat. Built about like Ellis Burks, he hit well in the low minors, but had an injury season in 1992, and hasn't yet hit at Double-A or above, not counting 37 at bats last fall. Grade C prospect; wouldn't be surprised if he makes a forward leap in '94.

YEAR	TEAM/LEVEL	G	AB	R	H	2B	3B	HR	RBI	BB	SB	AVG	OBP	SLG
1993	Pawtucket AAA	129	498	65	130	14	3	2	35	43	40	.261	.322	.313
1993	MLE	129	481	49	113	14	1	1	26	32	26	.235	.283	.274
1993	Boston	21	37	10	11	1	1	0	1	7	6	.297	.409	.378

BRIAN McRAE
Kansas City Royals
Center Field
$39

A September slump cost him a chance to hit .300. McRae is still young, the same age as Ryan Thompson and Bret Barberie and Cal Eldred, let's say, and 10 years younger than Brett Butler. In view of this we should probably assume that his improvement at bat is real, or partially real. A convert to switch hitting, he is still a vastly better righthanded than lefthanded hitter.

YEAR	TEAM/LEVEL	G	AB	R	H	2B	3B	HR	RBI	BB	SB	AVG	OBP	SLG
1992	Kansas City	149	533	63	119	23	5	4	52	42	18	.223	.285	.308
1993	Kansas City	153	627	78	177	28	9	12	69	37	23	.282	.325	.413
1994	**Projected**	**154**	**607**	**78**	**156**	**26**	**9**	**8**	**64**	**37**	**21**	**.257**	**.300**	**.369**

KEVIN McREYNOLDS
Kansas City Royals
Left Field
$19

He's been washed up for three years, and has now become the Whipping Boy of the Kansas City fans, who don't really understand why McRae (Mgr.) put him back in the lineup in mid-summer, after he complained about his playing time. He hadn't been playing because Gwynn was hitting .320, in addition to which McReynolds is too slow to play the outfield at Royals Stadium. Could have a marginally better season in a different park.

YEAR	TEAM/LEVEL	G	AB	R	H	2B	3B	HR	RBI	BB	SB	AVG	OBP	SLG
1992	Kansas City	109	373	45	92	25	0	13	49	67	7	.247	.357	.418
1993	Kansas City	110	351	44	86	22	4	11	42	37	2	.245	.316	.425
1994	**Projected**	**113**	**305**	**36**	**77**	**15**	**1**	**10**	**39**	**38**	**4**	**.252**	**.335**	**.407**

RUSTY MEACHAM

Kansas City Royals

Relief Pitcher

$18

After a wonderful 1992 season he developed a tender elbow, and was never able to pitch effectively. This was a critical failure for the Royals, as the bridge between their starters and Jeff Montgomery, which was so strong in 1992, completely broke through, allowing at least a dozen games to tumble into the abyss. If his arm is sound he will pitch well, but my mama always told me never to put my money on a sore-armed pitcher.

YEAR	TEAM/LEVEL	G	IP	W-L	SAVES	HITS	SO	BB	ERA
1991	Detroit	10	28	2-1	0	35	14	11	5.20
1992	Kansas City	64	102	10-4	2	88	64	21	2.74
1993	Kansas City	15	21	2-2	0	31	13	5	5.57

PAT MEARES

Minnesota Twins

Shortstop

$27

A 12th-round pick from Wichita State, he was slowed by injuries until last year. When Gagne fled and Leius got hurt he claimed the job, and hit over .300 into late July. A .186 average over the last months left him with stats which fairly reflect his ability .... Has decent range and a powerful arm, but is an inexperienced shortstop. No power, will swing at anything. He needs to improve to hold his job, and he might do it.

YEAR	TEAM/LEVEL	G	AB	R	H	2B	3B	HR	RBI	BB	SB	AVG	OBP	SLG
1992	MLE	81	296	36	72	19	0	2	20	8	4	.243	.263	.328
1993	Minnesota	111	346	33	87	14	3	0	33	7	4	.251	.266	.309
1994	**Projected**	**120**	**417**	**44**	**105**	**22**	**2**	**3**	**37**	**10**	**4**	**.252**	**.335**	**.407**

ROBERTO MEJIA

Colorado Rockies

Second Base

$26

In view of his youth (22 in April), speed, power and defensive position, he could become an extremely valuable player. The upside is, he could be the first middle infielder to reach 30-30. His strikeout/walk ratio is awful and his on-base percentage is unacceptable, so if he doesn't make it at second, he's an outfielder, and then he *has* to improve as a hitter just to play. He could be a poor man's Juan Samuel.

YEAR	TEAM/LEVEL	G	AB	R	H	2B	3B	HR	RBI	BB	SB	AVG	OBP	SLG
1993	MLE	77	268	29	64	10	0	7	27	10	7	.239	.266	.354
1993	Colorado	65	229	31	53	14	5	5	20	13	4	.231	.275	.402
1994	**Projected**	**140**	**478**	**58**	**113**	**23**	**5**	**12**	**45**	**22**	**11**	**.236**	**.270**	**.381**

JOSE MELENDEZ

Boston Red Sox

Relief Pitcher

$29

If he's healthy coming out of spring training, I recommend that you draft him. The Red Sox traded about 400 home runs to get him (Plantier), but he lost the first two months of the season to a sprained right thumb, then went out at the end of June with a strained neck muscle. He has pitched consistently well since coming to the major leagues, and should be a big help to the Red Sox bullpen in '94.

YEAR	TEAM/LEVEL	G	IP	W-L	SAVES	HITS	SO	BB	ERA
1991	San Diego	31	94	8-5	3	77	60	24	3.27
1992	San Diego	56	89	6-7	0	82	82	20	2.92
1993	Boston	9	16	2-1	0	10	14	5	2.25

BOB MELVIN

Boston Red Sox

Catcher

$8

He stays in the majors because people assume that a catcher who hits as little as he does must be some kind of defensive whiz. There is precious little independant evidence for this proposition, but in Boston, he qualifies as the good-hitting catcher . . . Assuming that major league owners are going to be cost-conscious in '94, as they claim, Melvin should stay in the league for at least one more year.

YEAR	TEAM/LEVEL	G	AB	R	H	2B	3B	HR	RBI	BB	SB	AVG	OBP	SLG
1992	Kansas City	32	70	5	22	5	0	0	6	5	0	.314	.351	.386
1993	Boston	77	176	13	39	7	0	3	23	7	0	.222	.251	.313
1994	**Projected**	**90**	**240**	**14**	**54**	**11**	**1**	**3**	**26**	**12**	**0**	**.225**	**.265**	**.317**

TONY MENENDEZ

Pittsburgh Pirates

Relief Pitcher

$14

Menendez has been in the minor leagues since 1984, originally in the White Sox system. He was released by them, and has been a minor league free agent four times, signing with Indianapolis, Texas, Cincinnati and Pittsburgh. He pitched well enough with Buffalo and Pittsburgh last year that he may actually have found a home on somebody's 40-man roster . . . Cuban born, is in excellent condition. Grade C prospect.

YEAR	TEAM/LEVEL	G	IP	W-L	SAVES	HITS	SO	BB	ERA
1991	Nashville AAA	50	107	3-5	1	98	92	47	4.05
1993	Buffalo AAA	54	63	4-5	24	50	48	21	2.42
1993	Pittsburgh	14	21	2-0	0	20	13	4	3.00

ORLANDO MERCED

Pittsburgh Pirates

Right Field

$30

Merced hit .362 before the All-Star break, .242 afterward. He's been in the league for three years and I'm still not sure what kind of a hitter he is, since he's always either hot or cold, but he does have a .372 career on-base percentage . . . Fielded .965 in the outfield, worst of any major league right fielder . . . Has career average of .311 with runners in scoring position.

YEAR	TEAM/LEVEL	G	AB	R	H	2B	3B	HR	RBI	BB	SB	AVG	OBP	SLG
1992	Pittsburgh	134	405	50	100	28	5	6	60	52	5	.247	.332	.385
1993	Pittsburgh	137	447	68	140	26	4	8	70	77	3	.313	.414	.443
1994	**Projected**	**143**	**458**	**71**	**124**	**22**	**4**	**8**	**61**	**73**	**6**	**.271**	**.371**	**.389**

HENRY MERCEDES

Oakland Athletics

Catcher

$9

A defensive catcher, won't hit enough to have a career. He's a Dominican native, strong, throws well. He lives in Santo Domingo, like Juan Marichal, the A's director of Latin American scouting, and was signed by Marichal in 1987. He had a lower back problem in 1988, and has never really hit anything. He wouldn't be on the 40-man roster if the A's had any good young catchers.

YEAR	TEAM/LEVEL	G	AB	R	H	2B	3B	HR	RBI	BB	SB	AVG	OBP	SLG
1992	MLE	85	236	27	47	7	1	0	15	20	0	.199	.262	.237
1993	MLE	85	244	27	49	10	0	2	24	23	0	.201	.270	.266
1993	Oakland	20	47	5	10	2	0	0	3	2	1	.213	.260	.255

LUIS MERCEDES

San Francisco Giants

Outfielder

$12

Two years ago he was a Grade B prospect, but his stock has slipped badly. His skills probably are not a lot different from those of Willie McGee, who has the job that he wants. He's a singles hitter, won't strike out or walk a whole lot, runs well. He's capable of hitting .300, but he's also 26, and if he's going to have a career it is time to get on with it.

YEAR	TEAM/LEVEL	G	AB	R	H	2B	3B	HR	RBI	BB	SB	AVG	OBP	SLG
1992	MLE	102	388	48	107	12	0	2	22	34	24	.276	.334	.322
1992	Baltimore	20	39	6	4	2	0	0	4	8	0	.103	.234	.154
1993	Two Teams	28	49	2	11	2	1	0	3	6	1	.224	.333	.306

KENT MERCKER

Atlanta Braves

Relief Pitcher

$29

A lefthander with a smoking fastball and a good curve, Mercker shot through the minor leagues, but has had some trouble establishing himself in the majors, blowing several opportunities to become the Braves' closer. He made six starts last year, pitching well as a starter (3.00 ERA), and may be in line to move into the Atlanta rotation should a spot ever become open. If that fails, he's a solid middle reliever.

YEAR	TEAM/LEVEL	G	IP	W-L	SAVES	HITS	SO	BB	ERA
1991	Atlanta	50	73	5-3	6	56	62	35	2.58
1992	Atlanta	53	68	3-2	6	51	49	35	3.42
1993	Atlanta	43	66	3-1	0	52	59	36	2.86

BRETT MERRIMAN

Minnesota Twins

Relief Pitcher

$9

He was in the California system, taken in the expansion draft and traded to Minnesota. He has had good ERAs for three years as a reliever, but with peripheral stats that aren't very good and also with unusual numbers of unearned runs—1.42 per nine innings, about three times the normal rate. This, along with his disappointing performance in his first major league action in '93, leaves me un-convinced that he can pitch. Grade D prospect.

YEAR	TEAM/LEVEL	G	IP	W-L	SAVES	HITS	SO	BB	ERA
1993	Edmonton AAA	22	32	1-3	4	31	15	10	1.42
1993	Portland AAA	39	48	5-0	15	46	29	18	3.00
1993	Minnesota	19	27	1-1	0	36	14	23	9.67

MATT MERULLO

Chicago White Sox

Catcher/DH

$10

He is not number one on the list, but he is among the players who might benefit from the Sox' release of their two designated hitters, Bell and Jackson. Merullo had his best minor league season at the age of 28, and got a week on a major league roster during somebody's injury. A lefthanded batter, probably not as good a hitter as his 1993 MLE would suggest.

YEAR	TEAM/LEVEL	G	AB	R	H	2B	3B	HR	RBI	BB	SB	AVG	OBP	SLG
1992	Chicago	24	50	3	9	1	1	0	3	1	0	.180	.208	.240
1993	MLE	103	336	39	101	25	0	9	51	22	0	.301	.344	.455
1993	Chicago	8	20	1	1	0	0	0	0	0	0	.050	.050	.050

JOSE MESA

Cleveland Indians

Starting Pitcher

$25

The Indians starting pitching is so awful (5.25 ERA for the year) that being healthy and able to win occasionally is all that it takes to stay in the rotation. Mesa was their best starter in '93, and that's as much as you can say for him—he's healthy and able to win once in a while. Used to throw a roundhouse curve; has junked that to work with his 90 MPH fastball, hard slider and a sharper curve.

YEAR	TEAM/LEVEL	G	IP	W-L	PCT.	HITS	SO	BB	ERA
1991	Baltimore	23	124	6-11	.353	151	64	62	5.97
1992	Two Teams	28	161	7-12	.368	169	62	70	4.59
1993	Cleveland	34	209	10-12	.455	232	118	62	4.92

HENSLEY MEULENS

New York Yankees

Outfield

$11

He's ready to move on after a miserable season, hitting just .204 in 75 games at Columbus, this on the heels of two years of failing to progress. Previous MLEs have shown him to be not a star hitter, but better than he has hit so far in the major leagues (.221, .344 slugging percentage). His defense . . . Well, he could be essentially described as a failed third baseman. Will probably be somewhere else in '94.

YEAR	TEAM/LEVEL	G	AB	R	H	2B	3B	HR	RBI	BB	SB	AVG	OBP	SLG
1992	MLE	141	513	76	126	24	1	19	79	47	10	.246	.309	.407
1993	MLE	75	272	32	50	12	0	11	37	26	4	.184	.255	.349
1993	New York	30	53	8	9	1	1	2	5	8	0	.170	.279	.340

DANNY MICELI

Pittsburgh Pirates

Relief Pitcher

$16

Micelli is an undrafted free agent who became the Kansas City Royals Minor League Player of the Year in 1992, when he struck out 90 men in 61 innings, posting a 1.92 ERA. He returned to Double-A in '93, although he had dominated that level in '92, and continued to register strikeouts. The Royals traded him to Pittsburgh as part of the Stan Belinda deal. Grade B prospect.

YEAR	TEAM/LEVEL	G	IP	W-L	SAVES	HITS	SO	BB	ERA
1993	Memphis AA	40	59	6-4	7	54	68	39	4.60
1993	Carolina AA	13	12	0-2	10	11	19	4	5.11
1993	Pittsburgh	9	5	0-0	0	6	4	3	5.06

MATT MIESKE

Milwaukee Brewers

Outfield

$11

Missed about half the season with a broken hand, which is fine now. According to the USA *Today Baseball Weekly* Mieske "could get a shot at the starting right field spot next season. Mieske . . . Is considered a top prospect." I would advise you to avoid him, bet on some other rookie. He runs well, but he's a .230 hitter, and is an old rookie at 26. Phil Garner could probably get 25 stolen bases out of him.

YEAR	TEAM/LEVEL	G	AB	R	H	2B	3B	HR	RBI	BB	SB	AVG	OBP	SLG
1992	MLE	134	499	59	115	24	6	13	56	28	9	.230	.271	.381
1993	MLE	60	210	28	48	12	1	6	17	21	4	.229	.299	.381
1993	Milwaukee	23	58	9	14	0	0	3	7	4	0	.241	.290	.397

BOB MILACKI

Cleveland Indians

Starting Pitcher

$10

Released by Baltimore, he went to spring training with Oakland, didn't make the team but signed with the Indians and was assigned to Charlotte. He worked as a swing man there (7 starts, 14 relief appearances), pitched well and was called up in September. He's only 29 and it's hard to say specifically why he can't win, but a pitcher with less than five strikeouts/game will always have a short career. Will get one more shot.

YEAR	TEAM/LEVEL	G	IP	W-L	PCT.	HITS	SO	BB	ERA
1992	Baltimore	23	116	6-8	.429	140	51	44	5.84
1993	Charlotte AA	21	72	4-3	.571	59	46	19	3.39
1993	Cleveland	5	16	1-1	.500	19	7	11	3.38

SAM MILITELLO

New York Yankees

Starting Pitcher

$16

After one of the best minor league careers in many years he pitched well in the closing weeks of the '92 season, and opened the year in the rotation. He was unable to throw well, was sent back to Columbus, where he went on the DL with pain in his shoulder, which the Yankees originally feared might be a rotator cuff. Apparently it wasn't, but he took the rest of the year off to let it heal.

YEAR	TEAM/LEVEL	G	IP	W-L	PCT.	HITS	SO	BB	ERA
1992	New York	9	60	3-3	.500	43	42	32	3.45
1993	Columbus AAA	7	33	1-3	.250	36	39	20	5.73
1993	New York	3	9	1-1	.500	10	5	7	6.75

KEITH MILLER

Kansas City Royals

Infield

$18

Miller was scheduled to be the Royals' regular third baseman, but started the season with a groin pull, later had a serious thumb injury and missed most of the year. He's never in his career gone very long without a serious injury of some sort, plus he doesn't have a defensive position, so it's hard to schedule him in. This is his free agent option year.

YEAR	TEAM/LEVEL	G	AB	R	H	2B	3B	HR	RBI	BB	SB	AVG	OBP	SLG
1991	New York NL	98	275	41	77	22	1	4	23	23	14	.280	.345	.411
1992	Kansas City	106	416	57	118	24	5	1	23	11	16	.250	.279	.307
1993	Kansas City	37	108	9	18	3	0	0	3	8	3	.167	.229	.194

KURT MILLER

Florida Marlins

Starting Pitcher

$22

A 6-5 righthander, originally drafted by the Pirates. Miller was one of the top pitching prospects in the Rangers' system; the Rangers traded Miller *and* Robbie Nen to Florida in exchange for Cris Carpenter, apparently because it was too much trouble to lock themselves in the garage and leave the engine running. Miller's record isn't awesome, but he's young and has been brought along quickly. Grade B prospect; lists "card collecting" as his hobby.

YEAR	TEAM/LEVEL	G	IP	W-L	PCT.	HITS	SO	BB	ERA
1992	Tulsa AA	16	88	7-5	.583	82	73	35	3.68
1993	Tulsa AA	18	96	6-8	.429	102	68	45	5.06
1993	Edmonton AAA	9	48	3-3	.500	42	19	34	4.50

PAUL MILLER

Pittsburgh Pirates

Pitcher

$10

A 53rd-round draft pick in 1987 who became a prospect by pitching well in 1990 and '91. Over the last two years his playing time has been limited due to shoulder troubles. He pitched well last year in Carolina (2.82 ERA) and so-so at Buffalo (4.47, but good control). The Pirates have many good young pitchers, and he is low on the list . . . Might not make 40-man roster.

YEAR	TEAM/LEVEL	G	IP	W-L	PCT.	HITS	SO	BB	ERA
1992	Pittsburgh	6	11	1-0	1.000	11	5	1	2.38
1993	AA and AAA	16	91	5-3	.625	88	58	26	3.77
1993	Pittsburgh	3	10	0-0	—	15	2	2	5.40

JOE MILLETTE

Philadelphia Phillies

Shortstop

$3

As I figure it, this guy is the antonym to Barry Bonds; everything Barry is, he isn't. Barry bats left, he bats right. Barry's an outfielder; he's an infielder. Barry is black, he's white. Barry can hit .330; he couldn't hit .230. Barry has power; he doesn't. Bonds can steal bases; he can't. Bonds draws 125 walks; he'll swing at anything. Barry's going to Cooperstown; he's going back to Scranton.

YEAR	TEAM/LEVEL	G	AB	R	H	2B	3B	HR	RBI	BB	SB	AVG	OBP	SLG
1992	Philadelphia	30	71	4	14	0	0	0	2	4	1	.197	.260	.197
1993	MLE	107	338	25	72	15	1	0	22	17	3	.213	.251	.263
1993	Philadelphia	10	10	3	2	0	0	0	2	1	0	.200	.273	.200

RANDY MILLIGAN

Cleveland Indians

First Base

$25

Joined the Indians August 17 and hit .426 in 19 games, saving his career. Cleveland has enough DHs and first basemen to stock an expansion team and two Cecil B. DeMille movies, and Milligan isn't the star of the gang: he's a 32-year-old righthanded batter who has a little power but can't get out of his own way. Still, he has a career on-base percentage of .393, and that *should* keep him in the league.

YEAR	TEAM/LEVEL	G	AB	R	H	2B	3B	HR	RBI	BB	SB	AVG	OBP	SLG
1991	Baltimore	141	483	57	127	17	2	16	70	84	0	.263	.373	.406
1992	Baltimore	137	462	71	111	21	1	11	53	106	0	.240	.383	.361
1993	Two Teams	102	281	37	84	18	1	6	36	60	0	.299	.423	.434

ALAN MILLS

Baltimore Orioles

Relief Pitcher

$27

Limited hitters to a .187 batting average when there were men on base, best in the American League . . . Has good fastball, best pitch is a slider. He's an athlete, bounces off the mound and gets to first in good shape. He's tough on right-handers, but lefthanders get a good rip at him . . . Often wastes his advantage when he gets ahead in the count. Solid pitcher, probably isn't going to move up.

YEAR	TEAM/LEVEL	G	IP	W-L	SAVES	HITS	SO	BB	ERA
1991	New York AL	6	16	1-1	0	16	11	8	4.41
1992	Baltimore	35	103	10-4	2	78	60	54	2.61
1993	Baltimore	45	100	5-4	4	80	68	51	3.23

NATE MINCHEY

Boston Red Sox

Starting Pitcher

$18

A 6-foot-7 righthander, Minchey was a second-round draft pick of the Expos in 1987, made slow progress in the low minors, and was included in two trades, which brought him to the Red Sox. He turned it around in 1991, and appears to be on the verge of landing a major league job. Grade B prospect; his opportunity is limited behind Clemens, Viola, Darwin and Sele, one of the league's better starting rotations.

YEAR	TEAM/LEVEL	G	IP	W-L	PCT.	HITS	SO	BB	ERA
1992	AA and AAA	30	179	15-6	.714	140	119	40	2.21
1993	Pawtucket AAA	29	195	7-14	.333	182	113	50	4.02
1993	Boston	5	33	1-2	.333	35	18	8	3.55

BLAS MINOR

Pittsburgh Pirates

Relief Pitcher

$20

His rookie season was neither a big success nor a clear failure. His strikeout/walk data was great, more strikeouts in the majors than the minors, with the same control rate, but he pitched poorly with men on base (.294 average) and runners in scoring position (.316), thus allowing 41% of his inherited runners to score. He didn't pitch well late in the season. Pittsburgh has an opening for a closer, but he's probably not the man.

YEAR	TEAM/LEVEL	G	IP	W-L	SAVES	HITS	SO	BB	ERA
1992	Buffalo AAA	45	96	5-4	18	72	60	26	2.43
1992	Pittsburgh	1	2	0-0	0	3	0	0	4.50
1993	Pittsburgh	65	94	8-6	2	94	84	26	4.10

GINO MINUTELLI

San Francisco Giants

Lefthanded Relief Pitcher

$12

Minutelli got into baseball by trying out with Tri-Cities, an independent team in the Northwest League. He had an 8.05 ERA but struck out 79 in 57 innings, and was purchased by Cincinnati. After seven years in their system he became a free agent, and signed with the Giants . . . Turns 30 in May. The Reds were using him as a starter, in which role he was no prospect; might have an outside shot as a reliever.

YEAR	TEAM/LEVEL	G	IP	W-L	SAVES	HITS	SO	BB	ERA
1992	Nashville AAA	29	158	4-12	0	177	110	76	4.27
1993	Phoenix AAA	49	54	2-2	11	55	57	26	4.02
1993	San Francisco	9	14	0-1	0	7	10	15	3.77

ANGEL MIRANDA

Milwaukee Brewers

Lefthanded Starting Pitcher

$25

Here's a switch: this guy was a reliever for years, and was converted to a starting role at Triple-A (1992). He pitched well for the Brewers, had a good rookie season. He had almost made the team in the spring, but a bout of shoulder trouble sent him out. He returned in June, was used as a spot starter and won a place in the rotation in July. **I like him.**

YEAR	TEAM/LEVEL	G	IP	W-L	PCT.	HITS	SO	BB	ERA
1992	Denver AAA	28	160	6-12	.333	183	122	77	4.77
1993	New Orleans AAA	9	18	0-1	.000	11	24	10	3.44
1993	Milwaukee	22	120	4-5	.444	100	88	52	3.30

KEVIN MITCHELL

Cincinnati Reds

Left Field

$35

Has had three straight years of serious injuries and declining playing time—113 games in '91, 99 in '92, 93 in '93. His 1993 injuries were a pulled hamstring in July and a sore left shoulder, which ended his season in August. He's the Danny Tartabull of the National League—a formidable righthanded power hitter who comes with enough baggage to require his own baggage handler. Still hoping to have one more big year, and might do it.

YEAR	TEAM/LEVEL	G	AB	R	H	2B	3B	HR	RBI	BB	SB	AVG	OBP	SLG
1991	San Francisco	113	371	52	95	13	1	27	69	58	2	.256	.338	.515
1992	Seattle	99	360	48	103	24	0	9	67	35	0	.286	.351	.428
1993	Cincinnati	93	323	56	110	21	3	19	64	25	1	.341	.385	.601

DAVE MLICKI

Cleveland Indians

Starting Pitcher

$10

His season was almost entirely lost following shoulder surgery, one of several serious injuries which have obstructed the Indians' efforts to rebuild their pitching staff. *One* of their problems, I think, is trying to skip Triple-A; they've tried that with Mlicki, Embree, Lopez, Nagy, and others, and they have nothing to show for it. Mlicki was Grade C prospect before, Grade D now.

YEAR	TEAM/LEVEL	G	IP	W-L	PCT.	HITS	SO	BB	ERA
1991	Columbus A	22	116	8-6	.571	101	136	70	4.20
1992	Canton-Akrn AA	27	173	11-9	.550	143	146	80	3.60
1992	Cleveland	4	22	0-2	.000	23	16	16	4.98

DENNIS MOELLER

Pittsburgh Pirates

Starting Pitcher

$9

A lefthanded finesse pitcher, a Grade D prospect. Pittsburgh got him from KC for Jose Lind. The good lefthanded finesse pitchers, the guys like Jimmy Key and Charlie Leibrandt . . . The thing those guys have, if you ever notice, is *grace*; they're extremely graceful, almost like dancers. Perfect balance. I don't see that in Moeller, and I'm skeptical about his future.

YEAR	TEAM/LEVEL	G	IP	W-L	PCT.	HITS	SO	BB	ERA
1992	Kansas City	5	18	0-3	.000	24	6	11	7.00
1993	Buffalo AAA	24	77	3-4	.429	85	38	21	4.34
1993	Pittsburgh	10	16	1-0	1.000	26	13	7	9.92

MIKE MOHLER

Oakland Athletics

Lefthanded Pitcher

$10

The A's skipped him across Triple-A, although frankly he hadn't pitched all that well in Double-A. He was awful, a major contributor to the A's 94-loss season . . . He really had no business being in the major leagues, I don't understand what he was doing there, and I don't really see how he can expect to develop unless he has some success . . . Lefthander, a 42nd-round draft pick, was an accounting major in college.

YEAR	TEAM/LEVEL	G	IP	W-L	SAVES	HITS	SO	BB	ERA
1991	Huntsville AA	8	53	4-2	0	55	27	20	3.57
1992	Huntsville AA	44	80	3-8	3	72	56	39	3.59
1993	Oakland	42	64	1-6	0	57	42	44	5.60

PAUL MOLITOR
Toronto Blue Jays
Designated Hitter/First Base
$60

Led American League in plate appearances (725), hits (211), batting average in the late innings of close games (.411), batting with men in scoring position (.384), average at home (.364). Apart from those kind of things he didn't do squat . . . Is now almost certain to get 3,000 hits, and could become the seventh player to score 2,000 runs. There are five now (Cobb, Ruth, Aaron, Rose and Mays), and Rickey Henderson will be the sixth.

YEAR	TEAM/LEVEL	G	AB	R	H	2B	3B	HR	RBI	BB	SB	AVG	OBP	SLG
1992	Milwaukee	158	609	89	195	36	7	12	89	73	31	.320	.389	.461
1993	Toronto	160	636	121	211	37	5	22	111	77	22	.332	.402	.509
1994	**Projected**	**147**	**587**	**92**	**172**	**31**	**4**	**13**	**74**	**71**	**20**	**.293**	**.369**	**.426**

RAUL MONDESI
Los Angeles Dodgers
Outfield
$20

The man who pushed the Dodgers to trade Eric Davis. He has impressive physical skills—is fast, throws well, generates considerable bat speed. The problem for him is going to be controlling the strike zone. He hit well last year in a 42-game trial, but I will be very surprised if he is ready to hit at that level for a full season. Grade B prospect.

YEAR	TEAM/LEVEL	G	AB	R	H	2B	3B	HR	RBI	BB	SB	AVG	OBP	SLG
1993	MLE	110	394	38	88	15	2	6	38	10	8	.223	.243	.317
1993	Los Angeles	42	86	13	25	3	1	4	10	4	4	.291	.322	.488
1994	**Projected**	**143**	**516**	**58**	**127**	**18**	**5**	**11**	**54**	**15**	**13**	**.246**	**.267**	**.364**

RICH MONTELEONE
New York Yankees
Relief Pitcher
$15

Comes in when the starter goes out early, which gives him a winning record because he has more chances to win games than chances to lose them . . . Has been in the Yankee bullpen for two-and-a-half years, pitched well until early July, when he hit a rough stretch. Gave up 14 homers in 86 innings last year; he'll be out of the league if he does that again . . . Juan Gonzalez is 1-for-13 against him.

YEAR	TEAM/LEVEL	G	IP	W-L	SAVES	HITS	SO	BB	ERA
1991	New York	26	47	3-1	0	42	34	19	3.64
1992	New York	47	93	7-3	0	82	62	27	3.30
1993	New York	42	86	7-4	0	85	50	35	4.94

JEFF MONTGOMERY
Kansas City Royals
Closer
$63

Tied Duane Ward for the American League lead in saves (45) and save opportunities (51) . . . Led American League relievers in fewest baserunners per nine innings (9.3) . . . For five straight years has pitched 63 to 73 games, 83 to 94 innings, with four of his five ERAs below 2.40. Few relief pitchers in history can match that consistency, and there is no indication that 1994 will be any different . . . Strikeout rates are declining gradually.

YEAR	TEAM/LEVEL	G	IP	W-L	SAVES	HITS	SO	BB	ERA
1991	Kansas City	67	90	4-4	33	83	77	28	2.90
1992	Kansas City	65	83	1-6	39	61	69	27	2.18
1993	Kansas City	69	87	7-5	45	65	66	23	2.27

CHARLIE MONTOYO
Montreal Expos
Infield
$10

Montoyo drew 156 walks for Stockton in 1988, when he was in the Brewers system. A career on-base percentage of .414 in the minors is not only the highight of his credentials, but pretty much the sum. He's a 28-year-old second baseman who doesn't have speed or power and can't play shortstop or third, which limits his usefulness from the bench, but as a Royals' fan, I'd rather have him at second base than Jose Lind.

YEAR	TEAM/LEVEL	G	AB	R	H	2B	3B	HR	RBI	BB	SB	AVG	OBP	SLG
1993	Denver AAA	84	259	40	84	7	4	2	34	47	3	.324	.429	.405
1993	Ottawa AAA	99	319	43	89	18	2	1	43	71	0	.279	.411	.357
1993	MLE	99	308	35	78	16	1	0	35	59	0	.253	.373	.312

MARCUS MOORE
Colorado Rockies
Pitcher
$7

A long-odds prospect; just a kid who throws hard. He was drafted by California in 1989 and went 16-5 for Quad Cities in 1990. California included him in the Devon White/Junior Felix trade after the season. He hasn't done anything since—a minor league record of 13-28 since 1990—and even at Quad Cities he walked 106 men in 160 innings. Grade D prospect; almost zero chance of being useful in '94.

YEAR	TEAM/LEVEL	G	IP	W-L	PCT.	HITS	SO	BB	ERA
1992	Knoxville AA	36	106	5-10	.333	110	85	79	5.59
1993	Colo Spri AAA	30	44	1-5	.167	54	38	29	4.47
1993	Colorado	27	26	3-1	.750	30	13	20	6.84

MIKE MOORE
Detroit Tigers
Starting Pitcher
$19

The Tigers scored 6.32 runs/nine innings for him, most in the league . . . Led the major leagues in home runs allowed, with 35, and also home runs per nine innings, 1.47. Has led the American League or tied for the lead in starts twice in a row, with 36 each year. He's a marginal pitcher, not as bad as his 5.22 ERA last year, but not able to win unless his team scores a lot of runs.

YEAR	TEAM/LEVEL	G	IP	W-L	PCT.	HITS	SO	BB	ERA
1991	Oakland	33	210	17-8	.680	176	153	105	2.96
1992	Oakland	36	223	17-12	.586	229	117	103	4.12
1993	Detroit	36	214	13-9	.590	227	89	89	5.22

MICKEY MORANDINI
Philadelphia Phillies
Second Base
$26

A better second baseman than Mariano Duncan, but a career .197 hitter against lefthanded pitchers (59-for-300), so there are good reasons to platoon him. Doesn't run a lot but is an 84% base stealer in his career (37 for 44) . . . Probably the best bunter on the Phillies . . . Will continue to play, will continue to platoon, isn't likely to have a big season.

YEAR	TEAM/LEVEL	G	AB	R	H	2B	3B	HR	RBI	BB	SB	AVG	OBP	SLG
1992	Philadelphia	127	422	47	112	8	8	3	30	25	8	.265	.305	.344
1993	Philadelphia	120	425	57	105	19	9	3	33	34	13	.247	.309	.355
1994	**Projected**	**132**	**447**	**55**	**114**	**18**	**6**	**3**	**36**	**36**	**12**	**.255**	**.311**	**.342**

MIKE MORGAN

Chicago Cubs

Starting Pitcher

$36

He missed some time in mid-season with a strained knee, which may or may not have contributed to his regression toward his pre-1991 level of performance. Continued to throw 69% ground balls and continued to pitch well in Wrigley Field, but control was so-so and ERA on the road was 4.95. His career won-lost record is now 93-127.

YEAR	TEAM/LEVEL	G	IP	W-L	PCT.	HITS	SO	BB	ERA
1991	Los Angeles	34	236	14-10	.583	197	140	61	2.78
1992	Chicago	34	240	16-8	.667	203	123	79	2.55
1993	Chicago	32	208	10-15	.400	206	111	74	4.03

HAL MORRIS

Cincinnati Reds

First Base

$35

Probably better cast as a platoon player than an everyday player. Like all Cincinnati Reds he has one or two serious injuries a year—a broken hand and a pulled hamstring in '92, shoulder surgery in '93. If he has a platoon partner such injuries are less damaging to the team, plus his platoon differential appears to be enormous. Over the last four years has hit .245 against lefthanders, .333 against righthanders.

YEAR	TEAM/LEVEL	G	AB	R	H	2B	3B	HR	RBI	BB	SB	AVG	OBP	SLG
1992	Cincinnati	115	395	41	107	21	3	6	53	45	6	.271	.347	.385
1993	Cincinnati	101	379	48	120	18	0	7	49	34	2	.317	.371	.420
1994	**Projected**	**120**	**421**	**54**	**125**	**23**	**1**	**9**	**54**	**44**	**6**	**.297**	**.363**	**.420**

JACK MORRIS

Toronto Blue Jays

Starting Pitcher

$5

Until he tore an elbow ligament, I wasn't totally convinced he was washed up. He still throws fairly hard and struck out 6.56 men per nine innings. The elbow obviously puts his future in severe doubt. If he recovers, he might be a decent pitcher again, but only if he and his managers realize that "knowing how to win" doesn't mean you can't adopt a pitch or inning limit.

YEAR	TEAM/LEVEL	G	IP	W-L	PCT.	HITS	SO	BB	ERA
1991	Minnesota	35	247	18-12	.600	226	163	92	3.43
1992	Toronto	34	241	21-6	.778	222	132	80	4.04
1993	Toronto	27	153	7-12	.368	189	103	65	6.19

JAMES MOUTON

Houston Astros

Second Base

$20

Mouton scored 126 runs at Tucson and was perhaps the best player in the PCL, in spite of which he a) was not called to the majors, and b) was not listed among the top prospects in the league by *Baseball America*. He's a converted outfielder who was playing second, and very badly; apparently there is a feeling that he may not make it at that position. The new Houston manager may take a very different view of him.

YEAR	TEAM/LEVEL	G	AB	R	H	2B	3B	HR	RBI	BB	SB	AVG	OBP	SLG
1992	Osceola A	133	507	110	143	30	6	11	62	71	51	.282	.376	.430
1993	Tucson AAA	134	546	126	172	42	12	16	92	72	40	.315	.397	.524
1993	MLE	134	505	79	131	33	6	9	57	45	26	.259	.320	.402

JAMIE MOYER

Baltimore Orioles

Starting Pitcher

$35

Moyer had shoulder surgery in 1989, and, in a perfect world, would have gone to the minors to work himself back. In the real world he bombed out of the majors, but recovered with a strong performance at Toledo in '92. The Tigers (how *do* those guys evaluate a pitcher?) cut him; he signed with Baltimore and had his best season. Posted a 2.44 ERA on the road, best in the league . . . Good chance of remaining effective.

YEAR	TEAM/LEVEL	G	IP	W-L	PCT.	HITS	SO	BB	ERA
1992	Toledo AAA	21	139	10-8	.556	128	80	37	2.86
1993	Rochester AAA	8	54	6-0	1.000	42	41	13	1.67
1993	Baltimore	25	152	12-9	.571	154	90	38	3.43

TERRY MULHOLLAND

Philadelphia Phillies

Starting Pitcher

$48

He was troubled much of the season with a sore foot, which may (or may not) have been aggravated because the Veterans Stadium grounds crew didn't properly maintain the pitcher's mound, causing his foot to land wrong . . . Opponents stole only one base against him in 1993, one in six tries. The six tries are the lowest attempt rate in the major leagues . . . Should have four-five more good years.

YEAR	TEAM/LEVEL	G	IP	W-L	PCT.	HITS	SO	BB	ERA
1991	Philadelphia	34	232	16-13	.552	231	142	49	3.61
1992	Philadelphia	32	229	13-11	.542	227	125	46	3.81
1993	Philadelphia	29	191	12-9	.571	177	116	40	3.25

BOBBY MUNOZ

New York Yankees

Relief Pitcher

$14

A part of the Yankees' basketball team, with Mark Hutton and Andy Cook. Munoz is 6'7", was a starter until last year, with poor control and a career record of 19 wins, 29 losses. The Yankees like his arm, and made him the closer at Columbus, where he had 10 saves and a 1.44 ERA over the first couple of months. Control troubles returned when he got to the majors. Grade C prospect.

YEAR	TEAM/LEVEL	G	IP	W-L	SAVES	HITS	SO	BB	ERA
1992	Albany AA	22	112	7-5	0	96	66	70	3.28
1993	Columbus AAA	22	31	3-1	10	24	16	8	1.44
1993	New York	38	46	3-3	0	48	33	26	5.32

MIKE MUNOZ

Colorado Rockies

Relief Pitcher

$7

Was the Tigers top lefthanded reliever in '92, but started out slowly last year, was designated for assignment and found himself the property of the Rockies. As I said last year, there really isn't much about him that would make you think he could sustain success . . . . Throws sinking fastball, slider, gets ground balls. Can succeed if he throws strikes, but hasn't done that consistently.

YEAR	TEAM/LEVEL	G	IP	W-L	SAVES	HITS	SO	BB	ERA
1992	Detroit	63	47	1-2	2	44	23	24	3.09
1993	Colo Springs AAA	40	38	1-2	3	46	30	9	1.67
1993	Two Teams	29	21	2-2	0	25	17	15	4.71

OSCAR MUNOZ

Minnesota Twins
Starting Pitcher
$15

Cleveland's fifth-round pick in 1990 out of the University of Miami, Munoz was traded to the Twins in the Sorrento deal. He struggled with injuries at the AA level before last year, finally got healthy and put in a good season at Nashville. He has a mid-80s fastball, also throws slider and knucklecurve, good strike-out rate, fierce competitor. The Twins need pitching, so he has an opportunity . . . Grade C prospect.

YEAR	TEAM/LEVEL	G	IP	W-L	PCT.	HITS	SO	BB	ERA
1991	Canton AA	15	85	3-8	.273	88	71	51	5.72
1992	Orlando AA	14	68	3-5	.375	73	74	32	5.05
1993	AA and AAA	25	163	13-6	.684	152	168	68	3.31

PEDRO MUNOZ

Minnesota Twins
Right Field
$25

Righthanded power hitter, only 25 years old. He ran well at one time, but has had knee problems which have taken his speed, and even put his career in jeopardy until he went on a home run/RBI tear late in the season (over half of his season's RBI were in September). No star potential now; will have to move his slugging percentage up from .400 in order to increase his playing time.

YEAR	TEAM/LEVEL	G	AB	R	H	2B	3B	HR	RBI	BB	SB	AVG	OBP	SLG
1992	Minnesota	127	418	44	113	16	3	12	71	17	4	.270	.298	.409
1993	Minnesota	104	326	34	76	11	1	13	38	25	1	.233	.294	.393
1994	**Projected**	**107**	**336**	**37**	**91**	**17**	**2**	**10**	**48**	**21**	**5**	**.271**	**.314**	**.423**

DALE MURPHY

Retired
Right Field
No Value

Murphy called it quits in May after getting about one hit a week. Murphy's last good year came when he was 31; after that, six years of trying to get it back . . . The most-similar player to Dale Murphy in all of baseball history is his last manager, Don Baylor. Murphy hit .265 in his career; Baylor, .260. Murphy hit 398 homers, Baylor only 338, but Murphy drove in 1,266 runs, Baylor 1,276.

YEAR	TEAM/LEVEL	G	AB	R	H	2B	3B	HR	RBI	BB	SB	AVG	OBP	SLG
1991	Philadelphia	153	544	66	137	33	1	18	81	48	1	.252	.309	.415
1992	Philadelphia	18	62	5	10	1	0	2	7	1	0	.161	.175	.274
1993	Colorado	26	42	1	6	1	0	0	7	5	0	.143	.224	.167

ROB MURPHY

St. Louis Cardinals
Relief Pitcher
$6

Has averaged 71 game appearances per season over the last seven years, despite often pitching poorly (3.68 ERA). In 1993 he allowed only four of 33 inherited runners to score (the norm is 32%), and was among the league leaders with 24 holds. I would have a hard time concluding that he had pitched well, but there is something about him that managers seem to like.

YEAR	TEAM/LEVEL	G	IP	W-L	SAVES	HITS	SO	BB	ERA
1991	Seattle	57	48	0-1	4	47	34	19	3.00
1992	Houston	58	55	3-1	0	56	42	21	4.07
1993	St. Louis	73	65	5-7	1	73	41	20	4.87

EDDIE MURRAY

New York Mets

First Base

$48

He adjusted to Shea Stadium, where the visibility is notoriously bad, by becoming more aggressive early in the count, so that he wasn't hitting in a hole, and drove in 100 runs for the first time in eight years (remarkably, he averaged 90 RBI/season from 1986 to 1992 without ever driving in 100) . . . Has aged exceptionally well, being about 88% as effective in his late thirties as he was in his twenties . . . Will get 3000th hit in 1995.

YEAR	TEAM/LEVEL	G	AB	R	H	2B	3B	HR	RBI	BB	SB	AVG	OBP	SLG
1992	New York	156	551	64	144	37	2	16	93	66	4	.261	.336	.423
1993	New York	154	610	77	174	28	1	27	100	40	2	.285	.325	.467
1994	**Projected**	**142**	**531**	**60**	**143**	**24**	**1**	**18**	**86**	**50**	**5**	**.269**	**.332**	**.420**

JOSE MUSSET

California Angels

Reliever

$16

A converted outfielder who throws sidearm and underhanded, and throws hard. His ERA at Midland was high, but his strikeout/walk data was good, and Midland is a pitcher's hell—they score like a thousand runs a year there. There is still a prejudice against a pitcher who pitches funny, and Musset will have to overcome that, but if Dan Quisenberry could do it throwing 78, this guy can do it throwing 88. Grade B prospect.

YEAR	TEAM/LEVEL	G	IP	W-L	SAVES	HITS	SO	BB	ERA
1991	Mesa A	10	14	1-1	2	14	10	5	3.21
1992	Quad City A	41	72	8-2	6	41	104	25	2.39
1993	Midland AA	59	62	2-6	21	59	59	32	5.49

MIKE MUSSINA

Baltimore Orioles

Starting Pitcher

$57

He was troubled by tendonitis and an unrelated back injury. He tried to pitch with the sore arm, but posted ERAs of 7.48 in both June and July. He finally went on the DL, and pitched better for a while on return, but then had a recurrence of the tendonitis, and ended his season early . . . A magnificent pitcher, but I would be wary of drafting him . . . Throws to first base less often than any other American League pitcher.

YEAR	TEAM/LEVEL	G	IP	W-L	PCT.	HITS	SO	BB	ERA
1991	Baltimore	12	88	4-5	.444	77	52	21	2.87
1992	Baltimore	32	241	18-5	.783	212	130	48	2.54
1993	Baltimore	25	168	14-6	.700	163	117	44	4.46

JEFF MUTIS

Cleveland Indians

Starting Pitcher

$10

A 27-year-old lefthander, a first-round draft pick in 1988, when the Indians had three picks in the first round. He has pitched consistently well in the minors (48-27, 2.99 ERA) but has struggled something fierce in the majors (3-11, 6.88). He's a finesse pitcher—low strikeout rates, good control—and I suspect that he is eventually going to be a rotation starter somewhere. Doesn't have a lock on a job for '94.

YEAR	TEAM/LEVEL	G	IP	W-L	PCT.	HITS	SO	BB	ERA
1992	Cleveland	3	11	0-2	.000	24	8	6	9.53
1993	Charlotte AAA	12	76	6-0	1.000	64	59	25	2.62
1993	Cleveland	17	81	3-6	.333	93	29	33	5.78

GREG MYERS

California Angels

Catcher

$19

Had about the same stats last year that he had for Toronto in '91. The Angels will probably open the season either with Chris Turner catching, or with Turner platooning with Myers. Myers is slow, even for a catcher, and his defense is not Ron Karkovice, but there has to be a place in the majors for a lefthanded hitting catcher who drives in 40 runs in less than 300 at bats.

YEAR	TEAM/LEVEL	G	AB	R	H	2B	3B	HR	RBI	BB	SB	AVG	OBP	SLG
1992	Two Teams	30	78	4	18	7	0	1	13	5	0	.231	.271	.359
1993	California	108	290	27	74	10	0	7	40	17	3	.255	.298	.362
1994	**Projected**	**112**	**326**	**26**	**81**	**17**	**0**	**7**	**40**	**22**	**2**	**.249**	**.297**	**.366**

RANDY MYERS

Chicago Cubs

Closer

$40

His season demonstrates just how vulnerable Thigpen's record is: there is a lot of space between 57 saves and the upper boundary of what is possible. Here's a pitcher having a good-not-great season for a fairly good team—but he saved 53 games in 59 tries . . . Only 28 years old; it's hard to remember that he was once traded for John Franco, who is about 73.

YEAR	TEAM/LEVEL	G	IP	W-L	SAVES	HITS	SO	BB	ERA
1991	Cincinnati	58	132	6-13	6	116	108	80	3.55
1992	San Diego	65	77	2-6	38	83	61	32	4.46
1993	Chicago	73	75	2-4	53	65	86	26	3.11

CHRIS NABHOLZ

Montreal Expos

Starting Pitcher

$25

He was stopped in mid-summer by a strained muscle in his left forearm, but returned in late September to pitch very, very well at season's close. The Expos have many young pitchers, but he still appears to be in possession of a starter's job. Throws good fastball, excellent sinker; isn't a quality pitcher and probably never will be, but wins as many as he loses.

YEAR	TEAM/LEVEL	G	IP	W-L	PCT.	HITS	SO	BB	ERA
1991	Montreal	24	154	8-7	.533	134	99	57	3.63
1992	Montreal	32	195	11-12	.478	176	130	74	3.32
1993	Montreal	26	117	9-8	.529	100	74	63	4.09

TIM NAEHRING

Boston Red Sox

Shortstop/Second Base

$24

At one time regarded as a infielder with a bat, Naehring had several years of back trouble, and bat trouble. He resumed hitting in September of '92, carried through in the minors and then the majors last year. The Red Sox infield is solid, and there's no obvious place for him, but I do believe he is a good hitter and a good fielder, and he may just shove somebody out of the way and take their job.

YEAR	TEAM/LEVEL	G	AB	R	H	2B	3B	HR	RBI	BB	SB	AVG	OBP	SLG
1992	Boston	72	186	12	43	8	0	3	14	18	0	.231	.308	.323
1993	Boston	39	127	14	42	10	0	1	17	10	1	.331	.377	.433
1994	**Projected**	**121**	**480**	**50**	**125**	**21**	**0**	**10**	**54**	**56**	**1**	**.260**	**.342**	**.367**

CHARLES NAGY

Cleveland Indians

Starting Pitcher

$20

One of the best pitchers in baseball in 1992, his arm went dead early in the season. A shoulder problem, originally diagnosed as tendonitis, was determined to be an impingement syndrome, meaning that there was so much tissue in his shoulder—so much muscle and cartilage and bone—that his arm was unable to rotate freely. He had surgery June 29. Pitchers have come back from this, but it's not going to be overnight.

YEAR	TEAM/LEVEL	G	IP	W-L	PCT.	HITS	SO	BB	ERA
1991	Cleveland	33	211	10-15	.400	228	109	66	4.13
1992	Cleveland	33	252	17-10	.630	245	169	57	2.96
1993	Cleveland	9	49	2-6	.250	66	30	13	6.29

ROB NATAL

Florida Marlins

Catcher

$10

Natal was taken from the Expos in the expansion draft. He is only eight months younger than the man he is backing up (Santiago), plus he is, like Santiago, a righthanded batter, so there's no platoon advantage to having him around. His defensive numbers in '93 were better than Santiago's, including a staff ERA of 3.83 with Natal, 4.14 with Santiago. He's a marginal prospect, but then, Santiago's a marginal player.

YEAR	TEAM/LEVEL	G	AB	R	H	2B	3B	HR	RBI	BB	SB	AVG	OBP	SLG
1992	Indianap AAA	96	344	50	104	19	3	12	50	28	3	.302	.359	.480
1992	MLE	96	325	36	85	16	1	7	36	20	2	.262	.304	.382
1993	Florida	41	117	3	25	4	1	1	6	6	1	.214	.273	.291

JAIME NAVARRO

Milwaukee Brewers

Starting Pitcher

$18

I urged you to avoid him last year, but then suggested you to look for a pitcher with a comparable won-lost record, "like Nagy or Smiley." Sorry 'bout that. A short summary of Navarro's 1993 season: he got the bejeezus beaten out of him. He led the American League in earned runs allowed, 127, and sacrifice flies allowed (17). The batting average against him on the first pitch was .423 (norm: .322) . . . 35%, 40% chance of a comeback.

YEAR	TEAM/LEVEL	G	IP	W-L	PCT.	HITS	SO	BB	ERA
1991	Milwaukee	34	234	15-12	.556	237	114	73	3.92
1992	Milwaukee	34	246	17-11	.607	224	100	64	3.33
1993	Milwaukee	35	214	11-12	.478	254	114	73	5.33

TITO NAVARRO

New York Mets

Shortstop

$16

As I mentioned, I like Tim Bogar, and think he's pretty good as shortstop prospects go. I'd say the same about Navarro. He played well at Double-A at age 20 (1991), but had a sore shoulder in the spring of '92, and had open (as opposed to arthroscopic) surgery to fix that, thus missed the '92 season. He's a .260 hitter, very fast, has a shortstop's feet and had a good arm before the surgery. Grade B prospect.

YEAR	TEAM/LEVEL	G	AB	R	H	2B	3B	HR	RBI	BB	SB	AVG	OBP	SLG
1991	MLE	128	467	57	124	8	3	1	35	52	31	.266	.339	.302
1993	Norfolk AAA	96	273	35	77	11	1	0	16	33	19	.282	.357	.330
1993	MLE	96	264	29	68	9	0	0	13	27	14	.258	.326	.292

DENNY NEAGLE

Pittsburgh Pirates

Lefthanded Pitcher

$20

Neagle had a first-rate minor league career before 1992, but didn't impress anybody in '92 or the first half of '93. After briefly re-acquainting himself with minor league hotel rooms he remembered some things like throwing strikes and using his slider to change speeds, and pitched much better after his return (3.38 ERA over the second half). I still think he can be an effective pitcher, either as a starter or in the bullpen.

YEAR	TEAM/LEVEL	G	IP	W-L	SAVES	HITS	SO	BB	ERA
1992	Pittsburgh	55	86	4-6	2	81	77	43	4.48
1993	Buffalo	3	3	0-0	0	3	6	2	0.00
1993	Pittsburgh	50	81	3-5	1	82	73	37	5.31

TROY NEEL

Oakland Athletics

DH/First Base

$40

His MLE from 1992 was .305 with a .478 slugging percentage, and his actual major league data were almost the same. If you do that in 120 games it's a nice little season, but if you do it in 600 at bats you can make a large pile of money. Neel is a big guy, and I'm not sure where he'll play when McGwire returns, but I'll tell you: he's going to play somewhere. Recommend that you consider him.

YEAR	TEAM/LEVEL	G	AB	R	H	2B	3B	HR	RBI	BB	SB	AVG	OBP	SLG
1992	MLE	112	370	47	113	29	1	11	57	46	1	.305	.382	.478
1992	Oakland	24	53	8	14	3	0	3	9	5	0	.264	.339	.491
1993	Oakland	123	427	59	124	21	0	19	63	49	3	.290	.367	.473

GENE NELSON

Texas Rangers

Reliever

$20

After having two straight miserable years he was having a very good year for the Angels' bullpen, but was released in September, supposedly to dump his salary (although why he would have a high salary, based on his 1991 and 1992 seasons, is a mystery to me). The Rangers picked him up to take a quick look at him, and he also pitched OK for them. A 33-year-old middle reliever, best pitch is a forkball.

YEAR	TEAM/LEVEL	G	IP	W-L	SAVES	HITS	SO	BB	ERA
1991	Oakland	44	49	1-5	0	60	23	23	6.84
1992	Oakland	28	52	3-1	0	68	23	22	6.45
1993	Two Teams	52	61	0-5	5	60	35	24	3.12

JEFF NELSON

Seattle Mariners

Righthanded Relief Pitcher

$10

He's a ground ball pitcher, and Piniella uses him to try to get a double play, so he *always* comes in with men on base. He had 95 inherited runners last year, an extraordinary total. Dennis Eckersley, pitching a comparable number of games, had 32 inherited runners. This makes Nelson a key member of the staff, because if he's not sharp, runs score in a hurry. He wasn't that sharp, and gave up 49 RBI in 60 innings. Ouch.

YEAR	TEAM/LEVEL	G	IP	W-L	SAVES	HITS	SO	BB	ERA
1991	Minors—2 Levels	49	61	7-4	33	62	60	24	2.67
1992	Seattle	65	80	1-7	5	71	45	44	3.49
1993	Seattle	71	60	5-3	1	57	61	34	4.35

ROBB NEN

Florida Marlins

Righthanded Pitcher

$14

Big righthander with a huge jaw, throws in the mid-90s. He has battled a variety of major and minor injuries, and his control has generally been poor, so the Rangers included him in the Cris Carpenter trade. At 24 he's a thrower, not a pitcher, and is out of options, so he'll have to learn his trade in the majors. Grade C prospect due to injury history and poor control.

YEAR	TEAM/LEVEL	G	IP	W-L	PCT.	HITS	SO	BB	ERA
1992	Tulsa AA	4	25	1-1	.500	21	20	2	2.16
1993	Okl City AAA	6	28	0-2	.000	45	12	18	6.67
1993	Two Teams	24	56	2-1	.667	63	39	46	6.75

MARC NEWFIELD

Seattle Mariners

Outfield

$26

This is one of the good ones, a young player who should be an MVP candidate about the year 2000, Lord willing and the creek don't rise. He was the sixth player taken in the 1990 draft, out of high school, and hit a 500-foot home run in his first pro game. He missed most of the 1992 season following surgery to remove a bunion from his big toe, but has hit well almost everywhere. Could be Rookie of the Year.

YEAR	TEAM/LEVEL	G	AB	R	H	2B	3B	HR	RBI	BB	SB	AVG	OBP	SLG
1993	Jacksonvil AA	91	336	48	103	18	0	19	51	33	1	.307	.374	.500
1993	MLE	91	322	38	89	17	0	15	41	22	0	.276	.323	.469
1993	Seattle	22	66	5	15	3	0	1	7	2	0	.227	.257	.318

WARREN NEWSON

Chicago White Sox

Right Field/DH

$23

Took most of the season off after his wife was seriously injured in a car accident. Newson has a career secondary average of .351, most of that accounted for by Eddie Yost-type walk ratios. A 5-foot-7 lefthanded line drive hitter, has some power, is an adequate outfielder and gives good effort . . . He's not destined for Cooperstown, but he's one of my favorite players.

YEAR	TEAM/LEVEL	G	AB	R	H	2B	3B	HR	RBI	BB	SB	AVG	OBP	SLG
1991	Chicago	71	132	20	39	5	0	4	25	28	5	.295	.419	.424
1992	Chicago	63	136	19	30	3	0	1	11	37	3	.221	.387	.265
1993	Chicago	26	40	9	12	0	0	2	6	9	0	.300	.429	.450

ROD NICHOLS

Los Angeles Dodgers

Reliever/Starter

$10

Nichols lost a game for the Dodgers in July, which gives him a career record of 11 wins, 31 losses. This wouldn't be a good batting average. He was cut loose by Cleveland, and signed with Albuquerque as a minor league free agent (have the Dodgers actually sunk to using the Cleveland Indians castoffs?). Anyway, he pitched OK for Albuquerque, and his major league career is probably **not** over.

YEAR	TEAM/LEVEL	G	IP	W-L	PCT.	HITS	SO	BB	ERA
1992	Cleveland	30	105	4-3	.571	114	56	31	4.53
1993	Albuquerque	21	128	8-5	.615	132	79	50	4.30
1993	Los Angeles	4	6	0-1	.000	9	3	2	5.68

DAVID NIED

Colorado Rockies

Starting Pitcher

$21

He was expected to be the ace of the Rockies staff after being the first player picked in the expansion draft, but his season was derailed by an elbow injury. He responded to treatment, and was throwing well late in the year. Elbow injuries are often serious and usually chronic, and *no* pitcher is likely to post a good record or a low ERA with the 1994 Colorado Rockies. He'll come back sometime.

YEAR	TEAM/LEVEL	G	IP	W-L	PCT.	HITS	SO	BB	ERA
1992	Richmond AAA	26	168	14-9	.609	144	159	44	2.84
1992	Atlanta	6	23	3-0	1.000	10	19	5	1.17
1993	Colorado	16	87	5-9	.357	99	46	42	5.17

JERRY NIELSEN

California Angels

Relief Pitcher

$9

A part of the Jim Abbott trade, he spent most of the summer at Vancouver, where he was not very impressive, and a month in mid-summer with the Angels, where he struggled. A late-round draft pick, he pitched well in the low minors in the Yankee system, where they bring pitchers along slowly. Grade D prospect, a candidate for the ever-popular role of lefthanded spot reliever.

YEAR	TEAM/LEVEL	G	IP	W-L	SAVES	HITS	SO	BB	ERA
1992	New York AL	20	20	1-0	0	17	12	18	4.58
1993	Vancouver	33	56	2-5	0	70	45	20	4.20
1994	California	10	12	0-0	0	18	8	4	8.03

MELVIN NIEVES

San Diego Padres

Outfield

$26

Nieves was the key player acquired by the Padres in the Fred McGriff trade. When an organization is forced to trade a Hall of Famer in mid-career there is no way they can expect to break even, but Nieves is a real quality prospect; he *should* be a fine hitter. He's a 200-pound switch hitter who throws well and runs all right, although he'll be slow at 30. He's only 22, and a **Grade A prospect**.

YEAR	TEAM/LEVEL	G	AB	R	H	2B	3B	HR	RBI	BB	SB	AVG	OBP	SLG
1992	MLE	100	343	50	92	21	2	18	63	33	3	.268	.332	.499
1993	2 Teams AAA	121	432	69	125	20	4	17	60	43	6	.289	.358	.472
1993	MLE	121	412	47	105	15	1	13	40	27	3	.255	.301	.391

DAVE NILSSON

Milwaukee Brewers

Catcher

$21

As a hitter he had exactly the same year that Greg Myers did, except that he walked a little bit more. He was the Brewers regular catcher, particularly over the second half, and his defense was not a pleasant surprise. He threw out only 23% of opposing base stealers, poorest in the American League, and there were other problems. As a hitter, he still has considerable potential. He could become one of the better-hitting catchers in the league.

YEAR	TEAM/LEVEL	G	AB	R	H	2B	3B	HR	RBI	BB	SB	AVG	OBP	SLG
1992	Milwaukee	51	164	15	38	8	0	4	25	17	2	.232	.304	.354
1993	Milwaukee	100	296	35	76	10	2	7	40	37	3	.257	.336	.375
1994	**Projected**	**131**	**419**	**53**	**119**	**25**	**2**	**7**	**61**	**42**	**6**	**.284**	**.349**	**.403**

OTIS NIXON

Atlanta Braves

Center Field

$40

Otis is a free agent at this writing. He needs to get into a grass park, where he can bunt. He hit .212 with men on base in '93, worst in the league, and this is not unexpected. With men on he tends not to bunt, and this takes away his best weapon. He played magnificently for three years in Atlanta, and I'm not unduly concerned about his age (35) because he's a speed player, and they age well.

YEAR	TEAM/LEVEL	G	AB	R	H	2B	3B	HR	RBI	BB	SB	AVG	OBP	SLG
1991	Atlanta	124	401	81	119	10	1	0	26	47	72	.297	.371	.327
1992	Atlanta	120	456	79	134	14	2	2	22	39	41	.294	.348	.346
1993	Atlanta	134	461	77	124	12	3	1	24	61	47	.269	.351	.315

MATT NOKES

New York Yankees

Designated Hitter/Catcher

$21

His defense has always been suspect, putting it kindly, and he hit the bench as soon as Stanley got hot. Nokes is a few months younger than Stanley, and until last year had been regarded as a better hitter. If Stanley cools off this year—more than a remote possibility—Nokes could re-take the larger share of the catcher's job. If not, Nokes should have years left as a bench player.

YEAR	TEAM/LEVEL	G	AB	R	H	2B	3B	HR	RBI	BB	SB	AVG	OBP	SLG
1992	New York	121	384	42	86	9	1	22	59	37	0	.224	.293	.424
1993	New York	76	217	25	54	8	0	10	35	16	0	.249	.303	.424
1994	**Projected**	**109**	**340**	**38**	**84**	**12**	**0**	**16**	**52**	**26**	**1**	**.247**	**.301**	**.424**

RAFAEL NOVOA

Milwaukee Brewers

Lefthanded Pitcher

$14

Novoa was originally with the Giants, where he shot from A ball to the majors in a single season (1990). The next year he developed tendonitis in his shoulder, and the Giants cut him from their 40-man roster, which left him free to make a deal. Milwaukee signed him and sent him back to do Double-A and Triple-A. He completed these assignments successfully, and might well be ready to pitch in the majors. Grade C prospect.

YEAR	TEAM/LEVEL	G	IP	W-L	PCT.	HITS	SO	BB	ERA
1992	El Paso AA	22	146	10-7	.588	143	124	48	3.26
1993	New Orleans AAA	20	113	10-5	.667	105	74	38	3.42
1993	Milwaukee	15	56	0-3	.000	58	17	22	4.50

EDWIN NUNEZ

Oakland Athletics

Relief Pitcher

$20

Since 1988 he has pitched for Seattle, the Mets, Detroit, Milwaukee, Texas and Oakland. LaRussa likes to hold on to his middle relief guys if they pitch well, and he pitched so-so. Opposing hitters hit .298 against him, but he gave up only two home runs, and his strikeout/walk data was good. Still throws very hard, although he has a tender arm. Tough to run on, pitches inside.

YEAR	TEAM/LEVEL	G	IP	W-L	SAVES	HITS	SO	BB	ERA
1991	Milwaukee	23	25	2-1	8	28	24	13	6.04
1992	Texas	49	59	1-3	3	63	49	22	4.85
1993	Oakland	56	76	3-6	1	89	58	29	3.81

SHERMAN OBANDO

Baltimore Orioles

Outfield/DH

$18

Opened the season as the righthanded part of a right field platoon, but the platoon broke up and he pulled a hamstring repeatedly, winding up with essentially a wasted season. He hit .272, but had more strikeouts than hits (26-25), and showed a secondary average of .163. He is young and he can hit some, but ranks well below Jeffrey Hammonds, a similar young player.

YEAR	TEAM/LEVEL	G	AB	R	H	2B	3B	HR	RBI	BB	SB	AVG	OBP	SLG
1992	MLE	109	367	58	93	17	1	13	46	22	2	.253	.296	.411
1993	Baltimore	31	92	8	25	2	0	3	15	4	0	.272	.309	.391
1994	**Projected**	**70**	**202**	**29**	**52**	**7**	**0**	**7**	**27**	**13**	**1**	**.257**	**.302**	**.396**

CHARLIE O'BRIEN

New York Mets

Catcher

$13

A righthanded hitting career backup catcher, will turn 33 in May. He is coming off his best season, having set career highs in hits (48) and batting average (.255), and is eligible to file for free agency, although I would guess he might return to New York. He is an exceptional defensive catcher, better than Hundley, and would have had a good career if he could have hit .255 consistently.

YEAR	TEAM/LEVEL	G	AB	R	H	2B	3B	HR	RBI	BB	SB	AVG	OBP	SLG
1992	New York	68	156	15	33	12	0	2	13	16	0	.212	.289	.327
1993	New York	67	188	15	48	11	0	4	23	14	1	.255	.312	.378
1994	**Projected**	**84**	**194**	**17**	**41**	**11**	**0**	**3**	**19**	**18**	**1**	**.211**	**.278**	**.314**

PETE O'BRIEN

Released

First Base

$1

He was released by the Mariners in July, having struggled through three-and-a-half years of a four-year contract, signed by a GM who must have been taking happy pills. He wasn't much of a player when he signed that contract at age 32, and is now 36. He might catch on somewhere as a lefthanded pinch hitter/defensive sub at first base, if he's willing to work for something near the minimum salary.

YEAR	TEAM/LEVEL	G	AB	R	H	2B	3B	HR	RBI	BB	SB	AVG	OBP	SLG
1991	Seattle	152	560	58	139	29	3	17	88	44	0	.248	.300	.402
1992	Seattle	134	396	40	88	15	1	14	52	40	2	.222	.289	.371
1993	Seattle	72	210	30	54	7	0	7	27	26	0	.257	.333	.390

JOHN O'DONOGHUE, JR.

Baltimore Orioles

Starting Pitcher

$18

A 6-foot-6 lefthander; when he pitches he always carries his father's baseball card in his pocket. He was a teammate of Ben McDonald's at LSU, but wasn't drafted out of college. The Orioles took a chance on him, and he has pitched well at every stop, a total of 497 innings. Grade B prospect; will eventually emerge as a rotation starter.

YEAR	TEAM/LEVEL	G	IP	W-L	PCT.	HITS	SO	BB	ERA
1992	AA and AAA	30	182	12-8	.600	138	134	59	2.62
1993	Rochester AAA	22	128	7-4	.636	122	111	41	3.88
1993	Baltimore	11	20	0-1	.000	22	16	10	4.58

JOSE OFFERMAN
Los Angeles Dodgers
Shortstop
$37

He made progress in every area of the game in '93, and is close to being a quality player. He improved his fielding percentage from .935 to .950, although he still led the league in errors, and still made 15 errors more than a typical major league shortstop with the same number of chances ... The Dodgers' double-play combination, Offerman and Reed, were first and second in the NL in sacrifice bunts, with 25 and 17, respectively.

YEAR	TEAM/LEVEL	G	AB	R	H	2B	3B	HR	RBI	BB	SB	AVG	OBP	SLG
1992	Los Angeles	149	534	67	139	20	8	1	30	57	23	.260	.331	.333
1993	Los Angeles	158	590	77	159	21	6	1	62	71	30	.269	.346	.331
1994	**Projected**	**155**	**575**	**73**	**150**	**16**	**5**	**2**	**46**	**73**	**31**	**.261**	**.344**	**.317**

BOBBY OJEDA
Cleveland Indians
Starting Pitcher
$5

Survived a tragic accident to return in August, pitching near his normal level. He's 36, and in a routine analysis we would expect his career to wind down soon. Highly traumatic events, however, change people in unpredictable ways; it might make him feel that there is more to life than baseball, or it might push him to a new level of dedication. It might make him more willing to experiment. His value depends on these unknown reactions.

YEAR	TEAM/LEVEL	G	IP	W-L	PCT.	HITS	SO	BB	ERA
1991	Los Angeles	31	189	12-9	.571	181	120	70	3.18
1992	Los Angeles	29	166	6-9	.400	169	94	81	3.63
1993	Cleveland	9	43	2-1	.667	48	27	21	4.40

TROY O'LEARY
Milwaukee Brewers
Outfield
$14

A 24-year-old lefthanded hitter, has paid his dues in the minors (672 games), was the Texas League MVP in 1992 and is looking to make the Brewers in '94. He probably won't hit enough to be a regular outfielder, nor is there an opening for him in the Milwaukee outfield unless Yount leaves, but he's a pinch hitter type (lefthanded line drive hitter) and runs well, which will help him until Garner gets fired.

YEAR	TEAM/LEVEL	G	AB	R	H	2B	3B	HR	RBI	BB	SB	AVG	OBP	SLG
1992	MLE	135	469	61	132	22	4	3	52	33	18	.281	.329	.365
1993	MLE	111	372	51	90	28	0	5	46	33	4	.242	.304	.358
1993	Milwaukee	19	41	3	12	3	0	0	3	5	0	.293	.370	.366

JOHN OLERUD
Toronto Blue Jays
First Base
$75

Hit far better on the road (.379 with 15 homers, 30 doubles, 59 RBI) than he did in Toronto . . . Hit .371 with runners in scoring position . . . I've compared him in the past to Rusty Staub. Staub in his parallel season (1967) hit .333 with 44 doubles ... I'm a great admirer of Frank Thomas, but I think Olerud was probably more valuable in '93 than the MVP. He's a better first baseman, and he created more runs.

YEAR	TEAM/LEVEL	G	AB	R	H	2B	3B	HR	RBI	BB	SB	AVG	OBP	SLG
1992	Toronto	138	458	68	130	28	0	16	66	70	1	.284	.375	.450
1993	Toronto	158	551	109	200	54	2	24	107	114	0	.363	.473	.599
1994	**Projected**	**154**	**550**	**92**	**170**	**36**	**1**	**24**	**92**	**99**	**1**	**.309**	**.414**	**.509**

JOSE OLIVA

Atlanta Braves

Third Base

$13

Traded to the Braves from the Rangers' system, Oliva didn't have a particularly good year in his first season at Triple-A, and has temporarily disappeared as a prospect. In view of his youth (23) and hitting ability, I think we'll see him again, although not necessarily as a third baseman. A strong righthanded hitter, he's taken criticism for his defense and attitude. Grade B prospect, won't play much this year.

YEAR	TEAM/LEVEL	G	AB	R	H	2B	3B	HR	RBI	BB	SB	AVG	OBP	SLG
1992	MLE	124	439	53	114	26	5	14	69	31	2	.260	.309	.437
1993	Richmond AAA	125	412	63	97	20	6	21	65	35	1	.235	.301	.466
1993	MLE	125	403	54	88	18	4	18	56	30	0	.218	.273	.417

OMAR OLIVARES

St. Louis Cardinals

Pitcher

$26

He was moved from a starting role to relief, except for nine games, and frankly did not pitch well; his ERA could easily have been higher than 4.17. He was bothered by a strained groin muscle, and also pissed off his manager by saying something to the media about his arm being tired after he had pitched several days in a row . . . He's still young; is liable to be pitching somewhere else and might bounce back strong.

YEAR	TEAM/LEVEL	G	IP	W-L	PCT.	HITS	SO	BB	ERA
1991	St. Louis	28	167	11-7	.611	148	91	61	3.71
1992	St. Louis	32	197	9-9	.500	189	124	63	3.84
1993	St. Louis	59	119	5-3	.625	134	63	54	4.17

DARREN OLIVER

Texas Rangers

Relief Pitcher

$13

The son of Bob Oliver, the outfielder/first baseman who drove in 99 runs for the Royals in 1970. He was drafted by the Rangers in the third round in 1988, but wasn't successful as a starter, and missed most of the 1990 and 1991 seasons due to an injury to his left (pitching) shoulder. He moved to the bullpen last year, and earned a major league look after a 1.96 ERA for Tulsa. Grade C prospect.

YEAR	TEAM/LEVEL	G	IP	W-L	SAVES	HITS	SO	BB	ERA
1992	Tulsa AA	3	14	0-1	0	15	14	4	3.14
1993	Tulsa AA	46	73	7-5	6	51	77	41	1.96
1993	Texas	2	3	0-0	0	2	4	1	2.70

JOE OLIVER

Cincinnati Reds

Catcher

$24

The trade of Dan Wilson seems to imply that the Reds will live or die with Oliver, unless there is another move coming. He's not much of a player, for a regular—a sub-.250 hitter who is slow even for a catcher, has a poor strikeout/walk ratio and just an average arm. He hits lefthanders very well (.280 in his career, .219 against righthanders). He hit well with men in scoring position in '93.

YEAR	TEAM/LEVEL	G	AB	R	H	2B	3B	HR	RBI	BB	SB	AVG	OBP	SLG
1992	Cincinnati	143	485	42	131	25	1	10	57	35	2	.270	.316	.388
1993	Cincinnati	139	482	40	115	28	0	14	75	27	0	.239	.276	.384
1994	**Projected**	**129**	**432**	**36**	**106**	**23**	**0**	**12**	**58**	**29**	**1**	**.245**	**.293**	**.382**

GREG OLSON

Atlanta Braves

Catcher

$19

He is sliding gradually toward a backup role, and the emergence of Javy Lopez may grease the skids a little. He's no kind of a hitter, but the Braves had a 2.92 ERA when he was catching last year (641 innings), the best of any major league catcher appearing in 70 or more games . . . Batted 51 times in double play situations, and grounded into 11 double plays, highest percentage in the National League.

YEAR	TEAM/LEVEL	G	AB	R	H	2B	3B	HR	RBI	BB	SB	AVG	OBP	SLG
1992	Atlanta	95	302	27	72	14	2	3	27	34	2	.238	.316	.328
1993	Atlanta	83	262	23	59	10	0	4	24	29	1	.225	.304	.309
1994	**Projected**	**60**	**162**	**15**	**38**	**7**	**0**	**2**	**15**	**18**	**1**	**.235**	**.311**	**.315**

GREGG OLSON

Baltimore Orioles

Closer

$40

You can't argue with a 1.60 ERA, but he is still not where he was two or three years ago. He allowed 48% of his inherited runners to score (15 of 31), the worst percentage in the American League, thus he was charged with only nine runs allowed, but 23 RBI . . . His season ended in early August due to a strained ligament in his elbow.

YEAR	TEAM/LEVEL	G	IP	W-L	SAVES	HITS	SO	BB	ERA
1991	Baltimore	72	74	4-6	31	74	72	29	3.18
1992	Baltimore	60	61	1-5	36	46	58	24	2.05
1993	Baltimore	50	45	0-2	29	37	44	18	1.60

PAUL O'NEILL

New York Yankees

Right Field

$35

Like Eddie Murray, he seemed to change his game plan last year, becoming much more aggressive early in the count. In an almost identical number of at bats, he reduced his walks by 33 and his strikeouts by 16, his strikeouts down 38 from two years ago. It seemed to work, as he picked up as many hits as he lost walks, and gained power. . . Fielded .988 in right field, best in the American League.

YEAR	TEAM/LEVEL	G	AB	R	H	2B	3B	HR	RBI	BB	SB	AVG	OBP	SLG
1992	Cincinnati	148	496	59	122	19	1	14	66	77	6	.246	.346	.373
1993	New York	141	498	71	155	34	1	20	75	44	2	.311	.367	.504
1994	**Projected**	**148**	**509**	**64**	**133**	**28**	**1**	**19**	**73**	**66**	**7**	**.261**	**.346**	**.432**

STEVE ONTIVEROS

Seattle Mariners

Relief Pitcher

$15

A 33-year-old righthander, pitched for Oakland in the mid-'80s. I believe he's been working in Japan or Egypt or someplace. He signed a Triple-A contract with Portland (Minnesota system), and Seattle, trying everything to patch the bullpen, traded for him. I saw him pitch, and he seemed to be throwing as hard as or harder than he did years ago, plus you have to like his minor league and major league record in '93.

YEAR	TEAM/LEVEL	G	IP	W-L	SAVES	HITS	SO	BB	ERA
1992	(Missed season with injury)								
1993	Portland AAA	20	103	7-6	0	90	73	20	2.87
1993	Seattle	14	18	0-2	0	18	13	6	1.00

JOSE OQUENDO
St. Louis Cardinals
Second Base
$18

He has been hobbled for two years by a bone spur on his heel, surgery for which ended his season in August. In the meantime, he has finally lost one of history's longest-running position battles, and must adjust now to a backup role . . . A switch hitter, but a much better lefthanded hitter (.276 to .238, over a period of five years) . . . He is now 30 years old, and has been in St. Louis for eight years.

YEAR	TEAM/LEVEL	G	AB	R	H	2B	3B	HR	RBI	BB	SB	AVG	OBP	SLG
1991	St. Louis	127	366	37	88	11	4	1	26	67	1	.240	.357	.301
1992	St. Louis	14	35	3	9	3	1	0	3	5	0	.257	.350	.400
1993	St. Louis	46	73	7	15	0	0	0	4	12	0	.205	.314	.205

MIKE OQUIST
Baltimore Orioles
Starting Pitcher
$14

A starting pitcher in the minor leagues, has had a good health record (no major injuries in five years) and has had excellent strikeout/walk ratios. Nothing else stands out about him. He throws a fastball, slider and change-up, gives up too many home runs (20 in 149 innings at Rochester) and has been a .500 pitcher (45-41 in the minors, 19-20 at Triple-A). Doesn't throw extremely hard.

YEAR	TEAM/LEVEL	G	IP	W-L	PCT.	HITS	SO	BB	ERA
1992	Rochester AAA	26	153	10-12	.455	164	111	45	4.11
1993	Rochester AAA	28	149	9-8	.529	144	128	41	3.50
1993	Baltimore	5	12	0-0	—	12	8	4	3.86

JESSE OROSCO
Milwaukee Brewers
Reliever/Closer??
$25

In August and early September he was the Brewers' closer, the first time in six years he has had that role. He has struck out more than one per inning for the last two seasons, re-building his credibility after a couple of years on the margins. His 1993 strikeout rate was by far the best of his career. He is 37 but in good shape, probably best used as the first left-hander in the pen.

YEAR	TEAM/LEVEL	G	IP	W-L	SAVES	HITS	SO	BB	ERA
1991	Cleveland	47	46	2-0	0	52	36	15	3.74
1992	Milwaukee	59	39	3-1	1	33	40	13	3.23
1993	Milwaukee	57	57	3-5	8	47	67	17	3.18

JOE ORSULAK
New York Mets
Outfield
$22

Played all three outfield positions for the Mets—66 games in left after Coleman blew up, 40 games in center, 23 in right. His consistency within his role is amazing. He has batted 379 to 413 times in seven of the last eight seasons, the other figure being 486. He has stolen five or six bases in each of the last five years, with batting averages staying in a 20-point circle (.269 to .289).

YEAR	TEAM/LEVEL	G	AB	R	H	2B	3B	HR	RBI	BB	SB	AVG	OBP	SLG
1992	Baltimore	117	391	45	113	18	3	4	39	28	5	.289	.342	.381
1993	New York	134	409	59	116	15	4	8	35	28	5	.284	.331	.399
1994	**Projected**	**118**	**305**	**37**	**83**	**13**	**2**	**4**	**27**	**20**	**4**	**.272**	**.317**	**.367**

JUNIOR ORTIZ
Cleveland Indians
Catcher
$8

Now in his mid-thirties, he established career highs in games played and at bats. See comment on Jesse Levis; I really don't understand why he was playing as much as he did. He's had on-base percentages *and* slugging percentages below .300 for three straight years, making him one of the worst hitters in baseball, plus he grounds into double plays all the time. He throws well, which is worth five or six runs, I guess.

YEAR	TEAM/LEVEL	G	AB	R	H	2B	3B	HR	RBI	BB	SB	AVG	OBP	SLG
1991	Minnesota	61	134	9	28	5	1	0	11	15	0	.209	.293	.261
1992	Cleveland	86	244	20	61	7	0	0	24	12	1	.250	.296	.279
1993	Cleveland	95	249	19	55	13	0	0	20	11	1	.221	.267	.273

LUIS ORTIZ
Boston Red Sox
Third Base
$14

Apart from his classic Dominican strikeout to walk ratio (74 strikeouts, 13 walks last year), Ortiz appears to be ready to hit major league pitching. He's 23 years old, an eighth-round pick in the 1991 draft, has played only 238 minor league games, and there's no job waiting for him in the Red Sox infield, where Cooper and Naehring can both play third. His best shot at playing time might be to move to right field.

YEAR	TEAM/LEVEL	G	AB	R	H	2B	3B	HR	RBI	BB	SB	AVG	OBP	SLG
1992	Lynchburg A	94	355	43	103	27	1	10	61	22	4	.290	.331	.456
1993	Pawtucket AAA	102	402	45	118	28	1	18	81	13	1	.294	.316	.502
1993	MLE	102	389	34	105	28	0	13	61	9	0	.270	.286	.442

JOHN ORTON
California Angels (Released)
Catcher
$10

Orton was released by the Angels at season's end; his ability to get another job will depend on other teams' eagerness to have a one-way catcher, a defense-only catcher. The Angels in '93 had a 3.26 ERA with Orton catching (268 innings), as opposed to 4.22 with Turner, 4.41 with Tingley and 4.74 with Myers, so there is certainly a reasonable argument that Orton's glovework justifies his bat.

YEAR	TEAM/LEVEL	G	AB	R	H	2B	3B	HR	RBI	BB	SB	AVG	OBP	SLG
1992	Edmonton AAA	49	149	28	38	9	3	3	25	28	0	.255	.379	.416
1992	California	43	114	11	25	3	0	2	12	7	1	.219	.276	.298
1993	California	37	95	5	18	5	0	1	4	7	1	.189	.252	.274

DONOVAN OSBORNE
St. Louis Cardinals
Starting Pitcher
$30

A lefthander who, like Arocha and Tewksbury and Cormier, rarely walks anyone. He was 8-3 at the All-Star break, apparently headed for 15 wins, but had an inflammation of his pitching shoulder shortly after that, and had a poor second half. He's only 24, he throws hard, and he knows how to pitch, so if healthy he is certain to have better seasons.

YEAR	TEAM/LEVEL	G	IP	W-L	PCT.	HITS	SO	BB	ERA
1991	Arkansas AA	26	166	8-12	.400	177	130	43	3.63
1992	St. Louis	34	179	11-9	.550	193	104	38	3.77
1993	St. Louis	26	156	10-7	.588	153	83	47	3.76

AL OSUNA

Houston Astros

Relief Pitcher

$18

After a good 1991 season he didn't pitch as well in '92, and started the '93 season at Tucson. On return he pitched better, allowing only 5 of 44 inherited runners to score, the best percentage in the National League. The new manager might have a different appraisal of him, and the Astros need a closer after Doug Jones's poor season. He may get a shot at the closer's job, but I'd be surprised if he kept it.

YEAR	TEAM/LEVEL	G	IP	W-L	SAVES	HITS	SO	BB	ERA
1991	Houston	71	69	7-6	12	59	68	46	3.42
1992	Houston	66	62	6-3	0	52	37	38	4.23
1993	Houston	44	25	1-1	2	17	21	13	3.20

DAVE OTTO

Released

Relief Pitcher

$2

A 6-foot-7 lefthander, he enjoys collecting baseball cards but is probably through appearing on them. Otto is very bright, graduated Magna Cum Laude from the University of Missouri with a degree in accounting. He has good control, but doesn't throw real hard, and his career was set back several times by knee injuries. He was waived by the Pirates on August 18.

YEAR	TEAM/LEVEL	G	IP	W-L	PCT.	HITS	SO	BB	ERA
1991	Cleveland	18	100	2-8	.200	108	47	27	4.23
1992	Cleveland	18	80	5-9	.357	110	32	33	7.06
1993	Pittsburgh	28	68	3-4	.429	85	30	28	5.03

SPIKE OWEN

New York Yankees

Shortstop

$17

Signed a three-year contract last year for a reported $7.1 million, and was the Yankees' shortstop the first half the season, but lost the job to Mike Gallego shortly after the All-Star break. He lost the job more because Gallego played well than because Owen played badly, but he is 33, and not a good enough player that one would expect him to be a regular in his mid-thirties.

YEAR	TEAM/LEVEL	G	AB	R	H	2B	3B	HR	RBI	BB	SB	AVG	OBP	SLG
1992	Montreal	122	386	52	104	16	3	7	40	50	9	.269	.348	.381
1993	New York	103	334	41	78	16	2	2	20	29	3	.234	.294	.311
1994	**Projected**	**118**	**362**	**39**	**85**	**16**	**3**	**3**	**25**	**39**	**5**	**.235**	**.309**	**.320**

JAYHAWK OWENS

Colorado Rockies

Catcher\Kansas Folk Hero

$9

Quoting from the Colorado media guide, "a player who manager Don Baylor can identify with, as Owens was hit by 11 pitches during the '92 season, upping his total to 32 over three seasons." They got him twice in 33 games in the majors . . . Grade D prospect, a 25-year-old catcher who can throw OK, but probably won't hit .250. Secondary average would be better than his batting average.

YEAR	TEAM/LEVEL	G	AB	R	H	2B	3B	HR	RBI	BB	SB	AVG	OBP	SLG
1992	Orlando AA	102	330	50	88	24	0	4	30	36	10	.267	.353	.376
1993	Colo Spr AAA	55	174	24	54	11	3	6	43	21	5	.310	.394	.511
1993	Colorado	33	86	12	18	5	0	3	6	6	1	.209	.277	.372

MIKE PAGLIARULO

Baltimore
(Free Agent)
Third Base
$25

Spent most of the season with Minnesota, hitting .292 with three homers in 83 games, then was traded to Baltimore for the stretch drive (Gomez was hurt) and hit .325 there with six quick homers. He's a free agent, and I wouldn't touch him with a 20-foot pole. He's 34 years old, and a career .242 hitter. It seems to me enormously unlikely that he will sustain his 1993 level of productivity, no matter where he plays.

YEAR	TEAM/LEVEL	G	AB	R	H	2B	3B	HR	RBI	BB	SB	AVG	OBP	SLG
1991	Minnesota	121	365	38	102	20	0	6	36	21	1	.279	.322	.384
1992	Minnesota	42	105	10	21	4	0	0	9	1	1	.200	.213	.238
1993	Two Teams	116	370	55	112	25	4	9	44	26	6	.303	.357	.465

TOM PAGNOZZI

St. Louis Cardinals
Catcher
$30

After a horrible start he had arthroscopic surgery on his knee in May, which explains the decline in playing time. He returned to play well, so that's not a concern for '94 . . . He is an excellent defensive catcher, has won the Gold Glove, and hits enough to hold off the competition. Has a multi-year record of hitting poorly in Busch Stadium.

YEAR	TEAM/LEVEL	G	AB	R	H	2B	3B	HR	RBI	BB	SB	AVG	OBP	SLG
1992	St. Louis	139	485	33	121	26	3	7	44	28	2	.249	.290	.359
1993	St. Louis	92	330	31	85	15	1	7	41	19	1	.258	.296	.373
1994	**Projected**	**116**	**377**	**29**	**95**	**19**	**1**	**4**	**39**	**25**	**4**	**.252**	**.299**	**.340**

LANCE PAINTER

Colorado Rockies
Starting Pitcher
$15

A lefthanded starting pitcher, originally from the San Diego system. I don't believe that any pitcher can be *expected* to post a winning record or a good ERA with this team in '94, although some pitcher will probably do it. Apart from that, I like everything about Painter. He throws reasonably hard, has good control, has good mechanics, and has been consistently successful since entering pro ball. If 1994 doesn't destroy him, he could be Bruce Hurst.

YEAR	TEAM/LEVEL	G	IP	W-L	PCT.	HITS	SO	BB	ERA
1992	Wichita AA	27	163	10-5	.667	138	137	55	3.53
1993	Colo Spr AAA	23	138	9-7	.563	165	91	44	4.30
1993	Colorado	10	39	2-2	.500	52	16	9	6.00

DONN PALL

Philadelphia Phillies
Relief Pitcher
$20

The Phillies acquired him September 1 in exchange for a player to be named, and he continued to pitch well in a setup role; they could have used him in the post-season if he had been eligible. After an off season in '92 he seemed to me (just watching on TV) to be using his curve more and the slider less; anyway, his strikeout/walk data were the best he has had in four years. Solid pitcher.

YEAR	TEAM/LEVEL	G	IP	W-L	SAVES	HITS	SO	BB	ERA
1991	Chicago AL	51	71	7-2	0	59	40	20	2.41
1992	Chicago AL	39	73	5-2	1	79	27	27	4.93
1993	Two Teams	47	76	3-3	1	77	40	14	3.07

RAFAEL PALMEIRO
Texas Rangers
First Base
$67

One of the three best first basemen in the league, with Frank Thomas and Olerud . . . Led the American League in runs scored, was fourth in total bases, fifth in homers, third in doubles, second in stolen base percentage (88%) . . . Sixth player in history to have 40 doubles, 30 homers and 20 stolen bases in a season (Chuck Klein, Willie Mays, Hank Aaron, Howard Johnson and Joe Carter) . . . Has filed for free agency.

YEAR	TEAM/LEVEL	G	AB	R	H	2B	3B	HR	RBI	BB	SB	AVG	OBP	SLG
1992	Texas	159	608	84	163	27	4	22	85	72	2	.268	.352	.434
1993	Texas	160	597	124	176	40	2	37	105	73	22	.295	.371	.554
1994	**Projected**	**160**	**616**	**106**	**178**	**37**	**3**	**25**	**88**	**75**	**9**	**.286**	**.364**	**.478**

DEAN PALMER
Texas Rangers
Third Base
$35

Made progress in some areas last year, but struck out more often (per at bat) than he had in '92, walked less often, had a poor year as a base stealer and made 29 errors at third base, most in the American League . . . More than 60% of his career home runs have been hit on the road—hence, the move to the new park is unlikely to decrease his power stats, and may improve them.

YEAR	TEAM/LEVEL	G	AB	R	H	2B	3B	HR	RBI	BB	SB	AVG	OBP	SLG
1992	Texas	152	541	74	124	25	0	26	72	62	10	.229	.311	.420
1993	Texas	148	519	88	127	31	2	33	96	53	11	.245	.321	.503
1994	**Projected**	**153**	**550**	**86**	**132**	**27**	**2**	**31**	**89**	**60**	**9**	**.240**	**.315**	**.465**

ERIK PAPPAS
St. Louis Cardinals
Catcher
$10

Pappas was the first-round draft pick of the California Angels in 1984, when he was just 18. He didn't make it with the Angels, or Cubs, or Royals, and was on the Louisville roster to start the '93 season. He caught a couple of breaks when Pagnozzi got hurt and Hector the Whale didn't hit, and took advantage of the opening. He's only 28, but not really a .276 hitter, and isn't likely to take Pagnozzi's job.

YEAR	TEAM/LEVEL	G	AB	R	H	2B	3B	HR	RBI	BB	SB	AVG	OBP	SLG
1992	Two Teams AAA	82	236	35	57	12	1	5	28	39	8	.242	.349	.364
1993	St. Louis	82	228	25	63	12	0	1	28	35	1	.276	.368	.342
1994	**Projected**	**82**	**227**	**28**	**56**	**13**	**0**	**5**	**28**	**32**	**3**	**.247**	**.340**	**.370**

CRAIG PAQUETTE
Oakland Athletics
Third Base
$18

He is also known as "Phil Hiatt"; I think you could trade them for one another and only their girlfriends would notice. Paquette got a chance to play when Lansford retired and Seitzer didn't play well, but he struck out 108 times in 105 games, without offsetting this with consistent power. He had also struck out 54 times in 50 games at Tacoma . . . May improve a little, but will be hard-pressed to hold a regular job.

YEAR	TEAM/LEVEL	G	AB	R	H	2B	3B	HR	RBI	BB	SB	AVG	OBP	SLG
1992	MLE	132	494	57	112	26	2	13	68	22	12	.227	.260	.366
1993	Oakland	105	393	35	86	20	4	12	46	14	4	.219	.245	.382
1994	**Projected**	**111**	**415**	**46**	**97**	**19**	**2**	**11**	**54**	**19**	**6**	**.234**	**.267**	**.369**

MARK PARENT
Baltimore Orioles
Catcher
$9

Spent most of the summer at Rochester, but was called up August 3, when Hoiles went on the DL with a back strain. He's a faint imitation of Lance Parrish—a big, slow, righthanded hitting catcher who throws well and has some power, but nothing else going for him. He's now 32, but he's as good a player as Bob Melvin or Junior Ortiz.

YEAR	TEAM/LEVEL	G	AB	R	H	2B	3B	HR	RBI	BB	SB	AVG	OBP	SLG
1992	Baltimore	17	34	4	8	1	0	2	4	3	0	.235	.316	.441
1993	MLE	92	320	36	70	12	0	11	43	31	0	.219	.288	.359
1993	Baltimore	22	54	7	14	2	0	4	12	3	0	.259	.293	.519

RICK PARKER
Houston
(Released)
Outfield
$10

Parker was sent to Tucson three times during the season, the third time August 21. *Baseball Weekly* reported that Art Howe felt very bad about sending him out, saying that "he gives you everything he's got, and he's got a lot of heart . . . he's just been a victim of circumstances." After the season, however, the Astros fired Howe and released Parker, so his future is unclear . . . 31-year-old righthanded hitter, good speed and defense.

YEAR	TEAM/LEVEL	G	AB	R	H	2B	3B	HR	RBI	BB	SB	AVG	OBP	SLG
1992	Tucson AAA	105	319	51	103	10	11	4	38	28	20	.323	.383	.461
1992	MLE	105	297	32	81	8	6	2	24	18	14	.273	.314	.360
1993	Houston	45	45	11	15	3	0	0	4	3	1	.333	.375	.400

DEREK PARKS
Minnesota Twins
Catcher
$20

Consider drafting him. Parks was the Twins first-round draft pick in 1986, and has bounced on and off the hot-prospect list for almost eight years. Despite this he is only 25 years old, and he is coming off his best minor league season, by far. He has cut his strikeouts sharply. Further, Brian Harper may be leaving as a free agent. The Twins, after a dismal season, may be re-building. Parks could be a building block.

YEAR	TEAM/LEVEL	G	AB	R	H	2B	3B	HR	RBI	BB	SB	AVG	OBP	SLG
1992	MLE	79	243	26	55	11	0	9	38	20	0	.226	.285	.383
1993	Portland AAA	107	363	63	113	23	1	17	71	48	0	.311	.392	.521
1993	MLE	107	348	47	98	21	0	12	53	36	0	.282	.349	.445

JEFF PARRETT
Colorado Rockies
Relief Pitcher
$7

Why a free agent pitcher coming off a 9-1 season would sign with an expansion team in a bandbox park, this I don't understand. Anyway, he did, and dealt with the conditions as well as can be expected, posting a 4.20 ERA on the road, which kept his overall ERA in the fives. He's been up and down (and over and out), and I know one thing. Don't expect miracles.

YEAR	TEAM/LEVEL	G	IP	W-L	SAVES	HITS	SO	BB	ERA
1991	Atlanta	18	21	1-2	1	31	14	12	6.33
1992	Oakland	66	98	9-1	1	81	78	42	3.02
1993	Colorado	40	74	3-3	1	78	66	45	5.38

LANCE PARRISH
Released
Catcher
No Value

Released by the Indians on May 30, probably bringing his career to an end. In the chart below I'll compare his career batting record per 150 games to those of Carlton Fisk and Gary Carter. He was a comparable hitter, as you can see, plus he threw better than either man, and blocked the plate better. His career was shorter than theirs, but longer than those of many Hall of Fame catchers. These are just observations, not an argument.

	AB	R	H	2B	3B	HR	RBI	BB	SB	AVG	OBP	SLG
Fisk per 150 games	526	77	141	25	3	23	80	51	8	.269	.341	.457
Parrish per 150 games	540	66	137	23	2	25	82	46	2	.253	.313	.445
Carter per 150 games	521	67	137	24	2	21	80	55	3	.262	.335	.439

DAN PASQUA
Chicago White Sox
Outfield/First Base
$12

Like Merullo and Newson, he might benefit from the Sox' release of Bo and Bell, or, on the other hand, they might release him, too. Pasqua hit 11 to 20 homers a year from 1986 through 1991, but has had hamstring problems over the last two years, hasn't played as much and hasn't hit much of anything. He's 32, might have one or two good years left.

YEAR	TEAM/LEVEL	G	AB	R	H	2B	3B	HR	RBI	BB	SB	AVG	OBP	SLG
1992	Chicago	93	265	26	56	16	1	6	33	36	0	.211	.305	.347
1993	Chicago	78	176	22	36	10	1	5	20	26	2	.205	.302	.358
1994	**Projected**	**53**	**123**	**17**	**29**	**7**	**1**	**4**	**17**	**18**	**1**	**.236**	**.333**	**.407**

BOB PATTERSON
Texas Rangers
Lefthanded Spot Pitcher
$18

Was hit hard a few times, but probably pitched better overall than his 4.78 ERA would suggest. Patterson mixes up an ordinary fastball and a pretty good curve, and also throws a screwball; he is regarded as an intelligent pitcher. Darren Oliver may push him for a job, but I suspect that he will be in the majors for several years yet.

YEAR	TEAM/LEVEL	G	IP	W-L	SAVES	HITS	SO	BB	ERA
1991	Pittsburgh	54	66	4-3	2	67	57	15	4.11
1992	Pittsburgh	60	65	6-3	9	59	43	23	2.92
1993	Texas	52	53	2-4	1	59	46	11	4.78

JOHN PATTERSON
San Francisco Giants
Second Base/Center Field
$8

Patterson had a serious knee injury in spring training, and missed most of the season. He's a 27-year-old switch hitter, runs well (or did, anyway, before the injury). He's a marginal prospect, almost no prospect. He's like Ted Wood: he's a good athlete, a good defensive player, and he hits .300 at Phoenix, so people who don't know any better figure he can hit some. Will never be a regular; might have career as a reserve.

YEAR	TEAM/LEVEL	G	AB	R	H	2B	3B	HR	RBI	BB	SB	AVG	OBP	SLG
1992	MLE	94	338	34	85	15	3	1	24	20	13	.251	.293	.322
1992	San Francisco	32	103	10	19	1	1	0	4	5	5	.184	.229	.214
1993	San Francisco	16	16	1	3	0	0	1	2	0	0	.188	.188	.375

KEN PATTERSON

California Angels

Lefthanded Spot Reliever

$10

Like most of the Angels' bullpen, he wasn't very good. Lefthanded hitters hit .276 against him, and he walked so many people, as he always has, that some of them had to score eventually. Steve Frey, when healthy, is the number-one lefty in the Angels' bullpen; Patterson may stay around as the other one, or they might give the job to somebody else.

YEAR	TEAM/LEVEL	G	IP	W-L	SAVES	HITS	SO	BB	ERA
1991	Chicago AL	43	64	3-0	1	48	32	35	2.83
1992	Chicago AL	32	42	2-3	0	41	23	27	3.89
1993	California	46	59	1-1	1	54	36	35	4.58

ROGER PAVLIK

Texas Rangers

Starting Pitcher

$31

One of the biggest surprises of 1993, spent the first six weeks of the year at Oklahoma City, but pitched a series of brilliant games for Texas late in the year, and appears to be the Rangers' number-two starting pitcher at the outset of 1994. He pitched 88 innings after August 1 with a 6-1 record and a 2.45 ERA . . . Had a major injury in 1991, and came back from it stronger than he was before.

YEAR	TEAM/LEVEL	G	IP	W-L	PCT.	HITS	SO	BB	ERA
1992	Okla City AAA	18	118	7-5	.583	90	104	51	2.98
1992	Texas	13	62	4-4	.500	66	45	34	4.21
1993	Texas	26	166	12-6	.667	151	131	80	3.41

BILL PECOTA

Atlanta Braves

Utility Player

$19

Here's another way to explain what's wrong with the Mets. Pecota was a fine backup player in Kansas City, went to the Mets, they stuck him in the lineup, where he was a disaster, and he went to Atlanta, where he again was a backup player, and he was great. The Braves used him at third and second, as a pinch runner and a pinch hitter against left-handed pitchers. Outstanding work habits.

YEAR	TEAM/LEVEL	G	AB	R	H	2B	3B	HR	RBI	BB	SB	AVG	OBP	SLG
1991	Kansas City	125	398	53	114	23	2	6	45	41	16	.286	.356	.399
1992	New York NL	117	269	28	61	13	0	2	26	25	9	.227	.293	.297
1993	Atlanta	72	62	17	20	2	1	0	5	2	1	.323	.344	.387

DAN PELTIER

Texas Rangers

Outfield

$17

Lefthanded line-drive hitter, doesn't have the power or speed of a regular outfielder, but throws well and could hit .270-.300 consistently, with good on-base percentages . . . He is among the players who could receive increased playing time if Palmeiro departs. His long-term future could be in the National League, where there is more demand for pinch hitters . . . Hit .406 in his career at Notre Dame.

YEAR	TEAM/LEVEL	G	AB	R	H	2B	3B	HR	RBI	BB	SB	AVG	OBP	SLG
1992	Okl City AAA	125	450	65	133	30	7	7	53	60	1	.296	.381	.440
1992	MLE	125	433	51	116	26	5	5	41	46	0	.268	.338	.386
1993	Texas	65	160	23	43	7	1	1	17	20	0	.269	.352	.344

ALEJANDRO PEÑA

Pittsburgh Pirates

Relief Pitcher

$5

Peña signed with the Pirates as a free agent in December, 1992, although his elbow was sore. The elbow went out in spring training, and he missed the season following surgery. He was throwing well enough late in the season that the Pirates put him on their roster, which means that they'll look at him in spring training. It seems a safe assumption that he's not going to be any *better* than he used to be.

YEAR	TEAM/LEVEL	G	IP	W-L	SAVES	HITS	SO	BB	ERA
1990	New York NL	52	76	3-3	5	71	76	22	3.20
1991	Two Teams	59	82	8-1	15	74	62	22	2.40
1992	Atlanta	41	42	1-6	15	40	34	13	4.07

GERONIMO PEÑA

St. Louis Cardinals

Second Base

$21

At season's end was still locked in a battle for the second base job. What's odd is that *both* Peña and Alicea can play, although Joe Torre has been harsh in his evaluations of them. The real problem isn't that they can't play; the problem is that Torre can't decide. Peña almost had the job, but went on the DL in July with a foot problem, and gave Alicea another shot. Good hitter, talented fielder but inconsistent.

YEAR	TEAM/LEVEL	G	AB	R	H	2B	3B	HR	RBI	BB	SB	AVG	OBP	SLG
1992	St. Louis	62	203	31	62	12	1	7	31	24	13	.305	.386	.478
1993	St. Louis	74	254	34	65	19	2	5	30	25	13	.256	.330	.406
1994	**Projected**	**93**	**249**	**40**	**66**	**16**	**3**	**6**	**30**	**26**	**15**	**.265**	**.335**	**.426**

TONY PEÑA

Boston Red Sox

Catcher

$10

The least productive near-regular in the major leagues in '93 . . . Peña has been in the majors for 14 years. His first three years his average was .301. The second three, it was .278; the next three, .259, the next three, .251, and the last two, .216 . . . His defense is still good, but his offense is unacceptable, and I doubt that he will be willing to take a pay cut and move into a backup role.

YEAR	TEAM/LEVEL	G	AB	R	H	2B	3B	HR	RBI	BB	SB	AVG	OBP	SLG
1992	Boston	133	410	39	99	21	1	1	38	24	3	.241	.284	.305
1993	Boston	126	304	20	55	11	0	4	19	25	1	.181	.246	.257
1994	**Projected**	**98**	**273**	**25**	**65**	**14**	**1**	**3**	**27**	**20**	**3**	**.238**	**.293**	**.330**

TERRY PENDLETON

Atlanta Braves

Third Base

$60

It is odd how closely his career parallels that of Bob Elliot, who was a run-of-the-mill National League third baseman in the 1940s, was traded to the Braves in 1947 and immediately won an MVP Award, hitting .317 with 22 homers (Pendleton hit .319 with 22 homers in his MVP year). Both had very strong follow-up seasons, and Elliott then hit .280 with 17 homers and 76 RBI in 1949. Elliot was outstanding in 1950.

YEAR	TEAM/LEVEL	G	AB	R	H	2B	3B	HR	RBI	BB	SB	AVG	OBP	SLG
1992	Atlanta	160	640	98	199	39	1	21	105	37	5	.311	.345	.473
1993	Atlanta	161	633	81	172	33	1	17	84	36	5	.272	.311	.408
1994	**Projected**	**153**	**596**	**76**	**161**	**28**	**2**	**14**	**75**	**38**	**6**	**.269**	**.313**	**.393**

BRAD PENNINGTON
Baltimore Orioles
Relief Pitcher
$12

Suppose that Ryne Duren was a lefthander. Suppose that Mitch Williams could throw even harder than he does, but that his control was even worse. Suppose that Steve Dalkowski had made the majors. Got the picture? Pennington can throw as hard as Randy Johnson, but the strike zone isn't a mystery to him; it's more like a rumor. I think that *eventually* Pennington may be good, but eventually might be five or seven years away.

YEAR	TEAM/LEVEL	G	IP	W-L	SAVES	HITS	SO	BB	ERA
1992	Minors—3 Levels	56	76	3-5	14	37	89	54	2.24
1993	Rochester AAA	17	16	1-2	8	12	19	13	3.45
1993	Baltimore	34	33	3-2	4	34	39	25	6.55

WILLIAM PENNYFEATHER
Pittsburgh Pirates
Outfield
$6

A wide receiver at Syracuse, he is a Grade D prospect, has just the faintest flicker of a chance to become a player. The scouts rave about his athletic ability, but after 607 professional games he doesn't really do *anything* well, even steal bases (he was 10-for-22 as a base stealer at Buffalo). His MLE for 1992 was better (.268 average), but that's the exception, rather than the rule. Awful strikeout/walk ratios.

YEAR	TEAM/LEVEL	G	AB	R	H	2B	3B	HR	RBI	BB	SB	AVG	OBP	SLG
1993	Buffalo AAA	112	457	54	114	18	3	14	41	18	10	.249	.277	.394
1993	MLE	112	439	41	96	15	2	10	31	13	7	.219	.241	.330
1993	Pittsburgh	21	34	4	7	1	0	0	2	0	0	.206	.206	.235

EDUARDO PEREZ
California Angels
Third Base
$27

Tony Perez's son, he was a first-round draft pick in 1991, and vaulted to the majors right away in '93, as soon as he began to hit a little bit. He is big for a third baseman, runs well now although he will probably lose that, doesn't have too much power now but will probably add that. Should hit .250 or better with double-figure homers, still learning at third but could be OK.

YEAR	TEAM/LEVEL	G	AB	R	H	2B	3B	HR	RBI	BB	SB	AVG	OBP	SLG
1993	Vancouver AAA	96	363	66	111	23	6	12	70	28	21	.306	.360	.501
1993	MLE	96	342	46	90	17	2	9	49	19	12	.263	.302	.404
1993	California	52	180	16	45	6	2	4	30	9	5	.250	.292	.372

MELIDO PEREZ
New York Yankees
Starting Pitcher
$26

Well, I've seen enough. I have always spoken well of Perez, but the fact is that he, far more than anyone else, kept the Yankees from beating Toronto. You can't just overlook that, and put him back out there to do it again . . . Opposing hitters hit .347 against him with runners in scoring position, worst in the league . . . He was supported by only four double plays in 163 innings, by far the least DP support in the major leagues.

YEAR	TEAM/LEVEL	G	IP	W-L	PCT.	HITS	SO	BB	ERA
1991	Chicago AL	49	136	8-7	.533	111	128	52	3.12
1992	New York	33	248	13-16	.448	212	218	93	2.87
1993	New York	25	163	6-14	.300	173	148	64	5.19

MIKE PEREZ
St. Louis Cardinals
Relief Pitcher
$27

If the Cardinals don't sign a free agent closer over the winter, this is the man to bet on. Perez, who has a mix of pitches in which nothing stands out, has gotten everybody out for two years in a setup role for Lee Smith, and with Smith gone is the obvious candidate to start collecting the saves. I would compare him now to Jeff Montgomery in 1990, when the Royals were still struggling to believe in Montgomery.

YEAR	TEAM/LEVEL	G	IP	W-L	SAVES	HITS	SO	BB	ERA
1991	St. Louis	14	17	0-2	0	19	7	7	5.82
1992	St. Louis	77	93	9-3	0	70	46	32	1.84
1993	St. Louis	65	73	7-2	7	65	58	20	2.48

GERALD PERRY
St. Louis Cardinals
Pinch Hitter
$19

My comment about him last year, oddly enough, was that he "will bat a hundred times, and anybody might have a good year in 100 at bats." His year goes a little beyond "good"; he was probably the best pinch hitter in the major leagues, him or Dave Hansen. Historically, players who have had great years as pinch hitters have had difficulty following up on that if they stayed in the same role.

YEAR	TEAM/LEVEL	G	AB	R	H	2B	3B	HR	RBI	BB	SB	AVG	OBP	SLG
1992	St. Louis	87	143	13	34	8	0	1	18	15	3	.238	.311	.315
1993	St. Louis	96	98	21	33	5	0	4	16	18	1	.337	.440	.510
1994	**Projected**	**94**	**02**	**12**	**25**	**4**	**0**	**2**	**13**	**12**	**4**	**.245**	**.325**	**.343**

ROBERTO PETAGINE
Houston Astros
First Base
$28

Petagine, only 23, is one of the best hitters in the minors today, and is perhaps the top prospect in the Houston system. Jackson has a *pitchers'* park—in fact, all four parks in the Eastern Division of the Texas League are pitchers' parks, for which reason Petagine was the first "Eastern" player since the league split into divisions in 1975 to win the batting title. There's no job for him, but he's a **Grade A prospect.**

YEAR	TEAM/LEVEL	G	AB	R	H	2B	3B	HR	RBI	BB	SB	AVG	OBP	SLG
1992	A and AA	107	377	60	111	26	4	11	61	53	4	.294	.386	.472
1993	Jackson AA	128	437	73	146	36	2	15	90	84	6	.334	.442	.529
1993	MLE	128	417	59	126	32	1	10	72	57	4	.302	.386	.456

MARK PETKOVSEK
Pittsburgh Pirates
Relief Pitcher
$6

A righthanded sinker/slider pitcher, Petkovsek was a star at the University of Texas, where he was 29-3. The Rangers made him their first-round pick in 1987, but he has failed to thrive in a pro environment, and nothing much is now expected of him. He left the Rangers as a six-year free agent, having gone 16-26 in two-plus years at Oklahoma City. He does throw strikes . . . A weak Grade D prospect.

YEAR	TEAM/LEVEL	G	IP	W-L	PCT.	HITS	SO	BB	ERA
1992	Buffalo AAA	32	150	8-8	.500	150	49	44	3.53
1993	Buffalo AAA	14	71	3-4	.429	74	27	16	4.33
1993	Pittsburgh	26	32	3-0	1.000	43	14	9	6.96

GENO PETRALLI
Texas Rangers
Catcher
$17

Has had a nine-year career as Texas' backup catcher, which is a rarity (the Jamie Quirk of the Rangers?) . . . Similar to Dan Peltier as a hitter—a lefthanded line drive hitter with a pretty good on-base percentage, but no power or speed. Rarely bats against a lefthanded pitcher . . . His decent 1993 season and the shortage of lefthanded hitting catchers will probably keep him where he is at least one more year.

YEAR	TEAM/LEVEL	G	AB	R	H	2B	3B	HR	RBI	BB	SB	AVG	OBP	SLG
1992	Texas	94	192	11	38	12	0	1	18	20	0	.198	.274	.276
1993	Texas	59	133	16	32	5	0	1	13	22	2	.241	.348	.301
1994	**Projected**	**57**	**102**	**9**	**25**	**5**	**0**	**1**	**11**	**12**	**1**	**.245**	**.325**	**.324**

J. R. PHILLIPS
San Francisco Giants
First Base
$10

He is approximately the same as Will Clark in terms of size, shape, color and position, plus he is a lefthanded hitter. Unfortunately, he's a lefthanded .225 hitter. He was in the Angels system, acquired on a waiver claim. He has real power—27 homers at Phoenix, and that's *not* a home run park. Throws well for a first baseman, but makes errors. Grade D prospect; will probably strike out too much to have a career.

YEAR	TEAM/LEVEL	G	AB	R	H	2B	3B	HR	RBI	BB	SB	AVG	OBP	SLG
1993	Phoenix AAA	134	506	80	133	35	2	27	94	53	7	.263	.336	.500
1993	MLE	134	480	56	107	26	0	20	65	36	4	.223	.277	.402
1993	San Francisco	11	16	1	5	1	1	1	4	0	0	.313	.313	.688

TONY PHILLIPS
Detroit Tigers
Utilityman
$70

I've been a baseball fan for a long time, and this guy is the best utility player I've ever seen, by a mile. He doesn't just play five positions; he plays five positions *well*, even spectacularly well. I've seen him dominate a game from right field, or from second base, or from third base. He's a switch hitter who hits .300 both ways, walks constantly, runs the bases well and has occasional power. The man is unbelievable.

YEAR	TEAM/LEVEL	G	AB	R	H	2B	3B	HR	RBI	BB	SB	AVG	OBP	SLG
1992	Detroit	159	606	114	167	32	3	10	64	114	12	.276	.387	.388
1993	Detroit	151	566	113	177	27	0	7	57	132	16	.313	.443	.398
1994	**Projected**	**145**	**551**	**102**	**144**	**21**	**2**	**8**	**53**	**105**	**12**	**.261**	**.380**	**.350**

MIKE PIAZZA
Los Angeles Dodgers
Catcher
$60

The most-similar season ever was by Joe Torre in 1966. Torre was also a catcher, and was essentially the same age at that time . . . Tied for NL lead in errors by a catcher (11) . . . Piazza is now the catcher on the All-Time Rookie All-Stars. Fred Lynn is the center fielder on that team, and Walt Dropo the first baseman. I doubt that Piazza can drive in 112 runs every year, but then, he doesn't have to.

YEAR	TEAM/LEVEL	G	AB	R	H	2B	3B	HR	RBI	BB	SB	AVG	OBP	SLG
1992	Los Angeles	21	69	5	16	3	0	1	7	4	0	.232	.284	.319
1993	Los Angeles	149	547	81	174	24	2	35	112	46	3	.318	.370	.561
1994	**Projected**	**155**	**550**	**71**	**171**	**26**	**2**	**27**	**94**	**45**	**3**	**.311**	**.363**	**.513**

HIPOLITO PICHARDO

Kansas City Royals

Starting Pitcher

$26

It is unclear whether he will start or what in 1993; the Royals front three is now Appier, Cone and Gordon, with at least four candidates for the other two spots. Pichardo is not a bad pitcher; he throws strikes and he throws ground balls, so he can get a lot of people out quickly when he is in a groove. He needs a better curve or change to move up a level, and he might well develop that.

YEAR	TEAM/LEVEL	G	IP	W-L	PCT.	HITS	SO	BB	ERA
1991	Memphis AA	34	99	3-11	.214	116	75	38	4.27
1992	Kansas City	31	144	9-6	.600	148	59	49	3.95
1993	Kansas City	30	165	7-8	.467	183	70	53	4.04

GREG PIRKL

Seattle Mariners

First Base/Catcher

$12

A hulking first baseman, approximately one-half the size of the Kingdome itself; knee injuries may have finished his career as a catcher. He is probably a major league hitter, and the injury to Tino Martinez creates at least a little bit of daylight for him. He is righthanded, slow, and never walks, but also doesn't strike out much and can probably hit the ball out of the Kingdome one-handed. Grade C prospect.

YEAR	TEAM/LEVEL	G	AB	R	H	2B	3B	HR	RBI	BB	SB	AVG	OBP	SLG
1992	MLE	138	490	41	119	27	1	12	46	15	2	.243	.265	.376
1993	Calgary AAA	115	445	67	137	24	1	21	94	13	3	.308	.329	.508
1993	MLE	115	416	45	108	20	0	13	63	8	2	.260	.274	.401

ERIK PLANTENBERG

Seattle Mariners

Righthanded Relief Pitcher

$10

The Mariners took him from the Boston system in the minor league Rule V draft, for reasons that aren't readily apparent (my guess would be that somebody saw something he was doing wrong that they thought they could correct). He had never done anything in the Red Sox system, but pitched well at Jacksonville and earned a late-season look. I would think he's at least a year away.

YEAR	TEAM/LEVEL	G	IP	W-L	SAVES	HITS	SO	BB	ERA
1992	Lynchburg A	21	82	2-3	0	112	62	36	5.18
1993	Jacksonville AA	34	45	2-1	1	38	49	14	2.01
1993	Seattle	20	10	0-0	1	11	3	12	6.52

PHIL PLANTIER

San Diego Padres

Right Field

$65

I don't believe any other player in baseball history has ever driven in 100 runs with as few as 111 hits. I think the previous record for 100 RBI on the fewest hits was by Rudy York in 1937, when he drove in a hundred with 115 hits . . . Had the highest ratio of fly balls to ground balls in the National League (154 to 99) . . . Hit just .185 against lefthanded pitchers, lowest in the NL.

YEAR	TEAM/LEVEL	G	AB	R	H	2B	3B	HR	RBI	BB	SB	AVG	OBP	SLG
1992	Boston	108	349	46	86	19	0	7	30	44	2	.246	.332	.361
1993	San Diego	138	462	67	111	20	1	34	100	61	4	.240	.335	.509
1994	**Projected**	**152**	**562**	**90**	**154**	**29**	**2**	**32**	**100**	**83**	**5**	**.274**	**.367**	**.504**

DAN PLESAC

Chicago Cubs

Relief Pitcher

$17

The Cubs signed him with the idea that he might emerge as the closer if Randy Myers didn't. Myers did, so Plesac's status is unclear. The Cubs had four lefties in the bullpen before Assenmacher was traded . . . 10 of the 74 hits against Plesac were home runs, and he gave up even more RBI (44) than runs scored (37). Fifty percent of his inherited runners scored (league average: 32%). He needs to pitch better.

YEAR	TEAM/LEVEL	G	IP	W-L	SAVES	HITS	SO	BB	ERA
1991	Milwaukee	45	92	2-7	8	92	61	39	4.29
1992	Milwaukee	44	79	5-4	1	64	54	35	2.96
1993	Chicago	57	63	2-1	0	74	47	21	4.74

ERIC PLUNK

Cleveland Indians

Middle Relief

$27

One of the four pitchers who sometimes served as the Indians' closer (with Lilliquist, DiPoto and Hernandez), Plunk is coming off the best season of his eight-year career. He's always been an underrated pitcher, which we can trace to several causes: he didn't pitch well his first couple of years, he doesn't look good on the mound, he has a funny name. May not have 15 saves again, but I think he'll continue to pitch well.

YEAR	TEAM/LEVEL	G	IP	W-L	SAVES	HITS	SO	BB	ERA
1991	New York AL	43	112	2-5	0	128	103	62	4.76
1992	Cleveland	58	72	9-6	4	61	50	38	3.64
1993	Cleveland	70	71	4-5	15	61	77	30	2.79

GUS POLIDOR

Florida Marlins

Second Base

$5

A 32-year-old Venezuelan, has had some playing time with California (1985-1988) and Milwaukee (1989-1990). He played for Edmonton in '85 and '86, in the California system, and was back there in '93, with the Marlins. Any playing time that he gets in the future will probably be, like that of 1993, strictly on an emergency basis.

YEAR	TEAM/LEVEL	G	AB	R	H	2B	3B	HR	RBI	BB	SB	AVG	OBP	SLG
1993	Edmonton AAA	72	249	26	71	16	2	3	40	17	1	.285	.335	.402
1993	MLE	72	233	18	55	12	1	1	28	11	0	.236	.270	.309
1993	Florida	7	6	0	1	1	0	0	0	0	0	.167	.167	.333

LUIS POLONIA

California Angels

Left Field

$29

Attempted to steal 43% of the time when he was on first base, the highest in the American League . . . Has led American League in caught stealing three straight years . . . May play somewhere else in '94. He has always hit poorly in California, much better on the road, and also his stolen base percentage is far better on the road, so if he does go somewhere else his overall performance might improve. Not much of a defensive player.

YEAR	TEAM/LEVEL	G	AB	R	H	2B	3B	HR	RBI	BB	SB	AVG	OBP	SLG
1992	California	149	577	83	165	17	4	0	35	45	51	.286	.337	.329
1993	California	152	576	75	156	17	6	1	32	48	55	.271	.328	.326
1994	**Projected**	**133**	**514**	**75**	**148**	**17**	**6**	**2**	**38**	**45**	**48**	**.288**	**.345**	**.356**

JIM POOLE

Baltimore Orioles
Relief Pitcher
$26

Poole, a 28-year-old lefthander who throws a fastball, sinking fastball and a change, has never been regarded as a prospect. The Dodgers got him from Texas in exchange for a talk-show host and a film director, and let him go to Baltimore on waivers, but I've always liked him because I figured anybody who strikes out 77 in 64 innings with a 2.40 ERA at San Antonio has *got* to be good. And he is.

YEAR	TEAM/LEVEL	G	IP	W-L	SAVES	HITS	SO	BB	ERA
1991	Two Teams	29	42	3-2	1	29	38	12	2.36
1992	Baltimore	6	3	0-0	0	3	3	1	0.00
1993	Baltimore	55	50	2-1	2	30	29	21	2.15

MARK PORTUGAL

Houston Astros
Starting Pitcher
$51

I don't think that anybody expects Portugal to go 18-4 again, but there also are not any obvious statistical flags here signaling a fluke. It's not like he's never pitched well before; he has. The Astros got him in 1988 for Todd McClure; since then he is 52-30 (30-9 in the Astrodome, 2.38 ERA; 22-21 on the road, 4.27). He has a complete set of tools—fastball, curve, slider, the famous change-up.

YEAR	TEAM/LEVEL	G	IP	W-L	PCT.	HITS	SO	BB	ERA
1991	Houston	32	168	10-12	.455	163	120	59	4.49
1992	Houston	18	101	6-3	.667	76	62	41	2.66
1993	Houston	33	208	18-4	.812	194	131	77	2.77

SCOTT POSE

Florida Marlins
Center Field
$12

Pose hit .342 for Chattanooga in '92, but didn't make the Reds' 40-man roster. The Marlins took him in the Rule V draft, utilizing a codicile in the expansion agreement which allowed them to take players in Rule V and farm them out. Pose played so well in spring training that he opened the season in center field, although that didn't last. Grade C prospect; could hit .300, but has clear weaknesses, and there's no job open.

YEAR	TEAM/LEVEL	G	AB	R	H	2B	3B	HR	RBI	BB	SB	AVG	OBP	SLG
1992	MLE	136	504	71	158	20	5	2	37	46	14	.313	.371	.385
1993	MLE	109	372	40	87	6	3	0	17	29	12	.234	.289	.266
1993	Florida	15	41	0	8	2	0	0	3	2	0	.195	.233	.244

DENNIS POWELL

Released
Relief Pitcher
$1

He was released by Seattle on August 13, Friday the 13th. His job was to get out lefthanders, and he was very good at that, limiting lefties to a .159 batting average last year (10-for-63), .236 over the last five years. But he was hit *so* hard by righthanders that it was dangerous to put him in the game . . . Got 10 double plays in only 40 double play situations, highest percentage in the American League. . . .

YEAR	TEAM/LEVEL	G	IP	W-L	SAVES	HITS	SO	BB	ERA
1991	Calgary	27	174	9-8	0	200	96	59	4.15
1992	Seattle	49	57	4-2	0	49	35	29	4.58
1993	Seattle	33	48	0-0	0	42	32	24	4.15

ROSS POWELL
Cincinnati Reds
Lefthanded Pitcher
$7

A starting pitcher, has a losing record and a so-so ERA in the minor leagues (41-45, 3.63), although his strikeout/walk data are fairly good. He gave up 27 homers in 180 innings at Indianapolis. A Michigan native and a graduate of the University of Michigan, he was a third-round draft pick in 1989. Grade D prospect.

YEAR	TEAM/LEVEL	G	IP	W-L	PCT.	HITS	SO	BB	ERA
1992	Nashville AAA	25	93	4-8	.333	89	84	42	3.38
1993	Indianapolis AAA	28	180	10-10	.500	159	133	71	4.11
1993	Cincinnati	9	16	0-3	.000	13	17	6	4.41

TED POWER
Seattle Mariners
Relief Pitcher
$10

He posted a 7.20 ERA in 20 games for Cleveland, but had pitched well for Piniella in Cincinnati, so the Mariners took a look at him in August, when Norm Charlton went out. He piled up 13 saves in seven weeks, and opens spring training as the Mariners' closer. I wouldn't be optimistic that he will keep the job, in that he is 39 and has been recycled more times than Tom Snyder, but we'll see.

YEAR	TEAM/LEVEL	G	IP	W-L	SAVES	HITS	SO	BB	ERA
1991	Cincinnati	68	87	5-3	3	87	51	31	3.62
1992	Cleveland	64	99	3-3	6	88	51	35	2.54
1993	Two Teams	45	45	2-4	13	57	27	17	5.36

TODD PRATT
Philadelphia Phillies
Catcher
$12

Pratt was in the Red Sox system for years, but they let the Phillies get him in the winter draft. You can't entirely blame them, as Pratt's defense does not draw raves, and he had never hit from 1985 to 1990. In the winter of 1990-91 he began to work out seriously, weight training and stuff, and his batwork vaulted forward. He doesn't get much work behind Daulton, but is perhaps the best-hitting backup catcher in baseball.

YEAR	TEAM/LEVEL	G	AB	R	H	2B	3B	HR	RBI	BB	SB	AVG	OBP	SLG
1992	MLE	82	248	32	75	13	0	10	45	43	1	.302	.405	.476
1992	Philadelphia	16	46	6	13	1	0	2	10	4	0	.283	.340	.435
1993	Philadelphia	33	87	8	25	6	0	5	13	5	0	.287	.330	.529

CURTIS PRIDE
Montreal Expos
Outfield
$15

Got a look as a pinch hitter and made a big impression, hitting a single, a double, a triple, and a homer in nine at bats, also stole a base. His 1993 MLE looks like Andy Van Slyke, making one wonder why it took him five years in the Mets system to get out of A Ball. His '93 season demands a place on the roster. I wouldn't bet on him to hit at the 1993 level, but it's a possibility.

YEAR	TEAM/LEVEL	G	AB	R	H	2B	3B	HR	RBI	BB	SB	AVG	OBP	SLG
1993	AA and AAA	119	442	106	143	17	7	21	61	46	50	.324	.395	.536
1993	MLE	119	421	83	122	14	4	15	48	34	26	.290	.343	.449
1993	Montreal	10	9	3	4	1	1	1	5	0	1	.444	.444	1.111

TOM PRINCE

Pittsburgh
(Released)
Backup Catcher
$9

He was released by the Pirates after the season; apparently they plan to use Goff as their backup catcher. Prince has a career batting average of .177 through 177 games. He lives on his defense, but his defensive stats aren't particularly good, either. Of course, that could be misleading; anyway, he's in the same boat as John Orton, except that Orton's defensive stats **are** good . . . Goes on an All-Star team with Duke Snider, Jeff King, Mel Queen.

YEAR	TEAM/LEVEL	G	AB	R	H	2B	3B	HR	RBI	BB	SB	AVG	OBP	SLG
1991	Pittsburgh	26	34	4	9	3	0	1	2	7	0	.265	.405	.441
1992	Pittsburgh	27	44	1	4	2	0	0	5	6	1	.091	.192	.136
1993	Pittsburgh	66	179	14	35	14	0	2	24	13	1	.196	.272	.307

KIRBY PUCKETT

Minnesota Twins
Center/Right Field
$71

Kirby swung at the first pitch 49% of the time, the highest in the American League . . . He had moved to right field, but returned to center in the closing weeks of the season. He continues to approach 3,000 hits at warp speed, has 1,996 hits in less than 10 years. Also continues to hit 60 points better in Minnesota than he does on the road . . . He's now 33; will hit .300 several more times.

YEAR	TEAM/LEVEL	G	AB	R	H	2B	3B	HR	RBI	BB	SB	AVG	OBP	SLG
1992	Minnesota	160	639	104	210	38	4	19	110	44	17	.329	.374	.490
1993	Minnesota	156	622	89	184	39	3	22	89	47	8	.296	.349	.474
1994	**Projected**	**151**	**604**	**86**	**182**	**33**	**4**	**16**	**87**	**40**	**11**	**.301**	**.345**	**.449**

TIM PUGH

Cincinnati Reds
Starting Pitcher
$16

The National League hit .303 against him, the highest against any National League pitcher. They hit .301 against Tewksbury, but that's OK, because Tewksbury has approximately zero walks. Pugh also allowed the highest on-base percentage, .363 . . . I doubt that he is as bad as he pitched in '93, but I also doubt that he's going to be too much better. The acquisition of Hanson, and his own poor performance, may drive him from the rotation.

YEAR	TEAM/LEVEL	G	IP	W-L	PCT.	HITS	SO	BB	ERA
1992	Nashville AAA	27	170	12-9	.571	165	117	65	3.55
1992	Cincinnati	7	45	4-2	.667	47	18	13	2.58
1993	Cincinnati	31	164	10-15	.400	200	94	59	5.26

HARVEY PULLIAM

Kansas City Royals
Outfield
$15

Spent the first half the season in Kansas City, not playing much, and the second half back at Omaha, not hitting much. It's a good guess that he will be somewhere else in '94 . . . he is symptomatic of the Kansas City problem: they won't give the kids a chance to fail. Harvey Pulliam is to Kevin McReynolds as Sean Berry is to Gary Gaetti, or as Jeff Conine is to Wally Joyner.

YEAR	TEAM/LEVEL	G	AB	R	H	2B	3B	HR	RBI	BB	SB	AVG	OBP	SLG
1992	Omaha AAA	100	359	55	97	12	2	16	60	32	4	.270	.338	.448
1992	MLE	100	346	44	84	11	1	10	48	25	2	.243	.294	.367
1993	Kansas City	27	62	7	16	5	0	1	6	2	0	.258	.292	.387

PAUL QUANTRILL

Boston Red Sox

Righthanded Pitcher

$22

Quantrill started the year in the bullpen, and moved into the rotation in mid-May, when Hesketh failed. In 14 starts he wasn't awful (3.87 ERA, excellent control), but didn't win (2-7), and returned to the bullpen so that Sele could move into the rotation. His stuff isn't great, but there is no reason he shouldn't have a substantial major league career . . . The Sox have the only two "Qs" in the majors right now, Quantrill and Quintana.

YEAR	TEAM/LEVEL	G	IP	W-L	SAVES	HITS	SO	BB	ERA
1992	Pawtucket AAA	19	119	6-8	0	143	56	20	4.46
1992	Boston	27	49	2-3	1	55	24	15	2.19
1993	Boston	49	138	6-12	1	151	66	44	3.91

CARLOS QUINTANA

Boston Red Sox

Right Field/First Base

$17

Coming back from a serious injury, he opened the year playing regularly between first base and right field. Mo Vaughn took over the first base job, and Quintana's bat drove him out of the lineup in July, when Deer was acquired . . . His ability will return if he works hard enough, but he's got a long way to go. You just can't live with an outfielder who hits five doubles and one homer in 300 at bats.

YEAR	TEAM/LEVEL	G	AB	R	H	2B	3B	HR	RBI	BB	SB	AVG	OBP	SLG
1991	Boston	149	478	69	141	21	1	11	71	61	1	.295	.375	.412
1993	Boston	101	303	31	74	5	0	1	19	31	1	.244	.317	.271
1994	**Projected**	**76**	**226**	**30**	**62**	**10**	**0**	**4**	**27**	**28**	**0**	**.274**	**.357**	**.372**

SCOTT RADINSKY

Chicago White Sox

Relief Pitcher

$24

Led the American League in relief wins, with eight . . . He's in a similar place to Mike Stanton of the Braves, a highly talented lefthander whose career has gone into reverse over the last two years, for no apparent reason; he just isn't getting quite enough hitters out. He's only 26 and still has a great arm; I expect his value to bounce up and down several times over the next 10 years.

YEAR	TEAM/LEVEL	G	IP	W-L	SAVES	HITS	SO	BB	ERA
1991	Chicago	67	71	5-5	8	53	49	23	2.02
1992	Chicago	68	59	3-7	15	54	48	34	2.73
1993	Chicago	73	55	8-2	4	61	44	19	4.28

TIM RAINES

Chicago White Sox

Left Field

$69

Raines missed the first two months, or most of them, following surgery to repair a torn ligament in his thumb, the injury suffered while sliding. It actually worked out well for the White Sox, as Raines's absence gave Joey Cora an opening to show what he could do, and Raines played at near an MVP level when he returned, playing the best he had since 1987. Made no errors . . . I believe that Raines *will* get 3,000 hits.

YEAR	TEAM/LEVEL	G	AB	R	H	2B	3B	HR	RBI	BB	SB	AVG	OBP	SLG
1991	Chicago	155	609	102	163	20	6	5	50	83	51	.268	.359	.345
1992	Chicago	144	551	102	162	22	9	7	54	81	45	.294	.380	.405
1993	Chicago	115	415	75	127	16	4	16	54	64	21	.306	.401	.480

MANNY RAMIREZ

Cleveland Indians
Outfield/DH
$38

Baseball America's Minor League Player of the Year, Ramirez is the best *hitting* prospect to come to the majors since Frank Thomas and Juan Gonzalez came up in 1990 (Gonzalez played briefly in '89). In projecting exactly how he will hit, we are dealing with an important unknown, which is the ballpark. A 21-year-old Dominican whose family came to the states when he was 13, righthanded hitter, nobody talks about his fielding.

YEAR	TEAM/LEVEL	G	AB	R	H	2B	3B	HR	RBI	BB	SB	AVG	OBP	SLG
1993	MLE	129	468	83	142	38	0	24	90	50	1	.303	.371	.538
1993	Cleveland	22	53	5	9	1	0	2	5	2	0	.170	.200	.302
1994	**Projected**	**147**	**515**	**87**	**149**	**35**	**0**	**26**	**94**	**51**	**1**	**.289**	**.353**	**.509**

KEN RAMOS

Cleveland Indians
Outfield
$10

The Indians have many candidates for jobs in the outfield and no openings, so Ramos probably isn't going to play for Cleveland this year. He might play somewhere. He's 26, a lefthanded singles hitter from the University of Nebraska, runs OK and has a career on-base percentage of .394 in the minor leagues. He won't be a regular, but could have a career as a pinch hitter/fifth outfielder.

YEAR	TEAM/LEVEL	G	AB	R	H	2B	3B	HR	RBI	BB	SB	AVG	OBP	SLG
1992	MLE	125	432	78	140	22	3	4	35	58	9	.324	.404	.417
1993	Charlotte AAA	132	480	77	140	16	11	3	41	47	12	.292	.353	.390
1993	MLE	132	460	59	120	14	7	2	31	36	8	.261	.315	.335

PAT RAPP

Florida Marlins
Pitcher
$15

Rapp had another impressive season in '93, and has pretty much narrowed down the questions concerning him to durability and consistency. Taken from San Francisco in the first round of the expansion draft, he was Edmonton's ace the first half the season, and pitched more than competently for Florida the second half. Righthander with good size, uses a standard selection of pitches. I like him.

YEAR	TEAM/LEVEL	G	IP	W-L	PCT.	HITS	SO	BB	ERA
1992	Phoenix AAA	37	121	7-8	.467	115	79	40	3.05
1993	Edmonton AAA	17	108	8-3	.727	89	93	34	3.43
1993	Florida	16	94	4-6	.400	101	57	39	4.02

DENNIS RASMUSSEN

Kansas City Royals
Starting Pitcher
$8

Rasmussen's career was hanging by a thread in August, 1992, when he was called to the Royals and pitched stunningly well, earning an award as American League pitcher of the week in there. He didn't follow up on that last year, is 35 years old and not much of an athlete, and there is little reason to expect that he will pitch in the majors again.

YEAR	TEAM/LEVEL	G	IP	W-L	PCT.	HITS	SO	BB	ERA
1992	Two Teams	8	43	4-1	.800	32	12	8	2.53
1993	Omaha AAA	17	106	7-8	.467	124	59	27	5.03
1993	Kansas City	9	29	1-2	.333	40	12	14	7.45

RANDY READY
Montreal Expos
Utilityman
$10

Spent most of the season at Rochester, was apparently released and signed with Montreal as a free agent. The Expos used him to cover second base during an injury, also looked at him at first and third. He played all right at second base and got on base regularly, which was as much as could have been hoped. He's 34 now, just looking for any opportunity to extend his career a month or two.

YEAR	TEAM/LEVEL	G	AB	R	H	2B	3B	HR	RBI	BB	SB	AVG	OBP	SLG
1991	Philadelphia	76	205	32	51	10	1	1	20	47	2	.249	.385	.322
1992	Oakland	61	125	17	25	2	0	3	17	25	1	.200	.329	.288
1993	Montreal	40	134	22	34	8	1	1	10	23	2	.254	.367	.351

JEFF REARDON
Cincinnati Reds
Reliever
$15

Pitched well the first half (2.08 ERA) but badly the second (6.67). This is a worrisome sign for a 38-year-old . . . Reardon has taken to throwing a knuckleball sometimes, how much I'm not sure; it must not be too much, or he'd have walked more than 10. The Reds need a closer, and Reardon obviously is not up to that, but taking the year as a whole he was still better than a hundred other pitchers.

YEAR	TEAM/LEVEL	G	IP	W-L	SAVES	HITS	SO	BB	ERA
1991	Boston	57	59	1-4	40	54	44	16	3.03
1992	Two Teams	60	58	5-2	30	67	39	9	3.41
1993	Cincinnati	58	62	4-6	8	66	35	10	4.09

JEFF REBOULET
Minnesota Twins
Utility Infielder
$17

Solidified his place on a major league roster by hitting .258, which is more than anyone would have expected him to hit. Reboulet can play shortstop with anybody in the league, plus he works the pitcher like Rickey Henderson, so if he would hit .258 every year, he'd be some player. He's more likely a .220 hitter, and at 30 is most likely to remain in a backup role.

YEAR	TEAM/LEVEL	G	AB	R	H	2B	3B	HR	RBI	BB	SB	AVG	OBP	SLG
1992	Minnesota	73	137	15	26	7	1	1	16	23	3	.190	.311	.277
1993	Minnesota	109	240	33	62	8	0	1	15	35	5	.258	.356	.304
1994	**Projected**	**113**	**278**	**30**	**62**	**13**	**1**	**2**	**23**	**41**	**4**	**.223**	**.323**	**.299**

GARY REDUS
Texas Rangers
First Base/Outfield
$21

Had another outstanding season as a fourth outfielder, playing almost regularly for two months while Canseco was out. Redus is a lower-case Rickey Henderson, a righthanded hitter who has power, speed, and also walks. In 1993 he hit .288 with a secondary average of .293; in his career has hit .252 with a secondary average of .389. He's 37 now, and will be pushed out of the league as soon as he has an off year.

YEAR	TEAM/LEVEL	G	AB	R	H	2B	3B	HR	RBI	BB	SB	AVG	OBP	SLG
1992	Pittsburgh	76	176	26	45	7	3	3	12	17	11	.256	.321	.381
1993	Texas	77	222	28	64	12	4	6	31	23	4	.288	.351	.459
1994	**Projected**	**95**	**231**	**33**	**58**	**14**	**3**	**5**	**23**	**26**	**10**	**.251**	**.324**	**.403**

JEFF REED
San Francisco Giants
Catcher
$14

A backup catcher, he out-homered Manwaring six to five in approximately one-fourth the at bats. He's never shown that kind of power before, and his secondary average, .311 last year, is .190 for his career. Virtually all of his at bats were against righthanded pitchers (he's a lefty), and there have been cases (Rance Mulliniks) where a player has truly become a better hitter when he was strictly platooned. More likely, it was just a fluke.

YEAR	TEAM/LEVEL	G	AB	R	H	2B	3B	HR	RBI	BB	SB	AVG	OBP	SLG
1991	Cincinnati	91	270	20	72	15	2	3	31	23	0	.267	.321	.370
1992	Cincinnati	15	25	2	4	0	0	0	2	1	0	.160	.192	.160
1993	San Francisco	66	119	10	31	3	0	6	12	16	0	.261	.346	.437

JODY REED
Los Angeles Dodgers
Second Base
$31

He suffered a bruised elbow in June, which cost him about 20 games, plus he didn't hit well until mid-August. Fielded .993 at second base, best in the National League, but his .151 secondary average was the poorest of any National League regular . . . He was never fast, and at 31 is slow enough for this to be a source of concern. He had 17 bunts last year, but still grounded into 16 double plays.

YEAR	TEAM/LEVEL	G	AB	R	H	2B	3B	HR	RBI	BB	SB	AVG	OBP	SLG
1992	Boston	143	550	64	136	27	1	3	40	62	7	.247	.321	.316
1993	Los Angeles	132	445	48	123	21	2	2	31	38	1	.276	.333	.346
1994	**Projected**	**146**	**543**	**67**	**146**	**34**	**1**	**5**	**46**	**55**	**5**	**.269**	**.336**	**.363**

RICK REED
Texas Rangers
Starting Pitcher
$17

A 29-year-old minor league veteran, has a distinguished minor league record (67-37, 2.94 ERA), but has had difficulty getting major league opportunities because he doesn't throw hard. He was a rotation starter for the Royals the second half of '93, but didn't get many wins because of bad luck and early exits. He is capable of winning 50 to 60 percent of his decisions as a major league pitcher.

YEAR	TEAM/LEVEL	G	IP	W-L	PCT.	HITS	SO	BB	ERA
199	Buffalo AAA	25	168	14-4	.778	151	102	26	2.15
1992	Kansas City	19	100	3-7	.300	105	49	20	3.68
1993	Two Teams AAA	24	163	12-7	.632	159	79	16	3.32

STEVE REED
Colorado Rockies
Relief Pitcher
$26

Carried a heavy load last year, saving seven games for Colorado Springs before the big team summoned; altogether he pitched 75 games, 97 innings. I have always loved this guy, as a prospect, and I still do, but the problem he faces is accurately reflected in two statistics. His 1993 ERA on the road: 1.60. His 1993 ERA at home: 6.39. If anybody can succeed despite this park, he's the man.

YEAR	TEAM/LEVEL	G	IP	W-L	SAVES	HITS	SO	BB	ERA
1992	Minors—2 Levels	56	60	1-1	43	45	63	10	2.10
1992	San Francisco	18	16	1-0	0	13	11	3	2.30
1993	Colorado	64	84	9-5	3	80	51	30	4.48

KEVIN REIMER

Milwaukee Brewers

Butcher

$26

He was taken in the expansion draft, by Colorado, and then traded to Milwaukee. About 70% of his at bats were as a designated hitter, which really is the only practical way to use him, but he didn't hit enough that you'd be happy with him as an everyday DH. It would be the understatement of the day to say that Reimer is not Phil Garner's type of player, but he is capable of better seasons.

YEAR	TEAM/LEVEL	G	AB	R	H	2B	3B	HR	RBI	BB	SB	AVG	OBP	SLG
1992	Texas	148	494	56	132	32	2	16	58	42	2	.267	.336	.437
1993	Milwaukee	125	437	53	109	22	1	13	60	30	5	.249	.303	.394
1994	**Projected**	**110**	**351**	**40**	**88**	**21**	**1**	**11**	**47**	**29**	**2**	**.251**	**.308**	**.410**

RICH RENTERIA

Florida Marlins

Second Base

$17

Renteria, who last played in the majors in 1988 with Seattle, had been released in 1991 and was playing God-knows-where until he won a job with the Marlins in spring training. He wasn't bad, hitting over .250 with a few walks, and committing only two errors in 45 games at second base. He also played 25 games at third, making no errors there. He is 32 (born on Christmas Day, 1961), but should keep his job.

YEAR	TEAM/LEVEL	G	AB	R	H	2B	3B	HR	RBI	BB	SB	AVG	OBP	SLG
1992	(Unable to locate any playing record).													
1993	Florida	103	263	27	67	9	2	2	30	21	0	.255	.314	.327
1994	**Projected**	**106**	**273**	**25**	**64**	**16**	**1**	**2**	**28**	**21**	**1**	**.234**	**.289**	**.322**

HAROLD REYNOLDS

Baltimore Orioles

Second Base

$31

Over the last two seasons he is 27-for-50 as a base stealer, so it's about time he stopped that, plus he hit .179 against lefthanders, the lowest of any regular player. Despite that I must say that I was far too hard on him last year; he was among the better second basemen. He led the majors in double plays, 111, and with a decent average and 66 walks, he's at least a participant in the offense.

YEAR	TEAM/LEVEL	G	AB	R	H	2B	3B	HR	RBI	BB	SB	AVG	OBP	SLG
1992	Seattle	140	458	55	113	23	3	3	33	45	15	.247	.316	.330
1993	Baltimore	145	485	64	122	20	4	4	47	66	12	.252	.343	.334
1994	**Projected**	**142**	**500**	**66**	**123**	**23**	**4**	**3**	**42**	**59**	**18**	**.246**	**.326**	**.326**

SHANE REYNOLDS

Houston Astros

Starting Pitcher

$18

Likely to start the '94 season in the majors but pitching long relief, behind the Astros outstanding starting rotation (Portugal, Harnisch, Kile, Drabek and Swindell, before the winter). There are other young pitchers trying to break that rotation. Leaving that aside, Reynolds looks very good. His control has gone from C+ to a straight A, and ERAs of 3.60 at Tucson are very creditable. Righthander, third-round 1989 draft pick, Grade B prospect.

YEAR	TEAM/LEVEL	G	IP	W-L	PCT.	HITS	SO	BB	ERA
1992	Tucson AAA	25	142	9-8	.529	156	106	34	3.68
1993	Tucson AAA	25	139	10-6	.625	147	106	21	3.62
1993	Houston	5	11	0-0	—	11	10	6	0.82

ARMANDO REYNOSO
Colorado Rockies
Starting Pitcher
$34

The Rockies' best pitcher. Reynoso pitched for years, and impressively, in the Mexican League, where many of the parks are at high altitudes, and the thin-air/curve-ball-won't-bite problem is endemic, so it is predictable (in retrospect) that he would be the man who could handle it. He seemed to understand that when the ball is jumping, the worst solution is to nibble, and add walks into the mix. He's a legitimately fine pitcher.

YEAR	TEAM/LEVEL	G	IP	W-L	PCT.	HITS	SO	BB	ERA
1992	Richmond AAA	28	169	12-9	.571	156	108	52	2.66
1993	Colorado Spr AAA	4	22	2-1	.667	19	22	8	3.22
1993	Colorado	30	189	12-11	.522	206	117	63	4.00

ARTHUR RHODES
Baltimore Orioles
Starting Pitcher
$30

Rhodes started very badly, and had arthroscopic surgery on his left knee in mid-May, which kept him out until the end of July. He said at the time that the knee had been bothering him for two years, although he had pitched well before then. After returning he pitched better, but really wasn't in mid-season form until mid-September. **His arm is fine, and he has Cy Young potential,** although probably not this year.

YEAR	TEAM/LEVEL	G	IP	W-L	PCT.	HITS	SO	BB	ERA
1992	Baltimore	15	94	7-5	.583	87	77	38	3.63
1993	Rochester AAA	6	27	1-1	.500	26	33	15	4.05
1993	Baltimore	17	86	5-6	.455	91	49	49	6.51

KARL (TUFFY) RHODES
Chicago Cubs
Outfield
$17

A veteran minor leaguer at the age of 25, has been in several organizations since he reached Triple-A in 1990. There has been a glass ceiling on him because he didn't hit for power, and after several seasons of hearing this, Rhodes bulked up and began hitting mass quantities of home runs—23 at Omaha, 7 for Iowa after being traded to the Cubs, and three more after being called up. Grade B prospect; I like his chances.

YEAR	TEAM/LEVEL	G	AB	R	H	2B	3B	HR	RBI	BB	SB	AVG	OBP	SLG
1993	2 Teams AAA	123	490	112	156	43	3	30	89	58	16	.318	.389	.602
1993	MLE	123	461	80	127	36	1	19	63	40	11	.275	.333	.482
1993	Chicago	20	54	12	15	2	1	3	7	11	2	.278	.400	.519

JEFF (WHITEY) RICHARDSON
Boston Red Sox
Second Base
$10

Another minor league veteran, 28-year-old Nebraskan. He has had previous trials with the Reds and Pirates. The Red Sox got him in a trade in April, kept him on the roster for a month, sent him down, brought him up, he played a little, and went out in mid-June with strained back muscles. A .260-range hitter with no power or speed, doesn't walk. Future is probably very limited.

YEAR	TEAM/LEVEL	G	AB	R	H	2B	3B	HR	RBI	BB	SB	AVG	OBP	SLG
1992	Buffalo AAA	97	328	34	95	23	2	3	29	19	5	.290	.329	.399
1993	Pawtucket AAA	9	28	2	9	1	0	0	1	1	0	.321	.333	.357
1993	Boston	15	24	3	5	2	0	0	2	1	0	.208	.240	.292

DAVE RIGHETTI

Released

Relief Pitcher

$5

Had a 3.94 ERA the first half, but collapsed after the break, and the Giants decided to make an entrée out of the last year of his contract. He is 35, and it is a fair guess that his career is over, although he might come back . . . He has triplets, you know. I wonder if he's the only major league player who ever had triplets? How about the only major league player who threw a no-hitter *and* had triplets?

YEAR	TEAM/LEVEL	G	IP	W-L	SAVES	HITS	SO	BB	ERA
1991	San Francisco	61	72	2-7	24	64	51	28	3.39
1992	San Francisco	54	78	2-7	3	79	47	36	5.06
1993	San Francisco	51	47	1-1	1	58	31	17	5.70

JOSE RIJO

Cincinnati Reds

Starting Pitcher

$84

A wonderful, wonderful pitcher; one can certainly make an argument that he is the best pitcher in baseball, although I go with Maddux. He has had ERAs of 2.84 or better for six straight seasons in a hitter's park, with winning records in each season. He led the National League in strikeouts, and had a strikeout/walk ratio almost 4-to-1 . . . Threw more pitches than any other National League pitcher, 4,052. And he's still young.

YEAR	TEAM/LEVEL	G	IP	W-L	PCT.	HITS	SO	BB	ERA
1991	Cincinnati	30	204	15-6	.714	165	172	55	2.51
1992	Cincinnati	33	211	15-10	.600	185	171	44	2.56
1993	Cincinnati	36	257	14-9	.609	218	227	62	2.48

ERNEST RILES

Boston Red Sox

Utility Player

$15

He's not as bad a player as the .189 average would suggest, because he played errorless ball at all three positions (second base, third base, a few innings at first) and his secondary average was .308 (multiply his at bats by four and you've got 32 doubles, 20 homers, 80 RBI, 80 walks). Still, .189 is .189; you've got to hit .200 or they're liable to cut you, no matter what your other accomplishments are.

YEAR	TEAM/LEVEL	G	AB	R	H	2B	3B	HR	RBI	BB	SB	AVG	OBP	SLG
1992	Tucson AAA	60	202	37	62	17	3	1	35	30	2	.307	.390	.436
1992	Houston	39	61	5	16	1	0	1	4	2	1	.262	.281	.328
1993	Boston	94	143	15	27	8	0	5	20	20	1	.189	.292	.350

BILLY RIPKEN

Texas Rangers

Second Base

$7

Ripken was the first player to get a chance at the Rangers' second base job after Jeff Frye was hurt. He hit .186 for 27 games by mid-May, then went on the DL with a strained hamstring, which bothered him the rest of the year . . . Hit .154 with runners in scoring position . . . He's a good fielder at second base, but that's the only thing he has going for him.

YEAR	TEAM/LEVEL	G	AB	R	H	2B	3B	HR	RBI	BB	SB	AVG	OBP	SLG
1991	Baltimore	104	287	24	62	11	1	0	14	15	0	.216	.253	.261
1992	Baltimore	111	330	35	76	15	0	4	36	18	2	.230	.275	.312
1993	Texas	50	132	12	25	4	0	0	11	11	0	.189	.270	.220

CAL RIPKEN
Baltimore Orioles
Shortstop
$45

I know nobody asked me, but if anybody does, I am completely opposed to putting personal goals ahead of the good of the team . . . Led American League in at bats . . . He still has probably the best arm among American League shortstops, and there aren't a lot of shortstops who can drive in 90 runs, but then, there aren't a lot of shortstops who ground into 20 double plays a year, either. Ripken will establish a career record for GIDP.

YEAR	TEAM/LEVEL	G	AB	R	H	2B	3B	HR	RBI	BB	SB	AVG	OBP	SLG
1992	Baltimore	162	637	73	160	29	1	14	72	64	4	.251	.323	.366
1993	Baltimore	162	641	87	165	26	3	24	90	65	1	.257	.329	.420
1994	**Projected**	**162**	**635**	**82**	**172**	**32**	**2**	**23**	**88**	**61**	**4**	**.271**	**.335**	**.436**

BILL RISLEY
Montreal Expos
Pitcher
$10

Righthanded non-prospect, pitched middle relief at Ottawa all summer and pitched three innings for Montreal in June. Well, he *was* a non-prospect; he struck out 74 in 64 innings at Ottawa, which is a prospect-type thing to do. The Reds were using him as a starting pitcher; the Expos moved him to the bullpen. There have been many pitchers (Eckersley, Gossage, Russell, Henke) who turned into outstanding relievers after failing as starters.

YEAR	TEAM/LEVEL	G	IP	W-L	PCT.	HITS	SO	BB	ERA
1991	Nashville AAA	8	44	3-5	.375	45	32	26	4.91
1992	Indianapol AAA	25	96	5-8	.385	105	64	47	6.40
1993	Ottawa AAA	41	64	2-4	.333	51	74	34	2.54

BEN RIVERA
Philadelphia Phillies
Starting Pitcher
$20

He led the NL in walks and baserunners allowed per nine innings (4.69 and 14.7), among men with 162 innings. The Phillies provided him with the best run support for any major league pitcher, so he escaped with a winning record . . . Mixed signals; he is probably a better pitcher than his 5.02 ERA, and may have been trying to pitch through an injury, but he's not going to win again unless he does pitch better.

YEAR	TEAM/LEVEL	G	IP	W-L	PCT.	HITS	SO	BB	ERA
1991	Greenville AA	26	159	11-8	.579	155	116	75	3.57
1992	Two Teams	28	117	7-4	.636	99	77	45	3.07
1993	Philadelphia	30	163	13-9	.591	175	123	85	5.02

LUIS RIVERA
Boston Red Sox
Shortstop
$11

He's lost his job but he's still here, waiting for the wind to blow him away. He's not a player that I would want on my bench because he doesn't do any one thing well enough that you would want to put him in the game to do it. He's no hitter, doesn't run real well, not a good enough shortstop that you would particularly want his glove in the game in the late innings.

YEAR	TEAM/LEVEL	G	AB	R	H	2B	3B	HR	RBI	BB	SB	AVG	OBP	SLG
1992	Boston	102	288	17	62	11	1	0	29	26	4	.215	.287	.260
1993	Boston	62	130	13	27	8	1	1	7	11	1	.208	.273	.308
1994	**Projected**	**75**	**203**	**23**	**45**	**11**	**1**	**2**	**19**	**18**	**2**	**.222**	**.296**	**.315**

KEVIN ROBERSON

Chicago Cubs

Outfield

$15

A big strong guy having his best minor league season, he ripped five quick homers after being called up. At this point major league pitchers realized he would lunge at a pitch off the plate, which forced him to cover a strike zone roughly the size of Kuwait, which forced him into a difficult transition. He's not a .189 hitter, and he does have power potential, but among the Cubs' legions of young outfielders, he doesn't stand out.

YEAR	TEAM/LEVEL	G	AB	R	H	2B	3B	HR	RBI	BB	SB	AVG	OBP	SLG
1993	Iowa AAA	67	263	48	80	20	1	16	50	19	3	.304	.356	.570
1993	MLE	67	252	34	69	17	0	13	35	13	1	.274	.309	.496
1993	Chicago	62	180	23	34	4	1	9	27	12	0	.189	.251	.372

BIP ROBERTS

Cincinnati Reds

Utilityman

$49

Went on the disabled list with a sprained thumb on July 2, came back for a couple of weeks, and then broke his ring finger. He should be 100% in '94 . . . He was the Reds' MVP in 1992, but the acquisition of Bret Boone seals second base, and the Reds have a good many outfielders, so it's not clear where he will play. I'd bet on a good year.

YEAR	TEAM/LEVEL	G	AB	R	H	2B	3B	HR	RBI	BB	SB	AVG	OBP	SLG
1992	Cincinnati	147	532	92	172	34	6	4	45	62	44	.323	.393	.432
1993	Cincinnati	83	292	46	70	13	0	1	18	38	26	.240	.330	.295
1994	**Projected**	**137**	**492**	**81**	**139**	**24**	**4**	**4**	**41**	**57**	**38**	**.283**	**.357**	**.372**

RICH ROBERTSON

Pittsburgh Pirates

Relief Pitcher

$8

A tall skinny lefthander, some people have said that he reminds them of John Smiley. He pitched well at Double-A in 1992, but poorly in Triple-A in 1993. This indicates one of two things: 1) that his stuff fools inexperienced hitters, but not the more experienced/less talented hitters in Triple-A, or 2) that something was wrong with his arm. Either way, I'd take a pass on him. Grade D prospect.

YEAR	TEAM/LEVEL	G	IP	W-L	PCT.	HITS	SO	BB	ERA
1992	Carolina AA	20	125	6-7	.462	127	107	41	3.03
1993	Buffalo AAA	23	132	9-8	.529	141	71	52	4.28
1993	Pittsburgh	9	9	0-1	.000	15	5	4	6.00

HENRY RODRIGUEZ

Los Angeles Dodgers

Outfielder

$10

He is only 26, but it is becoming increasingly apparent that he isn't going to get beyond the part-time outfielder status, at least unless somebody gets hurt. He's a lefthanded hitter and has 25-home-run power, but his strikeout/walk ratio is poor and not improving, and he doesn't have speed or defense to sell. He would have to hit .270 to crash the lineup, and .220 is a long way from .270.

YEAR	TEAM/LEVEL	G	AB	R	H	2B	3B	HR	RBI	BB	SB	AVG	OBP	SLG
1992	Los Angeles	53	146	11	32	7	0	3	14	8	0	.219	.258	.329
1993	Los Angeles	76	176	20	39	10	0	8	23	11	1	.222	.266	.415
1994	**Projected**	**66**	**200**	**20**	**47**	**9**	**1**	**5**	**23**	**10**	**1**	**.235**	**.271**	**.365**

IVAN RODRIGUEZ

Texas Rangers

Catcher

$59

Swung at 58% of the pitches thrown to him, highest in the American League . . . Has career batting average of .240 in Texas, but .292 on the road, so moving to a new park may help him. . . .The American League's All-Star catcher, based mostly on his defense. He is still young enough and strong enough to develop 20-home-run power, but then I would have said the same thing about Tony Peña at the same age.

YEAR	TEAM/LEVEL	G	AB	R	H	2B	3B	HR	RBI	BB	SB	AVG	OBP	SLG
1992	Texas	123	420	39	109	16	1	8	37	24	0	.260	.300	.360
1993	Texas	137	473	56	129	28	4	10	66	29	8	.273	.315	.412
1994	**Projected**	**140**	**470**	**49**	**128**	**24**	**2**	**9**	**57**	**23**	**3**	**.272**	**.306**	**.389**

RICH RODRIGUEZ

Florida Marlins

Relief Pitcher

$24

Hardworking lefthanded reliever, came to Florida as a throw-in in the Sheffield trade. He had a sinking spell right after the trade, which caused his ERA to balloon, but pitched well before and after that period, and can be expected to continue to. He's not a major talent, but a steady role player who is an important part of Florida's surprisingly deep bullpen (Harvey, Lewis, Rodriguez, Turner, and Aquino).

YEAR	TEAM/LEVEL	G	IP	W-L	SAVES	HITS	SO	BB	ERA
1991	San Diego	64	80	3-1	0	66	40	44	3.26
1992	San Diego	61	91	6-3	0	77	64	29	2.37
1993	Two Teams	70	76	2-4	3	73	43	33	3.79

KENNY ROGERS

Texas Rangers

Starting Pitcher

$30

Opened the year in the bullpen, but was forced into the rotation by injuries. He pitched fairly well, and "won" 16 games because Gonzalez and Palmeiro hit about a hundred home runs for him . . . In the end, Rogers wound up the year doing the job the Rangers had signed Lefferts to do, and Lefferts wound up with Rogers's assignment . . . Opponents stole four bases against him in 15 tries, the worst percentage (for the runners) in the American League.

YEAR	TEAM/LEVEL	G	IP	W-L	PCT.	HITS	SO	BB	ERA
1991	Texas	63	110	10-10	.500	121	73	61	5.42
1992	Texas	81	79	3-6	.333	80	70	26	3.09
1993	Texas	35	208	16-10	.615	210	140	71	4.10

KEVIN ROGERS

San Francisco Giants

Lefthanded Pitcher

$32

His fine rookie season greased the skids for Righetti. Rogers was a starter, and a good one, in the minor leagues; he might eventually become a starter in the majors. He throws quite hard, and throws a slider that moves. Since entering pro ball in 1988 he has never had a significant injury, and has never had an off season. His future could look a lot like Dave Righetti's past.

YEAR	TEAM/LEVEL	G	IP	W-L	PCT.	HITS	SO	BB	ERA
1992	Minors—2 Levels	27	171	11-8	.579	150	172	51	3.16
1992	San Francisco	6	34	0-2	.000	37	26	13	4.24
1993	San Francisco	64	81	2-2	.500	71	62	28	2.68

MEL ROJAS

Montreal Expos

Relief Pitcher

$28

After a brilliant performance in 1992 he opened the season as the Expos' temporary closer, while Wetteland was out with a broken toe. He had a tough time as a closer and continued to pitch so-so until the break, but posted a 2.04 ERA over the second half, winding up with good stats. He had only 10 saves in 19 opportunities, which is a) somewhat misleading, and b) still not very good. A strong middle reliever.

YEAR	TEAM/LEVEL	G	IP	W-L	SAVES	HITS	SO	BB	ERA
1991	Montreal	37	48	3-3	6	42	37	13	3.75
1992	Montreal	68	101	7-1	10	71	70	34	1.43
1993	Montreal	66	88	5-8	10	80	48	30	2.95

MARC RONAN

St. Louis Cardinals

Catcher

$7

A third-round draft pick in 1990, he got called up in September so he could see what a major league clubhouse looked like. He'll be back in the minors this year, and probably next year and the year after; the man can't hit. He swings left, which gives him an advantage on Pappas, in particular, and gives him an edge in the long run, but that doesn't matter if he doesn't hit at least a little bit.

YEAR	TEAM/LEVEL	G	AB	R	H	2B	3B	HR	RBI	BB	SB	AVG	OBP	SLG
1993	Arkansas AA	96	281	33	60	16	1	7	34	26	1	.214	.282	.352
1993	MLE	96	273	26	52	14	0	5	27	17	0	.190	.238	.297
1993	St. Louis	6	12	0	1	0	0	0	0	0	0	.083	.083	.083

JOHN ROPER

Cincinnati Reds

Starting Pitcher

$15

Roper had a good first start, made an indiscreet comment and didn't get anybody out the rest of the year. I made him a Grade A prospect last year, and I'm inclined to think now that was a mistake, but I think that among the Reds' young pitchers who pitched badly—Roper, Pugh, Powell, Luebbers—he has the best chance of turning it around . . . Lefthanded hitters hit .362 against him, highest in the National League.

YEAR	TEAM/LEVEL	G	IP	W-L	PCT.	HITS	SO	BB	ERA
1992	Chattanooga AA	20	121	10-9	.526	115	98	36	4.03
1993	Indianapolis AAA	12	55	3-5	.375	56	42	30	4.45
1993	Cincinnati	16	80	2-5	.286	92	54	36	5.63

RICO ROSSY

Kansas City Royals

Utility Infielder

$12

A 30-year-old utility infielder, plays all three spots (second, third, and short) well enough, also does some of the little things well. He's had a .400 on-base percentage twice in a row at Omaha, so he's not a wild swinger, but in Kansas City his batting average has been so low that his OBP is low, too . . . One of the Untouchables in the TV series was named Rico Rossy (or Rossi).

YEAR	TEAM/LEVEL	G	AB	R	H	2B	3B	HR	RBI	BB	SB	AVG	OBP	SLG
1992	Kansas City	59	149	21	32	8	1	1	12	20	0	.215	.310	.302
1993	Omaha AAA	37	131	25	39	10	1	5	21	20	3	.298	.400	.504
1993	Kansas City	46	86	10	19	4	0	2	12	9	0	.221	.302	.337

RICH ROWLAND

Detroit Tigers

Catcher

$18

Drafted in 1988, he shot through the system to Triple-A but stuck there, has been playing for Toledo since 1990. He is now 27, at his peak as a hitter, and he has real power, 30-homer power—basically his hitting stats wouldn't be a lot different than Tettleton's other than that he wouldn't walk as much. He also has an arm, perhaps the best throwing arm in the International League. Would be excellent backup to Kreuter.

YEAR	TEAM/LEVEL	G	AB	R	H	2B	3B	HR	RBI	BB	SB	AVG	OBP	SLG
1992	MLE	136	464	68	102	16	0	24	75	51	7	.220	.297	.409
1993	MLE	96	319	55	81	21	1	21	56	48	0	.254	.351	.524
1993	Detroit	21	46	7	17	4	0	0	5	11	0	.205	.295	.253

STAN ROYER

St. Louis Cardinals

Third Base

$12

The Cardinals acquired Royer in the Willie McGee trade. For three straight years he has gotten a few at bats and has hit, an overall average of .306. Now, he is *not* a .300 hitter—he's more like a .250 hitter—and the Cardinals kind of know that he isn't, but it's time for them to fish or cut bait, and it's hard to cut him loose when all he has done is hit. So it's a tough call.

YEAR	TEAM/LEVEL	G	AB	R	H	2B	3B	HR	RBI	BB	SB	AVG	OBP	SLG
1991	St. Louis	9	21	1	6	1	0	0	1	1	0	.286	.318	.333
1992	St. Louis	13	31	6	10	2	0	2	9	1	0	.323	.333	.581
1993	St. Louis	24	46	4	14	2	0	1	8	2	0	.304	.333	.413

KIRK RUETER

Montreal Expos

Lefthanded Starting Pitcher

$28

There is considerable reason here to suspect that the second time around the league will be a little different. I would compare Rueter to Randy Tomlin, who had similar stats in his first look in 1990 (chart below compares them), and who is still trying to solidify his position. Rueter struck out 31 in 85 innings, and there really aren't any good pitchers who have that kind of strikeout rate. Of course, he could be Bob Tewksbury.

YEAR	TEAM/LEVEL	G	IP	W-L	PCT.	HITS	SO	BB	ERA
1993	AA and AAA	16	103	9-2	.818	93	63	10	1.92
1993	Montreal	14	86	8-0	1.000	85	31	18	2.73
Tomlin in 1990		12	78	4-4	.500	62	42	12	2.55

SCOTT RUFFCORN

Chicago White Sox

Starting Pitcher

$32

The next one in line: McDowell, Fernandez, Alvarez, Bere, Ruffcorn. He was the Sox number-one pick in 1991 and has pitched well everywhere except for 10 innings with the big team, when his control deserted him. A 6-4 righthander from Baylor University, throws hard and throws strikes. A **Grade A prospect**, and the White Sox obviously know how to bring along a young pitcher.

YEAR	TEAM/LEVEL	G	IP	W-L	PCT.	HITS	SO	BB	ERA
1993	Birmingham AA	20	135	9-4	.692	108	141	52	2.73
1993	Nashville AAA	7	45	2-2	.500	30	44	8	2.80
1993	Chicago	3	10	0-2	.000	9	2	10	8.10

BRUCE RUFFIN

Colorado Rockies

Lefthanded pitcher

$30

Opened the year in the rotation, absorbing a 6.07 ERA in 12 starts. He moved to the bullpen, and was brilliant for four months, with a 2.50 ERA and 80 strikeouts in 86 innings. This ended a string of six losing seasons, during which he was 34-60. Red **Ruffin**g had a Hall of Fame career starting out 39-96, and Ruffin's strikeout rate was vastly better than it had been. I think his improvement is real.

YEAR	TEAM/LEVEL	G	IP	W-L	PCT.	HITS	SO	BB	ERA
1991	Philadelphia	31	119	4-7	.364	125	85	38	3.78
1992	Milwaukee	25	58	1-6	.143	66	45	41	6.67
1993	Colorado	59	140	6-5	.545	145	126	69	3.87

JOHNNY RUFFIN

Cincinnati Reds

Righthanded Pitcher

$24

If Dibble fails again, Ruffin would appear to be among those who could inherit the glory job. Ruffin was in the Chicago White Sox system, and was traded to Cincinnati in the Tim Belcher deal. He's a tall, skinny righthander, only 22, and struck out 69 men in 60 innings at Nashville. Throw in the fact that he pitched well for two months after being called up by the Reds . . . What's not to like?

YEAR	TEAM/LEVEL	G	IP	W-L	SAVES	HITS	SO	BB	ERA
1992	Birmingham AA	10	48	0-7	0	51	44	34	6.04
1993	Two Teams AAA	32	67	4-5	2	51	75	18	3.11
1993	Cincinnati	21	38	2-1	2	36	30	11	3.58

SCOTT RUSKIN

(Released)

Relief Pitcher

$14

Ruskin pitched four times for Cincinnati in September, getting a total of three men out, and was released after the season. Ruskin, a pitcher/outfielder for the University of Florida, entered pro ball as an outfielder/first baseman, switched to the mound in 1989, and made the majors just one year later. He pitched well at first, but has gone one step down every year. We'll see him again, but probably not in a starring role.

YEAR	TEAM/LEVEL	G	IP	W-L	SAVES	HITS	SO	BB	ERA
1991	Montreal	64	64	4-4	6	57	46	30	4.24
1992	Cincinnati	57	54	4-3	0	56	43	20	5.03
1993	Indianapolis AAA	49	56	1-5	28	60	41	22	5.14

JEFF RUSSELL

Boston Red Sox

Relief Pitcher

$48

A failed starter a long time ago (he led the National League in losses in 1983), he's become a consistent reliever, saving 30 to 38 games in four of the last five years. He's prone to elbow and ankle trouble, so any team that's depending on him needs to know what their backup plan is. His inability to pitch down the stretch in '93 contributed heavily to the Red Sox wipeout. He's only 32.

YEAR	TEAM/LEVEL	G	IP	W-L	SAVES	HITS	SO	BB	ERA
1991	Texas	68	79	6-4	30	71	52	26	3.29
1992	Two Teams	59	66	4-3	30	55	48	25	1.63
1993	Boston	51	47	1-4	33	39	45	14	2.70

JOHN RUSSELL

Texas Rangers

Catcher/Bullpen Coach

$1

Russell went to spring training as a non-roster player. He didn't make the roster, but was kept around as a bullpen coach, and was then activated to back up Rodriguez when Petralli was out for six weeks. He also got into a game at first base, one at third base and one in the outfield . . . Was released after the season, presumably to return to the bullpen.

YEAR	TEAM/LEVEL	G	AB	R	H	2B	3B	HR	RBI	BB	SB	AVG	OBP	SLG
1991	Texas	22	27	3	3	0	0	0	1	1	0	.111	.138	.111
1992	Texas	7	10	1	1	0	0	0	2	1	0	.100	.231	.100
1993	Texas	18	22	1	5	1	0	1	3	2	0	.227	.292	.409

KEN RYAN

Boston Red Sox

Relief Pitcher

$22

A minor league closer, he pitched respectably in '93, and is in line to get a chance at a closer job sometime, probably not now. Had 5.55 ERA in Fenway Park, 1.75 on the road, which doesn't mean much in limited innings. Has good fastball; strikeouts increased to more than one per inning after the All-Star break. With Russell, Melendez, Harris, Ryan and Quintana, Red Sox should have a better bullpen than they did last year.

YEAR	TEAM/LEVEL	G	IP	W-L	SAVES	HITS	SO	BB	ERA
1992	Minors—2 Levels	53	59	3-4	29	50	57	28	1.97
1992	Boston	7	7	0-0	0	4	5	5	6.43
1993	Boston	47	50	7-2	1	43	49	29	3.60

NOLAN RYAN

Retired

Starting Pitcher

No Value

Ryan wound up his career with 38% more strikeouts than any other pitcher in history—and 52% more walks. Steve Carlton is second in both categories . . . He is certainly not the greatest pitcher I have ever seen, but he is probably the most remarkable. He struck out 1,437 men after his 40th birthday . . . I won't miss him. The hero worship directed at him had become frankly embarrassing.

YEAR	TEAM/LEVEL	G	IP	W-L	PCT.	HITS	SO	BB	ERA
1992	Texas	27	157	5-9	.357	138	157	69	3.72
1993	Texas	13	66	5-5	.500	54	46	40	4.88
TYPICAL SEASON		41	273	16-15	.524	199	289	142	3.19

BRET SABERHAGEN

New York Mets

Starting Pitcher

$36

Over the last five years he is 14-5 with a 2.18 ERA in May and even better in August (11-1, 1.32), but struggles in mid-summer, and usually spends it on the DL. I don't mean to be patronizing, but managers can be astonishingly slow learners, so let me explain this: **PUT A PITCH LIMIT ON HIM. HE'S GOING TO KEEP GETTING HURT.** Seven innings, understand? Skip a turn in the rotation once in a while.

YEAR	TEAM/LEVEL	G	IP	W-L	PCT.	HITS	SO	BB	ERA
1991	Kansas City	28	196	13-8	.619	165	136	45	3.07
1992	New York	17	98	3-5	.375	84	81	27	3.50
1993	New York	19	139	7-7	.500	131	93	17	3.29

CHRIS SABO

Cincinnati Reds

Third Base

$35

Is eligible to file for free agency; at this writing it is unclear whether he will return in '94. The Reds have another young third baseman, Willie Greene, but are hardly in a position to throw away good players. Sabo is 32, so has probably had his best season (1991), but there's no reason to expect a sudden collapse. He has lost his speed after a series of ankle and foot problems.

YEAR	TEAM/LEVEL	G	AB	R	H	2B	3B	HR	RBI	BB	SB	AVG	OBP	SLG
1992	Cincinnati	96	344	42	84	19	3	12	43	30	4	.244	.302	.422
1993	Cincinnati	148	552	86	143	33	2	21	82	43	6	.259	.315	.440
1994	**Projected**	**136**	**500**	**71**	**129**	**33**	**2**	**17**	**67**	**40**	**9**	**.258**	**.313**	**.434**

ROGER SALKELD

Seattle Mariners

Starting Pitcher

$20

He was the Mariners' red-hot prospect in 1990, when a minor league manager described him as "the next Roger Clemens." With the pace that prospects march before us this seems like eons ago, but he is only 23. He missed all of the 1992 season and part of the '93 season following shoulder surgery, but returned to pitch well. He is 6-foot-5 and throws a fastball . . . well, at least a little like Roger Clemens.

YEAR	TEAM/LEVEL	G	IP	W-L	PCT.	HITS	SO	BB	ERA
1992		(Injured—Did not pitch)							
1993	Jacksonville AA	14	77	4-3	.571	71	56	29	3.27
1993	Seattle	3	14	0-0	—	13	13	4	2.51

TIM SALMON

California Angels

Right Field

$50

As to the question of great stardom . . . it seems to me that, the scope of his skills being limited (he doesn't run particularly well, although he is a superb baserunner, or hit .300), his chance of being a superstar would depend on hitting 35 or 40 homers a year. I doubt that will happen; I think he's more Mark McGwire than Frank Thomas. But he should provide the Angels with a solid cleanup hitter for several years.

YEAR	TEAM/LEVEL	G	AB	R	H	2B	3B	HR	RBI	BB	SB	AVG	OBP	SLG
1992	California	23	79	8	14	1	0	2	6	11	1	.177	.283	.266
1993	California	142	515	93	146	35	1	31	95	82	5	.283	.382	.536
1994	**Projected**	**151**	**548**	**94**	**147**	**31**	**1**	**28**	**92**	**81**	**8**	**.268**	**.362**	**.482**

BILL SAMPEN

Kansas City Royals

Relief Pitcher

$10

Sampen, who was among the Royals' fifteen protected players in the expansion draft, didn't get anybody out for two months, and was sent to Omaha in early June. He had a 3.41 ERA in 33 games at Omaha . . . 31 years old, doesn't throw hard, doesn't have any record of consistent success. Doesn't have a strikeout pitch. I'm sure he'll have a comeback season; I just don't see any reason to expect a *big* comeback.

YEAR	TEAM/LEVEL	G	IP	W-L	SAVES	HITS	SO	BB	ERA
1991	Montreal	43	92	9-5	0	96	52	46	4.00
1992	Two Teams	52	83	1-6	0	83	37	32	3.25
1993	Kansas City	18	18	2-2	0	15	9	9	5.89

JUAN SAMUEL
Cincinnati Reds
Utilityman
$14

He's running on empty, not so fast anymore, not much power left. The Reds used him at second base (70 games), also a few games here, there and yonder, but he didn't do anything to bring his career back to life, and will probably be moseying on down the road, since the Reds have traded for Bret Boone. He's not a very good second baseman, an awful outfielder, and not a good enough hitter to pinch hit.

YEAR	TEAM/LEVEL	G	AB	R	H	2B	3B	HR	RBI	BB	SB	AVG	OBP	SLG
1992	Two Teams	76	224	22	61	8	4	0	23	14	8	.272	.318	.344
1993	Cincinnati	103	261	31	60	10	4	4	26	23	9	.230	.298	.345
1994	**Projected**	**104**	**327**	**39**	**82**	**18**	**4**	**6**	**34**	**27**	**11**	**.251**	**.308**	**.385**

REY SANCHEZ
Chicago Cubs
Shortstop
$24

Getting some playing time due to the injuries of Dunston and Sandberg, he has played well but not as well as Vizcaino, and so remains in a backup role. He may play himself out of that role yet; over the last two years he's hit .284 against left-handed pitchers. His range factor at short was the best of any major league player, his fielding percentage average. Looks good.

YEAR	TEAM/LEVEL	G	AB	R	H	2B	3B	HR	RBI	BB	SB	AVG	OBP	SLG
1992	Chicago	74	255	24	64	14	3	1	19	10	2	.251	.285	.341
1993	Chicago	105	344	35	97	11	2	0	28	15	1	.282	.316	.326
1994	**Projected**	**112**	**355**	**35**	**93**	**11**	**2**	**1**	**28**	**19**	**5**	**.262**	**.299**	**.313**

RYNE SANDBERG
Chicago Cubs
Second Base
$73

Suffered a broken left hand in Arizona, putting him out of the MVP race before the season started. On returning to the lineup he fielded flawlessly and hit well, albeit not quite at his best level. At 34, one has to anticipate *some* decline. In his case, that means he can still have an MVP-candidate season, he just probably won't do it every year. He's got years left as a quality player.

YEAR	TEAM/LEVEL	G	AB	R	H	2B	3B	HR	RBI	BB	SB	AVG	OBP	SLG
1991	Chicago	158	585	104	170	32	2	26	100	87	22	.291	.379	.485
1992	Chicago	158	612	100	186	32	8	26	87	68	17	.304	.371	.510
1993	Chicago	117	456	78	141	20	0	9	45	37	9	.309	.359	.412

DEION SANDERS
Atlanta Braves
Center Field
$29

The departure of Otis Nixon clears the way for him to play every day, although the computer which projects stats (below) doesn't know that. If you add together his last two seasons you have 575 at bats, and a fairly good year—.290 with 14 homers and 20 triples. He's only 26 years old, but if he keeps playing football I would guess his career will probably be over within five years. I can't say that I'll miss him.

YEAR	TEAM/LEVEL	G	AB	R	H	2B	3B	HR	RBI	BB	SB	AVG	OBP	SLG
1992	Atlanta	97	303	54	92	6	14	8	28	18	26	.304	.346	.495
1993	Atlanta	95	272	42	75	18	6	6	28	16	19	.276	.321	.452
1994	**Projected**	**112**	**307**	**49**	**83**	**11**	**7**	**8**	**32**	**22**	**26**	**.270**	**.319**	**.430**

REGGIE SANDERS

Cincinnati Reds

Outfield

$45

He made it through the season without actually having to go on the DL, which was an upset. The Reds were forced to use him in right field, since they had Mitchell in left, but he doesn't have a right fielder's arm . . . He hit at the top of the order in '92, hit sixth or seventh last year; we must assume he is ready to move into the three or four spot, which means he could drive in 100 runs.

YEAR	TEAM/LEVEL	G	AB	R	H	2B	3B	HR	RBI	BB	SB	AVG	OBP	SLG
1992	Cincinnati	116	385	62	104	26	6	12	36	48	16	.270	.356	.462
1993	Cincinnati	138	496	90	136	16	4	20	83	51	27	.274	.343	.444
1994	**Projected**	**139**	**479**	**82**	**137**	**23**	**6**	**17**	**67**	**54**	**23**	**.286**	**.358**	**.466**

SCOTT SANDERS

San Diego Padres

Starting Pitcher

$24

A hard-throwing righthander born in Hannibal, Missouri, Sanders rarely makes top-prospect lists although he was a first-round draft pick and has struck out more than one per inning. The Padres' minor league parks favor hitters so much that the stats are slanted. Sanders's ERA at Las Vegas was actually pretty good; the Pacific Coast League ERA was 4.92, and Las Vegas is one of the best-hitting parks in the league. Grade B prospect.

YEAR	TEAM/LEVEL	G	IP	W-L	PCT.	HITS	SO	BB	ERA
1992	Las Vegas AAA	14	72	3-6	.333	97	51	31	5.50
1993	Las Vegas AAA	24	152	5-10	.333	170	161	62	4.96
1993	San Diego	9	52	3-3	.500	54	37	23	4.13

TRACY SANDERS

San Diego Padres

Outfield

$22

A Grade B prospect, a 200-pound outfielder who runs OK, is only 24 years old and a pretty good hitter. The Indians stole him with a 58th-round draft pick in 1990, and in 1992 he was the fourth-best prospect in the Eastern League, according to you-know-who. The Indians traded him to San Diego, and he took a liking to Dumont Stadium in Wichita (most lefthanded hitters do). A poor outfielder.

YEAR	TEAM/LEVEL	G	AB	R	H	2B	3B	HR	RBI	BB	SB	AVG	OBP	SLG
1992	MLE	114	375	55	86	10	2	18	73	55	1	.229	.328	.411
1993	Two Teams AA	119	402	64	115	19	6	18	67	65	10	.286	.389	.498
1993	MLE	119	388	51	101	16	3	14	54	44	6	.260	.336	.425

SCOTT SANDERSON

San Francisco Giants

Starting Pitcher

$29

Sanderson, now 37 years old, was released by the Angels, and signed with the Giants on August 3. He pitched very well for the Giants, going 4-2 with a 3.51 ERA, strikeout/walk ratio of 36/7 in 49 innings. It might be unrealistic to expect him to do that all year, but hey, he's won 56 games over the last four years, so who's to say he can't win 14 more this year? Or 16 more?

YEAR	TEAM/LEVEL	G	IP	W-L	PCT.	HITS	SO	BB	ERA
1991	New York AL	34	208	16-10	.615	200	130	29	3.81
1992	New York AL	33	193	12-11	.522	220	104	64	4.93
1993	Two Teams	32	184	11-13	.458	201	102	34	4.21

MO SANFORD
Colorado Rockies
Starting Pitcher
$15

He continues to wander in the wilderness, although at least it is now a major league wilderness. Sanford is a big guy and a good athlete, but his fastball is straight and his curveball is also known as Ball Three, so in the last three years he's gone from super prospect to pro suspect. He has a comeback in him, a big comeback, but it probably doesn't start until '95.

YEAR	TEAM/LEVEL	G	IP	W-L	PCT.	HITS	SO	BB	ERA
1992	Minors—2 Levels	29	149	12-8	.600	142	157	71	4.90
1993	Colorado Spr AAA	20	105	3-6	.333	103	104	57	5.23
1993	Colorado	11	36	1-2	.333	37	36	27	5.30

BENITO SANTIAGO
Florida Marlins
Catcher
$20

His .230 batting average was the second-lowest among National League regulars. His .214 average against righthanded pitchers was the lowest . . . Swung at the first pitch 49.4% of the time, the highest percentage of any major league regular . . . The average National League team got a .256 average from their catchers, with 17 homers and 77 RBI; the Marlins got a .222 average with 15 and 57. His throwing arm doesn't even begin to get him even.

YEAR	TEAM/LEVEL	G	AB	R	H	2B	3B	HR	RBI	BB	SB	AVG	OBP	SLG
1992	San Diego	106	386	37	97	21	0	10	42	21	2	.251	.287	.383
1993	Florida	139	469	49	108	19	6	13	50	37	10	.230	.291	.380
1994	**Projected**	**130**	**440**	**45**	**112**	**19**	**2**	**12**	**55**	**26**	**7**	**.255**	**.296**	**.389**

NELSON SANTOVENIA
Kansas City Royals
Catcher
$4

He spent most of the summer at Omaha, where he hit .237, and went 1-for-8 in a September callup. Santovenia is 32, was born in Cuba just before the gates closed, and lives in Miami. He played semi-regularly for Montreal in 1988-89, and was there when Hal McRae was the hitting coach. He throws very well but isn't a major league hitter.

YEAR	TEAM/LEVEL	G	AB	R	H	2B	3B	HR	RBI	BB	SB	AVG	OBP	SLG
1991	Montreal	41	96	7	24	5	0	2	14	2	0	.250	.255	.365
1992	MLE	91	271	19	64	13	0	4	33	29	0	.236	.310	.328
1993	MLE	81	266	26	57	11	0	9	33	9	0	.214	.240	.357

MACKEY SASSER
Seattle Mariners
Utility Player
$9

Sasser is now 31 years old, and his declining batting averages over the last four years (.307, .272, .241, .218) leave it unclear whether he will be in the majors when he's 32. He is built like a catcher and runs like a catcher, but he isn't. He doesn't hit for power, so if he hits .218, he doesn't do anything.

YEAR	TEAM/LEVEL	G	AB	R	H	2B	3B	HR	RBI	BB	SB	AVG	OBP	SLG
1991	New York NL	96	228	18	62	14	2	5	35	9	0	.272	.298	.417
1992	New York NL	92	141	7	34	6	0	2	18	3	0	.241	.248	.326
1993	Seattle	83	188	18	41	10	2	1	21	15	1	.218	.274	.309

DOUG SAUNDERS

New York Mets

Infield

$8

If Jeff Kent's career goes south Saunders is in line for a shot at the second base job. He's Doug Flynn, or supposed to be, a .245 hitter with no power, not much speed, but smooth as silk at second base. He's a career .247 hitter in the minor leagues, but at least he's consistent about it—.248 at Binghamton in '92, .247 last year. Grade D prospect.

YEAR	TEAM/LEVEL	G	AB	R	H	2B	3B	HR	RBI	BB	SB	AVG	OBP	SLG
1993	Norfolk AAA	105	356	37	88	12	6	2	24	44	6	.247	.334	.331
1993	MLE	105	346	30	78	10	4	1	19	36	4	.225	.298	.286
1993	New York	28	67	8	14	2	0	0	0	3	0	.209	.243	.239

STEVE SAX

Chicago White Sox

Utilityman

$14

Moved to left field during Tim Raines's injury, didn't play well there and couldn't get back in the infield after Raines returned, putting an end to 11-plus years of regular play. He's 34, and after two straight off seasons it would be optimistic to expect him to bounce back. Still runs well. Has a contract through 1995, which may get him an extra chance.

YEAR	TEAM/LEVEL	G	AB	R	H	2B	3B	HR	RBI	BB	SB	AVG	OBP	SLG
1992	Chicago	143	567	74	134	26	4	4	47	43	30	.236	.290	.317
1993	Chicago	57	119	20	28	5	0	1	8	8	7	.235	.283	.303
1994	**Projected**	**78**	**150**	**19**	**41**	**6**	**1**	**1**	**12**	**11**	**8**	**.273**	**.323**	**.347**

BOB (WATER-GATE) SCANLAN

Chicago Cubs

Relief Pitcher

$20

I warned you a year ago to lay off of him because, after pitching brilliantly the first five months of 1992, he was battered in almost every outing late in the year. His problems continued most of last year; he never really got started until mid-August, when he began to cut into his ERA a little . . . I don't think he has "closer" potential, but suspect he will have a better year in middle relief.

YEAR	TEAM/LEVEL	G	IP	W-L	SAVES	HITS	SO	BB	ERA
1991	Chicago	40	111	7-8	1	114	44	40	3.89
1992	Chicago	69	87	3-6	14	76	42	30	2.89
1993	Chicago	70	75	4-5	0	79	44	28	4.54

STEVE SCARSONE

San Francisco Giants

Infielder

$13

The Giants got him in exchange for Mark Leonard, and he spent the first half of the season on the disabled list after breaking a finger. Upon returning he hit exactly what his MLE said that he should, and played errorless ball in 20 games at second. The job of backup second baseman is critical to this team, because Thompson doesn't play 150 games a year. Scarsone is no regular, but could be a good backup for three-four years.

YEAR	TEAM/LEVEL	G	AB	R	H	2B	3B	HR	RBI	BB	SB	AVG	OBP	SLG
1992	MLE	112	395	50	98	22	3	10	54	26	9	.248	.295	.395
1992	Two Teams	18	30	3	5	0	0	0	0	2	0	.167	.219	.167
1993	San Francisco	44	103	16	26	9	0	2	15	4	0	.252	.278	.398

CURT SCHILLING

Philadelphia Phillies
Starting Pitcher
$62

Among the best pitchers in baseball, throws 90, has excellent split-finger fastball and change, good control, stays healthy. One can puzzle for hours about what it was that Baltimore and Houston didn't like about him . . . Throws to first base less often than any other major league pitcher, only 17 times in '93 (last among pitchers with 162 innings pitched) . . . Like many power pitchers, his record is dramatically better at night than it is in day games.

YEAR	TEAM/LEVEL	G	IP	W-L	PCT.	HITS	SO	BB	ERA
1991	Houston	56	76	3-5	.375	79	71	39	3.81
1992	Philadelphia	42	226	14-11	.560	165	147	59	2.35
1993	Philadelphia	34	235	16-7	.696	234	186	57	4.02

DICK SCHOFIELD

Toronto Blue Jays
Shortstop
$10

Opened the year as the Toronto shortstop, and played better than his .191 average announces. He's a good glove, and one of the few shortstops whose secondary average is better than his batting average. He's not Phil Rizzuto, and when he broke his forearm and the Blue Jays got Fernandez to replace him he disappeared forever from the Blue Jays' starting lineup. At 31, may get one more shot at an everyday job somewhere.

YEAR	TEAM/LEVEL	G	AB	R	H	2B	3B	HR	RBI	BB	SB	AVG	OBP	SLG
1992	Two Teams	143	423	52	87	18	2	4	36	61	11	.206	.311	.286
1993	Toronto	36	110	11	21	1	2	0	5	16	3	.191	.294	.236
1994	**Projected**	**41**	**97**	**11**	**21**	**4**	**1**	**1**	**8**	**13**	**2**	**.216**	**.309**	**.309**

MIKE SCHOOLER

Texas Rangers
Relief Pitcher
$1

His career is probably over. Schooler saved 33 games for the Mariners in 1989 and 30 more in 1990, but has since had a shoulder injury, tendonitis, and a strained bicep, and hasn't pitched well anywhere. The Mariners released him in March. The Rangers signed him, but the league hit .303 against him, and he was sent out on August 2. He didn't get anybody out at Oklahoma City, either, and was released again in September.

YEAR	TEAM/LEVEL	G	IP	W-L	SAVES	HITS	SO	BB	ERA
1991	Seattle	34	34	3-3	7	25	31	10	3.67
1992	Seattle	53	52	2-7	13	55	33	24	4.70
1993	Texas	17	24	3-0	0	30	16	10	5.55

PETE SCHOUREK

New York Mets
Lefthanded Pitcher
$12

Surrendered a .361 batting average with men on base, highest in the National League . . . In the five games that he won, which included his last two starts of the season, he really pitched well. He just got confused, like all of the Mets, and went three months in mid-summer without pitching any good games . . . A somewhat better pitcher than his record, but may not get another chance to prove it. No star potential.

YEAR	TEAM/LEVEL	G	IP	W-L	PCT.	HITS	SO	BB	ERA
1991	New York	35	86	5-4	.556	82	67	43	4.27
1992	New York	22	136	6-8	.429	137	60	44	3.64
1993	New York	41	128	5-12	.417	168	72	45	5.96

JEFF SCHWARZ

Chicago White Sox

Relief Pitcher

$18

Limited hitters to a .201 batting average, but walked seven men a game, making his rookie season about a wash. Schwarz will be 30 in May, a veteran of several minor league systems, and numerous trips to the disabled list. He was a starting pitcher until '92, had a minor league record of 40-67, with chronic control troubles. Made the majors after one good year in the bullpen, but will have short career unless his control improves.

YEAR	TEAM/LEVEL	G	IP	W-L	SAVES	HITS	SO	BB	ERA
1991	El Paso AA	27	142	11-8	0	139	134	97	4.89
1992	AA and AAA	44	75	3-4	9	42	95	40	2.05
1993	Chicago	41	51	2-2	0	35	41	38	3.71

DARRYL SCOTT

California

Relief Pitcher

$19

The Angels haven't tried him as their closer yet, but that would appear to be in the offing. Scott wasn't drafted out of college, and he must have been hurt because he throws pretty hard, or at least it looks pretty hard to me. Right-hander, excellent minor league record, was the closer at Vancouver most of '93. Grade B prospect; got his degree from a good small college.

YEAR	TEAM/LEVEL	G	IP	W-L	SAVES	HITS	SO	BB	ERA
1992	Edmonton AAA	31	36	0-2	6	41	48	21	5.20
1993	Vancouver AAA	46	52	7-1	15	35	57	19	2.09
1993	California	16	20	1-2	0	19	13	11	5.85

TIM SCOTT

Montreal Expos

Relief Pitcher

$15

Had the Tommy John surgery when he was 21 (1987), and took several years to get back to full strength. His record is inconsistent, but he has pitched well at times . . . Four-pitch pitcher, good strikeout rates. Over his two-year career has allowed a .196 average with none out/none on, but .281 with runners in scoring position. Because of this he allowed 55% of inherited runners to score (17 of 31), the worst percentage in the majors.

YEAR	TEAM/LEVEL	G	IP	W-L	SAVES	HITS	SO	BB	ERA
1992	Las Vegas AAA	24	28	1-2	15	20	28	3	2.25
1992	San Diego	34	38	4-1	0	39	30	21	5.26
1993	Two Teams	56	72	7-2	1	69	65	34	3.01

SCOTT SCUDDER

Cleveland Indians

Starting Pitcher

$10

Scudder is only 26; he just seems old because he pitched 100 innings for Cincinnati five years ago. He throws hard—who makes the majors at 21 if he doesn't throw hard?—and has a curve which scouts rave about, but batters hit. His control has always been poor, and he gave up 21 homers in 136 innings at Charlotte in '93, going 7-7 with a 5.03 ERA. He gets hurt every year. Grade D prospect.

YEAR	TEAM/LEVEL	G	IP	W-L	PCT.	HITS	SO	BB	ERA
1991	Cincinnati	27	101	6-9	.400	91	51	56	4.35
1992	Cleveland	23	109	6-10	.375	134	66	55	5.28
1993	Cleveland	2	4	0-1	.000	5	1	4	9.00

RUDY SEANEZ
San Diego Padres
Thrower
$2

Seanez is, roughly speaking, the worst pitching prospect in the history of the world. There is really nothing about his record that would cause a prudent person to suppose that he could pitch in the majors, but he throws hard, so he keeps getting chances. His control record is awful, and he's been hurt a lot, and he's never been effective anywhere.

YEAR	TEAM/LEVEL	G	IP	W-L	SAVES	HITS	SO	BB	ERA
1993	Colo Springs AAA	3	3	0-0	0	3	5	1	9.00
1993	Las Vegas AAA	14	20	0-1	0	24	14	11	6.41
1993	San Diego	3	3	0-0	0	8	1	2	13.50

DAVID SEGUI
Baltimore Orioles
First Base´
$26

The Orioles are asking around about first basemen, and Segui likely will be on the bench by spring. He isn't an awful player. He's a Gold Glove quality first baseman, and he's capable of hitting .300, although he hasn't yet. He had more walks than strikeouts. On the other hand, he is turriblc slow, doesn't have the power you want at first base, and hit .152 in the late innings of close games, worst in the league.

YEAR	TEAM/LEVEL	G	AB	R	H	2B	3B	HR	RBI	BB	SB	AVG	OBP	SLG
1992	Baltimore	115	189	21	44	9	0	1	17	20	1	.233	.306	.296
1993	Baltimore	146	450	54	123	27	0	10	60	58	2	.273	.351	.400
1994	**Projected**	**148**	**485**	**52**	**135**	**27**	**0**	**7**	**56**	**55**	**2**	**.278**	**.352**	**.377**

KEVIN SEITZER
Milwaukee Brewers
Third Base/First Base
$20

Seitzer went on a home run binge after joining the Brewers about August 1, which may save his career. He drove in 30 runs in 47 games for the Brewers . . . Doesn't have a third baseman's arm, doesn't run as well you would want your leadoff man to run, although he could do that. He's 32 now, and going to be out of the game soon if he doesn't go back to hitting .300.

YEAR	TEAM/LEVEL	G	AB	R	H	2B	3B	HR	RBI	BB	SB	AVG	OBP	SLG
1992	Milwaukee	148	540	74	146	35	1	5	71	57	13	.270	.337	.367
1993	Two Teams	120	417	45	112	16	2	11	57	44	7	.269	.338	.396
1994	**Projected**	**125**	**415**	**52**	**116**	**22**	**2**	**6**	**55**	**46**	**9**	**.280**	**.351**	**.386**

AARON SELE
Boston Red Sox
Starting Pitcher
$42

He fits the profile of a coming star so well it's disconcerting. An All-American at Washington State, he was a first-round pick in 1991. He struggled at first, but has pitched well everywhere for two years. He's a big (6-foot-5) righthander with a sweeping curve. There is every reason to expect him to be a star, except that young pitchers often slip suddenly into reverse . . . May lead the league in hit batsmen.

YEAR	TEAM/LEVEL	G	IP	W-L	PCT.	HITS	SO	BB	ERA
1992	A and AA	27	160	15-6	.714	147	141	61	3.60
1993	Pawtucket AAA	14	94	8-2	.800	74	87	23	2.19
1993	Boston	18	112	7-2	.778	100	93	48	2.74

FRANK SEMINARA

San Diego Padres
Starting Pitcher
$17

He opened the season in the rotation, but was sent to Las Vegas in May. I'm inclined to think that they pulled the plug on him a bit too quickly, as his ERA for the season wasn't that far from the National League norm, but he throws funny—if you can imagine somebody shot-putting a ball sidearm you'll have it—and people who throw funny don't inspire confidence from the management. A 50-50 chance of a comeback.

YEAR	TEAM/LEVEL	G	IP	W-L	PCT.	HITS	SO	BB	ERA
1992	San Diego	19	100	9-4	.692	98	61	46	3.68
1993	Las Vegas AAA	21	114	8-5	.615	136	99	52	5.43
1993	San Diego	18	46	3-3	.500	53	22	21	4.47

SCOTT SERVAIS

Houston Astros
Catcher
$22

The righthanded part of a platoon arrangement with Eddie Taubensee. Both showed similar improvement in '93, so they'll probably continue to share the job . . . between them they went from .229 with five homers, 43 RBI in 1992 to .252 with 20 and 74 last year. Taubensee throws a little better, but Servais is probably a better defensive catcher . . . Had .522 slugging percentage against lefthanded pitchers in '93, .292 against righthanders.

YEAR	TEAM/LEVEL	G	AB	R	H	2B	3B	HR	RBI	BB	SB	AVG	OBP	SLG
1992	Houston	77	205	12	49	9	0	0	15	11	0	.239	.294	.283
1993	Houston	85	258	24	63	11	0	11	32	22	0	.244	.313	.415
1994	**Projected**	**102**	**294**	**23**	**71**	**11**	**0**	**5**	**29**	**20**	**1**	**.241**	**.290**	**.330**

SCOTT SERVICE

Cincinnati Reds
Relief Pitcher
$17

Only 26 years old, he has ping-ponged around for eight years, pitching for Philadelphia, Montreal, Colorado and Cincinnati in the majors, and every team you can imagine in the minors. Based strictly on his age and ability, and overlooking the itinerant nature of his career, he looks like he can pitch. Throws hard, throws strikes, fastball moves. There is something here that people don't like, but I don't know what it is.

YEAR	TEAM/LEVEL	G	IP	W-L	SAVES	HITS	SO	BB	ERA
1992	Two Teams AAA	52	95	6-2	6	66	112	44	1.89
1993	Indianapolis AAA	21	30	4-2	2	25	28	17	4.45
1993	Two Teams	29	46	2-2	2	44	43	16	4.30

MIKE SHARPERSON

Los Angeles Dodgers
Second/Third Base
$19

The acquisitions of Reed and Wallach, the kids the Dodgers are building their future around, took most of Sharperson's playing time, despite his .300 season in 1992. He's 32 years old, a better hitter than Jody Reed and a *far* better hitter than Tim Wallach, but the Dodgers, like several other organizations, just have this thing for guys who make a lot of money. Will play more in '94, but will never be a regular.

YEAR	TEAM/LEVEL	G	AB	R	H	2B	3B	HR	RBI	BB	SB	AVG	OBP	SLG
1991	Los Angeles	105	216	24	60	11	2	2	20	25	1	.278	.355	.375
1992	Los Angeles	128	317	48	95	21	0	3	36	47	2	.300	.387	.394
1993	Los Angeles	73	90	13	23	4	0	2	10	5	2	.256	.299	.367

JON SHAVE
Texas Rangers
Second Base
$18

Managed the rare feat of having an on-base percentage lower than his batting average during his September callup . . . He is on the list of players who could be the Rangers' second baseman in '93, probably number one on the list, and could well wind up as a Rookie of the Year candidate. An unspectacular talent, 26 years old with no power and limited speed, but a good fielder with good work habits, and should hit around .275.

YEAR	TEAM/LEVEL	G	AB	R	H	2B	3B	HR	RBI	BB	SB	AVG	OBP	SLG
1992	Tulsa AA	118	453	57	130	23	5	2	36	37	6	.287	.343	.373
1992	MLE	118	446	53	123	21	4	1	33	28	4	.276	.319	.348
1993	Texas	17	47	3	15	2	0	0	7	0	1	.319	.306	.362

JEFF SHAW
Montreal Expos
Starting Pitcher
$12

I'm puzzled by why the Expos, who have many good pitching prospects, are wasting time with this guy. They tried him as a starter early in the year, but he wasn't very good (1-4, 3.96 ERA). He spent the rest of the year in the bullpen, where he limited the first batters he faced to a .103 batting average (4 for 39), the best in the major leagues, but wasn't any better overall.

YEAR	TEAM/LEVEL	G	IP	W-L	PCT.	HITS	SO	BB	ERA
1991	Cleveland	29	72	0-5	.000	72	31	27	3.36
1992	Cleveland	2	8	0-1	.000	7	3	4	8.22
1993	Montreal	55	96	2-7	.222	91	50	32	4.14

DANNY SHEAFFER
Colorado Rockies
Catcher
$18

A 32-year-old righthanded batter, had been catching in Triple-A since 1985, and had been in the minors since 1981. He signed with the Rockies as a free agent, went to spring training as a non-roster invitee. If he's a .280 hitter I'm the governor of New Jersey, but he can probably create as many runs as Joe Girardi, and you have to root for a guy who has paid his dues with treble damages.

YEAR	TEAM/LEVEL	G	AB	R	H	2B	3B	HR	RBI	BB	SB	AVG	OBP	SLG
1991	Portland AAA	93	330	46	100	14	2	1	43	26	2	.303	.360	.367
1992	Portland AAA	116	442	54	122	23	4	5	56	21	3	.276	.309	.380
1993	Colorado	82	216	26	60	9	1	4	32	8	2	.278	.299	.384

LARRY SHEETS
Milwaukee Brewers
Designated "Hitter"
$8

Sheets had a big year with Baltimore in 1987 (31 homers, 94 RBI. .316 average; it's one of the better fluke seasons in baseball history). He doesn't do anything but hit and didn't do enough of that, so he went to Japan in 1991, returning last year for a crack at the Seattle lineup. That failing, he went to New Orleans, to DH for the Brewers' Triple-A team. No future, but no worse player than Kevin Reimer.

YEAR	TEAM/LEVEL	G	AB	R	H	2B	3B	HR	RBI	BB	SB	AVG	OBP	SLG
1993	Seattle	11	17	0	2	1	0	0	1	2	0	.118	.250	.176
1993	New Orl AAA	127	457	60	128	28	1	18	98	31	3	.280	.329	.464
1993	MLE	127	446	54	117	24	0	19	89	28	2	.262	.306	.444

GARY SHEFFIELD
Florida Marlins
Third Base
$58

Made 34 errors at third base, giving him an .899 fielding percentage, the worst in the major leagues at any position in several years . . . I believe, from memory, that he is the fourth regular since 1920 to field less than .900 (at any position) . . . He was trying to play through a shoulder injury, of course. Had his best year as a base stealer, going 17-for-22.

YEAR	TEAM/LEVEL	G	AB	R	H	2B	3B	HR	RBI	BB	SB	AVG	OBP	SLG
1992	San Diego	146	557	87	184	34	3	33	100	48	5	.330	.385	.580
1993	Two Teams	140	494	67	145	20	5	20	73	47	17	.294	.361	.476
1994	**Projected**	**147**	**535**	**77**	**157**	**29**	**3**	**20**	**80**	**52**	**13**	**.293**	**.356**	**.471**

BEN SHELTON
Pittsburgh Pirates
First Base/Outfield
$10

A second-round selection in 1987, he has never really established himself as a prospect. I may be missing something, but my impression was that the only reason he was in the majors was that he is eligible to leave the Pirates as a minor league free agent, and Leyland wanted to take a look at him before he got away. Big, doesn't run, hasn't hit more than 15 homers in a season. Young enough to surprise (24).

YEAR	TEAM/LEVEL	G	AB	R	H	2B	3B	HR	RBI	BB	SB	AVG	OBP	SLG
1992	Carolina AA	115	368	57	86	17	0	10	51	68	4	.234	.362	.361
1993	Buffalo AAA	65	173	25	48	8	1	5	22	24	0	.277	.375	.422
1993	Pittsburgh	15	24	3	6	1	0	2	7	3	0	.250	.333	.542

KEITH SHEPHERD
Colorado Rockies
Relief Pitcher
$10

Another Rockies Pitcher Horror Show, posted a 3.00 ERA on the road, but 10.45 in Denver, which abbreviated his stay. Shepherd has never been a hot prospect, but has belonged to the Pirates, White Sox and Phillies, from whom the Rockies liberated him. I suspect he's a pretty good pitcher; anyway, he had a string of awfully good ERAs before Colorado got him. I also suspect it will be a year or two before his luck turns.

YEAR	TEAM/LEVEL	G	IP	W-L	SAVES	HITS	SO	BB	ERA
1992	Philadelphia	12	22	1-1	2	19	10	6	3.27
1993	Colorado Spr AAA	37	68	3-6	8	90	57	44	6.78
1993	Colorado	14	19	1-3	1	26	7	4	6.98

DARRELL SHERMAN
San Diego Padres
Outfield
$11

A little lefthanded batter who can run, he hit .332 at Wichita in '92, then played OK at Las Vegas, and opened the season on the major league roster. He plays within his skills—doesn't overswing, doesn't try to make impossible plays in the field or on the bases—and his managers like him, but his talents are modest. If Mike Felder is a poor man's Brett Butler, he's kind of a poor man's Mike Felder.

YEAR	TEAM/LEVEL	G	AB	R	H	2B	3B	HR	RBI	BB	SB	AVG	OBP	SLG
1992	MLE	135	454	68	115	13	0	6	29	47	30	.253	.323	.322
1993	MLE	82	256	33	56	6	0	0	7	24	28	.219	.286	.242
1993	San Diego	37	63	8	14	1	0	0	2	6	2	.222	.315	.238

TOMMY SHIELDS

Chicago Cubs

Infield

$9

You can list his name among the dozens of pretty good minor league veterans who are looking for the light. There was a crack opened up for him when Sandberg wasn't able to start the season, but Vizcaino hit about .370 the first few weeks of the season, which closed the door pretty quickly. He's 29 years old, running out of time, but there are worse players around who have jobs.

YEAR	TEAM/LEVEL	G	AB	R	H	2B	3B	HR	RBI	BB	SB	AVG	OBP	SLG
1993	Iowa AAA	84	314	48	90	16	1	9	48	26	10	.287	.351	.430
1993	MLE	84	300	37	76	13	0	7	37	20	6	.253	.300	.367
1993	Chicago	20	34	4	6	1	0	0	1	2	0	.176	.222	.206

ZAK SHINALL

Seattle Mariners

Pitcher

$9

Shinall, a 220-pound righthander, spent six years in the Dodger system, failing to make the roster despite good ERAs in tough parks. With the Mariners he pitched lousy at Calgary, but got one game in the majors anyway . . . A media guide says that his grandfather played for the Browns in 1941, but doesn't say who his grandfather was. If true, this means that three Mariners had grandfathers who played in the majors—Shinall, Boone and Salkeld.

YEAR	TEAM/LEVEL	G	IP	W-L	SAVES	HITS	SO	BB	ERA
1991	AA and AAA	54	96	4-4	10	101	51	31	2.92
1992	Albuquerque AAA	64	82	13-5	6	91	46	37	3.29
1993	Calgary AAA	33	47	2-1	5	55	25	18	5.01

CRAIG SHIPLEY

San Diego Padres

Utility Infielder

$14

A 31-year-old Australian who never walks, he has found his station in life as a backup infielder. He does two things well—he can run, and he can throw well enough to play shortstop or third base. This is enough to get you labeled a prospect, but not enough to keep you in the lineup. Shipley has survived that stage, where he was considered a disappointment, and can now be recognized as a useful reserve.

YEAR	TEAM/LEVEL	G	AB	R	H	2B	3B	HR	RBI	BB	SB	AVG	OBP	SLG
1992	San Diego	52	105	7	26	6	0	0	7	2	1	.248	.262	.305
1993	San Diego	105	230	25	54	9	0	4	22	10	12	.235	.275	.326
1994	**Projected**	**80**	**179**	**14**	**43**	**6**	**0**	**2**	**15**	**6**	**4**	**.240**	**.265**	**.307**

BRIAN SHOUSE

Pittsburgh Pirates

Lefthanded Relief Pitcher

$10

A 13th-round draft pick, short, doesn't throw particularly hard. He has pitched well in A ball and at Double-A, hasn't pitched well yet at Triple-A, but probably will. When he does that he can add his name to the seemingly endless list of left-handers who compete for the 40 or 50 available jobs as portside middle relievers. Grade D prospect.

YEAR	TEAM/LEVEL	G	IP	W-L	SAVES	HITS	SO	BB	ERA
199	Carolina AA	59	77	5-6	4	71	79	28	2.44
1993	Buffalo AAA	48	52	1-0	2	54	25	17	3.83
1993	Pittsburgh	6	4	0-0	0	7	3	2	9.00

TERRY SHUMPERT
Kansas City Royals
Second Base
$16

Shumpert hit .275 in 32 games in 1990, but got all mixed up at the plate in '91 and '92, winding up back in Omaha. He had a fine year with the bat and on the bases, and I will also say that I like him in the field, just my own observation. The Royals, however, never believe in their young players. It was hard for them to give him *one* chance; it may be impossible for them to give him a second.

YEAR	TEAM/LEVEL	G	AB	R	H	2B	3B	HR	RBI	BB	SB	AVG	OBP	SLG
1992	Kansas City	36	94	6	14	5	1	1	11	3	2	.149	.175	.255
1993	Omaha AAA	111	413	70	124	29	1	14	59	41	36	.300	.367	.477
1993	MLE	111	394	51	105	26	0	8	43	29	24	.266	.317	.393

JOE SIDDALL
Montreal Expos
Catcher
$4

The Expos two years ago were knee-deep in catching prospects, but have suffered a series of reversals . . . Natal lost in the expansion draft, Colbrunn had an injury and had to change positions, Goff chose to leave the organization. Laker hasn't hit. Siddall, who couldn't hit a baby in the butt with a fly swatter, got to the majors as a consequence of these things, to serve a couple of months as a backup catcher. No future.

YEAR	TEAM/LEVEL	G	AB	R	H	2B	3B	HR	RBI	BB	SB	AVG	OBP	SLG
1992	Harrisburgh AA	95	288	26	68	12	0	2	27	29	4	.236	.310	.299
1993	Ottawa AAA	48	136	14	29	6	0	1	16	19	2	.213	.306	.279
1993	Montreal	19	20	0	2	1	0	0	1	1	0	.100	.143	.150

RUBEN SIERRA
Oakland Athletics
Right Field
$59

Ruben Sierra is the first player in major league history to hit 20 homers, steal 20 bases, drive in 100 runs—and have a terrible season by his own standards. His .233 batting average was the lowest of any American League regular except Rob Deer . . . The standard explanation for his season is that he over-did his weight training in the off-season, and became muscle bound.

YEAR	TEAM/LEVEL	G	AB	R	H	2B	3B	HR	RBI	BB	SB	AVG	OBP	SLG
1992	Two Teams	151	601	83	167	34	7	17	87	45	14	.278	.323	.443
1993	Oakland	158	630	77	147	23	5	22	101	52	25	.233	.288	.390
1994	**Projected**	**148**	**594**	**87**	**164**	**31**	**5**	**22**	**97**	**50**	**17**	**.276**	**.332**	**.456**

DAVE SILVESTRI
New York Yankees
Shortstop
$15

He's an odd player, a shortstop who hits like Paul Sorrento or Steve Buechele or Ken Caminiti, hits more like a first or third baseman. He has more power than a typical shortstop, and draws more walks. When you see that your instinctive reaction is to assume that he's a marginal shortstop, out of position, but there's little independent evidence for this. Is 26 years old, Grade B or Grade C prospect.

YEAR	TEAM/LEVEL	G	AB	R	H	2B	3B	HR	RBI	BB	SB	AVG	OBP	SLG
1992	MLE	118	403	66	100	22	2	9	58	46	13	.248	.325	.380
1993	MLE	120	413	62	100	23	2	16	53	56	4	.242	.333	.424
Major League Total		14	34	7	10	1	2	1	5	5	0	.294	.385	.529

DON SLAUGHT

Pittsburgh Pirates

Catcher

$40

He became the Pirates' number-one catcher when his platoon partner, Mike LaValliere, reported out of shape. He hit .300 for the second straight season, the third time in four years, the other average being .295. 1993 was probably his best all-around season . . . The most-comparable major league player, by far, is Brian Harper. They're about the same age, similar hitters, similar fielders.

YEAR	TEAM/LEVEL	G	AB	R	H	2B	3B	HR	RBI	BB	SB	AVG	OBP	SLG
1992	Pittsburgh	87	255	26	88	17	3	4	37	17	2	.345	.384	.482
1993	Pittsburgh	113	377	34	113	19	2	10	55	29	2	.300	.356	.440
1994	**Projected**	**115**	**375**	**31**	**104**	**22**	**2**	**6**	**48**	**30**	**2**	**.277**	**.331**	**.395**

HEATHCLIFF SLOCUMB

Cleveland Indians

Relief Pitcher

$10

Slocumb was traded to Cleveland last June 1 and sent to the minors on July 5, keeping intact his streak of having spent at least part of every season in the minor leagues. Slocumb throws hard but not hard enough to live on it, so he has to do some other things. His control is poor, he is absurdly easy to run on, and his second and third pitches (a slider and a split-finger fastball) are just fair.

YEAR	TEAM/LEVEL	G	IP	W-L	SAVES	HITS	SO	BB	ERA
1991	Chicago NL	52	63	2-1	1	53	34	30	3.45
1992	Chicago NL	30	36	0-3	1	52	27	21	6.50
1993	Two Teams	30	38	4-1	0	35	22	20	4.03

JOE SLUSARSKI

Oakland Athletics

Starting Pitcher

$7

Slusarkski has a joke name, like Mickey Klutts or Charlie Frisbee or Drungo LaRue Hazewood. Despite this the A's made him a high draft pick, which was an obvious mistake, because when did you ever hear of a guy with a joke name becoming a good ballplayer? Compounding this, they brought him to the majors with essentially no Triple-A experience, and have been trying for three years to teach him how to pitch. It's probably a lost cause.

YEAR	TEAM/LEVEL	G	IP	W-L	PCT.	HITS	SO	BB	ERA
1992	Oakland	15	76	5-5	.500	85	38	27	4.45
1993	Tacoma AAA	24	113	7-5	.583	133	61	40	4.76
1993	Oakland	2	9	0-0	—	9	1	11	5.19

JOHN SMILEY

Cincinnati Reds

Starting Pitcher

$29

Developed a bone spur on his elbow, and had his most difficult season. I'm fairly confident that he'll come back; I would hate to speculate on how quickly. He has a good understanding of how to pitch, the sort of thing that looks instinctive; if healthy he will win, plus he has a contract that guarantees good money for a couple of years, so he'll get a full opportunity. Could be one of the steals of the '94 draft.

YEAR	TEAM/LEVEL	G	IP	W-L	PCT.	HITS	SO	BB	ERA
1991	Pittsburgh	33	208	20-8	.714	194	129	44	3.08
1992	Minnesota	34	241	16-9	.640	205	163	65	3.21
1993	Cincinnati	18	106	3-9	.250	117	60	31	5.62

BRYN SMITH

Colorado Rockies (Released)

Starting Pitcher

No Value

The Rockies signed him as a free agent, and released him on June 2, after the league had hit .362 against him. His career started late and lasted 13 years, so he's now 38. He was an underrated pitcher, a pitcher who didn't beat himself and could be counted on for 10 to 12 wins almost every year. If you can do that for five years in baseball, you can go fishing the rest of your life.

YEAR	TEAM/LEVEL	G	IP	W-L	PCT.	HITS	SO	BB	ERA
1991	St. Louis	31	199	12-9	.571	188	94	45	3.85
1992	St. Louis	13	21	4-2	.667	20	9	5	4.64
1993	Colorado	11	30	2-4	.333	47	9	11	8.49

DWIGHT SMITH

Chicago Cubs

Outfield

$32

After looking like a world-beater in 1989 he fell into a deep canyon, and couldn't get up. He began the long march back in mid-season 1992, and continued it with a slugging percentage almost .500 in '93. Among the Cubs' young outfielders there's Sammie Sosa, and then there's Derrick May, Smith and Glenallen Hill, and then there's a third group, not far behind. Whoever continues to hit will beat his way out of the pack.

YEAR	TEAM/LEVEL	G	AB	R	H	2B	3B	HR	RBI	BB	SB	AVG	OBP	SLG
1992	Chicago	109	217	28	60	10	3	3	24	13	9	.276	.318	.392
1993	Chicago	111	300	51	93	17	5	11	35	25	8	.300	.355	.494
1994	**Projected**	**133**	**371**	**50**	**101**	**19**	**4**	**8**	**43**	**28**	**11**	**.272**	**.323**	**.410**

LEE SMITH

New York Yankees

Closer

$46

The key facts here are a lot like Eckersley's. Both men are getting old for power pitchers, both have high ERAs but still are piling up saves, both still have great strikeout rates and strikeout/walk ratios, and both gave up too many home runs. In the case of Smith, you also have to worry about his weight and his knees, but I'm not ready to declare his career over. I think he may have a hundred saves left.

YEAR	TEAM/LEVEL	G	IP	W-L	SAVES	HITS	SO	BB	ERA
1991	St. Louis	67	73	6-3	47	70	67	13	2.34
1992	St. Louis	70	75	4-9	43	62	60	26	3.12
1993	Two Teams	63	58	2-4	46	53	60	14	3.88

LONNIE SMITH

Baltimore Orioles

Left Field/DH

$27

The Orioles picked him up from Pittsburgh for the stretch drive; who knows where he'll be playing this year. On the other hand, the son of a gun can still put runs on the scoreboard. If you project his stats over the last two years (combined) into 550 at bats, you'll see 95 runs scored, 20 homers with 9 triples, 87 RBI, 19 stolen bases, 98 walks. He's 38, but useful as a platoon DH.

YEAR	TEAM/LEVEL	G	AB	R	H	2B	3B	HR	RBI	BB	SB	AVG	OBP	SLG
1992	Atlanta	84	158	23	39	8	2	6	33	17	4	.247	.324	.437
1993	Two Teams	102	223	43	62	6	4	8	27	51	9	.278	.420	.448
1994	**Projected**	**107**	**243**	**39**	**61**	**16**	**2**	**5**	**32**	**40**	**6**	**.251**	**.357**	**.395**

OZZIE SMITH

St. Louis Cardinals

Shortstop

$51

Ozzie is 39, and has played more games at short than anyone except Aparicio. He isn't everything he once was, I suppose, but if you don't want him, give me a call. His range is still outstanding; he made a few errors, but an average shortstop would make more . . . Hit 282 ground-ball outs in '93, most in the majors . . . When he swung at a pitch he made contact 94.4% of the time, highest in the majors.

YEAR	TEAM/LEVEL	G	AB	R	H	2B	3B	HR	RBI	BB	SB	AVG	OBP	SLG
1992	St. Louis	132	518	73	153	20	2	0	31	59	43	.295	.367	.342
1993	St. Louis	141	545	75	157	22	6	1	53	43	21	.288	.337	.356
1994	**Projected**	**130**	**515**	**67**	**130**	**20**	**2**	**1**	**37**	**60**	**27**	**.252**	**.330**	**.305**

PETE SMITH

Atlanta Braves

Starting Pitcher

$19

The man primarily responsible for one of the greatest pennant races ever. Smith, after pitching well in April, went 0-5 with a 6.25 ERA in May and June, which helped put the Braves in a deep hole . . . I've always liked Smith, and always thought he was a good pitcher, but something always goes wrong for him, and he's going to run out of chances soon.

YEAR	TEAM/LEVEL	G	IP	W-L	PCT.	HITS	SO	BB	ERA
1991	Atlanta	14	48	1-3	.250	48	29	22	5.06
1992	Atlanta	12	79	7-0	1.000	63	43	28	2.05
1993	Atlanta	20	91	4-8	.333	92	53	36	4.37

ZANE SMITH

Pittsburgh Pirates

Starting Pitcher

$19

Smith had shoulder surgery in the 1992-93 off-season, and didn't pitch until June 16, then took September off with what was described as a tired shoulder. In between, he didn't get the ground balls which are essential to his success . . . He is 33, but in my opinion he will probably come back to pitch successfully again. He's got 78 wins; he'll get 110.

YEAR	TEAM/LEVEL	G	IP	W-L	PCT.	HITS	SO	BB	ERA
1991	Pittsburgh	35	228	16-10	.615	234	120	29	3.20
1992	Pittsburgh	23	141	8-8	.500	138	56	19	3.06
1993	Pittsburgh	14	83	3-7	.300	97	32	22	4.55

ROGER SMITHBERG

Oakland Athletics

Pitcher

$14

In 1987, Smithberg was a second-round draft pick of the Padres, who seem to have been intent on messing up his career. They had him as a starting pitcher, sent him almost immediately to Triple-A, let him fail there, then starting jerking him up and down the ladder. After four-plus years of this they released him, and he signed with the A's, who converted him to relief, and here he is. Grade C prospect.

YEAR	TEAM/LEVEL	G	IP	W-L	SAVES	HITS	SO	BB	ERA
1993	Huntsville AA	27	37	4-2	0	34	36	16	2.21
1993	Tacoma AAA	28	51	3-3	4	50	25	11	1.78
1993	Oakland	13	20	1-2	3	13	4	7	2.75

JOHN SMOLTZ

Atlanta Braves

Starting Pitcher

$68

For the future, I think I would rather have Smoltz than Glavine, not that I would kick either one off the 40-man roster. Strikeouts normally indicate career length . . . Smoltz over four years is 26-30 before the All-Star break, but 32-17 after . . . also over four years has limited righthanded hitters to a .194 batting average. Lefthanders have hit .265 against him.

YEAR	TEAM/LEVEL	G	IP	W-L	PCT.	HITS	SO	BB	ERA
1991	Atlanta	36	230	14-13	.519	206	148	77	3.80
1992	Atlanta	35	247	15-12	.556	206	215	80	2.85
1993	Atlanta	35	244	15-11	.577	208	208	100	3.62

J. T. SNOW

California Angels

First Base

$31

He blew hot and cold all year, hitting like an MVP in April (.343 with a .687 slugging percentage), then falling into such a terrible slump that he wound up in the minors, then coming back to be the American League's player of the week for the last week of the season. Switch hitter, good first baseman, should be a solid #5 hitter to back up Salmon until the end of the century.

YEAR	TEAM/LEVEL	G	AB	R	H	2B	3B	HR	RBI	BB	SB	AVG	OBP	SLG
1992	MLE	135	470	64	132	23	2	12	62	55	2	.281	.356	.415
1993	California	129	419	60	101	18	2	16	57	55	3	.241	.328	.408
1994	**Projected**	**148**	**528**	**78**	**143**	**28**	**2**	**18**	**77**	**66**	**3**	**.271**	**.352**	**.434**

CORY SNYDER

Los Angeles Dodgers

Outfielder/Third Base

$20

Led the league in strikeouts, with 147. Of course, nobody minds the strikeouts because he hits so many homers . . . He missed the ball when he swung 32% of the time, the highest percentage in the National League . . . His range factor (1.74) was the lowest of any right field regular . . . Defense at third is unacceptable. As an overall right fielder he ranks below Sosa, Walker, Gwynn, Justice, Bonilla, Anthony, Merced and whoever else happens to be playing the position.

YEAR	TEAM/LEVEL	G	AB	R	H	2B	3B	HR	RBI	BB	SB	AVG	OBP	SLG
1992	San Francisco	124	390	48	105	22	2	14	57	23	4	.269	.311	.444
1993	Los Angeles	143	516	61	137	33	1	11	56	47	4	.266	.331	.397
1994	**Projected**	**122**	**384**	**42**	**91**	**21**	**1**	**12**	**48**	**28**	**3**	**.237**	**.289**	**.391**

LUIS SOJO

Toronto Blue Jays

Second Base

$17

Sojo, who played well for California, was acquired by Toronto in exchange for Kelly Gruber. He's basically a second baseman, which, since Alomar rarely misses a game, wasn't much use to the Blue Jays, who needed a backup shortstop and somebody to play third if they pinch hit for Sprague. Sojo also had nagging injuries (strained muscles in his side), and was sent to Syracuse in July. He's a major league player, and should get a job somewhere.

YEAR	TEAM/LEVEL	G	AB	R	H	2B	3B	HR	RBI	BB	SB	AVG	OBP	SLG
1991	California	113	364	38	94	14	1	3	20	14	4	.258	.295	.327
1992	California	106	368	37	100	12	3	7	43	14	7	.272	.299	.378
1993	Toronto	19	47	5	8	2	0	0	6	4	0	.170	.231	.213

PAUL SORRENTO
Cleveland Indians
First Base
$33

Matched his 1992 season point for point, while improving his defense. He is 28 now, past the age at which players normally improve, although there have been cases where players needed a thousand at bats or so before reaching their full potential as hitters. He's hit only .221 (career) against lefthanders (31-for-140), which will keep him in the platoon box, while the addition of Ramirez could squeeze his playing time even further.

YEAR	TEAM/LEVEL	G	AB	R	H	2B	3B	HR	RBI	BB	SB	AVG	OBP	SLG
1992	Cleveland	140	458	52	123	24	1	18	60	51	0	.269	.341	.443
1993	Cleveland	148	463	75	119	26	1	18	65	58	3	.257	.340	.434
1994	**Projected**	**155**	**550**	**72**	**144**	**29**	**1**	**21**	**79**	**68**	**2**	**.262**	**.343**	**.433**

SAMMY SOSA
Chicago Cubs
Right Field
$42

For those of you who are still counting, there are now 23 seasons in history in which a player has hit 30 homers and stolen 30 bases, and it's been done by 14 different players (Kenny Williams, Mays, Aaron, Tommie Harper, Bonds Jr. and Sr., Dale Murphy, Hojo, Strawberry, Eric Davis, Joe Carter, Canseco, Gant and Sosa). It's been done by at least one player every year since 1987.

YEAR	TEAM/LEVEL	G	AB	R	H	2B	3B	HR	RBI	BB	SB	AVG	OBP	SLG
1992	Chicago	67	262	41	68	7	2	8	25	19	15	.260	.317	.393
1993	Chicago	159	598	92	156	25	5	33	93	38	36	.261	.309	.485
1994	**Projected**	**159**	**586**	**86**	**148**	**22**	**5**	**24**	**77**	**39**	**35**	**.253**	**.299**	**.430**

TIM SPEHR
Montreal Expos
Catcher
$14

One of many catchers to serve as Fletcher's backup; see comments on Siddall, Laker, McIntosh. Spehr is a hard-swinging, light-hitting catcher who is supposed to be good defensively, but committed nine errors in 242 innings in the field, five times the normal error rate. He did hit .350 after the All-Star break (14 for 40), which may fool people into thinking he can hit, which may give him a chance to redeem himself with the glove.

YEAR	TEAM/LEVEL	G	AB	R	H	2B	3B	HR	RBI	BB	SB	AVG	OBP	SLG
1992	MLE	109	324	38	73	20	0	10	33	49	2	.225	.327	.380
1992	Kansas City	37	74	7	14	5	0	3	14	9	1	.189	.282	.378
1993	Montreal	53	87	14	20	6	0	2	10	6	2	.230	.281	.368

BILL SPIERS
Milwaukee Brewers
Second Base
$19

In a nutshell: he had a surprisingly good season in 1991, had back surgery following the season, was replaced at shortstop by Listach, came back and had a very disappointing year, contributing heavily to the failures of his team. His .971 fielding percentage was the poorest of any American League regular at second base. I doubt that he can repeat 1991, but we'll see.

YEAR	TEAM/LEVEL	G	AB	R	H	2B	3B	HR	RBI	BB	SB	AVG	OBP	SLG
1992	Milwaukee	12	16	2	5	2	0	0	2	1	1	.313	.353	.438
1993	Milwaukee	113	340	43	81	8	4	2	36	29	9	.238	.302	.303
1994	**Projected**	**87**	**251**	**38**	**65**	**8**	**2**	**3**	**29**	**22**	**8**	**.259**	**.319**	**.343**

PAUL SPOLJARIC

Toronto Blue Jays

Lefthanded Starting Pitcher

$22

A lefthanded starting pitcher who throws hard and has a nice slider, and hopes to move into the Toronto rotation within a year or two. A native Canadian, he signed with Toronto as an undrafted free agent (I think Canadians weren't drafted then) and missed almost all of 1991 with a strained elbow or a broken ankle, depending on which source you believe, but has become perhaps the top pitching prospect in the organization.

YEAR	TEAM/LEVEL	G	IP	W-L	PCT.	HITS	SO	BB	ERA
1993	Dunedin A	4	26	3-0	1.000	16	29	12	1.38
1993	Knoxville AA	7	43	4-1	.800	30	51	22	2.28
1993	Syracuse AAA	18	95	8-7	.533	97	88	52	5.29

JERRY SPRADLIN

Cincinnati Reds

Relief Pitcher

$18

A 6-foot-7 righthander, didn't play baseball in high school and only one year of college, but the Reds took a flier on him, and it seems to be working out. Finesse pitcher, throws fastball, slider, split-finger and curve, has good control and his delivery is hard to read. The Reds have brought him along slowly because of his lack of a) experience, and b) a great fastball, but most of the markers about him are good.

YEAR	TEAM/LEVEL	G	IP	W-L	SAVES	HITS	SO	BB	ERA
1992	Chattanooga AA	59	65	3-3	34	52	35	13	1.38
1992	Indianapolis AAA	34	57	3-2	1	58	46	12	3.49
1993	Cincinnati	37	49	2-1	2	44	24	9	3.49

ED SPRAGUE

Toronto Blue Jays

Third Base

$29

Sprague would be a terrific bench player, but I'm not sold on him as a regular. He's big and slow (led American League in grounding into double plays, with 23), has a good arm but heavy feet. He doesn't walk, so his on-base percentage is low, and he scored only 50 runs despite playing regularly. He might double his home run count in his second year as a regular, and if he does obviously that's a different story.

YEAR	TEAM/LEVEL	G	AB	R	H	2B	3B	HR	RBI	BB	SB	AVG	OBP	SLG
1992	Toronto	22	47	6	11	2	0	1	7	3	0	.234	.280	.340
1993	Toronto	150	546	50	142	31	1	12	73	32	1	.260	.310	.386
1994	**Projected**	**142**	**519**	**58**	**136**	**26**	**2**	**16**	**70**	**45**	**1**	**.262**	**.321**	**.412**

RUSS SPRINGER

California Angels

Starting Pitcher

$14

With the late-season emergence of Leftwich and Magrane, there is limited room for anybody to break the Angels rotation (Finley, Langston, Magrane, Leftwich), plus there other candidates (Hathaway, Farrell, Lewis). Springer, who bombed in his mid-season opportunity, will probably have to go back to Vancouver and wait for another opening. It is too early to give up on anybody who can pitch as well as he has in Triple-A.

YEAR	TEAM/LEVEL	G	IP	W-L	PCT.	HITS	SO	BB	ERA
1992	Columbus AAA	20	124	8-5	.615	89	95	54	2.69
1993	Vancouver AAA	11	59	5-4	.556	58	40	33	4.27
1993	California	14	60	1-6	.143	73	31	32	7.20

SCOTT STAHOVIAK
Minnesota Twins
Third Base
$16

A 24-year-old lefthanded hitter from Creighton University, Stahoviak has some power, is a good baserunner, and walks a lot. He is big, 6'5", and his defense needs work. He was slowed by an elbow injury early in the year, but played well once healthy and earned a callup. The Twins are just surviving at third base, waiting for somebody good to show up, and he could very well be the man, but probably not this year.

YEAR	TEAM/LEVEL	G	AB	R	H	2B	3B	HR	RBI	BB	SB	AVG	OBP	SLG
1993	Nashville AA	93	331	40	90	25	1	12	56	56	10	.272	.375	.462
1993	MLE	93	324	32	83	24	0	10	45	39	7	.256	.336	.423
1993	Minnesota	20	57	1	11	4	0	0	1	3	0	.193	.233	.263

MATT STAIRS
Montreal Expos
Left Field
$10

Stairs, who was a hot prospect two or three years ago, disappeared from the Expos' roster in June. I'm not certain, but I think he signed with the Chunichi Dragons. Following the lead of Cecil Fielder, young players have been putting in a year or two in Japan to escape the clutches of a team which isn't giving them a chance to play. Stairs is only 25; I think we'll see him again.

YEAR	TEAM/LEVEL	G	AB	R	H	2B	3B	HR	RBI	BB	SB	AVG	OBP	SLG
1992	Montreal	13	30	2	5	2	0	0	5	7	0	.167	.316	.233
1993	Ottawa AAA	34	125	18	35	4	2	3	20	11	4	.280	.348	.416
1993	Montreal	6	8	1	3	1	0	0	2	0	0	.375	.375	.500

ANDY STANKIEWICZ
New York Yankees
Utility Infielder
$13

The Yankees tried to deal Gallego last spring, but had no takers, then Gallego got hot, which left them with an extra infielder. The result was that Stankiewicz, who was a pleasant surprise in '92, wound up back at Columbus, and didn't play very well there. He'll be out of options soon, and the Yankees will either have to put him in the majors or send him somewhere else. No star potential; will have more trials as a regular.

YEAR	TEAM/LEVEL	G	AB	R	H	2B	3B	HR	RBI	BB	SB	AVG	OBP	SLG
1992	New York	116	400	52	107	22	2	2	25	38	9	.268	.338	.348
1993	MLE	90	320	37	69	10	2	0	26	23	8	.216	.268	.259
1993	New York	16	9	5	0	0	0	0	0	1	0	.000	.100	.000

MIKE STANLEY
New York Yankees
Catcher
$39

The new Stan Lopata. Lopata was a career backup catcher in the 1950s, a righthanded hitter who exploded on the league in 1956, hitting 32 homers with 95 RBI. He was the same age as Stanley at the time. He got hurt the next year, never had another big year . . . Stanley led American League catchers in fielding percentage, at .996. He can hit. We'll see if he can stay healthy and stay hot.

YEAR	TEAM/LEVEL	G	AB	R	H	2B	3B	HR	RBI	BB	SB	AVG	OBP	SLG
1992	New York	68	173	24	43	7	0	8	27	33	0	.249	.372	.428
1993	New York	130	423	70	129	17	1	26	84	57	1	.305	.389	.534
1994	**Projected**	**125**	**419**	**59**	**110**	**17**	**1**	**15**	**64**	**68**	**1**	**.263**	**.366**	**.415**

MIKE STANTON

Atlanta Braves

Relief Pitcher

$25

Stanton's story is the same as Scott Radinsky's—a lefthander with real good stuff whose career isn't coming along the way I or many other people expected it to. Stanton is a little easier to understand than Radinsky because Stanton looks chunky . . . Don't expect 27 saves from him again this year; he lost the closer role in early August, and will have to earn his next shot at it.

YEAR	TEAM/LEVEL	G	IP	W-L	SAVES	HITS	SO	BB	ERA
1991	Atlanta	74	78	5-5	7	62	54	21	2.88
1992	Atlanta	65	64	5-4	8	59	44	20	4.10
1993	Atlanta	63	52	4-6	27	51	43	29	4.67

DAVE STATON

San Diego Padres

Left Field or First Base

$13

I've never seen this before: Staton played A ball, Double-A, Triple-A and the majors in '93, and had slugging percentages of .656 or better in all four places. The punch line is that he is really not much of a prospect—a slow 6'5" outfielder with a torn rotator cuff, who has some real power, but probably not the consistent power that would make him valuable. He's earned a chance to show us, though.

YEAR	TEAM/LEVEL	G	AB	R	H	2B	3B	HR	RBI	BB	SB	AVG	OBP	SLG
1992	Las Vegas AAA	96	335	47	94	20	0	19	76	34	0	.281	.353	.510
1993	Las Vegas AAA	11	37	8	10	0	0	7	11	3	0	.270	.317	.838
1993	San Diego	17	42	7	11	3	0	5	9	3	0	.262	.326	.690

TERRY STEINBACH

Oakland Athletics

Catcher

$37

His season was ended by a broken wrist in mid-August; he'll be fine for '94. He may have been having his best season. His .285 batting average is a career high, although he's always close to that, and his power was proportional . . . The A's ERA was 5.25 with Steinbach catching, 4.47 with Scott Hemond, which may or may not indicate something.

YEAR	TEAM/LEVEL	G	AB	R	H	2B	3B	HR	RBI	BB	SB	AVG	OBP	SLG
1991	Oakland	129	456	50	125	31	1	6	67	22	2	.274	.312	.386
1992	Oakland	128	438	48	122	20	1	12	53	45	2	.279	.345	.411
1993	Oakland	104	389	47	111	19	1	10	43	25	3	.285	.333	.416

DAVE STEWART

Toronto Blue Jays

Starting Pitcher

$37

He hasn't had a losing record since 1985, and I see no reason to think that he will in '94. If anything, I am more inclined to believe that he has completed his transition, and is ready to run off a couple of 17-10 seasons. He started '93 on the DL with a torn muscle in his elbow, and didn't pitch well until mid-August, but went 4-0 in September, and was MVP of the playoffs.

YEAR	TEAM/LEVEL	G	IP	W-L	PCT.	HITS	SO	BB	ERA
1991	Oakland	35	226	11-11	.500	245	144	105	5.18
1992	Oakland	31	199	12-10	.545	175	130	79	3.66
1993	Toronto	26	162	12-8	.600	146	96	72	4.44

DAVE STIEB

Kansas City (Released)

Starting Pitcher

$4

Has been plagued since 1990 by a herniated disk and a sore elbow. He started four times for the White Sox early in the season, ineffectively, and was released, then signed with the Royals, was sent to Omaha and didn't pitch any better then, earning another release. He's 36. There have certainly been pitchers who came back from this position, but the natural assumption is that his career is over.

YEAR	TEAM/LEVEL	G	IP	W-L	PCT.	HITS	SO	BB	ERA
1992	Toronto	21	96	4-6	.400	98	45	43	5.04
1993	Chicago	4	22	1-3	.250	27	11	14	6.04
1993	Omaha AAA	10	55	3-4	.429	71	21	14	6.09

KURT STILLWELL

California Angels

Second Base

$12

He won't be 30 for a year and a half, but his career appears to be almost over. He's not a bad defensive second baseman or shortstop, but a team can find somebody to do that job for minimum wage, and Stillwell doesn't do anything else well enough that it pays to keep him around and let him do it. Not real fast, no power, makes regular visits to the disabled list.

YEAR	TEAM/LEVEL	G	AB	R	H	2B	3B	HR	RBI	BB	SB	AVG	OBP	SLG
1991	Kansas City	122	385	44	102	17	1	6	51	33	3	.265	.322	.361
1992	San Diego	114	379	35	86	15	3	2	24	26	4	.227	.274	.298
1993	Two Teams	79	182	11	42	6	2	1	14	15	6	.231	.290	.302

KEVIN STOCKER

Philadelphia Phillies

Shortstop

$39

Stocker is not a .324 hitter, or anything close to that; he's probably going to hit in the .260-.270 range. This is more than enough: if he can hit .270 with 20 stolen bases, 60 walks and 30 doubles, which I think he can, that will make him one of the best-hitting shortstops in the league. Throw in excellent defense, what do you have? A package that will cost you at least $4 million a year.

YEAR	TEAM/LEVEL	G	AB	R	H	2B	3B	HR	RBI	BB	SB	AVG	OBP	SLG
1992	MLE	62	232	24	52	8	1	0	10	14	11	.224	.268	.267
1993	MLE	83	309	50	69	14	0	2	15	26	13	.223	.284	.288
1993	Philadelphia	70	259	46	84	12	3	2	31	30	5	.324	.409	.417

TODD STOTTLEMYRE

Toronto Blue Jays

Starting Pitcher

$21

He throws hard and looks good on the mound, and he's milked that for four-plus years in the starting rotation. He's an awful pitcher. After 156 starts, all of them with the best organization in baseball, he has a losing record (62-63). The league hit .292 against him, his strikeout/walk ratio is bad and gets worse every year, his career ERA is 4.41 and he misses a month every summer with an injury.

YEAR	TEAM/LEVEL	G	IP	W-L	PCT.	HITS	SO	BB	ERA
1991	Toronto	34	219	15-8	.652	194	116	75	3.78
1992	Toronto	28	174	12-11	.522	175	98	63	4.50
1993	Toronto	30	177	11-12	.478	204	98	69	4.84

DOUG STRANGE
Texas Rangers
Third Base/Second Base
$25

Went to spring training with the Rangers as a non-roster player and wound up the season as their regular second baseman. If he had had his 1993 season in 1989, when he got some playing time in Detroit, he would be a wealthy man now, but he hit .218 then and he's 30 now, so the Rangers will be looking at younger players. Good second baseman, and capable of hitting at the 1993 level again.

YEAR	TEAM/LEVEL	G	AB	R	H	2B	3B	HR	RBI	BB	SB	AVG	OBP	SLG
1992	MLE	55	202	22	55	13	0	3	18	6	1	.272	.293	.381
1992	Chicago NL	52	94	7	15	1	0	1	5	10	1	.160	.240	.202
1993	Texas	145	484	58	124	29	0	7	60	43	6	.256	.318	.360

DARRYL STRAWBERRY
Los Angeles Dodgers
Right Field
$19

The back injury which has cost him most of the last two years is obviously serious and probably chronic. His legal and emotional troubles, the odd tactless remark that makes headlines—those don't help. His rehab has supposedly gone well, and he's not old, so he could recover much of his ability. Back injuries have a mixed precedent. Dave Winfield recovered from his, but Dave Winfield is more the exception than the rule.

YEAR	TEAM/LEVEL	G	AB	R	H	2B	3B	HR	RBI	BB	SB	AVG	OBP	SLG
1991	Los Angeles	139	505	86	134	22	4	28	99	75	10	.265	.361	.491
1992	Los Angeles	43	156	20	37	8	0	5	25	19	3	.237	.322	.385
1993	Los Angeles	32	100	12	14	2	0	5	12	16	1	.140	.267	.310

WILLIAM SUERO
Milwaukee Brewers
Second Base
$13

A 27-year-old sometime prospect, probably will be in another organization in '94. Suero runs well and doesn't strike out, and might have a major league career if he could impress some manager as the kind of defensive player/clubhouse presence that nicely rounds out a roster. He's not going to be a regular, and I'll be a little surprised if he makes it even as a reserve.

YEAR	TEAM/LEVEL	G	AB	R	H	2B	3B	HR	RBI	BB	SB	AVG	OBP	SLG
1992	MLE	75	263	31	58	8	5	0	18	22	11	.221	.281	.289
1992	Milwaukee	18	16	4	3	1	0	0	0	2	1	.188	.316	.250
1993	Milwaukee	15	14	0	4	0	0	0	0	1	0	.286	.333	.286

B. J. SURHOFF
Milwaukee Brewers
Third Base/Catcher
$25

The Brewers have talked for several years about moving Surhoff to another position, and, emboldened by several successful shifts around baseball (Biggio, Zeile, Sprague), finally took the plunge in '93. They didn't derive any apparent benefits from it, as Surhoff didn't hit significantly better or steal any more bases. He was all right at third base, but doesn't hit as much as you would like your third baseman to hit. He's very consistent.

YEAR	TEAM/LEVEL	G	AB	R	H	2B	3B	HR	RBI	BB	SB	AVG	OBP	SLG
1992	Milwaukee	139	480	63	121	19	1	4	62	46	14	.252	.314	.321
1993	Milwaukee	148	552	66	151	38	3	7	79	36	12	.274	.318	.391
1994	**Projected**	**155**	**550**	**66**	**146**	**25**	**3**	**6**	**72**	**41**	**12**	**.265**	**.316**	**.355**

RICK SUTCLIFFE

Baltimore Orioles

Starting Pitcher

$18

His 5.75 ERA was the worst of any major league pitcher with 162 innings . . . Allowed 1.28 hits per inning, highest in the majors . . . Last in baserunners allowed per nine innings, 15.8 . . . His batting average allowed, .314, was also the highest in the majors, and his slugging percentage also, .496, and his on-base average allowed (.385) . . . He is 38. If he has a comeback left, it will be in a more limited role.

YEAR	TEAM/LEVEL	G	IP	W-L	PCT.	HITS	SO	BB	ERA
1991	Chicago NL	19	97	6-5	.545	96	52	45	4.10
1992	Baltimore	36	237	16-15	.516	251	109	74	4.47
1993	Baltimore	29	166	10-10	.500	212	80	74	5.75

DALE SVEUM

Oakland Athletics

First Base

$5

What *exactly* does Dale Sveum have to do to prove that he can't play major league baseball? How many times does he have to hit under .250 with no power? How many times does he have to hit under .200? (He's done that three times in four years.) How many defensive positions does he have to fail at? Do you want to try him at pitcher, just give him 150 innings or so to see if he's any good?

YEAR	TEAM/LEVEL	G	AB	R	H	2B	3B	HR	RBI	BB	SB	AVG	OBP	SLG
1991	Milwaukee	90	266	33	64	19	1	4	43	32	2	.241	.320	.365
1992	2 ML Teams	94	249	28	49	13	0	4	28	28	1	.197	.273	.297
1993	Oakland	30	79	12	14	2	1	2	6	16	0	.177	.316	.304

RUSS SWAN

Seattle Mariners

Relief Pitcher

$9

A 30-year-old lefthander, pitched well for the Mariners in 1991, not so well in 1992, poorly in '93. He was sent to the minors in June, recalled in August but almost immediately went on the DL with a hyperextended elbow. Has limited lefthanders to a .203 batting average in his career, but righthanders have hit .297 . . . Ground ball pitcher, could come back but I'm not betting on it.

YEAR	TEAM/LEVEL	G	IP	W-L	SAVES	HITS	SO	BB	ERA
1991	Seattle	63	79	6-2	2	81	33	28	3.43
1992	Seattle	55	104	3-10	9	104	45	45	4.74
1993	Seattle	23	20	3-3	0	25	10	18	9.15

BILL SWIFT

San Francisco Giants

Starting Pitcher

$68

He had his fourth consecutive outstanding season, and 20 wins to remove the last doubts. He's the most extreme ground ball pitcher in the majors, got 440 ground ball outs in '93 as opposed to 141 fly balls and pop outs, easily the highest ratio in the majors. The Giants turned 27 double plays behind him, most in the NL. He limited righthanded hitters to a .177 batting average, best in the majors by a starting pitcher.

YEAR	TEAM/LEVEL	G	IP	W-L	PCT.	HITS	SO	BB	ERA
1991	Seattle	71	90	1-2	.333	74	48	26	1.99
1992	San Francisco	30	165	10-4	.714	144	77	43	2.08
1993	San Francisco	34	233	21-8	.724	195	157	55	2.82

GREG SWINDELL

Houston Astros

Starting Pitcher

$54

A strained shoulder ruined his first season in Houston. He opened the season 4-1, but struggled through May and June. He probably should have gone on the DL sooner than he did, but he had taken a lot of money to pitch for the Astros, and has always taken pride in making his starts, so he tried to pitch through it. Returned to pitch well the final two months, and is among the better pitchers in the league.

YEAR	TEAM/LEVEL	G	IP	W-L	PCT.	HITS	SO	BB	ERA
1991	Cleveland	33	238	9-16	.360	241	169	31	3.48
1992	Cincinnati	31	214	12-8	.600	210	138	41	2.70
1993	Houston	31	190	12-13	.480	215	124	40	4.16

PAUL SWINGLE

California Angels

Righthanded Pitcher

$8

That is not a misprint: he really was called up in September after going 2-9 with a 6.92 ERA at Vancouver, apparently because the Angels were dead in '93, are serious about '94 and wanted to take a look at everybody they might need. He's 27 years old, a late-round draft pick who became a prospect by striking out a lot of people in A ball, but has yet to pitch effectively at any higher level.

YEAR	TEAM/LEVEL	G	IP	W-L	PCT.	HITS	SO	BB	ERA
1992	Midland AA	25	150	8-10	.444	158	104	51	4.69
1993	Vancouver AAA	37	68	2-9	.182	85	61	32	6.92
1993	California	9	10	0-1	.000	15	6	6	8.38

JEFF TACKETT

Baltimore Orioles

Catcher

$10

He is strictly a backup catcher, and his hold on that job is tenuous at best, since he ended the season at Rochester, with Mark Parent on the major league roster. He is a defensive catcher, and threw out 44% of opposing baserunners, which is excellent, although the ERA when he was catching was not good (4.75). My guess is that he will spend *part* of the '94 season on a major league roster, during somebody's injury.

YEAR	TEAM/LEVEL	G	AB	R	H	2B	3B	HR	RBI	BB	SB	AVG	OBP	SLG
1992	Baltimore	65	179	21	43	8	1	5	24	17	0	.240	.307	.380
1993	Baltimore	39	87	8	15	3	0	0	9	13	0	.172	.277	.207
1994	**Projected**	**42**	**101**	**11**	**21**	**3**	**0**	**1**	**9**	**11**	**0**	**.208**	**.286**	**.267**

FRANK TANANA

New York Yankees

Starting Pitcher

$26

Had exactly the same season that Warren Spahn had in '65, when Spahn was 44. Spahn pitched most of the year with a last-place Mets team, was traded late in the season to a pennant contender trying to bolster their pitching, pitched 198 innings with a four-plus ERA and wound up 7-16. He was released in spring training the next year . . . Tanana pitched better than the record suggests. But then, so did Spahn.

YEAR	TEAM/LEVEL	G	IP	W-L	PCT.	HITS	SO	BB	ERA
1991	Detroit	33	217	13-12	.520	217	107	78	3.69
1992	Detroit	32	187	13-11	.542	188	91	90	4.39
1993	Two Teams	32	203	7-17	.292	216	116	55	4.35

KEVIN TAPANI
Minnesota Twins
Starting Pitcher
$59

Only American League pitcher to give up 50 doubles (he gave up 56), and also led in stolen bases allowed by a wide margin (he gave up 42). Tapani struggled for four months, but fixed whatever was bothering him and pitched VERY well in September, going 5-2, 2.35. He's healthy and intelligent, he throws four pitches for strikes, and he is a very good bet to return to his previous form.

YEAR	TEAM/LEVEL	G	IP	W-L	PCT.	HITS	SO	BB	ERA
1991	Minnesota	34	244	16-9	.640	225	135	40	2.99
1992	Minnesota	34	220	16-11	.593	226	138	48	3.97
1993	Minnesota	36	226	12-15	.444	243	150	57	4.43

TERRIBLE TONY TARASCO
Atlanta Braves
Outfield
$28

Probably will inherit Otis Nixon's spot on the roster, and some of his playing time, either as part-time center fielder or backup outfielder. A lefthanded batter from California, he slipped through the draft and was signed by Atlanta as a free agent, which seems inexplicable since he has power, speed, and can throw. His MLE from '93 is better than previous seasons, but he is 23, so we'll assume this is real improvement. **Grade A prospect.**

YEAR	TEAM/LEVEL	G	AB	R	H	2B	3B	HR	RBI	BB	SB	AVG	OBP	SLG
1993	Richmond AAA	93	370	73	122	15	7	15	53	36	19	.330	.388	.530
1993	MLE	93	354	54	106	12	3	12	39	26	12	.299	.347	.452
1993	Atlanta	24	35	6	8	2	0	0	2	0	0	.229	.243	.286

DANNY TARTABULL
New York Yankees
Right Field/DH
$41

Had almost the same stats as Gil Hodges in 1952 (32 homers, 102 RBI, .254, .500 slugging percentage) . . . Hit only .210 in Yankee Stadium, the lowest of any American League regular in his home park, but had Frank Thomas numbers on the road . . . There are a lot of things he can't do, but a team needs a cleanup hitter. If he plays 140 games, he'll drive in 100 runs.

YEAR	TEAM/LEVEL	G	AB	R	H	2B	3B	HR	RBI	BB	SB	AVG	OBP	SLG
1992	New York	123	421	72	112	19	0	25	85	103	2	.266	.409	.489
1993	New York	138	513	87	128	33	2	31	102	92	0	.250	.363	.503
1994	**Projected**	**136**	**487**	**77**	**131**	**28**	**2**	**26**	**92**	**91**	**3**	**.269**	**.384**	**.495**

JIM TATUM
Colorado Rockies
Pinch Hitter
$16

Tatum pinch hit 71 times for the Rockies, and was fairly successful in that role, hitting .254 as a pinch hitter, usually for the pitcher. He hit .097 when he *wasn't* pinch hitting (3 for 31), which isn't how it's supposed to work. He is a good hitter, despite the .204 average; it's anybody's guess whether he will get another chance to prove it.

YEAR	TEAM/LEVEL	G	AB	R	H	2B	3B	HR	RBI	BB	SB	AVG	OBP	SLG
1992	Denver AAA	130	492	74	162	36	3	19	101	40	8	.329	.382	.530
1992	MLE	130	464	54	134	30	1	13	74	29	5	.289	.331	.442
1993	Colorado	92	98	7	20	5	0	1	12	5	0	.204	.245	.286

EDDIE TAUBENSEE

Houston Astros

Catcher

$23

Go read the Scott Servais comment, and I'll resume here. Taubensee is a couple of years younger than Servais, and he throws out 30% to 35% of baserunners, as opposed to about 25% for Servais. But the Astros' staff ERA has been significantly better with Servais catching, both years of the platoon arrangement . . . Taubensee is a good enough catcher that he could be a number-one man, but the platoon arrangement is probably the best thing for the team.

YEAR	TEAM/LEVEL	G	AB	R	H	2B	3B	HR	RBI	BB	SB	AVG	OBP	SLG
1992	Houston	104	297	23	66	15	0	5	28	31	2	.222	.299	.323
1993	Houston	94	288	26	72	11	1	9	42	21	1	.250	.299	.389
1994	**Projected**	**102**	**313**	**30**	**78**	**15**	**1**	**7**	**35**	**27**	**1**	**.249**	**.309**	**.371**

JULIAN TAVAREZ

Cleveland Indians

Starting Pitcher

$37

Skinny Dominican righthander, only 20 years old. The Indians in recent years have rushed numerous pitchers to the major leagues after they've pitched about two good months at Double-A, but in this case they didn't even wait for him to do anything at Double-A: they took him right out of the Carolina League. Excellent control, live arm, could be a fine pitcher when he grows up.

YEAR	TEAM/LEVEL	G	IP	W-L	PCT.	HITS	SO	BB	ERA
1993	Kinston A	18	119	11-5	.688	102	107	28	2.42
1993	Canton-Akr AA	3	19	2-1	.667	14	11	1	0.95
1993	Cleveland	8	37	2-2	.500	53	19	13	6.57

BRIEN TAYLOR

New York Yankees

Lefthanded Starting Pitcher

$28

His performance at Double-A was not without its warts. Control is supposed to be one of his assets, but he walked 102, threw 10 wild pitches, and raised some doubts about his pitching instincts. In two years in the minors he has committed 18 balks, a career's worth, and hit 19 batters. On the other hand, he is young, healthy, and throws 95 MPH. **Grade A prospect**, probably won't arrive this year.

YEAR	TEAM/LEVEL	G	IP	W-L	PCT.	HITS	SO	BB	ERA
1991	(Not in Organized Ball)								
1992	Ft Lauderdale A	27	161	6-8	.429	121	187	66	2.57
1993	Albany AA	27	163	13-7	.650	127	150	102	3.48

KERRY TAYLOR

San Diego Padres

Righthanded Pitcher

$19

Signed by the Twins as a free agent out of a Minnesota high school in 1989, Taylor was drafted by Padres under Rule V after a good year in the Midwest League in 1992. A fine athlete, throws low 90s fastball and has good movement on his curve. Grade B prospect, probably won't be in the majors this year. Last year was the year that he would normally have been in Double-A.

YEAR	TEAM/LEVEL	G	IP	W-L	PCT.	HITS	SO	BB	ERA
1991	Kenosha A	26	132	7-11	.389	121	84	84	3.82
1992	Kenosha A	27	170	10-9	.526	150	158	68	2.75
1993	San Diego	36	68	0-5	.000	72	45	49	6.45

SCOTT TAYLOR

Boston Red Sox

Pitching Prospect

$15

A sandy-haired 26-year-old lefthander, more of a survivor than an actual prospect. A 28th-round draft pick in 1988, he made a name in the organization by pitching brilliantly at Lynchburg (Class A) and New Britain (Double-A), but hasn't yet followed through at Pawtucket or Boston. If the Red Sox decide that Hesketh is finished, he probably will inherit Hesketh's job. Otherwise, he'll start the year at Pawtucket.

YEAR	TEAM/LEVEL	G	IP	W-L	PCT.	HITS	SO	BB	ERA
1992	Boston	4	15	1-1	.500	13	7	4	4.91
1993	Pawtucket AAA	47	123	7-7	.500	132	88	48	4.04
1993	Boston	16	11	0-1	.000	14	8	12	8.18

ANTHONY TELFORD

Baltimore Orioles

Righthanded Pitcher

$12

Telford is the Rodney Dangerfield of the Oriole organization, and may be ready to move on, see if somebody else will give him some respect. He was an All-American at San Jose State, but suffered a shoulder injury in 1988, and doesn't throw hard anymore. He does know how to pitch, and he got to the majors in 1990, after going 14-4 with a 1.86 ERA, but was a swing man at Rochester in '93.

YEAR	TEAM/LEVEL	G	IP	W-L	PCT.	HITS	SO	BB	ERA
1992	Rochester AAA	27	181	12-7	.632	183	129	64	4.18
1993	Rochester AAA	38	91	7-7	.500	98	66	33	4.27
1993	Baltimore	3	7	0-0	—	11	6	1	9.82

DAVE TELGHEDER

New York Mets

Righthanded Pitcher

$15

A 31st-round draft pick in 1989, he emerged as a prospect by going 18-7 in 1990, at two levels of A ball. He's continued to show well—hasn't been hurt, hasn't been thrown for a loop when he moves up a level, doesn't beat himself. He's 27, graduated from U-Mass before entering baseball, below-average fastball but seems to know what to do with it. Grade C prospect, ended the season in the Mets rotation.

YEAR	TEAM/LEVEL	G	IP	W-L	PCT.	HITS	SO	BB	ERA
1992	Tidewater AAA	28	169	6-14	.300	173	118	36	4.21
1993	Tidewater AAA	13	76	7-3	.700	81	52	19	2.95
1993	New York	24	76	7-3	.700	82	35	21	4.76

MICKEY TETTLETON

Detroit Tigers

Utility Regular

$63

Drove in 100 runs for the first time; he now has three consecutive seasons with 30+ homers and 100+ walks. He's no longer a catcher; he played 56 games last year behind the plate (mostly early in the season), 59 games at first base, 39 in right field, also played left and DH. He appears to be in great shape, and I wouldn't worry about his age yet (he's 33).

YEAR	TEAM/LEVEL	G	AB	R	H	2B	3B	HR	RBI	BB	SB	AVG	OBP	SLG
1992	Detroit	157	525	82	125	25	0	32	83	122	0	.238	.379	.469
1993	Detroit	152	522	79	128	25	4	32	110	109	3	.245	.372	.492
1994	**Projected**	**152**	**523**	**78**	**124**	**22**	**1**	**26**	**85**	**114**	**3**	**.237**	**.374**	**.432**

TIM TEUFEL
San Diego Padres
Infield
$19

Most of his playing time is at second base against lefthanded pitchers. He creates a good number of runs for a second baseman, and isn't charged with many errors, although he's not seen as a good glove. He has competition for a job in San Diego (Luis Lopez), but that's not terribly important, because he can catch on somewhere else. He's 35, so his career will end with his next major slump.

YEAR	TEAM/LEVEL	G	AB	R	H	2B	3B	HR	RBI	BB	SB	AVG	OBP	SLG
1992	San Diego	101	246	23	55	10	0	6	25	31	2	.224	.312	.337
1993	San Diego	96	200	26	50	11	2	7	31	27	2	.250	.338	.430
1994	**Projected**	**102**	**230**	**26**	**52**	**13**	**1**	**6**	**28**	**32**	**4**	**.226**	**.321**	**.370**

BOB TEWKSBURY
St. Louis Cardinals
Starting Pitcher
$58

The National League hit .301 against him, and he led the league in hits allowed, with 258. If he wasn't the best control pitcher in 70 years, this would worry you. He has pretty clearly established the ability to win if the league hits .300 against him, and to win big if they hit .270 . . . Handled 65 chances without an error, the best defensive performance in the majors. Will continue to win.

YEAR	TEAM/LEVEL	G	IP	W-L	PCT.	HITS	SO	BB	ERA
1991	St. Louis	30	191	11-12	.478	206	75	38	3.25
1992	St. Louis	33	233	16-5	.762	217	91	20	2.16
1993	St. Louis	32	214	17-10	.630	258	97	20	3.83

BOBBY THIGPEN
Philadelphia Phillies
Relief Pitcher
$14

Still throws hard and seems healthy. Fregosi, who managed Thigpen in Chicago, thought he might be able to bring him back, but hasn't yet. Lefthanded batters hit .333 against him last year; righthanders, .336. His contract has options for 1994-95 which almost certainly *won't* be picked up, but he is several steps away from being out of chances if he wants to push for them. He won't come back unless he develops a new pitch.

YEAR	TEAM/LEVEL	G	IP	W-L	SAVES	HITS	SO	BB	ERA
1991	Chicago AL	67	70	7-5	30	63	47	38	3.49
1992	Chicago AL	55	55	1-3	22	58	45	33	4.75
1993	Two Teams	42	54	3-1	1	74	29	21	5.83

FRANK THOMAS
Chicago White Sox
First Base
$95

His on-base percentage has gone *down* every season since he came up in 1990, and is still at .426. In every season of his major league career he has an on-base percentage over .400 and a slugging percentage over .500 . . . The most-similar season ever was by Mel Ott in 1932 . . . Frank was the first player since Ted Kluszewski in 1954 to hit 40 homers and also have twice as many walks as strikeouts.

YEAR	TEAM/LEVEL	G	AB	R	H	2B	3B	HR	RBI	BB	SB	AVG	OBP	SLG
1992	Chicago	160	573	115	185	46	2	24	115	122	6	.323	.439	.536
1993	Chicago	153	549	106	174	36	0	41	128	112	4	.317	.426	.607
1994	**Projected**	**157**	**560**	**110**	**186**	**37**	**2**	**35**	**121**	**130**	**4**	**.330**	**.457**	**.591**

JIM THOME
Cleveland Indians
Third Base
$37

Thome, like Mark Lewis, was hot cookies a couple of years ago, but returned to Charlotte to finish baking. He looks awfully good, a **Grade A prospect** by any analysis. He's only 23 now, a George Brett-type, a lefthanded hitter who has hit .373, .337, .336 and .332 in the minor leagues, and hit well enough in 47 major league games last year to alleviate some of the remaining doubts. Good glove at third base.

YEAR	TEAM/LEVEL	G	AB	R	H	2B	3B	HR	RBI	BB	SB	AVG	OBP	SLG
1993	MLE	115	391	65	117	18	2	19	78	58	0	.299	.390	.501
1993	Cleveland	47	154	28	41	11	0	7	22	29	2	.266	.385	.474
1994	**Projected**	**140**	**521**	**73**	**152**	**29**	**3**	**16**	**80**	**66**	**4**	**.292**	**.371**	**.451**

MARK THOMPSON
Colorado Rockies
Starting Prospect
$18

Thompson, the Rockies' second-round draft pick in 1992, has progressed rapidly, and will probably be thrown to the wolves (pardon, *called up*) by mid-season, if he continues to pitch well. He's a hard-throwing righthander from Russellville, Kentucky, pitched for the University of Kentucky. He has a minor league record of 14-6 with a 2.15 ERA.

YEAR	TEAM/LEVEL	G	IP	W-L	PCT.	HITS	SO	BB	ERA
1992	Bend A	16	106	8-4	.667	81	102	31	1.95
1993	Central V A	11	70	3-2	.600	46	72	18	2.20
1993	Colo Spr AAA	4	33	3-0	1.000	31	22	11	2.70

MILT THOMPSON
Philadelphia Phillies
Left Field
$21

A part of the Phillies tremendous outfield platoon, shares left field with Incaviglia. He drove in 44 runs, his best total since 1989, when he was a regular, but actually didn't hit as well last year as he is capable of hitting—his lowest average in three years. He's 35, and probably just has one or two years left. Still runs well and can still hit.

YEAR	TEAM/LEVEL	G	AB	R	H	2B	3B	HR	RBI	BB	SB	AVG	OBP	SLG
1992	St. Louis	109	208	31	61	9	1	4	17	16	18	.293	.350	.404
1993	Phildelphia	129	340	42	89	14	2	4	44	40	9	.262	.341	.350
1994	**Projected**	**110**	**291**	**39**	**78**	**12**	**2**	**4**	**29**	**30**	**14**	**.268**	**.336**	**.364**

ROBBY THOMPSON
San Francisco Giants
Second Base
$43

The best second baseman the Giants have had since they came to the Bay, probably the best they have had since they traded Frankie Frisch in December, 1926. He is among San Francisco's all-time top 10 in games, at bats, runs, hits, doubles and stolen bases, and close to the top 10 in homers and RBI. He's 32 and his back costs him 35 games a year, but as a hitter and fielder, he just gets better.

YEAR	TEAM/LEVEL	G	AB	R	H	2B	3B	HR	RBI	BB	SB	AVG	OBP	SLG
1992	San Francisco	128	443	54	115	25	1	14	49	43	5	.260	.333	.415
1993	San Francisco	128	494	85	154	30	2	19	65	45	10	.312	.375	.496
1994	**Projected**	**136**	**483**	**67**	**128**	**25**	**3**	**14**	**50**	**52**	**10**	**.265**	**.336**	**.416**

RYAN THOMPSON
New York Mets
Center Field
$22

The only real question here is whether he will strike out so much that he can't play. Thompson has athletic ability—a 6'3", 200-pound center fielder who can run and throw. If he hits .260, he's Dave Henderson, a player who'll have an seven- to nine-year career in center field, and help his teams. He's tried to shorten his stroke, but still struck out 81 times in 60 games at Norfolk last year.

YEAR	TEAM/LEVEL	G	AB	R	H	2B	3B	HR	RBI	BB	SB	AVG	OBP	SLG
1992	New York	30	108	15	24	7	1	3	10	8	2	.222	.274	.389
1993	New York	80	288	34	72	19	2	11	26	19	2	.250	.302	.444
1994	**Projected**	**140**	**505**	**65**	**124**	**22**	**4**	**15**	**50**	**36**	**11**	**.246**	**.296**	**.394**

DICKIE THON
Milwaukee Brewers
Utility Infielder
$15

Divided his time pretty evenly among shortstop, where Listach was often hurt, second base, where Spiers was coming back from an injury, and third, where Surhoff was just learning the position (helps us understand why the Brewers finished last, doesn't it?). He played well enough, but he is now 35, and just finishing up his career with piecework, like Uribe and Griffin.

YEAR	TEAM/LEVEL	G	AB	R	H	2B	3B	HR	RBI	BB	SB	AVG	OBP	SLG
1992	Texas	95	275	30	68	15	3	4	37	20	12	.247	.293	.367
1993	Milwaukee	85	245	23	66	10	1	1	33	22	6	.269	.324	.331
1994	**Projected**	**86**	**246**	**21**	**60**	**10**	**1**	**3**	**25**	**16**	**6**	**.244**	**.290**	**.329**

GARY THURMAN
Detroit Tigers
Utility Outfielder
$16

His main use with the Tigers is as a pinch runner and a defensive replacement in center field when Cuyler leaves the game for a pinch hitter. He is useful in that role, as he was 7-for-7 as a base stealer last year, and is an 80 per cent base thief in his career . . . Also a good outfielder, has good enough arm for right field.

YEAR	TEAM/LEVEL	G	AB	R	H	2B	3B	HR	RBI	BB	SB	AVG	OBP	SLG
1991	Kansas City	80	184	24	51	9	0	2	13	11	15	.277	.320	.359
1992	Kansas City	88	200	25	49	6	3	0	20	9	9	.245	.281	.305
1993	Detroit	75	89	22	19	2	2	0	13	11	7	.213	.297	.281

MIKE TIMLIN
Toronto Blue Jays
Relief Pitcher
$21

A righthanded Danny Jackson, throws a slider on the fists that looks like nobody would ever hit it, and if he gets in a groove can get three men out in a minute and a half. If he's not in his groove and the umpire doesn't give him the corner, he's useless. Has had elbow trouble and has failed to build on a fine rookie season, but is still capable of a big year.

YEAR	TEAM/LEVEL	G	IP	W-L	SAVES	HITS	SO	BB	ERA
1991	Toronto	63	108	11-6	3	94	85	50	3.16
1992	Toronto	26	44	0-2	1	45	35	20	4.12
1993	Toronto	54	56	4-2	1	63	49	27	4.69

RON TINGLEY

California Angels
(Released)
Catcher
$9

The development of Turner has pushed Tingley and Orton out of the catching picture in California. Tingley is 34 years old (35 in May), a righthanded non-hitter who spent the better part of 13 years in the minors waiting for his chance. I don't know who needs a .191 hitter, and I'm not sure that his defense is on the same level as Orton's, but if tenacity counts, we'll be seeing him again.

YEAR	TEAM/LEVEL	G	AB	R	H	2B	3B	HR	RBI	BB	SB	AVG	OBP	SLG
1991	California	45	115	11	23	7	0	1	13	8	1	.200	.258	.287
1992	California	71	127	15	25	2	1	3	8	13	2	.197	.282	.299
1993	California	58	90	7	18	7	0	0	12	9	1	.200	.277	.278

LEE TINSLEY

Seattle Mariners
Outfielder
$13

You might not believe that numbers can tell jokes, but Tinsley's records are actually funny, like Dalkowski's. In his early years he struck out with unbelievable frequency—177 times in 123 games for Madison in 1989—yet he has little power (six home runs that year). He also had, in his early years, many walks, many stolen bases, quite a few runs scored . . . A better hitter now, a switch hitter, 25 years old. Grade C prospect.

YEAR	TEAM/LEVEL	G	AB	R	H	2B	3B	HR	RBI	BB	SB	AVG	OBP	SLG
1993	Calgary AAA	111	450	94	136	25	18	10	63	50	34	.302	.372	.504
1993	MLE	111	424	64	110	20	10	7	43	34	22	.259	.314	.403
1993	Seattle	11	19	2	3	1	0	1	2	2	0	.158	.238	.368

FAST FREDDIE TOLIVER

Pittsburgh Pirates
Righthanded Pitcher
$10

A minor league veteran, 33 years old. Toliver went 7-6 for the Twins in '88, but lost the strike zone and went back to the minors, where he remained until last May. A skinny, wiry athlete, he has always had a good fastball but never gained command of a breaking pitch. The Pirates were using him as their Double-A closer, called him up for two months but then sent him to Buffalo.

YEAR	TEAM/LEVEL	G	IP	W-L	SAVES	HITS	SO	BB	ERA
1993	Carolina AA	33	40	2-2	12	32	48	24	3.15
1993	Pittsburgh	12	22	1-0	0	20	14	8	3.74
1993	Buffalo AAA	13	12	1-3	1	13	11	9	3.65

ANDY TOMBERLIN

Pittsburgh Pirates
Outfield
$9

A unique and interesting Grade D prospect. Undrafted, he signed with Atlanta from a 1985 tryout camp, as a pitcher. He was a so-so pitcher, wild, and converted to the outfield in 1988. When he reached Triple-A (1990) his MLEs showed him as a .280-.300 hitter who would walk, but with no power. Failing to reach the majors, he began swinging for the fences, resulting in more power, more strikeouts, but a lower average.

YEAR	TEAM/LEVEL	G	AB	R	H	2B	3B	HR	RBI	BB	SB	AVG	OBP	SLG
1992	Richmond AAA	118	406	69	110	16	5	9	47	41	12	.271	.348	.401
1993	Buffalo AAA	68	221	41	63	11	6	12	45	18	3	.285	.347	.552
1993	Pittsburgh	27	42	4	12	0	1	1	5	2	0	.286	.333	.405

RANDY TOMLIN

Pittsburgh Pirates

Starting Pitcher

$19

Tomlin posted a 2.55 ERA as a rookie in 1990, but this has gone up each year since then, putting his career in jeopardy. Tomlin is a described as a crafty lefthander, a change-of-speeds artist. His best pitch is his Vulcan change, which he jams back into his fingers so that it comes out like a wounded duck, but the hitters have got it timed . . . Best chance for a comeback might be in the American League.

YEAR	TEAM/LEVEL	G	IP	W-L	PCT.	HITS	SO	BB	ERA
1991	Pittsburgh	31	175	8-7	.533	170	104	54	2.98
1992	Pittsburgh	35	209	14-9	.609	226	90	42	3.41
1993	Pittsburgh	18	98	4-8	.333	109	44	15	4.85

SALOMON TORRES

San Francisco Giants

Righthanded Starting Pitcher

$32

A thin Dominican, Torres was one of the best pitchers in minor league baseball in 1991, but struggled with a "tired arm" in 1992. (This is a euphemism. It is impossible for an arm to be "tired"—fatigued—for longer than a week. If it doesn't come back then, it's something else.) Anyway, he was back on top of the world last year, and should be effective in the majors sometime before too long.

YEAR	TEAM/LEVEL	G	IP	W-L	PCT.	HITS	SO	BB	ERA
1993	Shreveport AA	12	83	7-4	.636	67	67	12	2.70
1993	Phoenix AAA	14	105	7-4	.636	105	99	27	3.50
1993	San Francisco	8	45	3-5	.375	37	23	27	4.03

STEVE TRACHSEL

Chicago Cubs

Righthanded Starting Pitcher

$24

A Rookie-of-the-Year candidate. Born on Halloween, 1970, Trachsel went to Long Beach State and was an eighth-round draft pick in 1991. They say he is a pitcher, as opposed to a thrower, and a three-to-one strikeout to walk ratio argues in favor of the proposition. Best pitch is a forkball, also throws average fastball and pretty good curve. Throws strikes. Grade B prospect; should be in the Cubs rotation this year.

YEAR	TEAM/LEVEL	G	IP	W-L	PCT.	HITS	SO	BB	ERA
1992	Charlotte AA	29	191	13-8	.619	180	135	35	3.06
1993	Iowa AAA	27	171	13-6	.684	170	135	45	3.96
1993	Chicago	3	20	0-2	.000	16	14	3	4.58

ALAN TRAMMELL

Detroit Tigers

Shortstop

$29

Trammell missed most of the 1991 and '92 seasons to a variety of knee and ankle injuries. Relatively healthy last year, he played extremely well, even recovering a large share of his lost shortstop job when it was decided that Fryman wasn't a shortstop. Trammell is 35, a good enough player to play another five years, but probably will never be able to put good seasons back to back again.

YEAR	TEAM/LEVEL	G	AB	R	H	2B	3B	HR	RBI	BB	SB	AVG	OBP	SLG
1992	Detroit	29	102	11	28	7	1	1	11	15	2	.275	.370	.392
1993	Detroit	112	401	72	132	25	3	12	60	38	12	.329	.388	.496
1994	**Projected**	**94**	**326**	**46**	**88**	**16**	**2**	**7**	**42**	**34**	**9**	**.270**	**.339**	**.396**

BRIAN TRAXLER
Los Angeles Dodgers
First Base
$9

Probably will leave the Dodgers as a minor league free agent, and may be in the majors with somebody next year. Traxler is a short, thick lefthanded hitter, looks shorter and heavier than his listed dimensions (5'10", 203). His batting records until last year look like nothing, a guy who would never hit, but if you see him he *looks* like a hitter, generates great bat speed with a short, violent stroke. Grade D prospect, 26 years old.

YEAR	TEAM/LEVEL	G	AB	R	H	2B	3B	HR	RBI	BB	SB	AVG	OBP	SLG
1992	MLE	127	363	35	89	18	1	6	35	22	0	.245	.288	.350
1993	Albuquer AAA	127	441	81	147	36	3	16	83	46	0	.333	.396	.537
1993	MLE	127	403	48	109	25	1	9	49	27	0	.270	.316	.404

JEFF TREADWAY
Cleveland Indians
Utility Infield
$21

Played third base for the Indians early in the year, while Thome was at Charlotte. He has little experience at third and can't throw, but did his best, and hit .300. An unusual utility infielder, he doesn't run well but is a classic pinch hitter—a lefthanded line drive hitter who doesn't strike out. That type of player is usually a first baseman/outfielder. Treadway's role in Cleveland is unclear, but he will be around for years.

YEAR	TEAM/LEVEL	G	AB	R	H	2B	3B	HR	RBI	BB	SB	AVG	OBP	SLG
1992	Atlanta	61	126	5	28	6	1	0	5	9	1	.222	.274	.286
1993	Cleveland	97	221	25	67	14	1	2	27	14	1	.303	.347	.403
1994	**Projected**	**104**	**246**	**25**	**69**	**15**	**1**	**3**	**25**	**16**	**6**	**.280**	**.330**	**.386**

RICKY TRLICEK
Los Angeles Dodgers
Relief Pitcher
$18

A 25-year-old righthander originally in the Philadelphia system, he was cut by Toronto after a poor year at Syracuse, signed with the Dodgers and made the major league team, for no obvious reason. He had had difficulty throwing strikes in '92, but solved that last year. He throws hard, and could make a career as a middle reliever.

YEAR	TEAM/LEVEL	G	IP	W-L	SAVES	HITS	SO	BB	ERA
1992	Toronto	2	2	0-0	0	2	1	2	10.80
1992	Syracuse AAA	35	43	1-1	10	37	35	31	4.36
1993	Los Angeles	41	64	1-2	1	59	41	21	4.08

MIKE TROMBLEY
Minnesota Twins
Reliever/Starter
$21

He's in the Mike Boddicker class. Trombley was a 14th-round draft pick, and looks the part; his fastball looks extremely hittable, and he throws what could only be described as a sloppy curve, which would destroy your timing for a week if you actually tried to hit it. He marched through the minors with a 43-24 record, one year, one level. He had some adjustment problems last year, but I wouldn't bet against him.

YEAR	TEAM/LEVEL	G	IP	W-L	PCT.	HITS	SO	BB	ERA
1992	Portland AAA	25	165	10-8	.556	149	138	58	3.65
1992	Minnesota	10	46	3-2	.600	43	38	17	3.30
1993	Minnesota	44	114	6-6	.500	131	85	41	4.88

GEORGE TSAMIS

Minnesota Twins

Lefthanded Relief Pitcher

$4

A starting pitcher in the minors, he made the majors as the second lefthander in the bullpen when the Twins traded Gary Wayne and then Guthrie got hurt. He doesn't have great stuff . . . as a matter of fact he doesn't seem to have anything, a sinking fastball and a mediocre breaking pitch. He moves stuff in and out and tries to stay away from the hitters, and was successful doing this in the minors . . . Nicknamed "The Animal."

YEAR	TEAM/LEVEL	G	IP	W-L	PCT.	HITS	SO	BB	ERA
1991	Portland AAA	29	168	10-8	.556	183	71	66	3.27
1992	Portland AAA	39	164	13-4	.765	195	71	51	3.90
1993	Minnesota	41	68	1-2	.333	86	30	27	6.19

GREG TUBBS

Cincinnati Reds

Outfielder

$8

A 31-year-old outfielder, has played 1,110 minor league games since signing with the Braves in 1984. He's a poor man's Rickey Henderson . . . well, actually he's more like a homeless man's Rickey Henderson. He's a short righthanded hitter who walks a lot—even last year, when he hit .186, his on-base percentage was pretty good—and steals some bases, 249 in the minor leagues. No prospect, but can play a little.

YEAR	TEAM/LEVEL	G	AB	R	H	2B	3B	HR	RBI	BB	SB	AVG	OBP	SLG
1993	Indianap AAA	97	334	59	102	21	4	10	45	42	15	.305	.383	.482
1993	MLE	97	320	47	88	18	2	7	36	33	10	.275	.343	.409
1993	Cincinnati	35	59	10	11	0	0	1	2	14	3	.186	.351	.237

SCOOTER TUCKER

Houston Astros

Catcher

$6

A 27-year-old righthanded hitting catcher, Tucker hit .274 in 98 games at Tucson, equivalent to about .225 in the majors. He has no power or speed, and is no prospect. The Astros platoon catchers, but if the righthander got hurt the best guess is that they would play Taubensee every day, rather than use Tucker to keep the platoon going. He'll probably stay around several years as a Triple-A backup/emergency callup.

YEAR	TEAM/LEVEL	G	AB	R	H	2B	3B	HR	RBI	BB	SB	AVG	OBP	SLG
1992	Houston	20	50	5	6	1	0	0	3	3	1	.120	.200	.140
1993	MLE	98	298	34	67	15	1	0	23	29	0	.225	.294	.282
1993	Houston	9	26	1	5	1	0	0	3	2	0	.192	.250	.231

BRIAN TURANG

Seattle Mariners

Outfielder

$13

Turang played left field for the Mariners over the last two months, and would like to hold that job for a number of years. The odds are against him; he probably is going to lose the job to Newfield, or Blowers, or somebody else. His MLEs don't suggest that he would create enough runs to be a regular left fielder, and at 26 he's probably not going to improve much.

YEAR	TEAM/LEVEL	G	AB	R	H	2B	3B	HR	RBI	BB	SB	AVG	OBP	SLG
1992	MLE	129	473	60	111	20	2	12	56	33	14	.235	.285	.362
1993	MLE	110	394	56	108	17	6	5	36	26	15	.274	.319	.386
1993	Seattle	40	140	22	35	11	1	0	7	17	6	.250	.340	.343

CHRIS TURNER

California Angels

Catcher

$16

A seventh-round draft pick in 1991, he got to the majors mostly with his defensive skills, and looked so good in September that the Angels are talking about him as a number-one catcher. I don't think he's Rookie of the Year material, and I suspect that his bat may be a disappointment, which will put him back into a platoon with Myers.

YEAR	TEAM/LEVEL	G	AB	R	H	2B	3B	HR	RBI	BB	SB	AVG	OBP	SLG
1993	Vancouver	90	283	50	78	12	1	4	57	49	6	.276	.382	.367
1993	MLE	93	268	35	63	9	0	3	40	34	3	.235	.321	.302
1993	California	25	75	9	21	5	0	1	13	9	1	.280	.360	.387

MATT TURNER

Florida Marlins

Righthanded Pitcher

$23

Turner, a veteran of the Braves and Astros systems, signed with the Marlins as a minor league free agent, and came to the big club after posting an 0.66 ERA in 12 games at Edmonton. He was impressive—throws hard, throws strikes; why he didn't make a better showing in the other organizations is a bit of a mystery. Is 27 years old; should have a solid future.

YEAR	TEAM/LEVEL	G	IP	W-L	SAVES	HITS	SO	BB	ERA
1991	Two Teams AAA	36	62	2-4	6	60	58	34	4.50
1992	Tucson AAA	63	100	2-8	14	93	84	40	3.51
1993	Florida	55	68	4-5	0	55	59	26	2.91

TOM URBANI

St. Louis Cardinals

Lefthanded Pitcher

$16

A 26-year-old lefthander. He's a control pitcher, although it hasn't shown up in the majors yet, has a fastball like anybody else's, a curve and change. He'll battle with Watson, Cormier, and others for a spot in the rotation . . . Grade C prospect, but I like him. He'll be a good pitcher if he increases his strikeout rate, and in the past he has improved dramatically in his second year at a level.

YEAR	TEAM/LEVEL	G	IP	W-L	PCT.	HITS	SO	BB	ERA
1992	AA and AAA	26	154	8-11	.421	141	87	52	3.51
1993	Louisville AAA	18	95	9-5	.643	86	65	23	2.47
1993	St. Louis	18	62	1-3	.250	73	33	26	4.65

JOSE URIBE

Houston Astros

Shortstop

$10

Once the Giants starting shortstop, Uribe spent the season backing up Andujar Cedeno, as he had spent 1992 backing up Royce Clayton. He's Alfredo Griffin, but without Alfredo's baserunning stunts—a 34-year-old switch hitter who was once a good shortstop, and can take the field and fill in there for a few innings or a few days. No hitter, career will end within a year or two.

YEAR	TEAM/LEVEL	G	AB	R	H	2B	3B	HR	RBI	BB	SB	AVG	OBP	SLG
1991	San Francisco	90	231	23	51	8	4	1	12	20	3	.221	.283	.303
1992	San Francisco	66	162	24	39	9	1	2	13	14	2	.241	.299	.346
1993	Houston	45	53	4	13	1	0	0	3	8	1	.245	.355	.264

SERGIO VALDEZ

Montreal Expos

Relief Pitcher

$18

Something is missing from the story here. Despite having pitched very well in 1992, Valdez was sent out during spring training in '93 (what part of that 2.41 ERA didn't you like?). He was called up in mid-summer for about three weeks, pitching three innings, but otherwise spent the summer at Ottawa, doing garbage work. Has been in several organizations . . . obviously there is something about him that his managers don't warm up to.

YEAR	TEAM/LEVEL	G	IP	W-L	SAVES	HITS	SO	BB	ERA
1991	Cleveland	6	16	1-0	0	15	11	5	5.51
1992	Montreal	27	37	0-2	0	25	32	12	2.41
1993	Ottawa AAA	30	84	5-3	1	77	53	22	3.12

JOHN VALENTIN

Boston Red Sox

Shortstop

$31

The new Eddie Bressoud, a righthanded hitting shortstop who had almost the same numbers for the Red Sox in '93 that Bressoud did in '62. He's an odd story, a guy who was in the minor leagues for several years before he began to hit, for which reason one should not *assume* that he will just continue to hit . . . Strong arm, good hands, range just average. Could hit anywhere from .230 to .300.

YEAR	TEAM/LEVEL	G	AB	R	H	2B	3B	HR	RBI	BB	SB	AVG	OBP	SLG
1992	Boston	58	185	21	51	13	0	5	25	20	1	.276	.351	.427
1993	Boston	144	468	50	130	40	3	11	66	49	3	.278	.346	.447
1994	**Projected**	**151**	**538**	**59**	**133**	**34**	**1**	**11**	**59**	**64**	**2**	**.247**	**.330**	**.375**

JOSE VALENTIN

Milwaukee Brewers

Shortstop

$15

A switch hitter, Valentin started in the Padres system and came to the Brewers in the Sheffield trade. He hit 17 homers at Wichita in 1991, but until he came to the majors hadn't hit anything since the trade. He's young (24), runs well and will take a few walks. He has the tools to be a good defensive shortstop, although he isn't yet. Grade C prospect; if Listach doesn't come back he might receive an extended trial.

YEAR	TEAM/LEVEL	G	AB	R	H	2B	3B	HR	RBI	BB	SB	AVG	OBP	SLG
1992	MLE	139	471	57	97	16	5	2	33	39	6	.206	.267	.274
1993	MLE	122	374	44	81	19	2	6	41	37	7	.217	.287	.326
1993	Milwaukee	19	53	10	13	1	2	1	7	7	1	.245	.344	.396

FERNANDO VALENZUELA

Baltimore Orioles

Starting Pitcher

$18

The only major league pitcher with 162 innings who had a strikeout/walk ratio less than even . . . His experience in Baltimore is similar to that of Rick Sutcliffe, which is that he pitched very well at first, looking like the Fernando of Old, rather than an Old Fernando. As soon as this happened, however, Johnny Oates proceeded to jump on his back and ride him as if he was Man O'War, with what seems to me a predictable result.

YEAR	TEAM/LEVEL	G	IP	W-L	PCT.	HITS	SO	BB	ERA
1991	California	2	7	0-2	.000	14	5	3	12.15
1992	Jalisco (Mex)	22	156	10-9	.526	154	98	51	3.86
1993	Baltimore	32	179	8-10	.444	179	78	79	4.94

JULIO VALERA

California Angels

Starting Pitcher

$10

He developed a sore elbow in spring training, so Rogers put him in the bullpen to nurse him back to health. He couldn't pitch effectively and the elbow finally blew out in June, leading to reconstructive surgery which cost him the rest of the season and probably 1994 as well. No way of accurately predicting his future . . . he was a fine pitcher before the injury, but will have to fight his way back.

YEAR	TEAM/LEVEL	G	IP	W-L	PCT.	HITS	SO	BB	ERA
1991	Tidewater AAA	26	176	10-10	.500	152	117	70	3:83
1992	California	30	188	8-11	.421	188	113	64	3.73
1993	California	19	53	3-6	.333	77	28	15	6.62

DAVE VALLE

Seattle Mariners

Catcher

$28

Valle hasn't filed for free agency at this writing, but is eligible, and since the Mariners have traded for another catcher, it must be assumed he is going to move on down the road. He is coming off his best major league season with the bat, but is 33 years old and a career .235 hitter, so whoever signs him may be riding for a fall . . . Led the major leagues in number of times hit by a pitch, 17.

YEAR	TEAM/LEVEL	G	AB	R	H	2B	3B	HR	RBI	BB	SB	AVG	OBP	SLG
1992	Seattle	124	367	39	88	16	1	9	30	27	0	.240	.305	.362
1993	Seattle	135	423	48	109	19	0	13	63	48	1	.258	.354	.395
1994	**Projected**	**133**	**374**	**41**	**84**	**16**	**1**	**9**	**41**	**37**	**1**	**.225**	**.294**	**.345**

TY VAN BURKLEO

California Angels

First Base

$6

A 30-year-old first baseman, he led the California League in RBI in 1986, then went to Japan in 1987. In 1988 he hit 38 homers, leading Seibu to the Japan championships, and was selected Japan's Player of the Year. Then he either was hurt or committed some horrible cultural atrocity; in any case he stopped playing, eventually returning to the Angel organization. He doesn't appear to be going anywhere.

YEAR	TEAM/LEVEL	G	AB	R	H	2B	3B	HR	RBI	BB	SB	AVG	OBP	SLG
1993	Vancouver AAA	105	361	47	99	19	2	6	56	51	7	.274	.364	.388
1993	MLE	105	341	33	79	14	0	4	39	35	4	.232	.303	.308
1993	California	12	33	2	5	3	0	1	1	6	1	.152	.282	.333

TODD VAN POPPEL

Oakland Athletics

Starting Pitcher

$15

He pitched several good games late in the season, providing hope that he may be ready. I remain skeptical. Although he was signed three and a half years ago, he still doesn't *really* have any experience—less than 400 innings—and he still doesn't throw strikes. He's out of options, so the A's have to keep him up or risk losing him, but when things start to go wrong for him, he's got no experience to fall back on.

YEAR	TEAM/LEVEL	G	IP	W-L	PCT.	HITS	SO	BB	ERA
1992	Tacoma AAA	9	45	4-2	.667	44	29	35	3.97
1993	Tacoma AAA	16	79	4-8	.333	67	71	54	5.83
1993	Oakland	16	84	6-6	.500	76	47	62	5.04

ANDY VAN SLYKE
Pittsburgh Pirates
Center Field
$49

Broke his collarbone crashing into a wall in mid-June, which put him out for eleven weeks. Until then it looked like any other season—he was hitting .300 with power and stealing bases and had made only one error in center field. He is 33—remember, Whitey Herzog used him to replace Keith Hernandez when he sent Hernandez to New York, which seems like a previous life. Anyway, the years will begin to catch up to him, probably.

YEAR	TEAM/LEVEL	G	AB	R	H	2B	3B	HR	RBI	BB	SB	AVG	OBP	SLG
1992	Pittsburgh	154	614	103	199	45	12	14	89	58	12	.324	.381	.505
1993	Pittsburgh	83	323	42	100	13	4	8	50	24	11	.310	.357	.449
1994	**Projected**	**129**	**484**	**71**	**134**	**22**	**5**	**13**	**67**	**53**	**10**	**.277**	**.348**	**.424**

JOHN VANDER WAL
Montreal Expos
Left Field/First Base
$16

I believe Vanderwal has some ability as a hitter, but it hasn't come forward in two seasons, and the Expos have other young players (Floyd, White, Pride and Montoyo) who may force him aside in '93. Vander Wal's 1993 season isn't as weak as it looks; his secondary average was .293, and he was playing in a pitcher's park and doing a lot of pinch hitting. Still, his career is in trouble.

YEAR	TEAM/LEVEL	G	AB	R	H	2B	3B	HR	RBI	BB	SB	AVG	OBP	SLG
1992	Montreal	105	213	21	51	8	2	4	20	24	3	.239	.316	.352
1993	Montreal	106	215	34	50	7	4	5	30	27	6	.233	.320	.372
1994	**Projected**	**100**	**250**	**33**	**61**	**15**	**2**	**5**	**29**	**31**	**3**	**.244**	**.327**	**.380**

GARY VARSHO
Cincinnati Reds
Utility Outfielder
$13

The Pirates released him after the 1992 season, and he signed with the Reds as a free agent. The Reds used him mostly as a pinch hitter for the pitcher, in which role he is somewhat miscast; he's not a *terrible* hitter, but there are better hitters available to do that job. He's an excellent baserunner and a good outfielder, although he lacks a strong arm.

YEAR	TEAM/LEVEL	G	AB	R	H	2B	3B	HR	RBI	BB	SB	AVG	OBP	SLG
1991	Pittsburgh	99	187	23	51	11	2	4	23	19	9	.273	.344	.417
1992	Pittsburgh	103	162	22	36	6	3	4	22	10	5	.222	.266	.370
1993	Cincinnati	77	95	8	22	6	0	2	11	9	1	.232	.302	.358

GREG VAUGHN
Milwaukee Brewers
Left Field
$39

His 1993 stats are extremely similar to those of Frank Robinson in 1973 (.266, 30 homers, 97 RBI, 82 walks.) Of course, Frank was 37 years old at the time . . . Vaughn was 27, the most common age for a player to have his best season. He's a pretty good fielder and runs well, though his stolen base percentage is poor. With his power and walks he can be expected to drive in and score around 90 runs.

YEAR	TEAM/LEVEL	G	AB	R	H	2B	3B	HR	RBI	BB	SB	AVG	OBP	SLG
1992	Milwaukee	141	501	77	114	18	2	23	78	60	15	.228	.313	.409
1993	Milwaukee	154	569	97	152	28	2	30	97	89	10	.267	.369	.482
1994	**Projected**	**153**	**559**	**89**	**136**	**25**	**3**	**27**	**91**	**77**	**10**	**.243**	**.335**	**.444**

MO VAUGHN
Boston Red Sox
First Base
$42

Mike Easler says that Vaughn will be better than Frank Thomas. He's out of his mind, but Vaughn is certainly a hitter (as I have said for years he would be). His defense, which was dismal in 1992, was better last year, although he still led the league in errors. His attitude was questioned in 1992, but when you drive in 100 runs your attitude improves. In 1993 we saw the real Mo Vaughn for the first time.

YEAR	TEAM/LEVEL	G	AB	R	H	2B	3B	HR	RBI	BB	SB	AVG	OBP	SLG
1992	Boston	113	355	42	83	16	2	13	57	47	3	.234	.326	.400
1993	Boston	152	539	86	160	34	1	29	101	79	4	.297	.390	.525
1993	**Projected**	**155**	**550**	**71**	**151**	**29**	**1**	**27**	**92**	**82**	**4**	**.275**	**.369**	**.478**

RANDY VELARDE
New York Yankees
Infielder
$22

Like almost all of the Yankee platoon players, he had his best season, despite a midsummer injury. The signing of Boggs pushed him off third base; Showalter used him in left field and at shortstop, occasionally at third base or DH. He is 31 now, beyond time of becoming a regular, but a good role player . . . Over the last five years has hit .301 against lefthanded pitchers, .247 against righthanders.

YEAR	TEAM/LEVEL	G	AB	R	H	2B	3B	HR	RBI	BB	SB	AVG	OBP	SLG
1992	New York	121	412	57	112	24	1	7	46	38	7	.272	.333	.386
1993	New York	85	226	28	68	13	2	7	24	18	2	.301	.360	.469
1994	**Projected**	**110**	**305**	**36**	**79**	**16**	**1**	**6**	**30**	**28**	**4**	**.259**	**.321**	**.377**

GUILLERMO VELASQUEZ
San Diego Padres
First Base
$15

Lefthanded line drive hitter, 26 years old; in the past I've compared him to Willie Montanez. He was asked to play first base after McGriff was traded, but isn't going to hit well enough to be a regular first baseman, and didn't hit as well as he is capable of hitting. His glovework is good . . . Staton or Plantier or Gwynn will play first for the Padres this year; Velasquez will try to establish some value as a pinch hitter.

YEAR	TEAM/LEVEL	G	AB	R	H	2B	3B	HR	RBI	BB	SB	AVG	OBP	SLG
1992	MLE	136	473	41	119	32	1	4	60	26	3	.252	.291	.349
1993	San Diego	79	143	7	30	2	0	3	20	13	0	.210	.274	.287
1994	**Projected**	**50**	**145**	**14**	**38**	**7**	**0**	**4**	**21**	**10**	**0**	**.262**	**.310**	**.393**

ROBIN VENTURA
Chicago White Sox
Third Base
$70

He couldn't be too much better than he is, a Gold Glove third baseman who scores 85-90 runs every year and drives in a few more than he scores. Lefthanded hitter, slow, more consistent than nature should allow. He's the best third baseman in the American League unless 1) Fryman plays there for Detroit (Fryman's skills are about the same as Ventura's), 2) Palmer hits 40 homers, or 3) Thome turns out to be everything he might.

YEAR	TEAM/LEVEL	G	AB	R	H	2B	3B	HR	RBI	BB	SB	AVG	OBP	SLG
1992	Chicago	157	592	85	167	38	1	16	93	93	2	.282	.375	.431
1993	Chicago	157	554	85	145	27	1	22	94	105	1	.262	.379	.433
1994	**Projected**	**158**	**588**	**88**	**162**	**28**	**1**	**19**	**91**	**98**	**3**	**.276**	**.379**	**.423**

HECTOR VILLANUEVA
Released
Catcher
$5

He drove in five runs in a game on June 3, but played only two major league games after that, and his career might be over; the Cardinals sent him to Louisville, where he hit only five homers in 40 games, and then released him. A big righthanded batter, prone to weight problems, he has to hit because he doesn't do anything else. Two years of not hitting might be enough to finish him.

YEAR	TEAM/LEVEL	G	AB	R	H	2B	3B	HR	RBI	BB	SB	AVG	OBP	SLG
1991	Chicago	71	192	23	53	10	1	13	32	21	0	.276	.346	.542
1992	Chicago	51	112	9	17	6	0	2	13	11	0	.152	.228	.259
1993	St. Louis	17	55	7	8	1	0	3	9	4	0	.145	.203	.327

FERNANDO VINA
New York Mets
Second Base
$8

A 25-year-old lefthanded hitting second baseman, in line behind Kent and Saunders. He wasn't on the 40-man roster last winter, and the Mariners claimed him under Rule V. He started the season on the Mariners bench, got into 24 games, but was reclaimed by the Mets when Seattle tried to send him down. Grade D prospect; basically just a kid who can run and can catch the ball.

YEAR	TEAM/LEVEL	G	AB	R	H	2B	3B	HR	RBI	BB	SB	AVG	OBP	SLG
1992	St. Lucie A	111	421	61	124	15	5	1	42	32	36	.295	.347	.361
1993	Seattle	24	45	5	10	2	0	0	2	4	6	.222	.327	.267
1993	Norfolk AAA	73	287	24	66	6	4	4	27	7	16	.230	.258	.321

FRANK VIOLA
Boston Red Sox
Starting Pitcher
$35

His season was ended by elbow surgery, and there is reason for concern. His strikeout/walk and strikeout/innings ratios continued to deteriorate, and it looked to me, subjectively, like he was struggling with both velocity and location. I still think he will pitch into his 40s, but he may be approaching an even more difficult phase in his career. He knows how to pitch . . . if anyone can adjust, he can.

YEAR	TEAM/LEVEL	G	IP	W-L	PCT.	HITS	SO	BB	ERA
1991	New York NL	35	231	13-15	.464	259	132	54	3.97
1992	Boston	35	238	13-12	.520	214	121	89	3.44
1993	Boston	29	184	11-8	.579	180	91	72	3.14

JOSE VIZCAINO
Chicago Cubs
Shortstop
$36

Once a prize prospect in the Dodger system, but lost out to Offerman as the Dodgers shortstop. With Sandberg and Dunston both unavailable early last year Vizcaino opened the season red-hot, slumped during the hot months, then closed with another rush, finishing with excellent offensive and defensive numbers. A switch hitter, needs a little work on the DP, but his play was nearly faultless, and he will probably hold his job even if Dunston is available.

YEAR	TEAM/LEVEL	G	AB	R	H	2B	3B	HR	RBI	BB	SB	AVG	OBP	SLG
1992	Chicago	86	285	25	64	10	4	1	17	14	3	.225	.260	.298
1993	Chicago	151	551	74	158	19	4	4	54	46	12	.287	.340	.358
1994	**Projected**	**155**	**550**	**58**	**145**	**13**	**3**	**3**	**46**	**38**	**10**	**.264**	**.311**	**.315**

OMAR VIZQUEL
Seattle Mariners
Shortstop
$34

Extremely good defensive shortstop, turns the double play well (he won the Gold Glove). He's not a *good* hitter (his .298 slugging percentage was the lowest of any major league regular), but he's a good bunter and will take a walk, so he's not an automatic out, either . . . A switchhitter, but a very weak righthanded hitter . . . Eligible to become a free agent after the season, unless he signs a multi-year this winter. An above-average shortstop.

YEAR	TEAM/LEVEL	G	AB	R	H	2B	3B	HR	RBI	BB	SB	AVG	OBP	SLG
1992	Seattle	136	483	49	142	20	4	0	21	32	15	.294	.340	.352
1993	Seattle	158	560	68	143	14	2	2	31	50	12	.255	.319	.298
1994	**Projected**	**150**	**506**	**53**	**128**	**14**	**3**	**2**	**34**	**45**	**12**	**.253**	**.314**	**.304**

JACK VOIGT
Baltimore Orioles
Outfielder
$20

A 27-year-old minor league veteran, he was called up as part of Baltimore's Great Right Fielder Hunt, and played well, splitting time between left and right. He played mostly against lefties, and jumped all over them: .352 average (32 for 91), .637 slugging percentage; all six of his homers were against lefthanders. He could be a classic Earl Weaver platoon player, in that his defense is fine and his secondary offensive skills are very strong.

YEAR	TEAM/LEVEL	G	AB	R	H	2B	3B	HR	RBI	BB	SB	AVG	OBP	SLG
1992	MLE	129	422	57	105	18	2	12	49	44	6	.249	.320	.386
1993	Baltimore	64	152	32	45	11	1	6	23	25	1	.296	.395	.500
1994	**Projected**	**83**	**259**	**40**	**67**	**12**	**1**	**7**	**30**	**33**	**4**	**.259**	**.342**	**.394**

PAUL WAGNER
Pittsburgh Pirates
Righthanded Pitcher
$26

Jim Leyland, who doesn't usually hype his players, seems to love this guy. I heard him say in an interview that Wagner had as much ability as any pitcher he had ever managed, and he told *Baseball Weekly* in September that "He has a great arm. If he doesn't turn into a good major league pitcher, he's missing a great opportunity." Has 90+ fastball, excellent slider, is working on a change, and needs to stay ahead of the hitters.

YEAR	TEAM/LEVEL	G	IP	W-L	PCT.	HITS	SO	BB	ERA
1992	AA and AAA	27	161	9-9	.500	155	120	61	3.63
1992	Pittsburgh	6	13	2-0	1.000	9	5	5	0.69
1993	Pittsburgh	44	141	8-8	.500	143	114	42	4.27

DAVE WAINHOUSE
Seattle Mariners
Relief Pitcher
$8

A Canadian citizen who has lived in Washington most of his life, he was the Expos' first-round pick in 1989, didn't progress rapidly and was traded to the Mariners for Frank Bolick. He started the year with the big team, but was sent out almost immediately, and pitched only 16 innings in the minors, so I'm assuming he was hurt. It wouldn't be the first time. Grade D prospect, 26 years old.

YEAR	TEAM/LEVEL	G	IP	W-L	SAVES	HITS	SO	BB	ERA
1991	AA and AAA	47	81	4-2	12	77	59	32	3.12
1992	Indianapolis AAA	44	46	5-4	21	48	37	24	4.11
1993	Calgary AAA	13	16	0-1	5	10	7	7	4.02

TIM WAKEFIELD

Pittsburgh Pirates

Starting Pitcher

$23

He ended the season pitching great again, throwing two straight shutouts after having pitched well before that. He hadn't been throwing the knuckleball very long before he had the baseball world roped and tied, as I suppose you know, and perhaps it was inevitable that his first rough stretch would send him reeling, since he didn't have a long history of success to fall back on. He's not a "safe pick," but I think he'll have a good career.

YEAR	TEAM/LEVEL	G	IP	W-L	PCT.	HITS	SO	BB	ERA
1992	Pittsburgh	13	92	8-1	.889	76	52	35	2.15
1993	Carolina AA	9	57	3-5	.375	68	36	22	6.99
1993	Pittsburgh	24	128	6-11	.353	145	59	75	5.61

MATT WALBECK

Chicago Cubs

Catcher

$17

To begin with, a switch-hitting catcher is going to have a job, unless he stinks. Walbeck doesn't stink; he's raw, but he has talent. He was called up in April during Wilkins's brief absence and hit well, but there was no place for him when Wilkins returned, so he went back to Iowa, where he didn't play particularly well. He doesn't have power and there's always the memory of Steve Decker, but he looks good.

YEAR	TEAM/LEVEL	G	AB	R	H	2B	3B	HR	RBI	BB	SB	AVG	OBP	SLG
1992	MLE	105	376	39	107	20	0	7	34	21	0	.285	.322	.394
1993	MLE	87	317	22	79	15	1	5	30	12	0	.249	.277	.350
1993	Chicago	11	30	2	6	2	0	1	6	1	0	.200	.226	.367

JIM WALEWANDER

California Angels (Released)

Pinch Runner

$6

Spent most of the summer at Vancouver, but was called up for three games in July as an emergency backup, then came back in September when the Angels were trying to see how many players they could use in a game. Since last we heard from him (Detroit, 1988) he's belonged to the Yankees and Rangers, stealing about 50 bases a year in the minor leagues but not doing anything else well enough to elicit interest.

YEAR	TEAM/LEVEL	G	AB	R	H	2B	3B	HR	RBI	BB	SB	AVG	OBP	SLG
1992	Ok City AAA	44	124	20	26	7	0	0	10	17	5	.210	.305	.258
1993	Vancouver AAA	102	351	77	107	12	1	1	43	60	36	.305	.416	.353
1993	California	12	8	2	1	0	0	0	3	5	1	.125	.429	.125

BOB WALK

Pittsburgh Pirates

Starter/Reliever

$17

He's been in Pittsburgh forever, but will be trying to get back where he used to be after delivering a miserable impression of a rotation starter. His 5.68 ERA was the worst in the National League, in addition to which he led the league in earned runs allowed, 118, had the worst strikeout/walk ratio and the fewest strikeouts/game. He was last in the league in both ERA at home and ERA on the road. He's 37.

YEAR	TEAM/LEVEL	G	IP	W-L	PCT.	HITS	SO	BB	ERA
1991	Pittsburgh	25	115	9-2	.818	104	67	35	3.60
1992	Pittsburgh	36	135	10-6	.625	132	60	43	3.20
1993	Pittsburgh	32	187	13-14	.482	214	80	70	5.68

CHICO WALKER
New York Mets
Utilityman
$18

Hit .122 in the late innings of close games, the worst of any major league player with 50 plate appearances (in that category) . . . he's 35, and the .225 average last year, combined with the Mets' desperate situation, may cost him his career. He's not a bad bench player, a switch hitter who can play the outfield or the infield, has some power and some speed. Over the last two years he is 22-for-23 as a base stealer.

YEAR	TEAM/LEVEL	G	AB	R	H	2B	3B	HR	RBI	BB	SB	AVG	OBP	SLG
1992	2 ML Teams	126	253	26	73	12	1	4	38	27	15	.289	.351	.391
1993	New York	115	213	18	48	7	1	5	19	14	7	.225	.271	.338
1994	**Projected**	**71**	**162**	**17**	**39**	**5**	**0**	**3**	**16**	**15**	**6**	**.241**	**.305**	**.327**

LARRY WALKER
Montreal Expos
Right Field
$65

After starting out red-hot he was slowed in midsummer by a strained rib cage muscle, and fell a little bit short of his fine 1992 season in the triple crown categories. He doubled his walks and almost doubled his stolen bases, so one can argue that he had his best season. The Expos cleanup hitter, needs to get to 100 RBI and/or 100 runs to be widely recognized as a star.

YEAR	TEAM/LEVEL	G	AB	R	H	2B	3B	HR	RBI	BB	SB	AVG	OBP	SLG
1992	Montreal	143	528	85	159	31	4	23	93	41	18	.301	.353	.506
1993	Montreal	138	490	85	130	24	5	22	86	80	29	.265	.371	.469
1994	**Projected**	**145**	**521**	**79**	**147**	**26**	**3**	**21**	**81**	**59**	**2**	**.282**	**.355**	**.464**

TIM WALLACH
Los Angeles Dodgers
Third Base
$20

Had the lowest batting average of any NL regular, .222, and the lowest on-base percentage of any major league regular, .271. The sad thing is that it **wasn't** an off year; that's his real level of ability . . . basically, he's washed up. He's still a good third baseman, but his glove cannot possibly carry his bat. Lord knows when or if the Dodgers will figure this out.

YEAR	TEAM/LEVEL	G	AB	R	H	2B	3B	HR	RBI	BB	SB	AVG	OBP	SLG
1991	Montreal	151	577	60	130	22	1	13	73	50	2	.225	.292	.334
1992	Montreal	150	537	53	120	29	1	9	59	50	2	.223	.296	.331
1993	Los Angeles	133	477	42	106	19	1	12	62	32	0	.222	.271	.342

DAN WALTERS
San Diego Padres
Catcher
$13

A huge, slow righthanded hitting catcher, won a shot at the catching job in '92, but has moved behind Ausmus and Kevin Higgins. He won a shot at the job by hitting .394 in 35 games at Las Vegas, then filling in well for Santiago during an injury. He lost it because he's not really that good—his .234 career average, through 84 games, is about what he's going to hit.

YEAR	TEAM/LEVEL	G	AB	R	H	2B	3B	HR	RBI	BB	SB	AVG	OBP	SLG
1992	San Diego	57	179	14	45	11	1	4	22	10	1	.251	.295	.391
1993	MLE	66	209	16	50	10	0	3	25	9	0	.239	.271	.330
1993	San Diego	27	94	6	19	3	0	1	10	7	0	.202	.255	.266

BRUCE WALTON

Montreal Expos

Relief Pitcher

$15

Walton was in the Oakland system 1985-92; he's now 31. He didn't do much through 1988, but seemed to adopt Eckersley's approach in 1989, pitched well at Tacoma in 1989-90, and then turned marginally amazing. He has followed through on this in the minors, but not yet in the majors (he has 29 major league innings over the last three years). The Expos are loaded with pitchers, but I'd like to see him get a real chance.

YEAR	TEAM/LEVEL	G	IP	W-L	SAVES	HITS	SO	BB	ERA
1991	Tacoma AAA	38	47	1-1	20	39	49	5	1.35
1992	Tacoma AAA	35	81	8-2	8	76	60	21	2.77
1993	Two Teams AAA	53	58	6-4	23	44	54	11	1.25

JEROME WALTON

California Angels

Center Field

$3

He was sent down April 22, hit .313 at Vancouver but was released anyway on August 20. We must suppose that his career is over, which means that it is time to ask: isn't he surely the worst player ever to get a book written about him? How about the worst player to win a Rookie-of-the-Year Award? How about the worst player to win *any* major award?

YEAR	TEAM/LEVEL	G	AB	R	H	2B	3B	HR	RBI	BB	SB	AVG	OBP	SLG
1991	Chicago NL	123	270	42	59	13	1	5	17	19	7	.219	.275	.330
1992	Chicago NL	30	55	7	7	0	1	0	1	9	1	.127	.273	.164
1993	California	5	2	2	0	0	0	0	0	1	1	.000	.333	.000

DUANE WARD

Toronto Blue Jays

Closer

$68

Took over the closer role after Henke went back to Texas, and was probably the best reliever in the American League. He finished 70 of the 71 games he came into, struck out 12.2 men per nine innings and just missed having twice as many strikeouts as hits allowed. He's been a terrific pitcher for years, just getting better and better, and I'd bet on him to save 200 games in the next five years.

YEAR	TEAM/LEVEL	G	IP	W-L	SAVES	HITS	SO	BB	ERA
1991	Toronto	81	107	7-6	23	80	132	33	2.77
1992	Toronto	79	101	7-4	12	76	103	39	1.95
1993	Toronto	71	72	2-3	45	49	97	25	2.13

TURNER WARD

Toronto Blue Jays

Utility Outfielder

$15

His number-one asset is defense in the outfield, but he's got to hit more than .192 to keep a job as a fifth outfielder. He's a switch hitter, but his career batting average is .341 against lefthanders (28-for-82), .209 against righthanders, so he may be the victim of somebody's misguided effort to "make use of his speed," like U. L. Washington and Mariano Duncan. Not a .192 hitter, but will never be a regular.

YEAR	TEAM/LEVEL	G	AB	R	H	2B	3B	HR	RBI	BB	SB	AVG	OBP	SLG
1992	Toronto	18	29	7	10	3	0	1	3	4	0	.345	.424	.552
1993	Toronto	72	167	20	32	4	2	4	28	23	3	.192	.287	.311
1994	**Projected**	**41**	**106**	**15**	**27**	**6**	**1**	**2**	**12**	**16**	**2**	**.265**	**.352**	**.377**

ALLEN WATSON

St. Louis Cardinals
Lefthanded Starting Pitcher
$35

He started out 6-0, winning six of seven starts, but didn't have *any* good outings after mid-August, so he will have to re-establish himself. He is comparable to Donovan Osborne: he throws fairly hard, has a good breaking pitch, and throws strikes. His minor league record is outstanding; he breezed through each level with no injuries. Outstanding hitter (one of the leading hitters in the country as a college player); **has definite star potential.**

YEAR	TEAM/LEVEL	G	IP	W-L	PCT.	HITS	SO	BB	ERA
1992	AA and AAA	16	109	9-5	.643	85	102	28	2.06
1993	Louisville AAA	17	121	5-4	.556	101	86	31	2.91
1993	St. Louis	16	86	6-7	.462	90	49	28	4.60

GARY WAYNE

Colorado Rockies
Lefthanded Relief Pitcher
$19

ERA on the road: 2.54. ERA in Colorado: 7.15. Wayne pitched well for Minnesota in '92, but was available at the end of spring training, when Kelly decided to go with Larry Casian as the second lefthander in the bullpen (Guthrie was the first). Wayne was traded to Colorado, where he did the same job, and actually pitched pretty well, although the overall ERA doesn't reflect this, and probably won't in '94, either.

YEAR	TEAM/LEVEL	G	IP	W-L	SAVES	HITS	SO	BB	ERA
1991	Minnesota	8	12	1-0	1	11	7	4	5.11
1992	Minnesota	41	48	3-3	0	46	29	19	2.63
1993	Colorado	65	62	5-3	1	68	49	26	5.05

DAVE WEATHERS

Florida Marlins
Starting Pitcher
$20

Weathers, pitching well at Edmonton, was called up in July to patch a leak in the bullpen, which he did not do well, and was recalled in September to try the starting rotation, in which role he was so-so (2-3, 4.58 ERA but 27 strikeouts, only 10 walks in 35 innings). The Marlins got him from the Toronto system, where he had pitched well in 1991. Grade B prospect.

YEAR	TEAM/LEVEL	G	IP	W-L	PCT.	HITS	SO	BB	ERA
1992	Syracuse AAA	12	48	1-4	.250	48	30	21	4.66
1993	Edmonton AAA	22	141	11-4	.733	150	117	47	3.83
1993	Florida	14	46	2-3	.400	57	34	13	5.12

LENNY WEBSTER

Minnesota Twins
Backup Catcher
$13

Like many of the Twins, he had a bad year. In his case, 1993 was probably more representative of his ability than the previous two seasons, when he had hit well. He can throw (threw out 37% of runners attempting to steal in '93) and has a reputation as a good defensive catcher. He might benefit a little bit if Harper leaves, but not really because he just isn't likely to hit enough to increase his playing time.

YEAR	TEAM/LEVEL	G	AB	R	H	2B	3B	HR	RBI	BB	SB	AVG	OBP	SLG
1992	Minnesota	53	118	10	33	10	1	1	13	9	0	.280	.331	.407
1993	Minnesota	49	106	14	21	2	0	1	8	11	1	.198	.274	.245
1994	**Projected**	**65**	**103**	**14**	**24**	**7**	**2**	**2**	**12**	**10**	**2**	**.233**	**.301**	**.398**

MITCH WEBSTER

Los Angeles Dodgers

Utility Outfielder

$13

Injuries continue to plague him, and it is hard to know how much the deterioration in his stats last season was due to age and how much was due to injuries. He has been a fine reserve outfielder, with some speed, some power, good defense. He'll be 35 in May, and if you're a baseball player, it is not good to have the words "has been" associated with your name.

YEAR	TEAM/LEVEL	G	AB	R	H	2B	3B	HR	RBI	BB	SB	AVG	OBP	SLG
1992	Los Angeles	135	262	33	70	12	5	6	35	27	11	.267	.334	.420
1993	Los Angeles	88	172	26	42	6	2	2	14	11	4	.244	.293	.337
1994	**Projected**	**65**	**103**	**14**	**24**	**7**	**2**	**2**	**12**	**10**	**2**	**.233**	**.301**	**.398**

ERIC WEDGE

Colorado Rockies

Catcher

$14

Spent most of the year on the disabled list, some of it at Colorado Springs. Wedge, now 26, is a pretty good hitter for a catcher, but has had arm trouble and elbow surgery, so it's questionable whether he is going to be a major league receiver. His best shot at the roster in '94 might be to take Jimmy Tatum's job, which is pinch hitting for the pitcher when the Rockies are down 6-1 in the fourth.

YEAR	TEAM/LEVEL	G	AB	R	H	2B	3B	HR	RBI	BB	SB	AVG	OBP	SLG
1992	MLE	65	203	20	55	8	0	8	29	23	0	.271	.345	.429
1992	Boston	27	68	11	17	2	0	5	11	13	0	.250	.370	.500
1993	Colorado	9	11	2	2	0	0	0	1	0	0	.182	.182	.182

BILL WEGMAN

Milwaukee Brewers

Starting Pitcher

$20

After pitching quite well for two years, he was bothered by an ulcer and a hiatal hernia. He didn't pitch well even when healthy, although maybe he was never really healthy, I don't know. Throws a slider and a pretty good fastball, and teaches us once again that you should never bet on a pitcher to be consistently successful with less than 4.5 strikeouts/game . . . His father was a high school teammate of Pete Rose.

YEAR	TEAM/LEVEL	G	IP	W-L	PCT.	HITS	SO	BB	ERA
1991	Milwaukee	28	193	15-7	.682	176	89	40	2.84
1992	Milwaukee	35	262	13-14	.481	251	127	55	3.20
1993	Milwaukee	20	121	4-14	.222	135	50	34	4.48

JOHN WEHNER

Pittsburgh Pirates

Utility Man/Third Base

$15

Wehner hit .340 in 37 games in 1991, which was a stone fluke. Since then he has hit .171 in 84 games, which is also sort of a fluke; he's not *that* bad. Jeff King has taken firm control at third base, and Wehner is trying to fit in as a utility infielder/outfielder. He runs well and has some line-drive power, and is said to be a hard-nosed competitor. No star potential.

YEAR	TEAM/LEVEL	G	AB	R	H	2B	3B	HR	RBI	BB	SB	AVG	OBP	SLG
1992	Pittsburgh	55	123	11	22	6	0	0	4	12	3	.179	.252	.228
1993	MLE	89	317	46	70	19	1	5	26	30	11	.221	.288	.334
1993	Pittsburgh	29	35	3	5	0	0	0	0	6	0	.143	.268	.143

WALT WEISS

Florida Marlins

Shortstop

$35

Healthy for the first time since 1990, he established career highs in almost everything—games, at bats, hits, walks, batting average. His defense was more along the lines of "solid" than "spectacular," but he was clearly the best shortstop any first-year expansion team has had . . . His .308 slugging percentage was the lowest for any National League regular, and his 79 walks were of limited value since he hit eighth.

YEAR	TEAM/LEVEL	G	AB	R	H	2B	3B	HR	RBI	BB	SB	AVG	OBP	SLG
1992	Oakland	103	316	36	67	5	2	0	21	43	6	.212	.305	.241
1993	Florida	158	500	50	133	14	2	1	39	79	7	.266	.367	.308
1994	**Projected**	**130**	**410**	**45**	**99**	**14**	**2**	**2**	**35**	**60**	**6**	**.241**	**.338**	**.300**

BOB WELCH

Oakland Athletics

Starting Pitcher

$10

He appears to be finished; I don't expect him to be on a major league roster in '94, or to pitch well if he is. His strikeout rate is very low, and his ERA was 6.08 after the All-Star break. He hasn't been able to stay healthy for two or three years . . . There are five pitchers in history who have truly similar records to Welch's—Dennis Martinez, Milt Pappas, Catfish Hunter, Dave Stieb and Vida Blue.

YEAR	TEAM/LEVEL	G	IP	W-L	PCT.	HITS	SO	BB	ERA
1991	Oakland	35	220	12-13	.480	220	101	91	4.58
1992	Oakland	20	124	11-7	.611	114	47	43	3.27
1993	Oakland	30	167	9-11	.450	208	63	56	5.29

DAVID WELLS

Detroit Tigers

Starting Pitcher

$30

Released by the Jays in the spring because Cito was tired of his overweight biker act, Wells signed with the Tigers and looked like a steal after a 6-1 start, but slumped in June and July and went down with a sore shoulder in August. He was healthy in September, though not pitching particularly well. He has a quick fastball and sharp breaking pitch, and has a good idea what to do with them.

YEAR	TEAM/LEVEL	G	IP	W-L	PCT.	HITS	SO	BB	ERA
1991	Toronto	40	198	15-10	.600	188	106	49	3.72
1992	Toronto	41	120	7-9	.438	138	62	36	5.40
1993	Detroit	32	187	11-9	.550	183	139	42	4.19

TURK WENDELL

Chicago Cubs

Starting Pitcher/Flake

$15

The Braves' fifth-round pick in 1988, he was traded to the Cubs at the end of 1991, and missed most of 1992 with an elbow injury. He pitched so-so last year, for Iowa and in the majors. He is known for his idiosyncracies. He chews licorice on the mound, brushes his teeth between innings, etc. A player who is destined to be good normally doesn't want attention for anything other than his performance. Grade C prospect.

YEAR	TEAM/LEVEL	G	IP	W-L	PCT.	HITS	SO	BB	ERA
1992	Iowa AAA	4	25	2-0	1.000	17	12	15	1.44
1993	Iowa AAA	25	149	10-8	.556	148	110	47	4.60
1993	Chicago	7	23	1-2	.333	24	15	8	4.37

BILL WERTZ

Cleveland Indians

Relief Pitcher

$19

A 6-foot-6 righthander, throws fastball and slider with average velocity. A Cleveland native, he was Academic All-Big Ten at Ohio State, and was drafted by the Indians in the 31st round in 1989. He went 15-8 as a starting pitcher, after which they moved him to middle relief, but he continued to move through the levels, and continued to pitch well on reaching Lake Erie. Grade B prospect.

YEAR	TEAM/LEVEL	G	IP	W-L	SAVES	HITS	SO	BB	ERA
1992	Canton-Akron AA	57	97	8-4	8	75	69	30	1.20
1993	Charlotte AAA	28	51	7-2	0	42	47	14	1.95
1993	Cleveland	34	60	2-3	0	54	53	32	3.62

DAVID WEST

Philadelphia Phillies

Lefthanded Relief Pitcher

$25

The Twins gave up on the huge lefthander after several frustrating seasons, and traded him to Philadelphia. The Phillies got him on a good conditioning program. He lost weight, went to the bullpen and put in a solid season in middle relief, holding batters to a .194 batting average. By the end of the season he had gained back all of the weight, and he looked tired in the World Series.

YEAR	TEAM/LEVEL	G	IP	W-L	SAVES	HITS	SO	BB	ERA
1991	Minnesota	15	71	4-4	0	66	52	28	4.54
1992	Minnesota	9	28	1-3	0	32	19	20	6.99
1993	Philadelphia	76	86	6-4	3	60	87	51	2.92

MICKEY WESTON

New York Mets

Starting Pitcher

$10

A 33-year old righthander, Weston throws about as hard as Queen Elizabeth, but with outstanding control. His minor league career record is 94-57, and he has led every minor league in ERA several times, exaggerating only a little bit. Despite this no one would give him a real chance in the major leagues, (his six innings with the Mets last year gave him a career total of 45) and he is losing his effectiveness in the minors.

YEAR	TEAM/LEVEL	G	IP	W-L	PCT.	HITS	SO	BB	ERA
1991	Syracuse AAA	27	166	12-6	.667	193	60	36	3.74
1992	Scranton AAA	26	171	10-6	.625	166	79	23	3.11
1993	Norfolk AAA	21	127	10-9	.526	149	41	18	4.24

JOHN WETTELAND

Montreal Expos

Closer

$69

His '93 season is one of the best that any reliever ever had. He had almost twice as many strikeouts as hits allowed. Dibble has done that, but with ERAs around 3.00. Wetteland's ERA was 1.37. Eckersley's done that, but not with 70 games or 85 innings. He allowed only six inherited runners to score. He blew six save chances, not many, and most of those were converted into wins . . . more of the same in '94.

YEAR	TEAM/LEVEL	G	IP	W-L	SAVES	HITS	SO	BB	ERA
1991	Los Angeles	6	9	1-0	0	5	9	3	0.00
1992	Montreal	67	83	4-4	37	64	99	36	2.92
1993	Montreal	70	85	9-3	43	58	113	28	1.37

LOU WHITAKER

Detroit Tigers

Second Base

$35

Despite the dropoff in his power totals, he was still an amazing player last season, posting a .371 secondary average. He still plays second base very well—in fact, I might argue that he's a better second baseman now than he was 10 years ago. He's strictly a platoon player now, hardly ever bats against a lefthander. Father time will catch him sooner or later, but there is *no* sign that it's ready to happen.

YEAR	TEAM/LEVEL	G	AB	R	H	2B	3B	HR	RBI	BB	SB	AVG	OBP	SLG
1992	Detroit	130	453	77	126	26	0	19	71	81	6	.278	.386	.461
1993	Detroit	119	383	72	111	32	1	9	67	78	3	.290	.412	.449
1994	**Projection**	**126**	**420**	**69**	**110**	**21**	**2**	**11**	**60**	**82**	**4**	**.262**	**.382**	**.400**

DERRICK WHITE

Montreal Expos

First Base

$15

A seventh-round draft pick in 1991, a California kid who went to school at the University of Oklahoma. He went to Double-A with very little prior experience, and had a decent enough year, didn't have a good year last year but was one of about a dozen people the Expos tried to fix the first base problem. He wasn't the worst of the dozen, but the emergence of Cliff Floyd obviously casts a shadow over his career.

YEAR	TEAM/LEVEL	G	AB	R	H	2B	3B	HR	RBI	BB	SB	AVG	OBP	SLG
1993	AA and AAA	88	328	46	88	16	1	6	41	25	12	.268	.328	.329
1993	MLE	88	314	35	74	13	0	3	31	18	8	.236	.277	.306
1993	Montreal	17	49	6	11	3	0	2	4	2	2	.224	.269	.408

DEVON WHITE

Toronto Blue Jays

Center Field

$57

Has developed into quite a player. The last three years he has stolen 33 to 37 bases each year, scored 98 to 116 runs, hit 15 to 17 homers, drawn 47 to 57 walks, and averaged 36 doubles. In '93 he was 34 for 38 as a base stealer, the best percentage of any major leaguer with at least 20 tries, and was second in the league in doubles, with 42. He's the best defensive outfielder in baseball.

YEAR	TEAM/LEVEL	G	AB	R	H	2B	3B	HR	RBI	BB	SB	AVG	OBP	SLG
1992	Toronto	153	641	98	159	26	7	17	60	47	37	.248	.303	.390
1993	Toronto	146	598	116	163	42	6	15	52	57	34	.273	.341	.438
1994	**Projected**	**151**	**624**	**98**	**168**	**28**	**5**	**16**	**52**	**54**	**35**	**.253**	**.313**	**.391**

GABE WHITE

Montreal Expos

Lefthanded Starting Pitcher

$29

Grade A prospect. White was drafted out of high school in 1990, part of the compensation for losing Mark Langston to free agency. He has been healthy all along and has pitched well everywhere, being named the seventh best prospect in the Eastern League by *Baseball America*. Throws a traditional repertoire—fastball, curve, change. The only thing not to like about him is that he may have been worked too hard too young.

YEAR	TEAM/LEVEL	G	IP	W-L	PCT.	HITS	SO	BB	ERA
1992	Rockford A	11	57	4-2	.667	50	42	12	2.84
1993	Harrisburgh AA	16	100	7-2	.778	80	80	28	2.16
1993	Ottawa AAA	6	40	2-1	.667	38	28	6	3.12

RONDELL WHITE

Montreal Expos

Voltigeur

$34

The fifth- or sixth-best prospect in the baseball world right now, behind Ramirez, Floyd, Chipper Jones and Carlos Delgado, possibly behind Alex Gonzalez. He is only 22 and his command of the strike zone is something that he must overcome, but he some power and speed and has hit .380 in 37 games of Triple-A. Will probably play left for Montreal because they have Grissom and Walker, although somebody may be traded. **Grade A prospect.**

YEAR	TEAM/LEVEL	G	AB	R	H	2B	3B	HR	RBI	BB	SB	AVG	OBP	SLG
1993	MLE	127	497	79	154	22	7	12	66	24	22	.310	.342	.455
1993	Montreal	23	73	9	19	3	1	2	15	7	1	.260	.321	.411
1994	**Projected**	**138**	**475**	**79**	**146**	**23**	**6**	**12**	**66**	**27**	**19**	**.307**	**.345**	**.457**

WALLY WHITEHURST

San Diego Padres

Starting Pitcher

$26

Part of the Tony Fernandez deal before the 1993 season, Whitehurst got a chance to be a rotation starter, and wasn't bad when he was healthy. He didn't win, mostly because of his team, and went on the disabled list three times with a strained rotator cuff. He's intelligent, throws strikes, has decent stuff for a third or fourth starter. He's never going to be a workhorse.

YEAR	TEAM/LEVEL	G	IP	W-L	PCT.	HITS	SO	BB	ERA
1991	New York NL	36	133	7-12	.368	142	87	25	4.18
1992	New York NL	44	97	3-9	.250	99	70	33	3.62
1993	San Diego	21	106	4-7	.364	109	57	30	3.83

MARK WHITEN

St. Louis Cardinals

Right Field

$32

Whiten and Zeile established that if your 1-2-3 hitters (Gilkey, Smith and Jefferies) are outstanding, the four and five hitters can drive in 100 runs even if they're *not* that good. Whiten is the five hitter, a right fielder with a famous throwing arm and a famous 12-RBI game, which could obscure the fact that he's basically just another ballplayer. He's OK, but he's a .250 hitter who has never hit 20 doubles in a season.

YEAR	TEAM/LEVEL	G	AB	R	H	2B	3B	HR	RBI	BB	SB	AVG	OBP	SLG
1992	Cleveland	148	508	73	129	19	4	9	43	72	16	.254	.347	.360
1993	St. Louis	152	562	81	142	13	4	25	99	58	15	.253	.323	.423
1994	**Projection**	**154**	**551**	**76**	**140**	**18**	**4**	**16**	**70**	**63**	**14**	**.254**	**.331**	**.388**

MATT WHITESIDE

Texas Rangers

Relief Pitcher

$24

Whiteside had a sensational minor league season in '92, and had a shot as the Rangers' closer late in the year. He was all right, but moved to a setup role when the Rangers acquired Henke, and was just fair in '93. He allowed only 15 of 59 inherited runners to score, which is a good percentage . . . Excellent control, best pitch is a sinking fastball, doesn't throw 90.

YEAR	TEAM/LEVEL	G	IP	W-L	SAVES	HITS	SO	BB	ERA
1992	Okla City AAA	12	11	1-0	8	7	13	3	0.79
1992	Texas	20	28	1-1	4	26	13	11	1.93
1993	Texas	60	73	2-1	1	78	39	23	4.32

DARRELL WHITMORE

Florida Marlins

Outfielder

$16

Listed by *Baseball America*, in one of their giddier moments, as the number-one prospect in the Pacific Coast League. He's 25 years old, too old to be considered a super-prospect, doesn't have outstanding power or speed, and his strikeout/walk ratio is Yugly. He's never hit anywhere other than Edmonton, where he hit .355, and even at Edmonton he was only 21% better-than-league in terms of productivity. Grade C prospect; will hit better than .204.

YEAR	TEAM/LEVEL	G	AB	R	H	2B	3B	HR	RBI	BB	SB	AVG	OBP	SLG
1993	MLE	73	256	37	80	20	1	6	44	15	7	.313	.351	.469
1993	Florida	76	250	24	51	8	2	4	19	10	4	.204	.249	.300
1994	**Projected**	**77**	**253**	**31**	**66**	**14**	**2**	**5**	**32**	**13**	**6**	**.261**	**.297**	**.391**

KEVIN WICKANDER

Cincinnati Reds

Lefthanded Relief Pitcher

$9

A close friend of Steve Olin, he was devastated by his friend's death, and found pitching in Cleveland an emotional burden. The Indians sent him to Cincinnati, but he continued to struggle . . . He has three good pitches, a fastball, a curve, and a cut fastball, but his control record is so bad that I question whether he should be in the majors.

YEAR	TEAM/LEVEL	G	IP	W-L	SAVES	HITS	SO	BB	ERA
1991	AA and AAA	32	37	2-2	2	33	31	18	3.41
1992	Cleveland	44	41	2-0	1	39	38	28	3.07
1993	Two Teams	44	34	1-0	0	47	23	22	6.09

BOB WICKMAN

New York Yankees

Starter/Reliever

$21

The worst 14-4 pitcher since . . . I dunno, Jim Coates or somebody. Showalter was smart enough to realize that his luck was going to run out sooner or later, and moved him to middle relief in the middle of the season. He's a ground-ball pitcher and not particularly vulnerable to a lefthander, so that worked out pretty well. I wouldn't rule out his chance of being a successful starter when he gets a little more experience.

YEAR	TEAM/LEVEL	G	IP	W-L	PCT.	HITS	SO	BB	ERA
1992	Columbus AAA	23	157	12-5	.706	131	108	55	2.92
1992	New York	8	50	6-1	.857	51	21	20	4.11
1993	New York	41	140	14-4	.778	156	70	69	4.63

CURTIS WILKERSON

Kansas City Royals

Utilityman

$14

After drifting near professional extinction he had a fine year as the Royals' top reserve infielder in 1992, his best season since 1988, but missed most of 1993 with a broken ankle. The key issue is whether his speed will return, or whether the ankle injury will cost him that. He is now 33, a switch hitter and a good second baseman, OK at short or third. He'll battle Howard, Miller and Wilson for spots on the KC bench.

YEAR	TEAM/LEVEL	G	AB	R	H	2B	3B	HR	RBI	BB	SB	AVG	OBP	SLG
1991	Pittsburgh	85	191	20	36	9	1	2	18	15	2	.188	.243	.277
1992	Kansas City	111	296	27	74	10	1	2	29	18	18	.250	.292	.311
1993	Kansas City	12	28	1	4	0	0	0	0	1	2	.143	.172	.143

RICK WILKINS

Chicago Cubs

Catcher

$46

One of the top surprise players of 1993, he wound up with the same slugging percentage as Mike Piazza (.561) and a slightly better on-base percentage (.376-.370). He's just one year older than Piazza, 26 to 25, and has the advantage of being a lefthanded hitter. He threw out 43% of opposition base stealers, best in the National League. Piazza was third, at 35%.

YEAR	TEAM/LEVEL	G	AB	R	H	2B	3B	HR	RBI	BB	SB	AVG	OBP	SLG
1992	Chicago	83	244	20	66	9	1	8	22	28	0	.270	.344	.414
1993	Chicago	136	446	78	135	23	1	30	73	50	2	.303	.376	.561
1994	**Projected**	**135**	**445**	**54**	**115**	**19**	**1**	**19**	**56**	**48**	**3**	**.258**	**.331**	**.434**

BERNIE WILLIAMS

New York Yankees

Center Field

$38

The Yankees had him leading off early in the year. In mid-season he was hitting .250 and had *no* stolen bases, despite his speed, so he dropped to the sixth spot, and played better. An excellent center fielder, he may be hurt by switch hitting—at any rate, he hasn't hit much from the left side. Like Pat Kelly, nobody is talking Cooperstown, but he's a good player now, and he's probably going to get better.

YEAR	TEAM/LEVEL	G	AB	R	H	2B	3B	HR	RBI	BB	SB	AVG	OBP	SLG
1992	New York	62	261	39	73	14	2	5	26	29	7	.280	.354	.406
1993	New York	139	567	67	152	31	4	12	68	53	9	.268	.333	.400
1994	**Projection**	**152**	**579**	**82**	**156**	**30**	**5**	**13**	**67**	**69**	**16**	**.269**	**.347**	**.406**

BRIAN WILLIAMS

Houston Astros

Starting Pitcher

$16

An outfielder and occasional pitcher in college. The Astros moved Williams to the mound after drafting him in 1990 due to his 90-mile-per-hour fastball and hard curve. So far, he has been unable to translate raw ability into major league success. He was moved through the minors very quickly, probably too quickly (40 games), and the new management in Houston might be doing him a favor by giving him a full season in Triple-A.

YEAR	TEAM/LEVEL	G	IP	W-L	PCT.	HITS	SO	BB	ERA
1992	Houston	16	96	7-6	.538	92	54	42	3.92
1992	Tucson AAA	12	70	6-1	.857	78	58	26	4.50
1993	Houston	42	82	4-4	.500	76	56	38	4.83

GERALD WILLIAMS

New York Yankees

Right Field

$15

He's like Hensley Meulens, Andy Stankiewicz, Dave Silvestri, Russ Davis—too old to be a prospect, as good a player now as he's ever going to be, but trapped in suspended animation by an organization that figures you can't possibly be a ballplayer unless you're past 30 and have had a couple of big years for Seattle or Cincinnati or somebody. Williams is a good outfielder, could hit .250-.260, steal 20 to 40 bases in a season.

YEAR	TEAM/LEVEL	G	AB	R	H	2B	3B	HR	RBI	BB	SB	AVG	OBP	SLG
1992	MLE	142	525	73	134	27	3	12	68	30	26	.255	.351	.406
1993	MLE	87	323	43	82	16	2	6	31	16	21	.254	.289	.378
1993	New York	42	67	11	10	2	3	0	6	1	2	.149	.183	.269

MATT WILLIAMS

San Francisco Giants

Third Base

$65

Third player in history to hit 30 homers and 30 doubles with less than 30 walks. The others were Felipe Alou and Butch Hobson, so I guess we can count on Matt being a manager someday, huh? . . . Extremely similar to Joe Carter, as a hitter. Led the National League in fly balls and popups hit (217), also led in slugging percentage against lefthanded pitchers (.683).

YEAR	TEAM/LEVEL	G	AB	R	H	2B	3B	HR	RBI	BB	SB	AVG	OBP	SLG
1992	San Francisco	146	529	58	120	13	5	20	66	39	7	.227	.286	.384
1993	San Francisco	145	579	105	170	33	4	38	110	27	1	.294	.325	.561
1994	**Projected**	**157**	**567**	**78**	**148**	**25**	**3**	**31**	**90**	**35**	**5**	**.261**	**.304**	**.480**

MIKE WILLIAMS

Philadelphia Phillies

Starting Pitcher

$15

A 25-year-old righthander, Williams was the Phillies' 14th-round pick in 1990 out of Virginia Tech. His stuff is average, but his control record in the minors is very good, and he has proven that he can succeed at the Triple-A level, going 18-3 the last two years. Grade C prospect; unlikely to start for the Phillies, but I would not be surprised to see him emerge as a middle reliever.

YEAR	TEAM/LEVEL	G	IP	W-L	PCT.	HITS	SO	BB	ERA
1992	Philadelphia	5	29	1-1	.500	29	5	7	5.34
1993	Scranton AAA	14	97	9-2	.818	93	53	16	2.87
1993	Philadelphia	17	51	1-3	.250	50	33	22	5.29

MITCH WILLIAMS

Philadelphia Phillies

Closer

$36

Williams has taken some heavy fan flak for not pitching well in the World Series, and has been the subject of numerous media stories for how he is handling it. Boiled down, there are two key questions: will Fregosi lose confidence in him (he will not), and will Williams be the same pitcher after the winter (yes, he will—because for one thing, he has been through this before after the 1989 playoffs). So his position is essentially unchanged.

YEAR	TEAM/LEVEL	G	IP	W-L	SAVES	HITS	SO	BB	ERA
1991	Philadelphia	69	88	12-5	30	56	84	62	2.34
1992	Philadelphia	66	81	5-8	29	69	74	64	3.78
1993	Philadelphia	65	62	3-7	43	56	60	44	3.34

WOODY WILLIAMS

Toronto Blue Jays

Reliever

$15

Williams is the Domingo Martinez of pitchers. He reached Knoxville in 1988, Syracuse in 1990, but was just sitting there killing time, pitching OK in a split role. He got the closer role at Syracuse early in the year and had a 2.20 ERA in 12 games, at which time the Blue Jays decided to bring him along. He wasn't bad, but there aren't millions of dollars in his future . . . A college shortstop at the University of Houston.

YEAR	TEAM/LEVEL	G	IP	W-L	SAVES	HITS	SO	BB	ERA
1991	AA and AAA	49	97	6-6	9	94	74	41	3.88
1992	Syracuse AAA	25	121	6-8	1	115	81	41	3.13
1993	Toronto	30	37	3-1	0	37	24	22	4.38

MARK WILLIAMSON

Baltimore Orioles

Reliever

$14

Williamson blew out his elbow in 1992, after several good years; 1993 was a rehabilitation season, and in a perfect world would probably have been done in the minor leagues. He gets ground balls with a sinking fastball, a palmball, and a slider, and as one would expect is ineffective on artificial turf. He didn't pitch well late in the '93 season (6.49 ERA after the break) . . . 30-35% chance of a comeback in '94.

YEAR	TEAM/LEVEL	G	IP	W-L	SAVES	HITS	SO	BB	ERA
1991	Baltimore	65	80	5-5	4	87	53	35	4.48
1992	Baltimore	12	19	1-0	1	16	14	10	0.96
1993	Baltimore	48	88	7-5	0	106	45	25	4.91

CARL WILLIS

Minnesota Twins

Middle Reliever

$26

Willis missed spring training '93 with an injury, then came back too quickly and was hammered. Once he worked into shape he was fine, posting an 0.72 earned run average after the break. His fastball moves and he has a very good vaseline sinker. He is among the most consistently effective middle relievers . . . Has a degree in parks and recreation managment from the University of North Carolina-Wilmington.

YEAR	TEAM/LEVEL	G	IP	W-L	SAVES	HITS	SO	BB	ERA
1991	Minnesota	40	89	8-3	2	76	53	19	2.63
1992	Minnesota	59	79	7-3	1	73	45	11	2.72
1993	Minnesota	53	58	3-0	5	56	44	17	3.10

CRAIG WILSON

Kansas City Royals

Third Base

$14

Traded to the Royals as part of the Jefferies/Felix Jose trade, Wilson made the Royals out of spring training, but went on the disabled list just as the season began with undisclosed personal problems. He returned to Omaha in June, where he hit .278 in 65 games, and made Kansas City late in the season. If his problems are behind him, he will battle Howard, Wilkerson and Miller for a utility spot.

YEAR	TEAM/LEVEL	G	AB	R	H	2B	3B	HR	RBI	BB	SB	AVG	OBP	SLG
1991	St. Louis	60	82	5	14	2	0	0	13	6	0	.171	.222	.195
1992	St. Louis	61	106	6	33	6	0	0	13	10	1	.311	.368	.368
1993	Kansas City	21	49	6	13	1	0	1	3	7	1	.265	.357	.347

DAN WILSON

Seattle Mariners

Catcher

$18

I probably said this in another comment, but to me, this trade (Wilson and Ayala for Hanson and Boone) is unfathomable. Wilson's a glove man, but he's not going to hit anything like what Bret Boone is going to hit, and probably won't hit enough to hold his job more than two-three years . . . Was a number-one draft pick of the Reds, and was named the best defensive catcher in his minor league several times.

YEAR	TEAM/LEVEL	G	AB	R	H	2B	3B	HR	RBI	BB	SB	AVG	OBP	SLG
1992	MLE	106	354	21	80	14	0	3	27	26	0	.226	.279	.291
1993	MLE	51	186	15	45	10	0	1	14	15	1	.242	.298	.312
1993	Cincinnati	36	76	6	17	3	0	0	8	9	0	.224	.302	.263

GLENN WILSON
Pittsburgh Pirates
Outfielder
$1

Thirty-five-year-old outfielder, best tool is, or was, his throwing arm. Wilson came up with Detroit in '82, played great for half a season, and battled unrealistic expectations for the rest of his career. He eventually made his way to Philadelphia, Seattle, Pittsburgh, Houston, the minor leagues, and now Pittsburgh again. He's slow, never walks, isn't a power hitter, and is unlikely to play in the majors again.

YEAR	TEAM/LEVEL	G	AB	R	H	2B	3B	HR	RBI	BB	SB	AVG	OBP	SLG
1991	Richmond AAA	29	100	13	27	4	0	2	15	13	1	.270	.351	.370
1993	Buffalo AAA	61	201	32	56	14	1	12	43	16	0	.279	.335	.537
1993	Pittsburgh	10	14	0	2	0	0	0	0	0	0	.143	.143	.143

NIGEL WILSON
Florida Marlins
Outfield
$23

In his September callup he went 0-for-16 and struck out 11 times, one of the least auspicious beginnings on record. Wilson was the first player taken by the Marlins in the expansion draft. His MLEs from '92 and '93 are very similar, and make it clear that he will be a .260 range hitter with a horrible strikeout/walk ratio, but slugging percentages in the high fours. Young enough to improve. Grade B prospect.

YEAR	TEAM/LEVEL	G	AB	R	H	2B	3B	HR	RBI	BB	SB	AVG	OBP	SLG
1992	MLE	137	514	76	136	32	5	25	61	25	9	.265	.299	.492
1993	Edmonton AAA	96	370	66	108	26	7	17	68	25	8	.292	.351	.538
1993	MLE	96	354	47	92	22	4	13	49	18	5	.260	.296	.455

STEVE WILSON
Los Angeles Dodgers
Reliever
$13

Wilson has a great arm, and pitches well for a few weeks at a time. Remember Brad Havens? Well, don't feel bad, nobody does, and in a few years those same people will remember Steve Wilson. Havens was a lefthander with the Twins in the 1980s. He threw hard, had a good curve, had good control, seemed to be intelligent, pitched well in the minors, but for some reason was never able to turn his tools into a career.

YEAR	TEAM/LEVEL	G	IP	W-L	SAVES	HITS	SO	BB	ERA
1992	Los Angeles	60	67	2-5	0	74	54	29	4.18
1993	Albuquerque AAA	13	51	0-3	0	57	44	14	4.38
1993	Los Angeles	25	26	1-0	1	30	23	14	4.56

TREVOR WILSON
San Francisco Giants
Starting Pitcher
$23

Went on the DL three times with tendonitis and inflammation in his throwing shoulder, and pitched only 20 innings after the All-Star break. With two 20-game winners on hand plus Black, Sanderson, Torres and Brantley, it appears unlikely that he will regain his place in the starting rotation, at least right away. Has become a marginal property; any chance of stardom is probably gone, but could be a good long reliever.

YEAR	TEAM/LEVEL	G	IP	W-L	PCT.	HITS	SO	BB	ERA
1991	San Francisco	44	202	13-11	.542	173	139	77	3.56
1992	San Francisco	26	154	8-14	.364	152	88	64	4.21
1993	San Francisco	22	110	7-5	.583	110	57	40	3.60

WILLIE WILSON
Chicago Cubs
Center Field
$14

He is probably through in Chicago, where they have young outfielders who are better than he is, and I wouldn't bet on him to be on a roster at the end of spring training. He can still run like the wind and rarely makes a mistake in center field, although he never could throw. That's enough to get him a backup job if a) he is lucky, and b) he's willing to play for the money they'll offer.

YEAR	TEAM/LEVEL	G	AB	R	H	2B	3B	HR	RBI	BB	SB	AVG	OBP	SLG
1991	Oakland	113	294	38	70	14	4	0	28	18	20	.238	.290	.313
1992	Oakland	132	396	38	107	15	5	0	37	35	28	.270	.329	.333
1993	Chicago	105	221	29	57	11	3	1	11	11	7	.258	.301	.348

DAVE WINFIELD
Minnesota Twins
Designated Hitter
$35

A few years ago we were assaulted by stories suggesting that there wouldn't be any more 3,000-hit players; Rose and Carew and Yastrzemski were supposed to be the last of them. Here's a prediction for you: between 1990 and 2010, the number of players with 3,000 career hits will double. I've followed this for 20 years, and I have never seen so many players so well-positioned to get 3,000 hits.

YEAR	TEAM/LEVEL	G	AB	R	H	2B	3B	HR	RBI	BB	SB	AVG	OBP	SLG
1992	Toronto	156	583	92	169	33	3	26	108	82	2	.290	.377	.491
1993	Minnesota	143	547	72	148	27	2	21	76	45	2	.271	.325	.442
1994	**Projection**	**123**	**456**	**55**	**114**	**20**	**2**	**14**	**61**	**50**	**3**	**.250**	**.324**	**.395**

BOBBY WITT
Oakland Athletics
Starting Pitcher
$36

His career is in a transition phase, the first phase having been extremely long and not particularly successful. Duncan is trying to work with him to get him to stop trying to make impossible pitches, and he is getting there. He still has a great arm, and he stays healthy, able to throw a lot of pitches in a season. His '93 season was good, and he was pitching very well at the end of the year.

YEAR	TEAM/LEVEL	G	IP	W-L	PCT.	HITS	SO	BB	ERA
1991	Texas	17	89	3-7	.300	84	82	74	6.09
1992	2 ML Teams	31	193	10-14	.417	183	125	114	4.29
1993	Oakland	35	220	14-13	.519	226	131	91	4.21

MIKE WITT
New York Yankees
Starting Pitcher
$10

He hasn't had an ERA below 4.00 since 1986, which you have to admit is a hell of an accomplishment, to keep earning a major league salary for seven years based on some good years in the distant past and an occasional run of a few strong outings. I'm being too harsh . . . Witt was pitching great last spring, but Paul Sorrento ripped a line drive off his elbow on June 1, which finished his season.

YEAR	TEAM/LEVEL	G	IP	W-L	PCT.	HITS	SO	BB	ERA
1990	Two Teams	26	117	5-9	.357	106	74	47	4.00
1991	New York	2	5	0-1	.000	8	0	1	10.13
1993	New York	9	41	3-2	.600	39	30	22	5.27

MARK WOHLERS

Atlanta Braves

Relief Pitcher

$29

Wohlers, who throws about a hundred miles an hour, pitched fairly well for the Braves in '92, but didn't hold the closer role and was sent to Richmond after an unimpressive spring training. He blew people away there for two months while the Braves sank slowly in the west, and was called up June 4 to help with the recovery. He pitched far better than his 4.50 ERA would suggest, and will again this year.

YEAR	TEAM/LEVEL	G	IP	W-L	SAVES	HITS	SO	BB	ERA
1992	Atlanta	32	35	1-2	4	28	17	14	2.55
1993	Richmond AAA	25	29	1-3	4	21	39	11	1.84
1993	Atlanta	46	48	6-2	0	37	45	22	4.50

TONY WOMACK

Pittsburgh Pirates

Infielder

$17

Womack is a 24-year-old lefthanded hitting shortstop, a seventh-round pick from a small college. He's got a good glove and has stolen 101 bases over the last two seasons. The Pirates gave him a look in September, but he's not going to take Bell's job or Garcia's, nor is it likely that the Pirates would want him sitting on the bench. Grade B prospect; his future could be bright, but it's a couple of years away.

YEAR	TEAM/LEVEL	G	AB	R	H	2B	3B	HR	RBI	BB	SB	AVG	OBP	SLG
1993	Salem A	72	304	41	91	11	3	2	18	13	28	.299	.331	.375
1993	Carolina AA	60	247	41	75	7	2	0	23	17	21	.304	.346	.348
1993	Pittsburgh	15	24	5	2	0	0	0	0	3	2	.083	.185	.083

TED WOOD

Montreal Expos

Outfielder

$10

His career is going nowhere. He started the year platooning in the Expos outfield, but didn't hit and was sent out in late April. He didn't do anything at Ottawa, either. . . . A lefthanded line drive hitter, supposed to be a good defensive outfielder, could have career as a fifth outfielder but isn't going to hit enough to be a regular.

YEAR	TEAM/LEVEL	G	AB	R	H	2B	3B	HR	RBI	BB	SB	AVG	OBP	SLG
1992	MLE	110	390	46	99	19	3	4	41	30	5	.254	.307	.349
1993	MLE	83	221	30	49	9	2	0	16	28	8	.222	.309	.281
1993	Montreal	13	26	4	5	1	0	0	3	3	0	.192	.276	.231

TRACY WOODSON

St. Louis Cardinals

Third Base

$8

The Cardinals' top righthanded pinch hitter, didn't have a good year and probably will not return this year. Stan Royer plays the same position(s) and is a similar hitter, and I'm guessing that Royer will get Woodson's job . . . Woodson's 31, was once a prospect in the Dodger system, and got a job with the Cardinals by combining a good year at Louisville, a .307 average in a callup, and a strong spring training. Limited future.

YEAR	TEAM/LEVEL	G	AB	R	H	2B	3B	HR	RBI	BB	SB	AVG	OBP	SLG
1992	MLE	109	393	46	103	19	1	9	44	18	2	.262	.294	.384
1992	St. Louis	31	114	9	35	8	0	1	22	3	0	.307	.331	.404
1993	St. Louis	62	77	4	16	2	0	0	2	1	0	.208	.215	.234

TIM WORRELL

San Diego Padres

Starting Pitcher

$25

You might want to draft him. He's Todd Worrell's brother, throws in the low 90s with a hard slider and good control. The Padres recalled him in June and put him in the rotation, where he struggled. Las Vegas, as you know, is a hitter's nirvana. His 89 strikeouts in 87 innings there are more indicitave of his ability than the high ERA. If his arm doesn't blow out before the Padres develop, he'll be a good pitcher.

YEAR	TEAM/LEVEL	G	IP	W-L	PCT.	HITS	SO	BB	ERA
1992	Las Vegas AAA	10	63	4-2	.667	61	32	19	4.26
1993	Las Vegas AAA	15	87	5-6	.455	102	89	26	5.48
1993	San Diego	21	101	2-7	.222	104	52	43	4.92

TODD WORRELL

Los Angeles Dodgers

Relief Pitcher

$12

Worrell, one of the best relievers of the late 1980s, discombobulated his elbow in 1989 and took three years to recover. He signed with the Dodgers because St. Louis wouldn't entrust him with the closer role, and the Dodgers didn't require him to take a physical. He went on the disabled list April 8, with, gasp, a sore elbow, which plagued him all year. When he did pitch, he wasn't very good. Has a 50-50 chance of a comeback.

YEAR	TEAM/LEVEL	G	IP	W-L	SAVES	HITS	SO	BB	ERA
1989	St. Louis	47	53	3-5	20	42	41	26	2.96
1992	St. Louis	67	64	5-3	3	45	64	25	2.11
1993	Los Angeles	35	39	1-1	5	46	31	11	6.05

RICK WRONA

Chicago White Sox

Catcher

$4

A decent defensive catcher, has lurked around the fringes of the majors for several years. He can't hit at all and his defense, while good, doesn't justify giving him a permanent roster spot, even as a backup, because a good organization can find a backup catcher who can hit a little, too. As long as his defense holds up, Wrona will have Triple-A jobs and will get occasional looks by teams that need a temp.

YEAR	TEAM/LEVEL	G	AB	R	H	2B	3B	HR	RBI	BB	SB	AVG	OBP	SLG
1992	Nashvill AAA	40	118	16	29	8	2	2	10	5	1	.246	.282	.398
1992	Cincinnati	11	23	0	4	0	0	0	0	0	0	.174	.174	.174
1993	Nashvill AAA	73	184	24	39	13	0	3	22	11	0	.212	.260	.332

ERIC YELDING

Chicago Cubs?

Outfielder

$14

He signed with the Cubs as a free agent a year ago and did a little bit of everything with them, everything except hit. He played the infield, outfield, pinch hit (huh?), pinch ran. I guess they signed him to replace Jerome Walton. He probably won't return to the Cubs in '93, but could show up somewhere in a similar role.

YEAR	TEAM/LEVEL	G	AB	R	H	2B	3B	HR	RBI	BB	SB	AVG	OBP	SLG
1992	Houston	9	8	1	2	0	0	0	0	0	0	.250	.250	.250
1993	Chicago	69	108	14	22	5	1	1	10	11	3	.204	.277	.296
1994	**Projected**	**57**	**153**	**14**	**37**	**4**	**1**	**1**	**12**	**9**	**9**	**.242**	**.284**	**.301**

ANTHONY YOUNG

New York Mets

Starter/Reliever

$22

One can easily find precedent for pitchers with similar records being successful within two or three years. Matt Keough was 2-17 in 1979, but 16-13 the next season. Camilo Pascual had records of 2-12 and 6-18 early in his career. Mike Parrott was 1-16 in 1980, and . . . well, maybe it's not a good example. Young's OK, not the best pitcher in the league, but should have some good years.

YEAR	TEAM/LEVEL	G	IP	W-L	SAVES	HITS	SO	BB	ERA
1991	New York	10	49	2-5	0	48	20	12	3.10
1992	New York	52	121	2-14	15	134	64	31	4.17
1993	New York	39	100	1-16	3	103	62	42	3.77

CLIFF YOUNG

Deceased

Lefthanded Pitcher

Was killed in a car wreck, November 4.

YEAR	TEAM/LEVEL	G	IP	W-L	SAVES	HITS	SO	BB	ERA
1990	California	17	31	1-1	0	40	19	7	3.52
1991	California	11	13	1-0	0	12	6	3	4.26
1993	Cleveland	21	60	3-3	1	74	31	18	4.62

CURT YOUNG

Oakland Athletics

Reliever/Starter

$3

The fourth-largest cause of skyrocketing health costs: trying to keep Curt Young in the Oakland rotation. Young pitches well for three weeks at a time, and LaRussa and Duncan are damned and determined to make a rotation starter out of him. One must admire their persistence; having failed 20 times to accomplish this, they go for 21. It isn't a question of whether this will work; it's just a question of when they're going to give up.

YEAR	TEAM/LEVEL	G	IP	W-L	PCT.	HITS	SO	BB	ERA
1992	2 ML Teams	23	68	4-2	.667	80	20	17	3.99
1993	Tacoma AAA	10	65	6-1	.857	53	31	16	1.93
1993	Oakland	3	15	1-1	.500	14	4	6	4.30

DMITRI YOUNG

St. Louis Cardinals

First/Third Base

$27

Probably will not reach the majors this year, but might if he whales the hell out of the ball at Arkansas. The fourth player taken in the 1991 draft, he has a Kevin Mitchell-type body and has been compared to him as a hitter, but is struggling to find a defensive position where he is not an absolute disaster. A **Grade A prospect**, based on his youth and hitting ability, but has some distance to go.

YEAR	TEAM/LEVEL	G	AB	R	H	2B	3B	HR	RBI	BB	SB	AVG	OBP	SLG
1992	Springfld A	135	493	74	153	36	6	14	72	51	14	.310	.378	.493
1993	St. Pete A	69	270	31	85	13	3	5	43	24	3	.315	.369	.441
1993	Arkansas AA	45	166	13	41	11	2	3	21	9	4	.247	.294	.392

ERIC YOUNG
Colorado Rockies
Second Base/Left Feld
$28

Young spent the first half-season as the Rockies' second baseman, but was pushed aside by Roberto Mejia, and went to left field, competing for playing time with Jerald Clark. He had a good year with the bat, at least for a second baseman, and could have scored 100 runs if he'd gotten enough playing time. Brett Butler-type hitter but righthanded, could draw 100 walks and steal 50 bases. I'm not sure how much he will play.

YEAR	TEAM/LEVEL	G	AB	R	H	2B	3B	HR	RBI	BB	SB	AVG	OBP	SLG
1992	Los Angeles	49	132	9	34	1	0	1	11	8	6	.258	.300	.288
1993	Colorado	144	490	82	132	16	8	3	42	63	42	.269	.355	.353
1994	**Projected**	**125**	**413**	**57**	**109**	**12**	**3**	**3**	**34**	**42**	**35**	**.264**	**.332**	**.329**

GERALD YOUNG
Colorado Rockies
Outfielder
$6

Opened the season as the Rockies' sixth outfielder, a pinch hitter/pinch runner/defensive sub, but was sent out in mid-May, having collected only one hit. Young, a 29-year-old from Honduras, hit .321 in half a season for the Astros in 1987, and has hit .300 several times since in the minor leagues (.298 last year), but has become progressively more futile as a major league hitter. Career is probably over.

YEAR	TEAM/LEVEL	G	AB	R	H	2B	3B	HR	RBI	BB	SB	AVG	OBP	SLG
1991	Houston	108	142	26	31	3	1	1	11	24	16	.218	.327	.275
1992	Houston	74	76	14	14	1	1	0	4	10	6	.184	.279	.224
1993	Colorado	19	19	5	1	0	0	0	1	4	0	.053	.217	.053

KEVIN YOUNG
Pittsburgh Pirates
First Base
$26

The under-achiever of the year; he's a .280 hitter, but fell into a slump, put pressure on himself, and didn't start to hit until September. He hit .192 with men in scoring position, worst in the National League. . . . The Pirates might give him a little more time to work through it, or they might move Merced to first, and give the outfield slot to Tomberlin or Cummings or Bullett or Pennyfeather. Young will have a comeback season sometime.

YEAR	TEAM/LEVEL	G	AB	R	H	2B	3B	HR	RBI	BB	SB	AVG	OBP	SLG
1992	MLE	137	467	70	131	25	4	5	50	51	12	.281	.351	.383
1993	Pittsburgh	141	449	38	106	24	3	6	47	36	2	.236	.300	.343
1994	**Projected**	**135**	**430**	**52**	**120**	**24**	**4**	**6**	**49**	**38**	**9**	**.279**	**.338**	**.395**

MATT YOUNG
Released
Thrower
No Value

A 1986 won-lost log of 8-6 prevented him from having a perfect record: more losses than wins in every season. His career record was 55-95, and over the last five seasons he has been 13-39. He's had ERAs over 5.00 four times in his 10-year career, others of 4.91, 4.58 and 4.47. His control started out OK, but gradually got worse and worse, reaching 6.9 walks per nine innings.

YEAR	TEAM/LEVEL	G	IP	W-L	PCT.	HITS	SO	BB	ERA
1991	Boston	19	89	3-7	.300	92	69	53	5.18
1992	Boston	28	71	0-4	.000	69	57	42	4.58
1993	Cleveland	22	74	1-6	.143	75	65	57	5.21

PETE YOUNG

Montreal Expos

Relief Pitcher

$14

A big righthander, only six feet tall but weighs 225. He played some third base in college, Mississippi State, was drafted by Montreal in 1989 and has drifted through the system, pitching fairly well everywhere. Grade C prospect, throws an OK fastball and a good slider. The Expos have lots of pitching prospects; in another year he may do something to distinguish himself from the herd.

YEAR	TEAM/LEVEL	G	IP	W-L	SAVES	HITS	SO	BB	ERA
1992	Montreal	13	20	0-0	0	18	11	9	3.98
1993	Ottawa AAA	48	72	4-5	1	63	46	33	3.73
1993	Montreal	4	5	1-0	0	4	3	0	3.38

ROBIN YOUNT

Milwaukee

(Free Agent)

Center Field

$25

At this writing, it is expected that he will continue to play. His batting averages over the last three years are in a group between .258 and .264, with on-base percentages and slugging percentages of equal consistency. We have to figure that that's his level of ability, but he is "only" 38 and in good shape apart from a nagging knee injury, and there have been many players in history who had comeback seasons at that age.

YEAR	TEAM/LEVEL	G	AB	R	H	2B	3B	HR	RBI	BB	SB	AVG	OBP	SLG
1992	Milwaukee	150	557	71	147	40	3	8	77	53	15	.264	.325	.390
1993	Milwaukee	127	454	62	117	25	3	8	51	44	9	.258	.326	.379
1994	**Projected**	**122**	**444**	**53**	**109**	**22**	**3**	**7**	**57**	**45**	**8**	**.245**	**.315**	**.356**

EDDIE ZAMBRANO

Chicago Cubs

Outfielder

$13

Zambrano is 28 and, until last year, no one had ever confused him with a prospect. He was signed by the Red Sox as an undrafted free agent, and signed with the Cubs last year as a minor league free agent. He had a big year at Iowa, which is *not* a great place to hit, although it's a good home run park. Hit .396 against lefthanded pitchers (at Iowa), so might be a platoon player. Grade C prospect.

YEAR	TEAM/LEVEL	G	AB	R	H	2B	3B	HR	RBI	BB	SB	AVG	OBP	SLG
1992	MLE	126	377	36	95	19	2	11	61	39	2	.252	.322	.401
1993	Iowa AAA	133	469	95	142	29	2	32	115	54	10	.303	.377	.578
1993	MLE	133	445	71	118	25	1	22	85	40	6	.265	.326	.474

GREGG ZAUN

Baltimore Orioles

Catcher

$14

A 5-foot-9 switch-hitting catcher, Zaun, whose nickname is "Turtle," is expected to back up Hoiles in the future, maybe as soon as 1994. He is the nephew of Rick Dempsey, and appears to have the good genes: he throws well and is an excellent handler of pitchers, cutting team earned run averages by almost a run each year in the minor leagues. Should have a long career as a backup, and might well be a regular.

YEAR	TEAM/LEVEL	G	AB	R	H	2B	3B	HR	RBI	BB	SB	AVG	OBP	SLG
1993	Bowie AA	79	258	25	79	10	0	3	38	27	4	.306	.373	.380
1993	Rochest AAA	21	78	10	20	4	2	1	11	6	0	.256	.302	.397
1993	MLE	100	322	27	85	11	1	2	38	22	2	.264	.311	.323

TODD ZEILE

St. Louis Cardinals

Third Base

$39

If you drive in a hundred runs people will stop talking about the things you don't do, or at least, other people will. Zeile has begun to fight third base rather than simply read and react; this is a normal stage, and he'll get by it in a year or two. He's not a true cleanup hitter, like Sheffield or Matt Williams, but is an average hitter for a third baseman, or maybe a tiny bit better.

YEAR	TEAM/LEVEL	G	AB	R	H	2B	3B	HR	RBI	BB	SB	AVG	OBP	SLG
1992	St. Louis	126	439	52	113	18	4	7	48	68	7	.257	.352	.364
1993	St. Louis	157	571	82	158	36	1	17	103	70	5	.277	.352	.433
1994	**Projection**	**151**	**560**	**74**	**149**	**29**	**3**	**14**	**80**	**74**	**11**	**.266**	**.352**	**.404**

ALAN ZINTER

New York Mets

First Base/Catcher

$7

Had a secondary average of .451 at Binghamton, all of it from power and walks. He was the Mets first-round pick in 1989, a catcher (then) from the University of Arizona. He didn't make it as a catcher and his minor league batting average is .248, so it's safe to say that the White Sox don't regret that they passed him over for Frank Thomas. Zinter's 26 in May, has yet to play Triple-A. Grade D prospect.

YEAR	TEAM/LEVEL	G	AB	R	H	2B	3B	HR	RBI	BB	SB	AVG	OBP	SLG
1992	Binghamton AA	128	431	63	96	13	5	16	50	70	0	.223	.337	.387
1993	Binghamton AA	134	432	68	113	24	4	24	87	90	1	.262	.386	.502
1993	MLE	134	417	55	98	20	2	18	70	61	0	.235	.333	.422

BOB ZUPCIC

Boston Red Sox

Outfield

$15

A good defensive outfielder on a team that needs defensive outfielders. A big righthanded hitter, he had a hot streak just after he came up, but the .241 average of last year is more consistent with his real ability . . . was reportedly offered a football scholarship by Penn State, but elected to go to Oral Roberts and play baseball . . . no star potential; suspect he won't play as much as the computer has projected.

YEAR	TEAM/LEVEL	G	AB	R	H	2B	3B	HR	RBI	BB	SB	AVG	OBP	SLG
1992	Boston	124	392	46	108	19	1	3	43	25	2	.276	.322	.352
1993	Boston	141	286	40	69	24	2	2	26	27	5	.241	.308	.360
1994	**Projected**	**129**	**347**	**43**	**81**	**23**	**1**	**5**	**37**	**32**	**4**	**.233**	**.300**	**.349**

HIGHEST-VALUED PLAYERS BY POSITION

CATCHER

Chris Hoiles $69
Darren Daulton $62
Mike Piazza $60
Ivan Rodriguez $59
Rick Wilkins $46
Mike MacFarlane $41
Don Slaught $40
Mike Stanley $39
Brian Harper $38
Terry Steinbach $37
Ron Karkovice $32
Chad Kreuter $3

FIRST BASE

Frank Thomas $95
Fred McGriff $78
John Olerud $75
Jeff Bagwell $72
Rafael Palmeiro $67
Mark McGwire $59
Mark Grace $58
John Kruk $58
Cecil Fielder $53
Will Clark $52
Greg Jefferies $52
Eddie Murray $42

SECOND BASE

Roberto Alomar $92
Carlos Baerga $85
Ryne Sandberg $73
Craig Biggio $65
Chuck Knoblauch $64
Delino DeShields $61
Robby Thompson $43
Brent Gates $42
Joey Cora $39
Bret Boone $37
Carlos Garcia $36
Lou Whitaker $35

THIRD BASE

Travis Fryman $70
Robin Ventura $70
Matt Williams $65
Terry Pendleton $60
Gary Sheffield $58
Dave Hollins $54
Edgar Martinez $54
Charie Hayes $48
Jeff King $44
Ken Camininti $42
Wade Boggs $41
Todd Zeile $39

SHORTSTOP

Jay Bell $75
Jeff Blauser $61
Barry Larkin $60
Ozzie Smith $51
Cal Ripken $45
Andujar Cedeno $42
Wilfredo Cordero $40
Tony Fernandez $40
Greg Gagne $40
Kevin Stocker $39
Jose Offerman $37
Jose Vizcaino $36

LEFT FIELD

Barry Bonds $100
Juan Gonzales $88
Tim Raines $69
Ron Gant $66
Albert Belle $65
Rickey Henderson $62
Bernard Gilkey $47
Luis Gonzales $47
Brady Anderson $45
Greg Vaughn $39
Moises Alou $38
Jeff Conine $37
Mike Greenwell $37

CENTER FIELD

Ken Griffey, Jr. $98
Len Dykstra $79
Marquis Grissom $65
Kenny Lofton $65
Brett Butler $60
Devon White $57
Andy Van Slyke $49
Shane Mack $47
Chad Curtis $42
Steve Finley $40
Otis Nixon $40
Brian McRae $39

RIGHT FIELD

Kirby Puckett $71
Phil Plantier $65
Larry Walker $65
Jay Buhner $64
Joe Carter $63
Dave Justice $63
Tony Gwynn $59
Ruben Sierra $59
Tim Salmon $50
Bobby Bonilla $46
Reggie Sanders $45
Darryl Hamilton $43

DESIGNATED HITTERS AND UTILITY PLAYERS

Tony Phillips $70
Mickey Tettleton $63
Paul Molitor $60
Bip Roberts $49
Danny Tartabull $41
Troy Neel $40
Julio Franco $37
Dave Winfield $35
Chili Davis $32
Mariano Duncan $32
Harold Baines $30
Mike Gallego $30

RIGHTHANDED STARTERS

Greg Maddux $95
Jose Rijo $84
Kevin Appier $83
Jack McDowell $74
Pete Harnisch $69
John Smoltz $68
Bill Swift $68
Roger Clemens $64
David Cone $62
Curt Shilling $62
Tommy Greene $59
Kevin Tapani $59
Bob Tewksbury $58
Kevin Brown $57
Mike Mussina $57
Andy Benes $56
Alex Fernandez $56
Denis Martinez $55
Tom Candiotti $54
Doug Drabek $53
Mark Portugal $51
Ben McDonald $45
Jason Bere $42
Daryl Kile $42
Aaron Sele $42
Pedro Astacio $40
Juan Guzman $40
John Burkett $39
Danny Darwin $38
Cal Eldred $37
Dave Stewart $37
Rene Arocha $36
Dwight Gooden $36
Jose Guzman $36
Mike Morgan $36
Bret Saberhagen $36
Bobby Witt $36
Willie Banks $35
Erik Hanson $35

LEFTHANDED STARTERS

Randy Johnson $76
Jimmy Key $70
Steve Avery $66
Mark Langston $66
Tom Glavine $59
Chuck Finley $55
Greg Swindell $54
Terry Mulholland $48
Wilson Alvarez $44
Greg Hibbard $38
Allen Watson $35
Frank Viola $35

CLOSERS

John Wetteland $69
Duane Ward $68
Bryan Harvey $66
Rod Beck $64
Jeff Montgomery $63
Roberto Hernandez $60
Tom Henke $55
Dennis Eckersley $53
Rick Aguilera $52
Jeff Russell $48
Lee Smith $46
Randy Myers $40
Gregg Olson $40

SET-UP MEN

Pedro J. Martinez $38
Xavier Hernandez $34

Kevin Rogers $32
Stan Belinda $30
Jeff Brantley $30
Jeff Fassero $30
Greg Harris $30
Greg McMichael $30
Bruce Ruffin $30

PROSPECTS

Cliff Floyd $44
Chipper Jones $40
Carlos Delgado $39
Manny Ramirez $38
Jim Thome $37
Alex Gonzalez $34
Rondell White $34
Javy Lopez $33
Scott Ruffcorn $32
Salomon Torres $32
Willie Greene $30
Bobby Jones $30
Rich Becker $29
Gabe White $29
Steve Karsay $28
Roberto Petagine $28
Tony Tarasco $28
Brien Taylor $28
Rick Helling $27
Kevin McGehee $27
Dmitri Young $27
Mark Newfield $26
Melvin Nieves $26
Mark Hutton $25
Benji Gil $24
Scott Sanders $24
Steve Trachsel $24
Carl Everett $23
Nigel Wilson $23
Kurt Miller $22
Midre Cummings $21